Canine Olfaction Science and Law

Advances in Forensic Science, Medicine, Conservation, and Environmental Remediation

Canine Olfaction Science and Law

Advances in Forensic Science, Medicine, Conservation, and Environmental Remediation

Edited by

Tadeusz Jezierski
Institute of Genetics and Animal Breeding of
Polish Academy of Sciences
Jastrzębiec, Poland

John Ensminger
Attorney, Stone Ridge, New York, USA

L.E. Papet
Executive Director
K9 Resources, LLC
Cincinnati, Ohio

CRC Press
Taylor & Francis Group
Boca Raton London New York

CRC Press is an imprint of the
Taylor & Francis Group, an **informa** business

CRC Press
Taylor & Francis Group
6000 Broken Sound Parkway NW, Suite 300
Boca Raton, FL 33487-2742

© 2016 by Taylor & Francis Group, LLC
CRC Press is an imprint of Taylor & Francis Group, an Informa business

No claim to original U.S. Government works

Printed on acid-free paper
Version Date: 20160126

International Standard Book Number-13: 978-1-4822-6023-6 (Hardback)

Visit the Taylor & Francis Web site at
http://www.taylorandfrancis.com

and the CRC Press Web site at
http://www.crcpress.com

Contents

SECTION I Anatomy, Genetics, Neurology, Disease, and Evolution

SECTION II   Chemistry and Aerodynamics of Odors

SECTION III   Behavior, Learning, and Training

SECTION IV   Uses in Forensics and Law

SECTION V Uses in Conservation and Remediation

SECTION VI   *Uses in Detection of Diseases and Medical Conditions*

Preface

WHY AN ENTIRE BOOK ON CANINE OLFACTION?

The value of human–canine relationships to humans is, in significant part, based on the ways in which the olfactory ability of dogs so greatly surpasses our own. This quality of the species was evident to us even in the first stages of domestication, and the uses we find for it continue to evolve. While this book discusses the history of canine olfaction in human society, it focuses particularly on the scientific study, legal analysis, and training of dogs for those applications that have been developed in the last century and that continue to be developed. This takes us into the fields of forensics and criminal law, medicine and disability law, conservation and protection of endangered species, eradication of invasive species and pests, and the training of dogs for these types of detection work. We make this journey with guides who are scientists, working in both pure and applied disciplines; trainers and handlers who have trained and deployed detection dogs; and lawyers who have evaluated evidence produced with the aid of detection and scent identification dogs. We discuss how recent applications of canine olfactory abilities were prefigured in the more traditional functions of dogs, such as tracking fugitives and hunting game.

The perspectives provided here are not static, and we will be the first to acknowledge that we can only give snapshots in time. Still, the amount of material assembled in this volume could easily have been larger and, frankly, is much greater than we expected two years ago when this project was nothing more than a proposal in the publisher's in-box. We hope the reader will agree that it is not too early to look at where this surprisingly active subject stands at present and to consider where it may be going.

WHO SHOULD READ THIS BOOK?

The 32 authors represented in this book provide a broad range of perspectives on canine olfaction, starting with aspects that might be called pure science, showing how the canine olfactory organ is built and how it works, followed by a section on odor chemistry and characteristics, and moving on to behavior as studied in the laboratory and as modified by the trainer and implemented by the handler. The final three sections include a series of chapters describing how canine olfaction is being applied in forensics, conservation, and medicine. The book will therefore be useful to scientists working in sensory research on dogs and other animals, as well as scientists developing technologies to supplement or replace the detection functions of dogs, veterinarians studying diseases affecting the nasal organ and sensory abilities, lawyers introducing or opposing the introduction of canine-based olfactory evidence or other evidence that may be corroborated by canine evidence, and expert witnesses preparing to testify concerning canine-based evidence.

The book contains much of value to trainers of all types of detection dogs (including narcotics, explosives, and accelerant detection dogs; cadaver dogs; dogs used in conservation; dogs used to detect and sometimes destroy pests and invasive species; dogs used in the increasingly investigated area of cancer detection) as well as trainers and users of service dogs with medical alert functions. We believe that administrators of law enforcement agencies with canine units will find the analysis of the scientific findings and legal limits of detection work of interest, as will conservation organizations seeking to determine the impact of human populations and environmental changes on endangered and threatened species. Administrators of hospitals and health care facilities should take note of the successes of dogs in detecting cancers and alerting victims of certain diseases concerning abrupt changes in their conditions. The fact is that the use of dogs for detection is pervasive in many areas of our lives today, and we are bold to say that some of these topics may even be of interest to the general public.

The "black box" label often given to canine olfactory results refers to the fact that we cannot ask the dog to tell us what it is smelling. This means that the dog's work is often considered anecdotal, random, and of dubious reliability. Yet such descriptions overlook the fact that an intense scientific effort has been underway for nearly a century to specify the parameters of the dog's dependability in performing olfaction-related tasks.

OLFACTION IN DOGS AND HUMANS

Olfaction and taste are forms of chemoreception that enable living organisms to receive, record, and use information about the presence of various chemicals in the environment. Olfaction—the sense of smell—is a ubiquitous modality of the animal kingdom and, in vertebrates, is mediated by specialized sensory (olfactory) cells of the nasal cavity. Many vertebrates, including most mammals, have a main olfactory system that detects volatile chemicals and an accessory olfactory system detecting fluid-phase chemicals (e.g., pheromones). Authors writing about different aspects of olfaction, e.g., Marchlewska-Koj (2011), point out that in some animal species sight and hearing become superfluous, but no animal species is lacking an ability to receive chemical stimuli from the environment. The importance of sensing molecules is demonstrated by the discovery that even plants are able to detect small molecules in their environments (Keller and Vosshall 2008).

The sense of smell provides animals with information essential for locating food, keeping aware of conspecifics and identifying their reproductive status, enabling mutual recognition of parents and progeny, and warning of predators and danger. The chemicals (odorants) that activate the olfactory system are generally present in the environment at very low concentrations. In the evolution of human–animal coexistence and interactions, humans learned to use animal species that proved to be cooperative, a process that, with changes in the species being used, is called domestication. Dogs, the first domesticates, became moving, real-time, and reliable odor detectors. Humans have always been fascinated with the canine ability to easily detect odorants even at long distances and, perhaps even in the Upper Paleolithic period but certainly by the Neolithic period, found this capacity useful in tracking game. Prehistoric tribes were also aware of the excellent warning function that comes from the canine's heightened sense of smell.

As just one example of how such skills are relevant to the research described in this book, Paleo-Eskimo cultures used their dogs to locate breathing holes of seals in sea ice (Arnold 1979), but now that canine skill is being used for preservation purposes so that ice roads for arctic oil drilling are laid out so as to avoid disturbing the subnivean lairs of ringed seals.

Under a perspective given to many of us in college biology courses even now, animals can be roughly divided into macrosmatic species, those equipped with an efficient and sensitive sense of smell, and microsmatic species, in which the sense of smell plays a minor role and is less efficient. To macrosmatic species belong insectivorous mammals, rodents, ungulates, and carnivores, while primates, including humans, were considered archetypically microsmatic. This distinction across the mammalian class, however, is now under reconsideration, as it has been found that the sense of smell plays a very important role in the lives of certain monkeys (Laska et al. 2000), and its value may have been seriously underestimated in humans (Jones and Rog 1998).

RECENT INCREASE IN INTEREST IN STUDYING OLFACTION

Until recently, the sense of smell was relatively neglected by scientists compared to sight and hearing, presumably because it is a less important sense for humans. Nevertheless, there were milestones in olfaction research, such as the discovery by Linda Buck and Richard Axel (1991) of the genes encoding odorant receptors and the subsequent sequencing of the human olfactory subgenome (Glusman et al. 2001; Zozulya et al. 2001). Even earlier, it was discovered that odors stimulate the production of cyclic adenosine monophosphate (cAMP) through olfactory-enriched adenylate cyclase (Pace et al. 1985; Sklar et al. 1986). Of extreme importance symbolically was the awarding of the 2004 Nobel Prize in Physiology or Medicine to Buck and Axel for their studies on G protein–coupled receptors selectively expressed in the olfactory epithelium, which coupled odor binding to the production of cAMP. Buck and Axel cloned olfactory receptors and estimated that there were approximately 1000 different genes for olfactory reception in the mammalian genome. This research opened the door to the genetic and molecular analysis of the mechanisms of olfaction.

The number of articles on olfaction in peer-reviewed journals seems to grow year by year, and many of these involve canine olfaction in both pure and applied disciplines. There are now journals and volumes devoted to olfaction and odors, and an increasing number of specialized conferences allow researchers to meet and discuss their findings. This book assembles many of those who write on canine olfaction and participate in international conferences where these developments are being discussed and debated.

The idea of devoting an entire book to the subject of olfaction is not new. In 1968, William McCartney wrote *Olfaction and Odours: An Osphresiological Essay*, devoted in significant part to canine olfaction. Earlier, in 1936, F.J.J. Buytendijk, a physiologist, had written *The Mind of the Dog*, with many chapters devoted to the dog's sense of smell. Animal behaviorists, such as Adam Miklosi (2007) and Alexandra Horowitz (2009), have devoted many chapters in books on dog psychology to olfaction, and editions of both their recent books featured close-ups of dog noses on the cover. *Canine Ergonomics: The Science of Working Dogs*, edited by William S. Helton (2009), has at least four chapters devoted almost exclusively to olfaction issues, but most of the chapters refer to the subject. *Human Scent Evidence*, by Paola Prada, Allison Curran, and Kenneth Furton (2015), provides an extensive discussion of how dogs are used in scent identification. There have also been countless popular books and training manuals on the specific uses of dogs in olfactory-focused work, particularly for narcotics and explosives detection. We are well aware that we join a parade in progress and can only hope that our efforts will further the study of and interest in the olfactory abilities of our best friend.

GOING FORWARD

More than 30 different specialties of sniffer dogs have been described in the scientific literature. The uses of canine olfaction in criminal investigations have brought courts into the discussions of how reliable dogs can be when taught to identify certain substances or match scents from crime scenes to those of suspects. Reports of strange reactions of pets to melanoma lesions in their masters have led to serious consideration of whether dogs can be deployed in clinical contexts for early recognition of certain kinds of cancers. The finding that dogs can more efficiently and more accurately survey certain endangered species than any other method has led agencies involved in wildlife preservation to accept and, in some cases, even mandate their use as a survey tool. This book looks across these various perspectives on canine olfaction in an effort to give as three-dimensional a picture as possible of where this subject is in the modern social context and where it may be going.

This book does not, however, provide an argument—much less serve as an advertisement—for a limitless expansion of canine olfactory functions. The chapter on the detection of volatile organic compounds mentions the development of portable technologies that may and probably should begin to replace certain functions of dogs. Legal commenters argue that there are limits to the uses of canine olfactory results in criminal prosecutions and that courts may sometimes have been lax in the extent they have admitted and permitted juries to rely upon canine-based evidence. Indeed, certain station and field procedures employed by a few police dog handlers, primarily in southern California and Texas, may be so flawed that the claimed scent identifications cannot reasonably be argued to have any validity as either scientific or legal evidence. Conservation work has been successful with some species but less so with others, and the expenses of deploying conservation detection dogs may effectively prohibit their use in certain environments that are difficult to traverse or extremely remote. Cancer detection by dogs may remain largely a curiosity unless it can be demonstrated that the approach surpasses other means of early detection by being less invasive or more reliable. Even if that threshold can be crossed, medical administrators are rightly concerned with how to tell patients that sophisticated laboratory technology could find nothing wrong with them, but a dog did.

Many of the issues discussed in this book remain unresolved, and in some cases controversial. We have not tried to smooth over the disagreements; the authors of various chapters inevitably take positions contradictory to others published by their colleagues, and what is stated in one chapter will, on occasion, be contradicted in another. We have tried to include cross-references so that readers can easily find the conflicting arguments that sometimes arise in such actively researched areas. Indeed, the coeditors—a scientist, a lawyer, and a trainer—happily acknowledge that we have even disagreed among ourselves on issues large and small. We see this not as a weakness in the volume but, rather, as one of its strengths. A book about olfaction that included only matters on which there is universal agreement would be short indeed, and one that insisted on general acceptance would not be much longer.

With these claims and cautions, we invite our readers to join us as we investigate this fascinating subject and hope they will find the analysis as interesting and provocative as it has been for us and the other investigators who participated in the creation of this book.

Tadeusz Jezierski, John Ensminger, and L.E. Papet

Acknowledgments

The concept of devoting an entire book to the subject of canine olfaction took root in a series of discussions the three of us had over the course of several years. Once we decided there was a book in the idea, however, we soon realized that we would need a great deal of help to bring the concept into print reality. We were fortunate that Mark Listewnik, senior editor of forensic science books at Taylor & Francis/CRC Press, took an early interest in the project and began helping us shape our idea into a book that we hope will be of interest and use to scientists, lawyers, trainers, and dog lovers the world over. It is not too much to say that without Mark's patience and encouragement, this book would never have happened. We also owe our deepest gratitude to Amy Blalock, who became the project coordinator inside Taylor & Francis, and whose efforts moved the project from manuscript to book. We would also like to thank Tara Nieuwesteeg, the project editor at Taylor & Francis, and Adel Rosario, who managed the typesetters who worked on the book.

In addition to the contributors, whose efforts produced most of the material in this book, we received research assistance and essential perspectives on canine olfaction from many collaborators and friends, the brief mention of whose names is hardly adequate thanks. These include Kingsbury Parker, Richard Hawkins, Brian Duggan, Yva Momatiuk, John Eastcott, Matt Johnson, Jim DeCamp, Craig Kuether, and James Harrison. We gratefully acknowledge that there were many others who helped us on various points and at various stages who are too numerous to list.

As anyone who has written a book learns sooner or later, spending long hours working on a manuscript can mean that family members and canine companions get less attention than they deserve. Tadeusz would like to thank his wife, Nina, for her patience and understanding, and allowing him the time to work on this book instead of being at home with her. John would like to thank his wife, Joan, for encouraging his efforts and tolerating his obsession with the canine world. L.E. Papet would like to thank his wife and soul mate, Sherri, for sharing a lifelong dream together accompanied by dogs for which they both hold extreme reverence. Lastly, we can never forget the companionship and love of Tadeusz's Awa, Siuch, Aramis, Portos Atos, Court, Bzik, Bexa, Gromit, Tytan, Oskar, Bis, and Cygun; John's Blackie, Sandy, and Chloe; and L.E. Papet's Alex, Katie, Wrex, Charmen, Toulouse, Runt, Sammy, Bear, Gibby, Powder, Sioux, Gatlin, Top, Roscoe, Bohann, Star, Zee, Blitz, Polly, Toby, and Page—whose sense of smell and other abilities have helped us in more ways than we could ever describe.

Tadeusz Jezierski, John Ensminger, and L.E. Papet

Editors

Tadeusz Jezierski is professor of agricultural science at the Institute of Genetics and Animal Breeding of the Polish Academy of Sciences. He has been a full professor at the institute since 1999 and is the head of the institute's Department of Animal Behavior. He is an internationally known author on a wide range of topics and has written papers on animal behavior, genetics, and animal welfare. His recent research interests include operant conditioning of sniffer dogs, behavioral genetics, human–animal interactions and the human–animal bond, genetic and environmental factors influencing social and sexual behavior of farm animals, feeding behavior, and emotional behavior and physiological reactions in farm animals. Professor Jezierski has written 73 peer-reviewed publications in scientific journals, 4 monographs, 4 handbooks, and 11 chapters in books. He has written 111 conference reports.

John Ensminger is an attorney who has practiced in the areas of constitutional law, mental patient civil rights, taxation of financial instruments, anti–money laundering and counterfinancing of terrorism, and most recently the law as it applies to skilled dogs. He has written over 30 papers on these topics, with articles on service and police dogs appearing in *Forensic Science International, Journal of Forensic Sciences, Journal of Animal and Natural Resource Law, New York Law Journal, Journal of Veterinary Behavior, Journal of Forensic Psychology Practice, Animal Science Papers and Reports, Deputy and Court Officer, Pets News,* and *Tax Notes*. He is a contributing editor for the website of the Animal Legal & Historical Center of the Michigan State University College of Law. He has written two books on specialized dogs, *Service and Therapy Dogs in American Society* and *Police and Military Dogs*.

L.E. Papet is the owner and operator of K9 Resources, LLC, a privately held licensed investigative firm that specializes in the use of detection canines. As a scientific data-driven canine trainer, handler, and consultant, his primary focus is the training, testing, and use of canines in olfactory disciplines such as (but not limited to) explosives, illicit drugs, humans (alive and deceased), pharmaceuticals, alcohol, accelerants, and many other forms of contraband and odor for both public and private sectors. Papet has trained hundreds of local, state, and federal officials; written over 170 protocols for the training, testing, safety, deployment, and implementation of detection canines; and received commendations for his work. He enjoys contributing to works involving working dogs employing the use of their olfactory skills. He resides just outside Cincinnati, Ohio, and may be contacted at lep@k9resources.com.

Contributors

David Bainbridge is a university clinical veterinary anatomist in the Department of Physiology, Development and Neuroscience in the School of Biological Sciences at the University of Cambridge. He is the director of studies in veterinary medicine at St. Catharine's College and at Trinity Hall. He has written numerous papers on zoology and veterinary medicine as well as popular books, including *Beyond the Zonules of Zinn*; *The X in Sex, Teenagers: A Natural History*; and most recently, *Curvology: The Origins and Power of the Female Body Shape*.

Danielle Bes has conducted research on Dutch scent identification procedures and DNA contamination of police gloves in cooperation with the criminal investigation unit of the Dutch police force and the Province of Zeeland in the Netherlands. She lives in Alkmaar, the Netherlands. She can be reached at daniellebes@msn.com.

Gudrun Brandes is group leader and senior lecturer in the Institute of Cell Biology in the Department of Anatomy at the Medical School in Hannover, Germany. She has conducted research in and taught cell biology, anatomy, biomedicine, and zoology. By using light and electron microscope techniques, she has studied characteristics of olfactory ensheathing cells and Schwann cells and is currently analyzing the interaction of cells with implant materials *in vivo*. She has written 51 peer-reviewed original articles and 3 review articles. She can be reached at brandes.gudrun@mh-hannover.de.

Bogusław Buszewski is chair of environmental chemistry and bioanalytics in the Faculty of Chemistry of Nicolaus Copernicus University in Torun, Poland. He has published 430 articles in areas such as environmental analysis, chromatography, and spectroscopy, and is currently conducting research on biomarkers and techniques of early cancer diagnosis, analytics of food products, and other chemical issues. In 2013, he published a book, *Electromigration Techniques: Theory and Practice* (Springer). He can be reached at bbusz@chem.umk.pl.

Megan A. Ferguson is an associate professor in the Department of Chemistry at the State University of New York–New Paltz. She is faculty adviser to the Environmental Geochemical Sciences program. Her research interests include environmental aquatic chemistry and surface chemistry, particularly as applied to bacteria of environmental relevance. She can be reached at ferguson@newpaltz.edu.

Francis Galibert is a professor emeritus in the Institute of Genetics and Development in the Faculty of Medicine of the University of Rennes in France. In the early 1970s, as a fellow in the group of Dr. Frederick Sanger in Cambridge (United Kingdom), he was deeply involved in the development of DNA sequencing methods. Then for more than 20 years, he participated in many international sequencing genome programs. He has published more than 200 papers, many of which have dealt with mammalian and canine genetics, and was a member of the team that, in 2005, described the genome sequence and haplotype structure of the domestic dog. He is a member of the European Molecular Biology Organization and has been elected to the National Academy of Medicine.

Nathaniel J. Hall is conducting postdoctorate research in the Department of Psychology at Arizona State University in Tempe, Arizona. He has published peer-reviewed articles on learning and cognitive development in dogs and wolves, odor discrimination, and canine behavior, including compulsive behavior. He can be reached at njhall1@gmail.com.

Aimee Hurt is a cofounder and director of operations of Working Dogs for Conservation in Missoula, Montana, and is one of the originators of the field of conservation detection dogs in North America. She has trained conservation detection dogs and teams for work in ecological monitoring, invasive-species management, and wildlife trafficking worldwide. She has worked with government agencies, conservation groups, and universities. She can be reached at aimee@workingdogsforconservation.org.

Keith P. Jacobi is a professor in the Department of Anthropology at the University of Alabama in Tuscaloosa, Alabama, and is a curator of human osteology for the Alabama Museum of Natural History. Through human osteology, paleopathology, and dental anthropology, he has investigated culture clashes at the time of contact. His most recent research has involved prehistoric Native American warfare and trophy-taking where it involves human body parts. He also has conducted research on decomposition of human remains and the taphonomy of skeletal remains. He has consulted on over 75 forensic cases and has conducted forensic workshops for high school and university groups as well as a Federal Bureau of Investigation Evidence Response Team. He has more than 35 peer-reviewed publications. He can be reached at kjacobi@as.ua.edu.

Thomas H. Jourdan is a professor of chemistry and assistant director of the Forensic Science Institute at the University of Central Oklahoma in Edmond, Oklahoma. He was formerly a supervisory special agent with the Federal Bureau of Investigation, where he worked, among other areas, in trace drug analysis, in particular, on environmental surfaces, encrypted drug ledgers, and currency. His current research interests include forensic toxicology and, specifically, the stability of synthetic cannabinoids in biological samples. He consults for the International Atomic Energy Agency and Interpol, and can be reached at tjourdan@uco.edu.

Patricia Kammeyer is in the Department of Pathology at the University of Veterinary Medicine in Hannover, Germany, where her research focus is in immunohistochemical characterization of olfactory neurons and glial cells in the canine olfactory epithelium. She won the Erich-Ahnelt-Gedachtnispreis in 2009.

Margie P. Lehnert is a lecturer in the Biology Department of Cuyahoga Community College in Parma, Ohio. She has studied and published numerous articles on insects, including bedbugs, specifically focusing on control strategies.

Sherri Minhinnick has been a canine trainer and handler for 20 years with experience crossing multiple disciplines of detection, including explosives, illicit drugs, human remains, live find, pharmaceuticals, and others while serving in both public (Ohio Task Force One [OHTF-1] and law enforcement) and private sectors. Minhinnick currently serves as director of operations for a licensed security firm specializing in detection services. She may be reached at sminhinnick@gmail.com.

Paul A. Moore is a professor in the Department of Biological Sciences at Bowling Green State University in Bowling Green, Ohio. He has conducted research on sensory ecology, measuring and quantifying the distribution of chemicals in diverse terrestrial and aquatic habitats and specifically examining the impact of anthropogenic chemicals on organisms in natural settings. A focus of his research has concerned how aquatic organisms locate the source of an odor stimulus. He has published over 80 peer-reviewed articles, and his book, *The Hidden Power of Smell: How Chemicals Influence Our Lives and Our Behaviors*, was published in January 2016. He can be reached at pmoore@bgsu.edu.

Mohamed Omar is a senior resident in the trauma department of the Hannover Medical School, where he is involved in patient care and research and teaching in traumatology. He has studied the morphological and functional characterization of the canine olfactory system and worked on comparative analysis of olfactory ensheathing cells and Schwann cell properties *in vitro* and *in vivo*. He won the evidence-based Medicine Prize awarded by the German Society of Orthopaedics and Trauma in 2014.

Cynthia M. Otto is executive director of the Penn Vet Working Dog Center and an associate professor in the University of Pennsylvania School of Veterinary Medicine. She has written 67 peer-reviewed articles on emergency medicine, disaster medicine, the impact of 9/11 on search-and-rescue canine health, and many other veterinary issues. Her current focus is on the health and performance of working dogs. She can be reached at cmotto@vet.upenn.edu.

Megan Parker is a cofounder and director of research at Working Dogs for Conservation. Her doctoral research at the University of Montana focused on the scent-marking behavior and chemistry of African wild dogs in Botswana. She has trained dogs to detect wildlife samples, including plants, animals, fish, scats, and wire snares, and wildlife contraband for antipoaching efforts. Her work with dogs and training handlers helps dwindling populations of wildlife in the United States, Asia, and Africa, and her research is focused on conservation impacts possible with dogs.

Alexandra Protopopova is an assistant professor in the Department of Animal and Food Sciences at Texas Tech University in Lubbock, Texas, where she is the director of the Human–Animal Interaction Lab. She is currently researching the behavior and welfare of companion animals and animals involved in animal-assisted therapy. She is an editorial board member of the *Journal of Applied Animal Welfare Science* and is a recipient of the Marian Breland Bailey Award for Applied Animal Behavior Research.

Pascale Quignon is an associate professor in the Institute of Genetics and Development at the University of Rennes in France. She conducted the first study on the polymorphism of canine olfactory receptor genes to search for correlations between polymorphism and olfactory abilities of dog breeds. She has written 30 articles on such topics as the mapping of canine genes, including olfactory receptor genes, as well as genes affecting dog morphology and genes implicated in canine genetic diseases. She is currently studying canine genes involved in genetic diseases homologous to human diseases.

Joanna Rudnicka is chair of environmental chemistry and bioanalytics, Faculty of Chemistry at Nicolaus Copernicus University in Torun, Poland. She has conducted research on the application of solid phase microextraction (SPME)–gas chromatography-mass spectrometry (GCMS) and sniffer dogs in the detection of cancer, and is currently focused on preparing samples for trace analysis of volatile organic compounds in exhaled breath. She has published 10 peer-reviewed articles in these areas and can be reached at joannarudnicka@vp.pl.

Leslie A. Shoebotham is a Victor H. Schiro Distinguished Professor of Law at Loyola University New Orleans College of Law, where she teaches in the fields of criminal procedure, criminal law, and torts. She is admitted to the bars of Texas, Louisiana, and the United States Supreme Court. She has written numerous law review articles on criminal and constitutional law issues and filed *amici curiae* briefs in the United States Supreme Court in cases involving canine sniffs. She can be reached at shoeboth@loyno.edu.

Marcello Siniscalchi is in the Section of Behavioral Sciences and Animal Bioethics in the Department of Veterinary Medicine of the University of Bari in Italy, where he lectures on veterinary physiology and ethology. His laboratory work has focused on the complementary specialization of brain hemispheres in canines, which has shown how lateralization of brain functions influences dog behavior. He is currently studying the relationships among emotion, cognition, and lateralization, looking specifically at whether dogs can detect the emotional state of a human being or another dog via smell. His work on tail-wagging responses to different stimuli was one of the subjects of a documentary on the National Geographic Channel. He can be reached at marcello.siniscalchi@uniba.it.

Keith Springer managed the Macquarie Island Pest Eradication Project for the Tasmania Parks and Wildlife Service, and now lives in Christchurch, New Zealand. His research and work have concerned invasive-species eradication from islands, on which he has written a number of articles. He was formerly a forest and national park ranger in New Zealand and worked in logistics management for the New Zealand Antarctic Programme. He can be reached at keith.springer@gmail.com.

Carol M. Stephenson is a behavioral scientist, retired from the Centers for Disease Control and Prevention, where she conducted behavioral research in workplace settings for more than 30 years. She is also a registered veterinary technician/member of the Society of Veterinary Behavioral Technicians, with over 20 years of experience in small animal practice. She owns a private canine consulting business, assisting clients with canine behavior issues, preventive puppy training, and various canine competition sports. She may be reached at buckeyecaninecollege@gmail.com.

Mark R. Stephenson has more than 40 years of experience designing, conducting, and managing applied research projects for the U.S. Air Force and the Centers for Disease Control and Prevention (CDC). He retired from the CDC in 2015 after having worked in the Division of Applied Research and Technology for 22 years. He has served as a consultant to the National Aeronautics and Space Administration (NASA), the National Academy of Engineering, and the National Academy of Medicine. He can be reached at mstephenson@fuse.net.

Emma N.I. Weeks is an assistant research scientist in the Entomology and Nematology Department of the University of Florida in Gainesville. Her research has focused on improving arthropod monitoring with an emphasis on identifying attractive semiochemicals for monitoring and trapping arthropods, including bedbugs and ticks. She is currently researching nonchemical control methods for medical and veterinary pests. She can be reached at eniweeks@ufl.edu.

Konstantin Wewetzer (wewetzer.konstantin@mh-hannover.de) is group leader and senior lecturer at the Department of Functional and Applied Anatomy of Hannover Medical School, Germany. He has studied the morphological and functional characteristics of the rat and canine olfactory systems and comparatively analyzed the regenerative capacity of olfactory ensheathing cells and Schwann cells. Currently, he is focusing on the role of neuron–glia interactions during lifelong turnover of olfactory sensory neurons. He is the author of 58 peer-reviewed original research and 6 review articles.

Deborah A. (Smith) Woollett is a cofounder and director of conservation of Working Dogs for Conservation in Three Forks, Montana. Dr. Woollett has trained and handled conservation dogs, designed and implemented conservation dog projects, and evaluated noninvasive monitoring methods to obtain key information on endangered populations. She is the author or coauthor of 16 published papers and 4 book chapters. She received the George Miksch Sutton Award in Conservation Research and can be reached at info@workingdogsforconservation.org.

Clive D.L. Wynne is a professor in the Department of Psychology at Arizona State University in Tempe, Arizona, and the director of the university's Canine Science Collaboratory. He is also director of research of Wolf Park, Battle Ground, Indiana. He has written more than 100 papers, of which about 30 concern canids. He is on the editorial board of *Behavioural Processes*.

Section I

Anatomy, Genetics, Neurology, Disease, and Evolution

The first section of this book deals with the theoretical basis showing how the olfactory organ is built and how it works, covering its anatomy, physiology, neurology, genetics, and evolution and the effects of disease on its condition and operation.

ANATOMY

The chapter on anatomy describes the gross structure of the canine nose and its evolutionary and developmental origin. Due to centuries of artificial selection for different functions and body shapes, dog breeds, as no other animal species, differ in head and muzzle shape. Long-headed breeds, such as borzois, have extremely long and narrow snouts, whereas bulldogs and other brachycephalic breeds with extremely short noses suffer from overly long palates in proportion to the head, which creates fluttering during breathing accompanied by a stertorous noise. This may have an impact not only on olfaction but also on the well-being of these dogs.

There are three types of cells in the olfactory epithelium and the cranial nerves. An unusual phenomenon of continuous and spontaneous regeneration of olfactory nerves has attracted the interest of neurologists as a model of how it may be possible to stimulate the regeneration of injured neurons of the spinal cord and brain. The author of the first chapter suggests that the size of the canine olfactory system may be evidence as to how the structure of a relatively big forebrain in mammals depends on the importance and complexity of the olfactory system. The author hypothesizes that an unusually direct access of the olfactory system to higher processing centers in the forebrain could explain why the perceptual phenomenon known as déjà vu often comes from odors, though it is not clear whether this phenomenon, known to humans, is present, or to what extent, in dogs.

WIRING OF THE OLFACTORY SYSTEM

The neuronal processes underlying olfaction are detailed in the chapter on the wiring of the olfactory system, which discusses the functional role of neurons and glia. The wiring of olfactory neurons is not established early in development once and for all, since olfactory neurons are regularly lost by cell death and replaced by neurogenesis. Olfactory neurogenesis is intriguing both from the anatomical and neurophysiological perspective and is discussed in several chapters.

Much of the chapter on wiring is devoted to cells of the main olfactory bulb and the accessory olfactory bulb of the vomeronasal organ, as well as to the olfactory ensheathing cells and Schwann cells. The olfactory ensheathing cells are a prime candidate to explain the repair of a damaged central nervous system, though this has not yet been confirmed experimentally. The authors underline that basic neural mechanisms are similar in different animal species, although the studies on rodent olfaction still outnumber those on dogs.

THE CANINE BRAIN AND OLFACTION

The chapter on brain function in canine olfaction makes us aware that canine behavior is in part driven by olfactory sensory information integrated and elaborated in neocortical areas of the brain. Raw olfactory stimulation in the olfactory bulb in the form of electrophysiological responses alone, without respective interpretation at higher cognitive levels, is not sufficient to steer the behavior of an animal. The author characterizes functional magnetic resonance imaging (fMRI) as a useful and promising tool to study how the olfactory information is processed and analyzed by the dog's brain. Some brain areas, such as the caudate nucleus, are involved in associations of an odor with positive expectations, including social rewards. The activation of these brain areas can be studied using fMRI. Another intriguing phenomenon is lateralization. In dogs, there is a right-nostril and right-hemisphere bias in response to threatening stimuli, whereas the left nostril and left hemisphere are specialized in processing familiar odor stimuli. The author suggests that evident asymmetries and lateralization of canine olfaction may be useful in developing new methods to train dogs to detect particular scents. Generally, the author states that the cognitive process that deals with olfactory information is still largely unknown.

GENETICS OF OLFACTION

The authors of the chapter on genetics of canine olfaction focus on three issues: perception of a volatile compound, discrimination, and identification. The chapter discusses the olfactory gene repertoire, the structure of olfactory receptor genes and proteins, genomic organization, as well as olfactory receptor gene polymorphism and expression. The authors suggest that the relatively limited knowledge of the principal factors influencing odor detection and discrimination may be a limiting factor in exploiting the olfactory ability of dogs and at least a partial explanation of some of the variability in results obtained in applied olfactory work. A fundamental question is why individual dogs, even within breeds used historically and presently for olfaction work, may be so varied in their detection abilities. How much of this variability is due to genetic makeup? How much to training? Studies on the genetic mechanism underlying canine olfaction may provide some answers. Genetic research may provide a means for selecting dogs for olfactory work so that lengthy and expensive training regimens can be more easily given to dogs genetically predisposed to becoming good detector dogs.

DISEASE AND OLFACTION

Numerous disorders can impair a dog's olfactory abilities. The author of the chapter on disease and olfaction describes three main categories of olfaction sensory impairment: anosmia, hyposmia, and dysosmia. Disorders of smell both in humans and especially in animals are less recognizable than disorders of other senses, for which validated tests are widely available. In veterinary medicine, there are no objective means to evaluate smell or taste in animals. The dog must first be trained to give a response to an odor, and on the basis of this response, one can only indirectly declare olfaction efficiency or a deficit. An alternative approach using habituation to familiar odors and then evaluating preference to a novel odor still requires validation and is not unequivocal, since it involves olfaction in terms of both odor perception and odor memory. The author explains how complete or partial loss of olfaction can be caused, paying particular attention to anosmia in dogs associated with canine distemper virus (CDV) infection. Concerning hyposmia in dogs, documented cases are limited to experimental settings.

The author points out that little is known about the effects of drugs, toxins, and medications on olfaction in dogs, and studies on these relate to human olfaction. The potential hazard for drug detection dogs that may be caused by exposure to cocaine is discussed, though the effect of subclinical exposure to cocaine on canine olfaction remains to be studied. There is as of yet no evidence of addiction in drug detection dogs. The author includes a list of classes of drugs that alter olfaction and a list of potential olfactory toxins.

EVOLUTION AND OTHER CANIDS

In the final chapter of this section, canine olfaction is considered from an evolutionary perspective, and its importance for wolves and other canids is discussed. The authors assume that the ecology of the wolf, especially due to the dispersal and relative low density of the prey odor, may explain some parallels with detector dogs searching for a target odor, e.g., drugs or explosives that are also dispersed and of low density. Another important parallel between searching for prey by wolves and searching for target odors by dogs is that both rely not only on olfaction but also on vision and hearing. This multimodality searching approach has both advantages and drawbacks. When tracking, for example, the ultimate goal is finding the source of the target odor, and it is not a problem if a dog uses other senses. If, on the other hand, a dog concentrates on visual cues from its handler and neglects olfactory stimuli during searching, this can be regarded as a disadvantage, an issue also discussed in the training and forensics sections of this book.

The authors describe several phenomena concerning wolves and canine olfaction that are still not well understood, such as wallowing by canines in objects emitting highly aversive odors to humans, such as putrefying meat. Regarding the evolution of olfaction, questions have been raised about how the acuity of the wolf's sense of smell compares to that of a dog. This has received little research attention, though olfactory receptor genome studies have shown that dogs, compared to wolves, have a nonsignificantly greater percentage of inactive olfactory receptor genes disrupted by mutations.

Assuming a greater acuity of the sense of smell in wild canids, Russian researchers and trainers have attempted to produce "superdogs" by crossbreeding wild canids and domestic dogs for odor detection functions. Such hybrids, as produced by Sulimov with dogs and jackals, were presented in mass-media reports as outperforming dogs in their detection ability, but this was not confirmed in rigorous scientific experiments. Interestingly, comparison of the olfaction acuity between dogs and wild canids revealed a seasonal variation of olfaction acuity in some wild canids, with a higher level of acuity apparent in spring months. (Crossbreeding of dogs with wild canids is known from ancient Egypt [Brixhe 1996] and Roman Palestine [Merlen 1971, p. 38], and has been confirmed genetically in certain lines of sheep-guarding dogs [Kopaliani et al. 2014].)

RESEARCH CONTINUES

The chapters of this section all acknowledge large areas where research has been lacking and thereby suggest where it may or should be going. There is inevitable overlap in the work of anatomists, physiologists, neurologists, behaviorists, and others, but a review of their topics also shows the gaps that need to be filled in, for a theoretical understanding of olfaction in dogs and their wild relatives, but also to improve our ability to use the dog's sense of smell in the real world.

Tadeusz Jezierski, John Ensminger, and L.E. Papet

1 The Anatomy of the Canine Nose

David Bainbridge

The olfactory abilities of dogs are famous, but the canine nose is a physiological compromise between at least six conflicting functions—respiration, vocalization, water balance, temperature regulation, recycling tears, and detecting odorant molecules. In addition, the canine nose was not designed specifically to carry out these functions but is instead the end result of hundreds of millions of years of natural selection and evolutionary chance. In this chapter, I will describe the gross structure of the canine nose but will emphasize its evolutionary and developmental origins, and also how its internal and external arrangement allows it to perform its various functions.

EVOLUTION OF THE NOSE

The sensory detection of chemicals—*chemoreception*—is readily divided into different modalities in dogs. These include smell or *olfaction* via the nose, taste or *gustation* via the taste buds, and *enteroception* of chemicals inside the body. However, tracing the evolutionary heritage of chemoreception through the backboned animals demonstrates that there has, at times, been considerable overlap between these modalities.

The first vertebrates were fish—aquatic forms whose entire body was continually bathed in a watery medium containing chemical signals. Because of this, many extant fish species still possess chemical-detecting cells throughout their mouth, throat, and gills, and spread over most of the surface of their body. However, even in animals with such a widely distributed chemosensory system, there always exist specialized olfactory organs: clusters of chemoreceptor cells that congregate on the snout, where they will encounter incoming chemicals "first." Thus, every vertebrate has a "nose."

Olfactory systems in fishes have three common configurations. In jawless fish, a single midline nasal duct may open out on the top of the head, in association with the pituitary. In cartilaginous fish, smell-sensitive cells are often clustered in a deep groove on the snout through which water is forced as the shark or ray swims forward. In bony fish, which are most closely related to land vertebrates, the nose often consists of a single short tube on each side of the head, with an inflow hole and outflow hole. Thus, some bony fish may appear to have two nostrils (*nares*) on each side of the head, and the olfactory receptor cells are entirely hidden along the tube connecting those nostrils (Kardong 2002).

When vertebrates migrated onto land, two major modifications occurred. First, the olfactory cells, which had previously evolved to function in water, now required continual bathing in fluid to allow odorant molecules to dissolve and be detected. Second, the olfactory pits or tubes on the snout developed a novel connection to the mouth cavity, so that the nasal cavities of all land vertebrates now open into the mouth or throat, as well as the outside world. The connection of the nasal cavities to the throat in mammals is via paired openings called the *choanae* (sometimes unhelpfully called the internal nostrils or nares).

The origins of the choanae remain uncertain, as does the fate of the "outflow nostril" of bony fish—although it is possible that the choanae actually *are* the outflow nostril, which migrated past the lips and teeth into the mouth (Zhu and Ahlberg 2004). Alternatively, the outflow nostril may have migrated backward into the eye socket to form the *nasolacrimal duct*, which now drains tears into the nasal cavity.

The olfactory system and muzzle were of central importance in the evolution of mammals, for several reasons. First, mammals evolved at a time when many of their potential predators were dinosaurs, which are thought to have been predominantly visual hunters active during the day. Thus, it is likely that many early mammals were nocturnal and that their evolution was focused on ecological niches requiring good senses of hearing and smell (Bainbridge 2008). Second, there is evidence that the relatively large mammalian brain evolved primarily to permit increased processing of olfactory stimuli (Rowe et al. 2011). Third, a distinctive anatomical feature of mammals is the *secondary hard palate*, which divides the nasal and oral cavities, meaning that the choanae open far back in the throat, rather than into the roof of the mouth as they do in birds or snakes. This arrangement provides the muzzle with great torsional rigidity, allowing mammals to exert extremely high forces via their intricately intermeshing teeth—to chew.

The dog has retained these distinctively mammalian features—it is intelligent with a large brain, it has a long strong muzzle, and most of all, it is a *macrosmatic* species, highly reliant on its excellent sense of smell.

EMBRYONIC DEVELOPMENT OF THE NOSE

The sensory parts of the nose develop initially from interactions between more than one cell type. Vertebrates are *triploblastic* animals whose body plans form from three layers of embryonic cells: the *ectoderm*, which forms the outer surface of the animal and the central nervous system; the *endoderm*, which forms the lining cells (*epithelium*) of the alimentary, urinary, and respiratory systems; and the *mesoderm*, which forms most tissues between the other two layers. Uniquely, vertebrate embryos also contain a fourth cell type, *neural crest*, which gives rise to many of their characteristic features.

The precursors of the left and right olfactory organs are the paired *olfactory placodes*, thickenings of the ectoderm on the surface of the snout. These interact with underlying brain tissue (also ectoderm derived), as well as nearby neural crest cells, to form the rudiments of the olfactory system— paired superficial *olfactory pits* on the snout connected to *olfactory bulbs* at the front of the brain, by the nascent *olfactory nerves* (Steventon et al. 2014).

The olfactory pits become progressively deeper, and soon, the thin membrane separating them from the oral cavity, the *oronasal membrane*, breaks down. At this point, the nasal cavities open directly into the mouth via the *primitive choana*, a situation perhaps akin to that seen in adult birds and snakes.

At this stage, the bony architecture of the muzzle starts to form. The skull is created by the fusion of many dissimilar bones, and the bones that form the nasal cavity are derived from two different sources. First, the bone at the back of the nasal cavity through which the olfactory nerves will pass to the brain is the *ethmoid* (or *mesethmoid*), and it initially forms in all vertebrates as a protective capsule for the olfactory sensory organ. It forms from a neural crest-derived cartilaginous precursor and thus is classified as part of the *chondrocranium* ("cartilage skull").

In contrast, all the other bones of the muzzle, which will be described in detail later, are derived from flat sheets of connective tissue and are classified as part of the *dermocranium* ("skin skull," also *dermatocranium*). As these develop, the olfactory pits gradually sink backward into the developing face, so that instead of being exposed on the surface of the snout, the sensory epithelium will be buried deep inside the nasal cavities that the dermocranial bones form.

For the final anatomical configuration of the nose to be completed, three further processes must occur (Figure 1.1a). First, shelves of connective tissue, and eventually bone, grow in from the sides of the muzzle to create the secondary hard palate which almost completely separates the nasal and oral cavities in mammals—leaving the nose connected to the throat (*pharynx*) via the *definitive choanae* far back in the mouth. The formation of the palate is occasionally deficient, and *cleft palate* (Figure 1.1b) is a relatively common congenital abnormality in dogs, but one that is sometimes amenable to surgical correction. As the palate forms, a second, midline, sheet of tissue grows down from the roof of the nasal cavity to form the *nasal septum*, which divides the nasal cavity into its left and right compartments. Third, swellings around the external nostrils (*nares*) are remodeled to create the distinctive morphology of the external nose (de Beer 1937).

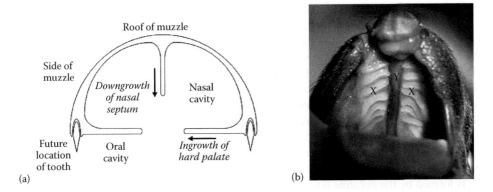

FIGURE 1.1 (a) A schematic cross section through the developing muzzle of a canine embryo showing the formation of the secondary hard palate and nasal septum. (b) An open-mouthed oral view of the palate of a stillborn crossbreed puppy with cleft palate, delivered by Caesarean section by the author. The animal's snout is at the top of the image, and its tongue (out of focus) is at the bottom. The ridged surfaces of the hard palate (X) are evident, growing inward from the sides of the muzzle but not meeting in the midline, leaving a fissure opening into the nasal cavity, through which the incomplete nasal septum (Y) may be seen.

SKELETON OF THE MUZZLE

Dogs' muzzles vary a great deal in shape, due to centuries of artificial selection to create canine faces that are either well-suited to their intended purpose or considered attractive (Figure 1.2). *Dolichocephalic* (long-headed) breeds such as the borzoi or saluki have extremely long snouts, while *mesocephalic* (or *mesaticephalic*) breeds such as the beagle have more moderately proportioned muzzles. *Brachycephalic* breeds such as the bulldog and the pug have extremely short noses and suffer many problems as a result—for example, their palates are often too long for their heads, causing them to flutter in the respiratory air stream, creating a stertorous noise. It should be noted that breed-related variation in snout length affects the entire skull, and brachycephalic breeds are more likely to suffer from other problems, too, such as eyeball prolapse and hydrocephalus (water on the brain). It is striking, however, that when the extremely brachycephalic skull of the cat evolved by natural selection, no such problems resulted.

Although it is formed from a set of thin, flat bones, the muzzle is extremely robust. Like the rest of the skull, it is configured into a series of struts, buttresses, and arches that dissipate forces

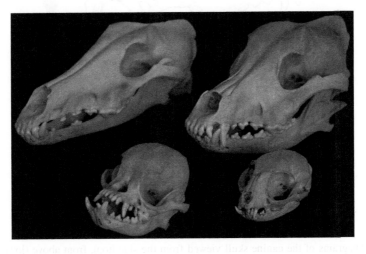

FIGURE 1.2 Skulls of dolichocephalic (borzoi, top left), mesocephalic (rottweiler, top right), and brachycephalic (Pekingese, lower left) dog breeds, and a cat skull (crossbreed, lower right) for comparison.

extremely efficiently. This strength evolved to resist the large forces developed during chewing, but it has also made the muzzle very resistant to accidental damage. Direct impacts may cause local buckling and fragmentation of the flat bones of the muzzle, but catastrophic failure usually only results from extreme impact forces, such as those in a high-speed road traffic accident.

The dermocranial bony elements that make up the skull are shown in Figure 1.3. Also shown are the terms used by anatomists to orientate structures toward the front (*rostral*), back (*caudal*), top (*dorsal*), bottom (*ventral*), sides (*lateral*), and midline (*medial*) of the head.

The opening to the bony nasal cavity is bounded laterally and ventrally by the *premaxilla* or *incisive* bone, which also contains the roots of the incisor teeth. Most of the nasal cavity is bounded laterally and ventrally by the large *maxilla* bone, which thus forms most of the hard palate (the floor of the nasal cavities) and contains the roots of all the other teeth. The caudal-most part of the hard palate is formed by the *palatine* bone. The roof of much of the nasal cavity is formed by the long, thin *nasal* bones, although the most caudal regions of the dorsal nasal cavities are enclosed by the large *frontal* bone (Pasquini et al. 1995; Konig and Liebich 2007).

One more dermocranial bone, the *vomer*, forms part of the nasal cavities, although its anatomy is complex and it is not shown in Figure 1.3. The vomer is a long thin bone that lies in the midline and runs obliquely from ventrally at the cranial end of the nasal septum to dorsally at the caudal end. At the cranial end, it is elaborated into distinctive V-shaped flaps, which protrude dorsally into the bony nasal cavity (Figure 1.4a), and the name of the bone refers to these flaps' similarity in shape to a plowshare (the Latin word which gives the bone its name).

Caudally, the nasal cavity is separated from the cranium by the *ethmoid*, a chondrocranial bone. One portion of this bone constitutes the *cribriform plate*, a domed bony partition between the nasal and cranial cavities, perforated by approximately 300 holes through which pass the many branches of the olfactory nerves. This plate is not visible externally on a skull, other than by viewing its caudal aspect through the large hole through which the spinal cord exits the back of the cranium, the *foramen magnum* (Figure 1.4b).

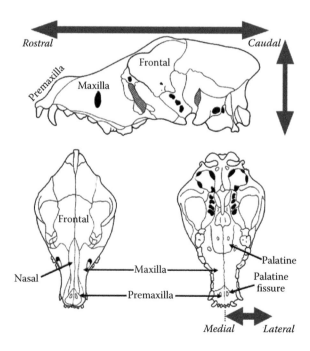

FIGURE 1.3 Diagrams of the canine skull viewed from the side (top), from above (lower left), and from below (lower right), with the bones forming the nasal cavities labeled. Also marked are the terms of orientation used by anatomists.

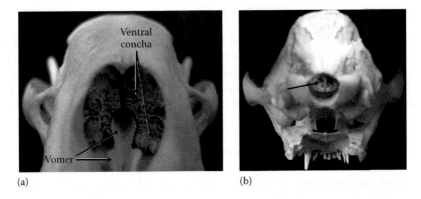

(a)   (b)

FIGURE 1.4   (a) A view through the bony nasal opening of the dog, showing the V-shaped vomer bone ventrally and the bony scrolls of the turbinates dorsally. (b) A view through the foramen magnum at the back of the skull, showing the perforations of the cribriform plate of the ethmoid bone through which the olfactory nerves run.

Thus, the bones of the muzzle create a strong, large, approximately tubular cavity through which air can pass on its way to the lungs and smell-sensitive cells. These thin flat bones are evident on a lateral radiograph of the canine head (Figure 1.5a), as are some of the other structures anchored to and contained within them.

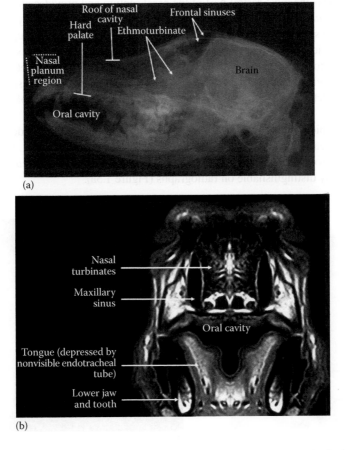

FIGURE 1.5   (a) A lateral radiograph of the canine head, showing the bones and soft tissues of the nose. (b) An MRI showing a transverse section of the canine nasal cavities.

NASAL PLANUM, CARTILAGES, AND MUSCLES

As air flows through the canine nose, the first structure it passes is the *nasal planum* (Figure 1.6a): the distinctive flat region of thickened skin surrounding the external nares. The skin is hairless (as in the cat, pig, and ox), although this hairless region does not extend ventrally to the upper lip (as it does in the ox). The skin bears a midline groove or *philtrum* (as in the cat and rabbit), but that groove does not descend as far as the opening of the mouth (as it does in the sheep, cat, and rabbit). The epidermis is unusually ridged (as in the ox) in a pattern that is unique to individual animals, just as fingerprints are in humans.

The planum is often moistened, although this is by fluids from inside the nose rather than from glands in the skin of the planum itself. A *wet nose* is sometimes said to be a sign of health in dogs, but there is much variation between individuals in this respect. However, a sudden reduction in wetness in an individual dog may indeed be a nonspecific sign of malaise. The planum and its boundary with the surrounding skin are predilection sites for autoimmune skin disease.

The external nares of the dog are often comma shaped, with the tail of the comma directed ventrally and laterally. Brachycephalic breeds are prone to congenital stenosis (narrowing) of the external nares, compounding their other respiratory problems—although this stenosis may be relieved surgically in some cases.

Dogs have the ability to widen their nostrils when exercising or savoring an odor, by the action of muscles that move the cartilages underlying the planum. The *nasal cartilages* of the dog are dermocranial in origin and, viewed rostrally, appear to almost entirely encircle the nares (Figure 1.6b). The midline, *septal part* is the most rostral part of the nasal septum and provides attachment for the *dorsolateral and ventrolateral parts* of the cartilages, which may be drawn laterally to flare the nostril.

Two layers of muscle act to move the cartilages (Evans 1993). The most superficial is the *levator nasolabialis*, which descends from its origin in the subcutaneous fibrous tissue along the dorsal midline of the nose to attach on the nasal cartilages. A deeper and thicker sheet of muscle, the *maxillonasolabialis*, originates in the connective tissue ventral to the eye and passes rostrally to insert on the cartilages. Between them, these muscles can pull the outer margins of the nostril dorsally and laterally.

The region occupied by the planum, cartilages, and muscles is entirely made up of nonbony tissue, and it can be readily manipulated from side to side in the living animal. For this reason, the region of the nose rostral to the premaxilla bone is sometimes called the *movable portion*. This region is also clearly distinguishable on radiographs (Figure 1.5a).

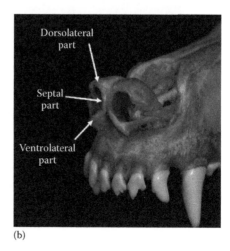

(a)   (b)

FIGURE 1.6   (a) The nasal planum of a dog. (b) Preserved specimen of the nasal cartilages of the dog.

VESTIBULE AND VOMERONASAL ORGAN

Once through the nares, air enters the *vestibule*. Unlike the equivalent region in humans, the canine vestibule is not entirely empty as it contains a rostral extension of some of the bony/membranous scrolls that fill the more caudal parts of the nasal cavity. For obvious reasons, the vestibule is a common site for foreign bodies to become lodged, especially in nasally inquisitive dogs.

Each side of the vestibule contains the egress of two ducts that convey the serous fluid that bathes the internal epithelium of the vestibule and also moisten the nasal planum. The first of these is the opening of the previously mentioned nasolacrimal duct, which drains tears from the medial aspect of the eye. Tears drain from the tear film on the anterior surface of the eyeball into two small holes, or *puncta*, one in the upper and one in the lower eyelid. The tears then drain through dorsal and ventral *canaliculi* into the *nasolacrimal sac*. From here, the epithelium-lined tube of the nasolacrimal duct, possibly homologous to the nasal tube of bony fish, passes through a bony canal in the maxilla bone to discharge into the vestibule of the nose. The function of the nasolacrimal system becomes clear when it becomes blocked, leading to tear overflow from the eye. Also, in healthy animals, dye introduced onto the surface of the eye is soon evident in the nostril on the same side.

The other duct draining into each side of the vestibule is the duct of the *lateral nasal gland*. This consists of secretory tissue, which also discharges a watery fluid into the vestibule. It is believed that this fluid is secreted to promote evaporative cooling (Blatt et al. 1972) and thus may be considered to be the nasal equivalent of panting.

On the ventral aspect of the vestibule lie the paired left and right *vomeronasal organs* (or *accessory olfactory organs* or *Jacobson's organs*). The vomeronasal organ is an additional site of odor detection present in many mammals and other vertebrates, but probably only present in vestigial form during embryonic life in humans. It has a different cellular morphology from the main olfactory epithelium of the nose and utilizes a different set of olfactory receptor genes. It has separate nervous connections to the brain and is possibly more involved in the detection of reproduction-related pheromones than the main olfactory organ. It has even been suggested that "vomerolfaction"—the detection of "vomodors"—should be dignified with its own terminology (Cooper and Burghardt 1990).

The canine vomeronasal organs each connect to both the nasal and the oral cavities, via the *incisive or nasopalatine duct*. This thin, membrane-lined tube passes through the hard palate via the much wider bony *palatine fissure* in the premaxilla bone (Figure 1.3), and its oral opening is often visible as a tiny slit on the lateral rim of the *incisive papilla*, a small mound of epithelium immediately caudal to the upper incisor teeth.

Immediately dorsal to the palate, a long, thin, blind-ending tube passes caudally from each nasopalatine duct. Cradled ventrally in two tiny troughs of cartilage, and sheltered by the overhanging laminae of the vomer bone dorsally, it is these paired left and right tubes that contain the vomeronasal sensory epithelium (Figure 1.7a). The two organs each give rise to the tiny fibers of the *vomeronasal component of the olfactory nerve*, which pass caudally in the nasal septum and converge immediately before passing through the ethmoid bone into the cranium and the *vomeronasal parts of the olfactory bulbs* of the brain.

Although dogs undoubtedly possess a well-developed sense of vomerolfaction, they make less dramatic facial expressions when drawing air into their vomeronasal organs than many species. These expressions are often called the *flehmen reaction* and are seen mainly in males. In horses, they entail dramatic upward curling of the lip, and in cats, a gawping open-mouthed facial expression.

NASAL CAVITIES AND PARANASAL SINUSES

Having passed through the vestibule, air is then conveyed into the central region of the nasal cavities, which are largely filled with elaborate scrolls of bone and cartilage covered with nonolfactory respiratory epithelium—called either *turbinates* or *conchae*. The bony cores of these scrolls are evident when viewed through the nasal opening of a canine skull (Figure 1.4a), but in life, they are extended by cartilage and thickened by a surface layer of pink respiratory epithelium.

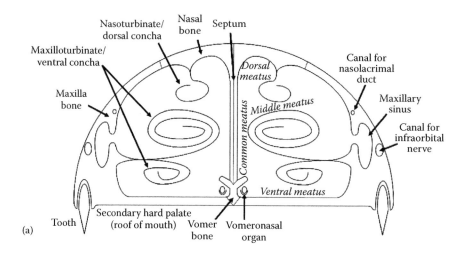

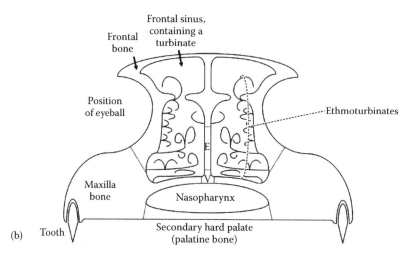

FIGURE 1.7 Schematic cross sections of the bony canine nasal cavities at (a) the level of the nonsensory nasal (dorsal) and maxillary (ventral) turbinates, and (b) the level of the sensory ethmoturbinates. E, ethmoid bone; V, vomer bone.

The dramatic folds and convolutions of the nasal turbinates have long been suggested to play a role in humidifying air on its way to the lower respiratory tract, and indeed, their complexity does appear to be increased in species that inhabit cold environments (Green et al. 2012). However, dogs can breathe through their mouths for long periods without any apparent ill effect, suggesting that the turbinates may have other roles. One likely possibility is that they filter out particulate matter from inspired air, as it adheres to the wet mucous layer that coats the turbinates. Another possibility is that they reduce water loss in cold environments. According to this theory, the turbinates are cooled as inspired air streams past. Then, as expired air at body temperature and saturated with water in the lungs passes over them in the opposite direction, the chilled turbinates cause a large proportion of the water vapor to recondense before it is lost into the atmosphere.

On each side of the rostral part of the canine nose (Figures 1.7a and 1.8), there are two turbinate scrolls. Ventrally lies the larger and more elaborate *maxilloturbinate* or *ventral concha*, which is an ingrowth of the maxilla bone. Dorsally, the smaller and simpler *nasoturbinate* or *dorsal concha* is suspended as a downgrowth of the nasal bone. As well as the intricate set of tiny airways between the individual folds of the turbinates, larger airspaces exist between these turbinates. These are the

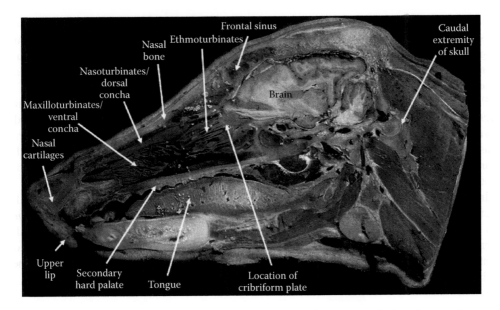

Frontal sinus
Ethmoturbinates
Nasal bone
Nasoturbinates/ dorsal concha
Maxilloturbinates/ ventral concha
Nasal cartilages
Caudal extremity of skull
Brain
Upper lip
Secondary hard palate
Tongue
Location of cribriform plate

FIGURE 1.8   A preserved canine head sectioned approximately in the midline.

ventral meatus between the palate and the ventral concha, the *middle meatus* between the ventral and dorsal conchae, the small *dorsal meatus* between the dorsal concha and the roof of the nasal cavity, and the *common meatus* between both conchae and the nasal septum.

Air flows through all the meati, but each has a particular role—much of the air destined for the lungs flows through the ventral and common meati, most of the air destined for the olfactory sensory cells passes through the common and middle meati, and the dorsal and middle meati represent the route by which air can reach the sinuses. Indeed, animals may consciously control the flow and destination of inhaled air. Much of the time, flow is predominantly laminar and passes through the ventral meatus into the lungs, but when dogs sniff, turbulent eddies of air are thought to be wafted more dorsally toward the olfactory epithelium.

In this central portion of the nose, another structure arises from the lateral aspect of the nasal cavity. The bilateral *maxillary sinuses* form as lateral air-filled outpouchings of the nasal cavity, which invade into the left and right maxilla bones (Negus 1958). Thus, these airspaces are largely surrounded by bone coated on its internal surface by respiratory epithelium similar to that seen in the rest of the nose. They open out into the nasal cavity via *nasomaxillary openings*. The bony separation of the maxillary sinuses from the nasal chambers is limited and appears so on radiographs—this has occasionally led to the sinuses being called the *maxillary recesses*, rather than the more discrete-sounding *sinuses*. However, in life, folds of nasal epithelium do partition these sinuses almost completely from the nasal cavity, and the nasomaxillary openings are quite small—which is why they can be clearly seen on MRI (Figure 1.5b).

The other *paranasal sinuses* in the dog are the more obvious *frontal sinuses*, which grow as paired bilateral dorsal diverticula of the more caudal region of the nasal cavities (Figures 1.7b and 1.8). They fill much of the volume of the frontal bones in the region between the eye sockets and are readily visible in many radiographic views, including the lateral (Figure 1.5a). Gentle percussion of a dog's head in this region elicits a humorously resonant sound, and these sinuses form a large structural barrier between the brain and the outside world. The frontal sinuses are occasionally fractured by high-energy impacts but usually heal well. In dogs, however, they are prone to infection by the fungus *Aspergillus*, which presumably gains access via the narrow *nasofrontal openings*.

The maxillary and frontal sinuses start to develop before birth, but only by skeletal maturity do they develop to their full extent, and thus, they are some of the latest-maturing anatomical structures in the entire body. The functions of the paranasal sinuses remain unclear, and many of the suggested roles are unconvincing, because they could just as well be achieved by solid soft tissues. The author suggests that the sinuses exist primarily to lighten the head—allowing bony sheets and struts to strengthen the skull without adding much additional weight. A minor additional role in creating resonant chambers for vocalizations is, however, possible.

Passing caudally into the caudal compartment of the nasal cavities, the ventral concha diminishes in size, leaving space for the hollow *nasopharynx* to convey air caudoventrally toward the larynx, trachea, and lungs (Figures 1.7b and 1.8). Conversely, the dorsal concha widens and transitions from the nasal to the ethmoid bone. As well as the cribriform plate previously described, the ethmoid bone contributes the most caudal parts of the nasal septum, and thrusts a complex array of tightly folded *ethmoturbinates* rostrally into the nasal cavity.

In dogs, there are usually 11 of these ethmoturbinate scrolls on each side, and they carry a large fraction of the olfactory sensory epithelium. They are sometimes subclassified into *endoturbinates* and *ectoturbinates*, but this refers to their spatial arrangement rather than to any fundamental differences in structure or function. Some of the ethmoturbinate scrolls even extend dorsally into the frontal sinuses. All in all, the ethmoid bones have perhaps the most complex shape of any bones in the body, and a hint of this complexity is sometimes evident on radiographs (Figure 1.5a).

OLFACTORY RECEPTOR CELLS AND THEIR CONNECTIONS TO THE BRAIN

The neurophysiology of smell is discussed elsewhere in this volume (see Chapter 2), but it is worth identifying some particular structural features of the structure and central connections of the olfactory epithelium.

As a macrosmatic species, the dog possesses an extensive olfactory epithelium, which covers much of the surface area of the ethmoturbinates but also encroaches into parts of the septum, roof, and wall of the nasal cavity. In fresh postmortem specimens, the olfactory epithelium may sometimes be discerned from surrounding normal respiratory epithelium by a slightly darker brown color, although the margins between the two epithelia are never sharp.

The sensory epithelium contains at least three cell types. The first of these is the *basal cell*, a stem cell that can divide, and its daughter cells differentiate into one of the other cell types of the epithelium (Leung et al. 2007). The second type is the *sustentacular cell*, which supports and nutrifies the sensory receptor cells and also secretes the watery fluid film in which odorants must be dissolved prior to detection.

The third cell type is the sensory *olfactory cell* itself. This takes the form of a *bipolar neuron*, with a central body or *soma* nestling amongst the sustentacular cells, and two thin cellular processes. The first, shorter process extends to the surface of the epithelium, where it bears between 10 and 30 hairlike projections, the *cilia*, and the olfactory receptor molecules themselves. The second, much longer process is the nerve fiber, or *axon*, which transmits electrical signals caudally to the olfactory bulbs of the brain.

Like the rest of the nasal cavities, the olfactory epithelium also contains nerve endings sensitive to touch and chemical irritation. However, these sensory modalities are not detected or perceived via the same anatomical pathways as smell itself, and indeed, these nerve impulses are not carried to the brain via the olfactory nerve. Instead, they travel via the nerve that conveys touch and chemical irritation from most of the face, mouth, and eyes, the fifth cranial nerve, or *trigeminal nerve* (for example, an extremely large branch of the trigeminal, the *infraorbital nerve* (Figure 1.7a), returns sensory information from the external surface of the canine nose).

Mammals are normally said to have 12 pairs of *cranial nerves*—peripheral nerves that directly exit the brain itself rather than the spinal cord, numbered I to XII. Because the olfactory nerve enters the brain rostrally to all the others, it is termed cranial nerve I. However, the olfactory nerve is an atypical cranial nerve in some ways. First, it does not enter the cranium as a single nerve trunk but, rather, as hundreds of small nerves, each representing a bundle of many olfactory cell axons, which passes through one of the many perforations in the cribriform plate of the mesethmoid bone. Second, the boundary between the peripheral and central nervous system, which is moderately easy to define in most peripheral nerves, is not at all clear in the olfactory system. Third, the olfactory nerve also contains a discrete component containing the longer axons formed by the olfactory cells of the vomeronasal organ.

The most remarkable feature of the olfactory nerve is that, uniquely among nervous system tissues, it continually spontaneously regenerates itself and is also capable of extensive repair following injury. Olfactory cells have a limited life span of probably no more than a few months, and they are continually replaced by proliferation and differentiation of basal cells. Each new olfactory cell must then grow a new axon along the olfactory nerve, navigate through the cribriform plate into the skull, and establish *de novo* connections with the neurons of the olfactory bulb (Roet and Verhaagen 2014).

So unusual is this continual regeneration and reconnection of a nervous structure that it has attracted a great deal of interest from researchers seeking to encourage regeneration of neurons following injury to the spinal cord or brain. It is possible that these remarkable regenerative abilities are supported by *glial cells* along the route of the olfactory nerve bundles. The olfactory nerve does not possess the glial cells that invest the axons of many nerve cell types with their insulating myelin sheath, but a special glial cell type is present—the *olfactory ensheathing cell*. Studies are underway to determine whether grafting these cells from the olfactory system to sites of spinal cord damage may encourage nerve regeneration in neuron types that are usually unwilling to regrow.

As described elsewhere, a great deal of olfactory processing takes place in the olfactory bulbs. These are much larger in the dog than in humans (Figure 1.9), and they fill most of the domed cavity

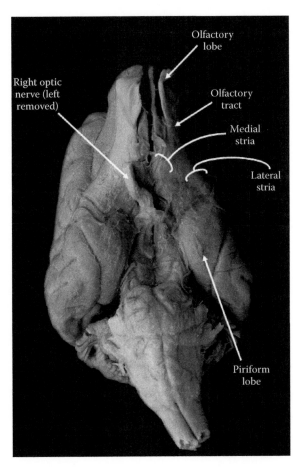

FIGURE 1.9 Ventral view of the canine brain, showing structures associated with the central olfactory pathways.

directly caudal to the cribriform plate. From the olfactory bulbs, sensory impulses spread throughout the brain, where they influence many aspects of behavior—especially food-seeking and reproductive behavior. However, as much of the content of this book makes clear, dogs can be trained to transmit their olfactory information to humans.

The gross structure of the central olfactory pathways may be discerned on the underside of the canine brain (Figure 1.9). From the olfactory bulbs, sensory information passes caudally through the large left and right *olfactory tracts*. Each if these then divides into the medial and lateral *olfactory stria*, which convey impulses to the opposite and same side of the brain, respectively. A major connection of the lateral stria is with the pear-shaped or *piriform cortex*, where yet more information processing takes place.

From all these structures, nerve fiber bundles ramify throughout the brain, including centers for conscious perception of smell. The sheer size of the olfactory system in dogs is evidence of how the structure of the huge mammalian forebrain was originally based on the importance and complexity of the olfactory system. Still today, the olfactory system has an unusual degree of *direct access* to higher processing centers in the forebrain, and it has been suggested that this is why smells may so readily induce strange perceptual phenomena such as déjà vu. It remains unclear, however, to what extent dogs' reliance on their impressive olfactory system means that they are continually perplexed by half-remembered echoes of their odorous past.

2 Wiring of the Olfactory System and the Functional Role of Neurons and Glia during Lifelong Turnover

Konstantin Wewetzer, Mohamed Omar,
Patricia Kammeyer, and Gudrun Brandes

The acuity and sensitivity of canine olfaction is widely recognized. To understand the basic principles underlying olfaction, it is crucial to identify the specific morphological, molecular, and physiological features of olfactory sensory neurons (OSNs; see Box 2.1 for abbreviations) and their neural connections along the olfactory pathway. One of the most intriguing aspects about the olfactory system is that the wiring of its neurons is not established early in development once and for all but is subject to lifelong turnover (Graziadei and Monti Graziadei 1985; Astic and Saucier 2001; Brann and Firestein 2014). This is in contrast to other regions of the nervous system and implies that during normal function, olfactory neurons are regularly lost by cell death and replaced by newly produced neurons (neurogenesis). Thus, understanding olfaction is not only a matter of molecular biology and physiology of an established neural network but includes also the analysis of processes that ensure adequate numbers and proper integration of adult-born neurons (Box 2.1).

Olfaction is mediated by OSNs that are localized in distinct regions of the olfactory system (Breer et al. 2006). OSN axon bundles are ensheathed by olfactory ensheathing cells (OECs), which vary with regard to localization and neural connections with the central nervous system (CNS). In dogs, OSNs are confined to the main olfactory epithelium (MOE) and the vomeronasal organ (VNO) (Read 1908; Dennis et al. 2003; Bock et al. 2009; Salazar et al. 2013), while they are absent from the septal organ and the Gruneberg ganglion characterized in mice (Gruneberg 1973; Fleischer et al. 2006; Barrios et al. 2014). The size of the MOE, which is localized along the ethmoturbinates and the septum, is dependent on dog breed (Read 1908; Wieland 1938; Muller 1955). The VNO, which is localized bilaterally in the nasal septum, is involved in pheromone detection (Barrios et al. 2014). OSN axons are connected with second-order neurons in the main olfactory bulb (MOB) via spherical synaptic relays called glomeruli, while vomeronasal neurons (VNs) terminate in the accessory olfactory bulb (AOB) (Nakajima et al. 1998). In dogs, the AOB is small and variable in size and located on the medial surface of the MOB (Salazar et al. 1992; Nakajima et al. 1998).

The olfactory system invokes an added level of complexity for understanding organization since it continuously regenerates at both the peripheral and central levels. This is much the same as the turnover in epithelia of the skin and intestine. However, distinct OSNs and VNs display highly specific neural connections with the MOB and AOB, respectively (Mombaerts 1996). Thus, replacement of these cells is much more complex than in other nonneuronal tissues. Neurogenesis in the adult olfactory system occurs both in the MOE/VNO of the nasal cavity and in the subventricular zone (SVZ), an area close to the brain's inner cavities, the ventricles (Altman 1969; Barber and Raisman 1978; Graziadei and Monti Graziadei 1985; Calof et al. 1996).

Whereas basal cells of the adult MOE and VNO continuously generate neurons that send their axons across the meninges into the brain, cells emerging in the SVZ differentiate into interneurons

BOX 2.1   COMMON ABBREVIATIONS IN CANINE NEUROBIOLOGY

AOB	accessory olfactory bulb
CNPase	2′,3′-cyclic nucleotide 3′-phosphodiesterase
CNS	central nervous system
GAP-43	growth-associated protein-43
HNK-1	human natural killer-1
MOB	main olfactory bulb
MOE	main olfactory epithelium
NCAM	neural cell adhesion molecule
OEC	olfactory ensheathing cell
ONF	olfactory nerve fibroblast
ONL	olfactory nerve layer
OR	olfactory receptor
OSN	olfactory sensory neuron
PNS	peripheral nervous system
PSA-NCAM	polysialic acid–coupled neural cell adhesion molecule
p75^{NTR}	neurotrophin receptor
RAG	regeneration-associated gene
SCI	spinal cord injury
SVZ	subventricular zone
TrkB	tyrosine receptor kinase B
VN	vomeronasal neurons
VNO	vomeronasal organ
VR	vomeronasal receptor

following migration into the MOB via the rostral migratory stream (Lois et al. 1996; Luskin 1998). While these events were originally recognized in rodents, several studies imply that they can be extrapolated to canines and humans (Kornack and Rakic 2001; Pencea et al. 2001; Bock et al. 2009; Malik et al. 2012). If there is continuous turnover of neurons, this means not only that neurons with specific connections get lost but also that newly produced neurons have to be integrated into the network without interfering with olfaction.

Taken together, the wiring of the olfactory system is not only remarkably complex, but it is also continuously rebuilt in the adult. In this chapter, we will summarize the basic processes underlying olfaction and focus on the events associated with neuronal turnover. The main emphasis is on the functional role of OSNs and OECs during these processes. Due to space limitations and the relatively simple cellular structure of the MOE, we will concentrate on the peripheral olfactory system, including OSNs and their axonal projections into the MOB (Schwob 2002). First will be an introduction to the morphology, localization, and physiology of OSNs and OECs during olfaction, and second will be a critical discussion of current concepts regarding the functional role of OSNs and OECs during neurogenesis, axonal growth into the brain, convergence onto specific glomeruli (glomerular targeting), and the relevance of OSN–OEC interactions. Finally, putative implications of the continuous OSN turnover for the treatment of CNS injury are addressed.

It is well established that olfaction is highly specialized in dogs, but its basic mechanisms are similar in different species. Despite the focus on the canine olfactory system, we will refer to rodent and human data, if necessary. This is due to the fact that the studies on rodents still outnumber those on dogs and that canine cells are more closely related to humans than rodents (Techangamsuwan et al. 2008; Wewetzer et al. 2011). This bears particular relevance for translational approaches aiming to transfer basic research into clinical practice (Rubio et al. 2008; Radtke and Wewetzer 2009).

CELLULAR CONSTITUENTS OF THE OLFACTORY SYSTEM

The main olfactory system consists of the olfactory mucosa and bulb. The mucosa contains the respiratory epithelium and the olfactory epithelium, which contains neurons expressing the olfactory receptors (ORs). The MOE is localized along the ethmoturbinates and the septum (Read 1908; Figueres-Onate et al. 2014) and covers an area of about 70–170 cm² depending on dog breed (Figure 2.1) (Wieland 1938; Muller 1955), compared to about 5 cm² in humans (Buck and Bargmann 2013). In dogs, the distribution of these two epithelia can overlap, and OSNs may also be found in the frontal and nasal sinus (Skinner et al. 2005). Macroscopically, the olfactory epithelium can be differentiated from the respiratory epithelium by its yellow color, which is due to pigmentation of the supporting cells. The major cellular elements of the peripheral olfactory system are OSNs of the MOE and OECs that ensheath bundles of OSN axons from the lamina propria of the MOE to the MOB.

OLFACTORY SENSORY NEURONS OF THE MAIN OLFACTORY
EPITHELIUM ARE CRUCIAL FOR ODOR PERCEPTION

OSNs are bipolar nerve cells with a single dendrite that extends from the apical end and gives rise to numerous thin cilia that protrude into the mucus that coats the nasal cavity (Schwob 2002; McEwen et al. 2008; Garcia-Lopez et al. 2010). The cilia not only have specific G protein–coupled ORs but also contain the transduction machinery required to amplify the sensory signals and transform them into electrical signals (McEwen et al. 2008; Buck and Bargmann 2013). OSNs reside in

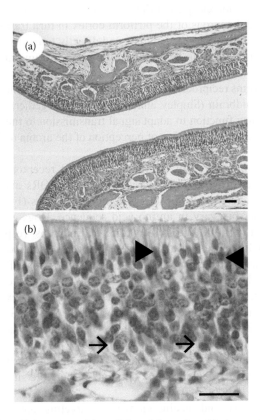

FIGURE 2.1 (a and b) The cellular composition of the adult canine olfactory epithelium after staining with hematoxylin/eosin. From basal to apical, there are basal stem cells (b, arrows), olfactory sensory neurons (OSNs), and supporting cells (b, arrow heads). Scale bar in a = 100 μm and in b = 20 μm.

a pseudostratified neuroepithelium that also contains microvillar cells, supporting cells, and basal cells (Figure 2.1a,b). Microvillar type I and II cells display a pyriform soma and are located in the apical third of the epithelium. They are 10–20 times less abundant than neurons. Whereas type I cells may be involved in chemoreception, the function of type II cells is unclear (Asan and Drenckhahn 2005).

Supporting cells are of cylindrical shape and span the entire width of the epithelium (Weiler and Farbman 1998). The oval nuclei of these reside in a single and narrow row in the apical region of the epithelium (Figure 2.1b). Besides stabilization of the epithelium, supporting cells may also be involved in chemoreception and phagocytosis of OSNs undergoing programmed cell death (Suzuki et al. 1996). Finally, there are stem cells, which in dogs and humans (but not in rodents) consist of a single-cell population, which is localized directly adjacent to the basal lamina (Figure 2.1b) (Hahn et al. 2005; Skinner et al. 2005). OSNs that make up 60–70% of the total cell number arise from basal cells and become shifted to the middle third of the epithelium during maturation discussed below.

After penetrating the basal lamina, OSN axons are grouped by 10–100 into fibrils that are ensheathed by OECs and project to glomeruli localized directly beneath the olfactory nerve layer (ONL). Projection of OSN axons into the glomeruli is characterized by a striking degree of convergence, which results in an approximately 100-fold decrease in the number of neurons transmitting signals (Mombaerts 1996; Buck and Bargmann 2013). OSNs are synaptically coupled to three types of neurons: mitral and tufted neurons are projection neurons connected with the olfactory cortex, while periglomerular cells are interneurons that may play a role in signal modulation (Shipley and Ennis 1996; Shepherd et al. 2011; Buck and Bargmann 2013). Signals are transmitted mainly to the olfactory cortex, which includes the anterior olfactory nucleus, the anterior and posterior nuclei of the amygdala, the olfactory tubercle, part of the entorhinal cortex, and the piriform cortex (Shipley and Ennis 1996). Pyramidal neurons of the piriform cortex in turn transmit the information indirectly to the orbitofrontal cortex via the thalamus and directly to the frontal cortex. The pathways to higher cortical areas are thought to be important for odor discrimination (Buck and Bargmann 2013).

The olfactory cortex forms reciprocal connections with the MOB, which also receives input from the basal forebrain and midbrain (Shipley and Ennis 1996). Together, these connections control output of the MOB and may function to adapt signal transmission to the physiological state of the animal. This includes, e.g., the heightening of perception of the aroma of foods when the animal is hungry.

Olfaction is based upon binding of odorants to odorant receptors (ORs) and vomeronasal receptors (VRs), expressed by OSNs and VNs, respectively. ORs and VRs have seven transmembrane domains characteristic of G protein–coupled receptors (Fleischer et al. 2009). They are related to one another but vary in amino acid sequence. Dogs express approximately 800 different ORs, compared to 1,000 and 300 in mice and humans, respectively (Buck and Axel 1991; Olender et al. 2004; Quignon et al. 2012). Since each OSN expresses only one OR, there are about as many distinct OSNs as there are ORs. OSNs of a given OR specificity are randomly dispersed in zones of the MOE, but the projection of axons to the glomeruli in the MOB is highly specific (Strotmann et al. 1994b; Strotmann and Breer 2006). OSNs expressing the same receptor converge onto the same glomeruli in the MOB (Mombaerts 1996; Strotmann and Breer 2006; Buck and Bargmann 2013). Studies in mice have shown that the axons from one epithelial zone converge onto two glomeruli on each side of the olfactory bulb and that the position of these glomeruli is mirror-imaged in the contralateral MOB (Buck and Bargmann 2013). The pattern of glomerular activation elicited by individual odorants is therefore similar in all individuals and bilaterally symmetrical in the two MOBs.

Convergence of OSN axons and specific glomerular targeting may optimize both detection of odorants present at low concentrations and the maintenance of neural maps for certain odorants in the brain over time. The two families of VR genes characterized in rodents do not seem to play a significant role in dog olfaction (Quignon et al. 2012). Whereas the VR2 gene family is completely degenerated in dogs, the VR1 gene family comprises only 10 members, compared to about 100 in rodents (Young and Trask 2007; Quignon et al. 2012). Compared to the MOB, the AOB contains a higher number of glomeruli, but the projection pattern is less stereotyped.

Binding of an odorant causes ORs to trigger the release of a guanosine triphosphate (GTP)–coupled G protein subunit and stimulates adenylyl cyclase III to increase production of cyclic adenosine monophosphate (cAMP), which in turn causes cation influx and a change in membrane potential of the ciliary membrane. Each odorant is recognized by a unique combination of different receptors because each OR that is exclusively expressed by a given OSN binds to several odorants (Buck and Bargmann 2013). Each odorant is therefore detected by a unique constellation of receptors that elicits a distinctive pattern of signals transmitted to the brain. The combinatorial coding of odorants greatly expands the discriminatory power of the olfactory system. The adaptation to odorants upon continuous exposure is based in part on modulation of the cyclic nucleotide-gated ion channel (Buck and Bargmann 2013).

OLFACTORY ENSHEATHING CELLS CLOSELY ASSOCIATE WITH AXONS IN THE LAMINA PROPRIA, OLFACTORY NERVES, AND OLFACTORY BULB

OECs are the nonmyelinating glial cells of the peripheral olfactory system that, like Schwann cells, arise from the neural crest (Forni and Wray 2012). Since OECs intimately associate with OSN axons from the lamina propria of the MOE to the glomeruli of the MOB (Ramon-Cueto and Avila 1998; Wewetzer et al. 2002), they are natural residents of both the peripheral nervous system (PNS) and CNS. Detailed ultrastructural studies in rodents revealed the morphological phenotype of OECs (Raisman 1985; Doucette 1991, 1993; Field et al. 2003); their functional role during olfaction and OSN turnover, however, is poorly understood. This is also true for the regenerative capacity of OECs after transplantation into the lesioned CNS (Franklin and Barnett 1997; Santos-Benito and Ramon-Cueto 2003; Radtke and Wewetzer 2009).

In rodents, OECs of the olfactory nerves generate fine cytoplasmic processes that encircle bundles of 10–100 OSN axons. The simplest fascicles of the lamina propria consist of a group of OSN axons ensheathed by a single OEC enclosed in a single basal lamina (Field et al. 2003). Further distally, the packing density of axons is increased, and several fascicles associate with larger nerves. Rodent OECs have an ovoid nucleus, which is generally located at the edge of the bundle. It was suggested that OECs may have two distinct surfaces: the inner surface encircles axon bundles (adaxonal), and the outer surface faces the basal lamina (abaxonal) surrounded by collagen fibers and covered by elongated olfactory nerve fibroblasts (ONFs) (Field et al. 2003). Due to the lack of ultrastructural evidence in the dog, it is not clear whether these data can be directly extrapolated. Light-microscopic visualization of canine OECs using 2′,3′-cyclic nucleotide 3′-phosphodiesterase (CNPase) as a marker, however, argues for a starlike appearance of OECs with a centrally located nucleus surrounded by flat fibroblast-like cells (Figure 2.2d) (Omar et al. 2011). Thus, OSN axons are only separated from the surrounding fibroblasts by a thin basal lamina, implying that canine OECs may lack two functionally distinct surfaces (Omar et al. 2011).

Upon entry of OSN axons into the MOB, the basal lamina surrounding the fascicles becomes continuous with the glia limitans (Doucette 1990). Thus, the basal lamina investment of peripheral olfactory fascicles begins where the olfactory axons exit the olfactory epithelium and ends where it coalesces with the glia limitans of the MOB. The structural features of the PNS–CNS transition zone were suggested to facilitate lifelong entry of OSN axons into the brain (Raisman 1985). Olfactory fascicles in the outer ONL are thought to be separated by interfascicular astrocytes and OECs (Barnett and Chang 2004). Several studies in rodents reported on the heterogeneity of the ONL based upon the differential distribution of molecular markers in the outer and inner part of the ONL (Franceschini and Barnett 1996; Barnett and Franceschini 1999; Au et al. 2002; Wewetzer et al. 2005; Brandes et al. 2011). Since the ONL is an area crucial for defasciculation of olfactory nerve fascicles, these data may be of functional relevance.

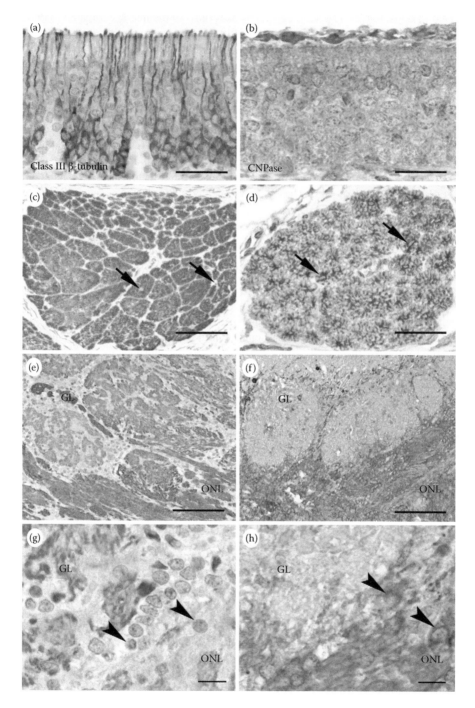

FIGURE 2.2 Visualization of adult canine olfactory sensory neurons (OSNs) and olfactory ensheathing cells (OECs) in (a–d) the olfactory mucosa and (e–h) the main olfactory bulb (MOB) using immunohistochemical detection of class III β-tubulin (a, c, e, and g) and 2′,3′-cyclic nucleotide 3′-phosphodiesterase (CNPase; b, d, f, and h). Class III β-tubulin is strictly confined to OSNs in the MOE (a), the olfactory nerve (c), and the olfactory nerve layer (ONL; e) OECs; c, arrows; g, arrows) visualized by CNPase immunoreactivity (arrows in d and h). OECs but not OSN axons are excluded from the glomeruli (GL; e and f). Scale bar in b = 50 μm (applies to a, b, g, and h). Scale bar in d = 100 μm (applies to c and d). Scale bar in f = 200 μm (applies to e and f).

Contrary to the morphological phenotype of OECs, little is known about their biology and functional role during olfaction. This is in striking contrast to the closely related Schwann cell. An activity shared by both OECs and Schwann cells is related to phagocytosis. Whereas Schwann cells are thought to participate in myelin clearance after peripheral nerve lesion (Fernandez-Valle et al. 1995), OECs may be involved in the removal of OSNs undergoing programmed cell death during development and in the adult (Wewetzer et al. 2005; Nazareth et al. 2015). Based on the capacity to ingest bacteria and viruses (Vincent et al. 2005b; Leung et al. 2008), OECs were suggested to be part of the innate immune response (Harris et al. 2009). Phagocytosis by OECs and the limited life span of OSNs may therefore be interpreted as an evolutionary strategy to prevent or minimize entry and spreading of neurotropic viruses (Detje et al. 2009; Kalinke et al. 2011).

It is a dogma in neurobiology that the function of neurons and Schwann cells is dependent on cell–cell interactions between both cell types. Whereas molecules such as neuregulin provided by axonal processes induce phenotypic differentiation of Schwann cells (Taveggia et al. 2005), Schwann cells were shown to preserve axonal integrity, slow axonal transport, neurofilament phosphorylation, and density (de Waegh and Brady 1990; de Waegh et al. 1992; Suter et al. 1993; Jessen and Mirsky 2002). Contrary to this, very little is known about reciprocal OSN–OEC interactions.

Although there is evidence that OSNs affect the phenotype of OECs (Wewetzer and Brandes 2006), it is not clear whether OECs exert similar influences on OSN axons nor if there is functional diversity among OECs from distinct sources, including the olfactory mucosa, the olfactory nerves, and the MOB (Au and Roskams 2003; Ramer et al. 2004). This may be due to several reasons. First, OECs display a complex morphology, which impedes light-microscopic immunolocalization of antigens. Sulfatide, for example, previously used as a specific cell surface marker for OECs on the basis of light-microscopic evidence (Franceschini and Barnett 1996), was subsequently detected on the surface of OSN axons using electron microscopy (Wewetzer et al. 2005). Second, there is a lack of molecular markers suitable for specific *in situ* detection of OECs. The neurotrophin receptor p75 (p75^{NTR}), for example, which serves as a marker for adult nonmyelinating Schwann cells *in situ*, is expressed by rodent and canine OECs only early in development and prior to downregulation in the adult stage (Franceschini and Barnett 1996; Wewetzer et al. 2005; Bock et al. 2007; Omar et al. 2011). Dissociation and culturing of OECs induces upregulation of p75^{NTR} in OECs (Wewetzer et al. 2005; Bock et al. 2007; Brandes et al. 2011), implying that cell–cell interactions crucially control p75^{NTR} expression *in situ* (Wewetzer and Brandes 2006). This idea is underscored by the finding that OSN–OEC interactions *in vitro* can block p75^{NTR} in OECs (Ramon-Cueto et al. 1993). Recently, it was noted that marker expression may be species specific. The enzyme CNPase, for example, is expressed by canine but not rat OECs *in situ* (Omar et al. 2011).

FUNCTIONAL ROLE OF OLFACTORY SENSORY NEURONS AND OLFACTORY ENSHEATHING CELLS DURING LIFELONG NEURAL TURNOVER

Maintenance of the adult olfactory system includes regular neuronal turnover. Thus, neuron production and cell death, axonal growth, and glomerular targeting have to be organized in a way to ensure proper production and integration of the novel neurons into an existing functional network. This includes interactions between OSNs and OECs as the major cellular elements of the olfactory nerves that are in close contact with each other. Despite continuous replacement of OSNs during adult life, the arrangement of inputs in the MOB remains stable, and therefore, its neural code for an odorant is maintained over time. This assures that an odorant previously encountered can be recognized years later (Strotmann and Breer 2006).

NEUROGENESIS AND PROGRAMMED CELL DEATH OF OLFACTORY SENSORY NEURONS

OSNs have a limited life span of between 4 and 8 weeks in rodents, and the total number of OSNs results from the balance between neuron production and loss (Robinson et al. 2002; Suzuki 2007). Distinct stages of OSN development occupy specific positions in the epithelium and display specific morphological features. Furthermore, they express stage-specific molecular markers that can be used for selective visualization (Bock et al. 2009). Although the majority of data refer to the rodent model, recent investigations in canines are confirmation of the main findings (Bock et al. 2007, 2009; Omar et al. 2011, 2013).

OSNs arise from basal cells that form a single row of cells directly above the basal lamina (Figure 2.1b). During differentiation, OSN cell bodies are displaced to the middle third of the epithelium, where the bulk of mature neurons are found (Figure 2.2b) (Bock et al. 2009). These neurons contain large and round nuclei with prominent nucleoli and stain positive for the olfactory marker protein (OMP) (Bock et al. 2009) (Figure 2.1b). Expression of OMP, which is found in all OSNs independent of OR specificity, is not turned on until axons have reached the MOB and established functional contacts (Verhaagen et al. 1990). Newly generated OSNs are positive for the glycoepitope (human natural killer-1 [HNK-1]), while the marker for immature OSNs includes tyrosine receptor kinase B (TrkB), growth-associated protein-43 (GAP-43), neurogenin-1, and Neuro D (Verhaagen et al. 1989, 1990; Bock et al. 2009; Omar et al. 2011). It is of particular relevance to note that these markers are also expressed by other neurons during development and after lesion (Van der Zee et al. 1989).

OSNs expressing a given OR are confined to distinct zones of the MOE in which they are randomly distributed (Strotmann et al. 1994b; Breer et al. 2006). Moreover, the adult rat and canine MOE consists of patches of "active" and "quiescent" zones that differ in abundance of mature and immature OSNs (Graziadei and Graziadei 1979; Verhaagen et al. 1989; Bock et al. 2009). Areas rich in mature OSNs have been shown to display a lower activity of basal cell proliferation, while areas with an increased number of immature OSNs not only stained preferentially with anti-HNK-1 and anti-TrkB antibodies but also contained a higher number of proliferating basal cells (Bock et al. 2009).

Clarification of the mechanisms underlying neural turnover is relevant for providing explanations as to the evolutionary advantages of this process. The life span of OSNs can be experimentally increased by preventing environmental exposure (Farbman et al. 1988; Stahl et al. 1990). Naris occlusion decreases neuron turnover and progenitor cell division and stimulates expression of the mature OSN marker OMP (Brunjes 1994; Waguespack et al. 2005; Suh et al. 2006). These data from rodents are in agreement with studies in the dog that reported preferential localization of immature OSNs in the rostral part of the epithelium (Bock et al. 2009). OSNs localized in a rostral region may be affected more severely by the nasal airflow than cells of the caudal region (Craven et al. 2007; Bock et al. 2009).

Together, these data may imply that the limited life span and turnover of OSNs is related to their unique distribution. Contrary to other neurons, OSNs have direct contact with the outer world via their terminal knob, which is immersed in the olfactory mucus (McEwen et al. 2008). This may result in increased damage of neurons, which in turn triggers increased production of neurons. Another consequence of the direct exposure of OSNs to the external environment may be increased susceptibility to infection with microorganisms. Neurotropic viruses have been shown to use the olfactory pathway as an entry route for infection of the brain (Mori et al. 2002; Rudd et al. 2006; Harberts et al. 2011). The limited life span of OSNs and phagocytic capacity of OECs may limit virus spread along the olfactory pathway (Loseva et al. 2009).

Finally, neuron turnover has been related to the function of the olfactory system (Lazarini and Lledo 2011). The majority of the studies focused on the role of SVZ neurogenesis. Genetic or pharmacokinetic ablation of adult-born neurons was shown to impair contextual and spatial memory and to alter the circuitry of projection neurons (Imayoshi et al. 2008; Cummings et al. 2014). Moreover, continuous postnatal neurogenesis may contribute to flexible associative learning (Sakamoto et al. 2014). This implies that adult-born neurons are crucial for stabilizing a brain circuit that exhibits high levels of plasticity (Gheusi and Lledo 2014).

AXONAL GROWTH OF OLFACTORY SENSORY NEURONS INTO THE MAIN OLFACTORY BULB

OSNs arise outside the CNS in the MOE. A prerequisite for proper functional integration into the olfactory pathway is their synaptic communication with mitral and tufted projection neurons inside the MOB. OSN axons therefore have to cross the meninges and navigate inside the CNS to establish functional contacts. Except the olfactory system, nowhere in the body is there entry of axons into the adult CNS. Axons of dorsal root ganglion neurons regenerating after dorsal rhizotomy, for example, stop growth at the CNS–PNS transition zone (Ramer et al. 2000; McPhail et al. 2005). Thus, the question arises as to how the olfactory system manages to override these growth-inhibitory influences.

The widely held belief is that OECs specifically promote entry and navigation of OSN axons in the CNS (Raisman 1985; Ramon-Cueto and Valverde 1995; Franklin and Barnett 2000) and may therefore be suitable for the treatment of CNS injury (Nieto-Sampedro 2003; Santos-Benito and Ramon-Cueto 2003; Barnett and Riddell 2007). This idea was originally based on several observations. Grafting of peripheral nerves was used to bypass nonpermissive optic tract lesions (Aguayo et al. 1981; Bray et al. 1987). Moreover, Schwann cells, but not oligodendrocytes or purified preparations of CNS myelin, promoted neurite growth in tissue culture (Bixby et al. 1988; Caroni and Schwab 1993). The conclusion from these experiments was that PNS Schwann cells but not CNS oligodendrocytes were effective inducers of CNS regeneration. This idea was underscored by the identification of growth-inhibitory molecules expressed by CNS oligodendrocytes, including Nogo-A (Chen et al. 2000b; GrandPre et al. 2000). Since the olfactory system is the only site that harbors OECs and displays lifelong axon growth into the CNS, it was suggested that both phenomena are causally related and that OECs display a unique intrinsic regenerative capacity (Ramon-Cueto and Valverde 1995). However, it still remains to be shown that OECs have, in fact, a unique regenerative capacity not shared by other regeneration-promoting glial cells, such as Schwann cells (Radtke and Wewetzer 2009).

Although many *in vivo* studies have reported on regenerative effects of OECs, it is not clear whether these are significantly superior to Schwann cells (Radtke and Wewetzer 2009). Even more important is the fact that the basic concept of axonal growth underwent significant alteration. While in the past, it was generally assumed that the glial environment crucially defines growth permissiveness, it has now become apparent that the regenerative properties of neurons are different and defined by the expression of regeneration-associated genes (RAGs) (van Kesteren et al. 2011; Finelli et al. 2013; Mar et al. 2014). Distinct neuron populations not only express distinct patterns of RAGs, but their expression is also altered following establishment of synaptic connections, which may, at least in part, explain the loss of regenerative properties observed during maturation. The absence of a coordinated RAG response in addition to an inhibitory extracellular environment is now considered the major reason for the regenerative failure of CNS neurons (Finelli et al. 2013).

Based on these considerations, it is instructive to reconsider the concept of OEC-guided growth of ORN axons into the MOB. What makes the olfactory system unique is that axon growth both under normal conditions and after lesion is initiated by newly produced and immature OSNs. As discussed, these neurons express markers typical of immature neurons, including HNK-1 and GAP-43, and expression of these does not cease until establishment of functional contacts (Verhaagen et al. 1989, 1990). Thus, the unique feature of the olfactory system is the continuous production of immature neurons in the adult stage. That OSNs are characterized by a strong inherent capacity for axonal growth that is independent of target tissue and/or glial environment can be deduced from experiments that ablated the MOB in adult rodents (Graziadei et al. 1978; Graziadei and Samanen 1980). In the absence of the MOB, OSNs did not only enter that brain but also formed ectopic glomerular-like structures in the frontal lobe (Graziadei and Graziadei 1979; Graziadei and Samanen 1980). This is a striking confirmation of the idea that OSN axons have a pronounced inherent capacity to enter the CNS and to organize novel areas to form synaptic sites typical of the olfactory bulb. If a bulbectomy is carried out early in development in neonatal rats, not only are glomerular-like structures formed, but there is also axon growth into the anterior olfactory nucleus correlated with odor discrimination as detected by precision olfactometry (Slotnick et al. 2004). Taken together, lifelong growth of OSN axons into the CNS is more likely based on the continuous supply of immature OSNs rather than on the putative regenerative properties of OECs. The implications of these findings are discussed under "Lessons From the Olfactory System" below.

Convergence of Olfactory Sensory Neuron Axons onto Specific Glomeruli

In mammals, OSNs of a given OR specificity are randomly distributed within distinct areas of the MOE, while their axons specifically converge onto two or three glomeruli of the MOB (Strotmann et al. 1994b). This arrangement is unique to the olfactory system. In other sensory systems, such as the visual system, the topographic map is closely conserved from the periphery to the CNS by maintaining the spatial relationships between the axons along their course (Cummings and Belluscio 2008). OR specificity of OSN axons is determined prior to axonal growth and the establishment of functional contacts (Nedelec et al. 2005). Olfactory nerves close to the MOE therefore contain a heterogeneous mixture of OSN axons, while axon bundles close to the glomeruli are of the same OR specificity (St John et al. 2002; Strotmann and Breer 2006). Thus, axonal growth to specific glomeruli includes heterogeneous fasciculation, defasciculation of heterogeneous axon bundles, and sorting of OSN axons, followed by homotypic fasciculation to specific glomeruli (Nedelec et al. 2005).

Investigations into the underlying mechanisms, which were mainly carried out in the rodent model, suggest that this complex process is governed by a hierarchical system of recognition and guidance molecules (St John et al. 2002). It is well established that the initial steps of this process, which include heterogeneous fasciculation of OSN axons in the proximal olfactory nerves and entry of axons into the CNS, are independent of the target tissue (St John et al. 2003; Chehrehasa et al. 2005). As discussed, ablation of the MOB does not prevent OSN axons from entry into the CNS (Graziadei et al. 1978; Graziadei and Samanen 1980). Subsequent defasciculation of OSN axons and homotypic fasciculation are thought to be controlled by a variety of adhesive and repulsive signals, which also include ORs in addition to adhesion molecules and glycoconjugates (John and Key 2005). Several studies suggest that ORs may play a dual role in odor recognition and glomerular targeting. Not only are ORs found in the axon terminals of OSNs (Strotmann et al. 1994a), but also, ablated expression of ORs in transgenic mice resulted in aberrant glomerular targeting (Wang et al. 1998). Thus, ORs may participate in the late homotypic fasciculation process.

Evidence that OECs are directly involved in this process is based on the fact that OECs express a number of different adhesion molecules and glycoconjugates, including neural cell adhesion molecules (NCAMs, polysialic acid–coupled neural cell adhesion molecule [PSA-NCAM]), L1, and laminin (Miragall et al. 1988, 1989; Miragall and Dermietzel 1992; St John et al. 2002). Although several studies reported on neurite-promoting effects of OECs *in vitro* (Kafitz and Greer 1998; Ziege et al. 2013), their concrete role in glomerular targeting has remained unclear. That OECs are in fact involved in this process, however, can be deduced from the targeted disruption of the Sox10 gene in transgenic mice (Barraud et al. 2010). The transcription factor Sox10 is expressed by neural crest cells and is required for specification and differentiation of OECs (Lee et al. 2008). Disrupted differentiation of OEC blocked glomerular targeting of OSN axons (Barraud et al. 2013). This implies that OECs during development play a major role in the establishment of specific neural connections of OSNs. Interestingly, Sox10 knockout mice display normal OSN axon growth into the CNS (Barraud et al. 2013). Thus, OECs may be dispensable for axon entry into the CNS in general, and OSNs display a striking inherent growth capacity. However, whether these developmental data are also true for the adult olfactory system remain to be shown.

It is likely that glomerular targeting during development and in the adult is at least in part governed by distinct signals. Whereas the establishment of glomeruli during early development may depend on molecular cues provided by OSNs and OECs, refinement of the connections during later stages may involve electrical activity. And although adult-born OSNs recapitulate many processes involved in early development, it is important to note that replacement of OSNs in the adult represents modification of an already existing system that is established early in development. Thus, adult-born OSNs will use molecular cues provided by OSNs of the same specificity. This may imply that homotypic signaling between OSNs may be more relevant in adults than in neonates.

Neuron–Glia Interactions and Determination of the Phenotype
of Olfactory Sensory Neurons and Olfactory Ensheathing Cells

Specific cellular functions are only conceivable on the basis of a specialized phenotype. After dissecting the functional role of neurons and glia during lifelong turnover, we will now concentrate on the question of how phenotypic properties of OSNs and OECs are determined. Cellular features may be either self-governed and autonomic (intrinsic) or dependent on environmental cues, including cell–cell interactions (extrinsic). The question of whether the OSN phenotype is preserved in the absence of OECs and vice versa is not only of academic interest but also crucial for cell transplantation.

An experimental paradigm suitable for studying the relevance of cell–cell interactions in the PNS is the crush injury, which transiently disintegrates neuron–glia interaction (Grothe et al. 1997). Under these conditions, both the axotomized neuron and the denervated Schwann cells undergo characteristic alterations of their phenotype (Grothe and Wewetzer 1996; Fu and Gordon 1997) that are, at least in part, indicative of their reciprocal influences under normal conditions. After lesion, neurons increase expression of RAGs at the expense of genes involved in transmitter metabolism, and myelin-forming and non-myelin-forming Schwann cells dedifferentiate into a common phenotype (Fu and Gordon 1997; van Kesteren et al. 2011). If regenerating axons reestablish contact with Schwann cells, there is restoration of the cellular phenotypes.

It is instructive to apply this model to the olfactory system. Similar to peripheral nerves, there is functional recovery after olfactory nerve lesion. However, OSNs deprived of interaction with OECs do not survive the lesion, and axonal regeneration is based on newly generated OSNs, the production rate of which is increased in response to the lesion (Roet et al. 2013). The fact that elimination of OEC-to-OSN signaling only accelerates neuron production compared to normal conditions and the presence of OECs argue against the idea that OECs crucially define OSN phenotypic properties relevant to axonal regeneration.

There is accumulating evidence, however, that OSNs, in turn, control the phenotype of OECs (Wewetzer and Brandes 2006). Elimination of OSNs either by olfactory nerve transection or by zinc sulfate inhalation has been shown to dramatically alter the molecular phenotype of OECs (Williams et al. 2004; Roet et al. 2013). As shown in rats using the DNA microarray technique, transection of olfactory nerves upregulates and downregulates hundreds of genes, whose expression is restored when regenerating axons from newly produced OSNs reestablish contact with OECs (Roet et al. 2013). Two molecules whose expression was studied also in canines are p75[NTR] and class III β-tubulin. P75[NTR] is not expressed by adult OECs *in situ* but becomes upregulated after olfactory nerve transection *in vivo* or by culturing of dissociated and organotypic slice cultures (Gong et al. 1994; Krudewig et al. 2006; Bock et al. 2007; Brandes et al. 2011; Omar et al. 2011). Class III β-tubulin is specifically expressed by canine OSNs *in situ* but becomes upregulated in OECs maintained *in vitro* in the absence of OSNs (Omar et al. 2013). These data are indirect evidence for the idea that the OEC phenotype is crucially determined via neuron–glia interactions (Wewetzer and Brandes 2006). This is reminiscent of the PNS, where myelin-forming and non-myelin-forming Schwann cells are guided into their phenotypes by axonal signaling (Jessen and Mirsky 2002, 2005).

If neurons define the specific glial phenotype, purified preparations of closely related cell types such as OECs and Schwann cells should have only minimal differences in gene expression (Wewetzer et al. 2002). Whereas DNA microarray studies in rats reported on major differences in the gene expression profile of OECs and Schwann cells (Vincent et al. 2005a; Franssen et al. 2008; Roet et al. 2011), the first report on the comparative analysis of cultured adult canine OECs and Schwann cells revealed, in contrast, overwhelming homology of both cell types (Ulrich et al. 2014). Only 10 out of approximately 40,000 gene probe sets analyzed were differentially expressed between OECs and Schwann cells, while both cell types displayed significant differences in the expression of 3,500 transcripts compared to fibroblasts (Ulrich et al. 2014). This, together with the fact that the morphological and molecular phenotype of adult canine OECs and Schwann cells displays significant differences only *in situ*, is in agreement with the idea that the specific OEC phenotype is determined via specific interactions with OSNs (Wewetzer and Brandes 2006). These data, together with evidence from bulbectomy and neural crest ablation experiments discussed here, are solid evidence for the notion that OSNs have a strong inherent axon growth capacity that is largely independent of their natural environment, including OECs. This does not exclude the possibility, however, that OECs may support certain not-yet-characterized functions of OSNs.

LESSONS FROM THE OLFACTORY SYSTEM FOR THE TREATMENT OF CANINE AND HUMAN CENTRAL NERVOUS SYSTEM INJURY

CNS injury associated with disruption of long fiber tracts results in paralysis and has a poor prognosis in canines and humans (Rowland et al. 2008; Olby 2010). The wide attention the olfactory system has received over recent years was also due to the idea to translate knowledge about the lifelong plasticity of OSNs into novel therapies for treating spinal cord injury (SCI) (Franklin and Barnett 2000; Mackay-Sim and St John 2011). Since the canine and human spinal cord and their reactions to injury as well as their cellular elements share close homology (Techangamsuwan et al. 2008; Spitzbarth et al. 2011), studies on the regenerative capacity of the canine olfactory system were considered to have major implications for the therapy of human patients (Wewetzer et al. 2011).

The dominant experimental approach that has made its way into clinical studies is the transplantation of *in vitro* expanded OECs isolated from the olfactory bulb or mucosa (Tetzlaff et al. 2011; Granger et al. 2012). In light of the vast number of studies, it is worth analyzing the experimental approaches in detail before offering a future vision. There is an extensive and impressive amount of literature on rodents, and the reported effects ranged from remyelination to the support of long-distance axon growth after CNS injury (Tetzlaff et al. 2011). On the basis of studies in rodents, it was concluded that OECs promote axonal regeneration and remyelination and that their effects on OECs were significantly better than those of Schwann cells.

Studies in canines and humans demonstrated that OEC transplantation in the injured spinal cord is a safe procedure but failed to reveal dramatic beneficial effects of OECs (Smith et al. 2002; Jeffery et al. 2005, 2006; Mackay-Sim et al. 2008; Granger et al. 2012; Mackay-Sim and Feron 2013). Nevertheless, these reports caused euphoric responses. However, there are a number of reservations. First and most relevant, OECs, in the majority of studies, were applied in comparison with noncellular controls, such as the culture medium used for cell expansion (Granger et al. 2012). Significant improvement of tested parameters may, therefore, be due to the complex cellular graft rather than to cell type-specific features of OECs. It is known that cells unrelated to OECs, for example, fibroblasts, can also promote regeneration (Lakatos et al. 2003). To define cell type-specific properties, it is essential to monitor their effects after transplantation under the same conditions. Second and surprisingly, there are only a few studies that used OEC and Schwann cell preparations generated under the same conditions and in the same purity for cell transplantation in the same study (Radtke and Wewetzer 2009). Thus, the hypothesis that OECs are superior to Schwann cells for CNS repair is still open (Franklin and Barnett 1997).

The comparative analysis of OECs and Schwann cells is further impeded by the fact that no cell type-specific markers are available that can be used for selective visualization of OECs and Schwann cells. Purified OEC cultures used for comparison with Schwann cells, therefore, may contain significant Schwann cell contaminations, as suggested by a recent study on adult canine OECs (Ziege et al. 2013). Using a novel two-step procedure to deplete canine Schwann cells from OEC preparations, Schwann cell–free preparations of OECs were established (Ziege et al. 2013). The characterization of these cell preparations will provide a solid basis on which cell type-specific effects of Schwann cells and OECs can be defined (Roloff et al. 2013; Ziege et al. 2013).

The discussion of the studies mentioned here does not generally argue against putative beneficial effects of cell transplantation. However, the conclusion that OECs have a unique capacity for CNS repair is, so far, not covered by experimental data. Moreover, even the conclusion that there is a cell type-specific regenerative capacity seems premature and requires comparative studies using well-defined cellular grafts and adequate controls (Radtke and Wewetzer 2009).

The plasticity of the olfactory system is based upon a striking inherent capacity of OSNs to organize their environment, which includes determination of the OEC phenotype. Learning from the olfactory system with regard to therapy of CNS injury, therefore will require strong efforts in understanding the special features of OSNs as well as the communication of OSNs with their environment.

3 Olfaction and the Canine Brain

Marcello Siniscalchi

Olfaction is believed to be dogs' most crucial sensory domain and, as a consequence, a fundamental starting point for the study of both social cognition and brain functions. Although the olfactory system is relevant for canine social life, apart from different works at genetic (Issel-Tarver and Rine 1996; Tacher et al. 2005; Robin et al. 2009), behavioral (Sommerville et al. 1993; Wells and Hepper 2003; Pickel et al. 2004), and cellular levels (Prince 1978; Nadi et al. 1980; Overall and Arnold 2007), at present, few studies have focused on the cognitive level. This is unfortunate since dog behavior is driven by olfactory information integrated and elaborated in neocortical areas (higher cognitive levels) rather than by raw olfactory stimulation in the olfactory bulb (i.e., electrophysiological responses from the olfactory epithelium receptors to different odorant mixtures).

FUNCTIONAL MAGNETIC RESONANCE IMAGING

A new promising technique to study how olfactory information is processed and analyzed by the dog brain is functional magnetic resonance imaging (fMRI). Using this functional neuroimaging procedure, it is possible to measure different brain areas' activities by detecting associated variations in blood flow, and particularly useful, fMRI can be applied on awake and conscious dogs (Berns et al. 2012, 2015; Cook et al. 2014; Jia et al. 2014). Despite being methodologically challenging, awake animal fMRI studies represent a valid approach to explore the dog's mind and to understand how sensory information is translated at the cognitive level since changes in blood circulation associated with neural activity are being monitored under more accurate physiological conditions (e.g., both cerebral activity and blood flow are affected by anesthesia). fMRI has been used to investigate the neural basis of olfaction in primates (Boyett-Anderson et al. 2003; Savic 2005) and rodents (Mori et al. 2005).

In a recent work, Jia and colleagues (2014) investigated brain activation in response to odorants of different concentrations in both anesthetized and conscious dogs using fMRI. In order to control accurately the extent and time of exposure of different odor stimuli to olfactory tissue, these authors built a custom device for the precise computer-controlled delivery of predetermined quantities of odorants over a precise time interval. Basically, they found that odor stimuli are processed by the dog's brain throughout the activation of an olfactory pathway similar to humans and that this activation is modulated by odor concentrations. The main brain areas involved in both anesthetized and awake dogs, and modulated by odor concentrations, were the olfactory bulb and the olfactory cortex (anterior olfactory cortex, piriform cortex, periamygdaloid and entorhinal cortices), while higher cognitive structures like the cerebellum (Barton 2012), and the superior, medial, and orbital parts of the frontal cortex, were activated mainly in awake dogs. The olfactory bulb has been implicated in certain types of olfactory learning and memory (Gheusi et al. 2000), discriminates odor cues in a complex olfactory environment (Doucette et al. 2007), and enhances sensitivity of odor detection (Jia et al. 2014). The olfactory information is primarily coded at the olfactory bulb level, and it is then transmitted via pyramidal neurons to the olfactory cortex (see Figure 3.1).

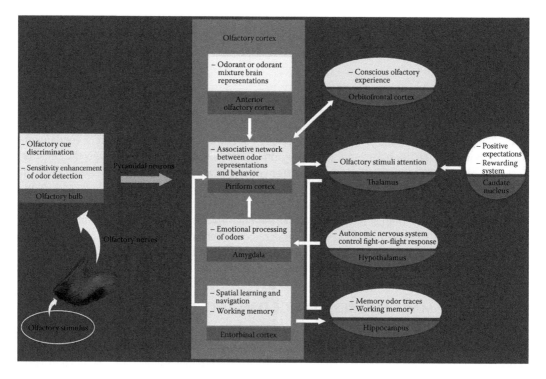

FIGURE 3.1   Diagram of the basic pathways of the canine olfactory network.

PATHWAYS OF OLFACTORY STIMULATION TO THE CANINE BRAIN

The anterior olfactory cortex plays a fundamental role in the cortical cascade, which provides a substrate for the analysis of the afferent pathway from the olfactory bulb to the brain. An intriguing hypothesis on the function of the anterior olfactory cortex as the "gestalt maker" (i.e., creating brain representations for odorants or odorant mixtures with properties that cannot be derived from the summation of single molecular features) has been derived from functional imaging and morphological studies (Wilson 2000; Haberly 2001; Jia et al. 2014). Haberly (2001) showed in humans that the anterior olfactory cortex receives a highly distributed projection from the olfactory cortex neurons, which is a necessary requisite neural circuitry to correlate activity from different odor feature inputs. The piriform cortex is closely involved in associative and behavioral level processes and is anatomically and functionally separated into anterior and posterior parts. The representations of odorants in the piriform cortex have been examined by electrophysiological recordings, imaging of intrinsic signals, and analysis of odorant-evoked gene expression (Illig and Haberly 2003; Rennaker et al. 2007; Stettler and Axel 2009), suggesting a model in which the piriform cortex works as an associative network that integrates and learns correlations between anterior olfactory cortex gestalts and behavioral, cognitive, and contextual information derived from a specially distributed network of brain areas (frontal, entorhinal, and periamygdaloid areas) (Haberly 2001; Jia et al. 2014). In particular, an important functional role of the piriform cortex could be a fast generalization of the threat significance of odor stimuli (e.g., predator associated odorant) that may elicit an unconditioned fight-or-flight response throughout the activation of the hypothalamic–pituitary–adrenal axis (Dielenberg and McGregor 2001; Haberly 2001). This hypothesis is based on direct olfactory bulb input to the piriform cortex that transports raw olfactory information that has particular significance for survival (Haberly 2001).

Olfactory stimulation can also directly activate amygdala and periamygdaloid areas, bypassing the primary olfactory cortex, and this is crucial for emotional processing of odor stimuli (Krusemark et al. 2013). In addition, there are a number of subcortical inputs to the amygdala that carry the output from the hippocampus, the hypothalamus, thalamic nuclei, as well as the nucleus of the solitary tract, which are important centers for control of the autonomic nervous system (Bennett and Hacker 2005) and for storing olfactory information items in the so-called working memory (Fransen 2005).

The autonomic nervous system largely determines a dog's behavior during emotional fight or flight. The entorhinal cortex is commonly perceived as a nodal point of cortical–hippocampal neural circuits, and it has been suggested that it serves as a temporal buffer of incoming information for the hippocampus (Hasselmo et al. 2002; Fransen 2005). In particular, the entorhinal cortex is involved in working memory for novel as well as for specific attributes of items (Otto and Eichenbaum 1992; Stern et al. 2001). Neurons in the entorhinal cortex exhibit greater activation during spatial learning and navigation (Sargolini et al. 2006; Jacobs 2012), which could be crucial for dogs during the use of airborne or waterborne odorants for navigation (e.g., following scents to sources or tracking and trailing).

The entorhinal–hippocampal system can be envisioned as a network that consists of a number of component areas performing an integrated set of operations (Haberly 2001). The hippocampal formation, in particular, is involved in the elaboration of odor traces related to episodic memory and also seems to support conscious event organization (i.e., it helps in specifying conscious perception of experiences as well as encoding "memory for conscious events") (Baars 2013; Baars et al. 2013). Furthermore, sustained activity in the entorhinal cortex could also be critical for effective encoding of long-term representation via synaptic modification in the hippocampal formation (Haberly 2001).

Most striking are studies on rat behavior that describe hippocampal "time cells" that fire briefly in sequence during periods between salient events (MacDonald et al. 2013). The work of MacDonald expands the generality of temporal coding of memories in the hippocampus, providing compelling evidence that time cells encode successive brief moments that compose the "flow of time" per se, even when spatial navigation and movements (e.g., locomotion, head movements, and speed) are eliminated. Because of the absence of direct thalamic relay between sensory neurons and the primary cortex, relatively little attention has been directed toward the thalamus in olfaction. However, recent human psychophysical and fMRI data suggest a role for the medial dorsal nucleus of the thalamus in an animal's attention to olfactory stimuli (Courtiol and Wilson 2014). In addition, the medial dorsal nucleus of the thalamus receives input from different olfactory structures including the piriform cortex, and there is now evidence that odorant presentation induces tightly related neural activities between the thalamus and the piriform cortex (Courtiol and Wilson 2014).

The hippocampal formation and thalamus relay information to the medial and orbitofrontal cortex, where the olfactory signal is subsequently interpreted (Shepherd 1994).

The medial and orbitofrontal cortex are neocortical elements that have a pivotal associative role in olfactory information processing, suggesting a possible functional link between these neural structures and conscious olfactory experience. Both of these structures are involved in integration of all sensory stimuli in relation to prior experiences at the cognitive level (Ramnani and Owen 2004; Li et al. 2010).

The caudate nucleus is another fundamental brain area involved in the analysis of olfactory stimuli (Curtis et al. 2007). A vast literature indicates that this region is involved in positive expectations, including social rewards. In particular, the caudate receives dopaminergic neuromodulation (i.e., excitatory inputs), by neuron structures from the brainstem, which acts as a signal of "rewarding prediction error" (Schultz et al. 1997; Berns et al. 2015). The novel information then goes from the caudate to the globus pallidus and the thalamus, where the input then provides feedback to the cortex. In other words, the caudate activity could play a role in transforming expected reward to change the animal's behavioral orientation to approach or consume the stimulus (Daw et al. 2011). The rewarding process associated with caudate activity includes both primary rewards (food, social) and, for humans, complex rewards like money, music, and more generally, art (Berns et al. 2015).

In dogs, Berns and colleagues (2015) recently studied the caudate activation in response to conspecifics and humans odors using fMRI in 12 awake subjects that had been trained to remain motionless, while unsedated and unrestrained, in the MRI (see Berns et al. 2012, 2013, for specific dog training during fMRI). Odor stimuli were self, familiar human, strange human, familiar dog, and strange dog. Human odors were collected from the armpit (sans deodorant), and dog scents were collected from the perineal–genital area using sterile gauze pads. Regarding the familiar-human stimulus, the authors preferred to use the odor of a member of the dog's household or a close friend instead of the dog's handler because handler odor could interfere with fMRI recordings. The familiar-dog stimulus was the odor collected from another dog in the household. Results revealed that the caudate was activated maximally with the familiar-human odor, suggesting that dogs have a positive association with it. The possible explanation given by the authors for the greater response of dogs' caudate to human familiar odor is that all of the dogs in the experiment were family pets and had been raised by humans since they were puppies. Whether this rewarding process to human odor (i.e., a "marker" to approach the familiar human) is based on food, play, or social hierarchy needs further investigation.

HEMISPHERIC SPECIALIZATION AND OLFACTION IN DOGS

Lateralization (i.e., asymmetry of the brain and behavior) has been observed in several animal models, including canine species (for extended review and references, see Rogers et al. 2013). In dogs, brain asymmetries have been described at both structural (Tan and Caliskan 1987a,b; Siniscalchi et al. 2011a) and functional levels (Quaranta et al. 2004, 2007; Siniscalchi and Quaranta 2014). Specifically, studies suggest the presence of a lateralized process of the dog's brain in the analysis of visual (Quaranta et al. 2007; Siniscalchi et al. 2010), acoustic (Siniscalchi et al. 2008, 2012), and olfactory stimuli (Siniscalchi et al. 2011b).

Lateralization of olfaction has been shown in both vertebrate and invertebrate species. In domestic chicks, for example, right nostril use has been associated with better discrimination of imprinting olfactory stimuli (Vallortigara and Andrew 1994; Rogers et al. 1998) and with a stronger behavioral response to a noxious odor (Burne and Rogers 2002). In honeybees, initial memory recall is facilitated when their right antenna was in use (Anfora et al. 2010). In mammals, horses showed a population bias toward using the right nostril to sniff at arousal stimuli (Siniscalchi et al. 2015).

In dogs, lateralization of olfaction was investigated by studying asymmetries of nostril use during sniffing at odors that differ in terms of emotional valence and degree of familiarity under unrestrained conditions (Siniscalchi et al. 2011b). The experiment involved presentation of dogs with different emotive stimuli (food, sweat of dogs' veterinarian, lemon, adrenaline, and estrous bitch vaginal secretions) presented on a cotton swab (Figure 3.2). The cotton swab, without any particular odor, was also presented as a control stimulus (neutral stimulus). Dogs were freely sniffing different odors, and nostril use was recorded using a digital video camera located on a tripod. A frame-by-frame analysis of the sniffing behavior revealed a consistent right nostril bias during presentations of clearly arousal stimuli like adrenaline and sweat odors of a veterinarian.

Given that in dogs, as with other mammals, olfactory neurons project back receptor information from each nostril to the olfactory cortex via the ipsilateral side, the previously described bias during sniffing of arousal stimuli suggests the involvement of the right hemisphere (Royet and Plailly 2004) (Figure 3.3). Studies in different animal models indicate that the right hemisphere responds to novel (unexpected) stimuli and takes control of behavior in response to arousal stimuli (Rogers and Andrew 2002, p. 660; Rogers et al. 2013). In dogs, right nostril bias in response to veterinarian odor supports the hypothesis of right hemisphere specialization in response to threatening stimuli. It should be specified that, although the odor of their veterinarian was likely to be quite familiar for dogs, it was associated with stressful activities like vaccine administration, blood sampling, and clinical examinations.

On the other hand, the preferential use of the right nostril in response to adrenaline stimulus is consistent with the idea that activity of the right hemisphere is directly related to sympathetic arousal (Craig 2005). In canine species, right hemisphere advantage in processing alarming stimuli

FIGURE 3.2   Right nostril use while sniffing adrenaline odor.

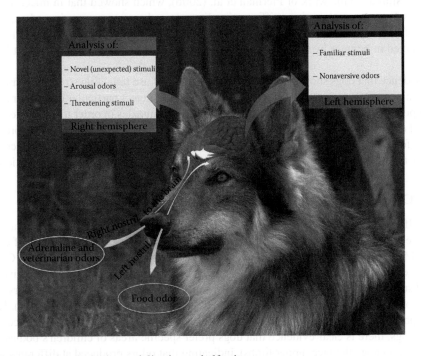

FIGURE 3.3   Dog's hemispheric specialization and olfaction.

has also been reported in visual (Siniscalchi et al. 2010, 2013) and auditory (Siniscalchi et al. 2008, 2012) sensory domains. For example, when threatening stimuli such as the silhouette of a snake (which seems to be an unconditioned alarming stimulus for most mammal species; see LoBue et al. 2008) were presented simultaneously to the left and right visual hemifields, dogs preferentially turned their heads to the left, confirming the right hemisphere's dominant role in processing fear (the lateral field of each eye of dogs projects mainly to the contralateral side of the brain: left lateral field → right hemisphere; see Fogle 1992, p. 203; Siniscalchi et al. 2010). In addition, the sight of a stimulus from which dogs wished to withdraw, such as an unfamiliar dog displaying an agonistic approach (presumably associated with negative emotions), produced a tail-wagging bias toward the dog's left side (right hemisphere activation) (Quaranta et al. 2007). Similarly, a striking left-orienting bias in the head-turning response (right hemisphere activation) was observed after thunderstorm playbacks (alarming auditory stimulus) (Siniscalchi et al. 2008).

By contrast, during sniffing at nonaversive odors (food, lemon, estrous bitch vaginal secretions, and the cotton swab), dogs showed initial right nostril use followed by a shift toward use of the left nostril when odor presentation was repeated. Hence, this particular pattern of sniffing suggests initial involvement of the right hemisphere followed by involvement of the left hemisphere. A very similar pattern has been reported in different species reflecting the right hemisphere's role in performing the initial broad scanning of stimuli followed by the left hemisphere's dominant role in the control of behavior when responses to stimuli became routine (i.e., familiarization, categorization) (reviewed in Vallortigara et al. 1999, 2011; Vallortigara 2000; Rogers and Andrew 2002, p. 660; MacNeilage et al. 2009) (Figure 3.3). In dogs, the specialization of the left hemisphere in processing familiar stimuli has also been reported in auditory response to familiar species-typical vocalizations (Siniscalchi et al. 2008, 2012).

Although there were no sex differences in hemispheric activation patterns by different odors, food and vaginal secretion olfactory stimuli induced different total odor investigation time in males and females. In particular, males tended to sniff estrous bitch vaginal secretions more than females did. This is similar to the work of Pierman et al. (2006), which showed that in mice, opposite-sex urine odors were more attractive sniffing stimuli compared to same-sex urine odors. Regarding food odor, female dogs tended to have higher total investigation time than males. Something similar has been noted in humans by Cain (1982), who reported a general female superiority at identifying food odors.

The evidence that dogs show clear asymmetries of nostril use reflecting striking lateralization of olfaction may open the door to new methods to train dogs to detect particular odors. For example, it might be possible in the future to develop new noninvasive muzzles in order to stimulate selectively one nostril during odor tracking. The general hypothesis is that the activation of the more appropriate nostril for a particular odor may enhance a dog's performance by reducing the distracting effects exerted by the other olfactory channel. This topic obviously deserves further investigation.

OLFACTORY CUES IN SOCIAL BEHAVIOR

In dogs, olfactory cues are important in social recognition. Different studies have established the importance of olfactory cues in the conspecific and interspecific relational systems of canids and humans (Millot 1994; Chen and Haviland-Jones 2000; Wells and Hepper 2000; de Groot et al. 2014). For example, conspecific odors play a fundamental role in signaling reproductive status in dogs, and subjects of both sexes are able to discriminate among organic chemical factors (i.e., pheromones) contained in urine, feces, the anal sac, and vaginal secretions (Miklosi 2007). Regarding the interspecific relational systems, although very little is known about the significance of human odors for dogs, there is clear evidence that dogs prefer specific areas of children's bodies for olfactory exploration (e.g., the face, upper limbs), indicating that odors produced at different anatomical parts could provide different specific information (Millot et al. 1987; Brisbin and Austad 1991) (see Chapter 19 herein).

What about the possibility that dogs could detect the emotional state of a human being or another dog by his/her smell? To evaluate this possibility, the author's laboratory is currently investigating the possible dogs' behavioral, physiological, and lateralized brain effects of presenting odors collected from both humans (armpit sweat) and other dogs (saliva, interdigital, and anal sac secretions) during different emotional conditions. For the dog, the situations are (1) a *disturbance* situation in which a stranger knocks on the window of the owner's car, (2) an *isolation* situation in which the dog is in a room of the house isolated from its owner, and (3) a *play* situation in which either two dogs or a human and a dog play together. For humans in the study, happiness and fear are induced by using emotion-eliciting movies. We expected these stimuli to be sniffed preferentially by one nostril (i.e., the left or the right) depending on the different activation of the two brain hemispheres by the emotional valence of the odors. Moreover, to test the different emotional responses of tested dogs, we are measuring change in subjects' behavior and cardiac activity.

The link between olfaction, cognition, and emotions represents a fascinating field of research, and the fact that alarming and higher emotional olfactory stimuli may act differently on the canine brain with the subsequent involvement of the hypothalamic–pituitary–adrenal axis (fight-or-flight response) is a topic that could have direct implications for both dogs' social communication and welfare.

CONCLUSIONS

Despite the well-known societal importance of canine olfaction for specialized activities, such as detecting cancers, explosive devices, and drugs, and following scented trails, and the evidence of the importance of olfactory cues in the relational systems between canids and humans, we know still very little about the cognitive processes that elaborate olfactory information at the brain level. This is unfortunate, not only because such understanding would enhance the basic knowledge of olfaction biology but also because a functional understanding of the canine olfactory system at the cognitive level would enhance human ability to improve canine detection capabilities. Noninvasive functional neuroimaging procedures such as fMRI, which could be applied also on awake and conscious dogs, coupled with behavioral studies represent promising and interesting tools for studying ever more deeply the cognitive processing of complex olfactory information in the dog brain.

4 Genetics of Canine Olfaction

Pascale Quignon and Francis Galibert

Olfaction, the ability to detect and identify a very large panel of molecules, mainly of small molecular size, either dissolved in water for the aquatic species or carried in air for terrestrial animals, has been developed to a great degree of sophistication during evolution. Thus, olfaction, as one of the five main senses, is essential for all animals but particularly for those living in the wild to survive. It allows them to find food and escape predators and dangers, but also to look for sexual partners and to reproduce. This sense is obviously not as important for domesticated animals, which usually do not have to care about finding food, protect themselves against predators, or choose the most appealing sexual partners. In that respect, it may be wondered whether this function has evolved differently or as successfully in the domesticated descendants of a species compared to its wild ancestors. Though perhaps in many cases, there has been a decline in the olfactory acuity of domesticated groups, dogs are probably an exception. Many breeds, from early in domestication, have been selected for hunting purposes, for which olfaction is of primary importance. Olfaction as a whole depends on several aspects:

1. *Perception*, the ability to detect the presence of a volatile compound in the air or water
2. *Discrimination*, the ability to distinguish different signals in a chemically complex environment
3. *Identification*, the ability to recognize a signal and compare it with previously memorized information

The first step of olfaction occurs in the nasal cavity. There, the odorant molecules are captured by specialized receptors expressed by specialized olfactory neurons. The role of these neurons is dual. Each of them must bind specifically to a small set of defined compounds, and through a complex downstream pathway (Figure 4.1), they must convert a chemical signal into an electrical signal sent to several brain areas. Ultimately, this last signal is converted into information that will be stored for further comparison. In the dog, the study of the genetics of olfaction has been mainly focused on the study of the olfactory receptor (OR) gene repertoire.

OLFACTORY SYSTEMS

Different olfactory systems have been identified in mammals, although not in all mammals: the main olfactory system, the accessory system, Masera's organ (also called the septal organ), and the Gruneberg ganglion (Figure 4.2) (Munger et al. 2009). These systems are made of several structures that are anatomically separated. They probably play different roles, even if the distinction between them is not well elucidated. Of these four, the first two are by far the most important and consequently the most studied.

MAIN OLFACTORY SYSTEM

The main olfactory system consists of the olfactory mucosa in the nasal cavity and the olfactory bulb in the frontal part of the brain, just behind the nasal cavity. The mucosa contains the respiratory epithelium and the olfactory epithelium (OE), or neuroepithelium, which contain neurons expressing[1] ORs (Tortora and Grabowski 2002). In the dog, these two epithelia cover the concha or

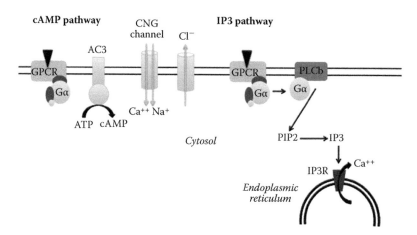

FIGURE 4.1 Schematic view of the two pathways through which a chemical odorant message is converted into an electrical message sent from the OSN to different brain regions, where it is decoded and stored. The cyclic adenosine 3′,5′-monophosphate (cAMP) pathway is by far the more important of the two. Once an odorant binds to its receptor, the alpha subunit of the G protein linked to the receptor activates an adenylate cyclase molecule (AC3), which in turn converts adenosine triphosphate (ATP) into cAMP. This induces the activation of a cyclic nucleotide-gated (CNG) channel and the entry of Ca^{++} and Na^+ ions then Ca^{++} activates a Cl^- channel. The inositol 1,4,5-triphosphate (IP3) pathway is also activated by the alpha subunit of the G protein. After the binding of an odorant molecule to its receptor, the alpha subunit activates the phospholipase beta (PLCb), which hydrolyzes phosphatidylinositol-4,5-bisphosphate (PIP2) and synthesizes IP3, leading to the release of Ca^{++} from intracellular storage. IP3R refers to an IP3 receptor.

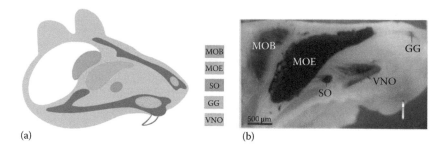

FIGURE 4.2 (a) Schematic drawing of a sagittal section of the rat nasal cavity showing the different organs implicated in olfaction. (b) Stained view of a sagittal tissue section. GG, Gruneberg ganglion; MOB, main olfactory bulb; MOE, main olfactory epithelium; SO, Masera's or septal organ; VNO, vomeronasal or accessory epithelium. (Image (a) courtesy of K9 Resources, LLC, http://www.k9resources.com.)

turbinates, large bones wound upon themselves. There are three turbinates in each nostril, one inferior, one middle, and one superior. They increase the surface of the respiratory epithelium and OE, which varies depending on the dog breed. The German shepherd has a mucosa spread over 200 cm^2, and the cocker, 67 cm^2, compared to the 5 cm^2 of the human OE.

Comparison of the olfactory mucosa in dogs and sheep reveals better structural refinement in the dog than in the sheep, with OE having greater thickness in the dog due to an increase in the number of olfactory cells (Kavoi et al. 2010). Olfactory sensory neurons (OSNs) represent 60–80% of the cells found in the OE. These are bipolar neurons composed of a dendrite, a cellular body, and an axon. The dendrite ends in a bud where several cilia emerge, increasing the surface of the epithelium, and the axon extends toward the olfactory bulb. Odorant molecules carried by the airflow are

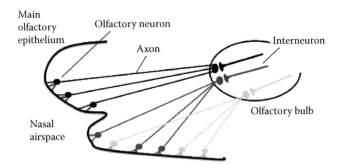

FIGURE 4.3 The main olfactory epithelium is divided into four regions within which olfactory sensory neurons (OSNs) expressing the same OR are grouped. The axons of OSNs expressing the same OR converge at the level of the olfactory bulb into the same glomerulus, where the first synapse is created.

dissolved in the mucus due to olfactory binding proteins (OBPs) and transported to two types of receptors to which they bind with high affinity, the ORs and the trace amine-associated receptors (TAARs). These two types of receptors are expressed by different OSNs. Through a complex cascade of reactions taking place in the body of the OSN, the chemical signals represented by the odorant molecules are converted into an electrical signal conveyed by the axons to the olfactory bulb.

The axons of the olfactory neurons are grouped into fibrils to constitute the olfactory fibers and then the olfactory nerve. This nerve goes through the cribriform plate and reaches the olfactory bulb. The bulb is organized in concentric layers. The periphery of the bulb contains glomeruli, spherical structures where axons of neurons expressing the same OR are grouped (Figure 4.3) (Mombaerts et al. 1996; Mombaerts 2001). In the glomeruli, the OSN apical dendrites make synapses with the apical dendrites of the olfactory bulb neurons, the axons of which form the lateral olfactory tract that reaches the cortex, where the electrical olfactory signal is analyzed. Thus, the olfactory bulb contains the first and unique synaptic relay between the OSN in the nasal cavities and the brain.

ACCESSORY OLFACTORY SYSTEM

The accessory olfactory system is made of the vomeronasal organ (VNO) and the accessory olfactory bulb. The VNO is located at the base of the nasal septum and is thus separated from the OE. The epithelium of the VNO is composed of three cell types similar to the ones found in the OE. The receptors expressed at the surface of the neurons are called vomeronasal receptors (VRs) (Dulac and Axel 1995).

MASERA'S ORGAN AND GRUNEBERG GANGLION

These two minor systems have been identified in rodents but not in the dog (Barrios et al. 2014). Masera's organ expresses a subset of the OR present in the OE (Kaluza et al. 2004; Tian and Ma 2004), whereas the Gruneberg ganglion expresses receptors found in the VNO but also the OE.

ODORANT RECEPTORS

Different types of odorant receptors have been described (Figure 4.4). The first ones were the ORs in 1991 (Buck and Axel 1991). The other entities that are involved in the odorant-sensory process are the VRs (Dulac and Axel 1995; Herrada and Dulac 1997; Matsunami and Buck 1997; Ryba and Tirindelli 1997) and the TAARs (Liberles and Buck 2006). VRs and TAARs are very few compared to the ORs. In the dog, nine V1Rs, no V2Rs, and two TAAR genes were identified, compared to more than a hundred V1Rs, a dozen V2Rs, and 17 TAAR genes identified in the rat genome (Table 4.1).

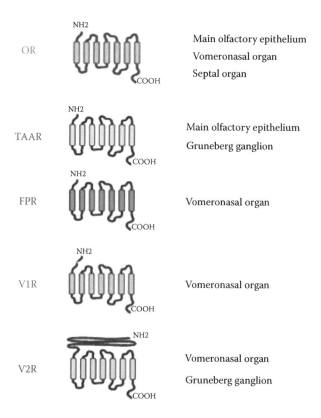

FIGURE 4.4 Schematic representation of the different receptors implicated in the binding of odorant molecules. Transmembrane domains are represented by cylinders. For all receptors, the COOH end of the protein is localized in the cytosol of the neuron. The names of the organs where the receptors are expressed are indicated on the right. FPR, formyl peptide receptor.

OLFACTORY RECEPTORS

A subset of OR gene transcripts were identified for the first time by Buck and Axel in 1991 in the rat OE. These belong to the superfamily of G protein–coupled receptors (GPCRs) and are coupled to specific G proteins, such as Ga(olf). Since their discovery, OR genes have been identified using bioinformatic tools in all eukaryotic genome species for which the genome sequences were determined. By far, ORs represent the largest gene family, with several hundred genes identified in the human genome (Malnic et al. 2004), 1,493 in the rat, and 1,094 in the dog genome (Quignon et al. 2005). Thus, the dog, mouse, and rat have 2.5–3.5 times more genes than humans. While it would be reasonable to believe that a larger number of receptors might favor the detection of a larger number of odorants, it seems that a higher sensitivity of detection allows these animals to detect odorants at very low concentrations not perceptible by humans, differentiating these two animals from humans.

VOMERONASAL RECEPTORS

Two families of GPCRs mainly dedicated to the detection of pheromones have been identified in rodents: V1R for vomeronasal receptor type 1 genes (Dulac and Axel 1995) and V2R for vomeronasal receptor type 2 genes (Herrada and Dulac 1997; Matsunami and Buck 1997; Ryba and Tirindelli 1997). V1Rs, as ORs, are coded by a unique coding exon, unlike V2Rs (Dulac and Axel 1995). The size of the V1R gene repertoire varies greatly among placental mammals (Grus et al. 2005).

TABLE 4.1

**Sizes of the Different Odorant Receptor Families
as Retrieved from Literature**

	OR	TAAR	V1R	V2R
Human	400[a]	9[b]	4[c]	0[d]
Rat	1,500[d]	17[b]	102[c]	90[e]
Dog	850[d]	2[e]	8[f]	0[d]
Cat	677[g]	–	21[g]	–
Tilapia	158[h]	44[h]	–	–
Zebra fish	143[i]	57[j]/109[k]	1[l]	>24/60[l]

Note: V1R, vomeronasal receptor type 1; V2R, vomeronasal receptor type 2.
[a] Malnic et al. 2004.
[b] Lewin 2006.
[c] Grus et al. 2005.
[d] Quignon et al. 2006.
[e] Zhang et al. 2010.
[f] Kaluza et al. 2004.
[g] Montague et al. 2014.
[h] Azzouzi et al. 2014.
[i] Alioto and Ngai 2005.
[j] Gloriam et al. 2005.
[k] Hashiguchi and Nishida 2005.
[l] Pfister and Rodriguez 2005.

Whereas rodents have more than 100 functional V1R genes, only 5 potentially functional V1R genes have been described in humans among a large number of pseudogenes (approximately 100 pseudogenes) (Rodriguez 2005). Similarly, the repertoire of functional V1R genes in dogs is small, with only 9 intact V1R genes (Young et al. 2005, 2010; Quignon et al. 2006), but slightly larger in cats, with 21 functional V1R genes (Montague et al. 2014). Moreover, dogs have a relatively thin vomeronasal epithelium and small accessory olfactory bulbs (Dennis et al. 2003). Interestingly, a recent study has shown that the dog V1R pseudogenes are also pseudogenes in wolves, leading to the hypothesis that the decline of the dog V1R repertoire did not occur in response to selective pressures imposed during domestication (Young et al. 2010).

TRACE AMINE-ASSOCIATED RECEPTORS

The search for new GPCRs involved in olfaction led to the identification of the TAARs (Liberles and Buck 2006). They are expressed in a subset of olfactory neurons scattered in the OE and in the Gruneberg ganglion (Gloriam et al. 2005; Lindemann et al. 2005; Zucchi et al. 2006; Fleischer et al. 2007). Then, it was also shown that TAARs respond to volatile amines present in urine (Hussain et al. 2009). This led to the hypothesis that TAARs could be involved in the ability of mice to determine the sex as well as the sexual or stress status of other mice (Liberles and Buck 2006). TAARs are found in most vertebrates but in very variable numbers: 17 in rats, 15 in mice, 6 in humans, 2 in dogs, and 109 in zebra fish (Gloriam et al. 2005; Lindemann et al. 2005; Liberles and Buck 2006; Zucchi et al. 2006; Hashiguchi and Nishida 2007).

THE DOG'S OR REPERTOIRE

In this chapter, we will consider the structure of canine OR genes and proteins and genomic organization of the OR genes, and discuss OR gene polymorphism and expression.

STRUCTURE OF THE DOG OR GENES AND PROTEINS

Like other chemoreceptors, ORs are GPCRs, and like all GPCRs, they are characterized by a seven-transmembrane structure, with an external N-terminus and a cytoplasmic C-terminus. But unlike many GPCRs, the receptors are encoded by a unique exon, at least in mammals, while the genes would be made of two exons, a first noncoding exon and a second one coding for the protein. Among the 1,094 retrieved canine OR genes, 872 encompass a complete open reading frame (ORF) able to code for a functional receptor, and the 222 remaining genes were considered as pseudogenes due to the presence of mutations leading to in-frame stop codons or frame shifts (Quignon et al. 2005).

Dog ORs have a mean size of 307 amino acids. They are characterized by a number of amino acid motifs located at specific locations regarding the transmembrane structures, such as the PMYLFGNLS (amino acid sequence) motif at the beginning of transmembrane domain II (TMII) or MAYDRYVAIC (amino acid sequence) at the end of TMIV and beginning of intracellular loop 2 (IC2). They are characterized also by a number of amino acids at defined positions, like tyrosine or cysteine. Although translocated to the cytoplasmic membrane, ORs are devoid of any classical peptide signal known to address the molecule at the membrane. Instead, a glycosylation site, Asn/X/Ser or Thr, which has been implicated in the translocation of the receptors, is present in all of them within the first 25 amino acids (Alioto and Ngai 2005; Azzouzi et al. 2014).

GENOMIC ORGANIZATION OF THE DOG OR GENES

The dog OR repertoire is distributed on 49 loci located on 24 out of the 38 + X and Y chromosomes composing the dog karyotype (Lindblad-Toh et al. 2005; Quignon et al. 2005). This organization in clusters is not specific to the dog, as it has also been observed in humans and mice (Glusman et al. 2001; Young and Trask 2002; Zhang and Firestein 2002) as well as fish (Azzouzi et al. 2014). The phylogenetic tree and computation at the level of amino acid identity allow the classification of OR genes into families and subfamilies, using criteria described by Ben-Arie et al. (1994). OR families are composed of ORs that have at least 40% amino acid identity, and subfamily members have at least 60% (Ben-Arie et al. 1994). Humans and dogs have a similar number of subfamilies (300), but nearly half of the human subfamilies are composed of pseudogenes, due to the higher number of pseudogenes in this species rather than from diversification of the OR repertoire (Quignon et al. 2005). Interestingly, the majority of ORs belonging to the same subfamilies are present in the same cluster, as observed for other species' OR repertoires (Malnic et al. 1999; Azzouzi et al. 2014). Despite being scattered into several chromosomes in every species, orthologous clusters, i.e., clusters made of orthologous genes, can easily be identified, showing that common ancestors must already have OR genes on multiple chromosomes. This supports the hypothesis of cis-duplication events at the origin of the OR family expansion and of the birth-and-death model (Sharon et al. 1998), in which new genes are created by successive duplications followed by divergence and maintaining of some duplicated genes or accumulation of deletions in others (Young and Trask 2002; Niimura and Nei 2005).

In addition to being classified into families and subfamilies, mammalian ORs are grouped into two classes, clearly separated in the phylogenetic tree. Class II OR genes were the first OR genes identified by polymerase chain reaction (PCR) with degenerated primers in terrestrial mammals. Class I OR genes were identified using the same method but in fish, and it was thought that class I ORs were specific to hydrosoluble odorants and class II to volatile odorants (Freitag et al. 1995, 1998). However, experimental results did not support this hypothesis. Indeed, about 100 genes in humans and about 200 in dogs belong to class I. Interestingly, all the OR genes belonging to this class are localized in only one cluster in the human, mouse, rat, and dog. In addition, this cluster does not contain any OR genes from class II. Also, the number of class I genes is quite similar in fish and in terrestrial mammals, and the number of pseudogenes in class I is smaller than in class II.

DOG OR GENE POLYMORPHISM

ORs are the first elements to be activated in the olfactory reaction cascade. Thus, polymorphisms of the OR genes able to modify their binding capacity could, at least in part, explain interindividual differences in olfactory sensitivity. Two types of genomic variations have been reported: single-nucleotide polymorphism (SNP) and copy-number variation (CNV). OR SNP polymorphism was first demonstrated in humans, revealing a high level of polymorphism in the coding regions (Gilad et al. 2000; Sharon et al. 2000; Menashe et al. 2002).

Dog OR gene polymorphisms within and between breeds were reported in two studies. In the first study, 16 OR genes from class I and II and various families and subfamilies composing the canine OR repertoire were resequenced in a cohort of 95 dogs belonging to 20 breeds (Tacher et al. 2005). This study revealed a total of 98 SNPs and four insertions/deletions (indels) and showed that all 16 genes were polymorphic, with 2–11 SNPs per OR gene. The minor allele frequency (MAF) of these SNPs varied from 0.5% to 50%, with 35 SNPs having a frequency less than 5% in the 95 dogs. Interestingly, more than half of the SNPs induced an amino acid change, with 30 involving a change of chemical group. Amino acid changes occurred in all parts of the OR protein. Additionally, five OR genes had an allele with an interrupted ORF, indicating that an individual dog may harbor a different subset of pseudogenes, as already observed in humans (Gilad et al. 2000; Menashe et al. 2002).

In the second canine study, 109 OR genes representative of a larger number of OR families and subfamilies and belonging to several clusters with high or low OR gene density, or even isolated OR genes, were sequenced in a cohort of 48 dogs of 6 breeds: German shepherd, Belgian Malinois, Labrador retriever, English springer spaniel, Greyhound, and Pekingese (Robin et al. 2009). A total of 732 mutations were identified: 710 SNPs, 17 short indels, and 5 long indels (6–74 nt). All but four of the 109 genes contained 1–22 SNPs, which confirmed the high level of polymorphism of the dog OR genes. Globally, OR genes are more polymorphic than any other coding exon or intron or even intergenic sequences with no known function. As in the previous study, the number of SNPs and their distribution within breeds vary significantly. At the whole population level, OR genes tended to be either weakly or highly polymorphic, with some exceptions: some genes were poorly or not polymorphic in one breed and highly polymorphic in the five other breeds. MAF varied from 1% to 50% globally, and the frequency within breeds could differ from the frequency across breeds. For example, some alleles were absent in all but one breed, where they were the major allele.

Interestingly, a correlation between the cluster size and the polymorphism level was observed. Indeed, the least polymorphic OR genes were preferentially localized in small OR gene clusters and the highly polymorphic OR genes in large OR gene clusters. Reciprocally, OR genes in small clusters tended to be less polymorphic than OR genes in large clusters. Of the 732 mutations, 307 were silent, 273 were missense (130 leading to the incorporation of an amino acid of a different chemical group), and 152 were nonsense (pseudoalleles). Amino acid substitutions were distributed all along the whole proteins: in its transmembrane, inner, and outer domains.[2]

Out of the 109 OR genes analyzed, seven were strictly pseudogenes, 86 were intact in all breeds, and 16 OR genes had both intact and interrupted ORF (pseudoallele). For each of these 16 OR genes, the frequency of pseudoalleles varied between breeds. Thus, at the whole dog population level, one OR gene cannot be called intact or pseudogene without doubt. This also suggests that pseudogene formation is still an ongoing process, as previously reported for human OR genes (Gilad and Lancet 2003). This *de novo* pseudogenization appears to be the counterpart of the acceptance of a large proportion of mutational events leading to the diversification of the OR repertoire and its continuous adaptation to a changing environment.

POLYMORPHISM AND ODOR PERCEPTION

A link between genetic variation in ORs and odor perception was first demonstrated by a positive correlation between the presence of two SNPs in the human OR gene OR7D4 and the perception of androstenone (Keller et al. 2007). Similarly, an association between isovaleric acid sensitivity and the genotype of the human OR pseudogene OR11H7P was shown (Menashe et al. 2007). The high polymorphism observed in the dog OR genes could thus affect the odorant detection capabilities and partly explain individual or breed olfactory differences. However, this highly expected relationship between OR polymorphism and dog olfactory performance is not supported by experimental data. In a preliminary study, Lesniak et al. (2008) analyzed 5 OR genes from 35 dogs (31 police sniffer dogs and 4 dogs trained to detect cancer markers), which were ranked according to their odorant detection performances. They detected 18 SNPs in the 5 genes, of which 10 induced amino acid changes. However, in the absence of information regarding the ligand specificity of these ORs and the chemical nature of the odorants used to rank the dogs, no correlation or suggestion linked canine olfaction performances and OR genetic polymorphism from these experiments.

A few years ago, CNVs were identified. They correspond to segments of the genome that may contain one or more genes and that are present in a variable number of copies in individuals. Analyses of the human CNVs showed that they would affect more ORs and V1R genes than other gene families and that two randomly chosen individuals showed, on average, a copy-number difference of approximately 11 in functional OR genes (Nozawa et al. 2007; Hasin et al. 2008; Young et al. 2008). Similar results were obtained with the first dog CNV map, showing that ORs and immunity-related genes are overrepresented in CNV regions (Chen et al. 2009). Another study showed that the 429 genes that are included in CNV regions were implicated in a wide variety of biological processes, including olfaction (Nicholas et al. 2009).

It would be important to perform more CNV analyses across breeds to detect correlations, if any, between the olfactory capabilities and the presence of CNVs. But the real asset regarding the impact of CNVs would be to correlate their presence with the number of genes and the level of expression of the corresponding ORs.

OR GENE EXPRESSION

Experiments performed with mouse, rat, and human tissues have shown that the level of expression varies considerably among OR genes. Depending upon the sensitivity of the technology used, just over one-third of the OR genes were shown to be expressed at a given time (Young et al. 2003), whereas by microarray hybridization, expression of up to 70% of OR genes could be detected (Zhang et al. 2004). It was also shown that a small number of OR genes were expressed in other tissues (e.g., testis, brain, and heart) (Feldmesser et al. 2006) and that 67% of human OR pseudogenes were expressed in the human OE (Zhang et al. 2007). Transcriptome comparison of rat OEs of different ages (adult, newborn, and aged) showed different levels of expression, with some ORs specifically expressed in each age group (Rimbault et al. 2009). This led to the hypothesis that for newborn rats that are blind and deaf, some ORs would be important for mother–newborn communication.

Almost no study has been performed regarding the analysis and determination of the genes expressed by the dog OE. Apart from ethical reasons that limit the use of tissues from live animals, there are also practical reasons that have limited the use of tissues from euthanized animals, as it is known from analyses performed with rat and mouse OE that OR expression is not uniform but regionalized, some OR genes being expressed in some regions and others elsewhere (Rimbault et al. 2009). Compared to rat and mouse OE, the dog epithelium is very large, too large to be sampled entirely at once, therefore limiting, if not preventing, its analysis. One alternative would be to recover by brushing enough cells from the nasal cavities, as has been done in human OR analysis.

Thus, studies of OR expression in dogs focused mostly on the expression in testis (Vanderhaeghen et al. 1993, 1997). Through degenerated PCR and cloning, these studies showed that most of the OR genes that were expressed in the testis had little or no expression in the olfactory mucosa. This restrictive expression pattern suggests that these ORs may play a role in the control of sperm maturation, migration, or fertilization. These hypotheses were confirmed by the study of one human OR gene that is implicated in sperm chemotaxis (Spehr et al. 2003). Indeed, spermatozoa expressing this OR gene migrate and accumulate at the maximal concentration of the bourgeonal odorant. In the mouse, one OR gene is implicated in the same way with respect to the lyral odorant molecule (Fukuda et al. 2004).

A COMBINATORIAL CODE

The first step of the olfaction process is the binding of an odorant molecule to its receptor. To date, very few ligand/receptor pairs have been identified. In the dog, *in vitro* experiments were performed for 47 dog OR genes belonging to family 6 of class II and for 22 genes of other class II families and class I (Benbernou et al. 2007, 2011). The canine OR genes were transiently expressed in a mammalian cell line expressing the specific G protein Ga(olf). The cells were then exposed to different odorant molecules belonging to C6–C13 aliphatic aldehydes, ketones, esters, fatty acids, and alcohols. The interaction of the odorant with the receptor was detected through calcium concentration measurements. Indeed, the stimulation of the Ga(olf) protein leads to a calcium influx through the opened nucleotide-gated channels (Nakamura and Gold 1987). These studies showed that two different aldehydes do not bind to the same set of ORs and that 28 of the tested ORs from family 6 recognized octanal, which reflects a complex combinatorial code combined with a nonadditive receptor code. These combinatorial codes allow the perception of many odorant molecules and a myriad of odorant mixtures in large excess compared to the number of receptors (Malnic et al. 1999).

DOG OLFACTION AND ITS PRACTICAL APPLICATIONS

The dog olfaction capabilities were first used by humans for hunting. Several dog breeds were then created to respond to different needs of hunting: blood scent, air scent, particular animal odor, etc. We can hypothesize that the creation of these different breeds was performed by selecting major genes implicated in all steps of olfaction. More recently, humans used the olfaction acuity of dogs for other purposes like drugs; explosives (Furton and Myers 2001); humans lost in avalanches, earthquakes, and fires (Migala and Brown 2012); and even currency. In the past few years, dog olfaction has been used to detect different human malignancies (Lippi and Cervellin 2012) (see Chapter 24 herein). As early as 1989, a report showing detections of melanoma by dogs was published (Williams and Pembroke 1989), and others followed in 2001 and 2013 (Church and Williams 2001; Campbell et al. 2013). Another study demonstrated that olfactory detection of human bladder cancer was feasible by trained dogs (Willis et al. 2004). By smelling urine, dogs are able to detect prostate cancer with a significant success rate (Cornu et al. 2011). The accuracy of lung (by urine or exhaled-breath screening), breast, and colorectal cancer detection by trained dogs was also proven (McCulloch et al. 2006; Sonoda et al. 2011; Bodedeker et al. 2012; Amundsen et al. 2014). Other studies also showed that a dog was capable of distinguishing different histopathological types and grades of ovarian carcinomas (Horvath et al. 2008, 2010, 2013). However, very limited success of breast and prostate cancer detection by dogs was reported (Gordon et al. 2008). Other uses can be illustrated by dogs used to locate live bed bugs and viable bed bug eggs (Pfiester et al. 2008) (see Chapter 21 herein), to locate live termites and discriminate them from nontermite material (Brooks et al. 2003), or to detect cows in estrus via the cow saliva (Fischer-Tenhagen et al. 2013). Also, one study showed that a trained dog could detect a patient infected with *Clostridium difficile* either by their stools or by a detection round in the patient rooms (Bomers et al. 2012).

CONCLUSION

The dog is certainly not the only species able to recognize a large spectrum of odors at very dilute concentration in the air. Most, if not all, wild mammals living in their own environment have probably developed exquisite odor detection performance through evolution, given the importance of this faculty for their survival. But dogs are more amenable than other mammals to be of human aid in the detection of illicit drugs, searches for people following earthquake disasters or avalanches, or cancer diagnosis, to cite a few of the possibilities.

The main problem in fully exploiting this exquisite canine odor detection capability is that too little is known about the many factors influencing odor detection and discrimination. This certainly explains why many studies produce very different results regarding the use of dogs to detect illicit drugs or to identify a criminal (as reported by Dunn and Degenhardt 2009; Ensminger 2012, pp. 117–146; Hickey et al. 2012; Jezierski et al. 2014). In fact, too many parameters in the setting of the trials are not taken into consideration, because of the absence of knowledge regarding their importance. Moreover, not all the breeds are the same, which is understandable given their different genetic backgrounds (vonHoldt et al. 2010). Moreover, within a given breed, different animals have different capabilities or perform differently. What makes a given dog or a given breed good at sensing odors? Is it its genetic makeup? Is it the training? Probably both. Or is it the proper aptitude of a dog to be trained and respond to the handler? Another set of questions relate to the nature of the odor detection problem with which a dog might be confronted. For example, there are fundamental differences between the detection of a given odor at a very dilute concentration, an odor toward which a dog can be trained, and the detection within a large spectrum of odors of only a specific one. It is not the same problem for a dog to search for humans after an earthquake and to identify from among different persons the perpetrator of a crime.

Fundamental studies to elucidate how much of a dog's olfactory ability depends on its genetic background, how much depends on its training, and what the genetic factors are that make a dog good at sensing odor are very much needed. Financial limitations, unfortunately, may mean that progress in these areas will not be as rapid as desirable.

ENDNOTES

1. In the neuron, the OR genes are transcribed into messenger RNA (mRNA), which then are translated into proteins that migrate to and are inserted in the membrane of the neurons.
2. The OR protein is a receptor located on the membrane of the neuron. The receptor goes through the membrane seven times and is thus classified as a transmembrane protein. The regions of the receptor that are in the membrane are called the transmembrane domains, the regions that are in the neuron are called the inner domains, and the regions that are in the external environment are called the outer domains.

5 Effects of Disease on Canine Olfaction

Cynthia M. Otto

Sensory disorders can impair a person or a dog's ability to function normally in society. It is clear that blindness and deafness are relatively easily recognized and quantified in humans. Even in animals, diagnostic tests to evaluate vision and hearing are validated and available. Furthermore, these tests do not require a training or learning component, as they are typically based on electrical stimuli. For example, an electroretinogram captures activation of the retina and is used to confirm blindness, whereas the brain stem evoked auditory response can be used to diagnose deafness.

In humans, disorders of smell and taste are less commonly recognized than other sensory disorders, and olfactory screening is rarely a part of a routine medical evaluation. In medical examinations of animals, there is no objective means to evaluate smell or taste. Most cases of abnormal olfaction in people are identified through patient reporting. Despite relative underreporting, disorders of olfaction are common, affecting between 1% and 20% of the human population (Bramerson et al. 2004; Fonteyn et al. 2014; Tuccori et al. 2011), whereas reports of confirmed olfactory dysfunction in the veterinary literature are rare (Myers et al. 1988a,b). The three main functional categories of sensory impairment are complete loss of smell (anosmia), a decreased ability to smell (hyposmia), and a distortion of the recognized odors (dysosmia) (Chaaban and Pinto 2012; Henkin et al. 2013). Dysosmias require patients to describe how the odor is abnormal, whether they are smelling odors that are not there (phantosmia) or the odor smells like something it is not (parosmia) (Chaaban and Pinto 2012; Henkin et al. 2013). Dysosmias currently cannot be diagnosed or characterized in dogs.

DIAGNOSIS OF OLFACTORY DYSFUNCTION

The diagnosis of hyposmia or anosmia in humans is typically made by testing the sensory response in a psychophysical test (Doty and Kamath 2014; Henkin et al. 2013). There are several "scratch-and-sniff" tests that allow either qualitative or quantitative measurement of odor recognition. For dogs, this type of approach is more challenging, in that the dog must first be trained to give a response to the odor. Failure of a dog to alert on a trained odor may result from (1) inadequate training; (2) improper or inadequate odor source; (3) environmental factors (e.g., air currents, heat, humidity, distractions); or (4) less commonly recognized medical conditions (e.g., systemic illness, hyposmia/anosmia). An alternative approach using habituation to familiar odors has been tested in a pilot study. Habituation to odor relies on both olfaction and memory. This study familiarized the dog to an odor by directing the dog to sniff each of two odor cards impregnated with urine, making this the familiar odor. The dog was then directed to sniff one odor card that contained the familiar urine and a second odor card that held urine from a different (novel) dog. Habituation was defined as a preference (time spent investigating) for the novel odor compared to the familiar odor (Salvin et al. 2012). This approach may provide an evaluation method for anosmia that can be utilized without prior odor training and may be able to estimate odor threshold, but this requires further validation. In order to determine if there is a medical explanation for a failure to alert or suspected hyposmia, all other training and environmental factors must first be considered. Systemic illness should be ruled out through a complete history and veterinary examination. A history of exposure to toxins or upper respiratory infections should be documented. If a dog has acutely lost its ability to detect odor and other medical conditions are not present, a complete assessment of olfaction is warranted.

Complete or partial loss of olfaction can result from either a disruption of odorant binding to olfactory receptors (e.g., a blockage of the nasal passage or rhinitis causing inflammation locally) or a failure of conduction of the impulse from the receptor to the brain (e.g., nerve disruption from head trauma or degeneration associated with aging) (Chaaban and Pinto 2012). As part of the evaluation, computed tomography of the head and rhinoscopy may identify structural factors that impair odorant binding. Magnetic resonance imaging may be able to identify structural abnormalities in the nerves and brain that impair conduction of the olfactory impulse (Henkin et al. 2013; Li et al. 1994). Options to evaluate olfactory function in dogs are generally limited to research settings but include electroencephalography, olfactory evoked potentials, and functional MRI (Berns et al. 2015; Ezeh et al. 1992; Flohr et al. 2014; Howell et al. 2011; Myers et al. 1984; Sato et al. 1996). In humans, evaluation of nasal mucus trace minerals, calcium, carbonic anhydrase VI, and cyclic nucleotides may provide insights into olfactory dysfunction (Henkin et al. 2013), but there are no data on nasal mucus composition in normal dogs or dogs with anosmia. The more difficult evaluation will be for a dog in which hyposmia is suspected. Diminished evoked olfactory potentials following infection with canine distemper virus (CDV) (Myers et al. 1988a) and an elevated odor threshold following canine parainfluenza infection (Myers et al. 1988b) have been reported in clinical cases and experimental studies, respectively.

CAUSES OF OLFACTORY DYSFUNCTION

In humans, the majority of cases of olfactory dysfunction are associated with postviral alterations, idiopathy, allergic rhinitis, or head trauma (Fonteyn et al. 2014; Henkin et al. 2013). The most common cause of anosmia in humans is congenital; however, head trauma resulting in shearing injury to olfactory nerves or scarring of nerve tracts is a common acquired cause of complete loss of smell (Fonteyn et al. 2014; Schofield et al. 2014). In dogs, the only report of anosmia was associated with CDV infection (Myers et al. 1988a). During active infection with CDV, similar to chronic rhinitis in humans (Henkin et al. 2013), the inflammatory response leads to nasal discharge, inflammation, changes in the physical character of nasal mucus, and decreased access to olfactory receptors (Myers et al. 1988a). Interestingly, several dogs that recovered from CDV had persistent impairment of olfaction. More recent studies have shown that CDV has a predilection for the neurons of the olfactory bulb (Rudd et al. 2010). This mechanism of anosmia/hyposmia may be similar to the postviral hyposmia commonly seen in humans, in which the impairment appears to be sensoneural (Chaaban and Pinto 2012; Riel et al. 2014). There are no reports of congenital or trauma-associated anosmia in dogs.

Hyposmia is more common in humans than anosmia and is most often associated with chronic rhinosinusitus and allergic rhinitis (Fonteyn et al. 2014). In dogs, although handlers of scenting dogs often perceive events that result in impaired odor detection (Myers et al. 1984), documented hyposmia is limited to experimental settings (Ezeh et al. 1992; Myers et al. 1988b) and one dog after recovering from CDV (Myers et al. 1988a). Canine diseases of the nasal passages, like parainfluenza (Myers et al. 1988b), create local inflammation, which, similar to human allergic rhinitis, can impair the binding of odorant to olfactory receptors (Chaaban and Pinto 2012; Gaines 2013). The mechanism of hyposmia in these cases has been proposed to include a decrease in the nasal cyclic guanosine monophosphate (cGMP) and cyclic adenosine monophosphate (cAMP), which serve as growth factors (Henkin et al. 2013), combined with local inflammation (Chaaban and Pinto 2012; Gaines 2013). In a model of allergic rhinitis in mice, eosinophilic infiltrates in the olfactory epithelium and excess mucin production were documented (Ozaki et al. 2010). Many of the human cases represent transient hyposmia, but, particularly with viral infections, there is the potential for more prolonged impairment associated with nerve injury.

Nonsinonasal causes of hyposmia were documented in a case series in humans; in that series, 37.9% of cases were postinfectious, and 33.1% were trauma related. Less commonly, idiopathic (16.3%), congenital (5.9%), toxic (3.4%), and neurological (3.4%) causes of olfactory dysfunction were diagnosed (Fonteyn et al. 2014). Similarly, in 5183 human patients evaluated in a Taste and Smell clinic, 27% were postinfectious, 16% were idiopathic, 15% had allergic disease, and 14% had head injury (Henkin et al. 2013). Less commonly, systemic disease has been implicated in human olfactory dysfunction. The list of diseases includes but is not limited to endocrine diseases (e.g., diabetes mellitus, hypoadrenocorticism, hypothyroidism); liver disease; neurodegenerative disease (e.g., Parkinson's, Alzheimer's); otolaryngeal disease; inflammatory bowel disease; and autoimmune disease (Bramerson et al. 2004; Chaaban and Pinto 2012; Henkin et al. 2013; Landis et al. 2004; Schubert et al. 2011; Steinbach et al. 2013). Obesity has been linked to decreased olfactory acuity in some studies, but the results have been inconsistent (Palouzier-Paulignan et al. 2012). Animal models have mainly focused on olfactory dysfunction in neurodegenerative diseases; variable results may be a function of the type of disease or the confounding impact of aging (Head 2013; Phillips et al. 2011; Wesson et al. 2011).

Effects of Trauma

Trauma-related olfactory loss has been reported in 60% or more of patients with traumatic brain injury (Gudziol et al. 2014; Schofield et al. 2014). The severity of injury appears to be related to the incidence of olfactory dysfunction (Gudziol et al. 2014; Schofield et al. 2014). Mechanisms for injury include direct damage to the sinonasal tract and shearing injury of olfactory nerves. Damage to the cribriform plate is likely to result in shearing or ischemia of olfactory neurons. Contusion and scarring in the olfactory bulb or processing pathways can also impair olfaction (Chaaban and Pinto 2012). Some patients with trauma-induced anosmia/hyposmia will regain olfactory function, with the majority of improvement occurring within 3 months of injury (Gudziol et al. 2014). The ability of olfactory neurons to regenerate is an important factor, not only in cases of trauma but also in response to inflammation and toxins; however, the extent of the recovery cannot be predicted. The impact of head trauma on olfaction in dogs has not been investigated; however, if a detection dog suffers trauma associated with loss of consciousness, evaluation of anatomic and functional olfactory pathways is indicated.

Compared to men, women are generally recognized as more sensitive in odor detection, and this finding has been reported in some animal studies (Doty and Cameron 2009). In women, alterations in odor perception have been reported during pregnancy. Changes include dysosmia with decreased odor recognition of specific but not all odors (Simsek et al. 2014) or heightened sensitivity (Doty and Cameron 2009) during the first trimester and a decreased odor threshold during the third trimester (Ochsenbein-Kolble et al. 2007). There are no studies of sex and odor detection sensitivity or the impact of gonadectomy (castration or ovariohysterectomy) on olfaction in dogs.

Effects of Age

A well-recognized factor in people is that olfactory function diminishes with age (Doty and Kamath 2014). It has been suggested that over 75% of people over 80 years of age have olfactory impairment (Doty and Kamath 2014). Even by the age of 65, half of the population is likely to experience some level of abnormal olfaction. For aging humans, this deficit can impact their safety and their life satisfaction. The cause of olfactory dysfunction is likely multifactorial and can be influenced by comorbidities, particularly neurodegenerative disease, but there are recognized structural aging changes that are key contributors. None of these changes have been characterized in the dog. Reported aging changes within the nose include changes in airflow patterns and mucus composition. In humans, these changes may be related to a higher prevalence of sinusitis and nasal disease and a decrease in mucociliary clearance (Doty and Kamath 2014). In addition, the cribriform plate, which is the gateway from the nasal epithelium to the olfactory bulb, is reported to undergo age-related sclerosis (Kalmey et al. 1998), resulting in ischemia or necrosis of olfactory receptor cells. Recent digital imaging studies have characterized the cribriform plate in carnivores but did not report on age effects (Bird et al. 2014) (see Figure 5.1).

The neuroepithelium also exhibits an age-dependent decrease in receptor number and cellular arrangement. The neuroepithelium is likely affected by a decrease in regenerative capacity and an increase in programmed cell death (apoptosis) (Doty and Kamath 2014; Robinson et al. 2002). Aging also impairs immune function and receptor cell signaling. Toxin exposure and damage may be cumulative, as suggested by the finding that environmental factors appear to outweigh genetic influences (Doty and Kamath 2014). In dogs, chronic exposure to air pollution has been shown to induce severe alterations in the nasal neuroepithelium (Calderon-Garciduenas et al. 2003). Brain changes with aging include a decrease in olfactory bulb size and atrophy of the frontal lobe, which may contribute to impaired olfaction (Doty and Kamath 2014; Head 2011; Tapp et al. 2006). The relationship between structural brain changes and olfaction has, however, not been tested in dogs. In addition, there have not been longitudinal studies of olfaction in dogs. In one pilot study of age-dependent odor habituation in police Labradors, a weak trend toward a decline in habituation with age was observed (Salvin et al. 2012).

In people, potential side effects of hundreds of medications include an altered sense of smell (dysosmia, hyposmia, or anosmia), but few drugs have been objectively tested (Doty and Bromley 2004). Based on a series of over 5000 human patients, nonanesthetic drug-related disturbances represent less than 1% of all smell and taste dysfunction (Henkin 1994; Henkin et al. 2013). A review of 136 drugs with potential smell or taste effects only identified 3 drugs (all angiotensin converting enzyme [ACE] inhibitors; see Table 5.1) that were associated with anosmia and 3 drugs (all antiarrhythmics; see Table 5.1) associated with smell disturbance in people (Doty and Bromley 2004).

EFFECTS OF DRUGS

Even less is known about the effect of drugs on olfaction in dogs. One published study documented impaired olfaction in dogs after 7 days of 2 mg/kg dexamethasone daily (Ezeh et al. 1992). This dose is in excess of the normal clinical applications and was used to simulate the endocrinologic disease of hyperadrenocorticism. In humans, the use of steroids has been associated with both treatment of smell dysfunction and the cause of smell disturbances; systemic steroids result in more

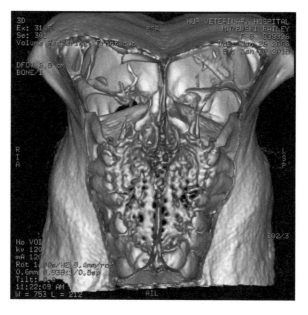

FIGURE 5.1 Digital imaging of the cribriform plate of a 9-year-old golden retriever. 3-D volume reformatted image from rostral region. (Image provided by Dr. Jennifer A. Reetz, DVM, DACVIM [LAIM], DACVR.)

TABLE 5.1

Classes of Drugs That Alter Olfaction

Type of Drug	Evidence for Anosmia or Smell Disturbance in Humans	Evidence in Dogs
Analgesics (pain medication)	Remifentanyl (Lotsch et al. 2012) Δ9-tetrahydrocannabinol (THC) (Walter et al. 2014)	
Anesthetics - general	Sevoflurane (Kostopanagiotou et al. 2011)	
Anesthetics - intranasal	Intranasal ketamine, lidocaine, tetracaine (Elterman et al. 2014)	
Antiarrhythmic	Tocainamide (Doty and Bromley 2004) Amiodarone (Doty and Bromley 2004)	
Antibiotics	Macrolides (clarithromycin, +/– azithromycin) (Tuccori et al. 2011) Doxycycline (Bleasel et al. 1990) Amikacin (Welge-Luessen and Wolfensberger 2003)	Metronidazole at high doses (Jenkins et al. 2014)
Antihypertensives/ cardiac medication	ACE inhibitors (enalapril) ACE inhibitors with diuretics (enalapril with hydrochlorothizide) ACE inhibitors with calcium channel blockers (enalapril with felodipine) Calcium channel blockers (For all inhibitors and blockers, see Doty and Bromley 2004)	
Anti-inflammatories	Nasal prednisone (Heilmann et al. 2004; Nguyen-Khoa et al. 2007)	Dexamethasone at high doses (Ezeh et al. 1992)
Chemotherapeutic agents	Cisplatinum, carboplatinum, cyclophosphamide, doxorubicin, 5-fluorouracil, levamasole, methotrexate (Ackerman and Kasbekar 1997; Doty and Bromley 2004)	

consistent improvement, whereas intranasal steroids have limited benefit or may impair olfaction (Heilmann et al. 2004; Nguyen-Khoa et al. 2007).

There are rare case reports of anosmia after antibiotic use, for example, one case after doxycycline (Bleasel et al. 1990) and one case after amikacin (Welge-Luessen and Wolfensberger 2003). In an Italian study of spontaneously reported adverse drug events, the macrolide antibiotic, clarithromycin, more commonly affected taste, but there were reports of abnormal olfaction alone or combined with altered taste (Tuccori et al. 2011). The olfactory disturbances were not characterized, so it is unknown if they were anosmias, hyposmias, or dysosmias. The majority of cases resolved with completion of treatment. Azithromycin is a macrolide antibiotic commonly used in veterinary medicine; there are no documented cases of azithromycin-induced hyposmia or anosmia in the human or veterinary literature.

A preliminary report investigating the olfactory effects of two commonly used antibiotics in explosive detection dogs showed no impact of doxycycline (5 mg/kg twice daily for 10 days) but did show that half of the dogs treated with metronidazole (25 mg/kg twice daily for 10 days) had a diminished odor threshold (Jenkins et al. 2014). This dose of metronidazole is higher than typical clinical usage and approaches doses associated with neurotoxicity in dogs (60 mg/kg per day) (Dow et al. 1989; Fitzgerald 2012).

Drugs and toxins share potential mechanisms by which they could impair olfaction. One potential mechanism is impairment of odorant binding, most commonly via altered mucus quality or quantity. Antihistamines and decongestants may impair olfaction through the drying effects on the mucosa (Nguyen-Khoa et al. 2007). In addition, antiproliferative drugs may alter the nasal neuroepithelium through inhibition of the normal turnover of olfactory sensory neurons, which are replaced regularly (Doty and Bromley 2004). In a recent review, the prevalence of smell abnormalities ranged from 5% to 60% of patients undergoing chemotherapy (Gamper et al. 2012); the large range was attributed to the predominance of self-reporting rather than psychophysical evaluation. Although decreases in smell may be anticipated based on the antiproliferative effects, increased sensitivity to odors associated with chemotherapy has also been reported (Bernhardson et al. 2009). In addition to the direct effects, chemotherapeutic agents often lead to indirect effects secondary to immunosuppression (Doty and Bromley 2004). There are no reports of the effects of chemotherapeutic agents on olfaction in dogs; however, dogs being treated with chemotherapeutic agents are not expected to be working in detection fields. Confirmation of olfactory discrimination and thresholds after completion of treatment is warranted for any dog that returns to work.

Drugs and toxins can also alter nerve conduction or cognitive perception (Doty and Bromley 2004; Henkin et al. 2013). Combined toxins and drugs represent approximately 3.4% of cases of nonsinonasal olfactory dysfunction in people (Fonteyn et al. 2014). Topiramate is used for control of some seizure disorders. Taste and smell impairment in one patient was reported during treatment but resolved after the drug was discontinued (Ghanizadeh 2009). This drug is not a first-line drug in seizure management in dogs but has been evaluated to have some potential benefit (Kiviranta et al. 2013).

Anesthetics have been implicated as a cause of smell dysfunction. Smell and/or taste dysfunction after anesthesia is rare and typically short lived (Elterman et al. 2014; Kostopanagiotou et al. 2011). Common features of anosmia cases include general anesthesia, intranasal delivery of local anesthetics, and surgical procedures (Elterman et al. 2014). Given that no individual drug is consistently implicated and that there are two case reports of resolution of long-standing anosmia after anesthesia (Cassidy et al. 2000; Cooper 1998), it is difficult to draw any conclusions about anosmia and anesthesia.

Many anesthetic and pain medications are also endogenous ligands for receptors in the brain. The olfactory system has recognized receptors for opioids and cannibinoids. Binding of an odor molecule to an olfactory receptor increases cAMP through G-coupled proteins; both opioids and cannibinoids activate inhibitor G-coupled proteins and decrease cAMP. Both the opioid remifentanyl and the cannabinoid Δ9-tetrahydrocannabinol (THC, 20 mg) increase odor threshold in volunteers (Lotsch et al. 2012; Walter et al. 2014). This THC-mediated olfactory impairment is in contrast to the role of endogenous cannabinoids in the olfactory bulb, where the actions appear to enhance olfactory sensitivity. This effect, however, might be dose specific or "state specific" (e.g., influenced by factors associated with fasting) (Soria-Gomez et al. 2014; Wang et al. 2012). The effect of exposure to cannabinoids or opioids on olfaction in dogs has not been evaluated.

Effects of Chemical Exposure

As recognized from occupational hazards in many industries, acute high exposure or chronic chemical exposure (see Table 5.2 for list) can impair olfaction through local injury, and degeneration of olfactory neurons and the neuroepithelium (Gobba 2006; Upadhyay and Holbrook 2004). There are no reports of acute exposure causing impaired olfaction in dogs; however, in the dogs that responded during 9/11, where acute exposure to high levels of dust and toxins was likely, there was no measurement of olfactory function (Slensky et al. 2004). It is unlikely that most dogs will reach the level of chronic exposure that can occur in industrial workers. In samples from search-and-rescue dogs and police canines that responded to the terrorist attacks of 9/11, toxins were not detected (Fox et al. 2008; Slensky et al. 2004). Although nickel and vanadium were detected in the nasal olfactory epithelium in dogs chronically exposed to air pollution, the values were not significantly higher than in control dogs (Calderon-Garciduenas et al. 2003). In a research study, zinc nanoparticles enhanced olfactory signaling *in vitro* (Moore et al. 2012); however, it is well recognized that high levels of zinc are neurotoxic to olfactory neurons in humans and dogs (Houpt et al. 1978; Jafek et al. 2004).

TABLE 5.2
List of Potential Olfactory Toxins

Dusts	Cement
	Hardwood
	Silicosis
Inorganic compounds (nonmetal)	Ammonia
	Carbon disulfide
	Carbon monoxide
	Chlorine
	Hydrogen sulfide
	Sulfur dioxide
	Methyl bromide
Metals	Aluminum
	Arsenic
	Cadmium
	Chromium
	Copper
	Lead
	Zinc
	Manganese
	Mercury
	Nickel
	Steel
	Zinc
Miscellaneous agents	Asphalt
	Menthol
	Oil of peppermint
	Pepper and spices
	Tobacco
Organic compounds	Acrylate and methacrylate
	Acetone
	Acetophenone
	Benzene
	Benzine
	Butyl acetate
	Chloromethanes
	Ethyl acetate
	Formaldehyde
	Hexane
	Pyrethrin
	Styrene
	Trichloroethylene
	Toluene
	Xylene

Source: Gobba, F., *Int. Arch. Occup. Environ. Health*, 79(4), 322–331, 2006; Upadhyay, U.D., and Holbrook, E.H., *Otolaryngol. Clin. North Am.*, 37(6), 1185–1207, 2004; Gobba, F., and Abbacchini, C., *Int. J. Med. Environ. Health*, 25(4), 506–512, 2012.

Repeated extended exposure to a room treated once with pyrethrin, 2-butoxiethanol, and 2-ethyl 6-propylpiperonyl ether dissolved in water resulted in acute nasal irritation that progressed to phantosmia and then anosmia, which persisted in an adult male (Gobba and Abbacchini 2012). The risk of repeated insecticide exposure is highest in dogs performing bedbug detection. Although these dogs are not routinely screened, guidelines for training include 4 h a week of maintenance training; therefore, any evidence of decreased olfactory performance should be observed. No reports of anosmia in pest-detection dogs are published.

EFFECTS OF SECONDHAND SMOKE

Cigarette smoke is frequently cited to alter olfactory function in humans (Ackerman and Kasbekar 1997; Doty and Bromley 2004; Katotomichelakis et al. 2007); however, the evidence for olfactory impairment is inconclusive (Bramerson et al. 2004; Hayes and Jinks 2012; Landis et al. 2004). In a study of human smokers, although no functional olfactory impairment was detected, the size of the olfactory bulb in smokers was significantly smaller than in nonsmokers (Schriever et al. 2013). Experimental studies in mice show a strain-dependent sensitivity of the olfactory epithelium to cigarette smoke (Matulionis 1974). It is unknown if there is a genetic factor that makes some individuals more susceptible with exposure to cigarette smoke. The effects of secondhand smoke are also unknown. In one study, children from smoking households were able to identify significantly fewer (71%) of 500 odors compared to children from nonsmoking households (79%) (Nageris et al. 2001), but odor threshold was not evaluated.

EFFECTS OF ALCOHOL AND ILLEGAL NARCOTICS

Alcohol is associated with smell disorders; in humans, acute alcohol ingestion impairs odor memory and discrimination (Doty and Bromley 2004). In honeybees, it was hypothesized that alcohol-impaired olfactory discrimination was a result of impaired olfactory processing (Mustard et al. 2008). Chronic alcohol ingestion can cause reversible and irreversible olfactory dysfunction (Doty and Bromley 2004). Dogs are more likely to have acute accidental alcohol toxicity than chronic alcoholism with its associated complications. Dogs intoxicated with alcohol will show clinical signs of impaired performance (Keno and Langston 2011) and will not be fit to work.

Cocaine exposure is a potential hazard for drug detection dogs in training or working. Intranasal cocaine can impair olfaction as a result of profound vasoconstriction and potential infarction of olfactory nerves (Ackerman and Kasbekar 1997). Cocaine-mediated nerve signal transduction deficits appear to be rapidly reversible (Tamari et al. 2013). In a series of cocaine abusers, permanent hyposmia/anosmia was uncommon (Gordon et al. 1990). Clinical cocaine toxicity appears to more likely affect pet dogs than working dogs (Thomas et al. 2014), although there are no studies of the effects of subclinical exposure on olfaction in dogs. There is no evidence of "drug addiction" in narcotic detection dogs; if anything, detection dogs are "addicted to the hunt," as evidenced by the search intensity of dogs regardless of the material they are taught to find.

CONCLUSIONS

Although there are numerous drugs and diseases that have been implicated to cause olfactory dysfunction in humans, the evidence for an effect in dogs is minimal. Regardless of the species, it is likely that the mechanism of olfactory dysfunction—disruption of odorant binding to olfactory receptors, or a failure of conduction of the impulse from the receptor to the brain—will be similar (Chaaban and Pinto 2012). The critical level of olfactory dysfunction needed to alter a dog's performance is unknown. Quantitative characterization of olfactory thresholds will allow evaluation of potential causes of a reduced threshold or discrimination of odors. Currently, the only way to provide evidence of olfactory performance is through training records.

6 Olfaction in Wild Canids and Russian Canid Hybrids

Nathaniel J. Hall, Alexandra Protopopova, and Clive D.L. Wynne

In this chapter, we consider canine olfaction from an evolutionary perspective. To do so, we will explore the functions of the olfactory sense for the dog's closest relative, the wolf. We provide an overview of what is known about wolf olfaction and how it aids survival. We then review whether wild canids have a better sense of smell than domestic dogs. We consider the little research that has been conducted on this topic and also explore Russian attempts to create hybrid dog–jackal odor detection canines.[1]

THE FUNCTION OF THE CANINE NOSE

Although dogs' remarkable sense of smell has been harnessed for human purposes with detection dog training, the dog's nose itself is not a human creation. A highly sensitive nose is present in the dog's wild counterpart, the wolf (Asa et al. 1986; Harrington and Asa 2003; Zimen 1981). The canid nose has several functions, and the detection of narcotics, explosives, and other substances of interest to humans is just a minor component of what the nose can do and is surely not its evolutionary purpose. Keeping in mind that the dog's nose has an evolutionary function focused on the acquisition of food, communication with conspecifics, and navigation might help overcome frustrations in training when the dog uses its nose for the detection of biologically relevant odors rather than human-intended targets.

To understand the evolutionary function of the dog's nose, we start by observing how the wolf uses its olfactory prowess. Unfortunately, the experimental evidence regarding wolf olfaction is limited; however, researchers have been systematically observing wolf behavior for several decades now and offer some relevant conclusions. The wolf is strikingly inclined to sniff. Asa et al. (1986) rendered wolves unable to smell through an olfactory pedunculotomy and found that these anosmic individuals continued to sniff and investigate their environment with their noses despite their inability to sense any odors. Thus, even when wolves receive no sensory feedback from sniffing, they continue to attempt to investigate their environment by sniffing (Harrington and Asa 2003). Olfaction appears to serve two primary functions for the wolf: first, the tracking and detection of prey and second, communication between conspecifics.

HUNTING

Wolves are known to hunt a variety of prey, ranging from the small hare to the large moose (Darimont et al. 2003; Milakovic and Parker 2011; Peterson and Ciucci 2003). Here, the contributions of vision and audition cannot be underestimated (see Harrington and Asa 2003 for a review). Vision is particularly important once the wolves are in close proximity to prey. However, wolves have to track their prey using olfactory cues because the prey are typically widely dispersed and are found in low density. This differs in part from other canids such as red foxes and coyotes, for whom vision seems to be the primary sense used in hunting (Harrington and Asa 2003). Wolves travel great distances in search of prey. They spend 28–50% of their day traveling in search of food and usually travel between 42 and 44 km between prey kills (Peterson and Ciucci 2003). During their search, wolves rely on a combination of chance encounters and tracking, scenting, and spotting prey. Wolves rely on their tracking and olfactory capacity in wooded areas, and their keen sight in open areas (Peterson and Ciucci 2003). Wolves have been observed spotting hares crouching in furrows from several meters away and simply walking up and grabbing the unsuspecting hare (Mech, unpublished data, cited in Peterson and Ciucci 2003).

Olfaction, however, still remains critical to the hunting wolf (Harrington and Asa 2003). Wolves' prey is widely dispersed, which puts pressure on them to travel and concentrate on senses other than vision. Here, the ability to track prey using olfactory cues becomes paramount because chance encounters are too rare to be sustainable, although the wolf is capable of going without food for 3–4 days (Lopez 1978; Peterson and Ciucci 2003). Thus, there are strong selection pressures on the ability to travel long distances and detect and locate sparsely populated prey as efficiently as possible.

This ecology of the wolf may in part be why the dog is such an excellent tool in detection work. The ecology of the wolf parallels the tasks we assign to detection dogs. We ask detection dogs to help us locate highly dispersed and low-density targets such as explosives, narcotics, and even wildlife, similar to the density of large prey items that wolves need to track to survive. A search dog is often assigned to search for long periods of time for a target that is unlikely to be found, or at least not found easily. Perhaps the ecology of the wolf has in part shaped the dog to be a good search companion. Another interesting parallel is that the wolf does not rely only on olfaction for prey detection. The wolf has keen senses of vision and hearing. The wolf does not ignore these senses when tracking and identifying prey but, rather, uses all available information. This is important to consider for the detection dog as well.

Although a trainer may focus on olfactory cues for a detection dog in training, the dog likely utilizes other senses to help find a target, if at all possible. For example, dogs very well might attend to visual cues from ground disturbances that could aid in the detection of improvised explosive devices. These cues could, in conjunction with olfactory cues, aid in the detection of explosives. The multimodality of search in the dog can also be a drawback, because dogs may also attend to visual cues from the handler or elsewhere that become associated with a reward. Thus, wolf ecology suggests that olfaction is a critical sense for dogs but not the only important one they possess. Instead, the wolf will use the cues available to track prey, and we hypothesize that the same is true of the dog.

COMMUNICATION

Despite its widely assumed importance in locating prey, relatively little research has been conducted on olfaction in this context. In contrast, much more research has focused on the use of olfactory cues in communication between wolves. Olfaction is a key source of communication for the wolf. Wolves likely can recognize individual pack members by smell, as they typically engage in low rates of anogenital sniffs and licks but will engage in increased investigation following prolonged periods of separation (Zimen 1981). Scent marking is an important use of olfaction in wolves that aids in navigating and maintaining territory, pair bonding, and mating. Scent marks can be made or placed with urine marks and scat. Urine and scat both have eliminative functions but also appear to serve as scent marks. Urine marks can be left in various ways. Raised-leg urination is typically made by high-ranking males and appears to function solely for scent marking (Rothman and Mech 1979). Squat urinations, on the other hand, appear to serve both eliminating and scent-marking functions. Scent marks are typically left in conspicuous areas that are well traveled, such as open roads, so that others can easily find them (Barja et al. 2004; Zimen 1981). Scat, in particular, is left in such places as on top of rocks or in clearings (Barja et al. 2004).

Scent marking is such an important behavior for the wolf that leaving scent marks occupies much of the animal's day for members of the pack that engage in it (Lopez 1978). On average, a scent mark is laid or sniffed every 2 min (Lopez 1978; Peters and Mech 1978), and a raised-leg urination scent mark is laid or encountered, on average, every 3 min (Peters and Mech 1978). The roaming wolf encounters or leaves a scent mark, on average, every 240 m (Peters and Mech 1978). Typically, however, only breeding pairs and dominant individuals make scent marks; low-ranking or lone wolves do not usually scent-mark (Rothman and Mech 1979).

One function of scent marking is to mark out territory. Scent marks are typically laid out circling a pack's territorial area (see Peters and Mech 1978 for details). The pattern of scent marks typically is heaviest in a bowl pattern surrounding the home territory. To maintain scent marks, areas are revisited, and new scent marks are laid on average every 3 weeks. In regions where two packs' territories are adjacent, scent marks are laid more often, yielding a thicker region of scent marks by both packs.

Lopez (1978) argued that the main purpose of scent marking is to aid the navigation of the region of the resident pack, and that marking out the pack's territory is a secondary purpose. Lopez suggests that the scent marks allow younger pack members to better navigate the territory and perhaps allows a separated pack member to locate other pack members, which has also been suggested by Peters and Mech (1978). In addition, Lopez notes that scat scent marking may have even more general communicative purposes to resident pack members, as wolves will scat-mark traps or poisoned baits, perhaps to warn other pack members.

While navigation and territory may be important functions of scent marking, it may also aid in mating and affiliation within a pack. Wolves are probably able to discern sex and sexual status of other wolves via olfactory cues in urine (Harrington and Asa 2003). The composition of volatile molecules in wolf urine does vary between sexes, across seasons, and with hormone levels, indicating that urine could serve as a signal of sexual status (Raymer et al. 1984, 1986). In fact, olfactory cues appear critical in the sexual development of male wolves. Male wolves that have been rendered anosmic prior to sexual experience fail to show interest in proestrous and estrous females (Asa et al. 1986). Interestingly, however, inexperienced females or sexually experienced males continue to copulate after being rendered anosmic (Asa et al. 1986).

The exact relationship between scent marking and pair bonding is not completely clear, but the two do appear to be related (Rothman and Mech 1979). Interestingly, scent-marking rates are highest immediately before and after breeding sessions (Asa et al. 1990; Rothman and Mech 1979). In addition, alpha pairs engage in a unique double-marking behavior. In double marking, the female and male scent-mark the same area, thereby double-marking the same region (Rothman and Mech 1979). Although it is not clear how, double marking appears to be important in pair bonding of the alpha pair in wolf packs, perhaps by providing information exchange via urine marks (Rothman and Mech 1979).

When discussing socially mediated olfactory cues, it is important to highlight that canids can sense via an accessory olfactory system known as the vomeronasal or Jacobson's organ (Adams and Wiekamp 1984; Harrington and Asa 2003). The exact nature and function of the vomeronasal organ remain elusive, but several studies have confirmed its importance in sexual behavior and the detection of pheromones (for a review of vomeronasal structure and function, see Doving and Trotier 1998; for a discussion of the anatomy of the vomeronasal organ, see Chapter 1 herein; for a discussion of the neural connections of the organ, see Chapter 2). Interestingly, however, what canids detect through the vomeronasal receptors and how important this vomeronasal odor perception is for canid behavior are largely unclear and require further study.

Zimen (1981) pointed out that one important difference in olfactory perception between humans and canids is that canids do not find aversive odors that humans find repugnant. In fact, canids appear to be attracted to odors such as putrefying meats. Wolves and dogs engage in a curious behavior known as *scent rolling* or *scent rubbing* (see Reiger 1979 for a review). This is a familiar behavior to many dog owners: on finding and sniffing an odor source that a human might find repulsive, the dog will begin to roll its face, neck, and side along the odor, transferring the odor to its coat. The function of this behavior is largely unknown and has received little experimental attention. One hypothesis is that scent rolling camouflages the predator's odor with odor from prey (Reiger 1979;

Zimen 1981). This seems unlikely, however, because wolves readily roll in other predator odors (Ryon et al. 1986), and odor camouflage is unlikely necessary to aid the wolf in hunting (Goodman 1978). Another hypothesis is that scent rolling allows an individual to become more familiar with a novel odor by "wearing" the odor (Fox 1971; Reiger 1979; Ryon et al. 1986).

Alternatively, scent rolling may be a social behavior (Fox 1971; Goodman 1978; Harrington and Asa 2003; Reiger 1978). For example, scent rolling on a novel and interesting odor may increase one's own social attractiveness (Fox 1971; Reiger 1979). Research in the spotted hyena (*Crocuta crocuta*) provides preliminary support for this hypothesis (Drea et al. 2002). We have also recently conducted some preliminary observations of scent rolling in dogs and wolves and have found that wolves will readily scent-roll in a wide range of odors, with a particular affinity to perfumes and colognes. Other researchers have made similar observations, noting that wolves will scent-roll on a wide range of novel odors (Goodman 1978; Ryon et al. 1986). Wolves will roll not only on novel odors that could be considered natural (e.g., predator feces) but also on odors they are unlikely to encounter in the wild (e.g., motor oil) (Ryon et al. 1986). In our observations, we have noticed that dogs show a reduced likelihood to scent-roll on novel odors compared to wolves. The wolf tends to show more investigation of novel odors and is much more likely to scent-roll than is the dog. It is unclear, however, whether the wolf is more sensitive to odors or simply shows greater interest. The question of relative odor sensitivity between dogs and wolves is the topic of the next section.

IS WILD CANID OLFACTION BETTER?

Various hypotheses about the acuity of the wolf's sense of smell have arisen in the scientific literature. One hypothesis is that the wolf is not very sensitive to faint odors but has a better capability than humans to discriminate between odors (Lopez 1978). In other words, the wolf is no different than humans in detecting low concentrations of an odor, but what a person smells as just "woods," the wolf smells as many different distinguishable odors (Lopez 1978). An alternative hypothesis is that the wolf's sensitivity to odors exceeds man's (Zimen 1981) and is very similar to that of the dog (Harrington and Asa 2003). Laska et al. (2000), however, provide evidence in favor of the contention that dogs' sensitivity to some odors is similar to that of primates. Whether dogs and wolves actually differ in their olfactory capability has received relatively little recent research interest.

One study, however, conducted by Southwest Research Institute (1974) explored the abilities of various mammalian species (including foxes and wolves, although data from wolves were not reported) as mine detectors. The aim of this project was to evaluate whether other species than just dogs might prove useful for mine detection work. In general, Southwest Research Institute concluded that pigs showed great potential, except for their propensity to root (not good around a mine!) and their unfortunate social stigma. Canid species other than the dog proved too fearful of humans for field use and were, therefore, not considered further. Figure 6.1 is adapted from Southwest Research Institute's final report and shows the mean detection accuracy for various breeds of dogs, wild canid species, and other noncanid species. The noncanid species showed promise in detection accuracy for the detection of land mines. Interestingly, only pigs (miniature and red Duroc) were able to detect mines buried at depths greater than 6 in., which exceeded the detection depth of all other species. Importantly, however, strong generalizations cannot be made from these data given the limited sample size of individuals from each species. Further testing of the olfactory detection capabilities was discontinued, which was explained by the authors thus:

> In working with exotic animals, the project staff was impressed with the olfactory acuity demonstrated by all species studied. It was the general consensus, however, that the demonstrated acuity would have been greater had it been possible to establish greater rapport with the "wild" animal species. Unfortunately, available project resources precluded the expenditure of an adequate amount of time for the socialization process. (Southwest Research Institute 1974, p. 11)

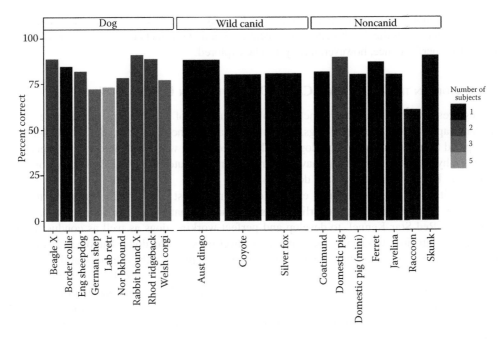

FIGURE 6.1 Performance of various breeds of dogs and noncanid species in detecting land mines. (Adapted from Southwest Research Institute, Olfactory Acuity in Selection Animals Conducted during the Period of June 1972–September 1974, Report AD787495, Southwest Research Institute, San Antonio, Texas, U.S., 1974.)

Overall, this preliminary work suggested that the few wild canids tested, and the handful of noncanid species, performed within the ranges observed for the dogs. This may not come as a surprise to modern olfactory researchers, who have learned over decades of research of the excellent olfactory acuity of rodents and a wide variety of other species (Passe and Walker 1985). In fact, giant African pouched rats (*Cricetomys gambianus*) have even been tasked with mine detection work (Poling et al. 2011a,b).[2]

Some more recent studies have looked at the canid olfactory receptor genome to identify differences in olfaction between dogs and wolves. Briefly, olfaction is thought to be governed in part by the binding of olfactants to olfactory receptors in the olfactory epithelium. Each olfactory receptor binds to only one type of odorant physiochemical feature, which depends on its genetic code (see Quignon et al. 2012 and Chapter 4 herein for a review of the genetics of canine olfaction). Animals that are thought to have a keen sense of smell, such as the mouse and the dog, tend to have a greater number of functional olfactory receptor genes, whereas microsmatic animals, such as humans, have fewer functional olfactory receptor genes and more nonfunctional olfactory receptor genes (pseudogenes) (Quignon et al. 2012).

Theoretically, by looking at the accumulation of different types of mutations in the olfactory receptor genome, we can begin to assess the selection pressure for olfaction in dogs and wolves. Using this theory, a couple of studies have investigated the number of pseudogenes and types of olfactory receptor polymorphisms that are present in the dog and wolf olfactory receptor genome. Zhang et al. (2011) showed that dogs had a greater percentage of their olfactory receptor genome disrupted by mutations (17.8%) compared to the wolf (12.1%), although this difference did not reach statistical significance. In a subsequent analysis, Chen et al. (2012) explored the accumulation of different types of mutations in the wolf, the Chinese village dog (CVD), and several different dog breeds. They found that the two animals that were less exposed to human-driven selective breeding—the wild wolf and the CVD—showed selection against deleterious olfactory receptor mutations, whereas modern breeding has led to purifying selection, removing the variability of different polymorphisms in the population, which likely was a result of breeding practices (i.e., artificial selection) in the dog breeds. The potential functional effects of these genetic differences on olfactory performance, however, have yet to be explored.

A Case Study in the Use of Wild Canid–Dog Hybrids in Detection Work

Although research offers no clear conclusion on the question of whether wild canids have superior olfactory capabilities to domestic dogs, work in Russia over the last several decades has aimed to develop and train superior detection dogs by selective breeding with wild canids. In this section, we review the hypothesis and work that have driven military institutes and applied working dog centers in Russia to breed hybrid animals for detection work.

The military of the Soviet Union expressed a keen interest in improving the performance of the military working dog from its earliest days, so much so that an experimental kennel was built in 1924, the Red Star Kennel, to develop and perfect working dogs as well as conduct research on training, nutrition, veterinary medicine, and novel uses of war dogs (Hudoleev 2014; Lulina 2014). Since the 1960s, there have been several attempts to improve the olfactory abilities of dogs, including even pharmaceutical approaches (Krushinsky and Fless 1959). The Soviet military experimented with different breeds and mixes of breeds but could not find one that did not require prolonged training. Researchers in the 1980s even attempted extreme measures to boost performance, such as sewing shut the eyes of puppies in a failed attempt to improve their olfactory acuity (Starovoitev 2013).

Due to increased frustration with the inadequate working ability of bomb and narcotic detection dogs, Klim Sulimov, senior research assistant at the D.S. Likhachev Scientific Research Institute for Cultural Heritage and Environmental Protection, was tasked with creating a "superdog" by experimenting with hybridization of dogs with their wild relatives (Sulimov 1995).

Russian scientists believed that wild canids have a better sense of smell due largely to an evolutionary account of the role of olfaction in the life of canids (Matychenko 2008; Sulimov 1995). The hypothesis that drove this work was that wild canids rely more on their sense of smell than do domesticated dogs because the ecology of the wild canid requires them to use olfaction to locate prey. The scientists hypothesized that this environmental selection pressure might result in animals that are ideal for detection work. Furthermore, the systematic attempts to eradicate wild canids carried out by people over thousands of years may have put further selective pressures on the population, thereby increasing the ability of wild canids to recognize and avoid human odor. The ability to detect tiny olfactory cues left by hunters can mean life or death for a wild canid (Sulimov 1995).

Sulimov, along with other Russian scientists, suspected that dogs, through domestication, may have been freed from the evolutionary pressures to keep up the acuity of their sensory organs, particularly the ability to use olfaction as well as their wild counterparts. He did, however, point out that an alternative hypothesis would suggest that dogs actually have a heightened ability to discriminate human odorants. The complete reliance of domesticated dogs on humans may have necessitated an ability to differentiate people. One person may be a food giver, whereas another may be dangerous. Another reason why domesticated dogs may benefit in being able to accurately track human odor is that trails left by people often lead to settlements with abundant food sources. Sulimov noted that it is common for a stray dog in the woods to follow a person and then abandon him or her when he or she reaches a town. These stray dogs almost never approach the person, suggesting that human odor may function more as a cue that leads the way to food.

Wild dogs, or village dogs (Coppinger and Coppinger 2001), may have retained their acuity for discriminating odors, but modern dogs, which are split into artificially selected breeds, may have reduced olfactory capacity. Sulimov argued that the constant destabilizing selection pressure on domestic dogs through the development of many breeds, with most of the selection driven by the appearance of the dog (or an ability to excel at a sport) as opposed to olfaction, has reduced the olfactory capabilities of domestic dogs. He noted that Belyaev, in his experiments with domesticated foxes, extensively discussed the destabilizing nature of domestication on certain traits of the animals. Even when dogs are supposedly bred for function, they are simply just bred to excel at a relatively artificial sport, in which the goal is to score points with judges. These sport dogs, Sulimov argued, are typically in a permanently hyperaroused state, which induces heightened body temperature and constant panting, which further interferes with successful odor detection.

Sulimov argued that modern breeds are too evolutionarily unstable for scent work, and instead, a more evolutionarily stable canid needs to be used—in his case, hybrids of the European jackal (*Canis aureus moreoticus*) and mixes of Laikoid dogs (a breed type developed in the Red Star Kennel by mixing spitz-type hunting dogs called Laikas with German shepherd dogs). A jackal, not a wolf, was chosen to bring hybrid vigor into the dog population for several reasons. First, Sulimov (incorrectly) believed that a jackal, not a wolf, is the wild animal most closely related to dogs; therefore, such a hybrid would bring the dog closer to its original evolutionarily stable form. Second, the smaller size and endurance to various climates of the jackal makes the animal especially useful for outdoor housing in the Russian climate. Third, Sulimov argued that the jackal has interesting behavioral traits that allow for better olfactory discrimination. For example, jackals in the wild actively seek out and feed on placentas left over by ungulates. He found in his own hybrids that with higher jackal content, the animals were better able to discriminate human gender. He suggested that this capability may be a remnant of the need of jackals to be able to track pregnant female ungulates and be able to discriminate between male and female odors.

Sulimov noted that another option may be to use the stray (or village) dogs that have not been destabilized by artificial selection. These dogs may still represent an evolutionarily stable animal, with natural selection exerting pressure to retain original olfactory capabilities. As mentioned, it may be quite beneficial for a village dog to be able to track human olfactory cues to lead it to settlements, and therefore food, and to be able to discriminate individual humans as friend or foe. Sulimov noted that there is already a precedent to using village dogs as working animals. They often excel at tasks, making them popular for circuses and even for flying into space. However, the use of these village dogs for a working dog breeding program is usually met with resistance from the public and officials. In Russian culture, as in much of the world, these dogs are considered unclean and inferior to modern established breeds.

A dog relatively close in size and temperament to a village dog is the Laika dog, used for hunting small game in Russia and parts of Europe. This breed has also not been traditionally attractive for working breeding programs, because of its relatively unknown heritage through the interbreeding of various working dogs. These dogs do have some anthrophobia (fear of people), but Sulimov noted that this can be overcome with just one generation of selective breeding. To further overcome anthrophobia and add traits of trainability and loyalty to the animals, Sulimov added fox terriers to his breeding program.

Sulimov reported that the best detection dogs were achieved by backcrossing a second-generation jackal hybrid with a mixed-breed dog (named Daika). The three offspring from this cross were even better detection dogs than either of the parents. In practice, Sulimov said that anything over 37.5% jackal could not be successfully used as a detection dog, but at 6.25% jackal, the animals acted like regular dogs. In Sulimov's dissertation, he presented data indicating that when experts were offered various dogs for work, and the hybrid content of the dogs was not disclosed, the 25% jackal hybrids were consistently chosen to be used more than any other dogs (see Figure 6.2). Sulimov claimed that with higher jackal content, the hybrids had better olfactory acuity; however, these high-content animals were not preferred for work, due to their high anthrophobia. Lesser percentages had less acuity—at least as evidenced by not being selected for work. Sulimov's results showed that jackal hybrids were significantly more likely to be selected for work and be employed for more years than were nonhybrid dogs. Sulimov has maintained his jackal–dog hybrid program, and these dogs are presently working as narcotic detection dogs for Aeroflot airlines at the Sheremetyevo Airport in Moscow (see Figure 6.3).

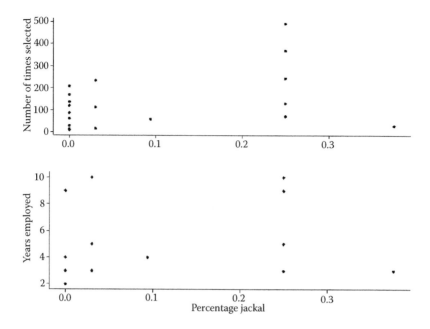

FIGURE 6.2 Number of times dogs and dog–jackal hybrids were chosen for detection work and the number of years they were employed. (Adapted from Sulimov, K.T., Kinologicheskaya identifikaciya individuma po obonyatel'nym signalam [Identifying individuals through olfactory cues using dogs], doctoral dissertation from the Institut Problem Ekologii i Evolucii imini A. N. Severtsova [A. N. Severtsov Institute of Ecology and Evolution], retrieved from DisserCat (accession number 03.00.08), available at http://www.dissercat.com /content/kinologicheskaya-identifikatsiya-individuuma-po-obonyatelnym-signalam, 1995.)

FIGURE 6.3 Jackal–dog hybrid that works as a detection canid for Aeroflot airlines at the Sheremetyevo Airport in Moscow. (Courtesy of C.D.L. Wynne.)

Sulimov's work on dog–jackal hybrids is not without its critics, however, even in Russia. Starovoitev, a close collaborator of Sulimov, noted that he does not find dogs to be systematically worse than the jackal hybrids (Starovoitev 2013). Starovoitev compared one of Sulimov's high-performing hybrids to the performance of a Laika-type dog on their ability to match a sample odor mixture from a selection of comparison odors. Both the hybrid and the Laika dog proved equally capable in this round of testing, suggesting that overall, the mixed-breed dog did no worse than the jackal hybrid. Critics of Sulimov have further noted, rather bitterly, that the idea that these jackal hybrids are better than regular working dogs keeps being repeated in the Russian media but that there have never been strong data or scientific literature to support the claim. Starovoitev brought up a time when a journalist from New York wrote of the wonders of Sulimov's dogs but could not get comments from any other scientists or biologists, due to a lack of data to support Sulimov's claims (Starovoitev 2013).

Partially as a response to the perceived success of Sulimov's enterprise, a biologist, Vecheslav Kasimov, attempted to breed the domestic dog with a wolf to create a superior detection dog (Kasimov et al. 2005). Kasimov crossed a tame hand-reared wolf, which was reported to show remarkable tolerance toward people, with a German shepherd dog. In an interview for a national news channel, Kasimov claimed that whereas a working German shepherd dog can search a location for narcotics in about 6 min, his "volkosob" (a Russian neologism, combining *volk* [wolf] and *sobaka* [dog]) can do so in less than 2 min (Ivanov 2007). Kasimov's volkosobs are currently patrolling the Chinese–Russian border (Ivanov 2007).

Unfortunately, most of the claims surrounding the performance of wild canids and hybrids compared to modern breeds have not been subjected to thorough scientific evaluation. Thus far, the most comprehensive study was conducted by Korytin and Azbukina (1986). They assessed the olfactory acuity of eight dogs (five Laika breed–type dogs, one English setter, one Russian sight hound, and one mixed-breed dog) and six wild canids [one wolf (*Canis lupus*), one red fox (*Vulpes vulpes*), two Arctic foxes (*Alopex lagopus*), one dingo, and one jackal–dog hybrid]. All the canids were given a simple test: A small piece of meat was hidden in one of three containers. The canid was allowed to inspect the containers and could choose a container by pawing or biting at it. To assess the acuity of the various canids, the researchers placed filters between the meat and the top of the container, thereby reducing the resulting odor plume. By increasing the number of filters, the researchers could systematically reduce the odor to identify when the canid could no longer detect the meat. Figure 6.4 shows the number of filters that were required until each canid could no longer detect the meat. The arctic foxes were able to detect the meat with the most filters, but dogs were not far behind and were comparable to the wolf, jackal–dog hybrid, and red fox. In addition, the researchers also evaluated seasonal variation in performance. Figure 6.5 shows the performance of the various species across seasons. Interestingly, most of the wild canids show clear seasonal influences, with a noticeable increase during the spring season, but the dog and perhaps the wolf show a relatively stable pattern all year. These results should be taken with caution, however, given the limited sample size for each species.

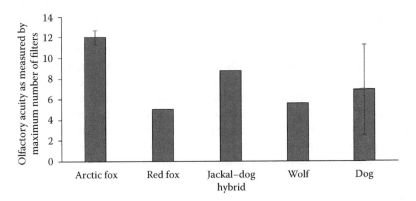

FIGURE 6.4 Olfactory acuity (as measured by the maximum number of filters through which a meat odor could be detected) across 2 years of monthly sessions. Bars show the mean maximum number of filters that were present with which the subject could still detect a piece of meat. Error bars show the standard deviation (SD) for canids for which there were multiple subjects. Only one red fox, one wolf, and one jackal–dog hybrid were tested.

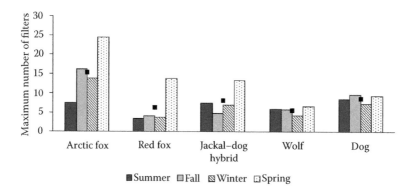

FIGURE 6.5 Seasonal variation in detection of meat for various canids. Bars show the maximum number of filters through which the canid could detect the meat across each season for a total of 2 years. Squares show the yearly average. No error bars were reported in the original data.

Although there has been considerable interest in Russia in hybridizing animals in order to create a superior working dog, not much research has been conducted comparing wild and domesticated canids in their olfactory capabilities. It seems that the assumption that wild canids are superior is not shown conclusively by any means with the presently available data, but there is some suggestion that jackal hybrids may be more successful as narcotic detection dogs (e.g., Sulimov 1995), or at least not worse than domesticated dogs (Starovoitev 2013). There is also some suggestion that arctic foxes have superior acuity in scenting food (Korytin and Azbukina 1986). Unfortunately, however, additional research is needed before any firm conclusions can be drawn regarding the performance of wild and hybrid canids.

CONCLUSIONS

In this chapter, we first reviewed the function of olfaction in the wolf. The wolf uses olfaction in the tracking and hunting of prey, and we highlighted how parallels, but also distinctions, can be noted to the task given to the search dog. We also suggested that wolves are not limited to olfaction when tracking and likely use acoustic and visual stimuli to aid performance, and that the dog is likely to do the same as well. We then covered the use of olfaction for communication, which is a critical function of the sense of smell for the wolf. Scent marking is crucial to the outlining of territories and probably navigation within territories. Olfaction is also important in pair bonding and sexual behavior.

Smell is, overall, a critical sense for the wolf, and many behaviors that are crucial for survival and reproduction depend on its function. In the last sections of this chapter, we reviewed the nascent and growing work that has tried to answer the question of whether wild canids may have superior olfactory capabilities to domestic dogs. The scientific evidence is minimal and equivocal. Applied detection work in Russia, however, has focused on breeding super detection dogs by creating hybrid strains of wild canids and domestic dogs. Some preliminary results and anecdotal evidence suggest that these programs might have achieved some success; however, to make any strong claims about the program, more in-depth and thorough research is required.

ENDNOTES

1. The authors greatly thank Drs. Valentin Petuskhov and Natalja Rodionova for assistance in finding and accessing the dissertations and research articles that are summarized in this chapter.
2. For the reader interested in the olfactory acuity of a wide variety of species, the authors recommend Passe and Walker (1985) as a starting point.

Section II

Chemistry and Aerodynamics of Odors

A study of canine olfaction by a single author or group of authors with a relatively unified focus might not have a section on the chemistry and properties of odor, or might raise such issues only as quick summaries of research lines too complicated for many authors or readers lacking backgrounds in organic chemistry or fluid dynamics. A contributed volume should not take such an approach, however, and we sought contributors who could discuss the chemistry and aerodynamics of odor. In this section, there is also a chapter on how the organic chemistry of odor overlaps with canine evidence in forensic contexts, an area where increasingly sophisticated studies of odor signatures produced by narcotics and cadavers may be able to refine our understanding of what drug and cadaver dogs may actually be sensing.

CHEMISTRY OF ODOR

The continuous development of analytical technologies and miniaturization of devices raises the possibility that in the future, some functions of detection dogs may be gradually replaced by machines. Chemists studying odor and its recognition by animals or devices want to know precisely what compound or combination of compounds may be found in a test sample, and to know which of these may be available to the sensory tool being studied. Dogs are not primarily used to detect individual chemicals (though this has been studied) but, rather, to identify materials that may release several compounds into the atmosphere, often in particular ratios that are described as odor signatures. There is, however, no simple relationship between the chemistry of volatile compounds and the odor impression perceived by the olfactory system of an animal. A compound may be pleasant at one concentration but unpleasant at a higher concentration. Odors of some compounds may dominate or even mask those of other compounds, or a new odor may emerge from the mixture. What odors and odor signatures dogs detect remains largely unknown and is the main reason why canine detection is often labeled as an unscientific "black-box" technology.

Gas chromatography coupled with mass spectrometry (GC/MS) is referred to in many chapters of this book, but the first chapter of this section (Chapter 7) focuses on this gold standard for the analysis of volatile organic compounds. The authors described the invention and development of these techniques in the last 50 years and the basic working principles that researchers use in performing these procedures. In contrast to canines, where a yes/no reaction is typically made without the handler knowing with which chemical compounds or at what concentration a behavioral reaction has been triggered, the output of the GC/MS analysis, after an appropriate interpretation, enables identification and quantitative determination of trace amounts of particular odorous chemical compounds.

Detector dogs, on the other hand, have the advantage of being mobile, self-directing, self-sampling, quick-response, real-time biosensors that use subtle changes in the concentration of odors to find an odor source under field conditions. The authors of the chapter on GC/MS technologies describe examples of the current use of this technique in forensic analyses of drugs and explosives and for human odor profiling, concluding that GC/MS can be helpful in better understanding how canine olfaction works and what its constraints are, an issue that is explored in the forensics context in the last chapter of the section (Chapter 9).

AERODYNAMICS OF ODOR

One of the crucial aspects of odor detection by canines is the need to understand how odor molecules move in an environment. The aerodynamics of odor helps explain why dogs may detect an odor source within seconds of deployment or, under unfavorable conditions, may not detect an odor at all. These issues are reviewed in the second chapter of this section (Chapter 8). It is important to be aware that the odor's movement has both spatial and temporal aspects. The author of this chapter finds much guesswork and even misinformation about the aerodynamics of odor, even in some peer-reviewed studies. Some research refers to "scent cones" as if this is a precise visual description of how odor travels, whereas an understanding of fluid dynamics of odor indicates that any simple reliance on a too-frequently-repeated catchphrase to describe the shape of an odor in a space is inevitably simplistic and frequently wrong. Errors from such reliance are not confined to scientific research but, unfortunately, extend even to courtrooms, where testimony about dogs moving in scent cones may say something about what the police dog handler sees in the animal's behavior but little about how the odor from a drug, an explosive, an accelerant, a cadaver, etc., is actually being carried in the air.

A Nebraska federal district court stated in 2008 that "[o]dors emanate from objects in a scent cone." This description of how odor disseminated from a suitcase in a bus station should no longer be accepted, which is not to say that the dog's alert was faulty or that the handler was incorrect, but only that the court's uncritical acceptance of the handler's description of the shape taken by an odor cannot be scientifically supported (*U.S. v. Johnson*, 2008 U.S. Dist. LEXIS 118503 [D.Neb. 2008]). It is all too common for investigators and courts to accept descriptions of odor that go so far as to specify its shape from the mere fact that a change in a dog's behavior indicates that a target odor has been encountered. This chapter describes odor movement in a way that will have to be taken into account in the future by the scientific community working on other aspects of odor, as well as lawyers, trainers, and handlers.

VOLATILE ORGANIC COMPOUNDS AND CANINE FORENSICS

The chapter on volatile organic compounds and canine forensics shows how olfactory detection of illicit substances or human cadavers by trained canines may be explained by chemical analysis. From a forensic and legal point of view, much uncertainty would be removed if it were possible to verify what chemical compounds and mixtures dogs deployed in investigations may actually be sensing. The murder trial of Casey Anthony in Florida involved the prosecution producing evidence of a cadaver dog as well as a chemical analysis of items in the car trunk where the body of the victim may have been placed. The evaluation of the chemical evidence turned into a battle of experts. The potential overlap of chemical and canine evidence in criminal investigations in the future is discussed in this chapter.

Chemical analyses are helpful in providing an objective explanation for canine alerting to objects that do not seem to be related to illicit activities. This issue arose with regard to currency that contained traces of cocaine but that may or may not have had any recent connection with the drug trade. The science of this issue is discussed in two chapters in this book, Chapters 9 and 17.

TECHNOLOGICAL ALTERNATIVES TO THE CANINE NOSE

Research on odor often includes mention of the possibility that dogs are likely to be detecting odors so slight that we as humans are incapable of detecting. While acknowledging the superiority of dogs in this regard, chemical research on odor has a twofold significance for the future of canine detection as a practical technique. On the one hand, although chemistry is telling us more and more about what dogs are detecting, it is, on the other hand, also resulting in technology (i.e., equipment and procedures) that may eliminate or severely curtail the need to deploy dogs for various olfactory functions. For forensic purposes, this would generally be desirable because the uncertainty of reaching judicial conclusions from the behavior of a police dog in the presence of a possible odor of evidentiary significance has created endless controversy that would, to a substantial extent, disappear if instrumentation could be developed to a sufficiently reliable level. For medical purposes, it would be desirable to use machines instead of dogs, at least in the clinical detection of diseases, because the industry of medicine would clearly be more comfortable with reaching diagnoses from standardized instruments and procedures.

Nevertheless, dogs will never be replaced entirely. Service dogs that may detect oncoming seizures are important to their owners not just because of this olfactory skill but also because of their companionship and perhaps because they are trained to respond to seizures by supplying aid after the seizure has begun. Dogs working in conservation are more mobile than even the most easily carried equipment and also warn their handlers of possible dangers. Police dogs that detect narcotics may also provide protection to their police handlers. In any case, the boundary between what is considered an appropriate use of a dog and what is considered the domain of a machine is not likely to remain static.

Tadeusz Jezierski, John Ensminger, and L.E. Papet

7 The Development of Gas Chromatography/Mass Spectrometry and Its Uses in Odor Analysis

Joanna Rudnicka and Bogusław Buszewski

While research on canine scent detection has been advancing, and the capabilities of dogs to distinguish various types of odors has been found to have forensic, medical, environmental, and other applications, the question remains as to what the dogs are actually smelling, what chemicals their highly attuned olfactory systems recognize in such small quantities.

Dogs have obviously developed an excellent sense of smell. (See Chapters 1 and 2 herein regarding canine nasal anatomy and olfactory cell physiology for a detailed description of the unique aspects of the canine olfactory system.)

Using trained canines for odor detection or identification, however, is often labeled as a "black-box technology" since it is not known what chemical compounds or mixtures of compounds the dogs respond to, and the dogs cannot tell us directly what odor impressions they smell. The analysis of volatile compounds using gas chromatography coupled with mass spectrometry (GC/MS) could help us to decipher what is triggering sniffer dogs' responses and what makes them give false alerts.

Meanwhile, chemical analysis has led to considerable progress in determining what can be measured in mixtures of chemicals, and which components of such mixtures can enter the air or surrounding liquids and could produce odor that might be recognized by a dog. Compounds are often present at such low concentrations that it is necessary to enrich them before analysis. The most common method of enrichment of volatile organic compounds (VOCs) is solid-phase microextraction (SPME) and sorption on solid sorbents, followed by thermal desorption (TD). Enriched volatile compounds can be subsequently analyzed by GC or GC/MS (Buszewski et al. 2012b). It is therefore important to discuss the primary chemical measurement system that has been developed over the last century to identify the components of odors. This takes us into the world of gas chromatography (GC) and mass spectrometry (MS). The authors will discuss the history and development of these two procedures and then review some of the uses to which they have been put.

BEGINNINGS OF GAS CHROMATOGRAPHY

GC has become an important technique in medical research, forensic investigations, and laboratories working on food control and environmental pollution. It permits both the qualitative analysis of a complex mixture and quantitative determination of its components.

The creator of chromatography (which comes from the Greek words for color and writing, respectively χρῶμα and γράφω) is considered to be the Russian botanist Mikhail Tswett, who investigated plant pigments and was the first researcher to divide the colored bands of plant extract on silica gel (Bielicka-Daszkiewicz et al. 2005). Tswett's initial work was published in 1905 (Tswett 1905), but rapid development of chromatographic methods occurred after the mid-twentieth century with GC. The theoretical basis for GC was first described in 1941 (Martin and Synge 1941). Practical application of the technique began in 1952 with the successful separation of fatty acid mixtures by gas–liquid partition chromatography (James and Martin 1952).

Chromatography includes a physical separation method that divides sample components in two phases: a stationary phase (solid or liquid on the carrier or gel) and a mobile phase (gas, liquid and gas, or supercritical fluid). GC is a technique for separating mixtures of volatile compounds into individual components. This technique can analyze the compounds at trace levels from parts per million (ppm) down to parts per quadrillion (ppq). Presently, GC is used exclusively for analytical purposes, though previously, it was used for preparation and purification of compounds. Substances to be analyzed by this method should be thermally stable and volatile and have a boiling or sublimation temperature no higher than 400°C. With nonvolatile compounds, derivatization reactions are used to modify the compound to increase volatility and allow for chromatographic separation (Witkiewicz and Hetper 2001).

Separation of compound mixtures in GC is based on differences in interaction of volatile compounds being carried by a carrier gas, called the *mobile phase*, through a column coated with a material commonly called a *stationary phase*. The attraction of the compounds carried in the mobile phase to the coating substance (stationary phase) varies, allowing for separation and identification of the components in the mixture being analyzed (analytes). If the stationary phase is a solid adsorbent, the process is referred to as gas–solid chromatography; if a liquid, the process is referred to as gas–liquid chromatography. In gas–solid chromatography, the principle of separation is adsorption, with mixtures separating by the degree of adsorption affinity of the components to the surface of the stationary phase. In gas–liquid chromatography, the mixture separates based on differences in the values of partition coefficients of the components in the mixture between the stationary (liquid) phase and the mobile (gas) phase (Rodel and Wolm 1992).

The value-distribution coefficient (or partition coefficient) for a particular compound depends on the stationary phase and temperature. If temperature is assumed to be constant, this partition coefficient is defined in Equation 7.1:

$$K_D = C_L/C_G \tag{7.1}$$

where
   K_D = distribution coefficient of compounds
   C_L = concentration of compounds (analytes) in stationary phase
   C_G = concentration of compounds (analytes) in mobile phase

THE GAS CHROMATOGRAPH

A gas chromatographic system consists of a carrier-gas container (or reservoir), a flow controller, cleaning filters (molecular sieve to remove impurities), an injector, a column, a thermostat (in which the column is placed), a detector, and a computer (Rodel and Wolm 1992) (Figure 7.1). After the detector, the gas is released into the atmosphere. The sample to be analyzed may be a gas, liquid, or solid that is injected, often by a microsyringe, into a heated vaporizer port at the head of the column. The sample then evaporates in a stream of carrier gas as it is being transferred to the column. In the column, the sample separates into individual components that pass through the column sequentially and then into the detector, where an electrical signal is generated. After amplification, signals are saved by a computer program as a chromatogram, with visible peaks (Witkiewicz and Hetper 2001).

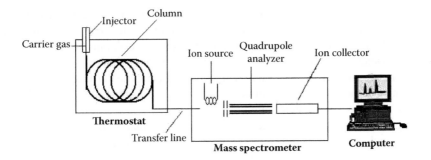

FIGURE 7.1 Scheme of gas chromatography/mass spectrometry system. (From Skoog, D.A. et al., *Principles of Instrumental Analysis*, 6th ed., Cengage Learning, Boston, 2006.)

Carrier Gas

A carrier gas should be chemically inert with respect to the stationary phases in the column and the components of the mixture being analyzed. Common carrier gases include helium, hydrogen, nitrogen, and argon (Bielicka-Daszkiewicz et al. 2005). The best carrier gas for most chromatographic systems is helium as it is nonreactive, nontoxic, and not explosive; changes only slightly in viscosity with increasing temperature; and conforms to the operational requirements of most detectors. Argon is also effective for many systems, exhibiting properties similar to helium, though viscosity changes are greater with increasing temperature, which requires taking pressure changes into account during the analysis. Nitrogen usually contains a certain amount of oxygen, which is unacceptable for analyzing mixtures at high temperatures and can lead to rapid oxidation and degradation of the stationary phase. Nitrogen can be used if deoxygenated or if special filters for oxygen are used. Hydrogen can act as a reducing agent, interacting with certain substances and thereby introducing errors in chromatographic analysis (Witkiewicz and Hetper 2001).

Injector

Injectors are devices to introduce the sample into a stream of carrier gas, which then carries components to the column. With capillary columns, which have a much lower sorption capacity than packed columns, smaller sample volumes are needed, and an injection splitter may be used so that only part of the sample enters the column while the remainder is carried out of the chromatograph system. This is needed for samples with high concentrations, but for samples with very small concentrations, splitless injection may be used. With splitless injection, the entire sample is directed into the column. Cool on-column inlets (cold injection) deposit the sample directly in the column and are used for analysis of substances at very low temperatures, which is useful in the analysis of thermally labile compounds (Bielicka-Daszkiewicz et al. 2005; Witkiewicz and Hetper 2001).

Columns

The column of a gas chromatograph can affect the quality of the separation of components in the mixture, so the type column and the packing used influence the results of a chromatographic analysis. Columns used in GC are of two types: packed and capillary. Among packed columns, three can be distinguished:

- Packed, analytical, with an inner diameter of 2–5 mm and length of 1–3 m
- Preparations (packed) with an inner diameter above 6 mm and length of 1–16 m
- Micropacked with an inner diameter of 0.8–1.2 mm and length of 0.5–2 m

The length of the column influences retention time (the longer the column, the higher the retention time), but it is improves compound separation. Therefore, the diameter of a column has a direct impact on the efficiency and sample's capacity in the column. Columns with a smaller diameter have greater efficiency than larger-diameter columns, but the latter have a greater sample capacity. Packed columns are made from material chemically and catalytically inactive in relation to the column packing and the substances separated in an analysis. Most packed columns are made from stainless steel, glass, copper, or aluminum.

Capillary columns are made from metal, molten glass, or quartz. They have an inner diameter of 0.1–0.6 mm and vary in length from 10 to 60 m. Capillary columns, depending on the kind of stationary phase, are divided into three types:

- Wall-coated open tubular column (WCOT)
- Porous-layer open tubular column (PLOT)
- Support-coated open tubular column (SCOT)

Common stationary phases for filling the columns are adsorbents (carbon adsorbent, silica gels, molecular sieves, porous polymers), as well as liquid stationary phases. Table 7.1 details characteristics of stationary phases used in GC (Witkiewicz and Hetper 2001).

DETECTORS

Substances separated by column chromatography are identified sequentially by a detector, which generates an electric signal from analyte traces as the carrier gas leaves the column. Detectors are divided into two types: (1) universal, for detection of many organic substances, and (2) selective, which are sensitive to a specific group of compounds (e.g., with specific structures or functional groups, such as halogenated compounds, or compounds with a specific element, such as phosphorus). Table 7.2 list detectors most commonly used in organic trace analysis. Detectors should ideally have high sensitivity and detectability, stable signal indications and baseline, a wide range of linearity, and the possibility of choosing for both selective and universal detection.

A thermal conductivity detector (TCD) detects all compounds, but since TCDs have high detection limits, they are not used for trace organic analysis. The flame ionization detector (FID) is the most widely applied detector in GC. In FIDs, a hydrogen flame is located between two electrodes. If only the carrier gas passes the flame, a constant ionic current of low intensity is produced, establishing a straight baseline measurement. When, together with the carrier gas, a substance is eluted from the column, the substance is ionized, and the increase in current can be measured (Equation 7.2).

$$CH^{\cdot} + O^{\cdot} \rightarrow CHO^{+} + e^{-} \tag{7.2}$$

where
$CH^{\cdot}$ = hydrocarbon radical
$O^{\cdot}$ = oxygen radical
CHO^{+} = formalism ion
e^{-} = electron

Detection and sensitivity of the detector depend on the ratio of the flow rate of the carrier gas, hydrogen, and air, which should be 1:1:10. FIDs are specific detectors and can be used to detect organic compounds. FIDs do not detect the presence of noble gases, oxygen, nitrogen, carbon monoxide, carbon dioxide, hydrogen sulfide, carbon oxysulfide, halogens, ammonia, nitrous oxide, formaldehyde, formic acid, water, or carbon disulfide. This detector has high sensitivity, high stability, and a large range of linearity (linearity indicates that the signal measured is proportional to

TABLE 7.1

Characteristics of Typical Stationary Phases for Analysis of Specified Organic Compounds in Gas Chromatography

Composition of Stationary Phase	Polarity	Maximum Temperature (°C)	Application
100% dimethylpolysiloxane	Low	340–360	Alcohols, aromatic hydrocarbons, esters, flavors and aromas, free fatty acids, glycols, halogenated hydrocarbons, hydrocarbons, ketones, organic acids, oxygenates, policyclic aromatic hydrocarbons (PAHs), pesticides, polymers, steroids, solvents, sulfur compounds
5% phenyl/95% dimethylpolysiloxane	Low	340–360	Alcohols, amines, hydrocarbons, bile acids, drugs, Environmental Protection Agency (EPA) methods, fatty acid methyl esters (FAME), flavors and aromas, glycerides, halogenated compounds, PAHs, polychlorinated biphenyls (PCBs), pesticides, steroids, sterols, sugars, sulfur compounds
5% diphenyl/95% dimethylpolysiloxane	Low	340–360	
6% cyanopropyl-phenyl/94% dimethylpolysiloxane	Midpolarity low	280–300	Organic volatiles and semivolatiles, aromatics, halocarbons, solvents
14% cyanopropyl-phenyl/86% dimethylpolysiloxane	Midpolarity low	300–320	Alcohols, aromatic hydrocarbons, organic acids, PAHs, pesticides, phenols, steroids
50% phenyl/50% dimethylpolysiloxane	Midpolarity	320–340	Drugs, pesticides
25% cyanopropyl/25% phenyl/50% dimethylpolysiloxane	Midpolarity high	260–280	Halogenated compounds, phenols, pyridines
Polyethylene glycol	High	250–260	Alcohols, aldehydes, anesthetics, antidepressants, aromatic hydrocarbons, esters, FAME, flavors and aromas, glycols, halogenated compounds, ketones, nitro compounds, PAHs, phenols, solvents, sulfur compounds
Cyclodextrin	Polar/ optically active	220–250	Separation of enantiomers, optical isomers of acids, alcohols, amino acids, aromatic hydrocarbons, diols, flavors, aromas, ketones, organic acids, phenols

Source: Varian, Inc., *Consumables and Supplies Catalog.* Posted at http://www.crawfordscientific.com/downloads /pdf_new/Varian-Catalogue-2010.pdf, 2010; Macherey-Nagel, *Gas Chromatography Application Guide/Technical Handbook.* Available at ftp://ftp.mn-net.com/english/Flyer_Catalogs/Chromatography/GC/GC%20Applis.pdf, 2015.

the concentration of the detected substance). It belongs to a group of destructive detectors since the sample is completely burnt in the flame (Westmoreland and Rhodes 1989; Witkiewicz and Hetper 2001).

The electron capture detector (ECD) consists of a chamber containing two electrodes and a radioactive source (^{63}Ni), which is less subject to change from contamination problems and can be operated at a high temperature. The carrier gas, argon or nitrogen (N_2), is ionized by the beta

TABLE 7.2

Detectors Commonly Applied in Gas Chromatography

Detection System	Type of Detector	Detection Limit (g/s)	Linear Range (g/s)
Thermal conductivity detection (TCD)	Universal	10^{-6} to 10^{-5}	10^5
Flame ionization (FID)	Selective (organic carbon compounds)	10^{-12}	10^7
Electron capture (ECD)	Selective (organic halogenated compounds)	10^{-13} to 10^{-14}	10^2
Thermal ionization (TID)	Selective (organic nitrogen and phosphorus)	10^{-13} N 10^{-14} P	10^3
Mass spectrometry (MSD)	Selective	10^{-12}	10^4

Source: Bielicka-Daszkiewicz, K. et al., *Zastosowania metod chromatograficznych* (English: *Application of Chromatographic Methods*), Wydawnictwo Politechniki Poznanskiej, Poznan, 2005; Witkiewicz, Z., and Hetper, J., *Chromatografia Gazowa* (English: *Gas Chromatography*), Wydawnictwo Naukowo-Techniczne, Warsaw, 2001; Macherey-Nagel, *Gas Chromatography Application Guide/Technical Handbook*. Available at ftp://ftp.mn-net.com /english/Flyer_Catalogs/Chromatography/GC/GC%20Applis.pdf, 2015.

particles (β) emitted from the source (Equation 7.3), generating positive ions of carrier gas $\left(N_2^+\right)$ and free electrons (e).

$$\beta + N_2 \rightarrow N_2^+ + e \tag{7.3}$$

When compounds with a high affinity for electrons are introduced into the ionization chamber, the compound (M) captures free electrons, forming negative ions (M⁻) (Equation 7.4). The ions collide with positive ions of the carrier gas and form neutral molecules (Equation 7.5); the number of free electrons reaching the anode decreases, resulting in a change in the current that can be observed. The change of current is recorded as a signal by the detector.

$$M + e \rightarrow M^- \tag{7.4}$$

$$M^- + N_2^+ \rightarrow M + N_2 \tag{7.5}$$

The ECD is a selective detector used to detect halogenated compounds, polyaromatic hydrocarbons, nitriles, nitro compounds, organometallic compounds, pesticides, and sulfur-containing compounds (Westmoreland and Rhodes 1989). This detector has been used to study explosives, with the objective of obtaining more information on what compounds dogs are detecting and for the development of training aids for explosive detection dogs (Harper et al. 2005).

The thermal ionization detector (TID; also referred to as the nitrogen–phosphorus detector [NPD]) is a modification of the FID detector. It is particularly effective in detecting compounds containing nitrogen (such as many drugs and explosives) and phosphorus (pesticides). It is somewhat more sensitive for compounds containing phosphorus than nitrogen (Westmoreland and Rhodes 1989). Cesium salts (for detection of phosphorus), rubidium salts (for detection of nitrogen), or potassium salts (for detection of organic halides) are introduced to a hydrogen/air flame. Under the influence of heat, ions are emitted from the salt (thermions), which react with compounds leaving the column.

MASS SPECTROMETRY

A mass spectrometer consists of a sample introduction system, ion source, analyzer ion, detector ion, and data system (computer) (Johnstone and Rose 1996).

ELECTRON AND CHEMICAL IONIZATION

The ion source creates ions from the analytes. The most commonly used methods of ionization include electron impact (EI) and chemical ionization (CI) (El-Aneed et al. 2009). In EI, analyte molecules (gaseous form) are bombarded with a beam of electrons. These electrons are emitted by the cathode and are accelerated as they move across the ionization chamber toward the anode by applying the appropriate voltage. Molecular ions are formed as a result of the bombardment, the ions then fragment, and these fragments may be further fragmented. 70 V is a standard for accelerating ions for fragmenting organic molecules (van Bramer 1997). The spectra recorded at 70 eV EI give comparable results, regardless of the spectrometer used, allowing for the creation of large databases to identify substances based on fragmentation profiles. These databases generally allow easy identification of substances being analyzed, but there are disadvantages in that the system needs a high vacuum, the sample compounds must be volatile, and the number of ions produced may be so high as to make interpretation difficult (Suder and Silberring 2006).

CI uses a reagent gas (methane, isobutane, ammonia) that reacts with the analyte in an ionization chamber. The reagent gas ionizes under the bombardment of a beam of electrons, and the ions thus formed collide with analyte molecules. Equations 7.6 to 7.11 show the ionization reactions that occur under CI, for example, with methane as a reagent gas (Johnstone and Rose 1996):

$$CH_4 + e \rightarrow CH_4^{+\bullet} + 2e \tag{7.6}$$

$$CH_4^{+\bullet} \rightarrow CH_3^+ + H^\bullet \tag{7.7}$$

$$CH_4^{+\bullet} \rightarrow CH_2^{+\bullet} + H_2 \tag{7.8}$$

$$CH_4^{+\bullet} + CH_4 \rightarrow CH_5^+ + CH_3^\bullet \tag{7.9}$$

$$CH_3^+ + CH_4 \rightarrow C_2H_5^+ + H_2 \tag{7.10}$$

$$CH_5^+ + M \rightarrow [M+H]^+ + CH_4 \tag{7.11}$$

The mass spectra obtained by CI are much easier to interpret than EI due to the fact that undesirable fragmentation is more limited, as well as because in EI, the sample must be evaporated before ionization. As in the electron ionization, the sample must be evaporated before ionization (Suder and Silberring 2006).

ANALYZERS

Ions separate on the basis of their mass-to-charge (m/z) ratio in the analyzer. The most common analyzers used are the quadrupole analyzer, the ion trap, and the time-of-flight (TOF) analyzer (Johnstone and Rose 1996). The quadrupole analyzer consists of four parallel metal rods. One diagonal pair of rods is connected to the positive side of a variable direct current (DC) source, and the other two rods are connected to the negative side. Variable radio-frequency (RF) alternating current (AC) is also applied to all four rods. By changing the ratio of the applied voltage, only ions of a certain m/z ratio will reach the detector, while other ions will be stopped. This analyzer has many advantages, including durability, small size, low cost, and ease of use (Buszewski et al. 2012b). Disadvantages include the limited range of mass separation to about 1,000 Da and unit m/z resolution (van Bramer 1997).

The ion trap analyzer is similar to the quadrupole analyzer. In the ion trap analyzer, instead of four electrodes, there are two endcap electrodes to which DC voltage is applied, and there is a doughnut-shaped ring electrode with an applied potential for an RF. A combination of RF and DC voltages is applied to create a quadrupole electric field. The mass spectrum is acquired by scanning the RF and DC fields to destabilize ions of a particular m/z ratio. Thereafter, the destabilized ions are ejected through a hole in one endcap electrode and reach the detector. The advantages of this analyzer, in comparison with the quadrupole analyzer, are higher sensitivity and better resolution. The disadvantage of ion traps, as with some other analyzers, comes from the modification of analytes by CI, as well as the difficulty in interpreting spectra for polar compounds such as alcohols, aldehydes, and ketones, all of which are components present in exhaled air (Buszewski et al. 2007).

The TOF analyzer permits separation of ions as a function of the time in which they reach a detector. Ions are formed in the ion source from neutral molecule analytes and are then directed to the mass analyzer by applying an electric field, which brings about their separation. The time to reach the detector depends on the m/z value. Ions of higher mass move more slowly after being free of the electron field and thus reach the detector later than lower-mass ions. TOF/MS records data quickly through multiple scans at high resolution and detects ions to masses above 100,000 Da. Deconvolution software can be used for chromatographic separation of substances being coeluted, providing a spectrum for each compound (Buszewski et al. 2007).

COMBINING TWO-DIMENSIONAL GAS CHROMATOGRAPHY WITH TIME-OF-FLIGHT MASS SPECTROMETRY (GC × GC-TOF/MS)

GC × GC-TOF/MS is a new tool for separating and analyzing complex mixtures, which can allow for the identification of a great number of VOCs in human breath (Phillips et al. 2013a) or, forensically, for determining ignitable liquids from fire debris (Frysinger and Gaines 2002). The technique uses two columns (with different kinds of stationary phases) to maximize sample resolution with two separation phases in a single analysis. The first column usually contains nonpolar stationary phases (100% dimethylpolysiloxane or 5% phenyl/95% dimethylpolysiloxane) and is 15–30 m in length with an inner diameter of 0.25 mm and a thickness of 0.25 μm. The separation mechanism in the second column must be different from that in the first column and so uses polar stationary phases (e.g., Carbowax: 50% phenyl/50% methylpolysiloxane). The second column is, at most, 1.5–2 m long, with an inner diameter of 0.1–0.25 mm and thickness of 0.25 μm. In the nonpolar primary column, VOCs are separated according to their boiling point, and in the polar secondary column (contained in the secondary oven), VOCs are separated based on their polarity. The separation in the first dimension takes longer than in the second. The VOCs being eluted are detected by TOF/MS. The most important element of the system is a thermal modulator, which connects the columns and allows collection and introduction of analytes to the second column (Phillips et al. 2013b) (Figure 7.2).

GC × GC-TOF/MS has been found to be particularly useful in analyzing complex matrices, such as decomposition odor (Brasseur et al. 2012; Dekeirsschieter et al. 2012; Forbes et al. 2014; Stefanuto et al. 2015), where part of the objective of the analysis is to determine what cadaver dogs recognize among the VOCs produced by decomposing human remains.

APPLICATIONS OF GAS CHROMATOGRAPHY/MASS SPECTROMETRY

Odorants are typically small organic molecules with masses less than 400 Da, though they differ in size, charge, shape, and functional group, including aldehydes, ketones, alcohols, esters, aliphatic acids, and compounds with aromatics or polycyclic or heterocyclic rings in their structures (Malnic et al. 1999).

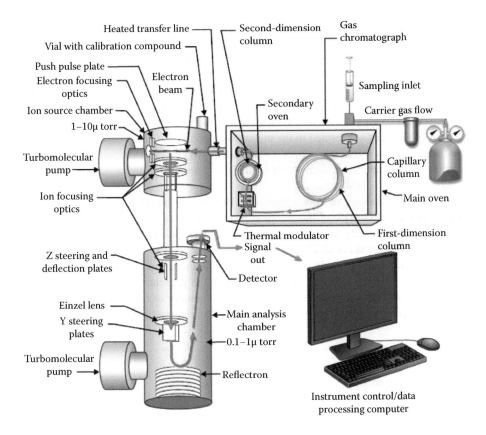

FIGURE 7.2 Scheme of GC × GC-TOF/MS. (From Leco Corp., Pegasus 4D GCxGC-TOFMS Brochure. Available at http://www.leco.com/component/edocman/?task=document.viewdoc&id=52&Itemid=0, 2014.)

GC/MS is the most widely applied system for the determination of mixtures of volatile and semi-volatile organic compounds in different matrices. The technique is characterized by high sensitivity and enables qualitative analysis, data retention (retention time and Kovats index), and quantitative analysis of peak areas (Mondello et al. 2008; Wang and Sahay 2009). MS allows for detecting low limits of compounds, including identification and quantitative measurement of VOCs in trace amounts, such as in human breath (di Francesco et al. 2005; van Berkel et al. 2008). Figure 7.3

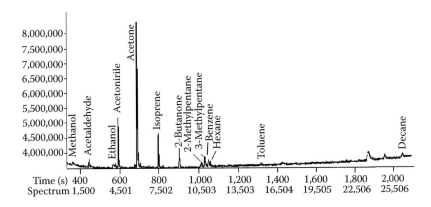

FIGURE 7.3 GC-TOF/MS chromatogram of breath of a healthy human (laboratory of authors).

shows a GC-TOF/MS chromatogram of exhaled air of a healthy human. Figure 7.4 shows mass spectra of acetone and isoprene.

VOCs are generated in the human body as products of the metabolic process (Buszewski et al. 2012a). Saturated hydrocarbons are mainly produced by peroxidation of polysaturated fatty acids, using reactive oxygen species (ROS). Isoprene is formed along the mevalonic pathway of cholesterol synthesis in the cytosolic fraction. Acetone is produced by hepatocytes via decarboxylation of excess acetyl CoA, which comes from fatty acid oxidation. Alcohols can be derived from metabolism of hydrocarbons. Aldehydes are formed in the metabolism of alcohol or as reduction of hydroperoxide by cytochrome p450 as a secondary product of lipid peroxidation. Compounds containing sulfur are generated by incomplete metabolism of methionine in the transamination pathway (Hakim et al. 2012; Miekisch et al. 2004).

The biochemical pathways of most compounds detected in breath have not been precisely and scientifically explained. Outside of biochemical processes, other sources of organic compounds in breath can be from respiratory factors, such as environmental pollution, or alimentary sources, such as food additives (Buszewski et al. 2012b).

VOCs in exhaled breath provide valuable information about the state of a human's health. The composition of the breath is variable and changes with the presence of some diseases. The sweet smell of acetone, for instance, indicates diabetes, while the odor of rotten eggs, which is caused by sulfur-containing compounds, suggests liver problems. Isoprene indicates problems with cholesterol

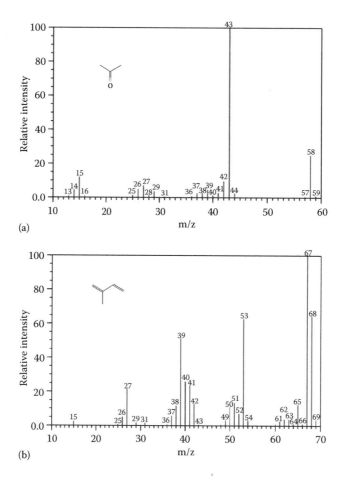

FIGURE 7.4   Mass spectra of (a) acetone and (b) isoprene, in selected-ion monitoring (SIM) mode with EI source.

metabolism, and compounds containing nitrogen point to uremia and kidney impairment (Rudnicka et al. 2011).

The most common methods to enrich VOCs for analysis are SPME and TD (Jones et al. 1995). After enrichment, samples are available for GC or GC/MS. VOCs have been detected in exhaled breath (Amann et al. 2010; Bajtarevic et al. 2009; Deng et al. 2004; Fuchs et al. 2010; Gaspar et al. 2009; Hyspler et al. 2000; Phillips et al. 2003a,b, 1999; Poli et al. 2010; Rudnicka et al. 2014; Yu et al. 2005), blood (Li et al. 2005; Miekisch et al. 2001), urine (Mills and Walker 2001; Mochalski et al. 2012), skin (Bernier et al. 1999; Gallagher et al. 2008), and saliva (Larsson 1965; Lochner et al. 1986), as well as on currency (Furton et al. 2002). Coupling SPME and spectrometry has also been used for detection of drugs and explosives at such locations as airports, thereby supplementing the work of drug and explosive detection canines (Joshi et al. 2009).

High selectivity, sensitivity, resolution, speed, accuracy, and precision have resulted in GC/MS becoming widely used in forensic science to analyze drugs, explosives, and ethanol, and for human odor profiling (Poole 2012) (Table 7.3).

The primary tool for quantitative and qualitative analysis of narcotics has been GC/MS and GC with FID (GC/FID) (Poole 2012). Products of *Cannabis sativa*—marijuana, hashish, and hash oil—are among the most commonly used illicit drugs in the world. The main psychoactive constituent of cannabis is Δ^9-tetrahydrocannabinol (Δ^9-THC), which is responsible for the hallucinogenic effects. Cannabinoids are extracted from cannabis by solvent extraction. Compound analysis should be performed after derivatization by silylating reagents. Samples can be analyzed by GC/MS or GC/FID (Lin et al. 2008; Musshoff and Madea 2006; Tomashefski and Felo 2004).

Heroin is a semisynthetic drug formed from opium or morphine (basic opium alkaloid included in *Papaver somniferum*). It always contains a mixture of alkaloids such as morphine, codeine, acetylcodeine, and 6-monoacetylheroin, and chromatographic analysis should be carried out after previous derivatization.

Cocaine is a natural alkaloid derived from the leaf *Erythroxylum coca* or *Erythroxylum novogranatense*. This drug is available in three principal forms: cocaine hydrochloride (soluble in water, degrades on heating); free base (formed by dissolving cocaine hydrochloride in water, adding a base, such as buffered ammonia, and extracting from aqueous solution with ether); and crack (cocaine hydrochloride dissolved in water with sodium bicarbonate and heated) (Boghdadi and Henning 1997; Tomashefski and Felo 2004). Cocaine samples often include ecgonine methyl ester, ecgonine, tropacocoine, benzoylecgonine, norocaine, cis- and trans-cinnamoylcocaine, and 3,4,5-trimethoxy-cocaine. As a result, profiling of cocaine requires derivatization (Boghdadi and Henning 1997; Musshoff and Madea 2006; Poole 2012).

Amphetamines are synthetic chemicals and are the major group of central nervous system stimulants. On the drug market, most are in the form of sulfates, while methamphetamine, methylenedioxyamphetamine (MDA), 3,4-methylenedioxymethamphetamine (MDMA), and 3,4-methylenedioxy-*N*-ethylamphetamine (MDEA) occur as hydrochlorides. Profiling of amphetamines has been carried out by GC/FID or GC/MS (Poole 2012; Raikos et al. 2003).

Illegal alcohols can be identified by GC/MS, which also permits identification of contaminants and classification of such illegal alcohols by group. GC is the basic method for investigating alcohol in fluids. The headspace technique allows for direct analysis of alcohol in matrices such as blood and urine (Boumba et al. 2008; Jones and Holmgren 2001).

GC can identify explosives and postblast organic residues of explosives. Organic explosive compounds can be classified into two groups: nitro-containing (trinitrotoluene, nitroglycerin) and non-nitro-containing (triacetone triperoxide, hexamethylene triperoxide diamine) explosives. Equipment used for this includes FIDs, NPDs, and GC/MS (Poole 2012).

Ignitable liquids can be divided into several classes: gasoline, petroleum distillates, isoparaffinic products, aromatic products, n-alkane products, dearomatized distillates, oxygenated solvents, and miscellaneous others. Substances can be identified by GC coupled with FID, ECD, or MS (Poole 2012).

TABLE 7.3
Exemplary Application of GC/MS

Compounds	Type of Sample/ Purpose of Detection	Technique for Detection of VOCs	Limit of Detection (LOD)	Limit of Quantification (LOQ)	Reference
Benzene	Breath/lung cancer	SPME-GC/FID	0.25 ng/mL	0.84 ng/mL	Yu et al. 2005
Styrene			1.26 ng/mL	4.20 ng/mL	
Propylbenzene			0.067 ng/mL	0.23 ng/mL	
Decane			0.012 ng/mL	0.04 ng/mL	
Undecane			0.027 ng/mL	0.08 ng/mL	
Propanal	Breath/lung cancer	SPME-GC/MS	1 pmol/L	3 pmol/L	Poli et al. 2010
Butanal					
Pentanal					
Hexanal					
Heptanal					
Octanal					
Nonanal					
Pentane	Breath/lung cancer	HS-SPME-GC-TOF/MS	0.18 µg/L	0.56 µg/L	Gaspar et al. 2009
Octane			0.20 µg/L	0.62 µg/L	
Nonane			0.11 µg/L	0.34 µg/L	
Decane			0.09 µg/L	0.28 µg/L	
Undecane			0.08 µg/L	0.23 µg/L	
Acetone			0.65 µg/L	1.96 µg/L	
Benzene			0.27 µg/L	0.81 µg/L	
Isoprene			0.30 µg/L	0.91 µg/L	
Hexanal			0.43 µg/L	1.29 µg/L	
Heptanal			0.43 µg/L	1.31 µg/L	
Propylbenzene			2.15 µg/L	6.50 µg/L	
Nonane	Breath/breast cancer	TD-GC/MS	ns	ns	Phillips et al. 2003b
5-Methyltridecane					
3-Methylundecane					
6-Methylpentadecane					
2-Methylpropane					
3-Methylnonadecane					
4-Methyldodecane					
2-Methyloctane					
Acetone	Blood/lung cancer	HS-SDME-GC/MS	0.62 nmol/L	ns	Li et al. 2005
Hexanal			0.24 nmol/L	ns	
Heptanal			0.32 nmol/L	ns	
Isoflurane	Blood	SPME-GC/MS	37.1 µg/L	ns	Mochalski et al. 2012
Hexane			25.2 µg/L		
Chloroform			14.1 µg/L		
Benzene			8.5 µg/L		
Isooctane			9.3 µg/L		
Toluene			4.1 µg/L		
Xylene			2.9 µg/L		

(Continued)

TABLE 7.3 (CONTINUED)
Exemplary Application of GC/MS

Compounds	Type of Sample/ Purpose of Detection	Technique for Detection of VOCs	Limit of Detection (LOD)	Limit of Quantification (LOQ)	Reference
Acetone	Urine	SPME-GC/MS	ns	ns	Kusano et al. 2011
2-Pentanone			ns	ns	
Dimethyl sulfide			11.48 ng	38.27 ng	
Pyrrole			11.63 ng	38.75 ng	
Toluene			10.92 ng	36.38 ng	
Hexanal			10.90 ng	36.35 ng	
4-Heptanone			10.96 ng	36.52 ng	
3-Heptanone			10.81 ng	36.03 ng	
2-Heptanone			10.47 ng	34.90 ng	
Benzaldehyde			11.72 ng	39.08 ng	
Phenol			12.61 ng	42.05 ng	
1-Octanol			11.63 ng	38.77 ng	
Octanoic acid			18.80 ng	62.65 ng	
Nonanoic acid			26.10 ng	87.00 ng	
Toluene	Blood	SPME-GC/MS	ns	ns	Kusano et al. 2011
Undecane			10.91 ng	36.38 ng	
1-Octen-3-ol			11.55 ng	38.49 ng	
1-Pentanol			ns	ns	
Hexanal			16.15 ng	53.83 ng	
2-Hepatanone			11.31 ng	37.70 ng	
Benzyl alcohol			12.11 ng	40.37 ng	
Nonanal			10.45 ng	34.85 ng	
Tetradecane			10.66 ng	35.53 ng	
1-Dodecane			11.03 ng	36.77 ng	
Toluene	Breath	SPME-GC/MS	ns	ns	Kusano et al. 2011
p-Xylene			4.57 ng	15.22 ng	
Styrene			3.79 ng	12.62 ng	
Benzaldehyde			2.03 ng	6.76 ng	
Phenol			1.37 ng	4.56 ng	
1,2-Dichlorobenzene			3.28 ng	10.93 ng	
2-Ethyl-1-hexanol			2.41 ng	8.04 ng	
Nonanal			2.66 ng	8.88 ng	
Dodecane			4.81 ng	16.03 ng	
Decanal			3.78 ng	12.61 ng	

(*Continued*)

TABLE 7.3 (CONTINUED)
Exemplary Application of GC/MS

Compounds	Type of Sample/ Purpose of Detection	Technique for Detection of VOCs	Limit of Detection (LOD)	Limit of Quantification (LOQ)	Reference
Hexanal	Buccal swab	SPME-GC/MS	3.61 ng	12.03 ng	Kusano et al. 2011
Benzaldehyde			6.29 ng	20.98 ng	
2-Pentylfuran			3.51 ng	11.71 ng	
Hexanoic acid			3.00 ng	9.99 ng	
(e)-2-nonenal			5.96 ng	19.88 ng	
(e,e)-2,4-nonadienal			7.52 ng	25.06 ng	
Decanal			4.79 ng	15.96 ng	
(e)-2-octenal			6.36 ng	21.19 ng	
Nonanal			5.75 ng	19.18 ng	
Acetophenone			5.49 ng	18.30 ng	
1-Octen-3-ol			5.53 ng	18.44 ng	
Nonanoic acid, methyl ester			4.18 ng	13.94 ng	
Amphetamine	Hair/drugs	GC/MS	0.045	0.151	Kusano et al. 2011
Methamphetamine			0.014	0.048	
3,4-Methylenedioxy-amphetamine (MDA)			0.013	0.043	
3,4-Methylenedioxy-methamphetamine (MDMA)			0.017	0.057	
3,4-Methylenedioxy-N-ethylamphetamine (MDEA)			0.007	0.023	
Cocaine	Hair/drugs	GC/MS	0.20 ng/mg	ns	Villamor et al. 2005
Heroin			0.10 ng/mg		
Morphine			0.20 ng/mg		
Amphetamine	Urine/drugs	SPE-GC/MS	10 ng/mL		Karacic and Skender 2001; Skender et al. 2002
Methamphetamine			3 ng/mL		
MDA			4 ng/mL		
MDMA			8 ng/mL		
MDEA			5 ng/mL		
Cocaine			5 ng/mL		
Morphine			3 ng/mL		
Codeine			5 ng/mL		
THCCOOH			7 ng/mL		
Cocaine	Blood/drugs	SPE-GC/MS	25.0 ng/mL	50.0 ng/mL	Da Matta Chasin and Midio 2000
Ethanol	Blood/ethanol	HS-GC-MS	0.005 g/dL	0.010 g/dL	Tiscione et al. 2011

Note: HS, headspace; ns, not specified; SPE, solid phase extraction.

In recent years, GC/MS has been used to analyze the human odor profile. Composition of human odor is dependent on the body's metabolism, hormonal control, bacterial interactions, and the presence of different VOCs (Kusano et al. 2011). Due to the low concentrations of compounds in human odor, it is necessary to enrich them before analysis by SPME, with sorption on solid sorbents. Sometimes, the human scent is collected on sorbent materials (cotton, polyester) by placing the material in a subject's hands, where it is in contact with skin for a definite time (See Figure 19.3 in Chapter 19). Next, the collection material is enclosed in a glass vial, and VOCs are then extracted into an SPME fiber and analyzed by inserting the fiber into the inlet of the GC. Here, the VOCs are thermally desorbed and separated in the chromatographic column. Human odorant collected on cotton sorbent from objects at crime scenes is often provided to trained sniffer dogs for identification of suspects (Poole 2012).

CONCLUSIONS

GC/MS has very quickly resulted in the development of sophisticated analytical techniques. It allows for identification and quantitative determination of trace amounts of odorant molecules and detection of organic compounds useful in medical research (e.g., cancer screening) and forensic science. GC/MS is characterized by high selectivity, sensitivity, and speed, and can provide perspective on the work of sniffer dogs in the detection of drugs, explosives, and even cancers.

8 Aerodynamics of Odor Plumes and Odor Plume Structures in Different Habitats

Paul A. Moore

Illicit substances, explosives, cancer cells, missing bodies, and various types of wildlife are just a few examples of what the keenly acute canine olfactory sense is used to detect (Cablk et al. 2008; Furton and Myers 2001; Lorenzo et al. 2003). Despite these diverse applications of canine olfactory behavior, all of these situations covered in this book require an understanding of how chemicals are dispersed and transported from the source of the chemical to the local vicinity of the canine's nose. Fortunately, the physical understanding of these processes is generally well quantified, but unfortunately, due to the difficulty of measuring small-scale chemical signals in air, direct quantification of the spatial and temporal nature of chemical signals is missing (Farrell et al. 2002; Jain et al. 2013; Zhu 1999). What is particularly amiss in the current state of knowledge is a lack of understanding of the odor dynamics at the spatial and temporal scale at which canines detect odor information.

The difficulties associated with extracting relevant behavioral information are immense and cannot be fully appreciated until the interaction between a sensory signal and the physical constraints of an environment are understood. This interaction produces the spatial and temporal nature of environmental information signals and can set limits on the types of possible behaviors (Moore and Crimaldi 2004; Vickers 2000). To understand the use of chemical signals by canines during searching procedures requires a knowledge of the physics involved in the movement and transport of chemicals through environments. For chemical signals, only two physical processes (turbulent advection and dispersion) need to be considered (Denny 1993). The reasoning for this statement can be seen by understanding the scale at which canine olfaction occurs.

The purpose of this chapter is to explain the set of physical factors that determine the movement of chemical signals within the different environmental conditions that are important for canine olfaction and to also provide some quantitative description of the spatial and temporal nature of aerial odor plumes. This is important as there is much guesswork about the structure of information in odor plumes in canine olfactory literature that is incorrect or lacking in regard to the physics of olfactory signals in these environments. Most studies concerning canine olfaction use one of two fundamentally flawed assumptions about aerial odor plumes without experimental or theoretical justification for those assumptions. First is that the plume is always symmetrically cone shaped as it expands downwind and that the edges of the plume are coherent and distinct (Cablk et al. 2008). Second is that at low wind velocities, odors tend to pool in small depressions in the ground and that diffusion plays an important role in these habitats (Lytridis et al. 2001). The theoretical and experimental work in this chapter will show that both of these assumptions are false and that more work within this area needs to be performed (Jezierski et al. 2014).

IMPORTANCE OF SCALE

Fundamentally, all of life resides within a fluid medium, whether that medium is air or water. Although the appearances of these media are exceedingly different, the underlying physical processes involved in the movement of chemicals are identical within these environments, except for scaling factors, such as density and viscosity (Denny 1993; Vogel 1994). (The viscosity of air is the resistance of air to deformation by outside stresses such as those that generate airflow.) Within each environment, the movement and interaction of air and water with physical features such as buildings and natural structures, like trees, determine the types of flows that are created, which, consequently, disperse the chemicals that are of concern (McAlpine and Ruby 2004). Approaching the problem of plume dispersal from a physical perspective allows one to recognize that two different situations (e.g., odors in an open plain versus an open patch of water) with comparable scaling factors will have very similar distributions of odor information.

The two scales that need to be considered when applying physical principles to the transport and transmission of behaviorally relevant odor signals are spatial and temporal scales. In addition, these scaling factors need to be considered as an order-of-magnitude phenomenon. This means that spatial scales of centimeters to tens of centimeters will have similar fluid dynamics (Vogel 1994). In an identical fashion, sampling odor signals from fractions of seconds to seconds will generate identical types of odor information. Thus, these scaling factors can help handlers and searchers begin to think about odor signals and information in different categories, such as large-scale phenomenon and small-scale phenomenon.

SPATIAL SCALE

Within the spatial scale, there are three intertwined and equally important size issues. First, one spatial aspect refers to the size range over which the canine's nose samples (Craven et al. 2007, 2009, arguing for a smaller range). This space over the nose (through fluid dynamics) and the brain (through neural connections) integrates a single sample. Odor patches that are smaller than this scale are smelled and processed as a single sample. Conversely, odor patches larger than this dimension are processed as two distinct odor samples. For most canines, the internaris distance is on the order of centimeters, and any side-to-side head movement is also on the order of tens of centimeters (Craven et al. 2007). This first scale sets the physical parameters of a single information sample.

The second spatial scale is the movement pattern of the searching canine. Again, this single scale can be separated into two distinct spatial scales. One movement scale refers to the vertical movement of the canine's head (Fiset and LeBlanc 2007). As a canine sniffs the ground (which can range from tiled floor to concrete to forested ground) or raises its head to sniff the air, the canine is actually moving its nose through aerodynamically different parts of the odor plume. Sniffs or odor samples near the ground will be fundamentally different in their informational value than those sniffs taken a meter off of the substrate. Perpendicular to the vertical movement, the horizontal movement scale refers to the movement pattern of the canine (and handler) through space. These scales can range from centimeters to kilometers as searches change from a localized drug search to a large-scale missing body search.

The final and third spatial scale is independent of the canine and its handler and refers to the space over which the odor is dispersed (Cablk et al. 2008; Hepper and Wells 2005). Along with the horizontal movement of the canine, the scale over which the odor plume is dispersed varies widely. The odor plume at close quarters (such as inside houses) has a significantly smaller dispersion scale than an outdoor missing body search. These scales can vary from centimeters to kilometers also.

TEMPORAL SCALE

The temporal scale, as opposed to the spatial scale, is significantly less complex. There are three important time scales to consider: the sniffing frequency of the canine, the integration time of the olfactory system, and the olfactory memory of the canine (Kepecs et al. 2006). The integration time of the olfactory system refers to the period of time where the chemical fluctuations are combined into a single event by the nervous system. Sniffing by vertebrates, and in particular canines, is a rapid inhalation of the air surrounding the naris. Given the aerodynamics of the nasal passage, canines are largely anosmic if they do not sniff. (There is some evidence that detection can occur through the vomeronasal organ in the back of the mouth.) Therefore, the frequency at which the canines sniff determines the discrete sampling of the odor signal. During a sniff, the canine inhales an odor sample, and the olfactory system processes that sample for information on intensity and the chemical makeup of the signal (Craven et al. 2009; Kepecs et al. 2006). During the brief period of time between sniffs, any changes in the external odor signal are lost or ignored by the canine. In other words, the sniff produces a digital sample of the analog odor signal. Canines typically sniff at a frequency of 4–7 Hz or 4–7 times a second (Craven et al. 2009). The frequency of this sniffing determines the range of temporal information available to the animal.

The second key component for temporal scales is the integration time of the brain and olfactory system of the canine. Even if sniffs produce independent samples of the external world, if the olfactory system integrates or averages two sniffs into a single sample, then the temporal resolution of the single sniff is determined by the brain and not by the sniffing. Information on the temporal resolution of terrestrial olfactory systems is quite limited, but by most estimates, the brain and olfactory system can detect distinct odor pulses at a frequency of around 10 Hz, which would match the sniffing frequency of most canines (Vickers 2000). The integration time is critical in understanding how many sniffs are averaged by the canine in order to detect concentration differences. The answer could be that each sniff is an independent sample. The final temporal scale that needs to be determined is the comparison time for the canine. The comparison time is similar to an odor memory in that the canine is able to compare the concentration of two different samples taken at two different time points. Searching for or attempting to localize an odor source requires the animal to compare both the chemical composition and the concentration of odor samples taken at two different time points. In essence, the canine is attempting to determine if the current odor sample is higher or lower in concentration than a sample smelled at a previous time. The critical scale in this comparison is how long the canine can remember the previous concentration in order to compare. Again, direct research in this area is rare, but the scaling factors are order-of-magnitude estimates. Most estimates in these areas put this comparison time on the order of minutes as the longest period (Head et al. 1995; Hepper and Wells 2005).

In summary, the spatial scales that are important for olfactory searching in canines range from centimeters (internaris distance and side-to-side head movement) to meters (vertical head movement and small-scale searching) to kilometers (large-scale searches). The temporal scales that need to be considered are on the order of seconds (sniffing and integration) to minutes (comparison between odor samples).

PHYSICAL CONSTRAINTS ON ODOR TRANSMISSION IN AIR

Once the scale factors are in place, it is possible to describe a set of parameters that can be used to quantify the transmission and movement of chemical signals in different habitats. These parameters are nondimensional parameters familiar within the fluid mechanics field but largely unknown outside of that field. A nondimensional parameter has no units associated with the value, which allows the parameter to be applied across different contexts. The value of nondimensional parameters is in the ability to categorize similar physical habitats together because the transmission and movement of chemical signals in those habitats will be similar. For example, a terrestrial and an aquatic habitat will have identical chemical signal patterns if these nondimensional parameters are the same despite the obvious difference in density and viscosity between air and water. Thus, two flows or environmental conditions that have overlapping sets of relevant nondimensional parameters will also have qualitatively similar plume transport characteristics. Conversely, habitats or flows with different nondimensional parameters will have dissimilar chemical signals. These parameters allow one to look past the superficial characteristics of habitats and understand chemical signal dispersion from a more abstract physical construct.

What follows is a development of plume parameters that is based on previously published work (Moore and Crimaldi 2004; Osterkamp 2011); however, the analysis has been altered to fit the specific interests of canines, their habitats, and the use of canines in searching paradigms. Fundamentally, the transport of a chemical from a source to the canine nose consists of two distinct physical processes: advection and dispersion. Advection is defined as the macroscopic, bulk chemical transport by the airflow. Advection is a dominant process in the movement of chemical signals even in extremely low wind conditions. On the other hand, dispersion is the result of three different physical processes. These are the turbulent interweaving of distinct fluid parcels (formally defined as *stirring*), molecular diffusion due to Brownian motion (formally defined as *mixing*), and spreading due to effects of shear in the mean velocity field (formally defined as *shear dispersion*). Shear can be thought of as two different *sheets* of air moving at different velocities. Shear occurs across the interface of these two sheets of air.

Turbulence is related to the fluctuation in velocity around a mean air movement vector. What is important for the consideration of chemical movement is the fluctuation of velocity rather than the mean air speed. The differences in air velocity over space create velocity gradients, and these fluctuating velocity gradients in turbulent flows deform, or stir, the spatial structure of the chemical field. Consequently, a homogenous chemical field is broken down or torn into thin filaments. This stirring, which turns a homogenous signal into filaments, does not directly produce chemical dilution. The concentration of odorant within the filament remains relatively unchanged. The stirring does promote molecular diffusion by increasing the surface area between parcels of fluids with differing chemical concentrations. As a result of this increased surface area, diffusion occurs and starts to dilute the chemical concentration. The result of these two processes, turbulent stirring and molecular mixing, is termed *turbulent mixing*. Within odor plumes, stirring is a process that redistributes chemicals and operates at large spatial scales. Mixing is a process that smears chemical gradients and operates at small scales. The relative rate of these two processes is determined by the spatial scales discussed.

Spatial gradients in concentration are blurred or eliminated by diffusion, which can be explained by the classic Fickian relationship (which indicates that flux is dependent upon molecular diffusivity and concentration gradients):

$$\vec{q} = -D_m \nabla C \tag{8.1}$$

By the process of Brownian motion, diffusion creates a movement of chemicals, called a flux, $\vec{q}$, in the direction from greater concentration to lesser concentration (in the direction of $-\nabla C$). A molecule's ability to diffuse in air can be quantified by the parameter molecular diffusivity, D_m, which has the unit of $L^2 T$—1. (Dimensional analysis is a mathematical process, which explains parameters by their basic dimensions, such a length, time, and mass.)

Chemicals relevant to canine searches (cadaverine, etc.) have a diffusivity on the order of 10^{-5} m^2/s in air. Although the exact diffusion coefficient changes based on which chemicals are being considered, the order-of-magnitude estimate of 10^{-5} m^2/s is sufficient for modeling purposes. The singular conclusion that can be drawn from this simple analysis is that molecular diffusion is an exceedingly slow process that needs to be considered only if there are large changes in chemical concentrations over extremely small distances (large ∇C). The average time required for a small particle (e.g., a molecule) to diffuse a distance L is $t_d = L^2 / 2D_m$. For example, for a molecule of interest to disperse 1 m from its source by the process of diffusion alone would take approximately 50,000 s or 14 h. Notice that diffusion time, t_d, is related to the distance L in a squared relationship. As spatial scales become larger (say from 1 to 10 m), diffusion becomes increasingly slow (1 m = 14 h diffusion time versus 10 m = 58 days).

The spatial scaling approach discussed demonstrates that diffusion can effectively be ignored for all canine searching conditions. For example, in situations that include buried bodies or sources within small confined spaces, the odor will diffuse through the soil or around the container, but as soon as the odor is liberated from the soil or container, small-scale air currents immediately act on the movement of the odor. As will be shown below under "High Mean Airflow," although diffusion has the potential to create concentration gradients, airflow tends to eradicate any larger-scale gradients in concentration. This is further proven by the use of the Péclet number. The Péclet number is a dimensionless ratio that quantifies the relative contribution of advection (velocity and length) and diffusion (diffusion coefficient) to chemical dispersion. If the mean flow velocity of any particular habitat is U, the time required for a chemical to disperse the same distance is $t_a = L/U$. Thus, the Péclet number is the ratio of the time required for advection compared to that required for diffusion to displace an odor of interest at a distance L from the source to the canine nose. Simplifying our equation by dropping the factor of 2 in t_d, the denominator, we have

$$\text{Pé} = \frac{t_a}{t_d} = \frac{U \cdot L}{D_m} \tag{8.2}$$

When Pé $\ll$ 1 (consider a day without wind or very short distances), chemical dispersion is dominated by molecular diffusion. When Pé $\gg$ 1 (larger distances and windy days), advection dominates. ($\ll$ and $\gg$ mean, respectively, significantly less than and significantly greater than.) For the purposes of this book, the question becomes at what wind or spatial scales diffusion can be ignored. This can be calculated by setting the Pé number to 1 and solving for a combination of wind speed and distance that balances the equation. For a light breeze (defined as 0.3 m/s on the Beaufort wind speed scale), diffusion is only important over spatial scales of a tenth of a millimeter). *Again, the conclusion that can be drawn is that for all canine search situations, diffusion can be ignored, and odor signals, as they are perceived by canines, are structured by advection* (Figure 8.1).

By ignoring diffusion, it becomes possible to focus solely on stirring as the major process that determines the dispersion of chemical signals for canine searches. The processes of stirring in air are governed by the nature and degree of the turbulence within the flowing medium. An order-of-magnitude estimate of the type of turbulence present in a flow is indicated by the Reynolds number. Similar to the Péclet number, the Reynolds number is a ratio of two different forces (inertial forces with viscous forces) that govern the generation of turbulence and gives a bulk measure of the turbulence. The inertial forces are the forces that are dominant at most macroscopic biological scales and represent the large, momentum-containing scales that sustain the turbulence. Sustaining turbulence

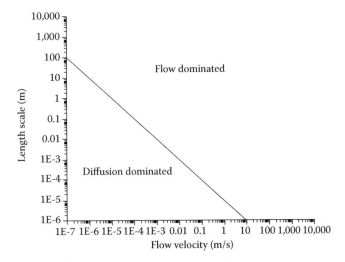

FIGURE 8.1 A graph of the Péclet number illustrating the differences between diffusion-dominated odor dispersion and advection-dominated dispersion. Most canine searches occur above the line, indicating that odor signals are structured by airflow and not diffusion.

is critical for chemical stirring. Conversely, viscous forces are those forces that tend to dominate in the microscopic world of biology and constitute factors that dampen turbulence. These forces are small-scale viscous processes that turn momentum into heat through the dissipation of energy. In the Navier–Stokes equations that govern in these situations, inertia is $\vec{u} \cdot \nabla \vec{u}$, or the velocity vector multiplied by the change in velocity over distance. In the nondimensional terms, inertia scales as $U \cdot U/L$. Viscous forces are $\nu \nabla^2 \vec{u}$, which scales as $\nu U/L^2$ (where ν is the kinematic viscosity of the fluid). Thus, the ratio of inertial to viscous forces forms the Reynolds number:

$$\mathrm{Re} = \frac{U^2/L}{\nu U/L^2} = \frac{U \cdot L}{\nu} \tag{8.3}$$

Similar to the discussion of the Pé, the discussion and analysis can be simplified to ratios that are much greater than and much less than 1. When $\mathrm{Re} \gg 1$, inertial forces are more important than viscous forces, and consequently, momentum in the flow is greater than viscous damping. In these situations, the flow is turbulent, and eddies are present. As the Re increases, inertial forces in relation to viscous forces also increase, and the level of turbulence within the flow is increased. As turbulence increases, a larger range of temporal and spatial scales are important in relation to the dispersion of chemical signals. As viscous forces increase, the Re number decreases. The dampening effect of viscosity overpowers the momentum of inertia, and turbulence in the system is dissipated. At low enough Re numbers, the flow becomes laminar. In laminar flow, the paths of the individual air particles do not cross each other, remaining parallel. In laminar flow, stirring is reduced compared to turbulent airflow.

The form of the Péclet number and that of the Reynolds number are the same in that they are both ratios of forces. These two simple equations can now be used to characterize the structure of information in chemical signals in different relevant habitats. Given the similar nature of both of these ratios, the interpretations of the Pé and Re numbers are analogous. For air at 20°C, the kinematic viscosity, $\nu = 15 \times 10^{-6}$ m²/s, is the denominator of the Re number and can be thought of as the molecular diffusivity of momentum within the fluid. Thus, ν is analogous to the molecular chemical diffusivity within the Péclet number. The Péclet number compares the rate of advective transport of the chemical (the numerator of Pé) to the rate of smearing (smoothing or eradication) of gradients and spatial structures in the chemical field (the denominator of Pé). In an analogous fashion, the Reynolds number compares the rate of advective transport due to momentum (the numerator of Re) to the rate of molecular smearing of velocity gradients (the denominator of Re). The two numbers are related through the Schmidt number:

$$\mathrm{Sc} = \frac{\mathrm{Pé}}{\mathrm{Re}} = \frac{\nu}{D_m} \tag{8.4}$$

where Sc is the ratio of the viscous diffusivity of momentum to that of the mass diffusivity. Typical at the spatial scales relevant for canine searches, chemical signals will have a Schmidt number in air on the order of 100–1000. These signals are considered to be weakly diffusive (relative to the diffusion of momentum).

In the interaction between diffusion and advection, diffusion acts to eradicate differences in chemical concentrations along spatial gradients (called mixing) at small scales. In other words, diffusion acts to homogenize the chemical signal, and as such, diffusive processes set a size limit for the smallest possible spatial gradient in concentration differences. This size limit is important in relation to the various spatial scales discussed. Any sampling by the canine at smaller spatial scales than this limit results in an identical odor signature. By sampling at a larger spatial scale, the canine will be able to detect concentration differences. Derivation of these scales is then critical in regard to canine olfactory searches. The spatial scales of the smallest velocity and chemical structures in any odor plume are controlled by the two diffusivities v and D_m derived previously. To determine the smallest spatial scale of chemical concentration differences, the smallest velocity structures within a flow need to be derived. The Kolmogorov microscale is a quantification of the smallest velocity structures within a flow. The Kolmogorov scale is

$$\eta = \left(\frac{v^3}{\varepsilon} \right)^{1/4} \tag{8.5}$$

where ε is the rate at which turbulent kinetic energy is dissipated into heat and v is the kinematic viscosity of the fluid. As Re increases by either increases in the flow velocity (and its variance), increases in length scales, or decreases in the kinematic viscosity, the flow becomes more turbulent. Concomitantly, the dissipation ε increases, and the smallest velocity structures in the flow, η, become smaller. Eddies within the turbulent flow can become smaller and smaller before they dissipate into heat.

In a similar derivation to the Kolmogorov scale, the Batchelor microscale is the scale of the smallest chemical heterogeneity within a flow. The Batchelor microscale introduces chemical diffusion into the calculation and is a measure of the smallest detectable differences within a flow. The Batchelor microscale is

$$\eta_B = \left(\frac{v D_m^2}{\varepsilon} \right)^{1/4} \tag{8.6}$$

Now the Schmidt, Kolmogorov, and Batchelor equations can be used to derive a single equation relating all three parameters, which is

$$\eta_B = \eta \, Sc^{-1/2} \tag{8.7}$$

The Sc number can be altered to interpret this relationship in terms of canine searches. As with all of the other parameters, these numbers and relationships are order-of-magnitude relationships and should not be considered precise numerical estimates. If the Sc number is larger than 1, then the scales of the smallest chemical concentration differences are significantly smaller than the smallest eddies. For typical terrestrial airflow patterns, the Kolmogorov microscale would be on the order of a micron, with the Batchelor microscale being approximately 30 times smaller (assuming Sc = 1,000).

BOUNDARY LAYERS

The final aspect of the constraints of the physics of chemical dispersion is termed a *boundary layer*. Odor dispersion is influenced by the interaction between airflow and a solid surface. (This interaction is defined as the "no-slip" condition, but is referred to as friction within the canine literature. While technically not true, the concept of friction is a useful analogy.) Within the terrestrial environment of concern for canine searching, boundary layers are generated as air flows over concrete, wood, grass, the sides of luggage, or any other surface that exists within the flow. When air flows around a solid structure, the interface between the solid structure and the airflow is called a *boundary layer*. At the surface of the structure, airflow is nonexistent, and as distance away from the structure is increased, the air velocity also increases. Thus, the boundary layer is a velocity gradient, and since chemical signals are dispersed primarily by air movement, the boundary layer has significant impacts on the spatial and temporal nature of chemical signals. Chemicals in this near-surface region, whether a wall, a floor, or the ground, exhibit a streaky, persistent characteristic (Crimaldi et al. 2002). Further from this surface, turbulent energy increases, and eddies become

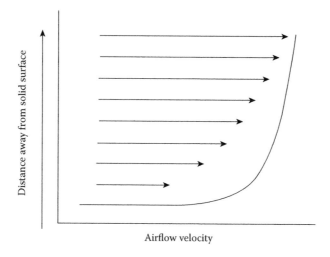

FIGURE 8.2 Graph depicting the airflow velocities within a boundary layer. Airflow is greatly decreased close to the solid surface and is zero at the surface's layer. The airflow velocity increases as distance away from the surface is also increased.

larger and larger. As eddy size increases, stirring intensifies, and chemicals are dispersed more rapidly. Smooth surfaces, such as floors or walls, will have larger boundary layers and more persistent chemical signals. Rough surfaces, such as driveways or grasslands, tend to increase energy and turbulence, causing signals to be more heterogeneous (Figure 8.2).

SUMMARY OF THE PHYSICAL CONSTRAINTS TO ODOR DISPERSION

This mathematical development of the physics of odor signals in air allows us to draw several important distinctions. First, at the spatial and temporal scales important for canine searches, odors are distributed by advection. This statement holds for open-field wildlife searches as well as confined room searches. Odor signals and the information contained within them are structured primarily by two processes: stirring, which serves to relocate odor patches within the larger plume, and shear dispersion, which serves to tear apart odor patches into smaller odor patches. Mixing, while important only for that small-scale distance between patches, serves to blur the edges of odor patches and nonodor patches. Finally, the distribution of odor information within an odor plume can be thought of as three distinct phases (Figure 8.3).

FIGURE 8.3 A picture representing the three different phases of plume growth. The black lines represent both the plume boundaries and the individual filaments of odor within the plume. The blue swirls represent airflow eddies. At the left-hand part of the diagram, the eddies are larger than the plume, and the plume meanders as a whole. As the plume expands to the same size as the eddies, the individual filaments begin to be stirred. As the plume is fully developed and the eddies become smaller than the plume, airflow serves to stir the filaments and homogenize the odor.

PHASES OF PLUME GROWTH

The first phase occurs when the odor patch is smaller than the smallest eddies within the airflow. This occurs when the odor is first being liberated from its source. The spatial distribution of the odor is localized around the source, and the airflow contains a wide range of eddies, all of which are larger than the odor plume. At this phase, the eddies serve to move the odor plume around as a whole. This causes meandering of the odor plume in space. Downwind, the canine will experience this as large shifts in odor concentration from exceedingly high levels to complete absence of the plume. It is expected that the canine will begin large lateral movements to locate the odor plume as the signal meanders over larger distances.

The second phase begins as the odor plume expands in size such that the plume is approximately the same size as the turbulent eddies within the airflow. At this point in time, shear dispersion is the dominant dispersal process and causes the odor patches to be torn apart and distributed in space as smaller and smaller patches. Rather than moving the plume as a whole, this phase causes the odor plume to form filaments of odors where there is still a very sharp concentration boundary between air parcels with odor and those without odor. Downwind, the canine experiences this phase as fast shifts in concentration over smaller spatial scales. The odor plume changes rapidly in concentration, but instead of the signal disappearing (as in phase 1), the signal rapidly fluctuates in concentration. At this point, the canine would be expected to perhaps stop and take several sniffs at a singular point in space as the signal fluctuates in concentration.

The final phase of plume development is where the odor plume is much larger than even the largest eddies and mixing becomes the dominant process. At this point, the concentration differences between odor-laden air packets and those without odor become blurred and eventually disappear as the plume becomes homogenous. At large distances downwind, the canine will experience this phase of plume development as a slowly fluctuating but fairly constant signal. Concentrations of odor rarely vary, and any differences in signal concentration across space are almost entirely absent.

ODOR LANDSCAPES AT VARYING SCALES

All of the processes outlined cause chemical sources to be dispersed in a three-dimensional distribution that is dynamic in both space and time. When considered from both the time and space perspective, the distribution creates a sensory landscape where the heights of the landscape (valleys and mountains) can be considered different concentrations and whose spatial distribution of valleys and mountains is dynamically changing over time. The exact nature of these changes depends upon the scale at which an organism samples the landscape. Canines, unlike swimming or flying organisms, are locked into a two-dimensional sampling of this landscape with a very limited vertical distribution. The process of stirring works to create and increase the height of the valleys and mountains, whereas mixing serves to homogenize the landscape (Figure 8.4).

For canines moving through the landscape at any pace, the odor information arrives in the brain as discrete samples processed by sniffs (Craven et al. 2009, although the exact neurophysiological work has not been done). The concentration of odorant between sniffs greatly varies because at the spatial and temporal scale of canine sniffing and movement, stirring is the dominant dispersal process. Wide shifts in concentration are present within the odor plume over relatively small distances. Even though concentration differences occur over smaller size scales, any consistent concentration increase toward the source of the odor is lost due to the dispersion of odors by turbulent eddies. Concentrations actually may be higher downwind rather than upwind at any moment in time. At these larger spatial scales, the processes of stirring and mixing need to be considered. Because the process of stirring is a much faster process than mixing, odor plumes are filaments of high-concentration odorants surrounded by spaces with very low chemical concentrations. Even in the most "wind-free" environments, such as closed spaces, stirring is dominant over mixing, and the sensory landscape consists of high peaks of chemical concentration surrounded by valleys with little to no chemical information present. Because

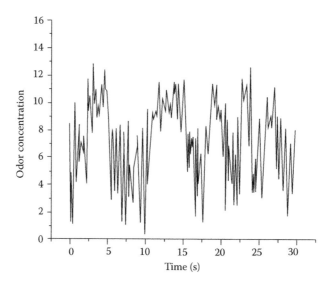

FIGURE 8.4 A typical turbulent odor signal that would be perceived by an animal sampling signals at the spatial and temporal scales of a canine. The concentration axis is arbitrary and is numbered only to show the relative extent of fluctuations in odor concentration.

mixing is relatively slow, these filaments of odor are very distinct, with sharp concentration boundaries. Finally, most importantly for canines performing searches (and for their handlers), the odor landscape is chaotic, with large unpredictable changes in concentration over time and space.

SEARCHING ODOR LANDSCAPES: ENVIRONMENT-SPECIFIC ODOR FIELDS

For canine searches, the exact distribution of the odor field will be highly dependent upon airflow for the environment being searched. Thus, each unique search habitat (open field, trunk of a car, open airport walkway, closed and confined basement) will have a different sensory landscape that fluctuates based on the amount of airflow present. It is important to point out that even in a very confined area, advection still distributes odors more effectively than diffusion. This section attempts to provide an overview of general habitats classified by different characteristics of airflow such that any specific situation can be placed within these general habitats.

When classifying habitats on their airflow, two main characteristics of habitats should be considered. First, the mean velocity of airflow is important. In general, higher mean airflow (or velocity) is correlated with higher levels of turbulence. The second factor that needs to be considered is secondary airflow. Secondary airflow is flow not correlated with the main or mean airflow. This airflow is often periodic and chaotic in nature and can be generated by the movement of objects within the habitat (such as other people, cars, and animals) or within buildings; changes in the activation of air-handling devices; or the opening and closing of room entrances. I will confine descriptions of typical odor signals to those canine situations where the location of the odor source is unknown and where there is some distance between the canine and the odor source. Situations where the source location is known (such as the human body for the determination of potentially cancerous cells) or where the distance is relatively short (such as the localized search of a suitcase or luggage) will not be covered.

High Mean Airflow with No Secondary Flow

Wide-open fields or large open indoor spaces would fall under this category of search habitats. A quick calculation of the Pé number indicates that for a mean wind velocity of 1 cm/s for a small search distance of 1 m, mean advection is 100 times more important for odor movement than molecular diffusion. Thus, in open habitats with little secondary flow, the mean airflow direction will determine the types of chemical information available for canines during searches. These habitats can have stationary natural obstructions, such as trees, grasses, or shrubs, or may have human-constructed obstacles such as furniture or pillars for large indoor spaces such as airplane hangars or the large hallways of airports. Within these habitats, the mean airflow is typically unidirectional, although the mean direction can vary slightly over time.

Odor plumes under these conditions can be viewed as an expanding amorphous shape emanating downwind from the odor source (Figure 8.5). Although the plume is thought to be cone shaped, it is not, as the edges of the plume are ephemeral and not clearly defined. The plume meanders as a whole; thus, the edges are constantly shifting in both the vertical and horizontal directions. Any attempt to "follow the edge" of the plume fails because this edge varies in its location. Within the plume, the three phases of plume growth discussed here are spatially short. The high wind velocity creates a high degree of turbulence. The increased energy in the air turbulence creates a large range of eddies that both move the plume as a whole (meandering) and also create stirring that shears the odor patches into long filaments. Phases 1 and 2 of plume growth occur quickly as turbulence further shreds odor patches into smaller and smaller filaments. The distance between filaments of odor-laden and clean air decreases to the point that diffusion will quickly homogenize the odor concentrations. Even here, the size scales are exceedingly small (microns) where diffusion acts quickly. At this point, the concentration of odorants may remain above the detection threshold for canines, but any directional or distance information on the source is lost (Moore and Crimaldi 2004; Vickers 2000).

As canines enter and move through the plume, the filaments will be detected through sniffs. The filaments of odor interspersed with filaments of clean air will arrive quickly to and move past the canine's nose. The signals will be sensed as a high-frequency odor signal, which means that the detection of odor will be quickly followed by clean air, which will be subsequently followed by odor-laden air, and so on. As the plume meanders largely from side to side or vertically, the canine may lose the scent as quickly as it detects it. Overall, the plume disperses quickly and has an ill-defined shape, and odorants may appear and disappear from the canine's sniffs at a chaotic rate (for example, see Figure 8.9).

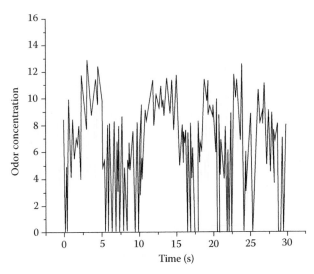

FIGURE 8.5 A representative odor plume signal that would be experienced by a canine in an environment with high mean airflow and no secondary flow. Odor signals are detected as high-frequency bursts with small no odor gaps in between high-intensity odor signals.

High Mean Airflow with Secondary Flow

Examples of habitats with a high mean flow rate along with second rates are similar to windy outside habitats near highways or within long indoor corridors in buildings with ventilation ports. The key point for the odor signals in these habitats is that the random movement of vehicles (as near a road) or the activation of an air-handling device (air-conditioning or heating) creates impulsive air currents that do not flow in concert with the main direction of airflow. These habitats are similar in physical structure to those described here and may even be the same environment habitats with slightly different conditions. As shown previously, a quick calculation of the Pé shows that advection (along with these random impulsive crosscurrents) is the dominant dispersal process.

Odor plumes found in these habitats have very similar characteristics to the signals described previously (Figure 8.6). The edges of the plume are ill defined and meander due to the high speed of the main airflow. Within the plume, canines will experience the same hit and miss of odor filaments at the same relatively high frequency. In addition, the three phases of plume growth are shortened as the high degree of energy in the turbulence of the mean airflow will quickly stir the filaments, causing the plume to homogenize at a relatively short distance from the odor source. The fundamental difference between these two odor signals is the degree and severity of the meandering. The periodic secondary flows created by objects moving through the odor plume or by the increase and decrease of crosswinds will cause the entire plume to move as a whole. The chaotic appearance of crosswinds will only move certain sections of the plume, essentially "offsetting" them from the main axis of the odor plume. This offset is similar to laying a large rope on the floor and then quickly shifting a middle piece of the rope. The two sections of the odor plume on either side of the moved piece remain relatively unchanged in their downwind progression, while the moved section is shifted in space by the crosswind.

The three phases of plume growth are essentially unchanged, but a piece of the entire plume is shifted in space. If the secondary airflow is created or moves in parallel with the main axis of the plume, the large-scale meandering of the plume as a whole remains unchanged. The turbulent energy contained within air moving the odor plume is suddenly increased, which serves to increase

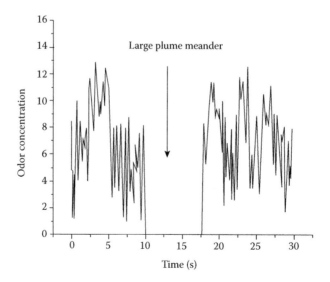

FIGURE 8.6 A representative odor plume signal that would be experienced by a canine in an environment with high mean airflow with impulsive secondary flow. Odor signals are detected as high-frequency bursts with large gaps in the signal as the secondary flow causes the plume to meander as a whole.

the rate at which the odor filaments are homogenized. In either case, the fine-scale structure of the odor filaments are altered such that a searching canine will quickly lose either the entire plume (such as a crosswind) or will detect concentrations within the plume that are suddenly homogenized. In either case, any directional or distance information carried by odor filaments is lost by the increased energy imparted to the airflow.

Low Mean Airflow with No Secondary Flow

Environments whose characteristics include low mean airflow and no secondary flow would include smaller indoor situations such as house or building searches or outdoor searches where the mean wind speed is less than 5 mph. In these conditions, advection is still the dominant dispersal process for odors, although molecular diffusion would begin to play a role in blurring the concentration gradients between odor filaments that are being moved by the mean wind flow. Inside buildings, small-scale air currents still exist and move odorants through rooms and open connecting areas. Even in really closed or confined search spaces (such as basements, attics, or heavily forested areas), air currents are still more important than any diffusional process. As in the previous no-secondary-flow habitat, these environments can have stationary structures (trees, pillars, furniture, stairways, etc.). Although the mean airflow can be unidirectional, this may not be the case inside buildings, where air-handling systems will move air through the structure, but not necessarily in an overall unidirectional way.

As in the previous two conditions, odor plumes under these conditions can be viewed as an expanding amorphous shape (Figure 8.7). The exact shape will be determined by the environment as the plume of odor may snake around stationary structures in the habitat. Unlike the previous two situations, the edges of the plume are relatively well defined such that a canine could potentially detect the edge of the odor plume. The turbulent energy of the airflow in these situations is high enough to move the plume away from the odor source but not high enough to begin to significantly shred the coherent odor patches into long thin filaments. As a consequence, the canine will not have long periods of time or space where the odor signal disappears. The canine, once in the plume, will

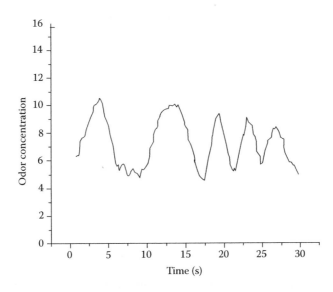

FIGURE 8.7   A representative odor plume signal that would be experienced by a canine in an environment with low mean airflow and no secondary flow. Odor signals are slowly changing peaks and valleys of concentration, with a constant presence of detectable signal in the plume.

be stimulated by odor, and the fluctuations of concentration over time will be smaller and slower than in the situations described. Within the plume, the three phases of plume growth are elongated as compared to the previous two situations. The filaments of odor stay coherent for a long distance away from the source, and the concentration gradient between clean air and odor-laden air is smooth and continuous. The canine will perceive these signals as slowly increasing and decreasing concentrations of odors. Overall, these slow valleys and peaks of odor will generally increase as the canine approaches the odor source.

LOW MEAN AIRFLOW WITH SECONDARY FLOW

Similar to the relationship between the environments described in the two situations in the previous section, this environment is closely related to the low-mean-airflow environment described previously (Figure 8.8). As with the other secondary-flow environment, the key difference between these two low-mean-airflow environments is the presence of periodic and sometimes chaotic secondary flows. These can be in the form of short gusts of wind in outdoor environments or the sudden opening or closing of entryways in indoor environments. Unlike the other secondary-flow environment, these sudden additions of airflow often contain more turbulent energy than the mean airflow. This sudden burst of turbulence will serve to significantly alter the odor distribution perceived by the canine during searching.

The odor signals produced under these conditions are significantly different from those described for plumes under low mean flow with no secondary flows. Because the secondary flow, such as gusts of wind, often has more turbulent energy than the mean flow, because of this sudden increase in the turbulent energy of the system the fine scale structure of the slowly changing peaks and valleys is completely disrupted. The plume as a whole is not shifted in space so much as that section of the odor plume, that is altered by the sudden secondary, flow becomes quickly stirred such that the odor filaments are significantly torn apart. The quick and intense stirring allows diffusion to act quickly to homogenize the signal because the spatial distances between clean and odor-laden air become exceedingly small.

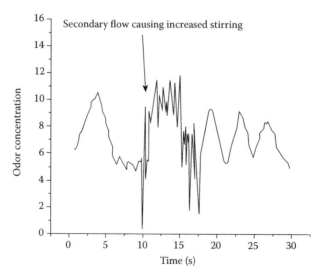

FIGURE 8.8   A representative odor plume signal that would be experienced by a canine in an environment with low mean airflow with impulsive secondary flow. Odor signals are slowly changing peaks and valleys of concentration, with large periods of intensely fluctuating signals as a result of increased stirring due to secondary airflow.

The three phases of plume growth are no longer applicable, due to the interruption of high-intensity secondary flows. These flows effectively stir the plume whether the secondary flow is parallel or perpendicular to the main flow. Canines searching plumes when these secondary flows impact the odor distributed will perceive these impacts as a sudden shift in odor dynamics. The signals will quickly change from slow and smooth chemical gradients to sudden large-scale changes in concentration. If the secondary flows stop or the canine moves away from the flow, the odor plume may become more coherent again. If this occurs, the plume edge is detectable again, and the concentration gradients become more smooth and predictable.

BOUNDARY LAYERS IN HABITATS

Every habitat described here has a boundary associated with the flow through that environment. Any time that airflow contacts a solid surface, a boundary layer is formed. These solid surfaces would include the ground in any outdoor habitat (grass, sand, small brush), concrete, carpeted floors, walls, or counters in indoor habitats. The dynamics of odor dispersion are fundamentally different within boundary layers as the relative contribution of advection and molecular diffusion changes closer to the solid surface. At the surface, molecular diffusion dominates, and far away, advection is the primary dispersal process. Thus, within the boundary layer, the movement of odorants transitions from advection to diffusion, which means that odor signals transition from highly chaotic with large fluctuations in concentration away from the solid surface to long-lasting, fairly constant concentrations at the surface/air interface. For the purposes of canine searches, odor gets "trapped" within this boundary layer (Figure 8.9). Any quick observation of canine sniffing patterns will show the animal periodically sampling these boundary layers for higher concentration of trapped odors. Sometimes, the canine will work its nose deeper into the boundary (particularly in grassy situations) because concentrations of odorants will be significantly higher and longer lasting near the surface. These signals provide little directional information for searching canines but can provide the ability to identify odors more precisely because of the increased concentration.

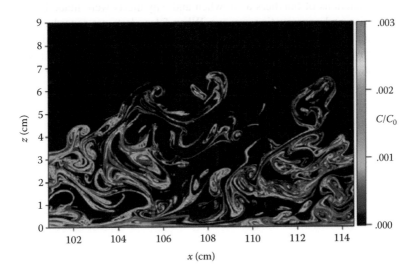

FIGURE 8.9 Image of a cross section through an odor plume illuminated with a laser. The color indicates the concentration of the odorant, where red is higher concentration, blue is lower concentration, and black is the absence of odor. The x- and z-axis values represent distance away from the odor source (horizontal axis, x) and distance above a solid surface (z). Notice the distribution of odor molecules trapped against the solid surface as opposed to the fluctuations apparent above the substrate.

SUMMARY

Odor signals for canine searches are highly dependent upon the airflow and the physical structures within the habitat. Because of this dependence, each odor signal will have a unique set of properties, including the spatial distribution, the temporal fluctuation in concentration, and any larger- or small-scale meandering. Despite these habitat-dependent signal structures, some general principles about odor signals as they pertain to canine searches can be drawn.

- The information contained within odor plumes and the types of odor plumes experienced by canines during searches are highly dependent upon the spatial and temporal scale of both the canine and the search area.
- Odor plumes, at the scales sampled and searched by canines, are structured primarily by the aerodynamics of airflow within the habitat. Diffusion is unimportant except in the microscale environment of boundary layers.
- In general, odor plumes contain chemical signals that fluctuate widely in concentration over time. The degree of the fluctuations in time or space is due to the intensity of the airflow of the habitat and the structural complexity of objects within that airflow.
- Despite the concept that odor plumes are unique to each habitat, general principles can be derived for the types of signals present under different flows.

This understanding of the aerial dynamics of odor plumes should help handlers during odor searches and provide some insight into what the canines are smelling and how their behavior may be dictated by this information. Particularly, assumptions of smooth increasing concentration gradients upwind are incorrect. Canines may periodically backtrack downwind because turbulent eddies have dispersed the odor such that downwind exhibits higher concentrations of odor than upwind. These eddies also may distribute odors in confined areas, where stable eddies are consistently being formed. Odors will be trapped in these eddies, and canines may consider them to be the most concentrated location of odors. Such an understanding is also important for scientists and others evaluating the explanations of handlers as to when and why alerts were made in such contexts as criminal investigation and conservation surveys. When false alerts are recorded, diffusion should not become a standard explanation of residual odor. The entire environment and the available evidence of air patterns must be taken into account when attempting to understand a specific canine's searching behavior.

9 The Practical and Legal Significance of the Chemical Analysis of Odor in Relation to Canine Forensic and Judicial Evidence

John Ensminger and Megan A. Ferguson

Chemical analysis of odor has a relationship with work of detection dogs in (1) identifying what chemicals and patterns of chemicals may be detected by dogs,[1] as well as identifying compounds they may not detect[2]; (2) designing optimal training aids that will most closely replicate the odors for which they are being deployed (see Chapter 18 herein); (3) improving existing chemical sensory procedures and instruments (see Chapter 7), and developing new technologies, including electronic noses[3]; (4) understanding the effect of environmental factors (seasonal, temperature, humidity, rainfall, etc.) on odor profiles (Meyer et al. 2013; Forbes and Perrault 2014; Forbes et al. 2014); (5) establishing comprehensive databases of chemicals associated with various events and items of interest in forensics, medical, and other scientific analysis (Vass et al. 2004); (6) evaluating training regimens for detection dogs (Harper et al. 2004, 2005); and (7) providing greater certainty as to the evidentiary value in criminal prosecutions of the reactions of trained detection dogs to odors of accelerants (Kurz et al. 1996) and individuals (scent identification as discussed in Chapter 19, cadavers in Chapter 16, and narcotics and explosives in Chapter 18).

This chapter will focus on two areas where chemical research has become evidence in such a way as to perhaps explain the significance of alerts of drug and cadaver dogs. The first concerns a murder prosecution in Florida where a cadaver dog alerted to the trunk of a car in which the body of a child may have been placed. A sample taken from inside the trunk of the car was analyzed with various chemical techniques (including gas chromatography/mass spectrometry (GC/MS) and laser-induced breakdown spectroscopy), and the results of that analysis were introduced at trial by the prosecution over objections by the defense. Although it will be argued that the trial court's admission of the chemical evidence was premature, given the considerable confusion between scientific groups on identifying a cadaver odor profile, it is likely that technology will continue to improve and a more specific profile will eventually become a matter of scientific consensus.

The second topic to be discussed here comes from the history of currency forfeiture in American law, where alerts of narcotics detection dogs were initially a basis for connecting currency to the illegal drug trade. After the recognition that most American currency was contaminated with cocaine residue, the alert of a drug dog was often held to be of little or no significance in making such a connection. When research indicated that dogs were not alerting to cocaine but, rather, to methyl benzoate (or a *profile* in which methyl benzoate was a significant component), the evidentiary value of a drug dog's alert came back into favor with courts because of findings indicating that the odor of methyl benzoate dissipates quickly, meaning the currency had to be in the proximity of drugs fairly recently before a dog alerted to it. Subsequent research indicating that currency-counting machines in banks might be accumulating cocaine and distributing it across bills has raised new questions as to the significance of canine alerts to currency (see Chapter 17).

VOLATILE ORGANIC COMPOUNDS AND THE ODOR OF HUMAN CADAVERS

In the 2011 trial of Casey Anthony,[4] charged with the murder of her 2-year-old daughter, Caley, the prosecution introduced evidence of both a cadaver dog and chemical analysis of a carpet sample from the trunk of a car to which the dog had alerted. The cadaver dog handler testified that his dog had indicated on the passenger area and trunk area of the vehicle where Casey's daughter's body was suspected of being placed, as well as to one spot in the backyard of the Anthony house. There was also evidence that the defendant's mother had called authorities to say that the vehicle smelled as if a dead body had been in it, and the scientist who performed the chemical analysis testified that, upon opening the can in which the carpet sample had been sent to him, the smell of a cadaver was overwhelming.

The defense argued that the evidence from the chemical analysis of the carpet sample should be excluded as unreliable, and the trial court held a hearing to determine whether such chemical evidence, not previously admitted by any American court, could satisfy the standard for admissibility for evidence derived from "new scientific principles or testing," as determined by a 1923 federal case, *Frye v. U.S.*,[5] and Florida case law interpreting *Frye*. *Frye* had long been the general standard for admissibility of new scientific evidence and continues to be so in some states, though many, including Florida subsequent to the proceedings in this prosecution, have adopted the standard accepted by the U.S. Supreme Court in the 1993 case of *Daubert v. Merrell Dow Pharmaceuticals, Inc.*[6] The trial judge ruled that the chemical evidence was admissible.[7]

EVIDENCE OF DECOMPOSITION EVENT FROM CHEMICAL ANALYSIS

The chemical analysis that the prosecution introduced was performed by Dr. Arpad Vass and his colleagues at the Oak Ridge National Laboratory.[8] Air from the can in which the carpet sample was shipped to the laboratory was analyzed by GC/MS without concentration, but "few compounds were observed in this sample (primarily chloroform) so it was deemed necessary to concentrate the sample in order to improve the signal-to-noise and to increase the sensitivity for lower abundance compounds (if present)." Therefore, cryogenic trapping was employed to "improve the detection limit for organic constituents in an air sample by a factor of 10 times or greater compared with direct sample injection into a GC/MS."[9] The GC/MS and cryotrapping procedures identified the 51 chemicals listed in the left column of Table 9.1.

Of the 51 chemicals found in the air sample by the GC/MS analysis, 41 were considered consistent with decompositional events because they were contained in the decompositional odor database of 478 chemicals associated with human decomposition that had been developed by the Oak Ridge National Laboratory pursuant to a government contract for the Federal Bureau of Investigation (FBI), Office of Victim Assistance.[10] According to Vass on cross-examination during the pretrial motion to exclude this chemical evidence, the agency declined to authorize release of the database to defense expert witnesses.[11] The correlation of the compounds identified through GC/MS analysis with the database, indicated in column 2 of Table 9.1, thus came solely from the report of the experts at the Oak Ridge National Laboratory and the pretrial and trial testimony of Vass. A significant number of the compounds identified as being in the database had not previously been otherwise identified in the peer-reviewed literature regarding human decomposition events, though some have been subsequently identified in papers and doctoral theses.[12]

The Oak Ridge analysis also eliminated as evidence of a decompositional event 17 of the chemicals as "known or possible gasoline constituents," because of the likelihood that gasoline would have been present in the trunk of the vehicle. Control samples tested in order to eliminate compounds

TABLE 9.1

51 Compounds Found in Trunk Sample from Cryotrapping Concentration and Gas Chromatograph/Mass Spectrometer Analysis

Compounds Identified in Odor from Florida Trunk Carpet Sample	Compound in Decompositional Odor Database[a]	Compound Found in Gasoline Vapors	Compound Found in Negative Controls[b]	Compound Found in Positive Control (Dead Montana Child)	Found in 30 Most Important for Decomposition (per Vass et al. 2008)[c] (Bold If Not Eliminated by Controls)
1-Methyl-ethyl benzene	Yes	Yes	No	No	No
1,2-Pentadiene	Yes	Maybe	No	No	No
1H-Indene, 2,3-dihydro	No	No	No	No	No
2-Butanone	Yes	**No**	Yes (pizza)	Yes	No
2-Chloropropane	No	No	No	No	No
2-Methyl furan	Yes	**No**	No (1)	No	No
2-Methyl hexane	Yes	Yes	Yes (trash bag)	No	No
2-Methyl propanenitrile	No	No	No	No	No
2,3-Butanediene	No	No	No	No	No
2-Methyl butanal	No	No	Yes (pizza, trip blank)	Yes	No
3-Methyl butanol	No	Maybe	Yes (pizza)	No	No
3-Methyl hexane	Yes	Maybe	Yes (trash bag, vehicle interior, garage air)	No	No
3-Methyl pentane	Yes	Yes	Yes (same as previous)	No	No
3-Methyl butanal	Yes	**No**	Yes (Knoxville carpet, pizza)	Yes	No
4-Methyl-2-pentanone	No	No	No	No	No

(Continued)

TABLE 9.1 (CONTINUED)

51 Compounds Found in Trunk Sample from Cryotrapping Concentration and Gas Chromatograph/Mass Spectrometer Analysis

Compounds Identified in Odor from Florida Trunk Carpet Sample	Compound in Decompositional Odor Database[a]	Compound Found in Gasoline Vapors	Compound Found in Negative Controls[b]	Compound Found in Positive Control (Dead Montana Child)	Found in 30 Most Important for Decomposition (per Vass et al. 2008) (Bold If Not Eliminated by Controls)[c]
Acetaldehyde (ethanal)	Yes	Yes	Yes (Knoxville carpet, pizza)	Yes	No
Acetic acid, methyl ester	Yes	No	No (2)	No	No
Acetone (2-propanone)	Yes	No	Yes (Knoxville carpet, pizza)	No	No
Benzene	Yes	Yes	Yes (multiple)	Yes	Yes (9)
Butanal	Yes	No	Yes (Knoxville carpet, trip blank[d])	Yes	No
Butanoic acid, methyl ester	Yes	No	No (3)	No	No
Carbon disulfide	Yes	No	No (but trace on Knoxville carpet) (4)	Yes	Yes (19)
Carbon tetrachloride	Yes	No	No (but trace on Knoxville carpet) (5)	Inconclusive	Yes (1)
Chloroethane	Yes	No	No (6)	No	No
Chloroform	Yes	No	No (trace on Knoxville carpet) (7)	No	Yes (12)
Chloromethane	Yes	No	No (8)	Yes	No
Decanal	Yes (trace)	No	No (9)	No	Yes (16) (not considered because trace level)
Dichloroethene	Yes	No	No (10)	Yes	No
Dichloromethane	Yes	No	No (11)	Yes	No
Dimethyl trisulfide	Yes	No	No (12)	Yes	Yes (15)

(Continued)

TABLE 9.1 (CONTINUED)

51 Compounds Found in Trunk Sample from Cryotrapping Concentration and Gas Chromatograph/Mass Spectrometer Analysis

Compounds Identified in Odor from Florida Trunk Carpet Sample	Compound Identified in Decompositional Odor Database[a]	Compound Found in Gasoline Vapors	Compound Found in Negative Controls[b]	Compound Found in Positive Control (Dead Montana Child)	Found in 30 Most Important for Decomposition (per Vass et al. 2008) (Bold If Not Eliminated by Controls)[c]
Dimethyl undecane	No	No	No	No	No
Dimethyl disulfide	Yes	**No**	No (but trace on vehicle interior) (13)	Yes	**Yes (7)**
Ethanol	Yes	Yes	Yes (Knoxville carpet, pizza)	Yes	No
Etheneamine	No	No	No	No	No
Ethyl benzene	Yes	Yes	No	No	Yes (13)
Hexane	Yes (trace)	Yes	Yes (Knoxville carpet, vehicle interior, pizza)	No	Yes (20)
Hexanol	Yes	**No**	**No (14)**	No	No
Isobutanal	Yes	**No**	Yes (pizza)	No	No
Isooctane	Yes	Yes	No	No	No
Limonene/pinene	Yes	**No**	Yes (trash)	No	No
Methanethiol	Yes	**No**	**No (15)**	Yes	No
Methanol	Yes	Yes	Yes (Knoxville carpet, pizza)	No	No
Naphthalene	Yes	Yes	Yes (trash bag)	No	Yes (5)
Octane	Yes	Yes	Yes (vehicle interior, garage air, trip blank)[a]	No	No

(Continued)

TABLE 9.1 (CONTINUED)

51 Compounds Found in Trunk Sample from Cryotrapping Concentration and Gas Chromatograph/Mass Spectrometer Analysis

Compounds Identified in Odor from Florida Trunk Carpet Sample	Compound in Decompositional Odor Database[a]	Compound Found in Gasoline Vapors	Compound Found in Negative Controls[b]	Compound Found in Positive Control (Dead Montana Child)	Found in 30 Most Important for Decomposition (per Vass et al. 2008) (Bold If Not Eliminated by Controls)[c]
Pentane	Yes	No	Yes (vehicle interior, pizza, garage air, trip blank)[a]	No	No
Tetrachloroethene	Yes	No	Yes (trash bag, garage air; found in degreasers)	No	Yes (4)
Tetrahydrofuran	No	No	No	No	No
Toluene	Yes	Yes	Yes (Knoxville carpet, vehicle interior, pizza)	Yes	Yes (2)
Trichloroethene	Yes (trace)	No	No (because garage air but less than carpet sample) (16)	No	Yes (22) (not considered because trace level)
Trimethyl pentene	Yes	Maybe	No	No	No
Xylene(s)	Yes	Yes	Yes (trash bag, vehicle interior, pizza)	No	No
Compounds under consideration: 51	41 (yes)	24 (indicated in bold)	16 (indicated in bold)	13 (7 of which not eliminated by prior steps are in list of 30)	5 (two eliminated as trace: numerical position in list of 30)

a   Vass case report (2009).

b   Highlighted numbers in parentheses indicate those chemicals still under consideration after others eliminated by controls, totalling 16 as indicated in summary in last row of table.

c   Bold entries indicate compound was among five used as evidence of human decomposition; numbers in parentheses indicate position of compound in Table 1 of Vass et al. (2008).

d   A trip blank is prepared prior to sampling using deionized water to identify contamination that might be present before samples are collected.

that could be explained as coming from sources other than a decompositional event included carpet samples from a vehicle found in a junkyard that was unrelated to the case; pizza (because pizza remains were allegedly found in trash in the subject car); laboratory air where the sample was stored (to see if there might be contaminants in the air that could explain any of the 51 chemicals found in the analysis, though there was no overlap from this); and samples from a roadkill squirrel allowed to decompose on a control carpet sample (because there could have been a nonhuman animal decomposing in the trunk). Testing was also conducted of the trash bags found in the subject car, the vehicle air, and the air of the garage where the vehicle was stored. A positive-control sample was obtained from a section of blanket in which a 3-year-old child had decomposed for approximately 3 months in Montana. Of the 24 compounds that did not overlap with gasoline constituents, 16 were left "whose source could not be potentially linked to any of the controls which were analyzed."

Of the 16 chemicals that had not been eliminated because of overlap with gasoline or controls,[13] seven were identified as "significant human decomposition chemicals" by comparison with a list of 30 such chemicals identified as such by Vass et al. (2008). Of these seven chemicals, two were eliminated as only being present in trace amounts. This identification means that Vass's forensic analysis chose to focus on those chemicals on a list published by Vass et al. (2008), which identified 30 "key markers of human decomposition" from buried bodies, though the body of Caley Anthony, if present in the trunk, was not buried. The 30 chemicals were identified as key markers not solely because of the amounts that might be detected, but through a "decision tree" that involved consideration of 10 factors[14]:

1. Reproducibility of detection (between burials and regardless of depth)
2. Detection of the compound as a component of human bone odor
3. Abundance of the compound
4. Longevity of detection
5. Background control concentrations
6. Whether the compounds were detected in surface decompositional events
7. Whether the compounds were detected in relevant areas other than the University of Tennessee's decay research facility (e.g., Noble, Georgia; morgues, forensic cases submitted to our laboratory, reports from other researchers)
8. Uniqueness of the compound
9. Chemical class trends
10. Effects of the environment (temperature, moisture, barometric pressure)

The decision tree thus incorporated quantitative and qualitative assessments, though the authors of the research stated that the "next logical progression in this study will be to develop/modify analytical instrumentation which can detect a significant proportion of these 30 compounds in the specified range of concentrations and chemical groupings."[15]

Virtually no analysis was provided by Vass of the positive-control sample, described in his expert witness report as "a forensic case in Montana where a 3 yr old child (decedent) was wrapped in a blanket and allowed to decompose over a 3-month period in the trunk of a car...." In Vass's table of compounds found in the analysis of the carpet from the suspect vehicle's trunk, he indicates that of the 51 compounds found in the carpeting, only 13 were found in the positive-control blanket. Of those 13, only 5 were found in the list of 30: benzene, *carbon disulfide, dimethyl trisulfide, dimethyl disulfide*, and toluene. The three chemicals in italics overlap with the five that Vass focused on after his elimination process with the trunk sample. If the positive-control results were included in the winnowing process, arguably, only these three chemicals should have been available to propose a human decompositional event from the trunk sample.

ARGUMENT AGAINST AN IDENTIFIABLE HUMAN DECOMPOSITION PROFILE

The defense obtained the services of Dr. Kenneth Furton as an expert. Dr. Furton's report stated the following:

> The methods employed by Vass and coworkers at Oak Ridge National Laboratory are still in the experimental stage and do not have sufficient databases of chemicals present in background materials and an insufficient number of decompositional materials and conditions to make ... scientific conclusions with reasonable degrees of scientific certainties using established statistical techniques. The data presented in the reports submitted does not allow for the calculation of error rates or the likelihood of false positive and false negatives under the conditions employed. Only a small fraction of the 478 "specific volatile compounds associated with burial decomposition" and the 30 chemicals Vass et al. (2008) have reported as "key markers of human decomposition" were present in the tested samples with five chemicals used to draw conclusions about the possibility of a decompositional event occurring (chloroform, carbon tetrachloride, carbon disulfide, dimethyl disulfide, dimethyl trisulfide). None of the fluorinated compounds Vass has reported to be specific for human decomposition were detected in the samples tested. Rather than interpreting that the lack of human specific fluorinated compounds as an indicator of a non-human decompositional event, Vass and coworkers speculated that this may indicate that their technique may not work for children. Similar speculation is found throughout the forensic report which ends with a conclusion that "a portion of the total odor signature" is "consistent with an early decompositional event that *could* be of human origin" with no reference to the degree of reliability of the method or statistical significance. The report does compare the compounds detected in the trunk samples and show that all of these compounds have been detected in animal remains as well.[16]

Vass et al. (2008) had acknowledged that their "study has shown that, for the most part, human decompositional end-products are not very unique in the chemical world," and Vass's report conceded that "an unusual variety of products or materials (not present in the trunk at the time of vehicle discovery) may have had some contribution to the overall chemical signature." Thus, he could not exclude the possibility that other events than human decomposition could explain the presence of the five chemicals, though he considered this at best a "remote possibility." In contrast, Furton argued in his expert witness report:

> The five chemicals used to draw conclusions about the possibility of a decompositional event are known to be present in cleaning products including bleach (chloroform and carbon tetrachloride) and in non-human decompositional events, including composting (carbon disulfide, dimethyl disulfide, dimethyl trisulfide). It is therefore critical to compare the concentrations/relative ratios of chemicals detected and compare these to databases of background materials and non-human decompositional events in order to determine if the levels detected are statistically significan[t].

Furton concluded:

> [I]t is my expert opinion that the use of characteristic chemicals to indicate a human-specific decompositional event has not been shown to be scientifically reliable to a level sufficient for use in forensic casework. At present, there is currently a lack of identified human-specific chemicals from decompositional events and an insufficient database of background materials and non-human decompositional chemicals to allow the reliability of this technique to be calculated.[17]

The defense moved to exclude

> Any testimony or evidence concerning any alleged identification of the chemical composition of human decomposition odor, any testimony regarding a test involving elemental analysis of Laser Induced Breakdown Spectroscopy, any testimony regarding quantification of chloroform, or reference to an alleged 'decompositional' odor analysis database....

TRIAL COURT RULING

In ruling on the motion, Judge Perry noted that the parties did not disagree that no case in Florida or, indeed, the United States had admitted evidence about "the chemical signature of the odor of human decomposition or the identity of the volatile chemical components of human decomposition." The judge summarized several of Vass's papers and quoted a statement from Vass's 2004 paper that "defining the chemical fingerprint produced by human decomposition is an attainable goal." He also cited prior Florida case law accepting evidence obtained by GC/MS,[18] and concluded that as long as the methodology was generally accepted, the opinions derived from use of the methodology did not have to be generally accepted. A 1998 Florida appellate case, *Berry v. CSX Trans., Inc.*,[19] had stated that "*Frye* allows opposite opinion testimony from experts relying upon the same generally accepted scientific principles and methodologies."[20] If there were defects in Vass's interpretations, as argued by Furton, this could go to the weight of those interpretations but need not make them inadmissible.

SEARCH FOR THE HUMAN DECOMPOSITION PROFILE

Regardless of whether the conclusion of the prosecution's expert in the Casey Anthony case is to be accepted—that the chemicals identified from the trunk were most conservatively explained as indicating a human decomposition event—research in the area has continued, and more scientific teams have published results listing chemicals and describing profiles of human and animal decomposition. Hoffman et al. (2009) identified 33 volatile organic compounds (VOCs) in 14 discrete types of human remains and determined that since the VOC profiles of different body parts could vary substantially, more care should be taken when choosing samples to train canines. Cablk et al. (2012), who used identical sampling and analytical procedures to Hoffman et al. (2009) but examined cow, pig, and chicken parts (bone, muscle, fat, skin) rather than human remains, found that 22 of those 33 VOCs were also detected during decomposition of one or more animal species. Of the remaining 11 compounds deemed to be unique to humans by comparison of these two studies, only 6 compounds remain unique upon comparison with more recent animal decompositions studies (Forbes et al. 2014; Perrault et al. 2014).

Unfortunately, very few studies have directly compared human and animal decomposition. Vass et al. (2008) examined human, deer, dog, and pig bones, aged 5–9 years old, by placing them in Tedlar bags and allowing 3 days for the headspace to equilibrate before sampling. Although only carbon tetrachloride and undecane were found to be unique to human bones, the authors reported that the relative contributions of different compound classes to the total VOC profile differed substantially between humans and the other animals studied. Vass (2012) later examined 186 headspace samples from soil collected at human or animal burial sites or from the soil surface where a decomposing body was found. This study corroborated that carbon tetrachloride and undecane were specific to human decomposition, added two other alkanes to the list of human-specific compounds, and postulated that the relative ratio of 2-methyl butanal to 3-methyl butanal could distinguish between human and animal remains. Finally, Stefanuto et al. (2015) compared surface decomposition of humans and pigs over the first 6 days of decay. Although their analysis suggested that there were fine distinctions between early human and pig decomposition, they concluded that more data were required before those distinctions could be made with confidence. Rosier et al. (2015) examined the decomposition of 6 human cadavers, one pig, and a host of other mammals, fish, amphibians, reptiles, and birds in a laboratory setting over a six-month period. Human and pig remains were separated by organ and tissue types, whereas the smaller animal carcasses were left intact. Human and pig remains could be distinguished from all other animal remains using a combination of eight VOCs. Despite the similarity in VOC composition between decomposing human and pig remains, the authors found that the pig and human data could be distinguished based on a combination of five esters. The authors stressed the need for further research, particularly on full bodies.

When Vass et al. (2008) published their list of 30 key markers of human decomposition, they stressed that most compounds were not unique in nature; indeed, 17 of the compounds were identified in control samples, albeit at concentrations that were typically at least tenfold lower than in decomposition samples. That only 5 of the 30 were found in the Casey Anthony trial and 7 of the 30 were found in the examination of animal remains by Cablk et al. (2012) might suggest that there was not a human body in the trunk, but the variability in results from different decomposition studies makes it clear that these disparities could easily arise if there was, in fact, a body in the trunk. Major variables among the different studies include whether the remains were whole or in parts; conditions of decomposition (e.g., in a body bag, buried, laid on bare soil, etc.); and decomposition time. One aspect that may be particularly relevant to understanding what cadaver dogs alert to and how to better train them is the sampling method prior to GC/MS analysis.

RELATING ANALYTICALLY DETERMINED DECOMPOSITION PROFILES TO CANINE SCENT ALERTS

GC/MS provides high-resolution, low-detection-limit identification of compounds with potential for quantification if additional standards are used, but its results are limited to what is physically injected into the GC column. There are multiple methods used to sample from decomposition sites, including sorbent tubes, solid-phase microextraction (SPME), direct headspace injection with cryo-focusing, and Scent Transfer Units (STU-100). Since canines sniff the headspace above or around a given sample, techniques that collect all compounds equally well would yield the best analytical foundation for investigating what dogs may be smelling.

Sorbent tubes are typically packed with two to three different granular materials that have high capacity for adsorbing various VOCs. Common adsorbents used for decomposition studies are Tenax TA (a porous polymer resin made from 2,6-diphenyl-p-phenylene oxide); a suite of graphitized carbon black products (e.g., Carbopack, Carbograph); and Carbosieve S-III (a porous carbon molecular sieve). A sampling pump pulls air through the tube, trapping volatile compounds on the adsorbents. Back in the lab, the tube is heated to drive off the VOCs before injecting into the GC/MS, often sending the heated gas sample that leaves the absorbent tube through a cryo-focusing tube prior to GC/MS injection. In cryo-focusing, the sample passes through a thin tube cooled by liquid nitrogen. This allows helium (the typical flow gas) and the primary components of air to pass through but traps analyte compounds, thus concentrating the sample and allowing for better separation.

In SPME, a fiber coated with one or more solid or polymeric compounds is inserted into the sample headspace, and VOCs preferentially partition from the air onto the fiber. The fiber may require 20 min or more in the headspace to adequately saturate with VOCs. The fiber is then placed directly into the heated GC/MS injection port, where analytes are desorbed.

Both sorbent tubes and SPME suffer from selective analyte partitioning from sample to collection device. Perrault et al. (2014) compared sorbent tubes and SPME with three common fiber coatings in a study of pig decomposition and found that, of 131 total detected compounds, only 36 were detected both by sorbent tubes and SPME. The remaining 95 compounds were fairly equally split between the two collection techniques, with sorbent tubes identifying most sulfur- and nitrogen-containing compounds and short-chain oxygenated compounds and SPME identifying most carboxylic acids, longer-chain acid esters, and monoterpenoid ketones. Thus, the odor profile that a cadaver dog sniffs on-site may differ significantly from that measured on GC/MS depending on the collection technique and adsorbent/coating materials chosen. Direct headspace injection, in contrast, allows no opportunity for analyte partitioning bias. In-line cryogenic focusing preconcentrates the sample to improve the detection limit. As of this writing, only one published study examining human decomposition has used this technique (Vass 2012).

A fourth sampling technique, the STU-100, uses a vacuum to pull air through a sterile gauze pad. VOCs adsorb into the pad, which is subsequently sealed in a plastic resealable bag until brought to the laboratory for desorption and injection onto GC/MS. The STU-100 has also been used to gather scent to present to detection dogs, including cadaver dogs. However, it too is limited due to variable adsorption of different VOCs to the scent pad. When a mixture of 39 standard VOCs with concentrations at 10 ppb by volume was examined using the STU-100 with cotton gauze pads, only 15 of the 39 VOCs were detected by GC/MS (Eckenrode et al. 2006). Eight of these detected compounds were associated with human decomposition in previous studies. DeGreeff et al. (2011) used the STU-100 to sample the air space around 21 recently deceased human bodies using three different types of sorbent pads. They reported 13 compounds relevant to decomposition. Here, too, 8 compounds had been reported in previous decomposition studies, but only one of those 8 compounds overlapped with those found in the previous study using the standard mixture of 39 VOCs. Of particular note was the lack of detected sulfides. Three sulfide compounds are on Vass's (2008) "top 30 human decomposition compounds" list; these are particularly relevant for relatively early decomposition, where tissue decay is still prevalent.[21]

PORTABLE GC/MS UNITS

Although GC/MS analysis has high specificity, sensitivity, and selectivity, the VOC profile it generates is dependent on the sampling method used in the field. Moreover, bringing samples back to the lab is time-consuming, and benchtop GC/MS analysis requires a trained technician. Portable GC/MS instruments can circumvent many of these drawbacks. Three person-portable GC/MS instruments are commercially available.[22] In-field direct sample processing times typically range from 3 to 8 min, and recent models have simplified the user interface so that operators require less training to obtain quality data (Smith 2012). These instruments have been used in various applications, including analysis of soil VOCs (Wirth et al. 2012b), disinfection of by-products in drinking water (Wirth et al. 2012a), explosives (Hunter and Riegner 2012), chemical warfare agents (Smith et al. 2004; Contreras et al. 2008; Bowerbank et al. 2009), and indoor air VOCs (Gorder and Dettenmaier 2011).

These portable GC/MS instruments are most commonly equipped with SPME introduction, consistent with many decomposition studies that analyzed samples with a benchtop GC/MS (Hoffman et al. 2009; Cablk et al. 2012; Perrault et al. 2014). However, to overcome the discrepancies between compounds that are present in the headspace and compounds that are adsorbed and released into the GC/MS by SPME, direct air injection can also be performed. Detection limits might suffer with direct injection due to the comparative concentration that SPME yields, but a small cryo-focusing unit, if necessary, would likely be feasible in the field.

COCAINE ON CURRENCY

After narcotics detection dogs began to provide forensic and judicial evidence regarding narcotics possession by suspects, canine alerts began to be introduced to establish a connection between large amounts of currency in possession or control of a suspect and illegal narcotics activities in which the suspect could be presumed to be engaged.[23] Forfeiture actions were often successful under federal legislation.[24] In the early 1990s, however, claimants of currency as to which forfeiture proceedings had been instituted began to argue that a drug dog's alert was meaningless in light of evidence that a high proportion of U.S. currency was consistently found to be tainted with cocaine.[25] Cases began to hold that a drug dog's alert could not provide the requisite probable cause to link currency to illicit narcotics activities.[26] Science seemed to provide strong support for this perspective (Oyler et al. 1996; Negrusz et al. 1998), though it was noted that levels of cocaine contamination were higher in currency seized in drug investigations than background levels of currency in general circulation.[27]

METHYL BENZOATE: A BREAKDOWN PRODUCT OF COCAINE

One strand of research, however, came to the rescue of police and prosecutors, with a series of papers indicating that dogs appeared to be alerting not to cocaine itself but, rather, to methyl benzoate, a volatile cocaine by-product. Furton et al. (1997a) tested volatile cocaine by-products and concluded that the dominant chemical in cocaine odor that was recognized by dogs was methyl benzoate, and that most dogs did not even alert to pharmaceutical-grade cocaine. The same team (Furton et al. 1999) concluded the following:

> We have studied in detail the diffusion of methyl benzoate from U.S. currency under different conditions. Whereas the parent cocaine molecule is non-volatile and can remain on currency for long periods of time, volatile decomposition products such as methyl benzoate dissipate quickly.... The evaporation rate of methyl benzoate from U.S. currency has been studied in detail. The amount of methyl benzoate on currency decreased exponentially. Evaporation rates varied considerably (2 to 2,000 ng/sec) depending on conditions, decreasing with increasing number of bills and covering of the currency.

Even within hours, the amount of methyl benzoate could drop below a level detectible by canines, and therefore, "circulated currency, innocently contaminated with μg quantities of cocaine would not cause a properly trained detection canine to signal an alert even if very large numbers of bills are present." In a subsequent paper (Furton et al. 2002), certain members of the same team stated more emphatically that "it is not plausible that innocently contaminated U.S. currency contains sufficient enough quantities of cocaine and associated volatile chemicals to signal an alert from a properly trained drug detector dog." This paper also noted that its results supported a U.S. patent described as "a method and product for providing the aroma of cocaine to the olfactory senses by volatilizing methyl benzoate ... whereby the aroma of street cocaine is perceived."[28]

Waggoner et al. (1997) found that "[w]hile training dogs to detect pharmaceutical cocaine, it became apparent they could detect only the highest concentration of this vapor that could be generated." Their dogs "did discriminate pharmaceutical cocaine from clean air, though with considerably less accuracy than they discriminated illicit cocaine vapor from clean air." Their evidence results suggested that "when dogs are trained to detect cocaine in the field, their discriminations probably depend on one or more constituents in the vapor sample in addition to cocaine HCl." Their results, however, were dramatically different from those of the Furton group:

> The average vapor sensitivity threshold for methyl benzoate vapor was 16 ppb compared to 0.03 ppb for illicit cocaine vapor.... This means that the highest methyl benzoate concentration in the illicit cocaine vapor was lower than the dogs' average threshold for methyl benzoate vapor. In other words, *the dogs were not apparently using methyl benzoate when detecting illicit cocaine under these laboratory conditions*. This suggests that compounds in cocaine other than methyl benzoate may be important in how dogs recognize cocaine [emphasis added].

Courts, however, recognized the Furton team's research and began to accept (again) that a drug dog's alert might indicate recent contact of the currency in question with narcotics activities.[29] In a 2005 federal circuit case, *U.S. v. $30,670*,[30] the government conceded that its forfeiture case turned on the dog alert evidence but argued that the dogs were alerting to methyl benzoate, which would evaporate in a "short period." The circuit court invited argument on "publicly available empirical information," and concluded that the "research of Dr. Furton and Dr. Rose established 'to a reasonable scientific certainty that a narcotics detection dog alerts to the odor of methyl benzoate as the dominant odor of illicit cocaine, and not to cocaine itself.'" An affidavit of Dr. Stefan Rose stating the cocaine "is a local anesthetic and as such blocks the transmission of nerve impulses" led the Seventh Circuit to conclude that "it seems that dogs cannot smell cocaine at all because the narcotic acts as an anesthetic that deadens olfactory senses." Citing and quoting from the various papers produced by Dr. Furton and his team, the court stated that "it is likely that trained cocaine detection dogs will alert to currency only if it has been exposed to large amounts of illicit cocaine within the very recent past." Therefore, the court concluded that "a properly trained dog's alert to currency should be entitled to probative weight."

In 2013, the Seventh Circuit again focused on the significance of canine alerts to currency in a case, *U.S. v. Funds in the Amount of $100,120*,[31] involving currency being carried by a passenger boarding a train in Chicago. Although the innocent-contamination argument had been rejected at earlier stages of the litigation, on a motion for summary judgment, the claimant offered the affidavit testimony of a forensic chemist, Sanford A. Angelos, who questioned the accuracy of Furton's conclusions as to the threshold for methyl benzoate detection by dogs (referring to Waggoner et al. 1997), and also argued, according to the circuit court, "that, so long as cocaine is present on the currency, the cocaine will continue to generate methyl benzoate and thereby replenish the methyl benzoate lost to evaporation." He also stated that cocaine residue could be trapped in currency and that, therefore, again according to the court, "innocently tainted, general-circulation currency contained significantly greater amounts of cocaine residue [than] assumed by Dr. Furton in [Furton et al. 1997b]."[32]

The court questioned the accuracy of Dr. Angelos's testimony as to the assertion that cocaine on currency would continue to generate methyl benzoate indefinitely, citing Dejarme et al. (1997) to the effect that "'pure' cocaine only continues to produce methyl benzoate for about 2,880 minutes (that is, 48 hours) depending on the temperature and humidity conditions. If so," the court continued, "it is difficult to see how the Funds, which Marrocco claims to have saved from years earlier, could still be producing methyl benzoate based on cocaine that allegedly tainted the Funds before Marrocco acquired them." It has already been noted that Furton et al. (2002) found that a 15-year-old sample of street cocaine was alerted to by most dogs in that study. Thus, a sufficiently large amount of residue on currency could presumably last longer than 48 h. The amount of cocaine on the currency in the 2013 Seventh Circuit case could not be established, because the money was no longer available for testing as "[p]resumably the government deposited the Funds into a bank account."[33]

SNAPDRAGONS: ODOR PROFILES WITH HIGH METHYL BENZOATE LEVELS

Additional questions arise from a 2015 paper by Cerreta and Furton, who evaluated "the odor profiles of various species of snapdragon flowers to assess how significantly methyl benzoate contributes to the total VOC profile or fragrance that is produced." These authors sought to determine the potential of the snapdragon to elicit alerts from narcotics detection dogs and stated that the 2013 Supreme Court case of *Florida v. Jardines*[34] called into question the selectivity and accuracy of drug detection dogs and specifically highlighted methyl benzoate, though the issue was raised in briefs, particularly in one written by Professor Leslie Shoebotham,[35] not in the decision of the Court. Cerreta and Furton (2015) noted that the 2002 study in which Furton was lead author had presented perfume samples containing methyl benzoate to trained drug dogs without the dogs reacting.[36] Now, presenting odors from various varieties of snapdragons, they found that again the dogs did not react despite the fact that "the percentage of methyl benzoate was exceedingly higher in the snapdragon flowers, than in the cocaine samples." As to how methyl benzoate in combination with other volatile chemicals might not be recognized by dogs trained to alert to cocaine, the authors state:

> The significant difference between the odor profiles of the snapdragon flowers and cocaine suggests that the pool of odor released from the flower aids in the canines' ability to differentiate between the snapdragon flowers and cocaine, even if the active odor is present in both samples. Since the active odor of illicit materials depends on the canines' olfactory receptor response, and is not necessarily the most prominent odor present,[37] it is possible that multiple odors produced by the snapdragons induce a canine's olfactory receptor response, while for cocaine, it is only methyl benzoate. This would allow for canines to interpret the odors produced by snapdragon flowers as entirely different than that of cocaine.

The relationship of these findings to the 1997 research of Waggoner et al. deserves another look at this point. At the very least, the work of Cerreta and Furton (2015) could be taken by drug kingpins as advice to surround cocaine and currency shipments with crushed snapdragons. It must also be questioned whether the cocaine odor profile has been too simplistically or too prematurely characterized as consisting almost exclusively of methyl benzoate, or if other explanations besides quantity of odor might explain why dogs did not alert to snapdragons.[38] It is possible that a new era of doubt as to the significance of drug dog alerts with respect to currency will begin.[39]

CONCLUSION

The threshold, the concentration of vapor that a dog can detect of a chemical (sometimes questionably referred to as the "absolute threshold"), varies depending on (1) the *chemical* [Furton and Myers 2001, providing a table of differing results as to acetic acid, propionic acid, and caproic acid, with some differences even between different papers by the same research teams; see also Johnston 1999, finding detection thresholds for methyl benzoate, cyclohexanone, and nitroglycerin to be on the order of tens of parts per billion, but for 2,3-dimethyl-2,3-dinitrobutane (DMNB), a detection taggant, to be at 500 ppt]; (2) the *breed of dog* (Walker et al. 2006); (3) *the individual dog* (Moulton 1975, noting that the threshold for detecting amyl acetate was lower than 10^{-7} and possibly as low as 10^{-9} for some dogs; Goth et al. 2003); and (4) the *training the dog used in an experiment had received* (Macias 2009; Macias et al. 2010, also noting different results in different trials of the same experiment).

In a table comparing the use of analytical techniques for detecting explosives with the use of dogs, Furton and Myers (2001) give the scientific foundation of the former as "electronics, computer science, analytical chemistry" but for dogs as "neurophysiology, behavioral psychology, and analytical chemistry." While this is undoubtedly an adequate comparison of the two approaches as viewed from the scientific literature, American courts considering canine evidence seldom investigate the neurophysiology, behavioral psychology, analytical chemistry, cognition, or other scientific issues that might provide a careful perspective on canine evidence, instead relying too frequently on platitudinous generalizations, often from the testimony of the handler of the dog involved, about how many parts per billion or trillion the dog can detect (*Jones v. United States Drug Enforcement Administration*[40]; *Farm Bureau Mutual Insurance Co. of Arkansas, Inc. v. Foote*[41]) and by what orders of magnitude dogs outperform machines (*California v. Sommer*[42]; *California v. Adams*[43]). The reason for this may often be placed on the manner in which the attorneys prepared for trial, given that American courts frequently rely on the disputants for the scientific sources they incorporate in their decisions.

While it might be argued that lawyers and judges cannot be expected to have a precise understanding of the complex scientific issues involved in odor detection, neither should a belief in canine superiority to equipment or humans create a presumption that such superiority comes with infallibility. This error becomes part of the logic by which courts have too easily accepted arguments that an unproductive alert is explained by the lingering of residual odor. As with the discussion of aerodynamics in Chapter 8 herein, a consideration of the scientific issues brings out many other possible explanations and may throw doubt on some of the currently popular legal reasoning in canine cases.

Comparisons of chemical sensors and canines often focus on the portability of the dog and its ability to move across landscapes and fearlessly enter dark spaces, including places where even the handler cannot or fears to go. For other functions, such as explosives detection, the urgency of developing alternatives to dogs is increasing as the range and complexity of explosives multiply.[44] For explosives detection and for search and rescue at disaster sites, the safety of both the dog and the handler also justifies the expense of research to develop portable chemical sensors. Yet, chemical research is helping to better train detection dogs, as well as contributing to the advancement of chemical sensory instruments. Indeed, some scientists are simultaneously working toward improving the functioning of detection dogs while also developing technologies designed ultimately to replace the need for such dogs.[45]

Understanding what detection dogs are reacting and alerting to makes their work less of a "black box." Humans have been satisfied with dogs as companions in the hunt for thousands, perhaps tens of thousands, of years without demanding that they explain themselves. Nevertheless, the needs of producing valid evidence for criminal prosecutions, certain diagnosis for medical applications, and better statistics for conservation applications will continue to spur science toward an ever-deeper understanding of the chemistry behind the practical uses of canine olfaction.

ENDNOTES

1. See Perrault et al. (2014); Hoffman et al. (2009), stating that "it is not known whether one chemical component, several components, or the whole VOC profile establishes the victim recovery (VR) canine's particular olfactory 'match' that elicits a trained response"; and Lorenzo et al. (2003), looking at what compounds "law enforcement certified detector dogs alert to when searching for drugs, explosives and humans."
2. See Joshi et al. (2009). Furton and Myers (2001) note that some explosive chemicals are not found in the headspace, and therefore may escape detection by instruments that rely on finding VOCs, as well as dogs.
3. Wilson (2015) describes recent advances in electronic nose technologies, noting:

   Electronic aroma detection (EAD) technologies encompass a wide array of electronic-nose (e-nose)-type technologies with many different gas-detection mechanisms and operating principles. The many types of e-nose instruments range from surface acoustic wave (SAW), quartz crystal microbalance (QMB), metal oxide semiconducting (MOS) and conducting polymers (CP), to the newer DNA-carbon nanotubes, and many others.

   Joshi et al. (2009) argue that electronic noses have a long way to go before becoming operational in the field and are insufficient compared to established analytical instruments such as GC/MS.
4. Case no. 48-2008-CF-15606-O. The case began in 2008 when the defendant's mother reported her granddaughter missing.
5. 293 F. 1013 (D.C. Cir. 1923).
6. 509 U.S. 579 (1993).
7. *Order Denying Motion to Exclude Unreliable Evidence*, Circuit Judge Belvin Perry, Jr., May 7, 2011. The chemical evidence was not admitted with any specific requirement to be corroborative or otherwise linked to the cadaver dog evidence, though the authors will consider some aspects of such a connection between the two types of evidence in a subsequent paper.
8. *Forensic Report* submitted to Detective Yuri Melich, etc., April 28, 2009 (hereafter "Vass's report").
9. Laser-induced breakdown spectroscopy (LIBS) was also used, according to Vass's report, "to determine if known inorganic components of decompositional events were elevated over the controls and also to determine if the relative abundance ratios of these elements could be used to determine a rough post-mortem interval."
10. DE-ACO5-00OR22725. Vass et al. (2004) state that the "current version of the database is presently being archived at the Federal Bureau of Investigation, Counterterrorism and Forensic Research Unit, Quantico, Virginia."
11. It must be questioned whether there is any continued justification for the FBI keeping the database proprietary to itself and those who developed it. Published papers have made many of the compounds in the database public, and the 2014 thesis by Caraballo lists at least 173 chemicals associated specifically with human decomposition from prior studies and adds 11 more from original research. Thus, nearly half of the database is likely now public.
12. A considerable amount of the cross-examination of Vass sought to emphasize differences between the results of Vass and his colleagues and those of Statheropoulos and his colleagues (Statheropoulos et al. 2005, 2007).
13. 2-Methyl furan, acetic acid methyl ester, butanoic acid methyl ester, carbon disulfide, carbon tetrachloride, chloroethane, chloroform, chloromethane, decanal, dichloroethene, dichloromethane, dimethyl trisulfide, dimethyl disulfide, hexanol, methanethiol, and trichloroethene.
14. A more precise description of the decision tree was not published with the 2008 paper, and a request to Dr. Vass to provide such documentation went unanswered.
15. This step may be indicated by Bilheux et al. (2014, 2015), research on which Dr. Vass was a coauthor.
16. Report of Kenneth G. Furton to Baez Law Firm, January 16, 2011.
17. DeGreeff and Furton (2011) note "a huge discrepancy in the reported compounds between different research groups." They state that their work "is the first to report VOCs obtained from a population of 27 individuals [cadavers] from multiple locations to determine similar volatiles." In summarizing this paper in a review paper, Furton et al. (2015) said that the comparison of human scent from living individuals differed from that collected from deceased remains in that with respect to the deceased remains, "there was less variation

between subjects signifying a more generalized odour." Agapiou et al. (2015) recently argued, in the context of establishing a VOC profile for search and rescue applications, that "significant effort and progress … is impeded because many studies report large numbers of candidate VOCs, are based on small numbers of participants, and use different analytical technologies, and standardized approaches to sampling data, normalization and validation have yet to be adopted." See also Perrault et al. (2014):

> Inconsistencies exist in the VOC profiles reported in published literature, which reflects variations in decomposition variables (environment, weather, soil type, cadaver/carcass size, geographical location, *etc.*) and/or analytical methods (collection technique, instrument used, instrument parameters, *etc.*) used in these studies. Variation-inducing factors are often associated with outdoor decomposition environments involving soil.

See also Stadler et al. (2012) and Dent et al. (2004).

18. *Florida v. Sercey*, 825 So.2d 959 (Fla. 1st DCA 2002).

19. 709 So.2d 552 (Fla. 1st DCA 1998).

20. The authors will argue elsewhere that judicial consideration of the admissibility of evidence of the sort accepted here should include statistical procedures used in filtering data. A general acceptance analysis would, in our opinion, reject filtering through a confidential database unavailable for scientific review, or comparison with a list of 30 key compounds only adopted in the research of the testifying expert and his colleagues. The analytical gap between data and expert opinion should not be overcome merely because the expert used conventional instrumentation and procedures to gather initial data.

21. The STU-100 has been shown to be successful for generating a scent aid for live human tracking (Harvey and Harvey 2003; see also DeGreeff 2010), but in this study, the human that was tracked was the source for the scent pad, as opposed to collecting scent pads from various corpses for training canines to find different corpses. Even if only a fraction of the VOCs on the live human were trapped on the scent pad, the tracking canine could follow that specific subset of compounds. If, however, a portion of VOCs associated with decomposition are trapped and there is substantial variability in compound breakdowns from one corpse to another, the efficacy of the scent pads may diminish.

22. Hapsite, by Inficon, and Guardion 7 and Tridion 9, both by Torion.

23. *U.S. v. $215,300*, 882 F.2d 417 (9th Cir. 1989); *U.S. v. $53,082*, 773 F.Supp. 26 (ED Mich. 1991), 985 F.2d 245 (6th Cir. 1993).

24. 21 U.S.C. 881; 18 U.S.C. 981.

25. *U.S. v. $639,558*, 955 F.2d 712 (DC Dir. 1992). "Axel alerted, all agree, to cocaine adhering to the cash in Bleichfeld's luggage. When some of the cash was later washed in a vat at the Drug Enforcement Administration, cocaine showed up.… In order to blunt the implications of this, Bleichfeld called an expert, Dr. James Woodford, who testified that 90 percent of all cash in the United States contains sufficient quantities of cocaine to alert a trained dog.… Officer Beard, the dog handler, suggested on the basis of hearsay that the number was lower, near 70 percent. (There is at least one study indicating that up to 97 percent of all bills in circulation in the country are contaminated by cocaine, with an average of 7.3 micrograms of cocaine per bill [citing Pool 1989].)" The court also referred to Ronald Siegel's book, *Intoxication*, which stated (p. 293) that "one out of every three bills in U.S. circulation is involved in cocaine transactions.…" See also *U.S. v. $53,082*, 985 F.2d 245 (6th Cir. 1993) (noting, "there is some indication that residue from narcotics contaminates as much as 96% of the currency currently in circulation"); *Jones v. U.S. Drug Enforcement Administration*, 819 F.Supp. 698 (MD Tenn. 1993) (referring to a Drug Enforcement Agency (DEA) chemist's finding that a third of randomly selected bills were contaminated with detectable cocaine); *Hetmeyer v. Virginia*, 19 Va.App. 103, 448 S.E.2d 894 (Ct. App. 1994) (dissent argued that although the dog had alerted to the currency, there was no evidence that the defendant was the source of its "contamination," but also cited *$53,082* and *Jones* regarding tainted currency in circulation).

26. *Muhammed v. DEA, Asset Forfeiture Unit*, 92.F.3d 653 (8th Cir. 1996) (finding a drug dog's alert "virtually meaningless [because] an extremely high percentage of all cash in circulation in America today is contaminated with drug residue"); *U.S. v. $30,060*, 39 F.3d 1039 (9th Cir. 1994) (probative value of dog's alert "is significantly diminished" because of the evidence of widespread currency contamination); *U.S. v. $506,231*, 125 F.3d 442 (7th Cir. 1997).

27. See Hudson (1989). ("Cocaine was present at background levels of less than 10 nanograms per note. In comparison, case samples were grossly contaminated with cocaine in the range from 50 to over 1,000 times the background levels determined for Sasktachewan.") Background levels of cocaine on currency may be increasing. See also Mesloh et al. (2002). Also, other drug residues are being discovered on currency. Luzardo et al. (2011).

28. W.J. Woodford. U.S. Patent 4,260,517. "Available Odor of Cocaine." April 7, 1981. Even though methyl benzoate dissipates quickly from the surface of currency, street cocaine itself apparently continues to emit volatiles for years as Furton et al. (2002) noted that "[i]nterestingly, 1 g of a 15-year-old street cocaine sample was confirmed to elicit responses from the majority of the detector dogs...."

29. *U.S. v. $22,474*, 246 F.3d 1212 (9th Cir. 2001) (noting that "the government presented evidence that the dog would not alert to cocaine residue found on currency in general circulation. Rather, the dog was trained to, and would only, alert to the odor of a chemical by-product of cocaine called methyl benzoate. Moreover, the government provided evidence that unless the currency Mahone was carrying had recently been in the proximity of cocaine, the detection dog would not have alerted to it. That evidence was not disputed."); *U.S. v. $242,484*, 389 F.3d 1149 (11th Cir. 2004).

30. 403 F.3d 448 (7th Cir. 2005).

31. 730 F.3d 711 (7th Cir. 2013).

32. Dr. Angelos died in 2011.

33. Nor did the court take into account the research of Jourdan et al. (2013). See Chapter 17 herein.

34. 133 S.Ct. 1409 (2013).

35. Brief of Amici Curiae Fourth Amendment Scholars in Support of Respondent, *State of Florida v. Joelis Jardines*, No. 11-564 (2013).

36. The possibility of drug dogs alerting to perfumes was raised in the case law as early as a Fifth Circuit case from 1982, *Horton v. Goose Creek Independent School District*, 690 F.2d 470 (5th Cir. 1982). This case continues to stand for this possibility. See Phipps (2014). Smith (2009), however, interviewed handlers who claimed that their dogs had never alerted to perfume, unless there were also illegal narcotics present.

37. The paper states:

   [I]n most cases, other compounds contributed more to the flowers' odor profile than that of methyl benzoate. For instance, the most abundant compound released from the Black Prince snapdragon was β-cis ocimene (63%), while both β-Myrcene (11%) and 2,6-dimethyl-2,4,6-octatriene (14%) contributed more than methyl benzoate (8%). The Rembrandt snapdragon's odor profile showed that acetophenone (42%) and β-cis ocimene (30%) were most dominant, with methyl benzoate contributing 26%. For the Maryland True Pink, methyl benzoate and β-cis ocimene contributed relatively similar amounts to the odor profile, at 41% and 45%, respectively. Conversely, methyl benzoate was the most dominant odor at 67% for Twinny Peach, but in general also the least odiferous type of snapdragon flower....

   See also Dudareva et al. (2000).

38. As noted in *U.S. v. $30,670*, some narcotics detection dog trainers use pseudococaine, primarily consisting of methyl benzoate, as "the only material used during training" for cocaine detection. See Edge et al. (1998), finding that a training aid for TNT, NESTT TNT, produced a dissimilar vapor from that of military-grade TNT. This research noted that the ratio of dinitrotoluene to trinitrotoluene in the training aid (8:1 in the static state) differed considerably from that in the military-grade TNT (39:1 in the static state), raising questions about the utility of the training aid (there was a similar discrepancy in the dynamic state, i.e., 4:1 versus 23:1). Differences were also noted in Lorenzo et al. (2003), in which Furton was a coauthor.

39. As of this writing, neither the scientific community nor the courts have had an opportunity to consider the significance of this latest research. See additional issues raised in Chapter 17 herein.

40. 819 F.Supp. 698 (1993).

41. 341 Ark. 105, 14 S.W.3d 512 (2000).

42. 16 Cal.Rptr.2d 165 (1993).

43. No. H030529, 2008 Cal.App.Unpub.LEXIS 4091 (Ct.App. 2008). In *Adams*, the handler referred to the "main lab" of the Bureau of Alcohol, Tobacco, Firearms and Explosives (ATF) in Maryland as having "super-duper top-secret" information. Throwing an aura of secrecy over canine work is unnecessary.

44. Harper et al. (2005) note that narcotics detection dogs "are expected to face a predictable line-up of 5 or 6 drug odors [but] the explosive detection canine is expected to face dozens of different explosive products during its service." This team also notes that
   While there are six principle chemical categories of explosives including aliphatic nitrates ($C-NO_2$), aromatic nitrates ($Ar-C-NO_2$), nitramines ($C-N-NO_2$), nitrate esters ($C-O-NO_2$), peroxides ($C-O-O-C$) and acid salts $\left(NH_4^+, NO_3^-\right)$, there are dozens of individual explosive chemicals which must be detected.
   Low vapor pressures of some explosive compounds complicate their detection.

45. See Patent no. US8726719 B2, Light-weight analyzer for odor recognition, invented by Arpad Vass and Marcus Wise, and using "the very specific and unique chemicals identified in the database of human decompositional odor... The detector is self-contained, portable and built for field use. Both visual and auditory cues are provided to the operator."

Section III

Behavior, Learning, and Training

TRAINING MEANS CHANGE

The pre-Socratic philosopher Heraclitus of Ephesus, who was active around 500 BC, is often credited with saying, "The only constant in life is change," which is a loose translation and possible paraphrase (Graham 2015; Wheelwright 1959, p. 29). It is clear that Heraclitus believed in a theory of universal flux. This thought is apropos for this section for several reasons, not the least of which provides a glimpse into the everyday life of a working dog. As we progress on the journey of understanding canine olfaction capabilities, the constant state of flux is evident for the dog, handler, trainer, or scientist as it correctly recognizes that change is the only constant in life when it involves a living, breathing being.

KNOWLEDGE DICTATES ADAPTATION

The varied aspects of dog training demand understanding of how dogs learn and adapt their behavior, which are elements of science well established and generally understood by anyone devoting the time necessary to comprehend such matters. In antiquity, harsh methods were probably assumed as the best, perhaps the only, way to train a dog. Arrian of Nicomedia, describing his favorite hunting hound, Horme, says that because as a puppy, "she was punished with a whip, if anyone even to this day [2nd century AD] should mention a whip, she goes up to the one who has said it and crouches down like one beseeching" (Phillips and Willcock 1999).

While much is known about dogs in general, we have only begun to understand some of the differences in learning, behavior, and training for dogs typically required to perform daily olfactory tasks and the associated duties that accompany the various disciplines in which dogs are deployed. Training a dog of this type often will result in training one aspect while witnessing legacy issues, some of which are unexpected. Whether it be trained to detect mercury, scat, corrosion, pharmaceuticals, alcohol, weapons, explosives, whale feces, or any number of the multitude of detection duties common today, the odor side of training is basically the same. However, it is often the nuances of training and deployment for such specifics that demand an understanding far different and are often comprehended the least. This section presents these issues in a clear, concise way while attempting to assist the scientist, trainer, lawyer, handler, or casual reader while simultaneously expressing a complete admiration of the dog and the work it can perform. The devotion to the dog is only surpassed by the expressions of a dog as stated by Charles Darwin when he said:

> But man himself cannot express love and humility by external signs, so plainly as does a dog, when with drooping ears, hanging lips, flexuous body, and wagging tail, he meets his beloved master. Nor can these movements in the dog be explained by acts of volition or necessary instincts, any more than the beaming eyes and smiling cheeks of a man when he meets an old friend. (Darwin 1873, p. 11)

HUNTING LEADS TO THE EXPRESSION OF EMOTION IN MAN AND ANIMAL

As a young man and into college age, Charles Darwin had great affection for his many dogs and often referred to them by name in correspondence. It is thought that throughout his life, Darwin may have owned some 12 dogs. However, it was his passion for hunting, often with his dog, on which Darwin spent exorbitant amounts of time. The keen insight he demonstrated in scientific observation led him to possess a clear understanding of the uniqueness that accompanied the animal he loved so much while on the hunting expeditions he enjoyed. It is thought the enthusiasm of hunting with his dog would have demonstrated proof of the ability to adapt to the environment and purpose of the human (Feller 2005, 2009). As discussed directly within this section, hunting for prey desired by man is at the heart of canine olfactory demonstration and forms the basis of the varied disciplines in which a dog is used today.

ACCEPTANCE OF CHANGE

This now brings us full circle to Heraclitus and his concept of flux or change. It is only through understanding the finite elements of training where the demonstrative ability to learn, modify, and adapt behavior forms the foundation of this section. The capacity of the dog to change, almost at will, is explored through the lens of proven scientific methods and experiential observations while exposing some of the most overlooked criteria of which any person employing a dog should be aware. Experiencing change throughout the course of daily life for a working dog dictates that the trainer, handler, lawyer, or scientist alike shall endeavor to exhibit knowledge necessary to maintain a highly performing specimen worthy of our most valued trusts, such as life itself. If any element of training, handling, or scientific study would be performed without absolute commitment to highest scientific standards and performance, it may well be centuries before we could truly understand, appreciate, and anticipate usage of such a fine animal to the full potential of which it is capable.

Further, it is the acceptance of change as a normal and customary event that will allow progress in utilizing the natural talent of the dog. A highly experienced trainer may gain insight into a certain dog psychological behavior being witnessed that may open the door to an alternative method of training. A novice search-and-rescue (SAR) handler could possibly learn to further motivate the dog by understanding the science behind reward delivery methods and timing. An attorney or law firm may realize that the 18-month-long study, which involves training a Bichon Yorkshire Terrier Mix and other dogs to locate scent (Hall et al. 2013), could be drastically different and may not be appropriate or apply to the months of training for the dog involved in their legal inquiries. The researcher may realize that a trainer may offer experimental and anecdotal analysis that could add to understanding to effectively reduce the time needed to design an experiment, thereby saving resources, or possibly offer guidance to improve performance making the research more valuable.

It is for these reasons and more that Section 3 offers something for everyone, novice to expert, observer or participant, all of which will aid in the furtherance of this wonderful animal and the multitude of ways the dog can positively affect human lives. Considering all that dogs do to enrich our lives on a daily basis, it seems that the least we humans can do is offer the very best that we have to them in return.

L.E. Papet, John Ensminger, and Tadeusz Jezierski

10 Canine Olfactory Learning and Behavior

Nathaniel J. Hall and Clive D.L. Wynne

A basic background in learning theory is critical for the understanding of canine olfaction. Recent research in olfaction emphasizes the importance of experience and learning on how olfactory stimuli are processed and perceived (Wilson and Stevenson 2006). The aim of this chapter is to provide a brief review of basic concepts in learning theory and explore phenomena that have been tested across a wide variety of species and sensory domains (including visual, auditory, as well as olfactory) indicating that the processes are generalizable across species. We will then extend these principles to olfactory learning tasks. Throughout we will highlight the small but growing literature that explores canine olfactory learning, and will highlight the implications of basic behavioral research for working odor-detecting dogs.

We will begin with a description of classical (Pavlovian) conditioning principles as they apply to canine odor detection. We will demonstrate how these factors influence generalization and discrimination, and then apply the findings of olfactory perception to dogs working on odor detection tasks.

CLASSICAL (PAVLOVIAN) CONDITIONING

Ivan Pavlov (1849–1936) was a pioneer in the study of physiology and medicine for which he won the Nobel Prize in 1904. His research subject was the topic of this book—the domestic dog. In his quest to understand the physiology of digestion, he became interested in the production of saliva when dogs were presented with food. As he repeatedly conducted studies with the same dogs, he noted that they began to emit what he originally called *psychic secretions* (Todes 2014). Salivation would commence before food was even placed in the animal's mouth if it could predict when the food was going to arrive. Sometimes simply the appearance of a researcher would be enough of a signal that food was on its way that the dogs would start to salivate. Curious about how the dogs could learn to produce saliva in the anticipation of food, Pavlov reoriented his laboratory away from the study of the physiology of digestion and toward the psychological questions of why the dogs began to salivate before the food was ever presented. This led ultimately to the discovery of what we now call classical or Pavlovian conditioning.

Probably the most commonly used example of Pavlovian conditioning derives from Pavlov's own research. To investigate how dogs could come to predict when the food was presented, Pavlov used stimuli that he could control and manipulate. One such stimulus was a metronome (contrary to generations of mistaken accounts, Pavlov likely never used a bell in his research; Todes 2014). When the metronome first sounds, the dogs surely do not salivate. A metronome has no meaning for a dog. If, however, the ticking of a metronome coincides with when food is presented, the sound of the metronome becomes associated with the presentation of food. Once this association occurs, the dogs begin to engage in behaviors that prepare them for the food whenever they hear the metronome. This typically includes starting to salivate.

Figure 10.1 exemplifies this relationship. At first, the metronome is called a neutral stimulus, as it has no meaning for the animal. This neutral stimulus then gets paired with the presentation of food. Food is an unconditioned stimulus, which means that it elicits an unlearned reflex. This reflex of interest that food elicits is salivation and is called the unconditioned response. After several pairings of the neutral stimulus (metronome) with the unconditioned stimulus (food), the metronome comes

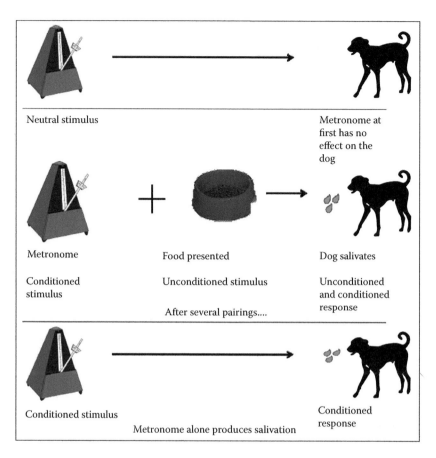

FIGURE 10.1 Outline of Pavlovian conditioning. The first row shows that, initially, a metronome has no effect on the dog. Next, the presentation of the ticking metronome is paired with the presentation of food. After several pairing trials, the metronome alone comes to elicit a response in the dog (the conditioned response), which in this case is salivation (bottom row).

to predict the food. The dog then begins to respond to the metronome by preparing for the food to come and starts to salivate. The metronome is then said to be a conditioned stimulus that elicits a conditioned response (which in this case is also salivation).

Although at first glance this may appear to have little relevance to odor detection, Pavlovian conditioning is very important in what professional trainers call the *imprinting* process (the term *imprinting* is used with a rather different meaning in the academic literature on animal behavior—see, e.g., Drickamer et al. 2008). During this initial training phase, trainers attempt to pair an odor with the delivery of food or a toy. Each trainer likely has his or her own unique method, but this stage generally involves the presentation of an odor followed rapidly by an unconditioned reinforcer such as a toy or food. In this case, the odor becomes a conditioned stimulus (equivalent to the metronome) and the food or toy is the unconditioned stimulus.

The conditioned response can vary but will likely depend in part on the unconditioned reinforcer. For food, the conditioned response may involve salivation, searching, scratching, barking, or possibly other food-soliciting behaviors, whereas for a toy, the conditioned response may involve some similar behaviors such as barking, scratching, searching, but may also include behaviors that would be directed toward a toy. The conditioned response will not be the desired alerting behaviors, such as a sit or down posture, which will be taught later, but will be behaviors directly related to the animal's anticipation of the food or toy unconditioned stimulus, which follows perception of the odor. Although this has not been directly demonstrated in dogs, evidence from a variety of species more commonly studied in experimental psychology laboratories indicates that animals engage in different conditioned responses depending on whether they are expecting food or some other kind of consequence such as water or warmth (Jenkins and Moore 1973; Wasserman 1973). Given the importance then of classical conditioning in the imprinting process, we next discuss several factors known to influence the strength of classical conditioning.

TIMING

One critical factor influencing classical conditioning is the timing of the relationship between the conditioned and unconditioned stimuli (in the case we are concerned with here, the relationship between odor and food or toy). Figure 10.2 sketches several different ways an odor and a consequence can be presented together. Laboratory studies over the past century have demonstrated that maximum conditioned responding is obtained with *delayed conditioning* (the top line in Figure 10.2). In delayed conditioning, the odor is presented and the food or toy is then presented while the odor is still present. A close second in terms of effectiveness is trace conditioning (second line in Figure 10.2), where the odor is presented, then removed for a period of time before being followed by the unconditioned stimulus (food or toy; for a review, see Gallistel and Gibbon 2000). It is just as well that trace conditioning produces less conditioned responding than delay conditioning because trace conditioning would be hard to implement with odor stimuli. It would take more elaborate technology than is usually available to rapidly and completely remove an odor once it has been released to where the animal can smell it.

One type of conditioning that produces even less conditioned responding than trace conditioning is simultaneous conditioning (e.g., Smith et al. 1969; bottom row of Figure 10.2). In this case, the odor and the unconditioned stimulus (toy or food) are presented simultaneously. Simultaneous conditioning produces less conditioned responding because the conditioned stimulus (odor) does not help the animal predict when the unconditioned stimulus will arrive.

Although not as effective, simultaneous conditioning is sometimes used when odors and unconditioned stimuli are paired by placing them physically together (placing odor and food in the same box, for example). To enhance the effect of this *co-hiding* procedure, the target odor should precede the unconditioned stimulus odor. This could be accomplished by having the target odor significantly more concentrated than the food odor. In this way, the odor of the target would reach the dog before the odor of the food.

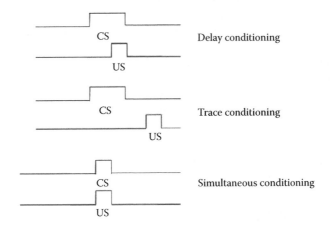

FIGURE 10.2 Timing arrangements of Pavlovian conditioning. Line diagram shows the temporal relationships of the conditioned stimulus (CS) and unconditioned stimulus (US) for the different types of Pavlovian conditioning. Time runs from left to right along each sketch. The square wave shows the onset, duration, and offset of the stimulus presentation.

TRIAL SPACING

Another important factor to consider in classical conditioning is trial spacing. Although it may seem logical to conduct as many imprinting trials (i.e., classical conditioning trials) during a training session as possible in order to maximize the use of available training time, numerous research studies indicate that increasing the time between pairing trials increases conditioned responding (e.g., Deisig et al. 2007; Menzel et al. 2001; Spence and Norris 1950). This is called the *trial spacing effect* (see Barela 1999 for a discussion of theoretical mechanisms underlying this effect). Thus, a trainers' time would likely be better served by conducting a few imprinting trials with several minutes break between each trial (perhaps interspersed with trials on other dogs) than conducting many trials back to back in one block of time.

A recent study with dogs has also suggested that spacing of training leads to enhanced learning (Meyer and Ladewig 2008). In this study, the researchers trained dogs either once per week or five times per week on a simple approach and paw touch task. Dogs that were trained once per week required significantly fewer training trials to reach a certain training level, suggesting that the spaced training led to stronger learning. It is important to note, however, that dogs trained five times per week were trained sooner overall, because they received five training sessions for every one training session the other dogs received (Meyer and Ladewig 2008).

Overall, the animal laboratory literature suggests that spacing trials several minutes apart is important for optimizing learning. The optimal training schedule for dogs that is appropriately spaced to enhance learning, yet sufficiently often to accomplish training goals efficiently, however, has yet to be studied in depth.

ODOR FAMILIARITY

The study of the role of the prior familiarity of an odor on imprinting success shows some conflicting findings. Some studies suggest that being more familiar with an odor may improve detection performance in rodents and humans (Dalton and Wysocki 1996; Escanilla et al. 2008; Mandairon et al. 2006; Yee and Wysocki 2001). Importantly, however, there is also a lot of research to indicate that exposure to stimuli before classical conditioning commences reduces the effectiveness with which they can become conditioned. This is such a well-established phenomenon that there is a name for it: *latent inhibition* (Lubow 1973).

Some of our own research has recently explored this topic (Hall et al. 2014). In our study, dogs were randomly assigned to one of four groups. Three of the groups were exposed to an odor for 5 days before detection training started, but the manner in which the exposure took place varied between groups (the final group was an unexposed control group). Group 1 was exposed to a target odor for 30 min per day for 5 days. Group 2 received six Pavlovian conditioning trials to the target odor per day. Group 3 received six Pavlovian conditioning trials per day to an odor irrelevant to later detection training. Group 4 received no odor exposure. All dogs were subsequently trained to detect the target odor. Dogs in Group 2, which had received the Pavlovian conditioning exposure to the target odor, learned the odor detection task significantly faster than all the other groups. Dogs in the exposure group (Group 1) learned the task no faster than dogs in the control group. This demonstrates that the simple passive exposure to the odor (as well as exposure to irrelevant odors) has no effect on odor-detection learning.

OPERANT CONDITIONING

Thus far, we have discussed classical conditioning. Classical conditioning is central to the phenomenon known in the odor-detection field as *imprinting*. It is likely pervasive throughout all of odor detection; however, it is not a procedure with which to get a desirable alerting behavior when a dog detects an odor. To achieve this aim, a different type of conditioning becomes very important: operant conditioning.

Operant conditioning differs from classical conditioning in how stimuli are arranged with respect to the subject's behavior (Skinner 1953). In classical conditioning, the critical features are the association between two stimuli, the conditioned stimulus and the unconditioned stimulus—odor and food or a toy. Although we expect to see a behavioral response, this type of conditioning does not require the subject to engage in any particular behavior. Instead, the subject comes to emit behaviors when the conditioned stimulus is present that are broadly speaking preparatory for the unconditioned stimulus. In operant conditioning, the subject's behavior is critical: without the appropriate behavioral response, the dog will not receive its reward. In operant conditioning, the food or toy can properly be called a reward for the behavior we wish to see. Operant conditioning is likely very familiar to the dog trainer who rewards or punishes a dog for alerting to a target or distractor odor.[1]

Operant conditioning is concerned with the relationship between a behavior and its consequence (Skinner 1953). In the operant context, stimuli that precede a behavior of interest and indicate whether a reinforcer is present or not are known as discriminative stimuli. They indicate whether food will be available. In the odor detection training field, the discriminative stimuli will be target odors, the behavior will be a trained alerting response (such as sit or down), and the consequence is the food or toy delivered by the trainer. There are several factors that can influence how odors can come to be discriminative stimuli or how reinforcers can reinforce an alerting response. In the section "Delivery of the Reinforcer," we will discuss how reinforcers are delivered and their effects on behavior. Subsequently, we will discuss how discriminative stimuli come to control behavior.

DELIVERY OF THE REINFORCER

The consequences of behavior that increase how likely it is that an animal will repeat that behavior are known by scientists as *reinforcers*—though *reward* means much the same thing. Several factors are important in modulating a reinforcer's effectiveness. Probably the most basic consideration is the animal's motivation for a particular reinforcer. This is often treated like a personality or dispositional factor and weighs heavily in the selection of dogs for training. Typical selection tests include an assessment of whether the candidate dog is strongly motivated by the kind of reward the trainer prefers to use—food or toys. Vicars et al. (2014) took selection of a food reinforcer even further by offering dogs a paired-stimulus preference assessment to identify each dog's most highly preferred food. They found that dogs' food preferences predicted the efficacy of that food as a reinforcer for a simple nose touch response. Several recent studies have begun comparing verbal praise, petting, and food as reinforcers for dogs. One pattern across studies is that food is generally a more effective reinforcer than petting or praise for most dogs (Feuerbacher and Wynne 2012, 2014; Fukuzawa and Hayashi 2013), and one recent study showed that petting is preferred to verbal praise (Feuerbacher and Wynne 2015). Unfortunately, no scientific work has directly evaluated the use of food or toys as rewards for odor-detection training and whether the choice of reinforcer can lead to better and more stable performance.

Since classical conditioning cannot be turned off even when we intend to work with operant conditioning, the factors noted above that influence behavior controlled by classical conditioning will also be relevant when working with operant conditioning. Thus, different rewards may produce different responses when an odor is detected. If dogs are trained with food, they may engage in food preparatory behaviors when the odor is found, whereas different behaviors may be emitted by a dog trained to detect the same odor by reward with toys. Despite the importance of odor-detection work with dogs, this idea, that different rewards will lead to different behavior patterns when a target is detected, has yet to be directly tested. Another potentially important difference between rewards is how quickly the dog will satiate to different reinforcers.

When food is used as a reward, motivation will gradually drop as the dog becomes satiated. How quickly dogs become satiated with toys, however, appears to differ greatly between dogs, and it is not clear how motivation changes for toys over repeated trials. The dog's motivation for the reward in use is always a critical consideration (Dean 1972). In one of our recent studies, we explored how odor-detection performance can be disrupted in dogs. In one condition, dogs that were trained using food were fed immediately before a testing situation. We noted significant variability in how disruptive pre-session feeding was for different dogs (Hall et al. 2015). Some dogs' performance was little affected by the prior feeding, but other dogs were completely disrupted and would rarely alert to the odor.

EXTINCTION

Another important concept that can severely disrupt performance is extinction. Extinction is a process in which the relationship between the dog's behavior and the delivery of the reward is disrupted producing a decrease in the previously reinforced behavior (Mazur 2006). Extinction is also a procedure in which the reinforcer for a previously reinforced behavior is withheld when the behavior is produced to reduce the occurrence of a target behavior. In odor-detection work, extinction can refer to the general training of a dog not to respond to specific nontarget stimulus. We will here restrict the use of the term *extinction* to situations in which a previously reinforced behavior no longer produces the reinforcer (i.e., the reinforcer is withheld). To maintain a response to an odor, alerts to an odor need to be continually reinforced. For example, if dogs are trained to alert to an illegal substance that after legislative action is no longer illegal, then to prevent the dogs from alerting to this now legal odor (e.g., marijuana in some states), extinction training could be conducted in which alerts to the odor are no longer reinforced. Figure 10.3 shows a learning curve and an extinction curve. (For more on extinction training, see Chapter 13.) Looking at Figure 10.3, it can be seen that if dogs are trained to the illegal odor and make more and more responses to it as training continues, then when extinction is initiated, the dog's alerts to the odor are no longer reinforced. With time, the dog becomes less likely to alert until alerting reaches near-zero levels. Importantly, extinction procedures can produce a lot of interesting side effects that we will now briefly describe.[2]

One interesting phenomenon that takes place when rewards are discontinued is known as the *extinction burst*. When extinction is first implemented, responding may actually increase initially before it decreases. In our example of extinction-training a dog so that it no longer alerts to an odor that has been legalized, it would not be unlikely for the dog to respond initially with increased intensity and strength of its alerting to the once illegal odor once it is no longer receiving a reward.

Extinction also has a tendency to induce behavioral variability (e.g., Antonitis 1951). The dog being trained to extinguish to a previously illegal odor might engage in new alerting behaviors or

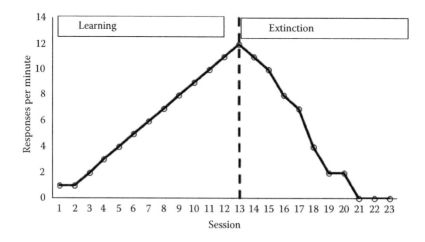

FIGURE 10.3 Acquisition and extinction. During the initial learning phase, the rate of response increases, but when extinction is implemented, the response rate decreases to zero.

attempt to alert to distractor odors. Frustration behaviors are also common during extinction. Dogs may start to bark or whine when the reinforcer is not delivered.

Another interesting and important component of extinction is spontaneous recovery. After a response is extinguished, responding will recover and occur spontaneously at later times, although it will again quickly extinguish. Returning to our example of the dog being extinguished for alerting to a now legal odor, the animal may spontaneously alert to the odor after a pause in extinction training, even though it had shown no response at all for an extended period. Thus, to effectively extinguish alerting behavior, it is important to continue conducting extinction training even after the dog seems to have ceased alerting to the odor. Keeping up extinction training will reduce spontaneous recovery until the behavior has completely extinguished, and should be followed by periodic retesting.

SCHEDULES OF REINFORCEMENT

So far, we have discussed rewarding every correct alert (continuous reinforcement) or none (extinction). This only covers the extremes of a continuum of possibilities. Correct alerts could be reinforced some—but not all—of the times they are presented. The way reinforcers are delivered for the occurrence of a behavior is called the schedule of reinforcement. There are several different types of schedules of reinforcement that have been studied in the animal laboratory; however, we will only discuss two that are most commonly used for detection dogs.

The first schedule we shall consider is the fixed ratio. This is simply a technical name for rewarding the dog after a certain number of correct responses are made (for more detailed discussions, see Catania 2007; Pierce and Cheney 2013). The simplest case is a fixed ratio (FR) 1—in which case every single correct response is rewarded. This is also known as *continuous reinforcement*. An FR 3 schedule indicates that the dog needs to make three correct alerts before a reinforcer is delivered. Schedules of reinforcement with larger FR values typically generate high rates of responding that follow a *break-and-run* pattern (Ferster and Skinner 1957). This means that animals tend to rest a while after a reward has been delivered (the *break*), and then respond in quick succession until they have produced enough responses to have earned the next reward (the *run*). For a detection dog, this pattern might show itself when a dog, after getting a reinforcer, is hesitant to start searching again until some time has passed, at which point it returns to a high level of search.

To generate more stable high rates of behavior, a variable ratio (VR) schedule of reinforcement might be more desirable. In this schedule, the number of correct alerts that are required to receive a reinforcer constantly changes. A VR 3 schedule would indicate that, on average, three correct alerts are required to receive a reinforcer. However, the precise number of alerts needed would vary all the time (while maintaining the stated average). Thus, the dog might sometimes be reinforced after one correct alert, sometimes after two, and sometimes after four or five alerts. The goal is to make the response requirement unpredictable from reinforcer delivery to reinforcer delivery, but ensure that it averages out to a predetermined value.

The key benefit of using a VR schedule is that it produces high rates of consistent behavior, but it has other benefits as well (Ferster and Skinner 1957). Typically, training may begin with a CR schedule, but as training progresses, the schedule can be gradually *thinned* (transitioned) to a VR schedule. The VR schedule allows the handler in the field to not reinforce alerts that occur under ambiguous situations when he or she is unsure whether an alert is a correct detection or a false indication. If the dog is trained with a continuous schedule of reinforcement, withholding a reward to an alert in the field would indicate to the dog that extinction is in effect. If, however, the dog was trained on a VR schedule prior to being declared deployment-ready, the dog would be accustomed to unrewarded alerts and would keep working. During deployment, the VR schedule allows the handler to maintain high performance without needing to indicate to the dog whether every alert was correct or false (see Chapter 13 for further discussion of VR training programs).

WHEN TO REWARD?

In discussing when to provide a reinforcer, we already discussed reinforcing every correct response (continuous schedule), what happens when the behavior is no longer reinforced (extinction), and two different ways reinforcers can be delivered intermittently (FR and VR). We advocated the benefits of the VR schedule over the FR and the continuous schedule of reinforcement. We have not yet discussed, given that a VR schedule is in use, how often reinforcers should be provided on average.

Some research has attempted to address this question. The answer appears to be *as often as possible*. The richer the schedule of reinforcement (the more often reinforcers are delivered) becomes, the better performance tends to be. Sargisson and McClean (2010) directly explored this question by manipulating the reinforcement rate for dogs detecting land mines using Remote Explosive Scent Tracing (REST). In this procedure, the odor of land mines is captured by using a vacuum pump to pull the air over land mines across a filter that captures the odorant molecules. The filter pads are then presented to the dogs indoors where they can assess whether an explosive odor is present or absent. Sargisson and Mclean (2010) evaluated the accuracy of their dogs as a function of the reinforcement rate. As the reinforcement rate increased for correct alerts, performance increased. Low rates of reinforcement yielded the poorest performances.

Some of our recent work confirms these results (Hall et al. 2015). In our study, dogs were trained on two different odor detections. For one odor, the dogs received additional odor exposures that were paired with a reward (classical conditioning). In a subsequent phase of testing, we attempted to disrupt the dogs' performance by placing distracting food odors around the odor stimuli and placing the dogs on extinction. The dogs maintained higher accuracies when exposed to the disruptors for the odor they had been trained to with the additional odor–reward pairings.

The finding that higher rates of reinforcement lead to greater detection rates supports a much broader theory in behavioral science, called behavioral momentum theory (Nevin and Grace 2000; Nevin and Shahan 2011). Behavior momentum is a concept that is inspired by classic momentum theory in physics (for a review, see Nevin and Grace 2000). The parallel here is that the strength of a behavior, or how resistant it is to being disrupted by other forces such as distractors or extinction, is directly related to the amount a behavior has been reinforced. The more rewards that have been delivered for detecting an odor, the stronger that behavior will be, and the more resistant it will be to other environmental distractors.

Together, these results and theory suggest that using as high a rate of reinforcement as practical for the objective will yield the strongest and least disruptable performances. This appears to contradict our prior suggestion, noted above, that intermittent schedules of reinforcement would be more desirable than continuous reinforcement. Reasons for this suggestion included that if a dog has only experienced reinforcement for every alert during training, but an operational situation arises in which it is undesirable or impossible to reinforce an alert, then the withholding of the reinforcer might signal to the dog that the situation has changed and the dog's responding may be negatively impacted. A dog accustomed to intermittent reinforcement during training would not find the lack of a reinforcer unusual and would therefore be less likely to suffer any influence on its behavior.

A situation such as this one, where laboratory studies lead to two somewhat contradictory recommendations for practitioners, underlines the urgent need for research that directly addresses the factors that might lead to the most stable performance across training and operational settings. At the present time, the best advice is to adopt a rich but intermittent schedule of reinforcement.

IMPORTANCE OF CONTEXT

Thus far, we have discussed the potential benefits of using VR schedules. We then discussed the research and behavioral momentum theory that suggests that trainers should provide rewards as often as possible on that VR schedule to maintain the strongest responding possible. Here, we discuss balances that the trainer needs to be aware of when deciding where to conduct training and when and where to reinforce dogs.

One important factor is the context in which training and real-world detection scenarios occur. Dogs can be very sensitive to the context in which training occurs. For example, Gazit et al. (2005b) explored context effects on explosive dogs' search behavior. At first, dogs were walked down two different paths: path A and path B. On path A, there were always explosives to find. On path B, however, explosives were never to be found. Very quickly, dogs learned that the different contexts were associated with different probabilities of a find and engaged in high rates of search activity on path A, but learned to not search the normally empty path B, even when explosives were present in subsequent experiments. This demonstration that context matters is widely confirmed in the animal laboratory (for a review, see Bouton 2004). An additional relevant contextual phenomenon that has been demonstrated in the laboratory but not yet in detection dogs is the finding that animals that experience extinction in one context show renewal of the extinguished behavior when moved to a new context.

These findings have several implications that the detection dog trainer should consider. For example, if dogs are always trained in one area where they receive rewards for finds but real-world detection always occurs in a novel area where finds are not rewarded, the dogs will likely show reduced search in the novel (real search) contexts. These decrements are particularly difficult to discover because a dog's performance will prove strong under test conditions in the typical training environment, but will only decrease when the dog is moved into a novel context where it is unknown whether there are any targets to be detected. The trainer should be cautious of the possibility that the dog learns that novel contexts indicate that rewards are unlikely to be delivered. Consequently, it is important to conduct training in a variety of contexts so that the dog cannot determine whether it is being trained (high probability of a find) or is in a real search (low probability of a find) scenario.

Analogous situations to those Gazit et al. (2005b) demonstrated could occur in explosives or land-mine detection in which one specific field is used for training, and a different field is the real search arena where alerts are not reinforced. Research on land-mine detection with the African giant pouched rat has shown a similar finding. The rats are trained to detect land mines in training areas where they are reinforced for correct detections. When searching in the field, where the presence of the land mine is unknown, the rats are run under extinction conditions (Mahoney et al. 2013). In their study, Mahoney et al. explored the detection rate of the rats when they are reinforced for every detection and when they are under extinction. They found that the rats adapted rapidly to the extinction conditions and detection performance become highly variable and unreliable. It then took several days of training with reinforcement to return the rodents to high and stable rates of performance.

Overall, this section has highlighted the importance of the questions of when and how reinforcers are delivered. We have highlighted the use of intermittent schedules of reinforcement and in particular the VR schedule. We have also mentioned the importance of maintaining rich schedules of reinforcement to help resist decrements in performance that might occur when extinction is in effect. Last, we discussed the importance of the context in which the animals are trained and how training in one context and expecting real-world detections in a different context might lead to performance decrements. In the section "Stimulus Control," we will move our focus more toward the stimulus, specifically the odor.

STIMULUS CONTROL

Stimulus control concerns how a stimulus can come to elicit or occasion behaviors of interest. In this section, we will explore how odors can come to control behavior and how changes in the stimulus (odor) alter behavior.

CUEING THE ALERT

We cannot discuss how odors come to control search dog behavior without first considering the possibility that dogs might not be responding to odors at all. Dogs are remarkably observant of human movements and are particularly sensitive to our communicative gestures (Miklosi et al. 1998; Udell et al. 2008b). Although dogs' remarkable attentiveness to people can often be a great advantage in a pet and a subject for training, it can, at other times, make us think that dogs are finding an odor when they are really just paying attention to the handler's movements. The scientific literature has demonstrated repeatedly that dogs, and even their closest relatives, wolves, are particularly skillful at following human communicative gestures (Miklosi et al. 1998; Udell et al. 2008a,b; Viranyi et al. 2008). Both dogs and wolves are even skillful in following humans' attentive state to indicate whether a reward is available (Udell et al. 2011). In addition, dogs have been shown to ignore olfactory information and will choose to look for hidden food where a human has gestured (Szetei et al. 2003).

Since the now famous case of Clever Hans (Pfungst 1911), in which a horse that was once thought capable of solving basic arithmetic was shown to be responding to the unintentional cues provided by the person asking it questions, the importance of critically assessing whether an animal is following the cues we believe it to be following must ever be paramount. The possibility that a dog handler might influence a dog's performance through subtle and unintentional cues is more than just conjecture. Lit et al. (2011) directly tested this possibility. Trained detection dog teams were sent out on a search. The handlers were told that the target odor had been hidden for the dog to find; however, no target odors were ever planted. Thus, any alerts were false alerts. In some conditions, the experimenter placed out markers that handlers believed indicated the location of a target odor. Handlers were more likely to indicate that their dog alerted if a marker indicated to the handler that a target odor was present. These results highlight the possibility that a dog might be responding to subtle unintentional cues from a handler. Thus, it is important to conduct testing in which the handler is blind to whether, and where, an odor is present to ensure that the dogs are alerting to the target odor and not cues given by the handler.

GENERALIZATION AND DISCRIMINATION

When a dog is trained to respond to a stimulus, in particular an odor, two important processes are in effect: generalization and discrimination. Generalization is the tendency of individuals to respond not just to the precise stimulus on which they were trained but also to stimuli similar to the trained stimulus (see Mazur 2006; Pierce and Cheney 2013). For example, if a dog is trained to alert to one quantity of an odor, the dog may also respond without additional training to similar untrained quantities of the odor. Furthermore, dogs that are trained on several varieties of smokeless powder may also respond to untrained varieties of smokeless powder with similar vapor profiles (Johnston and Williams 1999).

Discrimination is the reverse of generalization. Discrimination refers to an individual's ability to respond differently to stimuli that differ from the trained stimulus. Both generalization and discrimination are critical to the success of detection dogs, as these are the processes that govern whether a dog will respond or not respond to stimuli related to a target odor. In this section, we will cover important findings on generalization by framing them in the context of dogs working on an odor detection.

A generalization gradient shows how generalization follows a predictable pattern along a physical dimension of a stimulus. An animal's response is greatest to stimuli that are most physically similar to the stimulus to which they were trained (for a review, see Ghirlanda and Enquist 2003). This is easily demonstrated with visual and auditory stimuli. For example, an experimenter can train a pigeon to respond to a key light at a wavelength of 550 nm (a greenish-yellow color). Then, the experimenter can manipulate the wavelength of light and assess the wavelengths to which the pigeon will respond. As wavelengths that are further and further away from 550 nm are presented, responding decreases, typically following a Gaussian curve. This finding is readily generalizable to auditory stimuli (see Ghirlanda and Enquist 2003); however, few studies have investigated general-ization gradients with odor stimuli (see Cleland et al. 2009; Wright et al. 2008), and none have yet explored this with dogs.

Studying generalization gradients with olfactory stimuli is more complex because there is no easily accessible odor dimension akin to wavelength with light stimuli or frequency with auditory stimuli. There are a couple of dimensions, however, with which generalization gradients of olfactory stimuli have been studied. The first is using a series of chemically related odors (a homologous series of ali-phatic odorants) in which odors typically differ in the length of an unbranched carbon chain (Cleland et al. 2009). This stimulus dimension, however, may not be particularly relevant to detection dogs.

A more relevant stimulus dimension is the proportional composition of its components in odor mixtures. Wright et al. (2008) did just this with bees. They trained bees to respond to mixtures of 1-hexanol and 2-octanone that were either 10% or 90% hexanol. The bees generalized to odor mixture ratios of hexanol and octanone closest to the trained mixture but systematically decreased responding to odor mixtures less similar to the trained odor mixture. This could be similar to dogs' search tasks, as target odors are typically odor mixtures of various chemicals that may vary in their composition depending on their source (e.g., varieties of smokeless powders). Unfortunately, this kind of generalization of odor mixtures has not to date been thoroughly examined in dogs.

Another interesting dimension along which to consider generalization gradients is stimulus intensity/concentration. Generalization along stimulus intensity gradients, however, is typically biased and fails to show the more symmetrical Gaussian curve found in other dimensions. Typically, respond-ing is flat for a range of intensities around the trained stimulus or even higher for more intense stimuli, and then decreases for less intense stimuli (see Ghirlanda and Enquist 2003 for details). This has also been found for odor concentrations with bees (Bhagavan and Smith 1997). Bees that were trained to respond to a strong concentration of an odorant failed to generalize to the odor as the concentration decreased. Interestingly, however, bees that were trained at a low concentration did respond to the odor at a higher concentration. We are unaware, however, of published generalization research with respect to odor concentration in dogs, although it is important to consider that after training at one odor concentration, subjects may not spontaneously generalize to other, especially lower, odor concentrations.

Luckily, generalization gradients are not fixed: they are malleable to experience in predictable ways. Generalization gradients can be made broader or flatter by training subjects to respond to additional stimuli along the gradient (Ghirlanda and Enquist 2003). Wright et al. (2008) trained some of their bees to respond to two different mixtures of 1-hexanol and 2-octanone. Bees that were conditioned to respond to two mixtures showed significantly greater generalization than bees trained to just one mixture. In Figure 10.4, we show the expected generalization gradient in red had we trained a dog to a simple 50:50 odor mixture of hypothetical odorants. The blue line shows the expected effect when the dog is then trained to additional odor mixtures. It can be seen that this leads to a significantly broader generalization gradient. An opposite effect might be seen with over-training to one stimulus. Cleland et al. (2009) found evidence that increasing the number of training trials, increasing the odor intensity, and increasing the value of the reward all tended to narrow the generalization gradient, which caused greater responding to the target odor but proportionally less to chemically related odors. Thus, it might be important to consider that with repeated training, a trainer could be narrowing the range of odors a dog will respond to as shown in our hypothetical example in green in Figure 10.4. Again, direct research on this topic with dogs is lacking.

Another factor that can influence the generalization gradient is the training of nontarget odors along the stimulus gradient. Training *off* a nontarget odor (i.e., responses to nontarget odors are under extinction) causes a shift in responding away from the nontarget odor and moves the highest rates of responding to a novel stimulus: this is known as a *peak shift* (see Pierce and Cheney 2013 for further information). If multiple nontarget stimuli along the stimulus gradient are trained, then the generalization gradient will be narrowed (Ghirlanda and Enquist 2003). Wright et al. (2008) showed this in their study on generalization of bees to different mixtures of 1-hexanol and 2-octanone. They

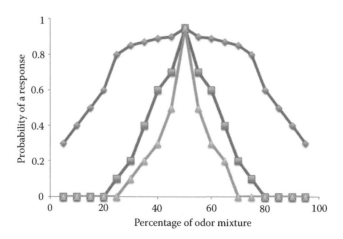

FIGURE 10.4 Generalization gradients. Red line shows a theoretical generalization gradient for a dog trained to a binary odor mixture (AB) that is 50% odor A and 50% odor B. Blue line shows theoretical generalization following training to multiple mixtures of different proportions. Green line shows theoretical generalization following overtraining to the 50:50 odor mixture or extinction training with multiple odor mixtures.

punished an additional group of bees for responding to a certain mixture and reinforced them for responding to a different mixture. This led to changes in the generalization gradient such that bees showed much less responding to nontarget odors and a narrowing of the generalization gradient. Although such work has yet to be replicated and extended with dogs, this research suggests that it is important to consider dimensions along which a target odor may vary. Might the dog encounter chemically related odors? Will the dog encounter the target odor in different concentrations? Will the dog encounter a target odor mixture in which the components might differ in proportional composition? If so, then training considerations could be made to broaden the generalization gradient or narrow it as desired.

SIMPLE ODOR MIXTURES

In this section, we will cover important topics relevant to training dogs to detect odor mixtures using simple (binary) mixtures as examples. In the next section, "Complex Stimulus Control," we will discuss further considerations for more complex odor mixtures.

BLOCKING

Blocking is a learning phenomenon found in a variety of species and across many sensory domains. First demonstrated by Kamin in 1969, it has since been extended to odorants in honeybees (Hosler and Smith 2000) and mice (Wiltrout et al. 2003). The basic phenomenon is demonstrated with two groups. The blocking or experimental group experiences an odor, odor A, paired with a food reward for several trials. They then receive further trials with an odor mixture containing the now familiar element A together with a new element we can call B. The AB mixture is paired with food reward. Finally, the subjects are tested for a response to odor B. In the control group, subjects just receive the AB odor mixture paired with food, without the prior pairings to A alone, and are subsequently tested for their response to odor B. Subjects in the blocking group show little to no response to odor B, whereas subjects in the control group readily respond to B. These results imply that the prior conditioning with A blocks the learning of additional redundant stimuli (element B). It is important to highlight, however, that demonstrations of blocking in olfaction are not always successful (e.g., in bees, see Gerber and Ullrich 1999; Guerrieri et al. 2005). Given the robustness, however, of blocking in the non-olfactory domain, it is worth considering potential situations in which blocking might arise in dog detection training.

A blocking situation could arise when dogs are trained to single odor during initial training and then later trained to a mixture containing that odorant. Consider a dog trained to pure trinitrotoluene (TNT). The dog is then transferred to commercial TNT, which is a mixture of mostly trinitrotoluene and dinitrotoluene (Lorenzo et al. 2003). From a blocking perspective, dogs would not attend to dinitrotoluene as they are blocked by the initial TNT training. Unfortunately, research along these lines has yet to be conducted in dogs to confirm whether a blocking effect would be observed in such a scenario.

OVERSHADOWING

Overshadowing is another compound stimulus effect that may be even more important than blocking when training odor mixtures. An overshadowing effect occurs when one stimulus is significantly more salient than the other stimuli in a mixture (see Pierce and Cheney 2013 for detailed information). In this situation, only the most salient stimuli become conditioned and the less salient stimuli gain little to no conditioning strength. In the animal laboratory, this might occur if a bright light and a quiet tone are presented at the same time and together predict when food is available. After the subjects become conditioned to this compound stimulus, one can test whether the light alone or tone alone will cause a response in the subject. With one stimulus significantly more attention-grabbing than the other, the subjects will only become conditioned to the salient stimulus and will ignore the less salient stimulus (the quiet tone). This phenomenon has been extended to olfactory stimuli (e.g., Kay et al. 2005).

Overshadowing is important to consider with odor mixtures in which the relevant stimuli may not be very salient. For example, in many explosives, the explosive component itself may have a very low vapor pressure, which means that it will only compose a small fraction of the odor headspace compared to contaminants that are significantly more volatile than the explosive itself. Thus, contaminants may come to easily overshadow the stimulus of interest (drug, explosive, etc.).

COMPLEX STIMULUS CONTROL

In this section, we explore in greater depth factors relevant to the olfactory system and more complex stimulus discriminations that are more akin to what the dog is expected to do in real-world situations. Very rarely are dogs asked to detect a pure odor or a binary mixture. Instead, the real world is a complex environment full of odor mixtures of many different compounds, and navigating through this world is all the more complex.

OLFACTION AS A SYNTHETIC SENSE

Ongoing basic research struggles with questions of how odor mixtures are perceived. In particular, when will odors be perceived configurally and when elementally? In configural odor perception, mixtures of odors yield a unique (synthesized) perception, such that odor A with odor B yields a new unique perception—odor C. Under an elemental or analytic processing scheme, odor A with odor B yields a mixture that is perceived as being composed of the components odor A and B. Although this is an active area of research, unfortunately, very little of this has been done with dogs. One study, however, showed that dogs trained to pure potassium chlorate (odor A) were unsuccessful in detecting a mixture of this odor with another odor—odor B (an undisclosed additive)—suggesting configural odor perception (Lazarowski and Dorman 2014). However, after dogs are trained to one potassium chlorate mixture, they can readily generalize to other potassium chlorate mixtures—in line with theories of elemental or analytical perception. This suggests that mixtures of potassium chlorate are not immediately recognized as containing potassium chlorate, but explicit training on mixtures can lead to elemental processing.

Waggoner et al. (1998) showed that dogs are adept at discriminating a target odor from background extraneous odors. In addition, dogs that are trained to detect explosive odors that are complex mixtures, the dog may only learn to respond to specific components of the target odor (see Oxley and Waggoner 2009). Unfortunately, very little work has been published in the scientific literature on the configural and elemental processing of odors in dogs, making broader generalizations about dog olfactory processing difficult.

Research from animal laboratories with other species, however, suggests that whether mixtures are perceived as configural or elemental will depend on the properties of and relationships among the odors themselves. From research on humans, we know that, generally, as the number of elements in a mixture increases, the probability that it will be processed configurally instead of elementally increases (for detailed information, see Wilson and Stevenson 2006). In addition, as the number of components of an odor mixture increases, humans become particularly poor at identifying the components of the mixture (Livermore and Laing 1996). Humans can readily identify the components of odor mixtures containing two components, but once the mixture contains four or especially five components, people fail to identify them, even if they are expert perfumers or flavorists (Livermore and Laing 1996). Whether or not dogs suffer a similar limitation on their perception of odor mixtures is a critical area for further research in the domain of explosive detection.

Recent research in mice with a different experimental paradigm gives some grounds for optimism that dogs may be able to at least identify a target odor in very complex background odors. Rokni et al. (2014) showed that mice could identify target odorants in a background mixture of up to 14 different nontarget odors. To achieve this, Rokni et al. trained the mice to a very large and highly variable set of stimuli. They were trained to detect a target odor from a mixture that varied from trial to trial and session to session. By constantly changing the background, mice were capable of being able to analytically assess whether the target odor was a component of the complex mixture.

CONDITIONAL DISCRIMINATION: THE DUAL FUNCTION DOG

Another area of interest for the detection dog is the idea of using a conditional discrimination to have the dog search for different odors on command. In a conditional discrimination, a cue indicates which discrimination task is in effect. For the search and rescue dog, an example could be a cue to the dog that indicates to search for living individuals, but a different cue would indicate to search for cadavers. Traditionally in animal laboratories, conditional discriminations are difficult to acquire and maintain at high rates of accuracy. The difficulty of the task shows in the research that has been conducted with such cross-trained dogs. Lit and Crawford (2006) showed that dogs trained to detect only live scent outperformed dogs that cross-trained with live and cadaver scent, especially when cadaver scent was present. These results are in part expected given the memory load that is required for this more complex training task. Thus, it may not be beneficial to attempt to have dogs respond to one command that indicates which scent to search for unless lower accuracy rates are acceptable.

MEMORY

Considering the memory burden of cross-training dogs leads to our final topic in this chapter: memory. Again, disappointingly, little work has been conducted exploring canine memory, though knowledge is growing. In particular, we are finding evidence of remarkable abilities. For example, Chaser, a border collie, has learned the names of over 2,000 toys (Pilley and Reid 2011). This displays a remarkable memory and learning capacity in this dog. Interestingly, however, dogs' capacity to remember odors has yet to be fully explored. Williams and Johnston (2002) provided some of the first work assessing the canine capacity to search for multiple odors. They trained a set of dogs to identify 10 different odors and showed that the dogs were readily able to accommodate 10 odors and alert to all 10 of them in a search task. Williams and Johnston, however, did not continue past 10 odors leaving the number of odors that a dog could learn to search for an open question. Given

Chaser's ability to search for a named toy from a set of 2,000, it seems likely that dogs will be found that can remember more than 10 odors. Rodents were highly successful in an odor recognition task (the odor span task) even when up to 70 odors were used (April et al. 2013). Together, these results suggest that the dog's capacity for recognizing odors is likely significantly greater than 10; however, no research has yet confirmed this.

Another component to memory that is largely unexplored is how long dogs will remember a trained odor. Lubow et al. (1973) did some initial exploration of this question. Using three dogs trained on several odor discriminations, the authors showed that the dogs retained relatively high levels of performance even after 69 days. Sixty-nine days was the longest delay tested, and thus it is quite possible that a dog could retain olfactory discriminations for longer periods of time. Similarly, reports suggest that dogs show little deterioration in performance across 4 months in identifying target odors from nontarget odors in a circle, which was the longest duration tested (Johnston 1999; Oxley and Waggoner 2009).

Relating odor memory to real-world detection scenarios, however, one must be careful as several potential processes could occur. One is extinction. If dogs are taken out for several searches and alerts are not reinforced, the behavior is undergoing extinction, which is quite different from forgetting. If dogs are sent out on several searches and no odor is ever found, the active search behavior will extinguish as discussed above. However, as soon as reinforcement is reintroduced into the situation, the performance may immediately rebound because the odor has not been forgotten; only the behavior that the dog uses to communicate with its handler ceased. Furthermore, across time, changes may take place in contexts, and testing environments as well as true forgetting, that may all influence the decay of a dog's performance with time. At this time, however, it is unclear the maximum length of time a dog can maintain an odor discrimination without intervening training to maintain its performance.

CONCLUSION AND FUTURE DIRECTIONS

In this chapter, we reviewed basic learning principles and how they apply to odor detection with dogs. We started off with an overview of classical and operant conditioning, and moved into the complex area of stimulus control. There we considered generalization gradients. Then we introduced behavioral phenomena related to compound stimuli such as blocking and overshadowing. Next we extended stimulus control to more complicated and varied odor mixtures, and ended with a discussion on canine memory. Throughout this chapter, we hope it has become clear how learning theory can aid the training and assessment practices for canine odor detection. We also hope that we have indicated the importance of learning and experiences on olfactory perception.

Throughout the chapter, it has become clear that, although the behavioral principles we have discussed are well established in typical laboratory species like pigeons, rats, and mice, there is a lack of scientific research on these topics with dogs. In some situations, we can easily extrapolate the behavioral principles demonstrated in rodents to dogs, but in other cases, as with memory, it becomes more difficult. In particular, there is a lack of scientific research on canine olfactory perception with simple and complex odor mixtures. Understanding how dogs can process odorants configurally or elementally could have important implications for understanding how best to train dogs to detect complex odors. We hope that this chapter is useful in the application of learning theory to detection dog training, but also encourages research and exploration into the several areas for which there is little information with dogs.

ENDNOTES

1. Several authors have published descriptions of operant training methods for odor detection dogs (and pouched rats), which are great resources (see Dean 1972; Jezierski et al. 2010; Poling et al. 2011b).
2. Additional texts on this topic include Mazur (2006) and Pierce and Cheney (2013).

11 Training Considerations in Wildlife Detection

Aimee Hurt, Deborah A. (Smith) Woollett, and Megan Parker

Conservation detection dogs are detection dogs trained to find targets valuable to the preservation of native species. While these targets may include poachers' tools such as snares and weapons, which can result in the illegal death of animals, or even invasive plants, which threaten to overtake an ecosystem, this chapter contends specifically with wildlife targets.

Conservation detection dogs are a unique niche among other detection dog disciplines (see Hurt and Smith 2009), and many of the training issues are shared. All detection disciplines require that the dog locate the trained target and clearly indicate the find to its handler, and that the handler recognize behaviors and respond accordingly. While touching on the commonalities among detection dog disciplines, this chapter aims to elucidate for readers the considerations at the core of conservation detection.[1]

There is a great deal of training that must happen before a team is deployed, and like humans, dogs are tractable beings and will always require training to remain proficient. Furthermore, training is intertwined with field deployment, and the objectives and parameters of fieldwork ought to inform the training plan from the outset.

DOG SELECTION

A desire to work and the ability to ignore distractions is a primary filter for detection dogs across disciplines (Maejima et al. 2007). Like their other working colleagues, conservation detection dogs exhibit high play drive, intense focus, and the ability and desire to work closely with a handler. Because conservation detection dogs tend to search in the environment in which imperiled wildlife persists, they have additional qualities that suit them to this endeavor (see Mackay et al. 2008; Hurt and Smith 2009; Woollett et al. 2014). For example, in areas where small mammals are plentiful, or where vistas may be wide with many ungulates or other animals, it may be necessary to work a dog with very low prey drive.

The varied environments where dogs are likely to work should also inform the choice of dogs, including size, coat type, and temperament. In many areas, a double- or thicker-coated dog may be less heat tolerant but may be more resistant to ectoparasites and biting insects. Larger dogs may have an easier time moving through downed timber or over boulders but may have a harder time moving through a low, thick bush or across some types of substrate. In some areas, larger dogs may appear as less achievable prey to predators such as pumas (*Puma concolor*).

Dogs may have additional considerations determined by their intended purpose. Searching for the temporarily buoyant scat of North Atlantic right whales (*Eubalaena glacialis*), Rolland et al. (2006) describe, "Given the demands of working on a boat, dogs that had good physical stability, persistence in locating samples and a calm disposition were selected."

HANDLER SELECTION

Handlers must possess the requisite tendencies and skill set to interpret dog behavior, be timely and appropriate in their responses, and be able to influence the dog (see Geneva International Centre for Humanitarian Demining 2003; Hurt and Smith 2009).

Handlers for conservation fieldwork need strong observation skills and optimally have a biological background so that they appreciate the value of samples, can recognize differences between species' signs, and have the training to communicate well with project personnel. Handlers should be well versed in orienteering and moving through backcountry areas with confidence and have the ability to return to a truck or camp without anxiety. Along with the ability to work in remote areas, handle a dog, and respond to changing conditions, handlers need to be physically fit and able to move their dog across downed trees, across creeks, and through all types of habitats safely.

Finally, as both dog and handler personalities and styles vary, it is important that the handler and dog are well matched to form a team. Smith et al. (2003) stressed "that the experience of the trainer and handler will play a crucial role in the success of each dog (Gutzwiller 1990). Inadequate training and handling, as well as personality conflicts between dogs matched to particular handlers, can cause a severe reduction in detection efficiency."

PASSIVE FINAL RESPONSE

Conservation detection dogs are used primarily for increasing the number of samples for hard-to-find, cryptic, small, rare, nocturnal, wide-ranging, and elusive species. When a sample is detected and recorded or collected, it is usually imperative that the sample maintain its integrity for biological study. If it is a scat sample, a live animal, a plant, or confiscated wildlife contraband, the sample may be needed for genetic, hormonal, or other additional study. Therefore, dogs ought to be trained with a *passive* final response (also called *alert* or *indication*). Passive indications include a sit, down, or stand at the target, as opposed to *active* indications, which involve scratching, barking, or pawing. Moreover, dogs should be trained to indicate on samples from a distance relevant to that particular type of sample. Live animals may be illegal or dangerous to touch, so pointing too closely with a dog's nose may be untenable. An indication trained a safe distance from the sample may be required for many reasons, and an active alert could endanger the sample, the dog, and ultimately, the study itself (see Figure 11.1). For example, live venomous animals such as Gila monsters (*Heloderma suspectum*) and venomous snakes could bite and injure the dog. Diseases such as chytridiomycosis and *Ranavirus* can be fatal to reptiles and amphibians; passive and distant indications would keep the dog from contacting the target directly, thus minimizing the risk of pathogen transfer between individuals.

On the island of Guam, dogs were used to detect invasive brown tree snakes (*Boiga irregularis*). The dogs were trained with an active alert because the study species, brown tree snakes, are an unwanted invasive species on the island and are nocturnal and arboreal (Savidge et al. 2011). A bark indication was trained, but as many frustration indications can accelerate into other frustration behaviors, the dogs sometimes pawed or bit at the snake, and even though the snakes were destined for euthanasia, the appearance of a dog pawing at a snake was unpalatable to program managers, and the dogs were retrained to a passive alert. Even the perception of a dog being aggressive or overly assertive with another species may be reason enough to train a passive alert.

TRAINING SAMPLES

To ensure success of a dog/handler team in the field, the acquisition and use of appropriate training samples is second only to the judicious selection of dogs possessing the requisite traits for detection work. However, the paradox of the conservation targets sought, often rare and elusive species, is that they themselves can be hard to find. Additionally, conservation dog trainers do not yet have the recourse of using artificial scent sources, unlike in other detection disciplines (e.g., pseudo scents in

FIGURE 11.1 When searching for live, endangered species, such as this geometric tortoise, it is imperative that the dog have low prey drive, that the trained alert be passive, and that the dog essentially ignore the
target once located while the handler or other team member records the data. (Courtesy of Working Dogs for
Conservation.)

cadavers, narcotics, etc.). As Woollett et al. (2014) discussed, any wildlife professional or manager
considering deploying conservation dogs must carefully reflect upon and identify the most appropriate and feasibly obtainable training samples, whether those are living animals, dens/nests or scat, or
plant matter. If it is utterly impossible to obtain the requisite training samples—for example if the
focal species is so rare that it does not even exist in captivity, then dogs may not be a viable monitoring tool, since they must first be exposed to suitable samples to learn the scent of the desired target.

SCAT

Fecal matter, or scat, is one of the target samples most commonly sought to obtain information on
wildlife populations. For years, biologists have collected scat to infer information about habitat use,
relative abundance, diet, and parasite loads of wild populations (Putnam 1984; Kohn and Wayne
1997). With advances in molecular genetics, it has also proven viable for DNA analysis to confirm
samples to species, individual, and sex levels, and to evaluate physiological stress, via corticosteroid
examination, all negating the need to capture or even visually observe individuals within a landscape.

Generally speaking, in regard to target safety, scat represents the lowest risk among common
conservation targets. While a passive alert will best protect the sample, inadvertently stepping on
the scat or getting some saliva on it will not render most scat samples unusable. Furthermore, any
risk there is limited to that sample, and the real target of interest (the animal depositing the sample)
is not in harm's way.

In recognition of the inherent difficulties in procuring naturally occurring training samples (i.e., of wild animals), the current and most mutual agreement among conservation dog trainers is that

[D]ogs must learn to generalize their search to include scat from any member of the target species, regardless of a particular animal's diet or other characteristics [and] dogs should be exposed to *at least* a dozen scats (ideally more) of varying dietary composition and ages and representing as many individuals of both sexes as possible. (Mackay et al. 2008)

Numerous studies have now demonstrated that offering dogs a variety of training samples allows them to generalize to scent common to all possible, and available, scats of the target species in the field, regardless of individual, sex, or reproductive status (Smith et al. 2003; Wasser et al. 2004; Vynne et al. 2011; Ayres et al. 2012).

It is imperative that any scats collected for training from the wild are authenticated as those of the study species. The individuals responsible for collecting scats for training should therefore, at the very least, be well versed in its physical characteristics and visual identification. All too often, scats from one species look very similar to another, sympatric species, and if this occurs during training, the dogs will be trained on all species presented to them. Often, collection of confirmed training samples will best be accomplished by experienced biologists with expertise in their particular species of interest. Confirmation at a genetics laboratory may be warranted. Also, once collected, care must be taken to avoid cross-contamination with nontarget training samples during storage (Vynne et al. 2011).

It is always preferable to gather training scats from the actual population and area for which surveys are planned. This facilitates the dog's transition from training samples to actual samples in the field (Working Dogs for Conservation, unpublished data). Wasser et al. (2004) obtained scats for dog training from multiple wild grizzly (*Ursus arctos*) and black bears (*Ursus americanus*), collected across seasons both at the study site and elsewhere, and introduced dogs to the scat of many different individuals, with a variety of natural diets. Smith et al. (2003) also used wild scats collected at actual San Joaquin kit fox (*Vulpes macrotis mutica*) study sites with a similar goal of teaching dogs to generalize to species, regardless of the characteristics of the animal that deposited it.

If collecting wild scats from the study region poses a problem, training scats can be sourced from another region or from captive animals (Mackay et al. 2008). While both, especially the latter option, are not considered ideal, they are often the only available recourse to acquire samples, particularly for secretive and low-density wildlife populations. In the absence of scat samples from wild bush dogs (*Speothos venaticus*), Dematteo et al. (2009) trained detection dogs to scats from 13 captive individuals (7 males and 6 females) at three different zoos, representing various stages of reproductivity and multiple diets. In a study where different target species were to be sought simultaneously, Vynne et al. (2011) initially trained dogs with scats from between six and eight captive and wild maned wolves (*Chrysocyon brachyurus*), jaguars (*Panthera onca*), and pumas. After confirming wild-collected samples found by the dogs via DNA analysis, they used a minimum of 12–15 samples for training prior to deployment in subsequent years. Though for their targets of giant armadillo (*Priodontes maximus*) and giant anteater (*Myrmecophaga tridactyla*), these authors trained dogs directly in the wild, in their study location, to visually identified scats (*n* = 4 for both species).

Long et al. (2007) successfully trained detection dogs to locate the scats of free-ranging black bears, fishers (*Martes pennanti*), and bobcats (*Lynx rufus*), using at least 20 training scats from each target species (representing numerous individuals and a wide range of food items) solicited from wildlife researchers, agency personnel, and rehabilitators across the United States.

Captive or nonlocal training samples meet the overall goal of providing the dog with a basic odor foundation. Their use then often necessitates more training in the field during the transition from training samples to genuine finds (see discussion in the section "Transition to Naturally Occurring Targets").

Indeed, the ability of dogs to generalize a subset of training samples to recognize natural targets makes them well suited to wildlife or conservation studies (Cablk et al. 2008; Woollett et al. 2014). Providing a diverse set of representative training samples will allow the dog to more quickly grasp the species (and range of associated scents) they will be called upon to indicate. For example, asserting that moldy or degraded scat *may* provide less scent, Mackay et al. (2008) suggested prioritizing training scats that vary in quality and quantity of odor—from degraded samples to large intact scat—which allows dogs to amass a broad scent perception relative to the target species.

Trainers must also bear in mind that factors they might have expected to come into play (and that may have influenced the types of training samples selected and provided) might turn out not to be representative of the scent scenario(s) the dog will actually encounter once in the field. For example, Ralls and Smith (2004) found no significant difference in the distances from which dogs detected single kit fox scats versus latrines despite the hypothesis that multiple scats should smell stronger than a single scat. Additionally, while provision of few or low-quality scat training samples can reduce accuracy (Vynne et al. 2011), dogs trained with only a few fresh scats, or other biological samples, have immediately recognized and detected large numbers of older, degraded samples during searches (Working Dogs for Conservation, unpublished data).

In studies of wildlife, whether San Joaquin kit fox or Cross River gorilla (*Gorilla gorilla diehli*), both fresh scats for genetic analyses *and* locations of older scats, which provide information on recent presence, distribution, dispersal corridors, or habitat use, are useful and illuminating (see Figure 11.2). To this end, the ability of dogs to generalize to *all* scats of a species that are available on the landscape regardless of samples available for training has proven important (Smith et al. 2006; Arandjelovic et al., unpublished data).

Data from published and unpublished field studies indicate that dogs have been focused on detecting scats on a species level rather than on the basis of sex, age, diet, or individual characteristics (see Smith et al. 2003). However, in the future, dogs may be deployed in natural settings to locate scats based on some of these other characteristics. When or if this becomes the case, training materials appropriate for these unique variables need to be considered in planning the study, similar to training sample considerations for species detection. To date, only laboratory-type controlled studies have trained dogs to match scat samples to individuals, with the idea of demonstrating that this dog application has the potential to reduce the need for follow-up confirmation genotyping of collected scats (Kerley and Salkina 2007; Wasser et al. 2009).

FIGURE 11.2 Fecal samples of various ages and conditions provide valuable information to wildlife researchers. Depending on age and condition, this Cross River gorilla dung sample in Cameroon underwent disease or genetic analysis, or both. (Courtesy of Romanus Ikfuingei.)

Finally, new prospects for future development of artificial scent sources (similar to pseudo scents available in cadaver, narcotic, and explosive detection disciplines; see Chapter 18 herein) for certain wildlife species and their characteristic scats have the potential to circumvent the difficulty of obtaining natural scat, thereby facilitating training and deployment of dogs in conservation and management programs. However, caution is nonetheless recommended since evidence exists to suggest there is, at least in some cases, no substitute for the actual target sample. Indeed, a recent study found that dogs trained on simulated explosives had low success in detecting the genuine target, and conversely, dogs trained on real explosives had low rates of detection for pseudoexplosives (Kranz et al. 2014b).

OTHER NONLIVING TARGETS

Using similar methods and principles as employed for scats, dogs have repeatedly demonstrated their ability to locate other sources of wildlife scent—like nests, dens or burrows, carcasses, and living animals (Dahlgren et al. 2012). Training a dog to locate the nests of species of interest (e.g., bees) can consist of sourcing nest material from commercially reared individuals and obtaining nests from the wild (Waters et al. 2011). However, similar to scat work, eventual training on a variety of nests—most importantly those produced directly in the wild—can most rapidly instill within the dog a complete scent picture in relation to the target.

When dens (or burrows) are sought, dogs are trained to be target specific (Theobald and Coad 2002). Similarly, carcass searches are generally highly exact, such as disease-detector dogs being trained to find only the carcasses of Sarcoptic mange-infected wild animals (Alasaad et al. 2012). Alternatively, the study objectives can instead dictate that a dog will need exposure to a range of targets that will allow broad generalization (i.e., carcasses of *all* birds and bats in an area versus just those of one species). In a study that aimed to demonstrate that dogs could be used to improve bird-strike mortality estimates at wind farms and other anthropogenic structures that cause bird fatalities worldwide, Paula et al. (2011) trained their dog to 17 different bird and bat species, collected during exploratory field surveys. They also recommend that future training involve provision of carcasses of differing decompositional states. Although carcass decomposition did not affect the dog's accuracy in field trials, a minor difference in detection time between fresh and decomposed carcasses occurred. The authors suggest that this is probably related to the intensity of odor a carcass emits during decomposition, pointing out that the dog was not trained to fresh carcasses, and since their odor may be less intense and of differing chemical composition, it could explain the reduction in the efficiency of the dog detecting fresh carcasses.

LIVE ANIMALS

The highest-risk searches, from the perspective of the target, are live animal searches. Cablk and Harmon (2011) explicitly and carefully discussed this for desert tortoises as an endangered species and also in light of the fact that domestic dogs are a noted source of predation for these animals. Surprisingly, even live targets that move slowly and do not resemble typical prey, such as snails, can elicit a predatory response (Working Dogs for Conservation, unpublished data). The temperament and characteristics that can be capitalized on to make good conservation detection dogs are often coupled with prey drive. The extent to which prey drive can be reliably controlled is widely variable among dogs. Size is sometimes an issue. For instance, because of vegetation, tall dogs will often be appropriate for searching for live animals.

Training to live animals can either consist of providing direct (but always safe) exposure to the target animal or be more of a two-phase process that incorporates all the potential or common and available scent sources to ultimately locate the species in the wild. For example, Stevenson et al. (2010) assessed the ability of a dog to counteract the difficulty (for humans) of locating live, hard-to-detect eastern indigo snakes (*Drymarchon couperi*) with other survey methods due to their extensive time spent in tortoise burrows and other underground refugia. Training consisted of initially exposing the dog to sections of shed skins collected from multiple eastern indigo snakes in the wild, followed by introduction to the odor of these live snakes via holding cages. While the dog used in this study successfully located both shed skins and live snakes in field trials, it had received greater exposure to shed skins and showed higher success in detecting this target, leading the authors to conclude that the dog would have benefited from additional training with live snakes.

Conversely, Savidge et al. (2011) trained heavily with live snakes and made extensive use of boxes, where a dog was encouraged to identify the box (or boxes) containing the target invasive brown tree snakes amid several other empty boxes. This was followed by handlers conducting blind searches for snakes secured in tubes or mesh bags and, finally, searches for wild snakes. Overall results suggested that dogs could be a viable monitoring tool for detecting brown tree snakes in refugia, particularly when compared to the performance of humans conducting daytime visual searches.

Reindl-Thompson et al. (2006) found that detection dogs show promise in detecting black-footed ferret (*Mustela nigripes*) presence in prairie dog colonies. These authors outlined that because they sought to indicate the presence of ferrets and not just the location of scats, their training program included multiple odor sources, initially scats from a captive animal and then bedding and a live ferret in a holding tube, thereby reinforcing for the dog the connection between the scats and the live ferret, and the fact that both scents represented a reward.

With rare or threatened wildlife, using live animals themselves for training may not always be practical, feasible, or legally permissible. As such, dogs can be trained to a proxy scent source, such as fabric or swabs that have been rubbed on captive animals or even permitted live wild, or some form of material (e.g., bedding) that has been housed with the target species and therefore contains the residual scent of that animal. Browne (2005) demonstrated in scent discrimination trials that dogs can be trained to detect Cook Strait tuatara (*Sphenodon punctatus*) scents with a high degree of specificity using cotton cloths prepared with tuatara scats, sloughed skins, or paper towels that captive individuals had sat on for several days within their enclosures. Prior to fielding, Cablk and Heaton (2006) trained dogs on the residual scent of the desert tortoise (*Gopherus agassizii*), with training aids prepared by wiping captive tortoises with sterile gauze only on the front fleshy parts (i.e., forelegs and neck), to teach dogs to specifically identify live tortoises rather than carcasses or feces. The dogs were then introduced to live captive tortoises under controlled conditions with both types of training samples (i.e., residual scent and captive animals), leading to success in locating wild unknown live individuals. Interestingly, Cablk and Heaton (2006) discussed how, without reinforcement in the field, the dogs ceased alerting on residual tortoise scent, refined their scent picture, and improved their ability to differentiate between burrows without and with tortoises, the latter being the ultimate purpose of deploying the dogs.

A multiphase training sample approach may often be necessary when the target species is invasive or noxious. Faced with quarantine issues and sample availability, Lin et al. (2011) were only allowed to use dead red imported fire ants (*Solenopsis invicta* Buren) in indoor training. Thus, dogs were initially exposed to dead and previously frozen ants. Subsequently, the dogs were taken to natural areas where various confirmed ant nests had already been identified first by visual inspection so they could learn the full, complex, natural scents of ant colonies in the wild. This allowed them to generalize to living organisms and in high densities.

Finally, in some cases, it will only be possible to identify the most appropriate target once dogs are actually on the ground, in a pilot training phase. Attempting to test the viability of dogs to survey for low-density and threatened Franklin's ground squirrels (*Poliocitellus franklinii*), Duggan et al. (2011) initially trained to scats only to find that the dog team was unlikely to encounter ground squirrel scat aboveground under natural conditions. As a result, they refocused training to detection of live Franklin's ground squirrels and burrows, using a multiphased approach. The final study results indicated that dogs could be used effectively in large-scale surveys for this species and illustrate the need for a creative training design that mimics actual conditions in the field (see Figure 11.3).

In summary, multiple stages of training, whether for scats, nests, burrows, carcasses, or living animals, are required for the dog to become fully functional.

FIGURE 11.3 To best prepare dogs for real-world conditions, creative training scenarios are often warranted. When training dogs to the scent of living Franklin's ground squirrels that live underground in burrows, polyvinyl chloride (PVC) tubing was used to create artificial burrows. Squirrels were contained at one end of the burrow, and length and turns were added to create increasingly complex scenting scenarios. (Courtesy of Working Dogs for Conservation.)

TRANSITION TO NATURALLY OCCURRING TARGETS

It is not uncommon for the odor associated with naturally occurring samples to differ markedly from the scent of the material presented to the dog in the initial, controlled training sessions, basically becoming a new variant of the target, which the dog must come to recognize in the field. When this is the case, and often it is, one can expect that the dog will initially hesitate upon smelling the target in the field. As a result, additional training is warranted until the dog learns to generalize odors to all variants of targets that may be encountered in the wild. It cannot be overstated that the transition from collected-type samples to naturally occurring targets is a pivotal step in successful training toward the end goal of the dog consistently performing an unprompted alert and maintaining fidelity to the target (Hurt and Smith 2009).

Contending with variations among targets happens not just between training and naturally occurring samples but also has been reported when dogs move between populations in the field. For example, Smith et al. (2003) described how when dogs trained on scats from wild (San Joaquin kit fox) populations were first exposed to scats from the urban population, which has a very different diet from the wild population, they initially hesitated before indicating that the scat was a kit fox, yet once rewarded, they became proficient at indicating kit fox scats from this population too.

Another valuable consideration is that once a dog is brought into the field environment, it has the potential to detect a residual scent from the target animal. Central to productive training is that dogs are rewarded only when they have located the scat, living animal, or other exact sample of interest rather than a residual scent (Mackay et al. 2008). Dogs have shown themselves to be quite capable of making this distinction, alerting to scats rather than dens of San Joaquin kit foxes (Woollett et al., unpublished data), and indicating burrows containing live tortoises versus vacant burrows with a residual scent (Cablk and Heaton 2006). However, sometimes the objective of a study, such as obtaining valuable information on presence of a rare species, can lend to broadening the training and reward from one target sample to others deemed important while directly in the field. For example, despite using scat samples collected from captive animals for training, Dematteo et al. (2009) found that a detection dog immediately recognized wild bush dog odor in the field, with the first confirmed den located during the first week of the study. In this instance, the researchers allowed the dog some leeway (e.g., to also generalize to hair and urine) because *any* data regarding location was seen to provide essential and rare insight into the bush dog's vulnerability and its role in tropical ecosystems.

Scat of certain species may be inherently distracting to a dog. One of the most important forms of olfactory communication, common in species of all carnivore families, is scent marking with glandular secretions, urine, or feces (Ralls and Smith 2004). Canids such as coyotes (*Canis latrans*), wolves (*Canis lupus*), and foxes (*Vulpes* spp), especially, are thought to use scats to mark territories and announce sex and status, with an accumulation of at least three scats or a latrine, functioning as a message center for canid social groups and conspecifics (Murdoch 2004; Ralls and Smith 2004) (see Figure 11.4). As such, particular scats are more than just a target to be found in return for a reward and actually impart chemical information to the dog. For instance, dogs first transitioning from training samples of San Joaquin kit fox scats to naturally deposited scats in the wild will often pause and carefully sniff scats, sometimes stalling out above the scat and forgetting to alert or slowly moving into a delayed alert (Working Dogs for Conservation, unpublished data). This concern is easily alleviated with repeated training in the field, but the majority of new trainers or handlers are often unaware of this issue in the wildlife detection arena.

Furthermore, a potentially problematic event occurs when even a highly effective scat detection dog responds *aggressively* to scat (e.g., attempting to eat, roll in, dig at, or urinate on it) or obviously avoids scat from a distinct target species (Mackay et al. 2008). Dogs have reacted negatively to wild-encountered scats from large carnivore species such as puma and wolf, seemingly responding to the chemical communication displayed by the animal that left it behind. In most cases, training can enable the dog to ignore the communication and focus solely on the target as an item that produces a

FIGURE 11.4 Canid latrines contain glandular secretions, which contain *information* of interest to many domestic dogs. Additional training and *in situ* experience may be required before a dog will ignore this information and immediately perform its trained alert. (Courtesy of Working Dogs for Conservation.)

reward. However, the reality is that it may not be possible to redirect some dogs, and these individuals simply will not be able to work effectively in the field on that target.

Moreover, sometimes the actual setting of genuine finds for a specific species will require a more complex training transitioning process. Rolland et al. (2006) trained dogs to North Atlantic right whale scat using previously collected scat samples from male and female right whales of varied ages, and that scent was added to dogs' repertoires through initial exposure using a scent box, followed by searches on land and then from the bow of a boat.

RESPONSIBILITIES OF THE HANDLER

Much of the focus in team preparation is on dog training, yet the handler has a great deal of influence over the dog and impacts the team performance. Handlers must not bring human bias into the search by expecting a target to be present in a given area (e.g., Lit et al. 2011) or being surprised to find a target in a location deemed unlikely. Bias can also impact where a team searches, especially when it is easy to conflate the types of places where targets are most likely to occur with the relative ease of seeing them in one area over another.

The handler's primary responsibility is safety (of oneself, other people, the dog, wildlife in the area). Second, the handler needs to direct the search such that the dog has the greatest opportunity to encounter the target while maintaining the study's methodology. This may involve more detailed searches of likely, complex habitats on a predetermined transect or may involve maintaining equal search effort across the search area. Third, the handler needs to support the dog so that it continues to alert to targets and ignore nontarget distractions in the search area.

Safety

Safety concerns are primarily dictated by climatic variables, physical attributes of the search environment, local disease and pest hazards, and wildlife present in the area. No matter where dogs are working, it is imperative that handlers and team members are well versed in noticing signs of heat exhaustion in dogs. Handlers can remain safe in hotter temperatures for a longer time than their dogs, so they need to be aware of panting behavior, tongue color, and saliva condition (see Mackay et al. 2008). Typically, conservation detection dogs and handlers are accompanied by one or more additional people. While these team members typically assist with navigation and data collection, the added safety benefit is notable.

Dogs will be safer if predetermined cutoff temperatures or search durations are established. In a desert environment, Nussear et al. (2008) noted that benefits of the dog outperforming human-only searches were somewhat diminished by the dogs not being able to work as long as humans. Nonetheless, handlers must not be goaded into overworking the dog. Highly driven dogs will typically not quit under their own volition and need their handlers to advocate for them.

Obedience is one safety measure that makes most hazards easier to mitigate. Common conservation dog industry commands focus on *heel*, *distance stop*, *recall*, and *down stay*, or variations of these, which ensure responsiveness of the dog and its safety on the landscape (e.g., encountering steep cliffs, waterfalls, etc.) as well as the safety of any wild animal, target or nontarget, that could be possibly encountered. Although dogs are a noninvasive or minimally invasive monitoring tool—often the least invasive of those available—they have the potential to act as agents of disturbance, which could also bring harm upon themselves. Therefore, all field-deployed dogs must consistently demonstrate highly functional obedience when the handler verbally issues a command (Woollett et al. 2014). Mackay et al. (2008) note that the New Zealand Department of Conservation's National Conservation Dog Programme (http://www.doc.govt.nz) has strict certification requirements for dogs working in conservation at the national level, and their interim certification alone focuses primarily on obedience and control work prior to dogs receiving full certification in field search skills (see Figure 11.5). Handlers must be able to demonstrate that they

FIGURE 11.5 Dogs in New Zealand's Conservation Dog Programme are certified in a multistage approach, with the first level based on obedience and safety around sensitive targets. (Courtesy of Working Dogs for Conservation.)

have control of their dogs with commands such as *heel, sit, come, stop, wait*, and *stay* (Theobald and Cheyne 2006).

Although national, state, or province-level certification is not yet the norm in the field of conservation detection, professional conservation dog trainers utilize highly stringent internal standards to assess a dog's ability to perform in a directed, controlled manner throughout a search (Hurt and Smith 2009; Woollett et al. 2014). Fitting a dog with an electronic collar, which can be engaged when necessary (e.g., a verbal command is not heard or heeded), secures an additional level of protection for both the dog and wildlife, especially where dangerous wildlife or domestic animals may appear suddenly and the risk of an encounter is high (Woollett et al. 2014).

GUIDING THE SEARCH

The handler is ultimately responsible for directing the search, whether the search parameters are strictly defined or intentionally loose. Strict parameters are described in Arnett (2006), where teams searched for bat carcasses on predetermined transect lines and dogs were permitted to search within 5 m on either side of the line. At the opposite end of the spectrum, Rolland et al. (2006) defined search lines for Atlantic right whale scat as merely needing to be parallel to the wind and downwind of pods of whales, resulting in an almost opportunistic search. Most reports fall in between these extremes, where handlers walk transect lines but the dogs can move freely around the handler (e.g., Smith et al. 2003; de Oliveira et al. 2012; Tom 2012), or a large area is defined within which the handler makes decisions in the moment as to where exactly to proceed (Thompson et al. 2011; Wasser et al. 2011, 2012).

These search parameters impact the skills that need to be developed during training. Dogs who will need to be tightly controlled must be highly responsive to directional commands given by the handler and/or be very well practiced at working on leash. However, while under frequent directional control, the dog must demonstrate intelligent disobedience (see Tachi et al. 1981) to ignore a directional command if it means leaving a target odor. At the same time, the handler learns to understand the dog's body language to avoid interfering while it is pursuing an odor. Conversely, in a search without much structure, there may be protracted periods without directional—or any other—commands; this maximizes the opportunity for the dog to investigate nontarget scents or get otherwise distracted. For this scenario, the handler must be very aware of what nontarget body language looks like and call the dog off of distraction quickly so that it maintains focus.

Lastly, not all conservation target scents are equally potent and thus are not equally detectable at the same scale, and consequently, this can repeatedly require different search scales and strategies (Woollett et al. 2014). It is imperative for trainers to remember this facet of target types, also strongly tied to scats being unequal among species, when embarking on successive odors.

MAINTAINING ALERT PERFORMANCE

When dogs perform a trained alert, or indication, it is the most definitive type of communication they can offer to the handler regarding the presence of the target. Alerts are exceedingly important to maintain the efficacy of searches as they reduce the chance of the handler misinterpreting or not seeing other on-scent behavior. This is vital in thick understory, when the handler and dog cannot always see each other. It also effectively pauses the active search and reduces the chance of a dog finding a target but then moving on before communicating the target's location to the handler.

Once a dog demonstrates its trained alert consistently while on deployment, if the alert degrades, it is most likely the fault of the handler. A common form of degradation is when the dog stays committed to the target but stands or stares at the handler instead of sitting or lying down (Cablk and Heaton 2006). Dogs may continue to effectively locate the target even though they no longer alert consistently, or the alert may further degrade to the point of the dog locating the target but then walking on without communicating the location of the target to the handler. Alerts typically degrade during deployment, and the handler must consciously make an effort to support alert behavior to minimize degradation.

NONTARGET ISSUES

When a dog alerts to something other than the trained target, it is off target or has *false-alerted* or *false-responded*. This is a *false-positive* result. Maintaining a dog's capacity to accurately differentiate a target from a nontarget scent is the primary ongoing training priority for conservation detection teams. The training plan to mitigate a loss of target fidelity will be informed by an understanding of the underlying cause of the error.

"LYING"

Through an anthropomorphic lens, humans frequently assume that a dog is lying to "cheat" its way into getting the desired reward. "Lying" in this context is considered to be the dog performing its trained alert when in actuality, it knows that the object to which it is alerting is incorrect. Disregarding the difficulty of determining what it is that a dog knows to be true, there are several reasons a dog may lie.

Perhaps the dog does not have sufficient search drive or work ethic to be well suited to the work and is jumping to the more "fun" parts of the job. Or it is a well suited dog but has not had its endurance built up enough in training to handle the duration of the search being conducted. Sometimes the density of the targets during deployment is less than the expectation that was set in training. Thus, the dog goes too long between intermittent reward opportunities to the degree of undermining its confidence in the search. All of these are actually errors made in dog selection and training, and lying is a symptom, not a cause.

HANDLER ERROR

Handler error is defined as "any action or cue that causes the canine team to perform incorrectly" (Scientific Working Group on Dog and Orthogonal detector Guidelines [SWGDOG] SC1:

Terminology). Common handler errors that cause the dog to indicate the presence of a target when, in fact, no target is present are inadvertent physical cues, such as tugging on the leash.

If the handler misreads the dog's behavior and believes the dog to be on scent, the handler may loiter in the area, which can cause an erroneous feedback loop where the dog searches harder because the handler is waiting and the handler continues to wait because the dog is working with increasing diligence. This erroneous feedback loop can also be started by the handler if he or she shows bias or expectation. Should a handler see what he or she believes to be a target and slow down, investigate, or point out the item to the dog, the dog may perceive this as the handler trying to tell the dog to search harder, or even to alert to this novel item (Mackay et al. 2008).

By far the most likely way to create an ongoing problem of the dog alerting to nontarget odors is to reward the dog for a nontarget. As noted in Vynne et al. (2011),

> Dogs will learn to search for scat that is not from study species if an inexperienced handler shows interest in scat that appears similar to scat of study species. Interest by the handler causes dogs to sit in apparent anticipation of a reward. The handler then believes the scat is from a study species, which increases the probability of repeating the mistake.

TARGET CONFUSION

Finally, nontarget issues emerge when the dog experiences legitimate confusion between samples and cannot tell the difference between a target and a nontarget. This almost invariably comes down to insufficient training; the dog does not know enough about the target to effectively distinguish it from others or know how to generalize to all variants of that target. Related to the prior discussion of training samples, if the naturally occurring sample is substantially different than training samples due to diet variation, or contamination of training samples, then the dog may not effectively be able to differentiate target from nontarget. See Box 11.1 for an example of when it may be beneficial to train dogs to alert to—rather than ignore—similar targets.

Though dogs have a remarkable ability to differentiate similar scents, without experience, they may be confused by a similar diet among target and nontarget species. Currently, the ability of dogs to distinguish among the scat of species that can hybridize is untested. Similarly, if a nontarget species overmarks (by urinating) on a target scat, or if a target species overmarks on non-target scat, legitimate confusion may ensue. This intermingling of scents is likely to occur when target and nontarget species use the same latrine. For example, joint latrines can result from coyotes responding to kit fox scats or kit foxes responding to coyote scats or both (Ralls and Smith 2004). When a dog is learning to locate naturally deposited scats of the San Joaquin kit fox, it often will encounter coyote scat at the same location. Hence, training must entail demonstrating to the dog that the kit fox is the target that produces the reward and the coyote scent is a neutral odor. Careful understanding of the study species is therefore crucial during training phases and prior to deploying dogs on actual searches.

Finally, although dogs are searching primarily by scent, if there is a strong visual component to the target, that might trigger the alert behavior prior to confirmation by scent. For example, when searching for living Franklin's ground squirrels, in training, the dog initially indicated to nontarget thirteen-lined ground squirrels when the squirrels were visible during the training scenario. When the squirrels were covered and no longer visible, the dog smelled each squirrel and readily discriminated between them (Duggan, Hurt, and Whitelaw, unpublished data).

DOG IS ACTUALLY CORRECT

Sometimes, a dog makes a decision that the handler believes is incorrect, but in fact, the dog is right. If the dog knows several targets, it may alert to the presence of any of those known targets, even if they are not relevant targets for the current study. It is important to consider which targets the dog is trained to in order to manage competing scents over the course of a dog's career. Tom (2012) noted the following:

> [P]rofessional detection dog agencies were hesitant to train for coyote scat detection because of this species near ubiquity throughout North America. As a result, future surveys conducted by dogs trained to locate coyote scats would encounter frequent nontarget detections.

Perhaps the dog is correctly indicating the presence of a target that the handler cannot readily see, as was the case with carnivore scat in Zambia, which was found to be under the surface of the ground after being buried by dung beetles (Working Dogs for Conservation, unpublished data).

Finally, sometimes, the dog is actually correct, but the metric against which it is being measured is imperfect. When searching prairie dog towns for the presence of black-footed ferrets, dog performance was measured against ongoing and historic spotlighting records (Reindl-Thompson et al. 2006). However, in one town without historic spotlighting records, the dogs indicated presence, while concurrent spotlighting surveys did not. However, subsequent trapping in the area where the dogs indicated ferrets proved that ferrets were, indeed, present.

MULTIPLE RELATED SPECIES WITH OVERLAPPING RANGES

BOX 11.1

Dogs excel at searching for more than one target at a time (Williams et al. 2001) and are frequently trained to search simultaneously for multiple animals of concern (Beckmann 2006; Long et al. 2007; Vynne et al. 2011). But what if the other species in the area are more common and are not sensitive species inherently of interest to the researcher?

In South Africa's Western Cape lives one of the most endangered species in the world, the geometric tortoise (*Psammobates geometricus*). Primarily due to habitat loss, there may be fewer than 300 individuals remaining. In order to find as many tortoises as possible in the remaining intact habitat, CapeNature biologists trained a detection dog to sniff out geometric tortoises (V. Hudson, personal communication). However, sharing the geometric range are the more common padloper (*Homopus areolatus*) and angulate (*Chersina angulata*) tortoises. While these other species are not of concern per se, the biologist chose to train to all species of tortoise because including all tortoise species allowed the following:

- More opportunity for reward in the field.
- Surrogates for training—training could occur with the less sensitive tortoises until the team was very well practiced.
- More training areas because the team has ready access to locations where the more common tortoises prevail.
- An assessment of relative density of each species. In fact, it has been determined that if there is an abundance of angulate tortoises occupying a site, there will likely be very few geometrics (Hudson and Hurt, unpublished data).

In this case, there was no risk to adding additional species to the cohort, because the geometric can be positively visually identified by the handler, once the tortoise is located by the dog. The imperative detail is that the trainer decided to include padloper and angulate tortoises as targets and trained the dog such that it was reliably indicating to all species of tortoise (see also Tom 2012). One cannot legitimately assess relative density if a dog is trained to alert to one target and may only occasionally be interested in another species.

MAINTAINING TARGET FIDELITY IN THE FIELD

Dogs can smell things people are unable to detect. Not only are they more sensitive to small amounts of odor, but they are also capable of a great deal of specificity. That is, they can differentiate between scents that humans cannot. This is one of the great benefits that detection dogs can offer research and conservation initiatives. But given the myriad of ways that a dog can get off target, how then to maintain target fidelity while deployed? The following are recommended:

- Set the dog up for success with lots of scent-imprinting training, with keen attention to training samples.
- Transition to the field in locations where dogs are likely to encounter naturally occurring targets.
- Ensure that the handler recognizes on-scent behavior and knows how to differentiate it from other behavior.
- During training, familiarize dogs with the concept of intermittent reward, so that they are not waylaid by not getting a reward in the field if the handler cannot confirm that the target is correct.
- Send samples to the lab for genetic analysis, to ensure that the teams are staying on target over time (Tom 2012).
- Train for the reality that will occur; the handler will not always know if the dog is correct. Do not be in the field the first time this occurs. Have a handling strategy practiced and in place (such as described in Cablk and Harmon 2011).
- If it takes time to determine if the target is correct, acknowledge the dog and move on; do not pay undue attention to a questionable target while the dog is watching.

Trust the dog, but know that mistakes are possible. If the dog is well suited to the work, assume that any mistakes are honest ones, which are heavily influenced by the handler and training practices.

CONCLUSION

In conservation detection, perhaps more than other detection disciplines, there is a great deal of variation among the types of targets, search areas, and search strategies employed to locate the target. All of these attributes must be considered in order to effectively train teams for field success.

Regardless of this complexity, many practitioners have enumerated the ways that dogs have made contributions to rare-species recovery, invasive-species eradication, and other applied conservation outcomes. Conservation detection dogs have become accepted tools alongside other noninvasive (and invasive) monitoring technologies, and their use continues to increase.

ENDNOTE

1. The authors thank Ngaio Richards, who graciously provided edits and comments.

12 Training Fundamentals and the Selection of Dogs and Personnel for Detection Work

Sherri Minhinnick, L.E. Papet, Carol M. Stephenson, and Mark R. Stephenson

A dog trained to perform olfactory surveillance to locate target odor may generally be referred to by many different names including detection dog, sniffer dog, scent discrimination canine, and other discipline-specific names (Lorenzo et al. 2003). Some believe that this type of usage dates back to their operation as hunting dogs 12,000 years ago (Davis and Valla 1978), but others suggest that this may date back to the Paleolithic period (Shipman 2015).

Training a detection dog to find a single odor can be an easy task and take relatively little time (Hall et al. 2013; Johnen et al. 2013; Walker et al. 2006). In fact, it is becoming a fast-growing sport for the masses (McCluskey and Small 2013; Parthasarathy 2011). However, training a highly reliable detection dog may take considerable time (Cornu et al. 2011; Fjellanger et al. 2002). Just as there are differing perspectives with regard to behavioral aspects of canine domestication (compare Udell and Wynne 2009 with Hare et al. 2010), opinions diverge on the best approaches to use in training detection functions. This disparity demands exploration of some of the key confounders to training, handling, and deployment of highly reliable detection dogs.

Trainers too have differences of opinion, which are displayed in the following adage: the only thing two dog trainers can agree upon is what the third trainer is doing wrong. The authors of this chapter are well aware that their colleagues training dogs for detection purposes may approach training differently or train an individual dog for a specific function using different methods, and will, as much as possible, try to ground the discussion here on the research conclusions that have appeared in the refereed scientific literature. We will also attempt to pay sufficient deference to the substantial history of training literature and lore that is often grounded on long and sound experience and passed from generation to generation as much of it has been passed to and, hopefully, retained by us.

Generally speaking "dogs are… easy and cheap to train and put into action" (Browne et al. 2006). While the act of training a dog comes easily to some, it can be extremely challenging for others, sometimes taking many months to perform (Cornu et al. 2011). This may be a result of dog selection, individual training methods, simple preferences, or other reasons. The one thing many trainers will agree upon is that when it comes to training a detection dog, the methods used by them to teach a dog to detect the initial odor will vary little from one odor to the next. In other words, odor is odor, provided that it is the correct odor, to the trainer. Within the confines of their methods, most initial odors will be taught the same way. Thus, for any given trainer, training a canine to detect scat or narcotics or explosives begins with similar basic training methods, and only after a base proficiency is demonstrated, verified, and tested will variables for discipline-specific trainings be introduced.

"It is generally believed that the most important feature for canine detection work is the acuity of a dog's sense of smell" (Lesniak et al. 2008). Nevertheless, in canine detection functions, one must also consider the dog in its entirety, the handler and the training he or she received, the trainer and training offered, what odor(s) the dog is being trained to detect, what distractors may inhibit the dog's performance, environmental conditions, application specifics, etc. One research team (Johnen et al. 2013) reported that with an "optimized training strategy," dogs could be trained to detect black tea with high sensitivity (92.1%) and specificity (97.4%) in a "short time," which was defined as no more than eight sessions, each lasting only a few minutes.

As a general observation, the authors will argue that aversive methods commonly in use today will not achieve such results. Haverbeke et al. (2008) noted in a study of Belgian military handlers that harsh training methods were widely used and verified that "low-performance dogs received more aversive stimuli than high-performance dogs." We assert that foundational positive training methods that are primarily focused on motivating the dog along with increased frequency of short training sessions focusing on these core principles should improve results.

IS TRAINING AN ART OR A SCIENCE?

Some scientists refer to dog training as an art (Plonsky 1998) as do many dog trainers. A variation of this was pointed out by Fjellanger et al. (2002), who note the following with respect to training in some parts of the world:

> Dog trainers often claim that the ability to train dogs is as much an art as a science. Unfortunately, mine detection dogs (whether for REST [Remote Explosive Scent Training] or field search) are routinely handled and even trained by nationals with little formal education, and who live in countries where dogs are not widely respected or kept as pets. If they are to train or work with dogs, such people must be given a detailed program to follow, and careful instruction in the basic principles of learning psychology. They are unlikely to have the background skills that are intrinsic to 'dog training as an art', but are capable of learning to apply relevant principles in an objective way (i.e., 'dog training as a science').

Looking at training as an art places the focus of developing training skills on learning by observation, detailed study, practice and more practice, recognition of ability from those passing on their skills, and becoming comfortable with calling oneself a dog trainer. Unfortunately, the *artistic* perspective sometimes brings with it a belief that protocols are optional or irrelevant, repeatability is tedious and unnecessary, and documentation of training methods and progress can be ignored altogether. Nevertheless, it must be acknowledged that people possessing scant understanding of scientific methods routinely train dogs with impressive results.

Regarding detection dog training as a science, on the other hand, puts the focus on the trainer's understanding and methods being aligned with scientific methodology and procedures, formal protocols, precise measurements, and replication, generally favoring the absolute over the arbitrary, the concrete over the abstract. A scientific approach assures defensible validity and reliability of performance, which are critical elements to detection dog training.

There may be a middle way. Rooney et al. (2007a) noted that "both objective and subjective assessment of behaviour have value in the assessment of behaviour." In assessing the efficiency with which dogs searched and located a range of target scents, this team used both subjective ratings by scientists who were nontrainer observers and objective ethological assessments provided by one ethologist, and found that "these measures correlated significantly" to the ratings of experienced trainers. Thus, there can be common ground between subjective and objective analysis, which might offer hope for similar correlation between artistic and rigorously scientific training approaches.

Of course it can be argued that science is, at least in part, an art. Science involving behavior is certainly not without intuition, without art. While discussing science as an art, behavioral psychologist B.F. Skinner of Harvard University (1956) said that science is not merely a matter of "statistics and scientific methodology." In describing how a psychologist learns to perform experiments and conduct research, Skinner notes that the "work habits which have become second nature to him have not been formalized by anyone, and he may feel that they possibly never will be."

Even if the scientists involved in a study can put on stolid *scientific* faces during experiments, this could be detrimental to overall dog performance thereby affecting modern canine research. Boredom is one symptom to be wary of; depression is another. Anhedonia, the loss of pleasure in normally rewarding stimuli, is a symptom of depression that is of great concern in dog performance. Repetitive nonstimulating actions brought on by routine trials might create this type of depression sometimes mistaken for boredom. As discussed while studying mink, Meagher and Mason (2012) stated that "[b]oredom can thus be operationalized and assessed empirically in non-human animals. It can also be reduced by environmental enrichment."

This might suggest the inclusion of trainers and handlers possessing an understanding and appreciation of the nuances for motivating the dog to aid in trials so as to ensure optimum performance during a study. Hecht and Rice (2015) have suggested that such individuals focused on motivation "do not typically consider the methods and technical issues that those conducting" the projects may have to keep in mind. Despite this, nonscientists can and should be integrated into methodologically sound scientific studies, as Hecht and Rice argue in their discussion of *citizen science* and canine behavior research. Ironically, this may even assist in holding down or reducing costs or possibly even yield results that a researcher "couldn't have dreamed of doing… without" (Bhattacharjee 2005).

In the typical scientific approach to training, a precise qualification criterion or baseline is set forth that the dog must meet or exceed to begin the study. The required criteria for qualifying a dog to be eligible for participation in a study may be in terms of trial design, environmental confounders, statistically sufficient number of testing trials, the number of target samples, distractor samples, negative trials, percentage of faultless trials, false alerts, misses, and more. This information is then used to evaluate dog performance based upon statistical analysis prior to entering the study. The acceptance or rejection of the dog prior to study inception is based upon analysis outcome strictly as a *sniffing device*. This same approach should be used for any detection dog training where reliability matters. However, in the standard approach to dog training as an art, the *trainer-artist* pays more attention to the dog's mood, changing motivation, etc., and generally will look at the dog as a living creature void of scientific evaluation. Additionally, while generally feeling all of the performance statistics are superfluous and rarely (if ever) performing any double-blind testing, the artist-trainer will intuitively know or feel that the dog is well trained. While such a trainer may feel that they know how to motivate the dog for best performance, we would suggest that any trainer not currently doing so should make simple adaptations to practices during the training of the dog in such a way as to scientifically validate the training provided. This can be done by performing periodic double-blind testing to accurately measure performance. By combining art and science into these practices, the trainer will produce a product (sniffing device) that meets the criterion necessary to surpass any scientific muster required.

Thus, the authors of this chapter respectfully suggest that there are elements of both science and art in effective training, especially of a highly reliable detection canine. The melding of two living, breathing, uniquely different beings, each initially possessing limited communication with the other, growing and learning to work together over time, into a team, a unit, is best understood through a perspective that has elements of both art and science. The team becomes something that neither component could ever become on its own. Nevertheless, the requirements of forensic routines, criminal trials, clinical examinations, conservation surveys, and other practical environments where detection dogs are deployed will constantly push for increased scientific certainty in all aspects, including training.

Ultimately the audience requiring the use of the canine team must also be taken into account. Audience requirements will impact dog selection, training focus, performance criteria, and reliability mandates. Records needed may vary by audience. Additionally, what information will be considered valid by each audience, how technically that information must be presented, and who might challenge the assumptions and conclusions of the work are impacted. Finally, not least in importance, successful consideration of the needs and influence of one's audience will impact future work and funding.

AXIOMS OF CANINE TRAINING

Some of the advice that the authors would offer to prospective and newly minted trainers will seem self-evident or obnoxiously basic to many who have been doing this work for a long time, but certain matters are important to emphasize and too often forgotten by those who should know better.

LET THE DOG BE A DOG

We humans use dogs for detection because of their superior sense of smell, because of their ability to follow odor to source, and because they can be trained relatively easily. Ferworn et al. (2006) correctly observe that "[p]erhaps the weakest link in the human–dog team is the human," while Fjellanger et al. (2002) note that a dog can function independently with very little input from the human side of the equation. Requiring a dog to perform human objectives is asking much, but allowing it to do so as closely as possible to its natural genetic and behavioral ability will make the process easier and more reliable. Unfortunately though, most odors that dogs are trained to detect are relevant from a humans' perspective but alien or irrelevant from the biological perspective of the dog. Therefore, the dog must somehow be nurtured and motivated to search for odors that may be not only irrelevant but also possibly even aversive in some circumstances. To accomplish this mission, a trainer will sometimes present an overwhelming human presence, micromanaging the actions of the dog or attempting in some way to force a dog into compliance. By attempting to alter the behavior in this manner, a trainer will be forcing the dog to understand the world from the perspective of the human. By forcing the dog into the human umwelt, stress is injected and the dog will lose motivation. This is most often noted when trainers teach obedience entirely too early, sometimes to a level of military precision that is imposed prior to any other training that the dog might enjoy.

However, there is another way. In dog training, the cornerstone is to comprehend and utilize the dog's umwelt, or universe, its way of interpreting the world in which it lives. Allowing a dog to enjoy the work, in a natural, unforced way, without coercion and intrusion by a human, permits the dog to cognitively discover successes on their own, which in turn adds further motivation and decision-making toward future training goals. While it is virtually impossible for a trainer to have complete understanding of the canine mind (Martinelli 2010), working to truly operate within this conceptual framework places the dog at ease and greatly reduces stress. This, in turn, unburdens the dog, allows for enjoyment in the work, and further motivates the dog for involvement in the training cycle. Applying this concept inevitably presents some difficulty for the trainer. Training is really nurturing in an attempt to change behavior. Understanding the dog's universe and attempting to blend in with it can be a challenge for any person, but doing so can yield extremely favorable results. By allowing the dog to be a dog and work within that world, quantified success will be the result simply by reducing stress (Rooney et al. 2005). "In general, a happy dog makes a good worker" (Rooney et al. 2009), which is exactly what is needed for training.

While there are many ways to train detection dogs, it is obvious that any best method should incorporate procedures addressing the concerns mentioned above while capitalizing on the natural abilities of the dog. It sounds simple, but training programs attempting to eliminate negative aspects of complex problems are rarely successful in completely addressing each individual element and sometimes revert to compulsive and aversive training.

Restrict Human Involvement and Limit Unnecessary Dependence

Evidence suggests that the *human factor* in olfaction dog training and deployment can be detrimental, as demonstrated dramatically with regard to handler cueing by Lit et al. (2011). Slabbert and Odendaal (1999) note that breeders can have a detrimental effect on well-meaning attempts to determine the ultimate suitability of a police dog:

> In cases where testing is used as a game, breeders will often obtain the services of a friend or colleague with little or no experience of puppy assessment and development. They follow a written test found in a dog magazine or book and open umbrellas, bang pots and call the puppies with great enthusiasm.

Unfortunately, the validity of this type of testing to predict suitability for any dog for any purpose may be poor because many of the activities used in these tests may result in changes in behavior among the pups during imprinting, which is the most critical time of life for any dog. Exposing a puppy to these sometimes-overwhelming events subjects the animal to unwanted or unexpected actions, all of which may be considered abnormal and stressful to the puppy, thereby altering the way a puppy will react to similar actions for the remainder of its life. Without ongoing training to overcome the changes induced by testing, the experiences could leave an indelible negative mark on the life of the dog.

A human handler may become so involved and crucial to execution of a behavioral sequence that it could render the dog ineffective when the human is removed. Kerepesi et al. (2005) found "strong support for long-term temporal sequences in dog–human interaction." They went on to determine that their "analysis has shown that during cooperative interactions there is a mutual dependency in dogs and humans, that is, their behaviour becomes organized into highly complex interactive temporal patterns." The study ultimately concluded that

> [I]n the course of the present cooperative task many task-related actions enacted by the partners became spontaneously organized into T-pattern [temporal pattern]. The repetition of the same sequence (...) allows the behaviour units to organize into a pattern that occurs every time when the dog picks up a building block. By its very nature the detected T-pattern does not only represent a sequential organisation but a temporal relationship among these units that is also relatively constant and gives a typical behavioural rhythm to the pattern.

The simple presence of a human can become a distraction to working dogs. Fjellanger et al. (2002) indicated that it became necessary to institute a protocol change in a study where they once allowed personnel in the room. In the revised protocol, they mandate that all personnel be removed from the area for all searches.

Human involvement in canine training and handling can create a problem. One such issue is the Clever Hans (Pfungst 1911) effect that was named after a horse purported to possess the mental ability to count. However, an investigation by the psychologist Oskar Pfungst (1874–1933) revealed that the truth behind the ability was Han's acute interpretation of unintentional behavioral cues from his handler and owner Wilhelm von Osten, as well as from others. This phenomenon involves two aspects that need to be considered when training a dog for detection work. The first part is the most talked about: the idea that a human can unintentionally and unknowingly cue an animal into an action. Certain training regimens are prone to exacerbate this issue as specific actions can affect the amount of communication that the dog seeks while performing a task. Marshall-Pescini et al. (2009) found that "human directed communicative behaviours are significantly influenced by their individual training experiences." Part two of the Clever Hans effect is that these cues provided by the handler or others can be extremely subtle and nuanced so as to be almost undetectable by anyone but the most advanced trainer or investigator. It is important that the Clever Hans phenomenon be considered in the training, handling, and testing of detection dogs, which can be trained to "ignore human cues" (Bentosela et al. 2008). Researchers have noted that this principle is valuable in the training of service dogs as well as explosives and drug detection dogs.

PROFICIENCY PROGRESSION VERSUS TIME-BASED COURT PREPARATION TRAINING

"A dog is a dog" and just as with people, each one is an individual (Burghardt 2003). While a dog in training may follow the general path of a prescribed syllabus, each animal will learn differently. The same can be said for their human counterpart. While each individual may expend the same effort to learn, training outcomes may vary due to their understanding of the task at hand. The nuances of adapting training to the individual can make the difference in ultimate proficiency and reliable actions. What takes a certain amount of time for one dog may double for another, and the same is true for people. A quick review of available training regimens will reveal that many are focused too intently on time-based training regimens geared more toward completion of a test or trial rather than absolute proficiency.

It is somewhat common for new handlers to attend training, which may range in time from a few short days to as much as a 12- to 16-week class or more. Further, it is common in some scientific trials for handlers to have very limited time to meet and work with a dog before progressing with the study. While more time should produce qualified results, such a result is uncertain unless built around proficiency progression.

Training (whether for canines or humans) is often logged as a culmination of total attendance time. In olfactory scenarios, one aspect that should be emphasized is the actual *nose time* of the dog as much can be learned by simply observing while the dog is working. By actually performing the function, either in training or in the field, the nuances of behavior become obvious and much easier to read. However, a problem is created when constraints are placed on the team to attend training defined solely by time instead of planning for mastery of skills and setting proficiency goals for the training. This issue is exacerbated once the dog and handler are deployed and begin routine maintenance training. These sometimes result in social events with post-training reports often indicating only arrival and departure times with very little recorded to illuminate the training information provided or learned.

The repeated demonstration of proficiency creates a more solid foundation for all subsequently acquired skills. This is not to say that the learning process must be linear. Progressing to a new skill requires clear proficiency being demonstrated on any aspect, which is part of the new skill. Some evidence suggests that a dog may learn a new task quicker by training that task less often (Meyer and Ladewig 2008). Problems associated with time-based training as opposed to proficiency training are potentially notable when a scientific trial uses a dog that has not been thoroughly vetted with distractor odors. Failure to demonstrate the ability to exclude confounders as reasons for false alerts or other issues in pretrial assessment and analysis limits the ability to ascertain true accuracy during trials due to the inability to understand the true detection capability of the dog. This, in turn, may raise questions about whether the experimental design can actually support the results claimed.

ANTHROPOMORPHISM AS A CONFOUNDER

Anthropomorphism is defined by Serpell (2003) as "attribution of human mental states (thoughts, feelings, motivations and beliefs) to nonhuman animals." This is commonly exhibited by humans, and as Serpell, citing Mithen (1996), suggests, without anthropomorphism, "neither pet keeping nor animal domestication would ever have been possible." In short, humans expect dogs to respond like humans in both action and thought. It might be suggested that this is due to a human perception of empathy being displayed by the animal. "The dogs' pattern of response was behaviorally consistent with an expression of empathic concern, but is most parsimoniously interpreted as emotional contagion coupled with a previous learning history in which they have been rewarded for approaching distressed human companions" (Custance and Mayer 2012).

While some people love dogs more than they do other people or simply compare the best and worst qualities of a dog to those of a person (Spady and Ostrander 2008), it is undeniable that anthropomorphic attribution is prevalent in our interactions with dogs. This is equally apparent in dog training and associated industries. Many working dog trainers, handlers, supervisors, researchers, and others ascribe human traits to the dog. Examples such as being an officer, family member, my boy, little girl, my buddy, pet parent, etc. abound. Some even claim that a dog can read "both our hearts and minds" (Sutter and Ostrander 2004).

Dogs have even breached the glass ceiling of scientific article authorship. Bhalla et al. (2001) included two dogs as coauthors, while among six authors of a paper written in 2000 in the *British Medical Journal* (Chen et al. 2000a), three were dogs with biographies: one a "junior research assistant," another an "intermediate research assistant," and the third a "senior research assistant."[1] Others may feel more grounded in the belief of their assistance.

> Although one of us (SG) [Simon Gadbois] has been using dogs in this capacity since the early 1990s, it was not until a student (Flannery and Gadbois, unpublished manuscript) decided to write a literature review on the topic that we realized the potential of this association between humans as field researchers and dogs as research assistants. (Gadbois and Reeve 2014, p. 24)

The problem presented by this interpretation is enormous. Whether it is a trainer training a dog, a handler deploying in the field, a certification official judging, a court weighing facts of a case involving a dog, or a researcher attempting to assist in the understanding, it must remain that such work should be objective. Failing to maintain objectivity taints results, regardless of expertise. This may be best summarized by Wynne (2007) as he concluded,

> Anthropomorphism comes very naturally to human beings. We must be continuously on our guard against it. Small children will label any self-propelled or animal-shaped object with human agency (Serpell 2003). The combination of both qualities creates objects that even adults have difficulty not interpreting in human terms. However, anthropomorphism must be resisted. Its drawbacks remain the same as they have always been: mentalistic folk-psychological accounts of animal psychology have no useful role to play in a modern objective science. They are non-material explanations which are the products of folk psychology and as such are not amenable to objective study. As I put it once before, 'the reintroduction of anthropomorphism risks bringing back the dirty bathwater as we rescue the baby'.... The study of animal cognition will only proceed effectively once it rids itself of pre-scientific notions like anthropomorphism.

ACTIONS AND INTONATIONS OF CUEING

While one research group acknowledges a dog's ability to interpret even the subtlest of human cues, they also feel that it is *unlikely* that a dog would have the cognitive ability to use it as a reference (Lakatos et al. 2012). However, it might be suggested that perhaps the most harmful human influence in detection work is cueing, signaling a dog to alert or engage in some other specific behavior in response to the handler's action and without a genuine reaction to the presence of an odor (Ensminger and Papet 2011a; Hauser et al. 2010). Cueing is a multifaceted problem in that it can increase dependency on the handler, thereby altering the decision-making process of the dog. "On the basis of our results, we argue that the decreased problem solving ability in the domestic dog is not due to their domestication but their strong attachment to humans" (Topal et al. 1997).

Cueing can be introduced either intentionally or inadvertently in each and every interaction with a dog, and working dogs are no exception. Each aspect of training, handling, and deployment, whether on the street, in the laboratory, or on the plains sniffing for scat, can be severely altered by the introduction of sometimes extremely minute actions or intonations that cause the dog to react. Often, the person inadvertently or unknowingly providing the cue or marker is oblivious to the distraction he or she is causing as the indicator may be a natural part of his or her interaction with the dog. "In a procedure that involves human communication, dogs show information-seeking behavior" (McMahon et al. 2010).

FIGURE 12.1 Directed sweep. Frame 1: handler facing dog and blocking with right knee; frame 2: handler pointing high; frame 3: handler pointing low, continues blocking; frame 4: handler pulling lead tight over the head of the dog.

One easily recognized example of a possible cueing event is a directed sweep (see Figure 12.1). This is a sweep whereby the handler maintains close physical proximity and interacts with the dog to precisely direct the dog's nose to a very specific spot for the dog to sniff. The handler will accomplish this via audible or visual actions used to entice the animal into place for the sniff. Key indicators of a directed sweep are as follows: a handler may stand in front of and facing the dog, a lead held tightly over the dog's head, the handler walking backwards, or the handler pointing to various items or locations (sometimes motioning in a *W* or *high-low* pattern) or constantly commanding the dog to *check*. Another example might include a handler directing the dog to sniff one very small tin in a row of tins while standing over the dog and either pointing or vocalizing directions. If this highly controlled approach begins during training, exercises, or deployments, it should be verified that the dog is providing indications in response to the actual odor detected, rather than merely responding to the handler's gestures and voice (Ensminger and Papet 2011b).

Clearly, in any *directed search* (Pickel et al. 2004) or sweep in which the dog is led or highly directed, potential exists for cueing due to human involvement. Some odor examination trials use canister placement via a *scent wheel* (Angle et al. 2014). If a dog is allowed to use these devices as nothing more than a receptacle for holding and presenting odor while the dog works independently, Angle et al. say that overall, "the scent wheel test appears to provide a valid measure of olfaction for testing accuracy and factors that might affect olfactory capabilities." However, any similarly constructed tool or pattern (generally Pickel et al. 2004), which demands use of a directed sweep in which a dog is led for training, testing, or while being deployed, should be a concern due to the possibility of cueing. Even if similar setups are used in training, Angle et al. concluded that it is still "prudent to teach dogs to perform their activities in 'real field' situations allowing the dogs to utilize and learn optimal ways to search environments to ensure success."

Marshall-Pescini et al. (2009), reviewing several studies, argued that

> [I]t appears that dogs with high levels of training, regardless of the specific type of trained activity/ sport, are more pro-active in problem solving situations and less dependent on their owners for a solution, since compared to untrained pet dogs, … they were more resilient in opening the box to obtain food, [and in a] second task they ignored their owner's misleading suggestions more than untrained dogs, thus obtaining a significantly greater food reward in the critical condition.

It is this perspective of independence that the present authors wish to emphasize as mandatory.

SELECTING DOGS FOR OLFACTION RESPONSIBILITIES

Volumes have been written on working dog selection. When selecting puppies, Volhard (Weiss 2002) and Campbell (Tataruca 2011) tests or others (Slabbert and Odendaal 1999) may sometimes be used. Generally, a dog selected for daily detection work should display many favorable behaviors

(Scientific Working Group on Dog and Orthogonal detector Guidelines [SWGDOG] SC3 2006). In a study investigating shyness and boldness for working dogs, Svartberg (2002) found that

> [T]he present study supports earlier results, and shows that in dogs there are general relationships between bold personality and ability to learn and perform well in tasks requiring varied training. Active, playful and bold dogs are more likely to learn more complex behaviour and perform well in situations requiring persistence. Fearless individuals may be less easily distracted and inhibited in novel situations, and the tendency to engage in play and chase may make the opportunity to engage in such activities more rewarding for these dogs.

Using this description of ideal traits required for a working dog equates to less time being needed to train a working dog, which may offer extreme benefits to the trainer. Maejima et al. (2007) "evaluated factors related to the aptitude of dogs that were trained in drug detection. Dogs were rated on seven behavioural traits that reflected two principal components: desire for work and distractibility" and then concluded that the "[d]esire for work was significantly related to successful completion of training."

In a study questionnaire developed to understand specific attributes of search dogs, Rooney and Bradshaw (2004) surveyed handlers and trainers using common vernacular and

> …identified 30 attributes generally considered to be important in the selection of specialist search dogs. When ranked by 180 dog handlers and trainers, the most important characteristics were: acuity of sense of smell, incentive to find an object which is out of sight, health, tendency to hunt by smell alone, and stamina. The importance of these attributes to the training and function of a specialist search dog is self-evident. The dog is trained to search for a training aid that is scented with a target odor. Thus, in order to be trainable, it must show a natural aptitude to search for hidden objects, use olfactory cues rather than vision, and possess an acute sense of smell. Once operational, a dog will be required to work for long periods and to carry out relatively complex searches. Good health and stamina are therefore paramount.

In this study, however, the single most important behavioral aspect of a detection dog was not queried. In querying trainers and handlers to rank *attributes* of which several are trained behaviors, statistical reliability (as a trained behavior) was strangely omitted.

BREED AS A PREFERENCE

Breed is often a priority in selection, though breed preferences are also highly variable. Limited work has delved into selection based upon breed. Various works have found that breed preferences differ.

> Rooney and Bradshaw (2004a) showed breed differences in behavioural attributes that are desirable for dogs used to locate explosives, weapons, or drugs; English Springer Spaniels and Border Collies scored significantly closer to ideal levels than Labrador Retrievers and cross breeds for 'agility', 'tendency to be distracted when searching', 'independence—ability to work without constant guidance', 'stamina', and 'motivation to obtain food.' (Maejima et al. 2007)

Alternatively, Jezierski et al. (2014) had a somewhat alternative perspective, noting the differences can be regional or even national:

> The suitability of particular breeds for detection tasks is of importance at procurement of dogs for the training and in operational work. The preference for a particular breed for detection may in different countries depend on a traditional choice of a breed, availability and current opinions. There is generally a lack of comparative scientific studies on suitability of particular breeds for detection tasks. In our study the German shepherds proved to be slightly superior to 3 other breeds and Terriers demonstrated on average relatively poorer detection performance. Terriers, on the other hand, have the advantage that they can fit into tight quarters and can be easily lifted to sniff areas difficult for other dogs to reach, such as narrow tunnels and inside cupboards.

A trainer may select a specific breed simply due to ample supply; a handler may have witnessed a specific breed perform well or want the dog to project a certain image to the public; a law enforcement or other agency may desire breed consistency within the department. Police dog trainers often prefer a specific breed, such as the German Shepherd (Adamkiewicz et al. 2013; Rolak 2000), possibly due to detection performance (Jezierski et al. 2014), or Belgian Malinois (Cornu et al. 2011) for doing detection work. Even preferred breeds sometimes experience program rejection rates exceeding 50%, which may explain why breeding programs are most often unsuccessful (Parmeter et al. 2000; Slabbert and Odendaal 1999; Wilsson and Sinn 2012). Additionally, there may be nothing inherently weak about the dog or its breed, and the failure may be related rather to the methodology used to train the dog, where "dogs may simply not be stimulated enough cognitively" (Gadbois and Reeve 2014, p. 11) or simply bored with the process. Different types of purebred dogs (Gordon et al. 2008), as well as mixed breeds and mongrels (Willis et al. 2004), sometimes from pounds and shelters (Weiss 2002), have proven effective as well.

DRIVE OR DESIRE

This is one area of dog training in which consensus has yet to be reached either in the scientific realm or dog trainer communities, as there exist many definitions and interpretations of *drive* in a dog. As explained by Cablk and Heaton (2006), "[d]rive is a motivational characteristic inherent in a dog. Drive cannot be trained, but is a required element of a working dog. Without drive, a dog has no motivation to perform or work." Alternatively, as suggested by the SWGDOG SC1 (2011), drive is defined as the likelihood of the dog to perform a set pattern of behavior based on a particular stimuli. Further, drives may be increased or decreased but not created or eliminated. In some training programs for olfaction work, three drives are typically discussed: *hunt*, which is the innate steadfastness and desire to investigate for prey; *prey*, defined as the instinctive desire to chase and catch something; and *retrieve* (or *play*) drive, which could be defined as willingness to bring something back once gathered (generally Cablk and Heaton 2006). For some programs, these three attributes are crucial in selection schemes as they greatly reduce the time and effort necessary to develop a scent detection canine.

While innate drive (desire) cannot be created, if present, it can be manipulated. An obvious strength in any drive can assist in the manipulation of another. Attempts to choose dogs based on various drives have been employed. Wilsson and Sundgren (1997) discussed prey drive ("also termed competitive drive or social competitive drive"). Desirable traits for selection may include qualities other than detection capability, such as "object focus, sharpness, human focus, and search focus," as studied by Sinn et al. (2010). Trainers often choose dogs exhibiting extremely high energy levels, which may have made the dogs unacceptable for work in some fields or as pets for owners incapable of handling them (generally, Marston et al. 2004), yet reduce training time and assist in capitalizing on the natural motor patterns used to train the dog.

CANINE AGE AS A SELECTION TOOL

Trainers consider the age of the dog in the selection process. Although correct imprinting and training of a puppy can produce a high-performing detection dog, most trainers have little desire for the added work involved. Trainers often seek dogs of approximately 12–36 months in age (Handy et al. 1961; Maejima et al. 2007). Dogs over 30 months are rarely chosen due to the lack of remaining working lifespan after training has been completed.

[Alexander et al. 2011] hypothesized that training larger and physically stronger dogs increases the likelihood of resorting to compulsive methods and harsher equipment such as choke chains, pinch collars and/or electronic collars to gain physical control of the dog to teach compliance to obedience commands as the dog matured. This was supported through the findings that as dogs matured and increased in age and size, the respondents utilized harsher equipment for training.

It could be concluded from Alexander et al. (2011) that training should begin at a much earlier age that would allow for proper conditioning long before an age when the dog has the size and strength to present an issue requiring compulsive measures. One recent study may serve to support starting dog selection with puppies.

A decade-long study tested 965 puppies, some as young as 7 weeks old, of which 206 (21%) could be traced to adulthood as trained police dogs. All the puppies had been given 10 tests, which included movement with and around the tester, reaction to distractions, negotiation of obstacles, making way into a room, interaction with a person, response to a new area, noise while left alone, sudden commotion, playing fetch, and tug of war. Of the 965 original puppies, only 206 trained police dogs could be traced. Out of the 206 traceable dogs, all serving as police dogs, 148 (72%) had passed the puppy test while 58 (28%) had failed. These findings indicate that suitability for becoming a working police dog can be predicted with some certainty, which further supports the findings of others (Svobodova et al. 2008).

ABILITY TO INTERACT BASED ON HANDLER PREFERENCES

Other factors that may be used in selection include the sex of the animal, physical appearance, size, and color. There is often a complete lack of objective information available regarding selection, such as results from social and environmental soundness testing, true physical condition, ability testing, etc. However, as Wilsson and Sundgren (1997) note, "[s]ubjective evaluation of complex behaviour parameters can be used as a tool for selecting dogs suitable as service dogs." Some handlers care more about the animal's ability to interact calmly with the handler than any other attribute. Thus, Rocznik et al. (2015) found that "[o]ften, a key determinant of adult working success is a dog's 'personality' or 'temperament'." The dog as well as the handler must be willing to adapt to the personality and temperament of the other to form a successful team.

DOMINANCE ASSOCIATION AS A SOCIAL RELATIONSHIP

Dominance is a topic that stirs strong emotion when discussing dogs. This may be in part due to some rather ancient paradigms that unfortunately may still be in use today. However, dominance as discussed here is more about the quality of relationship between social beings. Dogs—like their ancestors, wolves—are pack animals. Within a pack, hierarchy and associated positioning are present (Dagley and Perkins 2005; Handy et al. 1961), which, though not always recognized, can provide powerful tools for olfaction work. This is one primary factor often associated with the selection of working dogs in Europe and beyond.

With a dog and the handler creating a team, a hierarchy will exist (Akos et al. 2014). Pongracz et al. (2008) investigated whether a dog's dominance rank with other dogs affected its "social learning performance." They found that subordinate dogs "displayed significantly better performance after having observed a dog demonstrator in comparison to dominant dogs." There was less difference between high and low position dogs when the demonstrator was human.

As outlined by the many behavior and subjective ratings offered by Wilsson and Sinn (2012), a trainer could possibly evaluate many different aspects of the dog for any given program. Selection of a dog should include careful consideration of the discipline and tasks required. Hence, a conservation detection dog deployed sniffing for scat could require a uniquely different set of attributes than a dog being used in a set of relatively short duration "[b]ox tests" (Pickel et al. 2004) in a cancer study. However, in some cases, the same dog might fit the criteria for each discipline. While SWGDOG SC3 (2006) suggests certain criteria should be used, ultimately it may be a simple choice based on the trainer's opinion, which appears to be supported by Wilsson and Sundgren (1997) in which "[s]ubjective evaluation of behaviour characteristics may have some advantages." Selection is relatively task-specific and can vary greatly, even by any given trainer. Sometimes handlers will pick out the dog they want just by what is seen upon greeting the dog (Burghardt 2003). Ultimately, selection comes down to a "sort and cull process" (Coppinger 2014, at time 37:45) based upon the preferences of the selector.

FAST LEARNING VS. PROFICIENCY

Hall et al. (2013) determined that the method of delivering rewards could significantly affect training times for detection dogs. Johnen et al. (2013) stated that

> Our results demonstrate that dogs can learn quickly to perform a scent detection task as the indication of black tea. Dogs familiar with the training platform did not need more than eight training sessions to learn the correct indication of positive samples. With every training session lasting between 2 and 3 min, the overall training time on the platform took less than half an hour per dog and was completed in one day. During this time, each dog had approximately 300 reinforced contacts with the target scent.

Additionally, dog selection could weigh heavily on time required to train the animal. Not all training is equal or even comparable. Research "results demonstrate that naïve dogs can be trained to detect a novel odor using only discrete trials in a short period of time" (Hall et al. 2013), "less than half an hour per dog" (Johnen et al. 2013), or "less than 50 h to train a 3-year-old Small Munsterlander Pointer" (Walker et al. 2006). In contrast, in training cancer detection dogs, Cornu et al. (2011) reported that "total duration of the training phase for a Malinois, from the initial phase of learning through the unblinded exercises phase, was 16 [months]."

Ideally the dog selected must fit the confines of that trainer's understanding, capability, methodology, and preferences. Trainers attempt to meet the criteria of the training needed to accomplish the task for which the dog is being trained. Additionally, anticipating the unexpected is one element trainers are accustomed to confronting, as each dog is different. Training may start out well and end well, but it is really all about what happens in between that counts. Proficiency can take time, and that is something that should never be rushed.

CLASSICAL CONDITIONING, OPERANT CONDITIONING, AND LEARNING FROM SOCIAL STIMULI

Just like people, dogs learn in life through experiences. These experiences can be positive and negative. Training dogs, in general, and detection dogs, specifically, can benefit from an understanding of several aspects of learning theory. These provide an insight into the most effective, reliable, and repeatable methods known for training dogs. While one trainer may be better than another, all should possess a solid understanding of these principles. This understanding must begin with the two main learning methodologies.

The first is classical conditioning (Pavlov 1927). Under classical or as sometimes called respondent conditioning, a dog can be *trained* to offer a new automatic response, not normally given, for a stimulus. This form of training can only happen when the dog encounters a new stimulus paired closely in time with something that automatically elicits a normal, unconditioned, natural response. In Pavlov's original studies, he noted that dogs salivate normally to meat, but not to the sound of a bell. By pairing the presentation of the bell with the presence of meat, dogs quickly *learned* to salivate to the sound of the bell alone. Over a fairly short time, with sufficient pairing, a dog can be trained to exhibit a new behavior to some cue that was formerly neutral. Unfortunately, this learning method can backfire when an aversive situation is inadvertently paired with something during training resulting in undesirable responses from the dog. Undoing this unintentional aversive conditioning requires pairing positive consequences and minimizing or eliminating any further aversive pairings.

Operant conditioning is the second training method that is important to clearly understand (generally Most [1954] 2014; Skinner 1953; Thorndike [1911] 1988). Operant conditioning promotes learning based upon actions that an organism chooses to take, connecting those actions to the consequences of those actions. This form of training relies upon observable behavior from the dog that is then either reinforced (increasing the likelihood of that behavior occurring again), ignored (decreasing the likelihood that the behavior will occur again), or punished (which stops behavior in its tracks, but does not by itself result in new learning). Further, reinforcement can be either positive or negative. Positive reinforcement occurs when something pleasurable happens after the dog offers a behavior—in essence, the dog receives a reward for the offered behavior. Negative reinforcement *is the withdrawal of something aversive* in response to a behavior offered by the dog. In this instance, removal of something that the dog does not like is the reward for the offered behavior.

A word about punishment is in order. Punishment is *applying* something aversive to the organism. It is important to be clear about the difference between negative reinforcement (the dog does something to remove an aversive stimulus) and punishment (the handler inflicts an aversive stimulus on an animal). The value of punishment is that it can stop whatever behavior is occurring in its tracks; however, punishment by itself does *not* teach a dog (or any organism) what the desired response should be. It simply teaches that the current behavior is *not* okay. It is up to the handler to subsequently provide other options reinforced by positive or negative reinforcement to indicate to the dog what a correct response can be.

There are other well-researched methods by which organisms learn besides classical and operant conditioning. Social learning theory suggests that organisms learn from others through observation, modelling, and imitation. Thus, it is not necessary for a dog to personally experience every consequence of every behavior in order to learn. Many trainers can attest that dogs observe each other being rewarded (or punished!) and adjust behavior accordingly. Many young dogs learn social manners and simple obedience by observing and imitating older dogs. Pongracz et al. (2003) and McKinley and Young (2003) noted, "dogs are social animals and should be predisposed to learn from social stimuli." *Stimulus enhancement* was described by Cracknell et al. (2008) as learning via observing the behavior of others with a stimuli. Slabbert and Rasa (1997) reported social facilitation in which one dog was encouraged or facilitated to also engage in behavior that another dog performed. Price (2008, pp. 63–64) noted imitation learning in which one dog mimicked the behavior of another dog. Topal et al. (2006) and Fugazza and Miklosi (2014) have also investigated imitation learning, which is commonly used in the hunting industry using dog packs for finding prey.

There are additional physiological and behavioral phenomena relevant to detector training. One specifically important to training detection dogs is the perceptual characteristic present in all organisms known as habituation. Perception happens in the brain and involves processing and understanding sensory input. Because the brain experiences an endless stream of stimuli to process and sort out, by necessity, not all sensory input can be attended to by the organism. The dog, like other mammals, has evolved to attend most intently to new stimuli or to stimuli that stand out above the background chatter of everything going on in the immediate environment. This means that when a stimulus is present and persistent, but remains relatively unchanged over time, the brain will automatically begin to tune it out or give it less attention. This is sensory habituation.

One aspect of habituation was noted by Price (2008, p. 51) who described it as "the persistent decrease in frequency and (or) intensity of a response due to repeated stimulation in the absence of reinforcement and punishment." Price related this to a training method also called *desensitization* (Mills 2005) that is commonly used to eliminate reactive behavior in dogs. Rooney et al. (2007a) also noted this phenomenon. Additionally, *extinction training* (Gazit et al. 2005b) may be used. "Extinction can be defined as the waning of a learned response due to the lack of reinforcement" (Price 2008, p. 60). This can be vital in detection work utilizing distractor training.

Two additional types of learning believed to occur include latent and insight learning. Latent learning involves observational learning to a point of apparently knowing what to do, but not yet having the opportunity to demonstrate that knowledge until the environment is right to allow the behavior to be demonstrated. Insight learning is a form of cognitive learning where a sudden reorganization of thought promotes new understanding of a situation creating the *ah-ha* moment. All of these approaches to learning are used or witnessed to varying degrees in detection dog training.

In summary, classical and operant conditionings are sometimes used independently, sometimes together, and occasionally in conjunction with other methods of learning to form the impetus for training a reliable detection dog. "Both autonomic (involuntary) and non-autonomic (voluntary) responses are subject to conditioning" (Price 2008, p. 52).

VETERINARY EVALUATION

Before a dog is accepted for training, a full veterinarian work-up should be performed and documented. Wilsson and Sinn (2012), in their study examining predictive validity of two behavioral measurement methods, noted that "[t]he sample we present here consisted initially of 496 German shepherd dogs that were bred from 91 litters at the SAF kennel between the years 2005 and 2009." Of the 496 dogs, only 383 were deemed medically fit, and of those, 70% were used in their study.

Their analysis provides insight into health issues and sensory limitations of some dogs, which may get worse with age. The veterinary evaluation should include a complete health screening, which may require follow-up procedures because health issues (like allergies, genetic anomalies, etc.) can weigh heavily on future canine olfactory work. It has also been suggested that medications such as glucocorticoids and doxycycline (Jones et al. 2004) may also affect a dog's sensory capacity. Semiannual checkups should be performed as Hirai et al. (1996) have noted that age-related changes may affect the canine olfactory system.

SELECTION AND APPOINTMENT OF A HANDLER

Various attributes are needed to be a good handler such as integrity, work ethic, teamwork, flexibility, trainability, confidence, responsibility, judgment, dedication, initiative, physically sound, etc. (SWGDOG SC5 2006). Other traits needed are dexterity, fleet of foot, compassion, empathy, able to quickly gather and analyze data to make decisions, and having an understanding of canine behavior and the science of canine olfaction. It is always best if a handler has also had training and experience as a trainer. Handlers without a thorough understanding of canine behavior and learning theory, and who have not also engaged in training experiences with many different dogs, will struggle to manage difficulties handling the dog in novel or unusual situations that may arise.

Alexander et al. (2011) noted gender differences in receptivity to scientifically validated positive training methods. For example, "[t]he majority of paid military working dog handlers and law enforcement dog handlers are men" and "female [handler-] trainers had a preference towards positive reinforcement training methods over men." Aside from standard detection dog training, more time may be required for the dog and the handler to adapt to each other. In a review of gender differences in human–animal interaction, females generally display "higher levels of positive behaviors and attitudes toward animals...whereas men typically have higher levels of negative attitudes and behaviors" (Herzog 2007). However, there has been little research comparing the effectiveness of handlers or trainers based upon gender (Kotrschal et al. 2009). Many police handlers are appointed based upon length of service, rank, political motive, request, or other reasons that should be largely irrelevant to successful training and deployment of detector dogs.

> Other programs, including many municipal police programs, are organized locally for local requirements and are loosely affiliated with other programs th[r]ough professional associations (e.g., National Narcotic Detector Dog Association, United States Police Canine Association). In these programs, the municipality usually acquires trained or untrained adult dogs on an 'as needed' basis to match with a specific canine handler. (Burghardt 2003)

For law enforcement purposes, handlers selected generally have been in law enforcement for some time and have had some sort of previous experience with canines, although not necessarily with law enforcement dogs. A common belief is that handling a working canine is a lifestyle choice that requires constant care so handlers should have proper facilities to house the dog and a family committed to dealing with the issues associated with a working canine (Eden 1985). It should also be noted that working with and handling professional dogs may be detrimental to the handler's health. Handlers may theoretically be exposed to zoonotic diseases that can be carried by dogs in general (e.g., sarcoptic mange, lice, visceral larva migrans from intestinal worms, rabies). Reid et al. (2004) found that while there was no significant difference in hearing loss between dog handlers and controls, "dog handlers may need to be placed on a hearing conservation programme" simply due to sound levels exceeding the European Union Physical Agents (Noise) Directive. This can be due to barking dogs (especially in kennel environments) and typical military or police weapons training. Other issues affecting the health of canine handlers and trainers include dog bites. "K-9 training does have potentially dangerous elements. Class members, for example, kept a 'stitch count' to mark dog bite injuries to handlers during the training cycle" (Burghardt 2003; Sanders 2006).

SELECTION OF A TRAINER OR A VENDOR

Being an effective trainer, especially for specialized olfaction dogs being deployed daily, requires abilities and knowledge not often considered in prior recommendations. The best trainers will possess a wide range of knowledge and be continually working to increase the depth and breadth of that expertise. This is exemplified by a willingness to adapt to new knowledge as it becomes available. Fruitful topics worthy of study and mastery by detection dog trainers include dog-specific information related to working dog selection, basic canine health and welfare, nutrition, general care, medical and first aid, managing a kennel, disease prevention strategies, canine learning, training techniques, proper use of training equipment, critical thinking and problem-solving skills, reinforcer timing and delivery, critical developmental stages, scientific principles used in training, and flexibility to adapt training based on the dog. Additional knowledge relevant to detection dog training and handling includes environmental conditioning, organized record-keeping skills, and information about application-specific odors being used. This specialized knowledge includes information about needed licensing, as well as knowledge and skills related to acquisition, storage, handling, placement, and transport of source material. Legal and supervisory requirements must also be well understood.

Trainers may work well with dogs, but a trainer must also possess the capability to train handlers. This is often more difficult than training the dog and requires dog trainers to acquire some knowledge of human adult learning theory in order to be truly effective. Trainers must impart enough information for the handler to become essentially a novice trainer. An excellent dog trainer may be completely capable of training dogs, but have poor *people skills* and thus fail to train the handler to work optimally with the dog. Failing to produce a reliable competent team will often manifest as a breakdown of some sort during the working life of the team. New handlers should be paired with a dog that has already been trained. This allows the new handler to witness proper operational techniques and understand appropriate performance from the dog, under supervision, long before they are expected to perform as a team in the field. In these authors' experience, some trainers choose to train novice dogs and novice handlers together. While this may result in an economy of effort on the part of the trainer, this combination is not ideal and can easily produce inferior results, as novice handlers will make some handling mistakes more often than an experienced trainer, thus confusing the dog and lengthening training time.

One unfortunate observation of the professional detection dog training community is that some trainers seem to be reluctant to share training knowledge and can be extremely secretive with what they consider their *secrets of training*. Some have speculated that this might be an effort to keep handlers dependent upon trainers or that it is perceived to be an economic necessity—if one gives away all of one's training tips to others, there would be no need to employ the dog trainer in the future. This is particularly problematic to institutions or departments needing the services of detector dogs, but having budget restrictions that barely permit paying for enough training to get a team semi-operational. Based on an informal examination of police curricula and guidelines, many programs are more concerned with officers learning how to justify their actions in court by structuring testimony a certain way rather than training the dog and handler to produce quality operational performance that would limit the need to testify (SWGDOG SC5 2006). It is our contention that too many programs focus strongly on potential legal issues of dog handling, but rarely bother to emphasize the acquisition of knowledge and skills in their handlers that reflect the science behind canine olfaction and detection.

A prominent trend in the canine training industry for military and police dogs, including odor detector dogs, often involves obtaining dogs that are already partially or completely trained, sometimes from vendor trainers in foreign countries. This has been true for decades (Handy et al. 1961). Many of the largest training facilities routinely purchase and import pre-trained dogs. Certainly, some of these dogs may require and receive additional training prior to being sold for specific work environments. Additionally, an individual trainer may function primarily as an importer and purchase dogs from a breeder or trainer outside the United States that specializes in providing police-type dogs (Burghardt 2003). As legal challenges of detection canine teams continue, a court may not be receptive to the argument that a dog performs reliably if a handler receives a pre-trained dog from such a broker and then claims the dog was trained locally. In many cases, there may actually be no traceable information as to who trained a dog or how the dog was trained. This could become important if any performance or behavioral issues arise or if the dog's performance is questioned in a legal proceeding. Assuredly, a local trainer who has experience correcting performance or behavior problems could be engaged to resolve problems that develop, but that could consume time and sometimes funding that is not readily available. The handler and the department may find themselves in a difficult situation if legal issues arise regarding the training and performance of a dog that is not working up to expected standards.

One question that needs to be asked is, when is the trainer really the trainer? It is not uncommon for a trainer to acquire dogs from several sources. Many times a trainer may import dogs from another canine trainer source. A dog may actually go through several kennels prior to being sold to a department. Sometimes dogs are acquired from companies or individuals specializing in training dogs for police or ring sport. A dog purchased may be a green dog, pre-started, or in some cases a completely trained dog. This is presumably done for financial reasons tied to time constraints, as it may cost less to acquire a pre-trained dog and require less time and effort before the dog is sold compared to selecting a dog and performing all the training. It is increasingly important to know the complete training history and performance of the dog so as to be defensible in court. This would mandate knowing exactly who trained the dog, and in some cases, it may actually turn out that several trainers actually trained the dog. This information is important to document whenever possible.

SUMMARY AND CONCLUSIONS

In summary, we have explored the idea of detector dog training being a complex mixture attributed in part to both art and science. Building upon the extensive body of published, validated work from the early behaviorists (e.g., BF Skinner) to more modern cognitive-behavioral scientists, learning theorists, and data-driven canine trainers, we proffer that effective dog training is the art of applying structured scientific principles and protocols in an individualized and nuanced fashion to efficiently and effectively change or shape desired behavior of the dog. We have attempted to throw light upon the fact that while a dog may be initially chosen for detector work based upon its inherent olfactory ability, it is important for the trainer to engage in partnership with the dog through training. We recommend training that specifically limits human interaction during odor detection work and minimizes demands upon the dog so as to not interfere with and negate the intrinsic nature and enthusiasm of the dog. While scientific work progresses, current research seems to indicate that minimizing human guidance during training and deployment of detector dogs should produce more valid and reliable results. Handlers should focus instead on motivating the dog for superior results.

Clearly, there is very little published, validated research on those factors that most impact the practical selection of the detector dog, handler, and trainer. The field would benefit from a thorough competency analysis of the knowledge, skills, and abilities needed for both detector dog trainers and handlers that are crucial to successful training and performance. Such an analysis could be based upon validated assessment techniques used by vocational psychologists to examine factors leading to success in other professions.

With all the knowledge, skill, and training necessary to field a proficient and reliable detection team, we suggest that, generally, training should be done individually. For example, the dog should be trained by a qualified proficient trainer first, the handler should learn handling techniques with a well-trained dog and an experienced mentor trainer as a guide, and only when a desired level of proficiency has been demonstrated by both should they be brought together to learn to work as a team. This strategy is not new—it is a successful approach that has been studied, validated, and utilized in the training and deployment of guide dogs for the blind since the first U.S. program was set up in 1929 by Morris Franks and The Seeing Eye (Moody et al. 2006, p. 10).

ENDNOTE

1. Gareth Williams, one of the contributors to the paper, noted to John Ensminger (personal communication) that it was perhaps not irrelevant that the particular issue of BMJ was a Christmas issue, which may have disposed the journal's staff toward a certain though perhaps temporary joviality.

13 Training a Statistically Superior Scent Discrimination Canine
Where Trainer Wisdom Meets Scientific Validation

L.E. Papet and Sherri Minhinnick

This chapter briefly discusses complex aspects incorporated into the scientifically based, pragmatic, and efficient training of highly reliable scent discrimination canines.

ACCLIMATION

Acclimation is defined as the act of an individual dog becoming accustomed to new conditions and surroundings. Goals of acclimation position the dog to increase overall well-being and pleasurable experiences, which reduces stress, thereby helping the dog adapt to the day-to-day interactions it will experience. In a scientific setting, this can also "minimize experimental variability" (Meunier 2006). Accomplishing acclimation is similar to any other training process and must be approached thoughtfully, carefully, and with the utmost focus on the difficulties, which present challenges confronting the needs of the dog.

> Stressors such as noise, immobilization, training, novelty, transport or restricted housing conditions have been reported to elicit responses in behavioural, cardiovascular, endocrine, renal, gastro-intestinal, and haematological parameters. These and other parameters that change during stress may thus be indicative of poor welfare. (Beerda et al. 1997)

A new canine trainee should be provided ample time to adjust to new surroundings, particularly upon arriving at a training facility. Acclimation time may vary for each dog. Allowing sufficient time for the dog to become comfortable with people, surroundings, patterns, food, temperatures, etc. is vital in reducing stress and improving welfare. Agencies sometimes require a "letter of acclimation from the dog's veterinarian" (USDA 2012) anytime a dog is transitioning from one locale to another. Maejima et al. (2007) discussed the acclimation period as taking approximately 1 month, though this did include more than getting used to the surroundings.

Typical routines and schedules may vary as each dog adjusts differently. Increased numbers of dogs in a kennel result in longer acclimation times. During acclimation, the trainer should schedule a few minutes of physical contact with the dog to take place several times a day. Interaction should be positive while remaining somewhat separated emotionally from the animal. Routine positive contact with the dog can significantly reduce stress as evidenced by studies of dogs in shelters (Hennessy et al. 1997; Coppola et al. 2006). Contact can be as simple as brushing, rubbing the chest, checking the pads, the tail, or ears, or other physical contact, while making certain that each interaction involved stays positive. Minimal talking should be permitted as verbalizing is reserved for communication carrying specific meaning to the dog. Feeding by hand several times a day during acclimation promotes a positive connection. These engagements develop the dog's positive association, which may also assist in scientific study. Meunier (2006) seems to have struck the right balance in saying a "goal of a comprehensive dog care program is to develop appropriate socialization, acclimation, and training regimens that minimize stress and distress, thereby leading to improvements in the quality of scientific data."

A fully trained dog may need less acclimation, as the U.S. Army's (2005) Military Working Dogs field manual indicates that a military working dog (MWD)

> is medically fit for regions and missions with a minimal requirement for acclimation to heat or physical stress where complete veterinary support is available. The MWD is fit for short duration deployments. There are no significant limiting or compromising factors. Medical problems may exist which slightly limit performances but are controllable.

The military also recognizes that leaders should understand these issues and veterinary care should be available. Failure to do so can present risks, such as heatstroke, as discussed by Andress and Goodnight (2013) and Boxall et al. (2004).

Living in a home is often the choice made for housing the dog, though kenneling is also used. Dogs living in a domicile with people are subjected to the normal human movement about the home as well as many different social cues provided by various family members. Citing the work of Erdohegyi et al. (2007), Lit et al. (2011) stated a "[d]ogs' biases for utilizing human movements or social cues impair decision-making and reasoning abilities," which indicates that this could impact performance in the field. Meanwhile, dogs living in kennels should be exposed to auditory stimulation such as classical music as it may reduce stress (Kogan et al. 2012). Udell et al. (2008b) observed that "[h]umans control access to many reinforcers, thereby making interaction with humans essential. This likely results in dogs spending a greater proportion of their time watching humans and responding to their behavior than in species not domiciled with humans." Alternatively, Hare et al. (2002) noted in a study evaluating social cognition that when comparing two groups of puppies, one family reared and the other littermate reared, there was no difference in performance.

However, outside the laboratory, opinions seem to differ.

> Prior to the initiation of training, the handler must completely rid himself of the notion that he is dealing with a household pet. A land mine/booby trap detector dog is a working dog and must be treated as such. It is almost universally agreed among professional trainers that the role of household pet and working dog can seldom be combined effectively, and the detector animal, whether still in training or an accomplished performer, *must not be allowed to share the handler's quarters at any time*. It would appear obvious that if an animal receives a large amount of fussing and attention outside the working situation, then his performance in the working context is likely to decline. In other words, best performance will result if praise and attention are made contingent upon good working performance. (Mitchell 1976) (emphasis added)

MARKERS AS REWARDS, REINFORCERS, MOTIVATORS, AND COMMANDS

The nature and personality of most high-energy dogs used for olfaction functions certainly demand the use of a reinforcer (or reward). One thesis study, Stokke (2014), indicated that male dogs prefer Kong® rewards over food, and the opposite was true for females. That work also revealed that preferred rewards may increase false alerts. Vicars et al. (2014) noted that "using positive reinforcement as a training strategy depends largely on its effectiveness, which is a direct function of the stimuli delivered as consequences or rewards." While this study discussed using only consumables, reinforcers used in olfactory training routinely fall into six categories, which are physical, tactile, audible (tone), verbal, visual, and consumable. Each category contains multiple options, presenting the opportunity for selection based upon individual preference determined by the dog, the trainer, or both. By using multiple reinforcer types either individually, in combination, as primary or secondary (conditioned reinforcer or bridge stimulus), or as a marker, the trainer can enhance their effectiveness by substituting one for another at will. This creates a form of generalization on rewards and motivational tools, which can be critical for motivation and in deployment situations where factors such as time, location, and safety can influence the type of reward given.

Research is limited on the use of various working dog rewards or the training techniques that employ different categories of reinforcers (see Table 13.1). Dogs have shown preferences when presented with choice, and this selection may vary over time (Vicars et al. 2014). Allowing a dog to choose an initial reward and then routinely incorporating reinforcer-type changes, or even experimenting with different types or categories of these tools, is good practice as it provides variation, alleviates initial boredom, and sets the foundation for advanced training.

The option of using different types of reinforcers provides operational flexibility as to which reward to use and under what circumstances. The work performed by Meagher and Mason (2012) investigating mink found that "[t]he insights yielded by these data were critically dependent on using a diverse array of stimuli. Indeed, this is the first experiment of its kind to systematically investigate how enrichment affects responses across stimulus types." A complete and thorough exploration using a variety of working dogs could assist in understanding this very important issue. Overall, these various forms of communication with the dog provide a language unlike any other. Whether intended to motivate, reinforce, correct, command, or simply mark an act, each being used in multiple aspects of training is similar to certain words in any language that possibly have more than one meaning. A single communication with a dog only differs by the conditioning associated with its use. The authors of this chapter recommend that a dog be conditioned to receive more than one of the six types (and varieties within the types) of rewards during training or deployment. While mainly for motivation and advanced training, this can also serve as part of a safety protocol. A dog being conditioned to accept a secondary reinforcer is one

TABLE 13.1
Common Primary Motivational Tools Along with Common Couplings

Reinforcer Description	Common Reinforcer Types and Couplings							
	Category							
	Audible	Verbal	Tactile	Physical	Consumable	Visual	Simulate	Marker
Hard tube	s	s	+	**P**	–	s	–	–
Soft tube	s	s	+	P/s	–	s	+	+
Jute toy	s	s	+	P/s	–	s	+	+
Tennis ball	s	s	s	P/s	–	s	+	–
"Good dog"	s	P/s	s	s	–	s	–	+
Arms waving	s	s	–	s	–	P/s	–	+
Yodel	P/s	s	s	s	–	s	–	+
Treat	s	s	s	–	**P**	–	–	–
Whistle	P/s	s	–	s	–	s	–	+
Petting	s	s	P/s	–	–	s	–	+
Chest rub	s	s	P/s	–	–	–	–	+
Yelp	P/s	s	–	s	–	s	–	+
Tone	P/s	s	–	s	–	s	–	+
Food	–	s	s	–	P/s	–	–	–
Clicker	P/s	–	–	–	s	–	–	**P**
Narc bag w/ towel	s	s	s	P/s	–	s	+	+
Dummy throw	s	s	s	P/s	–	s	+	+
Kong ball/throw	s	s	s	P/s	–	s	+	–
Clapping	P/s	s	s	s	–	P/s	–	+
Rolled towel	s	s	s	P/s	–	P/s	+	+

Legend: P = primary reinforcer use, s = secondary reinforcer use, (+) = may be used, (–) = generally no or limited use.

way this can be accomplished. Having this availability to reinforce behavior with different rewards depending on the situation would be paramount in any best practice, as it allows a handler to adapt to current events in the field. An example might be a dog alert on a busy highway. The standard reward for that dog may be a large rubber Kong, which bounces around in extreme capricious movement, but circumstances surrounding the location of where the reward will be presented prevent a bouncing ball on the roadway full of vehicles even if the dog is on lead. Instead, the handler could reward with a verbal, visual, tactile, consumable, or audible reward without fear of the dog running into harm's way.

Porritt et al. (2015) investigated an issue plaguing working dog trainers and handlers worldwide, which involves the meme of some unknown dog trainer: "Train like you work and work like you train." Specifically, the concern noted was decreased performance from target-rich environments to target-free environments for working dogs. Moving from one area to another constantly sniffing, while not appearing difficult to the casual onlooker, is extremely taxing for a dog. During continued sweeps, a dog can grow tired and become bored if not able to occasionally experience a bit of motivation by finding odor and receiving positive reinforcement. One obvious solution mentioned was placement of target odor for the purpose of detection by a *scent detecting dog* (SDD), which would create the scenario where a dog alert would allow for reinforcement, thereby motivating the dog to continue working. The problem generated was the placement of *hides* could create a "logistically difficult, dangerous, or impractical" situation. The solution chosen for investigation involved training dogs to detect noncontraband target stimuli, which eliminated the problems while providing easy placement of alternative training aids to assist in motivating the dog for continued work and effectiveness.

> Our findings have consequences for many contexts in which scent detecting dogs are employed. Without the opportunity to find rewarded targets in repetitive search environments, scent detecting dogs will become ineffective after a short period, and this performance decrement is hard to reverse. Meanwhile, a co-trained, non-contraband odour, secreted in a dog's working environment and contingently reinforced upon being found, acts to maintain performance in finding contraband target odours that would be rarely encountered during a dog's working life.

As discussed, working dogs need to be motivated to continue working, sometimes for extended periods, and one way to do this is to create target-rich environments for the dog to alert and receive a reinforcer. Additionally, the fact that actual training materials and training aids can create extreme difficulties (discussed in Chapter 18) is an issue. Extensive research and discussion is currently underway for simulate, pseudo, nonvolatile, nonhazardous training odors and aids, and it seems a comparison of strategy might be inevitable and worthwhile. Endeavoring to offer a comparison of divergent strategies between an innocuous vs. pseudo vs. simulate odors would present thought that Porritt et al. (2015) have a compelling idea, which is presumably simple, possibly solves a problem, and could be easily implemented by trainers.

However simple, using a co-trained, noncontraband odor secreted in a dog's working environment and contingently reinforced upon being found is not without difficulties. The first issue could present a large obstacle for implementation. When training a dog to find an illegal drug, the dog should locate only illegal substance odor. A potential concern that will need to be addressed is that adding an odor of a legal substance for the dog to locate, strictly for motivational purposes, undermines the foundation of a legal system. A dog trained to locate a legal substance and odor could easily alert on the presence of that motivating odor in deployment. This act alone would make it very difficult for any officer to receive a search warrant based on a dog alert from an animal trained to find grandmother's favorite cake ingredient, especially considering it could be easily argued to be a violation of the U.S. Constitution. This specific issue has been discussed for decades. A quick look may reveal some discussion currently ongoing concerning drug dogs alerting (or not) to different legal substances and odors such as methyl benzoate and others commonly found in many everyday items including foam, plastic, makeup, deodorant, and snapdragon flowers (Cerreta and Furton 2015; Furton et al. 2015).

The length of time a dog can work without external motivation is dependent upon many factors. Trainers routinely train dogs to increase the working time they can endure. Each aspect of training can alter working time. Condition of the dog such as overall physical fitness, boredom, ailments, etc., can impact this work time. Training aids have much to do with work time as well. The placement location, soak time (time needed to saturate hide location with odor produced from the source material), search time, number of hides placed, sequencing of the hides placed, number of times a day hides are placed, reinforcer schedule, etc. all play a role in the work rate experienced. Agencies and companies employ handlers who work their dogs for extended periods and use very few training aid placements. The dog, the handler, the methods used to train the dog, the methods used by the handler, the target placement scheme utilized for any given dog, the environment, ambient conditions, etc. all play a critical role in extending work time.

One thing is clear, however, and that is the length of time a dog can work can be increased over time with proper training. Key elements to being a good handler are knowing when the dog should be motivated, testing to see if it is working, or querying other related issues to ensure effectiveness. One extremely oversimplified cardinal rule taught to every handler is *trust your dog*. However, this needs a slight adjustment to more closely address the responsibility. Every handler should learn to *trust and verify your dog*. While the handler can have a tremendous impact on the issue of the dog working for extended periods of time, little research has focused on this issue.

VISUAL MOTIVATION

A dog readily accepts and interprets communication from humans, and a myriad of studies have advised us that dogs read our nonverbal visual cues very well. Additionally, it is well known that dogs have used visual acuity to recognize one item from another (McKinley and Young 2003), even by name. It is for this reason that visual communication in the form of command, correction, and motivation is possible and can be very effective in dog training. Provided that they can be seen, simple non-audible actions can send a well-received message as people visually demonstrate excitement, frustration, fear, or any other emotion visually, which the dog can see and interpret. This can be exampled in dog training by simple hand signals to issue commands, wild flailing arm actions to imitate excitement, or simple fast-paced movement of the hands or legs to elicit a general sense of approval.

VERBAL AND AUDIBLE PRAISE AND ENCOURAGEMENT

Audible communication is any sound or word uttered to the dog and is the most prevalent communication method used in training and handling. It could be recognized as a command, distraction, correction, reward, motivator, encourager, or simple attention gatherer. When discussing this type of communication, it is generally divided into two subgroups: tone and verbal. It is worth noting that verbal is the single most used communication and requires segregation from tone. Mitchell and Edmonson (1999) found that "people talk to dogs repetitively during play (and in other contexts) to get their attention and otherwise exert control," which is often exacerbated in detection dog training and deployment. It has often been said that it "may not be what you said but rather how you said it" that makes a difference. This is especially true in dog training, as nuance is more critical than many realize.

While the dog is becoming comfortable in the processes of investigating odor, locating the reward, and returning to the trainer, it is acceptable to add needed communication by selectively adding certain word associations that will become an integral part of the daily working life. Verbal communication is the most common audible method used with a dog; some trainers and handlers talk to the dog incessantly, and unfortunately, overcommunicating with the dog is common among many trainers and handlers. This can desensitize the dog to any communication from that person and cease being an effective tool for communication. This communication element should be implemented sparingly to eliminate overuse as it can easily create a dog dependent on human direction. Words used should be limited in length to single or double syllables. Verbal commands should only be used when absolutely necessary for an act to be accomplished.

Tone communication is a less popular form of communication with the dog. This type of expression can be a highly effective tool depending on delivery, with inflection and tone alone controlling either the correct or incorrect message. Praise, encouragement, and motivation are crucial to the dog and can come in many forms. Most green dogs require substantial motivation, which eases the learning process and association. Audible reinforcers can be used when the dog is doing something well and preferably when not looking at the trainer or handler. Any audible motivator should be delivered in high octave with great excitement, which can be difficult to master, especially for men.

Any communication marker implementation should be synchronized with assessment to ensure that the dog somewhat comprehends or associates the use of the marker prior to additional markers being added. Motivation markers should end with a high pitch syllable that is excitedly amplified. Conversely, commands or directives should be monotone lower pitch intonations exuding authority and demanding compliance. Volume when using a motivator adds excitement or compliance when adding range to a command. Increasing range requires proficiency at shorter distances before introducing greater separation from the handler. As range increases, so should volume to ensure audibility by the dog.

An example of a verbal encouragement marker might be *good boy* (Most [1954] 2014) offered in high octave voice immediately upon grab bite *mouth on* engagement. To increase the value of this reinforcement, adding another simultaneous audible marker could be crucial as these rest as clues of approval, which motivate the dog. After the dog has complete understanding of the term and acceptance across all uses of the word or tone, a reduction in use of the word should take place. Ensuring limited use of this single term adds value of the marker for the dog. Overuse could desensitize the dog to use or create complacency. Also by reducing the use, the dog can begin to generalize the use as determined by context. Braem and Mills (2010) noted that a dog can generalize a command that is already known easier than a new command. The same is true of any communication issued to the dog. The key aspect of verbal (and all) communication is delivery.

Any communication with the dog should be limited to that which is essential and especially any verbal dialog must be used sparingly. Other audible (tonal) sounds can be used as well. Yodel, whistle, yelp, and clap are common audibles. These can be implemented just as any other communication. While not as popular as they once were, some disciplines still use them very effectively. Some audible tones cannot be heard by a human but can be successfully used with a dog.

FOOD REWARDS

Food is obviously a motivation for dogs. As noted by Feuerbacher and Wynne (2012), "[t]he greater efficacy of food as a reinforcer parallels the evolutionary origins of dogs as scavengers of human refuse [citing Coppinger and Coppinger 2001] and supports the use of food as a reinforcer for training." Relatively few working detection dog programs use food as the primary reward, though at least one governmental agency continues the practice (Strobel et al. 2001). One aspect of using food is that it mandates daily training to ensure that required training and nutrition are received by the dog. This method of reward also entices limited movement of the dog once an alert is declared, and thus, it compels the dog to remain stationary to receive the reward. However, even with food reward training methods, trainers are finally beginning to understand the importance of allowing the dog to operate independently from the person. In such cases where a dog would alert at some distance from the handler, the handler will sound a whistle to indicate to the dog it is acceptable to return to the handler for the food reward.

TACTILE MOTIVATION AND SUPPORT

Tactile rewards, just as other types of reinforcers, can be excellent motivators. The method in which the dog is approached to engage in contact can impact the delivery of the reinforcer (Vas et al. 2005), which is a sign of the confidence, or lack thereof, currently displayed by the dog. Some dogs seem to prefer physical engagement over verbal encouragement (Feuerbacher and Wynne 2012). Tactile reinforcers make very good secondary rewards for some dogs. "Stroking and patting the dogs were the most frequently used rewards," which were used in one investigation by Haverbeke et al. (2008). As a practical matter, the use of tactile motivation can be employed in most aspects of olfaction training. Specifically, this method of reinforcement offers a calming effect upon the dog, which can assist the dog in refocusing effort. Although it can be used as a primary reinforcer, use as a supporting action (secondary reinforcer) is more common. For these reasons, tactile reinforcement plays a critical role in detection dog training.

Toys and Other Physical Reinforcers

For any person ever having owned a dog, remembering their friend accompanied by a favorite toy is a great memory. Most rewards in use today are physical objects. A piece of polymerizing vinyl chloride (PVC) pipe, jute toy, narc bag (which is a duck cloth bag with Velcro closures at one end and commonly filled with a soft material such as a hand towel), tennis ball, Kong, or a multitude of other items all serve well as reinforcers. To a dog, texture matters in a physical reward. This is exampled by the use of PVC pipe used as a reward for a dog. One dog may accept this hard dense object, while another may prefer something less firm such as a narc bag with a towel inside. Lore has it that hard items teach a dog to have a *hard mouth*, while conversely, a narc bag teaches a *soft mouth*, which generally only matters in the hunting world when retrieving downed prey. However, this may actually be a result of the breed typical motor patterns (or faults) specifically dealing with a hypertrophied kill-bite in a foraging pattern.

Using different types, styles, shapes, sizes, materials, and colors of reinforcers during training is important. The main goal of this is to create an array of interesting motivators for the dog, which help eliminate boredom. When a dog is interested, it is motivated to perform. Having the flexibility of using different toys (or other reinforcers) assists the trainer in maintaining dog motivation. An additional flexibility associated with the use of multiple rewards is that some items may be used as odor carriers, while an identical twin, such as an identical PVC pipe, will be used as a distractor odor source to ensure that the dog will not alert to clean PVC pipe. Using this concept with reinforcers removes problems later in training by introducing discrimination in an intuitive way and greatly reducing the need for dedicated distractor or extinction training.

Commands and Obedience

Adding obedience is mandatory, although this is where a dog may experience some difficulty. Many trainers immediately begin obedience as the very first training process, sometimes utilizing compulsion training. Waiting as long as possible to add this guidance communication is critical for it allows the dog to first associate the act of hunting for odor independently while being extremely motivated. By adding commands, actions will now be dictated to the dog, which can induce stress. If added too soon, this can actually cause a dog to be removed from training. The trainer sometimes attempts absolute control through obedience when very little is actually needed. The trainer must remember to be resolute in training obedience communication while being somewhat forgiving in initial implementation. This allows the dog to remain motivated in investigating odor. If the command is worth giving, it is worth enforcing and reinforcing. However, one major problem is the overuse of commands and even more overuse of enforcement. There should be a balance that can only be achieved if both are performed sparingly.

There are many ways to train obedience commands, some of which work well. Although not the preferred method, one example of a marker sometimes used in detector training today is the clicker (generally, Cornu et al. 2011), which is not highly accepted in detection dog training. Commands should be added once the dog demonstrates the action as part of conditioning and odor recognition training. One effective method is to look for key times when the dog is already demonstrating the desired action and begin a conditioning and association of that action with the language desired. By using this predisposed act to add association of verbal communication, the dog will readily accept within very few repetitions. Other commands can be added in similar fashion as needed. Commands should be firm, guttural utterances, while encouragers, motivators, and reinforcers should be markers of excitement, which mandates highly variable octave emissions, which sometimes takes significant effort to master, particularly for men. Some people unfamiliar with detection dogs believe that the dog is taught commands in a foreign language to prohibit another person, not understanding the language taught, from being able to control the dog. The reality is that many dogs are taught the trainer's native language, and when the dog is sold, it already understands that language so the new handler adapts to the dog. Typical commands used for the dog are to guide the dog to perform a certain action. Most common detection dog commands are sit, down, stay, heel, here, leave it, no, and check, or some version thereof. Most are self-explanatory except for the *no* command, which is the most overused command today. Many use this term very loosely while the opposite should be true. The *no* command should be used only under extreme circumstances when it is imperative that the dog must absolutely stop whatever action is currently underway. An example would be a dog placing itself directly in harm's way.

Obedience commands should be trained one at a time until proficiency has been attained. Force or compulsion should not be used as waiting for the dog to exhibit the action demonstrating the desired behavior is favorable. Any command action (e.g., sit, down, stay, here, heel, etc.) can be further reinforced by adding secondary markers such as verbalizing praise, such as "Sit...Good boy." Additional secondary rewards could include a pat on the head, rubbing an ear, patting a chest, etc. This creates a generalization of command structure and approval, which is beneficial.

An example of a needed command might be instruction to release a reinforcer held in the dog's mouth. If the dog is prone to relinquish the toy, a trainer could issue the desired release command followed by praise once the dog releases. However, if the dog exhibits any refusal to relinquishing a toy, an easy way to teach this action is to employ the use of opposites. The dog possesses the toy (prey) and begins to shake the item violently, which mimics a kill. With the toy representing the prey, it therefore exhibits traits of escape such as movement. The trainer can mimic this radical movement by placing hands firmly on the toy and gently beginning a side-to-side movement, which the dog will enjoy countering. This should be supported with the praise marker, "good boy." After a couple of seconds, all movement should be immediately ceased until the reinforcer is being held absolutely still with neutral pressure. Since the dog has already demonstrated refusal, this can again be expected.

The trainer should now enact the single most critical portion of this exercise of negating any attempt by the dog to maintain possession by ensuing in a game of tug of war. The trainer's role is to not permit the dog to feel pressure of the toy in its mouth during this time. If the dog pulls or pushes, the trainer should immediately follow the action to neutralize any force felt by the dog. In other words, do not fight the dog for the toy. Rather, follow the toy so that the dog does not feel the tug in the mouth, so that the game is no longer present. The elimination of pressures calms the dog and immediately upon seeing this reaction, a release command, such as *mine*, should be issued until such time as the toy is released. Upon release, offer exuberant verbal and tactile reinforcers in support. It should be noted that many handlers use extreme play with a dog in which they grab the toy and swing the dog off the ground by a rolled towel. This action is more for the benefit of the handler than the dog and absolutely should not be allowed due to the possibility of inadvertently hurting the dog.

MOTIVATION DELIVERY TIMING, CONDITIONING, AND SCHEDULES

Maintaining motivation is vital in detection dog training and use. Delivery and timing is critical when communicating any type of message to a dog, especially motivation. The effectiveness of the reward is based upon when the delivery of the reinforcer takes place. If the timing is correct, training can progress quickly. Alternatively, poor use of timing can produce extreme delays in the training or even cause setbacks substantial enough to necessitate starting over. If delivery is too early, the dog may be distracted, be confused, or not understand why the delivery was made, and conversely, if too late, the dog may not recognize it as associative of the action for which it was delivered. The critical factor in using the classical conditioning theory (Pavlov) is dictated by one of three conditioning scenarios, which are simultaneous, delayed, and trace conditioning. Of these, simultaneous conditioning is least effective, and delayed conditioning is most effective as "the conditioned stimulus overlaps in time the unconditioned stimulus" (MacLean et al. 1955; see also Chapter 10 herein).

The next area of importance is the delivery schedule of the reinforcer (generally Hilliard 2003). One process used to deliver the reward is a continuous schedule. Continuous or constant ratio (CR) 1:1 schedule implies that a reinforcer will be delivered for each and every correct alert (1 reinforcer: 1 alert) and some trainers use only this strategy. Another option is the fixed ratio (FR) schedule, which implies an FR of reinforcement for a specific number of alerts. An example might be 1 reinforcer delivered for each 3 correct alerts, or a 1:3 ratio. This also is common practice in training. Yet another option is a variable ratio (VR) schedule, which employs numerous different FR schedules that can be changed periodically. VR schedule of delivery is when the reinforcer is delivered on a varying rate of correct alerts. Using this schedule permits a moving target of reinforcer delivery where 1 reward is being delivered for each 1 alert (equating to a continuous schedule) in one series, 1 reward is being delivered for each 3 alerts (equating to an FR schedule of 1:3) in another series, and 1 reward is being delivered for each 4 alerts (equating to an FR schedule of 1:4) in yet another series. In other words, the delivery can be altered to any number of reinforcers for any number of correct alerts for any series of events at any time as permitted by the trainer in an effort to respond to the needs of the dog at a particular point in time. Some research has investigated reinforcer delivery (see Chapter 10 herein).

The criteria for selecting the reinforcement delivery schedule (hence frequency) should take into account the actions of the dog, the handler, and the team, as well as the conditions under which the team is working. An example might be an explosives detection dog going through initial basic training and receiving rewards utilizing a continuous schedule. The dog advances in training using an FR schedule and is now being deployed in the field. As the team progresses in ability, a VR schedule should be implemented and maintained in deployment. In certain conditions while on deployment, a bomb dog would not be rewarded in typical fashion for fear of exacerbating circumstances in the environment. Conditions can change seldom or rapidly, even minute by minute, and adapting to the dynamic circumstances of daily operations is paramount; thus, these delivery schedules are guidelines that must maintain some flexibility. However, to accept this type of adaptation, a dog must be properly conditioned.

Initial training should employ a continuous schedule (1:1) to establish effective conditioning and association. As the team develops, ratios can and should change to an FR, which can be altered from time to time. As the team continues improving, handlers and trainers should use a much more flexible VR schedule, which can be extremely capricious at times, thus enabling a knowledgeable handler capable of reading the behavior of the dog to react based upon circumstances in the field. Hilliard (2003) noted that

> Variable reward schedules also encourage persistence in the face of extinction. That is, variable schedules teach the dog to be persistent and stubborn in trying to obtain its reward through instrumental behaviour, even when the reward rate is low. Many studies have shown that variable reward schedules produce more persistent conditioned behaviour than fixed schedules. A simple explanation of the variable reinforcement phenomenon is this: when the dog never knows how many times (or how long) it will be required to perform before being rewarded, it 'loses track' of how many or how long and concentrates on performing persistently, convinced that if it tries hard enough it will eventually get the reward. This is highly desirable behaviour in a detector dog.

Best practice should include the use of a CR schedule during basic training, adjusting to an FR schedule for advanced training as consistency increases, and then possibly to a capricious VR delivery schedule for an experienced team as a VR schedule in the field motivates for search endeavors (Fjellanger et al. 2002). Should a problem be discovered at any time, training should revert to a continuous (1:1) ratio, which can assist in correcting problems. If doing so, it must be remembered that "the dog is often being trained to alert to a scent associated with the item rather than the item itself" (Furton et al. 2002), and since odor is not readily visible, reading the dog's behavior accurately is of extreme importance prior to delivering a reward.

Hunting and Liking Odor as the Reinforcer for Detection Dogs

Obviously, the primary goal as a trainer should be to condition the dog to focus on the act of locating target odor as everything else becomes moot should the dog not possess this ability. However, training programs often begin with the most boring and tedious aspects for the dog such as obedience. Typically, after some time, odor recognition training begins as an immediately chained conditioning pattern consisting of odor exposure, recognition, response, and reinforcement. The result is a dog being challenged to remain interested while attempting this process long before it can realize the internal motivation and enjoyment associated with performing the exciting part of training exercises.

Rarely discussed is the conditioning necessary to assist the dog in realizing odor, or more correctly stated, the act of hunting odor, is more important and enjoyable than the reinforcer offered when finding odor. When employing this type of training, the acquisition of target odor can become the reward to the act of hunting, wanting, and locating odor. In this light, a properly trained dog will readily leave a typical reinforcer behind in search of odor which has become a higher probability intrinsic motivation (Premack 1959). As stated by Killeen (2014), "[w]hen the instrumental action becomes habitual, it may come to be preferred over the contingent behavior." The dog may use a reinforcer as a release signal, but the true desire is the act of hunting odor. An experienced dog trained in this method will often voluntarily leave behind a reinforcer to again search for odor. This type of training decreases the distractor and extinction training as it focuses the dog on the only constant in the entire training process, which is the target odor.

Another way of looking at this is the dog desires the hunting of odor, effectively wanting the odor more than it desires the reinforcer (Berridge and Robinson 1998; Berridge 2004; Berridge et al. 2009). A properly trained canine can readily search for odor, without the need of a typical reinforcer as commonly used. As discussed previously in Porritt et al. (2015), the goal was to entice the dog to work longer periods without the need of constantly placing aids to serve as a method of the dog receiving a reinforcer. This trained behavior can be one of several methods used to motivate the dog and conditioning it to work for extended periods. Some neurological research argues that rewards for dogs being trained to detect odor might best be kept to items, such as food, that have an odor stimulus so that the dog is encouraged to resume work by using the same part of its neurological system (Berridge and Robinson 1998; Berridge 2004; Berridge et al. 2009), hence the foraging model.

Training on the use of multiple rewards facilitates this training method. While conditioning the dog to use multiple rewards, it is common to have reinforcers scattered about in a training venue within easy view of the dog. As the dog continues searching for odor and ignoring the visible reinforcement items scattered about, the dog willfully steps over and around these tools. While it is not difficult to train the dog, it is not necessarily one aspect of training that produces this result but rather a series of training actions. The one key element in this training is starting with a dog that will display independence.

Under some conditions, preexposure to two similar events appears to increase the ease with which they can be discriminated. The effect has typically been demonstrated in experiments that make use of conditioning procedures and in which the critical events are used as conditioned stimuli (CSs). (Blair et al. 2003)

Ultimately, this is a complex mixture of conditioning, motivation, desire, wanting, liking, discrimination, extinction, and many other aspects of detection training or work.

PREEXPOSURE

Preexposure is the act of exposing the dog to a desired target odor prior to initial discrimination training. This is not to be confused with prescenting, which has a slightly different context and meaning. Prescenting is defined by Scientific Working Group on Dog and Orthogonal detector Guidelines (SWGDOG) (SC1) as "[a] sample target odor that is presented to the dog prior to deployment. The dog's objective is to match the prescented odor to the target odor. Operational use: This is commonly used in tracking/trailing and/or scent discrimination line ups." Prescenting as described by SWGDOG is used where a trained dog is exposed to target odor, possibly via a scent item left at the scene of a crime, prior to initiating a track, trail, or scent identification (ID) process. Prescenting has been used for many years and continues today in the disciplines mentioned. While exceedingly rare, it has been used in disciplines such as dogs trained for narcotics or cadaver work.

Conversely, preexposure is the act of exposing an untrained dog to target odor prior to training. This can be a powerful tool in training detection dogs and unfortunately is not in wide use today. In doing so, care should be taken to prevent contact between the dog or the trainer and the target odor source due to safety concerns.

Illuminated as one of the most *laborious* (Hall et al. 2014) portions of the training process, *initial odor acquisition* can present challenges. While Hall et al. used preexposure as part of conditioning as well as an exposure process to accomplish the work, preexposure can be incorporated in almost all training functions. Regardless of methodology, a relatively short amount of time is necessary to produce positive results. In the case of Hall et al., they used delayed conditioning to perform only six trials a day for 5 days. The findings speak volumes for the effectiveness.

> Five of the eight dogs in the Pavlovian-relevant group alerted to the target odorant correctly on more trials across the three days of training than did any of the 24 dogs in the remaining three groups. The Pavlovian-relevant group had a median of 70% correct on the first training session, whereas no other group exceeded 52%. By the end of three training sessions, the Pavlovian-relevant group's median was 93% correct, whereas the remaining groups' medians ranged from 53% to 68% correct…. No other group showed systematic differences from the control group.

A similar adaptation to the delayed conditioning can be accomplished by saturating a reward or reinforcer with odor to be used in training. Depending on the specific target odor and other environmental conditions, necessary saturation time can range from minutes to weeks as sizeable odor amounts must be available for acquisition by the dog during initial training. However, regardless of specific methodology employed to exercise preexposure, the effect can be sizeable by reducing training time and increasing effectiveness.

PRECONDITIONING AND INITIAL ODOR RECOGNITION TRAINING

Preconditioning is the act of physically conditioning the dog to prepare it for training that it is about to undergo. Preconditioning is an element of canine performance seldom discussed or used and falls in line with final stages of acclimation. There are two main aspects to preconditioning: physical and mental. While preconditioning prior to initiating a training regimen is rare, it sets the tone for all training that follows. As an example of the effectiveness, Altom et al. (2003) concluded that "[p]hysical conditioning of canine athletes prevented a reduction in olfactory acuity following one hour of treadmill exercise." Training is an extremely taxing regimen of physical and mental dexterity requiring exacting precision at times. Ensuring the dog's overall wellness prior to starting a training program is paramount to success as performance can be impacted. The harder the dog has to work physically, the higher the body temperature will go, which could impact overall detection performance. A dog in peak condition will be less stressed, will be more consistent in action, and will generally perform better. A dog that is foggy in thought or has a difficult time adapting to the mental aspect of training will struggle. A well-conditioned dog that is quick to adapt to changing scenarios will learn faster and be more consistent.

Trainers often argue that a dog has limited or restricted time they can work before needing a rest and often use 15–30 min as a rule. The acceptance of this self-imposed duty cycle lore is one not befitting the working dog and more likely generated as a result of work opportunities than capability. As examples, a police dog in a small town may have very little work availability, whereas a similar dog working a major border checkpoint could have a comparatively high work availability load. According to Gazit and Terkel (2003b), the lore may have some validity. However, these authors also say that a dog can be conditioned to remove such limitations when they suggested, "it is both possible and essential to properly train the dogs in order to achieve optimum adjustment to working under extreme physical conditions." A properly trained dog can investigate successfully for extended periods of time, often longer than a handler is willing or sometimes capable of working before needing to rest.

Overall performance is dependent upon the ability of the dog to work efficiently and effectively in the environment in which it is deployed. Thus, it is the increased ability to adapt to the conditions through preconditioning and training that will benefit detection. For this reason, training should actually begin with both physical and mental conditioning. A simple program of building the physical and mental acuity of the dog lays the proper foundation for the complex training regimen to follow and assists the dog in adapting and maintaining the interest critical for a detection dog.

Respiratory Rate and Cardiovascular Fitness

Detection work requires superior health, excellent cardiovascular conditioning, and overall physical fitness. Trainers, handlers, doctors, and scientists often refer to their dogs as *canine athletes* (Zink and Schlehr 1997; Wendelburg 1998; Gillette 1999; Toll and Reynolds 2000; Steiss 2002; Altom et al. 2003), yet it is rare for a training program to incorporate a regimen to increase and maintain the peak physical condition of the dog. After acclimation, the first step in the training of a detection dog is to make certain that the dog is of superior health and physically fit as possible.

Sniffing in detection work is a strenuous task that requires relatively stable respiratory rate. High respiratory rate can create difficulties and loss of effectiveness, so "[c]onditioning is used to maintain the dog's metabolism so that it can handle the ongoing activity levels and prepare the dog for potential metabolic extremes" (Gillette 1999). Economic and practical considerations in the deployment of detection dogs require that their working abilities be weighed against limitations of restricted duty cycles and training time and combined with other factors such as dog and handler distress (Agapiou et al. 2015).

Cardiovascular conditioning is critical to establishing the proper physiological condition necessary for highly reliable detection work. Altom et al. (2003) found that "utilization of a moderate physical conditioning program can assist canine athletes in maintaining olfactory acuity during periods of intense exercise." Huntingford et al. (2014) suggest "that hunting dogs behave physiologically more like endurance dogs rather than like sprinting Greyhounds or agility dogs …." Gillette (1999) argues:

> The trained and conditioned canine athlete or working dog's metabolism performs at a different level than the pet dog. Some variation can be related to the breed of the dog, but a healthy, conditioned athletic dog can exhibit metabolic variants that have the potential to confuse the general practitioner or anyone not accustomed to these peculiarities.

Thus, those training and working with detection dogs must become familiar with the physiological parameters and extremes to which the work will sometimes push them.

In concept, a conditioning program is easily devised by using routines similar to those of professional athletes (Zink and Van Dyke 2013). After completing a veterinary checkup and consulting and discussing any potential problems with the veterinarian, the safest way to implement a program is to establish a baseline for current conditioning. This baseline will serve as measurement criteria by which all future evaluations will be compared. Design of the program should be with assistance from a canine sports medicine or rehabilitation specialist or possibly a trainer with significant experience in a similar regimen. The program should be identical in frequency, rest periods, time of day, duration, and intensity. A warm-up and cool-down period should be included just as a professional athlete would experience. The program should start slow and remain constant until a dog has acclimated to the base program. Monitoring should begin even during the first workout to establish baseline making certain to document the findings and key observations. Demonstrating acclimation to the workout allows increased difficulty to be added one element at a time and allows the dog to adapt to the increased performance requirement. Documenting the performance changes and comparing to previous results allow for acclimation before the next change. Decline in demonstrated ability would mandate reduction of difficulty to a point of stabilization and consultation with a veterinarian.

An excellent method of preconditioning the dog is swimming. This is something to which most dogs have little exposure. Implementing an initial swimming regimen will work the dog not only physically but mentally as well. Simply have the dog swim in a pond, pool, lake, or virtually any body of water. Once the dog is swimming, the trainer should slowly begin to walk around the edge of the body of water. The dog will use mind and body in an attempt to follow the trainer and, by doing so, will be both mentally and physically challenged; this will prepare the dog well for future training.

Nutrition

Another vital element in conditioning is nutrition, which should be discussed with a veterinarian. Some working dogs eat once a day as in the study by Lefebvre et al. (2008), while many trainers and veterinarians would recommend twice daily. Some findings indicate feeding in the morning as this improves cognitive performance (Miller and Bender 2012). Actual deployment scenarios may present issues that can cause difficulty, such as gastric torsion or bloat (USDA 2012). Thus, a feeding regimen must consider typical working schedules and routines. Regardless of the frequency, feeding should be immediately followed by a rest period of at least 2 h for initial digestion to begin, thereby reducing the possibility of negative health effects.

Nutritional requirements are greater in all working dogs than pets. Most nutrition research has been performed by commercial producers of dog food, resulting in somewhat limited data being available from other sources. Interestingly, however, a nutritional study by Angle et al. (2014), which investigated detection of source odor in the 20–100 mg range, concluded that "[f]rom a practical point of view, the dogs' detection thresholds being this low makes the effects of diet insignificant unless the scent capabilities need to be in the low milligram quantities." Alternatively, Altom et al. (2003) found that "data derived from this study suggest that high levels of saturated fat can further reduce the odorant-detecting capabilities of poorly conditioned canines." In choosing nutrition for the dog, sources for protein, fat, and fiber are critical along with additives that can further support the dietary needs of the canine. Some dogs have allergies, which can affect olfaction, and attention should be given to excessive scratching, ear infections, or other medical issues that may be caused by certain foods. A dog may need supplementation of the normal diet to eliminate or prevent problems associated with diet as advised by a veterinarian.

Monitoring Technique

As the dog works through the preconditioning routine, monitoring during the event is crucial. Goldberg et al. (1981) examined panting due to heat and exercise, and found that as a dog's exertion increases, the internal method of evaporative cooling changes. A dog will start by first inhaling and exhaling through the nose. In the next stage, the dog will begin inhaling through the nose and exhaling through the nose and mouth. Finally, the dog will adjust yet again to inhale through the nose and mouth and exhale through the nose and mouth. Goldberg et al. went on to say that "[p]anting is the major avenue of evaporative cooling in dogs exposed to heat and/or exercise." Since the mouth and tongue are the most prevalent aspects visible during this monitoring, checking a dog's mouth and tongue is one way to monitor in the field and during training.

The various stages seen in dogs are mouth closed; mouth open; and tongue retracted, flaccid, slightly spatulated, slightly extended, fully spatulated, fully extended, pulsing, curled, and rolled, although not necessarily in that order. Obviously varying degrees of each position are possible as are combinations of the conditions. The way each dog exhibits exertion is different, and the way the tongue will demonstrate these positions will change accordingly. Generally, as exertion increases, the mouth will begin to open, and the tongue will extend and begin to spatulate. An absolute stopping point for any novice dog is when tongue spatulation is evident. Until the trainer recognizes and understands all the stages of exertion and how to interpret the meaning for each dog worked, this should be a stopping point.

A regimen may be increased in difficulty by adjusting frequency, duration, intensity, and complexity while making certain to adjust one single element of the routine at a time and allow for acclimation before making any other adjustments. As physical fitness improves, overall conditioning will be demonstrated in muscle tone, time to exertion, recovery time, etc. Over time, the dog will have increased cardiovascular fitness as well as overall physical and mental capabilities, which will enhance olfactory performance.

TRAVEL AND TRANSPORTATION

Although seldom considered, travel is an integral part of daily life for a working dog and is an especially powerful stressor for dogs (Meunier 2006). While some dogs are natural travelers, not all dogs travel well and may exhibit signs of nausea such as bile discharge, vomiting, confusion, stress, panting, anxiety, and other reactions. These conditions demand recovery time and could include removal from service or reduced effectiveness. Travel training is vital to detection to prevent such episodes (Slabbert and Odendaal 1999).

Travel training can begin by teaching the dog to enter a vehicle, which many dogs will readily perform and couple this with other positive aspects of training. Once in, the vehicle should be moved a short distance and stopped. After removing the dog from the vehicle, the trainer should immediately begin an activity such as the conditioning regimen. This general type of acclimation makes the routine fun and enjoyable for the dog. Care should be demonstrated by making certain to maintain positive outcomes while increasing distances. Incrementally increasing the length of the trips allows the dog to adapt to the moving vehicle over time with no negative consequences, which could set back training. Increasing airflow over the dog can also help eliminate potential nausea or other discomfort and can decrease travel acclimation time. Prohibiting trips that could induce negative effects such as a winding road is critical in all stages of this training.

For travel, a working dog needs to be crated. When the dog is placed in a crate, the temperature inside the crate should be watched for 10–15 min as temperatures can rise significantly, causing a dog to stress and become sick. As travel training progresses, it can be incorporated into environmental soundness conditioning by visiting new and different locations as a confidence builder. Exposing the dog to unusual or unique surroundings will further improve in desire and motivation and will improve travel.

TRAINING FOR RELIABILITY

Training a dog is not difficult, but training a scent discrimination canine team requiring reliability beyond reproach for day-in, day-out deployment requires a very special dog that can be almost impossible to handle on the best of days. Dogs are chosen for olfactory work for three basic reasons, including the genetic ability to detect odor, the ability to follow that odor to source, and lastly, ease of training. Most training is a simple, straightforward process of conditioning behavior, though as Starling et al. (2013) state, "[a]nimal training relies heavily on an understanding of species-specific behaviour as it integrates with operant conditioning principles." While operant conditioning is attributed to Skinner, it seems to have been foreshadowed decades earlier.

> Colonel Konrad Most, a police commissioner at the Royal Prussian Police Headquarters, anticipated many of Skinner's key concepts in his book, Training Dogs (Most 1954). A pioneer in animal training, Most showed an understanding of the key elements of operant conditioning including primary and secondary reinforcement, extinction, shaping, fading, chaining, and negative conditioning (punishment). (Burch and Pickel 1990)

Any discussion of compulsion training can send chills through people due to the varying definitions imposed. Eliminating compulsion and permitting a dog to gently find its own way using cognitive and olfaction ability allow training to come more naturally to the dog. As pointed out during their investigation, Haverbeke et al. (2008) noted that "low performance dogs received more aversive stimuli than high-performance dogs." Dogs easily discern the difference between a happy and an angry face (Muller et al. 2015), and thus, a trainer should always approach the event with enjoyment because "the use of stimulating working methods during training… would exploit the natural instincts of dogs" (Tataruca 2011). This allows the dog to achieve the goals of a human handler by capitalizing on instinctive behaviors within the dog.

We still have little understanding of the true limits of canine olfaction; however, permitting the animal to investigate independently has been demonstrated to produce a highly reliable detection dog. In fact, Steen et al. (1996) argued that a dog can even detect odor with mouth open running at full speed as "dogs can divert the stream of air through nose or mouth or both according to the needs of the moment. They can switch from air searching with a continuous airstream inward through the nose to a 200 breaths min^{-1} sniffing within a second." Interestingly though, a thesis by Parnafes-Gazit (2005) found "an inverse ratio between rate of panting and efficiency of the dog's olfactory work, with increase panting resulting in significant decrease in explosives detection. The decline in efficiency was also expressed in longer duration of search period."

As training progresses, the dog should intrinsically react to the task by hunting for odor as a preoccupation just as it is genetically guided to do. This would allow the dog to focus less on behaviors that generate undesirable results for the handler. Removal, to the greatest degree possible, of mundane, forced, boring simplistic and disengaging repetitive methods of training is mandatory. Converting the training syllabus into a cognitive game induces anticipation and motivation enjoyed by the dog and makes the animal want more (Berridge 2004). Berridge and Robinson (1998) state that

> [D]opamine may be more important to incentive salience attributions to the neural representations of reward-related stimuli. Incentive salience, we suggest, is a distinct component of motivation and reward. In other words, dopamine systems are necessary for 'wanting' incentives, but not for 'liking' them or for learning new 'likes' and 'dislikes.'

By keeping the dog motivated and exercising these routines daily, extreme desire to perform the task becomes commonplace (Berridge et al. 2009). Further, Parnafes-Gazit (2005) correctly sums up the situation:

> [D]espite findings in the literature that suggest the importance of sniffing rate for successful olfactory detection, I suggest here that the influence of the dog's motivational level on its detection performance dominates that of the olfaction variables (i.e. sniffing frequency). Under motivated situations the dog will recruit all of its resources in order to fulfill the assigned task successfully, by fully focusing its attention on the olfactory cues available for detection of explosives. Consequently, a demonstrated motivation to work should be the main factor under consideration when selecting a detection dog.

A solid foundation of training is vital to supporting long-term success of a detection dog program. Studies have shown that the type of training and degree to which a dog is trained affect its problem-solving capabilities (Osthaus et al. 2003, 2005; Marshall-Pescini et al. 2008, 2009). Range et al. (2009) summarize this well by stating, "[w]e found that better trained dogs showed significantly better problem solving abilities." However, incorrect training often begins a downward spiral that damages this foundation. There are many ways to train a dog, but unfortunately, not all of them work well or provide superior outcomes. As noted by Haverbeke et al. (2008), some training regimens actually incorporate difficulties that cause lowered performance. Compulsion and aversion training are such methods that, as noted by Alexander et al. (2011), are too commonly used in working detector dog training.

Some trainers use shock (or E-) collars, especially in police, military, and search and rescue (SAR)-type training, often with little, no, or improper training in the use of the device and with little regard of the dog's welfare. The use of these devices in some cases could be considered excessive punishment, or in some cases abuse, especially if the trainer is upset or mad. These collars should be used only as a last resort by someone properly trained to use them. Schilder and van der Borg (2004) found that use of such collars induced body and ear positions in dogs that suggested that fear and pain resulted from this technique.

Human Involvement and Boredom in Training

The archenemy of detection dog success is boredom. As correctly noted by Wemelsfelder (1985), "[a]ccepting that boredom is an adverse state, it can be regarded as a form of stress for the animal." This general lack of interest, which is thought of as stress, can be driven by many factors but is most often the result of actions brought about by human interaction in training. Meagher and Mason (2012) stated that boredom can be "assessed empirically in non-human animals. It can also be reduced by environmental enrichment." Ultimately, for a dog to achieve the high standards placed upon it and of which it is capable, absolute interest demonstrated by the canine is paramount. This means that *motivation is the key element* as described earlier by Parnafes-Gazit (2005). The omission of something interesting for the dog to do creates boredom and prevents achievement of these goals (Slabbert and Odendaal 1999). As mentioned earlier, multiple rewards or reflex forming stimuli are critical and eliminate boredom. Tataruca (2011) argued for "the use of an extremely large variety of reflex forming stimuli, so that the possibility of negatively influencing the performance of the dog to be close to zero." Even though validated, multiple rewards (of varying categories and types) are not in wide use in training or deployment programs.

One of the most frequently presented issues confronted in training is evidenced by humans injecting themselves into the training too soon and sometimes in overwhelming volume. This is routinely demonstrated when trainers too often begin by teaching the dog obedience as the very first act, normally employing some degree of compulsion training. Once basic obedience has been trained, a typical strategy is to elevate the obedience of the canine to a precision level. While teaching these maneuvers may be good for advanced control of the dog, it is most often administered in ways that produce a negative effect (Schilder and van der Borg 2004) and can begin a downward spiral of training. Also, aversive and compulsive approaches force the dog to rely on the human, creating dependence and influencing decisions made by the dog.

Another avenue of overindulgence by a human is in the conditioning portion of the training involving odor recognition. Sometimes this involvement is to such degree that the dog is conditioned to associate the human with the action of finding the odor. This type of mundane compulsion used in training becomes boring for the dog, and this act of intentional or sometimes unintentional (Vynne et al. 2011) overindulgence can create cueing (Ensminger and Papet 2011a), and many other negative dependency issues, which can become the death knell of a detection dog program.

Over-involvement in odor recognition training is also sometimes demonstrated in the use of a scent wall. A scent wall is essentially a façade with holes, commonly placed in *W* or *high–low* pattern, in which an odor source can be placed. The holes sometimes allow for delivery of a rein-forcer as well. Many departments use similar homemade *walls*, and various trainers also produce a proprietary version carrying their name. A trainer will begin by placing an odor source inaccessible to the dog inside one of the holes. The placement simultaneously allows target odor availability on which the dog can be enticed to react while restricting access to the source. As the dog is guided to the odor source location by the trainer, generally walking backward while demonstrating a pointing gesture and verbally enticing the dog to *check* a specific location, the trainer will essentially cue the dog to locate the odor or demonstrate an alert. These actions can inherently instill an association and dependency cueing, which are unnecessary and counterproductive for the dog's education. It is also not uncommon to have several trainers or helpers located in close proximity to the odor source, sometimes connected with leads to the dog, which could create human interference or dependency (Herstik 2009).

Dutch Box and Other Shaping Devices

Similar training is performed using *Dutch box* containers that are sometimes referred to as *scent* or *scratch* boxes. Similar derivations may be found using various names (usually that of a trainer), which claim improvement in design over a device that has been in use for decades. This training device is a container that allows for placement of source material to produce odor availability while safely restricting access. Certain designs even incorporate a reinforcer delivery mechanism. Some of these devices have a shield behind which the dog can see the reinforcer but acting as a secondary method of preventing access to the reinforcer.

The odor source is placed in a compartment of Dutch box allowing odor to escape while protecting the source. While being controlled by one or more trainers, the reward, generally a ball on a rope, is dangled in the area occupied just above the odor source compartment so as to tease the dog. The canine can easily see the reward while smelling the odor. The construction of the device is such that the trainer can decide when reinforcement delivery is appropriate and simply drop the rope or reward using another ball. As the dog first sees the toy and then smells odor, the trainer will be standing beside or behind the box. The trainer will tease the dog and may allow a quick grab at the toy while making certain to permit the dog to actually bite the toy acting so as to tease the dog. As the dog moves closer to the source odor, it enters an area deemed to be appropriate by the trainer (who generally cannot smell the odor). Access to the reward (reinforcer) is allowed when the human believes that the dog has correctly indicated the source location. The similarities between this method and those previously described in the scent wall demonstrate that this method also requires overwhelming visibility and focus on a human during the odor locating or recognition period, thus possibly creating an unintended conditioning association. There are many different types of training tools offered today that assist in shaping behavior (see Chapter 14). While each may have benefits, there is not one single answer for all training.

Limiting Human Involvement for Independence

Scientists work diligently to study ways of understanding and possibly improving canine detection capabilities (see Chapter 3). Similarly, the authors of this chapter believe that the dog will excel in detection when and only when humans learn to allow the dog to perform the necessary cognition and learning to understand target odor and what is desired as a result of that odor, independently and with only minimal human interference or involvement. This is evidenced when Topal et al. (1997) concluded, "[o]n the basis of our results, we argue that the decreased problem solving ability in the domestic dog is not due to their domestication but their strong attachment to humans."

A proper environment, which presents necessary conditions for the dog to utilize cognition to learn while severely limiting human involvement, is critical when training a detection dog, especially when the team is judged based upon work performed. To create an effective basis of acclimation, preconditioning, and training, mimicking an instinctual set of foraging rules and motor patterns, which naturally follow, is most effective. As Blumstein (2000) aptly said, "Ask anyone who has trained their dog, or ask a circus trainer; training works by enhancing pre-existing motor patterns." Using genetic motor patterns combined with severely restricting human involvement in training, especially during odor acquisition and reinforcement, results in the dog learning to locate the desired target odor disassociated from the human. One aspect of Guthrie's (1935) work still has applicability, as noted by Mangalam and Singh (2013):

> The manifestation of a new behaviour involves the perceptive appreciation of the prospective affordances of an object or a situation prior to the solution being discovered by an individual. Thereon, the animal keeps discarding the irrelevant motor movements, which make the behaviour more skillful with experience, i.e., variation decreases and effectiveness increases. This kind of motor pattern refinement has been referred to as the 'one-trial learning' process.

This allows for more consistent replication of action using the dog's olfactory skills and cognitive ability, and ultimately the dog will itself alter foraging behavior (from survival odor) to the new paradigm of the desired (target odor) outcome. As noted again by Mangalam and Singh (2013):

> In nature, animals presumably always face the distinct but complementary challenges of identification and optimization of foraging returns. The decision making mechanisms combine information from the motivational states and the environment, and enable animals to exercise choice among the possible alternative behavioural strategies in a foraging situation.

A "dependent relationship with the owner prevents a dog from completing the task successfully" (Topal et al. 1997) and thus should be restricted. Hare and Tomasello (2005) found that young puppies already possess skills that are necessary to read human pointing and gaze and "were nearly perfect in the basic tests." From their work, it could be concluded that less human contact in foundation training is critical to eliminate dependence on the human gestures.

The Foraging Model

Standard training trials use heavy human interaction (Figure 13.1) to teach initial odor recognition and discrimination, which can be taxing on the dog and the trainer alike. As stated by Hall et al. (2014), "One important and laborious component of the training process is acquisition of the initial odor discrimination." However, training that utilizes the natural sequence of foraging motor patterns can remove the mundane and labor-intensive portion of the training and actually compel it into a motivator simply because the dog is rewarded by and enjoys the act of executing the pattern. The sequence described as "orient, eye, stalk, chase, grab bite, kill bite" (Coppinger and Coppinger 2001; generally, Coppinger 2014 at time 33:40) is hard-wired within the canine and provides an avenue of intrinsic action performed by the dog from which it receives tremendous pleasure. This is much more than a retrieval game as not all dogs are retrievers but all dogs exhibit some form of foraging motor patterns. By utilizing the foraging model of training (Figure 13.2) patterns and teaching the dog to accept target odor as replacement for survival odor, it highlights the intrinsic behavior in each dog while focusing on the new paradigm. It should be noted that "training animals works by increasing the likelihood that an individual performs a pre-existing motor pattern" (Blumstein 2002) and human intervention is not an inevitable part of that sequence.

Establishing Target Odor Recognition and Self-Rewarding

Utilizing the foraging model, a practical description of training starts as conditioning, which includes initial target odor recognition drills using an odored toy in a *context-independent* (Gazit et al. 2005b) self-rewarding process that the dog can enjoy. This begins with the naive dog secured for a short

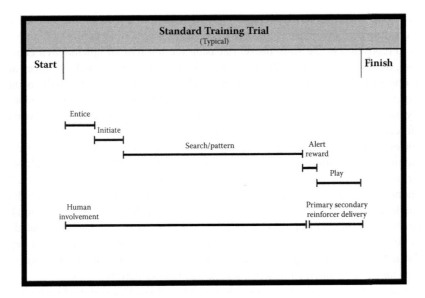

FIGURE 13.1 Standard training trial.

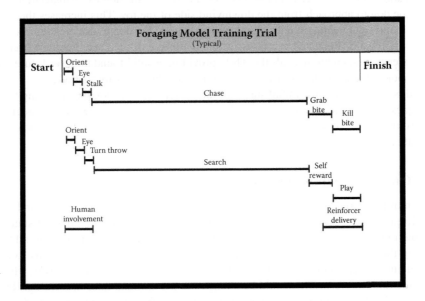

FIGURE 13.2 Foraging model training trial.

period in an area to witness other dogs performing the tasks. After a few repeated exposures, the naïve dog is turned released off lead and free to roam within large open areas containing interesting terrain and various obstructions, both natural and man-made. The trainer is located where the prescented reward can be easily thrown to different points upwind of the trainer and the dog. Care should be taken to always maintain a general downwind position from where the reward will be projected.

As the trainer holds a prescented reward, the dog will begin to look in the direction of the person and the toy; it becomes "less distracted" (Haverbeke et al. 2008) and begins to orient itself within close proximity to the handler. As the dog makes visual contact with the toy and begins to focus (eye, per Coppinger's stages of foraging), a slight movement of only the toy spurs the dog to focus on the item while excluding the person. Rotation of the person (hence the toy that the dog is actually watching) in either direction in an attempt to slightly hide the toy will cause the dog to begin to reposition, creating best advantage (stalk, per Coppinger's stages of foraging) of the toy. Just as the dog begins to reposition in the stalk phase, releasing the toy into an upwind area entices the dog to give chase, the fourth element in the foraging sequence. As the toy lands, bounces around, and settles, the dog approaches. Since the dog is approaching from downwind, it will encounter a dispersing (target) odor plume prior to locating the toy. When the dog intercepts the odor plume and then exactly locates the source, the grab bite is initiated creating a self-reward. A secondary audible (tone) reinforcer can be provided to enhance reinforcement.

This type of odor and reinforcer presentation is sometimes confusingly referred to as simultaneous conditioning. In this training method, the toy actually presents the target odor, along with other odors, prior to the dog initiating the grab bite, which in turn provides the (self) reward. This action clearly demonstrates delayed conditioning rather than simultaneous conditioning, which is the most effective method of classical conditioning and reinforcing Pavlovian behavior (generally Roberts 2002). After the grab bite, a kill bite (sixth in motor pattern sequence) may be executed by the dog shaking its head back and forth with the reinforcer in its mouth. It is possible (dog dependent) to demonstrate an additional motor pattern sequence by lying on the ground and chewing, which mimics dissecting and consuming the toy, a possible seventh motor pattern behavior.

During preconditioning and odor recognition training, this process should be replicated two to three times daily for best results. In successive repetitions, a capricious trajectory of the throw to a different location should be used to maintain or add interest for the dog while understanding that the goal is for the dog to approach from the downwind side of the toy. This increases the opportunity for the dog to intersect the target odor plume and encourage the dog to use olfaction as the method of locating the reward. Repeated exercises in this manner will increase the dog's overall fitness, physical dexterity, and endurance, all the while providing a solid foundation for future odor training. Care should be taken to not overtrain the dog beyond the limits for that dog.

It should be noted that in the initial stages of these exercises, the dog may be using visual locating techniques rather than olfaction. The goal is that within very few repetitions to begin secreting the throw so that it becomes less visible causing the dog to primarily resort to olfaction for locating and acquisition.

RECALL IN ODOR RECOGNITION TRAINING

In detection training, recall is a dog's return to the handler or trainer once a command (or marker) is given. To prepare for recall, a trainer should lower posture to reduce physical stature, spread the arms out to the side, and entice the dog to return. During recall, the trainer should try audibly encouraging the dog to further reinforce the desired behavior. As the dog begins to return, the trainer could use a recall motivator in high octave, while motioning with one's arms, which further motivates the dog to return. This could be changed to a command later in training. Reacquiring the toy should be done with positive methods keeping the fun and playful mood of the hunt and recall, thus increasing the motivation of the dog to return to the handler and give up the reward. As with all training, care should be taken to recognize the mental and physical aspects of the dog and should stop while the exercise is still fun and enjoyable. After completion of the exercise, the dog should be placed in a cool kennel and allowed to completely recover and rest. The main role of the trainer or new handler is to learn to read, understand, and even predict the dog's actions in this scenario.

There are many other ways to teach a dog to recall if the dog demonstrates hesitancy to return. Two of the most common employ tools such as a long line to reel the dog in or a fenced system essentially feeding the dog into a long narrow run with one end open where the trainer occupies the open end. Both of these methods use a stimuli to lure the dog away from the trainer and a reward (which can vary by dog) to return to the trainer.

CONTEXT INDEPENDENCE IN ALL ASPECTS

During the entire preconditioning, odor recognition, and training trials, care should be taken to change virtually each context in which the dog is trained. To rephrase the important matter, each element that can be varied should be. By altering every single aspect in training, the only constant will prove to be target odor. One such example should be to change the reinforcer type. By adding a variety of reinforcer types in training, the dog becomes less accustomed or dependent upon the odor produced by one specific reinforcer item or type, making it easier and less time-consuming to discriminate the odor of that reward from the target odor thereby making it easier to extinct. The same holds true for all odors used in training including trainer odor. Varying trainers (providing that the methodology used is identical) present uniquely different trainer and associated odors for the dog, thereby building less dependence on any single trainer's odor, again allowing for ease of extinction. Altering the training locations, the obstacles in which hides are maneuvered, location of the hides, confounding obstacles and odors, and even the people in and around the training environment is fundamental in training.

Performing this sort of training adapts the dog to constant change and to accept the only constant as target odor. Blind and double-blind evaluation should be performed routinely to ascertain benchmarks for performance analysis. The person(s) performing the evaluation should change as should the context, location, odors used, etc., which again creates a firm understanding of true capabilities. Further, since odor is involved, a simple series of double-blind trials, which tests the success of simple odor recognition and discrimination, should be routinely executed to validate the odor detection alone aside from all other capabilities that the team may have.

READING ODOR RECOGNITION

In preconditioning and training, initial odor recognition is sometimes mistakenly referred to as imprinting. After initial odor recognition has been successfully trained and tested to ensure ability, the next stage involves increasing the difficulty of access to odor placement. This will further reinforce olfactory training for the dog but is specifically focused to teach the trainer to read the nuances in behavior of the dog. The finesse of this type of training can be quite complex. Reading the dog's action accurately is the highest priority for the trainer in this stage due to the need of being able to communicate this to any new handler, which could require up to 2 years before the dog and the handler understand the behavior of the other (Bird 1996). While somewhat difficult to implement due to the goals required, it should be pointed out that this training allows for the human to use the same series of actions simplifying training matters, increasing repeatability, and increasing the speed with which the trainer, handler, and dog can learn. As well, it continues the use of the exact model utilized for conditioning, which mimics foraging motor patterns of the dog—Coppinger's stages as previously discussed.

Instead of tossing odored rewards in places somewhat easily accessed or in certain cases even visible to the dog, the goal is to now work the odored item into a location where the dog thinks that it may be in one location when in fact it has been located elsewhere. Additionally, the item should still be accessed by the dog although not necessarily easily. A trainer can begin by tossing the odored reward into a stand of shrubbery, where it may come to rest off of the ground, close to the end of a drainage pipe, inside the bed of a pickup truck, underneath a vehicle, etc., all in an effort to increase difficulty in locating and accessing the reward. In some cases, a dog may attempt to solicit assistance from the trainer on the more difficult odor locations. The trainer should always refrain from offering any assistance in these exercises as the dog will quickly learn that it can turn to the human for intervention in the effort. It would not be uncommon in this scenario to pull up a chair and have a seat as it could take some time. The benefit is that the dog learns to think through the problem, and when done so correctly, the dog finally does get the toy at which time it will be visibly more confident. It is also worth noting that at no time should the odor be placed for that would then present an option for the dog to track to the odor defeating the whole purpose of the drill.

DEPRIVATION AS MOTIVATION

A preferred method for building desire is the use of deprivation training, which withholds that which the dog desires. When used as a motivational tool, short-term deprivation immediately prior to the training event can be particularly effective. Restricting a dog from participating in training activities while placed in a position of observance of others in training is uniquely motivating to the dog. This process quickly exposes the innate desire within the dog and generally only takes one or two sessions for major changes to be witnessed. A word of caution is that deprivation training can alter a dog's otherwise normal behavior and should only be used sparingly and with proper guidance. This may be associated with model-rival techniques demonstrated in retrieval-selection (McKinley and Young 2003) tasks, which have indicated improvements similar in nature.

ENSURING PROFICIENCY BY TESTING, TESTING, TESTING

As training progresses, difficulty is increased incrementally making certain to test the dog each step of the way to ensure proficiency. Eliminating steps or individual stages in training may be possible but should not be attempted by a novice with limited experience of only a few dozen dogs. Further, most of this foundational work is performed outdoors to assist in separating the human from the equation to the fullest extent possible and to create a less restrictive training environment, building independence.

As odor locating difficulty is increased, incremental testing should be performed regularly using four different methods. The first testing mark is for the trainer to witness to a point of complete satisfaction each action performed by the dog, where the dog can routinely demonstrate exact replication of the act. A second testing mark would dictate the dog being removed from the area, with odor reward being thrown (not placed) where even the trainer cannot be certain of the exact location, and then reintroduce the dog while the trainer is watching from a distance so as to have no influence. This too must replicated numerous times to a point of complete satisfaction. The third type of testing is single-blind testing where an unbiased person hides odor for the dog to find, which again must be replicated to satisfaction. The last and the only real test of ability involves using a double-blind process. This dictates that neither the dog, the handler (trainer), nor the evaluator has any knowledge of whether a placement exists or not or the location if one does exist. Care should be maintained to eliminate placement issues, which could allow the dog to track or otherwise manipulate the outcome. In a discussion of the use of dogs in prostate cancer detection, Elliker et al. (2014) note that, "double blind testing illustrates that these rigorous tests are vital to avoid drawing misleading conclusions about the abilities of dogs to indicate certain odours."

Concerning proficiency, it should be mandated that baseline olfactory double-blind examinations utilizing target odor, distractor odor, and blanks (negatives) take place prior to performing scientific study utilizing olfaction. The use of previously *certified* (Kranz et al. 2014b) dogs, whether by the agency employing the dog or a national organization, as a qualifier to replace statistical analysis does not pass the muster of scientific exploration and can greatly skew findings due to the extreme bias that could be present in certification organizations.

DIVERSITY IN TRAINING

As the dog understands commands, subsequent training is built upon continuing the methodology of mimicking foraging behavior, while adding interest and difficulty. Some changes might include adding or varying the distance, partially obscuring the toy, fully obscuring the toy, changing environmental conditions, multiple reinforcers, multiple and changing distractors, witnessed placement and faking of placement, witnessed action with unknown or no placement, unexpected placement, changing height of placement, training in different light conditions, traveling to different training environments, etc. This is all part of the contextual independence that the dog must learn, which conditions the dog to understand that odor could be present anywhere (Gazit et al. 2005b). For a properly trained dog, the time it takes to locate odor does not vary in differing light conditions (Gazit and Terkel 2003a). When increasing the difficulty, sequential change or additions are important with only one element in the equation changing at a time and maintaining the target odor as the only constant. Once proficiency has been demonstrated and tested, progression to the next element is in order. Maintaining a list of each baseline performance evaluation is critical for future comparison (Gazit et al. 2005a,b).

SUMMARY

As a dog gains experience, performance improves, proving that effective training has been given. This is generally due to the dog having "refined their sense of smell," the dog having "learned to detect anomalous odours, which do not belong in the setting," and the fact that "[y]ears of actual work experience and training improved a dog's capability in any task it is trained for" (Hayter 2003).

Three precursor elements must be accepted for success:

1. Severely restrict any human involvement to the absolute minimum in the training and handling processes.
2. Allow the dog to be a dog and experience extreme enjoyment in doing that which only a dog can do, naturally.
3. Objectively evaluate all skills learned by the dog and the handler (past, present, and future) for improvement.

The basis for this thought is the expansion from *trust your dog* to *trust and verify the canine team*. Most of what is denoted here has been practiced for centuries by hunters using dogs to locate prey. Although this work does not contain secret, magic, or otherwise proprietary information, it is rare to find these and other necessary attributes compiled into one single training program today.

14 Statistical Reliability Confounders and Improvement in Advanced Dog Training

Patterns, Routines, Targets, Alerts, Distractors, Reinforcement, and Other Issues

Sherri Minhinnick

Advanced training is the combination of the improvement of previously acquired skills and the adding of skills that further enhance statistical performance in deployment. To begin advanced training, the dog should have demonstrated a consistent and reliable ability to locate the *odored toy* (see Chapter 13). As confidence and capability increase, so should difficulty, and this chapter will illuminate several of the key parameters necessary for a dog to become deployment ready.

INDEPENDENT SNIFFING AND PATTERNING DURING SEARCH ROUTINES

As training progresses, confidence and capability should increase. Simultaneously, difficulty should increase and one aspect of increasing difficulty is teaching the dog to pattern. While it might sound as simple as teaching a dog to walk around an object, in detection work, pattern training is the act of teaching the dog to independently investigate various yet specific areas or items in a methodical *search pattern* (Cormier et al. 1995), thereby increasing the likelihood of encountering target odor if present. Training the dog to pattern can be difficult and create either positive (decreased stress) or negative (increased stress) outcomes, and should be approached similarly like all other trainings—in small steps. By maintaining positive training, the dog will be less stressed thereby enhancing welfare (Deldalle and Gaunet 2014). Pattern training involves chaining individual actions into patterns where the dog will perform them automatically. Whether it is a row of vehicles, a set of cabinets, a circle of canisters for a planned trial, or virtually anything else, the act of patterning allows the dog to independently follow a sniffing regimen around the myriad of items and obstacles encountered on a daily basis. By teaching the dog this maneuver, it greatly enhances the autonomy with which the dog can perform the sweep while simultaneously reducing the need for human intervention.

When dogs have received little to no pattern training, it is easily recognizable. A handler will generally be heavily involved in the actions of the dog in a directed search. This may be exampled by a handler sometimes standing still, facing the dog in order to block its forward movement. The handler will then begin to walk backward or very closely alongside the dog while holding the lead tightly, sometimes above the dog's head, and pointing closely at a precise spot. This pointing may take the form of tapping at various places, usually in a *W* or high/low pattern while instructing the dog to "check here" (Ensminger and Papet 2011b; Chapter 13 herein). However, this type of directed search could take many forms. One investigation used a circle of cans, sometimes called a *scent wheel*, and directed searching.

> During testing, each dog was guided around the circle of cans by his or her respective handler. The dog was presented each can and allowed to sniff it.... Upon reaching the end of the circle, the direction was reversed, and the dog was presented each can a second time, this time going counter-clockwise instead of clockwise. (Kranz et al. 2014a)

This type of human input can be detrimental as outlined by Szetei et al. (2003): "In the case of contradictory cues, dogs prefer to rely on the human communicative signaling (pointing) when they have only olfactory information about the hiding place." Similarly, Cooper et al. (2003) state that, "Dogs give preference to social cues (other dogs and humans) over abstract non-social cues as information sources about reward location." Many trainers teach guided forms of pattern work, yet few, in the author's experience, teach pattern work to be performed independently, whether on lead or off. Independent patterning reduces human involvement in training and deployment and provides greater repeatability and reliability. An excellent example is demonstrated in Fjellanger et al. (2002):

> Dogs were trained to enter at one of the doors, make one circuit of the stand sniffing at each box or filter, and exit at the same door. For any one search, zero, one or two trainers could be in the room, either hidden behind the blind or in the open (we note that as a result of experiences in the program described here, our current procedure is to remove or hide all personnel for all searches). For the dog, the only constants on any search event were the presence of the circular stand and the room itself. Dogs searched the stand with no support or assistance from the trainers, except for the whistle reward when correct positive alerts were given.... If the dog correctly determined that there were no positives on the current trial (i.e., it gave no alert), it was rewarded once it was outside the door.

Pattern training should begin in extremely calm conditions, preferably outdoors, often in early morning or late evening, using identical containers. Identical containers are important in certain investigations as it reduces the possibility of a cue or residual odor for an inexperienced dog. "Seven controls, each made up of 1 mL of mineral oil, were deposited in identical sterile containers. Each set of containers were used only in one session and subsequently discarded" (Concha et al. 2014). However, for properly trained animals, it should be noted that containers of glass, metal, plastic, and wood have been used and "in cases in which the dogs could have used both olfaction and vision, they chose to use only olfaction" (Gazit and Terkel 2003a).

It could be suggested that pattern training can begin with 20 open top containers (boxes, buckets, or similar containers) that are easily recognizable as nearly identical in shape, size, and color. The top of the container should be at the approximate height of the dog's neck, which will allow the dog completely free and easy access to interior portions of the vessel. The trainer should place each container in a straight row with the sides touching. With the dog slightly restrained while in a position to observe, the trainer will place the odored toy approximately 6 in. above the first container in the row to establish a starting point. The trainer will then move the odored toy along the top of the containers in the row leaving an odor trail for the dog to follow. Upon arriving at the last container in the row, the trainer will drop the odored toy into the open topped vessel.

Next, the trainer should escort the dog to an area approximately 3 ft. short of the first container and release the animal with a *check* command. The dog will begin following the odor along the row of containers, while the trainer's role is to move slightly away from the area allowing the dog to search independently until locating and grabbing the toy. When the dog actually grabs the toy, the trainer should immediately offer a verbal secondary reinforcer and motivator. With the trainer repeating this action several times in quick succession, the dog will immediately adapt to checking this simple row of containers. Once the dog consistently follows the row of containers and successfully gathers the toy, difficulty should be increased. The trainer should next vary the container in which the toy is dropped. Upon success working through this series of trials, additional complexity should be contemplated with the trainer increasing the distance between containers incrementally up to approximately 2 ft. As the dog routinely demonstrates the ability to locate and obtain the odored toy in this enhanced series of trials, the trainer must now increase the difficulty further in order to teach the *trained final response* (TFR) or alert (Alexander et al. 2015).

BEHAVIOR CHANGES AND ALERT RESPONSES

The term *alert* has diverse meanings to different people. Alerts are often called by many other names including *hit* (Kranz et al. 2014a), *interest* (Moser and McCulloch 2010), *body language* (Cablk and Heaton 2006, distinguishing trained alert from untrained body language), *positive response* (Kranz et al. 2014a; Lazarowski and Dorman 2014), *indicate* (Long et al. 2007), *behavioral response* (Furton et al. 2002, "behavioral response of a drug dog [i.e., the dog alerting]"), *changes in dog behavior* (Engeman et al. 2002), *interest, final response, indication* (Scientific Working Group on Dog and Orthogonal detector Guidelines [SWGDOG] SC1 2011), and more. There is considerable debate along the range of practical, scientific, and legal disciplines as to what constitutes an alert, who may call an alert, where alerts should be in relation to odor source, etc. SWGDOG SC1 (2011) describes an alert as a "characteristic change in ongoing behavior in response to a trained odor, as interpreted by the handler." However defined, the litmus test should be poignantly overt in that an alert should be clearly recognizable by any person (not just a trainer or handler) witnessing the act as indicative of an obvious change from prior behavior.

Handlers are often taught that certain natural dog behaviors may be included as part of an alert. These behaviors indicate a change in dog body posture, speed or direction, ear position, hackle position, tail position or movement, abrupt head turn, breathing change, sniffing change, or any number of other possibilities. Alerts may not be called and items may be missed due to the observer not witnessing a change in behavior. Engeman et al. (2002) concluded that

> Of the 16 planted snakes that were missed during the inspections monitored by a concealed observer in 1998, 10 were missed due to a lack of a behavior change by the dog that would indicate the presence of a snake....

Some trainers and handlers believe an alert could actually be a fluid event where a dog could demonstrate different actions at different times, all of which would qualify as an alert. In other words, a dog could sit on one alert, bark on another, stare at yet another, and so on, which courts have sometimes accepted (*South Dakota v. Lockstedt*, 695 N.W.2d 718 (2005); *U.S. v. Holleman*, 743 F.3d 1152 (8th Cir. 2014)). As an alert is currently defined by SWGDOG, this could be interpreted as possible and even acceptable.

In theory, an alert is an identifier declared exclusively by the handler (though it should be evident to other observers) in response to witnessing a change of behavior (COB) followed by a TFR being demonstrated by the dog upon locating the highest concentration of odor or source. Some authors define allowable distances from the source within which a dog should alert (Lazarowski and Dorman 2014), while others measure the distance from the alert to the source (Savidge et al. 2011). However, on occasion, difficulties may be presented in the demonstration of the alert. One possible problem is that an alert may occur at the highest concentration available to the dog, which may or may not be the source. A *fringe response* as discussed by Cormier et al. (1995) may be possible. A fringe alert is one demonstrated by the dog along or in the odor plume but some undefined distance away from the highest odor concentration or source. Further difficulties may lie in the fact that there are numerous other reasons why a dog may not exhibit a typical TFR. These include an unstable or moving surface, the surface temperature of the area being too extreme, such as hot asphalt, or physical space limitations in the area. When these difficulties are encountered, often the dog will reposition in order to demonstrate a TFR that may be as close as possible or simply convenient.

TYPES OF ALERTS AND INDICATIONS

Alerts displayed by a dog can be one or more various trained actions or may be more intrinsic such as pointing (Spady and Ostrander 2008). The two most typical types of alerts are *passive* and *active* (Furton and Myers 2001), the latter of which is sometimes referred to as assertive or aggressive. It has long been believed that active alert dogs are more accurate. Passive alerts generally include a sit or a down, sometimes accompanied by a stare (occasionally at source), though a stare can also serve as an independent alert. Passive alerts are generally considered to be nondestructive or noncontinuous actions. Active alerts generally require continuous actions such as scratching or barking. In the case of Search and Rescue (SAR) dogs, a unique alert is the *refind* (Jones et al. 2004), where the dog locates a target and returns to the handler in an attempt to guide the handler to the target. A variation of this is the *bringsel*, a padded (sometimes jute) stick fashioned to be carried by the collar. "When a SAR dog is trained in this fashion and finds its target, it holds the bringsel in its mouth and returns to the handler" (Jackson et al. 2013). Each alert can be trained independently or sometimes combined.

Trainers often train an alert simultaneously with initial odor recognition by first confining odor in a container. A dog is then directed to a container or series of containers and commanded to check or sniff the container. Once the trainer *believes* the dog is smelling odor (sometimes for the first time), the trainer will either initiate a command to perform the desired alert action such as sit or down at which time a reinforcer will be delivered, or the trainer may actually issue a reinforcer without the desired action. If the latter is used, a series of similar trials will be conducted slowly convincing the dog to display the desired alert and being rewarded for doing so. This type of alert training contains a series of major concerns or flaws that should be evaluated. First, the trainer cannot smell the odor, at least not to the degree of which a dog is capable. Next, the trainer does not know where the odor is actually located and thus the assessment of location is an assumption at best. As the dog begins to encounter odor, conditioning will begin as the trainer reinforces desired actions that are impossible for the human to determine with absolute certainty. At this point, the human, incapable of using either visual or olfactory means in detecting such, is being made an intrinsic part of the pattern in establishing behavior instead of an element separated from the behavior.

A suggestion might be to train the alert only after the dog has repeatedly demonstrated proficiency in independently locating odor of its own volition. In other words, the *former method* compels a dog to locate odor as determined by someone incapable of discerning the location, while the *suggested method* allows the dog using its natural keen sense of smell to locate the odor that will naturally cause a natural behavior change, which is evident to the trainer. With a dog already recognizing odor, and pattern training allowing the dog to acclimate to both expected and unexpected encounters (Kranz et al. 2014a; a dog's previous unfamiliarity with trial setup required a lineup to acclimate the dog), trainers can capitalize on these to implement the conditioning necessary to train an alert as described.

Most trainers have a preferred alert and then train accordingly. However, one optimum method of alert training is allowing the dog to choose the alert, which produces a more reliable, repeatable alert. A trainer must have patience to train this type of alert as it often entails waiting for the dog to make a decision. Most dogs will display a natural reaction that will generally be a sit, down, scratch, or bark. While remaining motionless, the trainer should wait for the dog to demonstrate the behavior and quickly reinforce with a physical, audible, and tactile reward. If the dog begins exhibiting behavior that would be unsuitable for deployment purposes, such as a scratch for an explosives detection dog, the trainer should simply issue a subtle command for the ideal alert desired, such as sit. Unfortunately, this requires patience and time not often afforded or considered worthwhile for many trainers. Ultimately, any alert is acceptable if reliability is demonstrated, it is clearly identifiable, and the action does not present legacy issues in deployment.

An alert is preceded by a natural COB as the dog captures scent. Sometimes this is equated to a human hearing tires squeal on pavement and immediately turning to see what is going on. A dog will react similarly when encountering a target odor, which can be witnessed as current behavior different from that by which it was immediately preceded and can be something as simple as a head turn, change in direction, change in tail wagging, etc.

> Body language is a change in the dog's behavior upon encountering scent or the target, indicating that the dog has scent or has located the target. This is natural behavior, not trained, and is an alternative, albeit not preferred, means of communicating encounter with target scent to the handler. (Cablk and Heaton 2006)

Many handlers and some trainers refer to a COB as *interest*, although this term is, in the experience of the author, extremely overused, especially when handlers do not understand the actions of their dog and may simply *feel* the dog is in odor. An alert should not be called based upon this interest being exhibited by the dog. An alert should consist of a COB followed by a TFR that is clearly identifiable.

A well-trained dog should exhibit an alert that any observer can clearly conclude is overt, decisive, and highly repeatable. While conditions occasionally exist preventing an obvious alert such as limited physical space, the majority of alert problems involve training, handling, or other human involvement such as alert selection, alert reinforcement, odor threshold training, cueing, lead control, blocking the dog, etc. (Ensminger and Papet 2011a). Unfortunately, it may sometimes take an extremely trained eye to identify behaviors causing these problems.

FALSE ALERTS MUST BE ADDRESSED

A *false alert* (Vesely 2008) occurs when a dog has demonstrated a behavior change followed by a TFR when target odor is absent. Some evidence suggests that this is closely related to lack of sniffing (Concha et al. 2014), although experience would suggest that cueing is the culprit due to the fact that the dog has no need to sniff if trained to cue. Two very common causes for false alerts arise from unique novelty odors or odor sometimes associated with the trainer, handler, environment, equipment, etc., which are commonly called distractors (Lazarowski and Dorman 2014), or from cueing, an action either purposefully or inadvertently interfering with the dog's interpretation of odor, usually caused by humans (Miklosi and Topal 2013), and will only become exacerbated if not corrected with rigorous foundational training for both the dog and the handler. *Extinction* (Skinner 1953, p. 53, commenting on the work of Pavlov; Skinner 1974, p. 58; see Chapter 10 herein) training may also need to be involved if extraneous odor is involved. "To ensure scientific validity, important evaluation issues include identifying what items might cause false alerts and exposing these items in training and testing" (Furton and Myers 2001). Once discovered, both the dog and the handler should undergo immediate retraining.

> Measurements should be conducted in a double-blind fashion with impartial evaluators and the results evaluated to determine reliability. Also, tests should include positive controls…. and negative controls (no sample or potentially interfering or distracting samples). (Furton and Myers 2001)

This should include strong foundational training while reinforcing canine independence. Habituation training may also be needed, which can be accomplished in as little as one session (Salvin et al. 2012).

RESIDUAL AND LINGERING ODOR, WHAT'S LEFT BEHIND

Alexander et al. (2015) state that, "Residual odor is defined as odor originating from a 'target substance that may or may not be physically recoverable or detectable by other means' [citing SWGDOG SC1]." This is sometimes referred to as lingering odor. U.S. courts have accepted a dog's alert "to residual scents lingering for up to four to six weeks" (*Jennings v. Joshua Independent School District*, 877 F.2d 313 [5th. Cir., 1989]).

Some research recommends training a dog on a very low concentration of odor.

All detection tasks require that dogs respond to the lowest detectable concentrations of the target odor because it is such initial samples that can then prompt them to move in directions that lead to higher concentrations. Although trainers and handlers tend to focus on the quantity of training aids used as defined by weight, dogs respond to training aids in terms of the vapor concentration of signature compounds, not weight. It is therefore important that all dogs be trained to pay attention to a range of concentrations, including even the faintest whiff of target odors, regardless of differences in search scenarios. The findings from these sensitivity studies suggest that this approach will make the best use of dogs' impressive olfactory sensitivity. (Johnston 1999)

The lower a dog's odor detection threshold is, the more likely it is to alert to residual odor. If not tightly monitored and controlled, this can lead to two distinctly different problems. On one end of the scale is the false alert (discussed previously) where, due to the extremely low threshold capability combined with scent generalization, it could be suggested that such minutia creates an environment where false alerts can happen. This is especially harmful as it can consume a massive amount of time and effort in the field where false alerts still demand searches be executed. On the other end of the spectrum is *fringing* (discussed previously) where a dog will alert some distance away from a source, once again causing a search. The only difference between the two would be that, on the false alert, a search would yield nothing, while on the fringe alert end, it may yield nothing or, worse yet, it could be overlooked due to the alert distance from the source. In general, a well-trained police dog should not alert on residual or lingering odor after the source has been removed, especially after a short period of time.

The percentage of indications of residual hashish odor after 24 h was even higher than for fresh odor emitted by samples that were present at the searching site.... A significantly lower detection rate was found for residual odor of heroin, with almost no detection after 48 h. (Jezierski et al. 2014)

Exceptions do exist for certain areas of law enforcement, however. This is exampled in Browne et al. (2006), quoting Katz and Midkiff (1998): "Accelerant-detection dogs are trained to locate the residual scent of flammable products used as accelerants by arsonists...." There may be an even greater concern for cadavers. As noted by Alexander et al. (2015), "residual odor of human remains in soil can be very recalcitrant and therefore detectible by properly trained and credentialed [Human Remains Detection] HRD dogs" up to 667 days after body removal. It should be noted that the soil was not tested for presence of volatile organic compounds, which may be present in such conditions.

Alerting to residual odors often arises from training where relative odor availability is not closely monitored such as a trainer allowing use of target odor in limited concentration, extremely small source size, or making continual improper odor placements, which often derive from the use of odor-only (sans source) placement model. A major contributing factor is the lack of understanding of odor availability as compared to odor source weight. While some work is investigating the development of systems that control such issues, there are currently very few ways for a trainer to quickly and precisely adjust available odor concentrations.

Some research states that the vomeronasal organ (VNO), part of the olfactory system, "essentially allows a dog to 'taste' a smell, thus strengthening its ability to detect odours" (Barone et al. 2015) and especially minute odor. In deployment of a drug dog, this is sometimes demonstrated by a dog licking at odor on a door handle of a vehicle just prior to an alert even though no substance appears to be present. The marijuana odor residing on the hands of the person can be transferred to the door handle of the vehicle leaving enough odor to cause the alert (David and Lewis 2008; Florida v. Harris, 133 S. Ct. 1050 2013; Parmeter et al. 2000).

Properly training a dog to ignore residual or lingering odor dictates discipline in the training process. Correction of this issue involves use of severely oversized target odor for a period of time until successful testing has abated residual odor alerts. The dog will learn that the odor available is so large it becomes extremely easy to locate. Casual reduction of this over time slowly allows adjustment to normal values.

HONORING FOR ALERT IMPROVEMENT

Honoring is the act of steadfastness once a change in behavior followed by a TFR has been provided by the canine. An easily recognizable example of honoring is a hunting dog pointing a bird. The dog will not move until it is released, even when the hunter flushes the bird and it flies away, often only inches from the dog. Another example of honoring might be demonstrated when a dog is sniffing target scent in a vehicle door seam, then detects what it believes to be the highest concentration of odor and displays a TFR (sit). Once this happens, the dog remains with that location until released by the handler. Some dogs have demonstrated such steadfastness that movement cannot be forced or, if moved, they will return to the point of the TFR to maintain position again and again.

Training an act of honoring involves a precise sequencing and use of a continuous schedule delivery for the reinforcer, which transition to a VR schedule delivery, both employing delayed conditioning timing. Once reliable, the delivery timing again slowly changes by extending trace conditioning thereby increasing the time of reinforcement. This method should be implemented only after high repeatability and reliability can be demonstrated. A dog properly trained in honoring will seek odor to what it believes to be source and demonstrate a COB followed by a TFR. At that point, the dog will not move away from the area prior to a release.

DEPLOYMENT READY PATTERNING

Once the dog reliably demonstrates basic odor recognition and can reliably demonstrate an alert, further enhancement of pattern training now continues. To train this action, a trainer should revert to the initial pattern training trial design previously discussed with the exception of restricting access to all odor *source material* (hides) by the dog. To add difficulty, the trainer could increase distance between containers or replace straight lines with progressively more radical serpentines, right angles, circles, squares, or any other number of options. Each of these steps should be incrementally practiced until routine and then tested until extreme reliability has been demonstrated in each new formation.

Additional improvements in patterning should now include objects that vary from the originals by height. Short sport field border cones may be used to teach a dog much lower patterns only several inches high. Trainers may use tall barrels to teach taller patterns where a dog may need to stand on its hind legs and *check high* to access the area. In teaching pattern improvement, the trainer should take care to use items where the dog will have only one way to access the area to be sniffed. To describe it differently, if the idea is to train a dog to sniff a row of shelves containing multiple levels, train the dog on each level to a point of proficiency prior to moving on to the next row height.

Advanced patterning training on associated items of specific interest (based upon deployment) such as shelves, cabinets, desks, aircraft, wilderness areas, automobiles of various types, etc. should only begin after alert training and testing has proven successful with double-blind testing (DBT). A double-blind test should include altering the line from a straight line to a serpentine and then to other shapes such as square or circle.

Additionally, while patterning, the trainer should simultaneously be focusing on hide placement. Each new type of location (desk, vehicle, cabinet, etc.) where a hide is placed will be remembered by the dog. Changes in odor availability, duration and frequency of placement, location type, environment in which training is performed, etc. are all fundamental in lengthening the time and improving the way a dog will search. Placing too many aids will make it too easy for the dog and reduce the desire and performance. Not placing enough hides may lead to the dog becoming bored and quit working. Finding the balance of these aspects can ensure that the dog will work for extended periods without the need for constant reinforcement.

Reinforcer Timing and Placement

Reinforcement timing and placement are the most difficult elements for the trainer to learn and teach. Yamamoto et al. (2009), following Coppinger et al. (1998), argue that with service dogs, timing must be precise. Timing may be defined in scientific or mathematical terms and equations, which are important to know, but this does very little to prepare a handler to work with these elements in training. Timing and placement particularly involve delivery of information that the dog uses to put tasks in sequence and tie them together. Timing and placement can be critical to a command, correction, reinforcement, removal, punishment, and other situations. Using incorrect timing or placement of reinforcers can have an extremely negative impact in the training (and handling) of a dog.

> A dog's response to commands is influenced not only by the relationship with its owner, but also the owner's dog handling ability. Professional dog trainers can sometimes control dogs better than their owners, and often dogs obey the trainers' commands better even during their first interaction. This finding suggests that there is a skill to giving commands, and appropriate rewards or punishment, to elicit desired behavior from dogs. (Yamamoto et al. 2009)

One area of timing and placement that is extremely difficult to master is reward or reinforcer delivery. While a very experienced canine may accept more leeway in delivery timing, the training of a novice or green dog does not allow for such fluctuation. As we are dealing with the dog detecting something that cannot be seen by the naked eye, we must learn to interpret the dog's body language to know when, how, and where to place the reinforcer. This is difficult to learn when interacting with only one dog but becomes increasingly so when additional dogs are introduced with new and different requirements. Without the benefit of having experienced the timing and placement needs of many dogs over time and the behaviors that accompany those needs and actions, it is difficult for a handler to develop this skill properly.

> Efficient training requires reinforcement at precisely the right moment. Experience shows that a dog will easily make the link between the sound of the whistle or 'clicker' as a reward and the desired action. It may seem frustrating when a dog interrupts desired action to get reinforcement, but a precisely given reward will result in the dog immediately returning to the same situation/action in an attempt to manipulate the trainer to give more 'rewards'. Timing is essential! (Fjellanger et al. 2002)

Poor timing causes massive confusion for the dog as associations or connections are not made, and this may be one of the leading causes for dogs failing training programs. Yamamoto et al. (2009) cite numerous studies that "have indicated that delayed reinforcement and punishment will retard classical conditioning in dogs and rabbits... and operant conditioning in dogs, rats, pigeons, and humans...." It is for this reason the author believes that this intrinsic, self-reward training method establishes a sound foundational footing on which a trainer, handler, scientist, or behaviorist, whether novice or experienced, could easily succeed in building a foundational program.

DISTRACTORS, DETECTION TO DISCRIMINATION

Distractor training is an integral necessity in scent work. Distractors are *nontarget stimuli* (SWGDOG SC1 2011) or odors that the dog may encounter in the course of deployment and should encounter during training. Distractor training is sometimes called *discrimination training* (Dean 1972). Unfortunately, distractor training is the most often overlooked aspect of scent discrimination training, even though it is foundationally vital in confirming statistical reliability (Elliker et al. 2014; Macias et al. 2008; McCulloch et al. 2006).

Just as target odor is placed for locating, this training process involves the placement of distractor or nontarget stimuli for the purpose of confirming that the dog will not exhibit an alert. Salvin et al. (2012) and others have correctly noted that exposing the dog to many odors in the training process assists and enhances the sourcing of target odor and increases performance, as well as habituating the dog to a novel nontarget odor after one exposure. For this reason, distractor training basics begin in the conditioning phase.

For a detection dog to become a scent-discrimination canine requires that it develop the ability to locate desired target odor while simultaneously excluding nontarget or extraneous odor that could be present. Both odor trials must be performed correctly to establish reliability as each element is equally important. It is not until distractor training has been begun that a dog transitions from scent identification to scent discrimination. As Johnston (1999) aptly notes, it "may be that dogs' ability to discriminate among target and non-target odors is even more impressive than their sensitivity." Some distractors may be chosen due to emitting similar odor to that of the target odor as demonstrated by Kranz et al. (2014a).

> Twenty-six everyday items were chosen—some because they were hypothesized to be potential emitters of 2E1H, some purely out of the curiosity of the author. The items included five samples of PVC tile ('Chalet', 'Chatsworth', 'Ebony Marble', 'Eurostone', and 'Twilight Blue' designs); three types of PVC pipe (Charlotte, Genova, and Lasco brands); three types of electrical tape (Grainger, Lowes, TrueValue brands); three types of plastic food wrap (Glad Cling Wrap, Saran Wrap, and Ziplock Perfect Portions Wrap); a Glad trash bag; a Ziplock freezer bag; a plastic lid to a soda fountain cup; bubble wrap; a plastic milk jug; a credit card; a lottery ticket; a movie ticket; a plastic notebook divider; a Wal-Mart shopping bag; a shower curtain; and a playing card.

A best practice for distractor training should include odors commonly associated with the working environment, the handler, the dog, training equipment, transport vehicle, storage, and handling, along with many other associated items, This should include deploying the dog to sniff blank controls as well, a procedure sometimes not used even in research projects (McCulloch et al. 2006). Additionally, this training should be inclusive of odors to dispel common myths or misunderstandings about the effectiveness of canine olfaction. The distractor odors should be slowly and incrementally introduced into the environment during conditioning and initial odor recognition training. By adding odors with this method, the dog learns that novelty odors abound, and there is no benefit associated with them. This method requires patience to allow the dog to investigate without interruption. Additionally, if distractor training is incorporated into training early on, use of an assertive verbal banishment command (leave it) eliminates the need for further correction when removing the desire of the dog to alert upon a distractor odor.

Some trainers defer this training to the end of the training cycle and use avoidance training to correct errors. It is not recommended as this method can use compulsion and create discrimination/detection issues in deployment. However, if distractor odors present issues, a simple process to correct this problem would be to introduce an extinction process by returning to a basic pattern training setup and include a straight row of noncontaminated containers. Within each, one distractor odor is placed. It is not necessary for the trainer or handler to know the locations of odors. No target odor should be present in the environment. A trainer should allow the dog to sniff each container to determine if the dog displays any behavior change or TFR to the distractor odors. If no COB or TFR is witnessed, the trainer should move on to additional tests with different odors commonly encountered or associated with the program. However, should a dog attempt to demonstrate any behavior change, simply removing the reinforcer will assist in correcting this behavior.

Worth noting is that if a dog is inclined to show a COB on any distractor, the dog may desire to stay with the odor, awaiting reinforcement. This is another time to simply wait for the dog to leave the area and issue verbal praise followed up by an immediate trial presenting target odor upon which the dog will be paid for an alert. However, as Bentosela et al. (2008) commented, extinction training can result in behavioral changes, some of which are unwanted that might include moving back and away from the experimenter, lying down, vocalizations, or rearing.

Additional Target Odors

Although the maximum number of odors a dog has been trained to detect has no real apparent value (Johnston 1999), most detection dogs are trained to detect more than one odor. Adding a new target odor is accomplished by replicating the initial conditioning and initial odor recognition training with a new odor. Care should be taken when adding new odors in overly quick succession as it can lead to problems as the dog may quickly adapt to thinking that any new or novel odor encountered is a new target odor. A best practice would be to allow significant time delay in sequencing of new odor placement.

> Further, the sequence of odors trained for detection plays no role in reliability of detection. The more odors added, the easier it seems to be for a dog to learn. The amount of training required when more odors are added generally does not increase. Dogs can learn a new odor in one pass and the amount of training required to refresh detection performance and to train new odor discriminations tended to decrease as more odor discriminations were trained. (Williams and Johnston 2002)

Overwhelming Distractor (Masking) Odor Training

Once the dog has demonstrated proficiency in alerting on target odor and not alerting to nontarget odor (generally Lazarowski and Dorman 2014), advanced distractor training should begin. This is sometimes referred to as *masking* odor training, a misnomer as it is not teaching how to mask but rather how to ensure the dog will alert when distractor odors are comingled with target or when used to prevent detection. As mentioned by Waggoner et al. (1998),

> [A]lthough the detection performance of dogs is susceptible to being perturbed by the presence of an extraneous odor, it takes a large or even very large amount of this odor in relation to the amount of target odor for this effect to be realized. The extent of this effect depends on the nature of the substances.

In the field, target odor will undoubtedly comingle with extraneous odor of all kinds. This training involves placement of a small amount of target odor masked by an overwhelming amount of distractor odor(s). The training has three goals. The first goal is to confirm that the dog is capable of locating target odor and displaying a proper alert. The second goal is to ascertain whether the dog will exhibit any behavior change to the distractor odor(s) being used to conceal target odor. The third one is to investigate whether the dog will issue an alert on the container with both target and overwhelming nontarget odor(s) present. This type of training takes patience and requires that one allow the dog to make a decision and initiate a slight change in behavior before interfering.

A very effective method for training is to use a simple straight-line pattern of, say, 15 (or more) containers in which odor can be placed while simultaneously restricting access to the odor source. The trainer should make certain that airflow is highly restricted to limit odor movement. The containers are divided into five groups of three containers each. The container groups on each end are devoted to target odor on one end and target odor being masked on the other. The middle group (set of three containers) is restricted to masking (distractor) odor only. The two remaining groups of containers are used as buffers between canisters containing odor. The trainer should make the placements on each end in containers placed in different positions. In other words, if target odor is in vessel three from the end, the masked target odor on the other end of the line should use a container different from three from the end. Doing this helps the trainer keep track of odor location without presenting an identical setup for the dog. By running this setup, confirmation of alert on target odor will be established, confirmation of no alert on masking agent will be confirmed, and

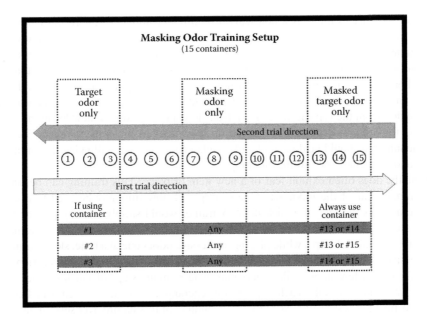

FIGURE 14.1 Masking odor training setup.

finally, it will present the masked target odor and possibly result in alert by the canine. This avails the opportunity to work on all the confounders in the maze with one setup (see Figure 14.1).

By presenting this line to the dog for investigation, the trainer should remember that there should be two alerts, one on each end of the line with no alert in the middle. Next the trainer should repeat the trial from the opposite end of the line, which will place all odors in different positions from before. As long as the dog correctly demonstrates the appropriate response, proceed to the next set of odors while discarding these training odors, which should not be used again. If the dog indicates on a distractor, extinction training should immediately commence. If the dog fails to alert to target odor or target plus distractor odor, remedial training should commence to reinforce an alert on the containers carrying target odor.

WELL-BALANCED DOG AND ENVIRONMENTAL SOUNDNESS

Another training approach sometimes omitted is environmental soundness training, which prepares the dog for the encounters of external stimuli that may be experienced in the course of deployment. Reactivity to slippery floors, people walking about or talking, loud noises such as gunfire, vehicle traffic, horns blowing, etc., which are all part of everyday life for a working dog, are unacceptable and training can solve these issues. Enabling the dog to encounter, negotiate through, and continue to perform amidst these issues is crucial, which makes environmental soundness key for a successful detection dog.

This training is vitally important (Lopes et al. 2015) and multifaceted. First, as hard as one tries, not all possible environmental anomalies can be trained for and many new experiences are inevitably encountered in the field. Therefore, it is incumbent upon the trainer to prepare a dog to encounter the unknown. By providing this training, a dog's internal confidence will grow considerably and reduce overall stress in the dog. When a trainer provides this training without any negative consequences, the confidence and trust the dog has in the trainer will grow as well, spurring even more trust and growth. This trust is easily transferable to a new handler when the time comes.

Many training regimens do not include environmental soundness conditioning. This can be evidenced by a dog that works well in the training environment but does not perform well outside that environment. Another example is a dog fearful of *slippery floors* (Slabbert and Odendaal 1999). Ultimately, the dog should be able to function well regardless of location, whether known or not. A well-conditioned dog can go to a location never seen and operate with complete confidence.

Early on, while learning to travel, the dog was exposed to some new environs that provide a head start. For best practice, with target odor now being a primary driver for the dog, that odor can be used as an enticement for learning new environments. To accomplish this, the trainer simply removes the dog from the typical training environs to expose the dog to new locations. Prior to the dog entering the area, hides should be placed in new locations or on new item(s). Each new hide location encountered should be done with only slight encouragement, allowing the animal to freely seek, find, and then enjoy the reward for doing so.

Additionally, dogs often exhibit fear of a new item or place. This training can be used to completely eliminate fear of the unknown. One example of how this may be used to overcome this would be to address the fear of a slick floor. A trainer would simply start by placing target odor outside the area with a slick floor and allow the dog to locate and then receive the reward. Next, in a series of very incremental steps, while placing successive odors one at a time, slowly transition each hide progressively deeper inside the area with the slick floor. Depending on the reaction of the dog, this may take only a few steps while others may require many steps of much smaller increments. Care should be taken to make each exploration, encounter, reward, and removal from the area extremely positive for best results. Successive encounters of this nature over several days can easily remove fear and replace it with confidence and mental strength for deployment. This type of training is also routinely overlooked in scientific study (see Smith et al. 2003, noting "[i]deal candidates were unable to look away from the object regardless of distractions within the testing area….").

CONTINUOUS IMPROVEMENT IS MANDATORY

In a typical training scenario, when a dog misses an odor, the handler will assist the dog into the proper location and cue the dog, and it is generally documented as a positive find. Dog training and handling is not a perfect art or science and therefore always provides room for improvement.

> Industry-wide adoption of an ethos of continuous quality improvement, voluntary welfare accreditation and certified training qualifications will result in a degree of difference occurring between service providers – both within and between industry sectors. Market forces will influence the adoption of best practice by this industry. (Branson et al. 2012)

While some detector dog teams are highly proficient and have proven reliability, sometimes apparently achieving 100% reliability (Brooks et al. 2003), some canine teams may be good but far from perfect. It is for this reason that teams should implement a continuous improvement process (CIP) for training to increase the overall reliability of the team.

> Although few additional studies have critically examined the efficacy of detection teams, improved training, certification and maintenance protocols have been developed by various government agencies and private certifying organizations. To ensure scientific validity, important evaluation issues include identifying what items might cause false alerts and exposing these items in training and testing. Measurements should be conducted in a double-blind fashion with impartial evaluators and the results evaluated to determine reliability. Also, tests should include positive controls (known explosive scents free from potential contamination) and negative controls (no sample or potentially interfering or distracting samples. (Furton and Myers 2001)

Training is the act of teaching the dog or the handler, or both, the requisite information and techniques to accomplish the job assigned. During training, a typical scenario would dictate that the trainer places odor and allows the odor to reach equilibrium in the location, and then the various teams take turns running the scenario in a single-blind test. If a problem is presented such as a miss (dog does not locate odor) or a false alert during the deployment, the trainer works with the handler and the dog to assist in locating the odor and conclude with a positive outcome. That scenario would generally be documented as a positive find in training records even though a miss or false alert occurred. Unfortunately, this type of training often thrusts the handler into not only learning his job but also attempting to read the dog, which can be overwhelming to some and is conducted far too often in detection dog work.

A different perspective is to approach training as just what it is—teaching. One of the most effective methods of teaching is say, see, and do type of training (Felder and Silverman 1988). Using this method would dictate that the trainer, handler, and any other witness possess knowledge of all necessary criteria and possible actions, including expected outcomes, prior to running the scenario. The handler would then watch as the trainer (or someone else) runs the dog through the scenario to see if it matches the expected outcome. If not, discussion satisfies reasons as to why the scenario differed from expectations and the scenario is rerun. If the first pass is as expected, the handler is then provided an opportunity to run the scenario with the dog. If outcomes match, everyone can move on to another scenario. If not, a complete and thorough discussion to understand why outcomes failed to match expectations should take place, during which modifications are possible. At this point, the scenario is rerun until such time as expectations coincide with outcomes. This allows all parties present to constantly and immediately compare what is expected to what is seen. When a handler is able to describe to the trainer what they are seeing as it is happening, this greatly increases learning (Felder and Silverman 1988). Allowing the handler to learn how the dog will react in constantly changing circumstances and scenarios is paramount for the handler to improve by providing a comparison between what is expected and what was observed. Described another way, when a dog is searching independently, it allows the handler a position of observation where they can see what the dog is doing instead of being directly involved in an action where they are concentrating on their own actions as well as the dog actions.

This type of instruction increases learning and can only be compounded by running more scenarios, which translates into demonstrated proficiency. This equates to a higher reliability due to the handler being able to better read the dog in differing circumstances as well as removing the human element from the search. It also better prepares the handler to walk into most any scenario, in training or in the field, and quickly sum up expectations that can then be instantly compared as the dog is deployed. Additionally, experiential knowledge accumulated allows the handler to learn without having negative consequences thrust upon the dog needlessly while exposing areas of potential improvement.

SINGLE-BLIND AND DOUBLE-BLIND TESTING

There are generally two types of testing used to evaluate dogs and handlers. These are single-blind testing (SBT) and double-blind testing (DBT). SBT is most often used as the be-all and end-all when, in fact, it should only be used in a training program after proficiency has been demonstrated to the trainer, as it is simply a litmus test for progression. With this testing, only the trainer knows the particulars of each scenario, and the handler and the dog operate in single-blind fashion. Single-blind tests are used far too frequently as part of a training day and act as a disservice by allowing the handler to make mistakes long before demonstrating proficiency, which the dog also experiences, adding to confusion and having an opposite impact of those desired. This type of testing should be implemented only when the team has displayed complete command in the training and used only to expose issues and build confidence.

DBT is the true testing method used experimentally to qualify a team for deployment. A double-blind test routinely is basic in scientific analysis and mandates that no one in the testing environment be aware of the placement of target odor, nontarget odor, or blanks (no odor at all). DBT requires a minimum of three people to execute properly. A handler is required to manage the dog during the exercise. An evaluator documents the outcome of the actions performed by the dog and the handler.

Neither of these people have any knowledge of the trial setup, whether odor is used or not, and where any odor may be placed. An experimenter sets up each aspect of the trial(s) including targets, distractors, and masking odor(s) along with determining where blanks are placed. This type of testing is as close as one gets to real-world working conditions. DBT should be implemented only when complete proficiency has been repeatedly demonstrated in each segment of training and should be used annually to determine the actual deployment reliability via scientific method.

Although "no systematic deterioration in detection performance for up to four months" (Johnston 1999), or some other period, may be claimed, routine maintenance training should be mandatory for detection dog teams. Although no standard has been imposed by any national certification organization, most teams adopt a regimen of 16 h per month (Cormier et al. 1995), usually broken down into one training day every other week. A problem with this structure is that training sessions routinely result in a get-friendly, get-together, resulting in more socializing than training.

Training with others is important, but it is equally important to maintain momentum for improvement. One way to accomplish this is to train more frequently in smaller buckets of time, allowing for others to participate and witness ongoing successes and failures. Instead of building a training day into a schedule, insert training into a workday. Work as you train and train as you work. As stated by Ericsson (2008),

> The best training situations focus on activities of short duration with opportunities for immediate feedback, reflection, and corrections. Each completed trial should be followed by another similar brief task with feedback, until this type of task is completed with consistent success.

INTRODUCING NEW TECHNOLOGIES OR STANDARDS

As technology is developed to aid the canine or team in their work, training must take place to introduce the new technology. Inevitably, Weilenmann and Juhlin (2011) are correct in observing that "the relationship between dogs and humans change when new technology is introduced." Whether a simple microphone (Thesen et al. 1993) or "a wireless device that is worn by the off-leash working dog which lets the handler know whether the dog is sniffing sufficiently as it moves through the area" (Gazit et al. 2003), a dog-mounted camera system (Ferworn et al. 2006), technology that removes the dog from the field for remote sniffing (Fjellanger et al. 2002; Schoon et al. 2014), or possibly bio-inspired devices (Nguyen and Kemp 2008), technology will continue to evolve and the dog must be trained to adapt to these new ideas.

RECORDKEEPING INTEGRITY

Implementing a CIP allows honest assessment of weaknesses, which exposes areas of performance to be dedicated for improvement. While most legal systems routinely experience challenges to canine reliability, many trainers and handlers continue to operate with information based somewhere between pure assumption and flawed data. Whether the method of capturing data is a hand-written report or a sophisticated computer program capable of easily furnishing any type of report one could imagine, this problem is created due to the lack of accurate and honest documentation. In addition to failing to require reports for each and every alert as a unique stand-alone event in training, testing, certification, and field deployment, it is even suggested by some best practices being offered today that one can have an *unconfirmed alert* (SWGDOG SC1 2011). Many claim that technology does not exist to allow a confirmation or deny the presence of residual or lingering odor in this type alert, and therefore it should not count either for or against the team. The reality is every alert counts. There may be times when residual odor is documented in police reports, even though no confirmation statement was made to the officer indicating the recent presence of the target odor substance. Other times, residual or lingering odor or shake (residue) may be documented, even though no evidence was collected or even witnessed that would indicate the recent presence of target odor substance (*Huff v. Reichert*, 744 F.3d 999 (7th Cir., 2014)). Still yet, it could happen where these types of alerts are left undocumented due to having inconclusive results. Aside from the injustice of accountability for actions, this type of acceptance of the unknown is, in the opinion of the author, undermining the honesty needed for improvement.

Alerts are commonly overlooked when teams of K9 units use group-training days to deploy canine teams in schools. A dog may alert on five uniquely different items, which may be documented on one form, if documented at all. Another example might be a typical traffic stop where a dog alerts to a vehicle and no contraband is located, which results in no documentation of an alert. The lack of these honest data limits the usefulness of any information gathered, as what is in existence is skewed at best.

To rectify this, each and every alert must be documented. Each alert must be classified to establish whether an alert was successful in discovering evidence (positive attribution for the team), either physical or in a statement made by the individual to the handler directly (hearsay not permitted), or whether no evidence was discovered in the search (negative attribution for the team). Only by comparing the two segments of data can true reliability begin to be established. Without honest assessment, improvement is but a dream. Unfortunately, an attitude of secrecy persists in record-keeping. One such example is a prosecutor in Ohio recommending the destruction of records avoiding disclosure to defense attorneys (Ensminger and Papet 2014).

CERTIFICATIONS

Instead of training to maximum proficiency, trainers often train *to* a certification. Certifications are required by most agencies using scent discrimination dogs today. Unfortunately, many certifications are inherently flawed and may do more harm than good as they often use subjective measures, which may be altered depending on the handler, handler's agency, dog, trainer, evaluator, and organization or association being used. In its simplest form, these previews of performance may take as little as a few minutes with others requiring 40 h to complete, although it should be noted that time is not a measure of difficulty or adequacy.

While many different organizations or associations exist that can provide a certification, some only certify law enforcement officers, such as the United States Police Canine Association (USPCA), while others certify civilians, such as the North American Police Work Dog Association (NAPWDA), in disciplines such as SAR work. There are others that test both prequalified civilian teams as well as law enforcement in narcotics and explosives.

A certification may encompass various aspects of the canine team performance, with the team displaying obedience, scent work, tracking, apprehension, etc., while others are only interested in odor work. While all aspects of a certification may be important, some of the most disturbing issues with current certification practices often deal directly with olfaction.

Predetermined bias is far too common in certification testing. Most dogs involved in olfaction work are deployed in law enforcement circles, and the common belief is certification events should be limited to law enforcement only. This means that the scenarios from target odor placement, distractors, masking odors, scenario design, etc. are established, set up, monitored, documented, and judged by fellow officers. Further, the handler may work in a department with or that has close ties to the evaluator, who happens to be a fellow canine officer, often the same officer supplying backup in time of need, possibly inviting a go-along, get-along mentality sometimes associated with embattled law enforcement departments. Additionally, certifications are sometimes adjusted based upon promises to correct deficiencies. Obviously these issues individually or combined can create overwhelming bias, which courts routinely ignore (Ensminger and Papet 2014).

Even more important is the lack of scientific standards being considered in testing criteria. Certifications routinely use SBT and, sometimes worse, intentionally or inadvertently exposing hide locations to participants. Subjective evaluation is routinely used when it comes to accuracy on sourcing odor. A simple best practice should include a series of trials of various difficulty using double-blind evaluations by an unbiased person. To increase transparency to the people served, qualified visitors should be allowed to witness these trials without being visible to the team.

Additionally, all scientific study should adopt the practice of establishing an entry baseline for dogs entering a study rather than relying upon a preexisting *national organization* or other certification. This one simple act of adding a series of simple double-blind tests prior to initiating the study will add extreme credibility to a study for reason outlined above.

SUMMARY

Training and working a detection dog can be extremely demanding, both physically and mentally, often far beyond the scope of what is normally seen in a well-behaved animal at the end of a lead. Many split-second decisions must be made in the midst of a complex and dynamic environment in order to support the opportunity for successful completion, regardless of the outcome. To accomplish this task, a variety of elements must coalesce into one formidable team. A breakdown of any element at any point and disaster can strike. This is exactly why excellent training is so absolutely vital, for anything less is not worthy of conversation. And to improve requires exploration and research with handlers and trainers assisting in the development of priorities (SWGDOG SC7 2010).

This all starts with the typical three-legged stool being composed of the right dog, the handler, and the trainer. Even an inferior dog can perform to the incredibly high standards demanded in daily detection work if excellent training is provided. Similarly, a naïve handler can look like a seasoned professional providing excellent training guides along the way. In other words, starting with something less than ideal can reach extreme heights provided that the right instruction is given. However, should training begin with an inferior trainer, training principle, or process, one should be prepared, at best, to accept the accolade of mediocrity. This is exactly why excellent training is very important.

Some believe that training has a beginning, middle, and end when, in reality, it is a journey, for once training starts, it should never end for the entire working life of the dog. There should exist a foundation of continuous improvement for the simple fact that mistakes will be made and must be corrected for anything less is a state of complete denial. A certification is nothing more than a snapshot of performance on any given day and does nothing to measure or substantiate findings that happen in a real world, with real people, with real lives, some of which could be harmed by the false presumption of competence, proficiency, and statistical performance.

Dogs are amazing animals that are capable of achieving monumental tasks when properly trained to extremely high statistical standards. They, in turn, search for hours and work for long periods of time (Garner et al. 2001), with very little needed, and then do it all again the very next day, no questions asked. It is only hoped that the trainer and the handler can live up to the expectations of the dog.

Section IV

Uses in Forensics and Law

That dogs can recognize the scent of individuals was known to Homer, who describes Argos as a hunting dog once "very clever at tracking," recognizing Odysseus, his master who has been missing for 19 years, though no one else in the palace is able to do so. The poet's emphasis on the dog's once keen sense of smell, and the fact that the king of Ithaca looked so different after his extended absence that even his wife did not know him, suggest that odor was how Argos recognized his master. Argos, the first dog given a name in western literature, would have been 21 years old. The knowledge of his master's return allowed the long-neglected but ever faithful animal to slide peacefully into the "doom of dark death" (*Odyssey* 17.290-327, Lattimore translation 1975; Lilja 1976, p. 29).

Even in antiquity, dogs tracked not only game but also humans. In the fourth century BC, King Philip of Macedon is said to have used dogs to track enemies in the Balkan mountains (Forster 1941). A fourth century Christian writer, Basil, described dogs as capable of thought and compared their tracking ability to finding the true argument:

> When the dog is on the track of game, if he sees it divide in different directions, he examines these different paths, and speech alone fails him to announce his reasoning. The creature, he says, is gone here or there or in another direction. It is neither here nor there; it is therefore in the third direction. And thus, neglecting the false tracks, he discovers the true one. What more is done by those who, gravely occupied in demonstrating theories, trace lines upon the dust and reject two propositions to show that the third is the true one? (Nicene and Post-Nicene Fathers II.viii, 350)

In 1808, a dog was credited with finding the body of a missing child by refusing to move from a location in a wood shed (Anselm von Feuerbach 1808, p. 9), yet formal cadaver dog work only began in the 1970s. Teaching dogs to recognize odors of narcotics, explosives, and other items dates from the late 1960s and early 1970s, although, during World War II, the British Army taught dogs to recognize "'unexploded' explosive scent" from landmines buried from 3 to 12 in. deep (Lloyd 1948; for a general timeline of initial deployments by police departments of dogs with specialized functions, see Ensminger 2012, pp. 5–6).

COMPARING CANINE EVIDENCE WITH OTHER FORENSIC TECHNIQUES

Canine behavior must be considered from numerous angles in training and using dogs in law enforcement functions. Variables in behavior can be assessed qualitatively in terms of specific body movements and reactions, and quantitatively in terms of frequency, mean duration, standard deviation, and range. In biology, it is taken for granted that exceptions or deviations from typical behavioral patterns will occur, and such variations are normal phenomena. Law enforcement tasks assigned to dogs include subduing suspects and controlling crowds, tracking and identifying perpetrators, detecting illicit substances and contraband, finding human bodies, rescuing victims in avalanches and disasters, and sometimes comforting people in distress. Those functions that involve the police dog's sense of smell raise questions of reliability and accuracy that police administrators are required to consider and lawyers in courtrooms will raise in prosecuting or defending those accused of crimes. Labeling canine olfactory work as unscientific, or more disparagingly, as junk science, is, however, going too far in categorizing such work. Results of hundreds of papers in peer-reviewed journals demonstrate that despite the fact that canine indications are not 100% accurate, most results are statistically far better than chance.

High-technology methods, such as DNA testing, and thoroughly vetted forensics techniques, such as fingerprint analysis, have deservedly achieved wide acceptance and easy admission as trial evidence, but should not be seen as requiring by comparison that canine work and other statistically less reliable forensics techniques be jettisoned altogether. On the other hand, neither should canine evidence be accepted based solely on testimony, tradition, and police experience built up over more than a century as to tracking evidence and half a century as to contraband detection evidence. Far too much of the judicial history of canine evidence has been controlled by police trainers and handlers as witnesses, either for the prosecution or the defense, without comparing such testimony to the growing body of scientific literature on the reliability of canine detection either in the laboratory or the field.

It is worth noting that forensics is one area where other species than dogs are being deployed for olfactory work, though generally in very restricted situations. This includes bees for detecting drugs (Schott et al. 2015) and pouched rats for finding land mines (Poling et al. 2011a,b; see also Chapter 10 herein). It has also been posited that elephants may recognize the scent of landmines and even warn conspecifics of the threat, and may be trained to recognize the odor of other explosives (Steyn 2015). Research being conducted at the University of Witwatersrand, South Africa, in collaboration with Adventures with Elephant and the U.S. Army Research Office shows that in the detection of TNT, elephants have demonstrated 95.1% specificity and 99.7% sensitivity (Miller et al. 2015).

SCIENTISTS VS. LAWYERS VS. TRAINERS VS. HANDLERS

Chapters in this section of the book differ depending on the professional profile of the author, whether lawyers, some scientists, or trainers. Lawyers build their arguments largely on judicial concepts as developed by courts and law school and academic analysis of canine evidence. The legal focus is often on how field evidence and scientific research can be correlated with legal concepts of proof and admissibility of evidence in courtroom settings. Is a sniff of a dog to be considered a search under a country's concept of a suspect's rights? On the other hand, scientists writing here, as elsewhere in this volume, are more interested in verifying the significance of experimental results by applying statistical tests.

CONFLICTING CONCEPTS OF RELIABILITY AND DIFFERENT TYPES OF FAILURE

Referring to canines, if sniffer dogs used systematically for forensic purposes are correct in 90% of trials, a statistical test would warrant a finding that dogs are able to detect or identify the odor, but from a legal point of view, there is still a concern about the 10% failure rate. An attorney would claim that his or her client belongs to the 10% where the identification or detection procedure is erroneous. Although such an error rate would probably not satisfy a legal standard such as guilt beyond a reasonable doubt, if the judge takes an all-or-nothing view as to the reliability of a dog, the evidence may nevertheless be admitted.

The author of the chapter on scent lineups, a biologist, backs his arguments and opinions with his own experimental results and those of other researchers, using statistical tests. Dogs, as living creatures, cannot be compared with machines. In particular, it is relatively easy to assess when a machine is out of order, whereas dogs can make mistakes without clearly identifiable reasons. Considering trained canine sniffing from a biological perspective, used for purposes that are relevant for humans and irrelevant for canine biology, such as narcotics or explosives detection, it is easily acknowledged by the scientist that mistakes or failures may occur. In nature, predators make numerous mistakes and often fail in hunting for prey, yet success in hunting is crucial for the survival of predators.

There are two broad kinds of canine errors. The first is a false alert (false positive) when a dog alerts but no trained target odor is present. The second is a miss (a false negative indication) when the dog does not alert to a target odor that is present. The frequency of these mistakes determines the accuracy of the dog. Reasons for the two kinds of errors can be quite different. They may, for instance, result from an insufficient operant conditioning when poor training has created a vague association among the target odor, the trained response, and the reward or has, to some degree, extinguished the association. The dog may be bored or motivation for a reward may be poor, resulting in a dog being temporarily uninterested in searching. Mistakes can also be related to temporary deterioration of acuity or discrimination ability. (See Chapter 5 on the effects of disease.)

Some reasons for failure cannot be fully ascribed to the dog but rather to the handler or the search circumstances. For example, due to specific airflow at the searching location, the odor may be blown downwind and away from the source while the dog is operating upwind of the source, which means that no possibility exists for odor molecules to contact the dog's olfactory organ. (That air flow is not always correctly described, even in the scientific literature, was argued in Chapter 8 on aerodynamics.)

A false alert, on the other hand, may appear to occur when a dog alerts to the residual target odor of an illicit substance that was present sometime before the search but which was moved prior to the time of the search. From the dog's perspective, it is correct, but in a courtroom setting, a lawyer may insist on calling it a false alert. The question of what produces the odor, and how long it lingers, can be particularly complicated with some illicit substances, as discussed in Chapters 9 and 17.

Legal consequences of dogs' false alerts and misses can differ depending on the kind of search, material, and situation. If, for example, the customs officer at a border checkpoint is authorized to request passengers to open their luggage and no detection dogs are deployed, the officer would make a detailed check of randomly selected luggage. If dogs are deployed, and a request to open the luggage is made because of a false alert of a dog and no illicit material is found, there may be no legal consequences. More serious consequences may follow when results of a scent identification by dogs are presented in court as evidence of guilt, which with corroborative evidence, may lead to a conviction. If conclusive exonerating evidence is later found, perhaps years after the defendant has been incarcerated, it may be realized that the corroborating evidence was weak and the canine identification should never have been admitted in the first place. Thus, in identifying a perpetrator on the basis of odor, eliminating false alerts and all other forms of error should be paramount.

OTHER CONSIDERATIONS IN CANINE DEPLOYMENT

Legal issues and consequences of using detection dogs may be quite unexpected, as was shown by Australian research, which found that detection and deterrence rates remained low despite deployment of detection dogs (Dunn and Degenhardt 2009; Dray et al. 2012; Hickey et al. 2012). Negative effects included reports of some suspects hastily consuming large amounts of drugs upon seeing a dog, raising health concerns. Thus, determining the social value of deploying police dogs for detection functions is not restricted solely to the quality of the detection dog's behavioral repertoire.

Tadeusz Jezierski, John Ensminger, and L.E. Papet

15 Canine Drug-Detection Evidence

Admissibility, Canine Qualifications, and Investigative Practices

Leslie A. Shoebotham

The right of the people to be secure in their persons, houses, papers, and effects, against unreasonable searches and seizures, shall not be violated, and no Warrants shall issue, but upon probable cause, supported by Oath or affirmation, and particularly describing the place to be searched, and the persons or things to be seized (U.S. Constitution, 4th Amendment).

BACKGROUND AND CANINE SNIFF DOCTRINE

As the U.S. Supreme Court has explained, "the ultimate touchstone of the Fourth Amendment is 'reasonableness.'"[1] When law enforcement officials engage in a *search* within the meaning of the Fourth Amendment, "reasonableness generally requires the obtaining of a judicial warrant."[2] The Court recently reiterated that "[i]n the absence of a warrant, a search is reasonable only if it falls within a specific exception to the warrant requirement."[3] Critically important to the analysis of most canine sniffs—i.e., those sniffs performed on objects located in a public area—the Court has concluded that a drug-detection sniff by a reliable detection dog is *not* a "search" under the Fourth Amendment.[4] Therefore, in determining the admissibility of a warrantless canine alert, justifying the sniff under a particular warrant exception is not necessary, or even appropriate, because the sniff is not a "search" in the first place.

The Court first considered the constitutionality of a warrantless canine drug-detection sniff in *United States v. Place*.[5] There, agents seized Place's luggage on the basis of reasonable suspicion in order to subject the bags to a canine sniff.[6] The question in *Place* was whether *Terry v. Ohio* supported a brief seizure of *personal property* on the basis of reasonable suspicion—as contrasted with the detention of an individual that the *Terry* Court upheld.[7] Although *Place* expanded *Terry* to allow law enforcement to briefly seize personal property on the basis of reasonable suspicion,[8] the detention of Place's luggage violated the Fourth Amendment because the agents held onto Place's luggage for too long—90 min—before subjecting the bags to a canine sniff.[9] Despite rejecting the luggage seizure in *Place* based upon its length and intrusiveness, *Place* nevertheless went on to address the warrantless canine sniff to which Place's luggage was eventually subjected.

Justice O'Connor, writing for the majority, explained that a canine sniff of luggage located at an airport is not a search because the sniff is "much less intrusive than a typical search"—i.e., the sniff does not require opening the luggage—and the information revealed by the sniff is "limited" in that it "discloses only the presence or absence of narcotics, a contraband item." Based on the limited information disclosed—the existence of contraband and nothing else—the *Place* Court concluded that a "canine sniff by a well-trained narcotics detection dog ... did not constitute a 'search' within the meaning of the Fourth Amendment."[10]

Place's authority was bolstered just a year later in *United States v. Jacobsen*,[11] in which the Court considered two issues: the scope of the so-called private search doctrine and whether the Fourth Amendment required officers to obtain a warrant to field test suspected contraband.[12] In upholding the warrantless field-testing, *Jacobsen* concluded that because contraband is illegal, an individual lacks a legitimate expectation of privacy in possessing it.[13] After *Place* and *Jacobsen*, then, the critical question became whether the *circumstances* of the contraband's possession—i.e., the contraband's location in a high privacy area, like a home—might make a difference in determining whether a warrant is required to perform a canine sniff of that location.

After *Place*, modern law enforcement has increasingly relied on canine drug-detection sniffs.[14] From a law enforcement perspective, one of the primary advantages of the canine sniff technique is the sheer speed with which an individual's luggage or vehicle can be screened for the presence of contraband. That speedy canine alert allows law enforcement to make quick decisions about whether further investigation of an individual or a vehicle is appropriate, thereby ensuring that the detention required (to perform the sniff) remains within lawful limits.

CANINE SNIFFS OF VEHICLES

Despite questions concerning the accuracy of drug-detection sniffs,[15] after *Place* the Court has expanded—with two notable exceptions[16]—law enforcement's authority to use warrantless canine sniffs. In *Illinois v. Caballes*, the Court held that a canine sniff of a vehicle during a lawful traffic stop was not a "search" for Fourth Amendment purposes.[17] *Caballes* involved a routine traffic stop for speeding. While a warning ticket was being written (and while Caballes was seated with the officer in the squad car), a second officer arrived and deployed a drug-detection dog to perform a canine sniff of the exterior of Caballes's vehicle. The dog alerted on the vehicle's trunk. Based on the automobile exception to the Fourth Amendment's warrant requirement,[18] the detection dog's alert provided probable cause to perform a warrantless search of Caballes's vehicle.[19] Upon opening the trunk, the officers found the marijuana for which Caballes was arrested.

In addition to reaffirming the validity of the canine sniff technique, *Caballes* is important because the Court upheld law enforcement's authority to perform a canine sniff of a vehicle at an ordinary traffic stop[20]—i.e., a traffic stop in which the officers *lacked* reasonable suspicion to believe that Caballes was transporting drugs in his vehicle.[21] *Caballes* also introduced the requirement that a drug-detection dog must be "well-trained"[22] in order for the dog's alert to establish probable cause to search the vehicle. Finally, critically important in *Caballes* was the fact that the traffic stop—i.e., the seizure—had been lawful and that the duration of the stop was not extended to accommodate performing the canine sniff.[23]

DRAGNET SNIFFS OF PARKED VEHICLES

Caballes was also important for what the opinion did not say. The *Caballes* majority did not elaborate on whether authority exists for law enforcement to perform suspicionless drug-detection sniffs of *parked* vehicles—i.e., dragnet drug-detection sniffs of vehicles parked, for example, at a public shopping mall or other public location. The *Caballes* dissenters clearly feared that *Caballes* would be read to support dragnet canine sniffs, however.[24] Justices Souter and Ginsburg, in their respective *Caballes* dissents, argued that suspicionless dragnet drug-detection sniffs would be too intrusive to be treated as non-searches under the Fourth Amendment. So, dragnet drug-detection sniffs of vehicles parked at public locations would, at the very least, be controversial and would likely be subject to a strong challenge by a defendant seeking suppression of any contraband found in a vehicle search performed as a result of the sniff. With that said, however, there is one type of dragnet drug-detection sniff that lower courts have *upheld*: canine sniffs of students' vehicles parked in their school's parking lot.[25] Although the Court has yet to address this narrow school-sniff issue, dicta—i.e., statements not necessary to reach a court's holding—in some of the Court's school-search cases arguably provide support for this particular dragnet practice.[26]

EXTENDING A COMPLETED TRAFFIC STOP TO PERFORM A CANINE SNIFF

Since *Caballes*, the Court's interest in the canine sniff technique has not waned. The Court has decided three canine-sniff cases.[27] Like *Caballes*, the newly released case, *Rodriguez v. United States*, also arose out of a canine sniff performed at a traffic stop and asked the Court to decide important questions left unresolved by *Caballes*. The traffic stop in *Rodriguez* was initiated after a patrol officer, who had been tailing Rodriguez's vehicle, observed the car briefly veer off the highway onto the road's shoulder and then return to the traffic lane—a traffic violation under Nebraska law. Unlike the traffic stop in *Caballes*, however, the canine sniff of Rodriguez's vehicle was performed 7 to 8 min *after* the patrol officer issued Rodriguez a warning ticket for the lane change violation. Importantly, the delay in performing the canine sniff was seemingly not due to any lack of diligence on law enforcement's part.[28] And, as a final piece to the puzzle, although the patrol officer had a *hunch* that Rodriguez was transporting drugs in his vehicle, the magistrate found that reasonable suspicion to detain Rodriguez to investigate a drug crime was *lacking*[29]—a finding that the district court and U.S. Eighth Circuit did not disturb in upholding the canine sniff of Rodriguez's vehicle as valid under the Fourth Amendment.[30]

In upholding the canine sniff of Rodriguez's vehicle, the Eighth Circuit concluded that the 7 to 8 min extension of Rodriguez's already completed traffic stop did not invalidate the otherwise lawful stop.[31] In the Eighth Circuit's view, the extension was no more than "a de minimis intrusion on Rodriguez's personal liberty." The U.S. Supreme Court granted Rodriguez's petition for certiorari to address a circuit split on this issue: whether law enforcement's suspicionless extension of a traffic stop to investigate other crime—even for a short (i.e., de minimis) period of time—violates the Fourth Amendment.[32]

In a 6–3 decision authored by Justice Ginsburg, the Court held that "a police stop exceeding the time needed to handle the matter for which the stop was made violates the Constitution's shield against unreasonable seizures. A seizure justified only by a police-observed traffic violation, therefore, 'become[s] unlawful if it is prolonged beyond the time reasonably required to complete th[e] missions' of issuing a ticket for the violation."[33] As the majority saw it, the problem with the sniff was not that it was unrelated to the reason for the traffic stop—*Rodriguez* expressly reiterated that the Fourth Amendment was not violated by "unrelated investigation that did not lengthen the roadside detention."[34] Instead, the canine sniff violated the Fourth Amendment because the sniff was performed *after* the time reasonably required to issue the ticket. In so finding, *Rodriguez* rejected the government's argument that a de minimis extension of a traffic stop in order to perform a canine sniff was a minor intrusion that was offset by the government's strong interest in interdicting contraband.

As *Rodriguez* explained, the canine sniff fell outside the routine scope or *ordinary incident* of a traffic stop, and could not be "fairly characterized as part of the officer's traffic mission"—a mission that was noted to include "checking the driver's license, determining whether there are outstanding warrants against the driver, and inspecting the automobile's registration and proof of insurance."[35] In response to the *Rodriguez* dissenters' cynical prediction that officers would simply perform the canine sniff *prior to* issuing the traffic ticket, the majority explained that the key inquiry was an officer's *diligence*; "[t]he critical question, then, is not whether the dog sniff occurs before or after the officer issues a ticket, as Justice Alito supposes, but whether conducting the sniff prolongs—i.e., adds time to—the stop."[36] Although *Rodriguez* created a bright line of Fourth Amendment protection, it remains to be seen whether the decision provides a meaningful limitation on suspicionless canine sniffs of vehicles at traffic stops. Or instead, might *Rodriguez* be circumvented, as the dissenters predicted, by simply performing the canine sniff at the outset of the traffic stop and then rolling the dice—i.e., hoping that the trial court finds the overall length of the stop was not prolonged to accommodate the sniff. Only time will tell.

VEHICLE-SNIFF LIMITATIONS

A canine sniff of the exterior of a lawfully stopped vehicle does not violate the Fourth Amendment because the sniff itself is not a search.[37] In addition to *Rodriguez*'s limitation on suspicionless extensions of completed traffic stops, the authority to perform a vehicle sniff has an *additional* restriction. In the absence of probable cause—which is generally lacking prior to the drug-detection dog's alert—the Fourth Amendment is violated if the detection dog *physically enters* the vehicle while performing the sniff.[38] This rule has an important exception, however. If the detection dog's entry into the vehicle was "*instinctual* rather than orchestrated" by law enforcement, the dog's warrantless physical entry will not violate the Fourth Amendment and the dog's subsequent alert to the presence of contraband within the vehicle is admissible (assuming that the detection dog is found to be reliable).[39]

In determining whether the canine handler or patrol officer *facilitated* the detection dog's entry into a vehicle, federal courts look to whether the officer (1) placed the dog inside the vehicle or encouraged the dog to enter;[40] or (2) asked the vehicle's occupants to provide an entry point for the detection dog, such as by opening the vehicle's windows, doors, or hatchback, which the dog then uses to gain entry into the vehicle.[41] In a recent case, the U.S. Tenth Circuit relied on a patrol car's dashcam video in concluding that the detection dog's entry into the suspect's vehicle was facilitated by law enforcement—because the patrol officer had *prevented* the vehicle's occupants from closing the doors after they were asked to exit the vehicle.[42]

CANINE SNIFFS OF HOMES

Prior to *Rodriguez*, the Court decided two canine-sniff cases—*Florida v. Jardines*[43] and *Florida v. Harris*[44]—cases that have had a substantial impact on the canine-sniff practice area. In *Jardines*, the Court considered whether the Fourth Amendment was violated by a warrantless canine sniff of a private home—a sniff that was made possible by the officers and detection dog's physical entry onto the home's curtilage[45] (Jardines's front porch).[46] A *search* occurred, *Jardines* explained, because police had "gathered … information by physically entering and occupying the [curtilage of the house] to engage in conduct not explicitly or implicitly permitted by the homeowner." Importantly, *Jardines* did *not* analyze the Fourth Amendment question under the so-called *Katz* test,[47] an approach adopted in the late 1960s requiring consideration of Jardines's privacy expectations in the information that the canine sniff revealed.[48] Instead, *Jardines* relied on *United States v. Jones*[49] in holding that the canine sniff of Jardines's home was a *search*—because the government's physical intrusion into a constitutionally protected area (the home's curtilage) was done to *gather evidence*.[50]

Jardines distinguished between, on the one hand, a physical entry to gain evidence—which *Jardines* held requires a search warrant—and, on the other, an officer's entry to knock on a person's door simply to engage the home's occupant in conversation.[51] Because the officers and detection dog's entry exceeded "background social norms," the Fourth Amendment was violated.[52] *Jardines* defended its reliance on an "unlicensed physical intrusion" to answer the Fourth Amendment question, rather than applying *Katz*, by explaining that its "property-rights baseline" had the "virtue" of "keep[ing] easy cases easy."

Justice Kagan, writing on behalf of two other Justices, concurred to make the point that the case could just as easily have been decided based on *Katz*.[53] In the concurring Justices' view, *Kyllo v. United States*[54]—a case that applied *Katz*'s reasonable-expectations test—controlled the canine sniff question.[55] Similar to the thermal imager at issue in *Kyllo*, Justice Kagan described drug-detection dogs as "highly trained tools of law enforcement, geared to respond in distinctive ways to specific scents so as to convey clear and reliable information to their human partners."[56] The concurring Justices clearly believed that, based on *Katz* and *Kyllo*, the canine sniff of Jardines's home violated Jardines's reasonable expectation of privacy and for *that* reason was a Fourth Amendment *search*. The outcome under either of *Jardines*'s two Fourth Amendment analyses was the same, however: a warrant was required to perform a canine sniff of a home.[57]

WARRANTLESS CANINE SNIFFS OF APARTMENTS

The divergence between the *Jardines* majority and concurring opinions may lead to different outcomes in at least one context, however. The *Jardines* majority based its Fourth Amendment analysis on law enforcement's unlicensed physical entry onto Jardines's curtilage to perform the canine sniff, not the privacy interests undermined by the sniff itself.[58] Therefore, *Jardines* does not address the constitutionality of canine sniffs of a person's living space that can be accomplished *without* an intrusion onto curtilage—i.e., canine sniffs of apartments or public housing projects performed from the facilities' common-area hallways.[59] After *Jardines*, courts have applied *Jardines*'s property-rights analysis to warrantless canine sniffs of apartments—sniffs performed from the apartments' common hallways—and have reached *opposite* results.[60] Importantly, however, in upholding a warrantless apartment sniff in *North Dakota v. Nguyen*, the North Dakota Supreme Court *ignored* Justice Kagan's *Kyllo*-based concurrence in *Jardines* in concluding that the sniff of the defendant's apartment did not intrude on the defendant's legitimate privacy expectations.[61] Notwithstanding *Nguyen*, however, the outcome of a *Kyllo*-based privacy analysis involving a canine sniff of a home or apartment remains an open question. And, it is almost certainly a mistake to assume that Justice Kagan's *Jardines* concurrence—which treats a detection dog as a "sense-enhancing tool" similar to the thermal imager in *Kyllo*—offers nothing to the *Kyllo*-based analysis of a canine sniff of a residence.[62]

Moreover, it seems inevitable that the validity of a warrantless apartment sniff will be challenged based upon Justice Kagan's *Kyllo*-based concurrence in *Jardines*.[63] To impose a warrant requirement on an apartment sniff, *Jardines*'s property-rights baseline can only be stretched so far before it risks defacing the very property concepts on which *Jardines* relies.[64] Consider, for example, *Illinois v. Burns*, an Illinois intermediate appellate court decision that successfully threaded the needle in applying *Jardines*'s property-rights baseline in requiring a warrant to sniff the defendant's apartment.[65] In *Burns*, even though the apartment sniff was performed in the apartment's common hallway, the court required a warrant because law enforcement performed the apartment sniff in the middle of the night.[66] Although properly decided,[67] *Burns* has likely stretched *Jardines*'s property-rights analysis about as far as it can legitimately go. Aside from middle-of-the-night apartment sniffs, to require a warrant under *Jardines*'s property-rights analysis courts will be required to draw subtle distinctions regarding *apartment curtilage*—decisions that will be, at best, only tenuously supported by the commonly held property-based societal understanding described in *Jardines*.[68]

GOOD FAITH EXCEPTION TO THE EXCLUSIONARY RULE

After *Jardines*, the good faith exception to the exclusionary rule[69] has become important in determining the admissibility of canine sniff evidence in cases where the canine sniff was performed *prior* to *Jardines*, but the case was not yet final at the time *Jardines* was decided. Based on the good faith exception, even though the pre-*Jardines* warrantless home-sniff violates the Fourth Amendment, the canine sniff evidence may nevertheless be admissible. Here, courts apply *Davis v. United States*,[70] the Court's recent decision on the good faith issue holding that when police "conduct a search in reliance on binding appellate precedent," the evidence is admissible under the good faith exception.[71] In applying *Davis* to pre-*Jardines* canine sniffs, courts first look to whether, prior to *Jardines*, binding state or circuit precedent existed that authorized a warrantless canine sniff of a person's residence.[72] Not surprisingly, differences in state and circuit precedent have produced opposite outcomes on whether the good faith exception is available for a pre-*Jardines* canine home-sniff.[73]

Public Property versus Private Property

The Minnesota Supreme Court quite properly concluded that *Jardines* could not be boiled down to a simple *private property* versus *public property* litmus test in determining whether a warrant is required to perform a canine sniff.[74] In *Minnesota v. Eichers*, the Minnesota Supreme Court was asked to impose a warrant requirement on a canine sniff of personal property—a mailed parcel—that was located on private property—a UPS mailing center—at the time of the sniff. In upholding the warrantless parcel-sniff, the court in *Eichers* contrasted the high expectation of privacy in one's home—the location sniffed in *Jardines*—with the location and the object sniffed in *Eichers*. Important in *Eichers*, both the defendant and the general public were *excluded* from accessing UPS's interior mailroom. Therefore, *Eichers* concluded that the defendant lacked a legitimate expectation of privacy in that private property location.

DETECTION DOG CERTIFICATION, TRAINING, AND FIELD PERFORMANCE RECORDS

Courts use certain documentation in determining a detection dog's reliability, including the dog's (1) certification, (2) training records, and (3) field performance records (when field performance records are available and the court finds them to be probative of canine reliability). Most drug-detection dogs receive their original training for contraband detection from private vendors,[75] which *certify* the dog's competency for drug detection.[76] The private certification process is controversial, however; no national or regulatory guidelines exist that establish best-practices standards for canine drug-detection certification.[77] Instead, detection dogs are certified in accordance with each private vendor's own internally generated certification standards—standards that differ significantly from agency to agency.[78] With that said, however, efforts are in place to establish an industry-wide certification and training guideline for drug-detection dogs. The Scientific Working Group on Dog and Orthogonal detector Guidelines (SWGDOG)—"a partnership of local, state, federal and international agencies including private vendors, law enforcement and first responders"[79]—was established to bolster the reliability of drug-detection dogs by creating a best-practices guideline, which could be voluntarily adopted by certifying agencies.[80]

Once a police agency purchases a drug-detection dog, responsibility for maintaining the dog's detection proficiency falls on the dog's canine handler—who is expected to implement a regular *training* program.[81] Training activities take place in a controlled environment—one that the canine handler creates in order to conduct drug-detection *exercises* with the dog. In addition to conducting exercises, a canine handler's responsibilities include documentation of those exercises in training records—which document important information, such as the "type and amount of drug used, number of searches, type of exercise done, location where the drug was hidden, time lapse of find, location of training environment, and whether the location of the drugs was known to the handler."[82] Also, to maintain the dog's status as a *certified* drug-detection dog, the dog is expected to undergo yearly recertification.[83] If the dog is not recertified, however, courts may nevertheless accept the dog as reliable if law enforcement conducted regular training with the dog during that period.[84]

And, finally, documentation concerning the detection dog's field accuracy—the dog's track record for locating contraband in the field—is set out in the detection dog's *field performance* records.[85] Although keeping and maintaining field performance records is the recommended practice,[86] not all police groups do so. Importantly, however, most courts have not required the government to produce field performance records and, additionally, have refused to draw an adverse inference on canine reliability if law enforcement did not keep records of the detection dog's accuracy in the field.[87]

DETERMINING CANINE RELIABILITY FOR CONTRABAND DETECTION

In *Florida v. Harris*,[88] the U.S. Supreme Court considered the critically important issue of canine reliability—i.e., how courts should determine whether a detection dog's alert is sufficiently reliable to establish probable cause.[89] Like *Caballes*,[90] *Harris* involved a drug-detection sniff of the exterior of a lawfully stopped vehicle.[91] Upon stopping Harris's truck, the patrol officer (Officer Wheetley) observed that Harris was "visibly nervous" and had an open beer can in the truck's cup holder. The officer asked for Harris's consent to search the truck, but Harris refused. The officer then retrieved his detection dog, Aldo, from his patrol car and deployed the dog for a "free air sniff" of the exterior of Harris's truck. Aldo alerted on the driver's-side door handle. A search of Harris's truck followed—a search that revealed "200 loose pseudoephedrine pills" and other precursor ingredients for the production of methamphetamine. Although Harris admitted to the officer that he "cooked methamphetamine at his house and could not go more than a few days without using it," the search of Harris's truck did not turn up any drugs.[92]

Harris was charged with possession of pseudoephedrine with intent to use it to manufacture methamphetamine. While out on bail, Harris, strangely enough, had a *second* run in with Officer Wheetley and Aldo. During this second traffic stop, Aldo again alerted to the driver's-side door handle, but the ensuing search of Harris's truck revealed "nothing of interest." Harris moved to suppress the evidence found in his vehicle during the first traffic stop, on the ground that the detection dog's alert had not established probable cause to search his vehicle.

At the suppression hearing, Officer Wheetley testified about both his and Aldo's training in drug detection. The Court described that testimony as follows:

> In 2004, Wheetley (and a different dog) completed a 160-hour course in narcotics detection offered by the Dothan, Alabama Police Department, while Aldo (and a different handler) completed a similar, 120-hour course given by the Apopka, Florida Police Department. That same year, Aldo received a one-year certification from Drug Beat, a private company that specializes in testing and certifying K-9 dogs. Wheetley and Aldo teamed up in 2005 and went through another, 40-hour refresher course in Dothan together. They also did four hours of training exercises each week to maintain their skills .... According to Wheetley, Aldo's performance in those exercises was 'really good.' The State introduced 'Monthly Canine Detection Training Logs' consistent with that testimony: They showed that Aldo always found hidden drugs and that he performed 'satisfactorily' (the higher of two possible assessments) on each day of training.[93]

Although Wheetley had not maintained complete field performance records for Aldo—i.e., Wheetley only documented Aldo's alerts that resulted in an arrest, not the alerts where a physical search failed to uncover any contraband—the trial court concluded that probable cause existed to search Harris's truck. The Florida Supreme Court reversed, however, adopting a *requirement* that police agencies maintain detection-dog field performance records and produce those records for the trial court's use in determining canine reliability.[94]

Despite calling its analysis a totality-of-the-circumstances test, the Florida Supreme Court was clearly requiring the State to introduce specific items of canine-reliability evidence, including field performance records, in every case involving a canine drug-detection sniff. The U.S. Supreme Court granted certiorari and unanimously reversed the Florida Supreme Court's decision.[95]

Justice Kagan, writing for the Court, framed the issue broadly, explaining that the Court was considering "how a court should determine if the 'alert' of a drug-detection dog during a traffic stop provides probable cause to search a vehicle." The Court rejected the Florida Supreme Court's "strict evidentiary checklist"—an approach that the Court emphasized was inconsistent with a totality-of-the-circumstances determination of probable cause.[96] And, in requiring a preset list of canine-reliability evidence, *Harris* declared that the Florida Supreme Court had "flouted" the Court's precedents on totality determinations.[97]

Harris instead found that a detection dog's reliability was properly established by more limited information—i.e., the detection dog's "satisfactory performance in a certification or training program …." To highlight the disjunctive nature of this canine-reliability showing, *Harris* explained that *either* certification from a "bona fide organization" *or* successful completion of a training program would satisfy the canine-reliability requirements necessary to establish probable cause.[98] The Court based its conclusion on law enforcement's *strong incentive* to use reliable drug-detection dogs.[99]

On the issue of field performance records, *Harris* emphatically rejected the Florida Supreme Court's valuation of this evidence.[100] As *Harris* explained, field performance records were hardly *the gold standard* for canine reliability:

> Making matters worse, the decision below treats records of a dog's field performance as the gold standard in evidence, when in most cases they have relatively limited import. Errors may abound in such records. If a dog on patrol fails to alert to a car containing drugs, the mistake usually will go undetected because the officer will not initiate a search. Field data thus may not capture a dog's false negatives. Conversely (and more relevant here), if the dog alerts to a car in which the officer finds no narcotics, the dog may not have made a mistake at all. The dog may have detected substances that were too well hidden or present in quantities too small for the officer to locate. Or the dog may have smelled the residual odor of drugs previously in the vehicle or on the driver's person. Field data thus may markedly overstate a dog's real false positives.[101]

Yet, *Harris* was reluctant to give the government too much leash in establishing canine reliability. *Harris* explained that the defendant "must" have an "opportunity"—which the Court described as "a probable-cause hearing"—to challenge the government's canine-reliability evidence. At this hearing, *Harris* contemplated that the defendant could challenge the detection dog's reliability by "cross-examining the testifying officer or by introducing his own fact or expert witnesses." To challenge the government's canine-reliability showing, *Harris* envisioned that a defendant might (1) "contest the adequacy of a certification or training program, perhaps asserting that its standards are too lax or its methods faulty"; (2) "examine how the dog (or handler) performed in the assessments made in those [certification or training] settings"; and (3) present "evidence of the dog's (or handler's) history in the field …."[102] This third canine-reliability challenge is interesting. Despite *Harris*'s earlier criticism of the Florida Supreme Court's reliance on field performance records in a canine-reliability determination, the Court nevertheless confirmed that field performance records were "sometimes … relevant," "although [this evidence is] susceptible to the kind of misrepresentation we have discussed [above] …." Although *Harris* does not require police agencies to create or maintain field performance records, the Court noted that, if the canine handler testified, the defendant would be allowed to ask the handler about his or her dog's field accuracy.[103]

Harris described the hearing regarding a drug-detection dog's reliability as "proceed[ing] much like any other [probable-cause hearing]."[104] First, the government introduces evidence of the detection dog's certification or training. Second, the defendant may introduce evidence to challenge the government's canine-reliability showing "by disputing the reliability of the dog overall or of a particular alert …." If the defendant fails to contest the government's canine-reliability evidence, then the inquiry ends and the detection dog will be found to be reliable.[105] Third, if the defendant challenges the government's evidence, then the judge must weigh the competing evidence.[106] Similar to any other probable-cause determination, *Harris* instructs that the issue of canine reliability addresses whether a detection dog's alert, when "viewed through the lens of common sense, would make a reasonably prudent person think that a search would reveal contraband or evidence of a crime."

CANINE-RELIABILITY DETERMINATIONS AFTER *HARRIS*

Harris is relatively new; it remains to be seen how broadly lower courts will construe the decision. After *Harris*, a drug-detection dog's valid credentials—proof of satisfactory performance in a certification or training program—is enough to justify a presumption that the detection dog's alert provided probable cause to search a suspect's vehicle. And, based on *Harris*'s admonition, courts should address detection-dog reliability by viewing the totality of the circumstances "through the lens of common sense."

After *Harris*, federal circuit courts have placed the initial burden on the government to produce evidence regarding the detection dog's qualifications—evidence of the detection dog's certification or training.[107] Although field performance records have not been required, courts have considered them if the records are available.[108] Thereafter, the defendant may introduce evidence to challenge, or impeach, the detection dog's or handler's reliability.[109] Although *Harris* stated that a defendant *must* have an opportunity to challenge reliability, at least one court, the U.S. Fifth Circuit, has questioned this requirement.[110]

Prior to *Harris*, the Fifth Circuit had a rule that if a canine sniff was used to establish probable cause for a vehicle search, the government was *not* required to introduce evidence regarding the detection dog's certification or training.[111] After *Harris*, the Fifth Circuit's rule has been called into question because *Harris* seemingly *requires* the government to make a threshold showing on the detection dog's reliability.[112] That showing could be made by introducing evidence of the dog's certification from a "bona fide organization" or "successful[] complet[ion of] a training program"—evidence that the defendant could then challenge. However, in a post-*Harris* decision, *United States v. Thompson*, the Fifth Circuit questioned what a defendant is required to show to secure an evidentiary hearing challenging canine reliability.[113] In *Thompson*, the Fifth Circuit explained that the defendant was not entitled to a probable-cause hearing on canine reliability because "he gave no supporting detail or explanation of the dog's alert in this case and he did not request either discovery about the dog's training and reliability or an opportunity to cross-examine the handler."[114]

While it may seem ironic to identify specific documents that the government and the defendant should either provide or request, especially in light of *Harris*'s admonition against strict evidentiary checklists in probable-cause determinations,[115] the fact remains that *Harris*, itself, identified several ways to challenge the reliability of a drug-detection dog's sniff.[116] The key to applying *Harris* is not to *require* each and every potentially relevant shred of evidence, but instead to view all of the available evidence, including testimony, through the "lens of common sense."[117]

TYPES OF CANINE-RELIABILITY EVIDENCE SUBMITTED

Gleaning what we can from the limited number of post-*Harris* cases reveals the types of evidence that law enforcement should anticipate providing in connection with a defendant's canine-reliability challenge. Courts have approvingly cited the following evidence as sufficient to establish canine reliability for contraband detection:

- Initial training records[118]
- Pre-deployment and annual certification records[119]
- Periodic training records[120]
- Annual recertification records[121]
- Expert testimony confirming reliability[122]
- Officer testimony about the sniff in question,[123] as well as the dog and handler's training and certification[124]

The purpose of the government's evidence is simple: establish the drug-detection dog's reliability through the "totality of the circumstances." After the government submits training and certification records, the defendant likely faces an uphill battle in impeaching the detection dog's reliability.[125] In *Harris*, the Supreme Court specifically noted that a defendant could cross-examine the government's expert or introduce his own fact and expert testimony.[126] Further, the Court confirmed that case-specific evidence—such as evidence of a canine handler's cueing—could be used to challenge a detection dog's reliability.

The *Harris* Court left little doubt that field performance records are not required to establish canine reliability. Nonetheless, defendants still request—as they should—copies of field performance records. Little mileage will be made from arguments based on a dog's poor field performance, however. For instance, the Fourth Circuit determined that a 25.88% to 43% field performance success rate, when combined with a training and certification record demonstrating a 100% controlled-environment success rate, is still sufficient to establish the dog's reliability.[127]

Considering the Court's statements in *Harris*, as well as the cases decided since *Harris*, it appears that the defendant should seek discovery of, and possibly proffer, the following evidence:

- Expert testimony refuting reliability[128]
- Factual witness testimony concerning the circumstances of the sniff[129]
- Any training or certification records showing poor performance in controlled settings[130]
- Information describing the methods and instruments used to train the drug-detection dog, especially if those methods may be considered inadequate[131]
- Evidence regarding the entity or association that certified the drug-detection dog[132]
- Testimony and evidence, such as video, depicting the sniff in question[133]
- Field performance records or performance logs[134]

It goes without saying that the records provided to the defendant about the drug-detection dog's reliability must be complete and genuine. Heavily redacted records have been criticized for failing to give the defendant a meaningful opportunity to test reliability through contradictory evidence and cross-examination.[135] And, not surprisingly, the government's failure to produce an authentic certification document for the drug-detection dog creates its own set of problems, including potentially undermining the court's view of the detection dog's reliability.[136]

Other Post-*Harris* Canine-Reliability Challenges: Handler Cueing and Unfamiliar Circumstances

After *Harris*, even if the government produces the drug-detection dog's credentials—i.e., the dog's certification document or training log—an additional avenue for challenging the dog's reliability remains. As *Harris* explained, a defendant may challenge the reliability of an otherwise reliable drug-detection dog based on "circumstances surrounding a particular alert … if say, the officer cued the dog (consciously or not), or if the team was working under unfamiliar circumstances."[137] Handler cueing occurs when a drug-detection dog reacts to its human partner's "specific body language that is usually ritually repeated that indicates the location of the target odors the canine[] [is] looking for."[138] Handler cueing may be either inadvertent or intentional.[139] Important here, in a well-known study by Lisa Lit, and others, it was shown that the canine handlers' *beliefs* concerning the presence of contraband influenced the drug-detection dogs to alert even in the absence of the target odor.[140] In other words, the Lit study's findings show that even a highly trained drug-detection dog will react—i.e., alert—in response to the canine handler's belief that the dog will likely encounter a target odor upon deployment.[141]

Because the court's credibility determination will almost always favor law enforcement, establishing handler cueing will be difficult in the absence of bodycam or dashcam video. Additionally, most people either will not observe the handlers' cueing or, because they are not themselves canine experts, will not appreciate the significance of what they did see.[142] Bodycam and dashcam video could be a game changer for defendants' cueing-based challenges, however. With a video, an expert will then be positioned to identify both intentional handler cueing as well as any inadvertent cueing of which the canine handler is presumably unaware.

And finally, *Harris* referenced the possibility of a canine-reliability challenge based on the drug-detection team's "working under unfamiliar circumstances."[143] For now, we have little guidance on the meaning of this particular challenge or how broadly courts will interpret it. *Harris*'s reference to the drug-detection *team* may be no accident, however. If courts parse the phrasing of *Harris*'s comment, then this particular challenge could be limited to circumstances where the *team* is working under unfamiliar circumstances—i.e., where a drug-detection dog trained on street drugs is instead used to screen currency to determine whether the money has been in recent contact with cocaine.[144] Limiting this challenge in this manner makes little sense, however, since consideration of inadequacies or omissions in the drug-detection dog's training is already considered as challenges to the dog's certification and training. Instead, the "unfamiliar circumstances" challenge should include, for example, situations where an otherwise reliable drug-detection dog is working with a new human partner or the drug-detection dog is deployed to sniff under unfamiliar conditions, such as sniffing of cargo containers when the detection dog has been trained and used for close-proximity sniffs.

DAUBERT CHALLENGES TO CANINE SNIFF EVIDENCE AFTER HARRIS

Since *Harris*, the government has taken the position that the *Harris* decision closed the door on science-based challenges to the reliability of canine sniff evidence. In other words, after *Harris*, while an individual detection dog's reliability was open to challenge—i.e., because the dog was not certified, was not properly trained, or was cued to alert during the deployment at issue—the canine sniff technique itself was presumed to be reliable, and therefore not subject to a *Daubert* challenge[145] concerning the technique's scientific basis. And, for canine sniffs of vehicles or close-proximity sniffs of luggage and parcels, courts have generally agreed with the government's interpretation of *Harris*. With that said, however, an inroad may be developing—an argument that *Harris* did not preempt courts from considering the scientific legitimacy of canine sniff evidence in every context.

CANINE SNIFF EVIDENCE IN CIVIL FORFEITURE CASES: THE CLASSIC BATTLE OF THE EXPERTS

In civil forfeiture cases, the government seeks forfeiture of currency based upon the money's connection to a drug crime.[146] To properly seize currency, however, the money must be uncovered in a lawful search—which oftentimes involves a canine sniff. A canine alert may be used both as a justification for a warrantless vehicle search (which uncovers the currency) and, important in civil forfeiture cases, to establish that the currency was recently in contact with illegal drugs, regardless of how the currency was lawfully uncovered.

In a traffic stop, a canine alert to the vehicle provides probable cause to conduct a warrantless search of the vehicle. If the search turns up cash *and* contraband, the currency's owner generally does not challenge the money's connection to a drug crime; the currency is therefore forfeited and no judicial forfeiture proceeding occurs. On the other hand, if the physical search reveals only currency—i.e., no contraband—in addition to uncovering the currency, the canine sniff will likely be instrumental in establishing the currency's connection to a drug crime. Alternatively, the canine sniff may occur only *after* the currency's discovery—i.e., after a consent-based search reveals the currency. Here again, the canine sniff will likely be used to establish the currency's connection to a drug crime. Whether used to discover currency or to establish that the currency had recently been in contact with contraband, canine sniff evidence is critically important in civil forfeiture cases.

In cases where the currency's owner requests a judicial forfeiture proceeding—a proceeding at which the currency's owner must establish a lawful source for the money in order to recover seized funds—prior to *Harris*, the claimant often asserted the so-called currency contamination theory to disprove the government's case. Here, the claimant argued that a canine alert to circulated money did not establish the currency's connection to drug activity because most circulated U.S. currency is contaminated with trace amounts of drug residue.[147] And, the claimants supported their argument by pointing to published scientific studies that established the widespread presence of drug contamination on circulated U.S. currency. The presence of this drug residue—usually cocaine—meant, the claimants argued, that a detection dog's alert was not a reliable indicator that the currency had recently been in contact with street drugs.[148] Based on the currency contamination argument, some courts did not view canine sniff evidence as a reliable indicator of the currency's recent contact with contraband, and accordingly returned the seized funds to their owners.

That was not the end of the story, however. To rebut the currency contamination argument, the government looked to other scientific studies to bolster its case. The government came to rely on scientific research by Dr. Kenneth Furton and others that concluded that drug-detection dogs do not, in fact, alert to the drug residue present on most circulated U.S. currency.[149] Instead, the research showed that drug-detection dogs alerted to a volatile cocaine byproduct—methyl benzoate—that is produced when cocaine is exposed to humid air.[150] Dr. Furton's research stated that because methyl benzoate evaporates quickly from the surface of currency, a drug-detection dog's alert meant that the cash had *recently* been exposed to cocaine.[151] Therefore, in Dr. Furton's view, canine alerts to currency generally proved that the bills had recently been in contact with cocaine—a conclusion that was fatal to the claimant's recovery of the seized cash.

Although *Harris* has seemingly foreclosed generalized arguments regarding the reliability of canine *drug-detection* sniffs for purposes of a probable cause hearing, the reliability of *currency* sniffs may be treated differently. For example, in a post-*Harris* civil forfeiture case, the claimants established a basis for a *Daubert* hearing to contest the reliability of currency sniffs.[152] In *$100,120.00*, the claimants offered expert affidavit testimony that "created a dispute of material fact regarding whether the government has proved by a preponderance of the evidence that drug-dog alerts to currency are in general … reliable evidence that the currency recently has been in contact with illegal drugs." The claimants introduced the affidavit testimony of a forensic chemist, Sanford A. Angelos, who challenged the following premises of the government's case:

- Drug-detection dogs alert only to methyl benzoate when sniffing currency.[153]
- Drug-detection dogs alert only to currency that has recently been in contact with cocaine because of methyl benzoate's rapid evaporation rate.[154]
- The threshold level of methyl benzoate that must be present for a drug-detection dog to detect cocaine on circulated currency.[155]

The claimants additionally introduced the affidavit of Dr. Lawrence J. Myers, who holds degrees in zoology, ethology, neurophysiology, and veterinary medicine. Dr. Myers opined that "there is no scientific evidence demonstrating that a drug dog's ability to detect cocaine translates into the ability to detect cocaine residue on currency." And, the claimants introduced the affidavit of a "certified drug dog training and behavior consultant," David Kroyer. Kroyer opined that the detection dog at issue had not been properly trained to perform currency sniffs; that the dog's certification was problematic because the dog had been certified in-house, rather than the "industry standard" of certification through an outside agency; as well as describing problems with the dog's post-certification training and field performance. Based upon what can only be described as the claimants' substantial showing, the Seventh Circuit remanded the case to the district court for a *Daubert* hearing to determine whether the drug-detection dog's alert demonstrated that the currency at issue had recently been in contact with illegal drugs.[156]

The *$100,120.00* remand[157] will likely serve as a tutorial on how the government should *not* litigate currency sniff cases. The district court noted the tension between the claimants' currency contamination theory and the government's "Furton theory."[158] Yet, on remand, the government did nothing to prove its case other than rely on "publicly available empirical information."[159] This tactic was plainly insufficient to rebut the expert evidence previously offered by the claimants, and the district court concluded that the government had "forfeited any objection to the admissibility of [the claimants' expert] evidence under Rule 702."[160] Instead, the government should have submitted "expert evidence concerning Dr. Furton's theory."[161] Moreover, the district court was unimpressed with the government's assumptions that "dog-alert evidence is reliable as a given," determining that the Seventh Circuit had not previously foreclosed "any challenge to the probative value of a drug dog's alert to currency."

The government approached the remand by resting on its laurels, and it did so—perhaps—based on a misunderstanding of *Harris*.[162] The district court distinguished *Harris*, noting that *Harris* involved a probable cause hearing, which required a lesser standard of proof than a civil forfeiture action under the Civil Asset Forfeiture Reform Act. Consequently, the government's reliance on *Harris* as a talisman that somehow shielded currency sniffs from a canine reliability challenge was misplaced. All things considered, the post-remand district court decision in *$100,120.00* teaches civil forfeiture litigants that *Daubert* hearings may be available to challenge the reliability of canine sniff evidence. And that expert evidence—not merely "publicly available empirical information"—must be introduced to support the scientific theories advanced in support of or against a civil forfeiture claim.

RETIREMENT OF MARIJUANA-TRAINED DETECTION DOGS IN STATES WHERE MARIJUANA POSSESSION AND USE HAS BEEN DECRIMINALIZING

Legalization of marijuana use and possession in some states, as well as the adoption of medical marijuana laws in many more, has led to questions about the continued use of marijuana-trained detection dogs.[163] In fact, some police agencies in the state of Washington—a state that voted to legalize marijuana—have chosen to *retire* their marijuana-trained dogs rather than face the inevitable canine-reliability challenges related to alerts from marijuana-trained dogs.[164] Other police agencies have resisted retiring their marijuana-trained dogs, suggesting instead that marijuana-trained dogs can be retrained—through so-called "extinction training"—to teach the dogs to refrain from alerting to the odor of marijuana.[165] Retirement of marijuana-trained detection dogs will be expensive, so it is understandable that police agencies might prefer to try extinction training as a means of recouping their substantial investment in detection canines. Unfortunately, however, the science behind extinction training provides little support for the proposition that drug-detection dogs can be conditioned to lose the dogs' marijuana response on a consistent basis over time.

Extinction training conditions an animal to *refrain* from responding to stimuli or smells to which the animal was either originally conditioned to respond or that the animal has come to associate with the conditional response.[166] Prior to the decriminalization of marijuana, courts addressed extinction training in connection with canine training to eliminate certain nuisance behaviors that drug-detection dogs sometimes picked up. For example, extinction training was used to teach the detection dog to ignore *dead* scents,[167] residual odors,[168] and "odors from objects regularly accompanying controlled substances, such as coffee or packaging materials."[169] With legalized marijuana, however, the scope of the proposed extinction training is far broader—i.e., more fundamental—with the goal being to rehabilitate a marijuana-trained detection dog by eliminating a core concept of the dog's training.[170]

As the behavioral literature makes clear, extinction is "a highly complex phenomenon"[171]—with studies relying on environmental manipulation and observation of rats and rabbits (not canines).[172] While one might assume that extinction training causes the *destruction* of what was originally learned, "this is not true; much of the original learning survives extinction."[173] Instead, new learning *inhibits* old learning and leaves the organism with "two available 'meanings' or associations" with the old learning.[174] In other words, "extinction training" leaves the target organism with an *ambiguity* about a particular thing or behavior—an ambiguity that is heavily dependent on the *context* for selecting between the conflicting meanings.[175] And, the behavioral literature describes various extinction phenomena—i.e., the "renewal effect,"[176] "spontaneous recovery,"[177] "rapid reacquisition,"[178] and "reinstatement"[179]—which suggest that it is likely a mistake to assume that extinction training is an easy fix for marijuana-trained detection dogs.[180] In view of the substantial body of scientific literature concerning extinction, if a simple "extinction-training certificate" was used to establish a marijuana-trained dog's reliability, the trial court may well be faced with a legitimate *Daubert*-based conflict between, on the one hand, the Court's clear concerns regarding junk science[181] and, on the other, *Harris*'s instruction that courts should find reliable detection dogs certified by a "bona fide organization."[182]

CANINE SNIFF OF A PERSON

Another canine sniff question concerns whether a canine sniff of a person—as contrasted with a sniff of unattended personal property or a vehicle's exterior—is a *search* for Fourth Amendment purposes.[183] Unless the canine sniff takes place at an international border,[184] the answer to this question may well boil down to whether, in performing the sniff, the drug-detection dog makes *physical contact* with the sniffed individual.[185] Close-proximity canine sniffs—i.e., sniffs involving physical contact with the detection dog—have been described as intrusive and offensive.[186] Both the U.S. Fifth and Ninth Circuits have rejected close-proximity canine sniffs of schoolchildren as *searches*,[187] in part because the drug-detection dogs "put their noses right up against the children's bodies."[188]

In contrast, canine sniffs where the dog's nose is merely *near* the person—without making physical contact—have been upheld.[189] For example, in *Jones v. Texas*, a Texas intermediate appellate court recently upheld a canine sniff of a person where the drug-detection dog was located "an arm's length away" from the defendant and performed the canine sniff without making physical contact.[190] Importantly, however, reliance on a *physical-contact* test likely oversimplifies the Fourth Amendment question. While a detection dog's physical contact during a canine sniff certainly qualifies as a Fourth Amendment search and seizure, courts should not overlook the intrusiveness and offensiveness of close-proximity *noncontact* sniffs.[191] Therefore, the critically important question of "how close is too close" has yet to be decided.

ACKNOWLEDGMENT

The author would like to thank her research assistant, H. Rick Yelton, for his research skills and excellent assistance in preparing this chapter.

ENDNOTES

1. *Brigham City v. Stuart*, 547 U.S. 398, 403 (2006).
2. *Vernonia School District 47J v. Acton*, 515 U.S. 646, 653 (1995).
3. *Riley v. California*, 134 S. Ct. 2473, 2482 (2014).
4. See *U.S. v. Place*, 462 U.S. 696, 707 (1983).
5. 462 U.S. 696 (1983). In a case decided just 3 months prior to *Place*, the Court presaged that it would uphold warrantless canine drug-detection sniffs of luggage at airports. See *Florida v. Royer*, 460 U.S. 491, 505–506 (1983) (plurality) ("The courts are not strangers to the use of trained dogs to detect the presence of controlled substances in luggage … . If [a canine sniff] had been used, Royer and his luggage could have been momentarily detained while this investigative procedure was carried out.").
6. *Place*, 462 U.S. at 702. The agents developed reasonable suspicion based on Place's behavior at the airport, discrepancies between the address tags on Place's luggage, and the fact that, upon investigation, the agents discovered that the addresses listed on Place's luggage did not exist and that his telephone number belonged to a third address.
7. See *Terry v. Ohio*, 392 U.S. 1, 27–28 (1968) (upholding the brief detention of a person—described as a *stop*—based on reasonable suspicion that the detained individual was preparing to commit a crime and a *frisk* based on reasonable suspicion that the individual was armed and presently dangerous).
8. *Place*, 462 U.S. at 706 ("[S]ome brief detentions of personal effects may be so minimally intrusive of Fourth Amendment interests that strong countervailing governmental interests will justify a seizure based only on specific articulable facts that the property contains contraband or evidence of a crime.").
9. *Place*, at 709–10 (declining to place an "outside time limitation" on a valid *Terry* stop, but noting that the Court had never upheld a 90 min detention of a person under *Terry*). In addition, the agents' failure to provide Place with clear directions about the storage and return of his luggage exacerbated the intrusiveness of the seizure.
10. *Id.* (describing the canine sniff technique as "*sui generis*" in that "[w]e are aware of no other investigative procedure that is so limited in both the manner in which the information is obtained and in the content of the information revealed by the procedure").
11. 466 U.S. 109 (1984).

12. In *Jacobsen*, a Federal Express employee discovered white powder—i.e., suspected cocaine—after accidentally damaging the parcel in which the powder had been packaged for mailing. FedEx turned the parcel over to law enforcement agents who, without a warrant, performed a field test on the white powder. Importantly, the field test was capable of revealing only that the powder was cocaine, but no other information about the powder—i.e., "not even whether the substance was sugar or talcum powder." *Id.* at 124.

13. See *Jacobsen*, at 124 ("Here, as in *Place*, the likelihood that official conduct of the kind disclosed by the record will actually compromise any legitimate interest in privacy seems much too remote to characterize the testing as a search subject to the Fourth Amendment."). In considering whether the warrantless field-testing intruded on Jacobsen's legitimate privacy expectations, *Jacobsen* applied the *Katz* test. See *Katz v. U.S.*, 389 U.S. 347 (1967).

14. Drug-detection canines have traditionally been described as "*narcotics* detection dogs," and that terminology is often still used. When used in this way, the term *narcotic* is intended to convey that the detection dog has been trained to alert to illegal drugs or contraband. However, from a medical or scientific perspective, the term *narcotic* has a narrower meaning—the term is descriptive of an *opiate* drug or medication. The term *narcotic* is therefore not a generic description for an illegal drug. Because drug-detection dogs are typically trained to alert to both opiates and some non-opiate drugs (i.e., methamphetamine), this chapter uses the term, *drug-detection dogs*. And, the Court used this naming convention throughout the recent *Florida v. Harris* decision, describing the detector dog at issue there as a "drug-detection dog."

15. See, e.g., *Illinois v. Caballes*, 543 U.S. 405, 411 (2005) (Souter, J., dissenting) ("The infallible dog, however, is a creature of legal fiction."). Justice Souter cataloged lower court cases in which surprisingly high error rates failed to result in a finding of unreliability. See also Dery III (2006), at 403–406 (addressing various factors affecting accuracy of drug-detection dogs); Shoebotham (2009), at 838–842, 866 (examining whether drug-detection dogs alert to contraband or, instead, to chemical byproducts of contraband—molecules that are present in both contraband and noncontraband substances); Brief of *Amici Curiae* Fourth Amendment Scholars in Support of Respondent, *Florida v. Jardines, cert. granted*, 132 S. Ct. 995 (No. 11-564) (Jan. 6, 2012), 2012 WL 2641847, 7, 19–32 (same); Lit et al. (2011) (finding "that handler beliefs affect working dog outcomes, and human indication of scent location affects distribution of alerts …").

16. See *Rodriguez v. U.S.*, 135 S. Ct. 1609, 191 L. Ed. 2d 492 (2015); *Florida v. Jardines*, 133 S. Ct. 1409 (2013).

17. 543 U.S. 405, 409–10 (2005). Prior to *Caballes*, the Court discussed, in dicta (statements not required to reach the decision), a warrantless canine drug-detection sniff of a vehicle performed at a drug interdiction checkpoint. See *Indianapolis v. Edmond*, 531 U.S. 32 (2000). Although the checkpoint-seizure of Edmond's vehicle violated the Fourth Amendment—because the checkpoint's primary purpose was indistinguishable from a general interest in crime control—*Edmond* refused to treat the vehicle sniff as a Fourth Amendment *search*. See *id.* at 40: "The fact that officers walk a narcotics-detection dog around the exterior of each car at the Indianapolis checkpoints does not transform the seizure into a search. Just as in *Place*, an exterior sniff of an automobile does not require entry into the car and is not designed to disclose any information other than the presence or absence of narcotics."

18. The automobile exception authorizes law enforcement to perform a warrantless probable cause-based search of a vehicle. *California v. Carney*, 471 U.S. 386, 392 (1985). The rationales for this warrant exception include the ready mobility of vehicles as well as society's reduced expectation of privacy in vehicles due to vehicles' pervasive regulation. Further, police are not required to obtain a search warrant to perform a probable cause-based search of a vehicle even if police have time to seek the warrant and no exigency exists that prevents them from doing so. See *Maryland v. Dyson*, 527 U.S. 465, 467 (1999) (per curiam), rejecting, as "squarely contrary to our holdings," the view that the automobile exception "requires a separate finding of exigency in addition to a finding of probable cause …."

19. *Caballes* assumed, without deciding, that the canine alert established probable cause to search Caballes's vehicle. See *Caballes*, 543 U.S. at 406 (describing the case's background facts: "The dog alerted at the trunk. Based on that alert, the officers searched the trunk …"). After *Caballes*, courts equated a canine alert with probable cause to perform a warrantless vehicle search under the automobile exception. See *U.S. v. Bowman*, 660 F.3d 338, 345 (8th Cir. 2011), finding that a detection dog's certification and training established probable cause to search a vehicle; *U.S. v. Parada*, 577 F.3d 1275, 1282 (10th Cir. 2009), finding that "a dog's alert to the presence of contraband is sufficient to provide probable cause" even without the detection dog's "final indication" regarding the presence of drugs; *U.S. v. Sundby*, 186 F.3d 873, 875–76 (8th Cir. 1999): "Assuming that the dog is reliable, a dog sniff resulting in an alert on a container, car, or other item, standing alone, gives an officer probable cause to believe

that there are drugs present."; *U.S. v. Ludwig*, 10 F.3d 1523, 1527–28 (10th Cir. 1993), finding that a detection dog's alert provided probable cause for police to open and search a vehicle's trunk. And, in the Court's recent canine-reliability decision, *Florida v. Harris*, the Court again assumed that a canine alert by a reliable detection dog established probable cause to search a vehicle. See 133 S. Ct. 1050, 1057 (2013): "If a bona fide organization has certified a dog after testing his reliability in a controlled setting, a court can presume (subject to any conflicting evidence offered) that the dog's alert provides probable cause to search." However, the issue of whether a drug-detection dog's alert, by itself, established probable cause to search was not before the Court in *Harris*, only the issue of how courts should determine canine reliability. See Brief for Respondent 1, *Florida v. Harris, cert. granted*, 132 S. Ct. 1796 (Mar. 26, 2012) (No. 11-817), 2012 WL 3864280. Nevertheless, *Harris* treated those issues as one and the same. Because probable cause has traditionally been determined under the totality of the circumstances, this *Harris* dicta—that a reliable detection dog's alert, by itself, established probable cause—is surprising. Cf. *Illinois v. Gates*, 462 U.S. 213, 238 (1983), applying a totality-of-the-circumstances analysis, which requires the magistrate "to make a practical, common-sense decision whether, given all the circumstances … there is a fair probability that contraband or evidence of a crime will be found in a particular place."

20. See *Caballes*, at 410: "A dog sniff conducted during a concededly lawful traffic stop that reveals no information other than the location of a substance that no individual has any right to possess does not violate the Fourth Amendment." In addition to *Place*, *Caballes* relied heavily on *Jacobsen*'s conclusion that individuals lack a legitimate expectation of privacy in possessing contraband. See *id.* at 408: "[A]ny interest in possessing contraband cannot be deemed 'legitimate,' and thus, government conduct that *only* reveals the possession of contraband 'compromises no legitimate privacy interest,'" quoting *U.S. v. Jacobsen*, 466 U.S. 109, 123 (1984).

21. See *Caballes*, 543 U.S. at 407: "[W]e proceed on the assumption that the officer conducting the dog sniff had no information about respondent except that he had been stopped for speeding …." In contrast, prior to seizing the luggage in *Place*, the agents had developed reasonable suspicion to believe that Place was carrying contraband in his bags. The seizure of Place's luggage violated the Fourth Amendment, however, because the agents detained the luggage for too long and in too intrusive of a manner based upon *Terry*.

22. See *Caballes*, 543 U.S. at 409: "[T]he use of a well-trained narcotics-detection dog—one that does not expose noncontraband items that otherwise would remain hidden from public view—during a lawful traffic stop, generally does not implicate legitimate privacy interests" (citation and internal quotation marks omitted).

23. See *Caballes*, 543 U.S. at 407: "A seizure that is justified solely by the interest in issuing a warning ticket to the driver can become unlawful if it is prolonged beyond the time reasonably required to complete that mission."

24. See *Caballes*, at 410–411 (Souter, J., dissenting), calling for reexamination of canine sniff doctrine because in situations where police deploy drug-detection dogs without first detaining a person in a *Terry* stop or seizing a vehicle in a traffic stop, "the Fourth Amendment [would be rendered] indifferent to suspicionless and indiscriminate sweeps …"; *Caballes*, at 422 (Ginsburg, J., dissenting): "Today's decision … clears the way for suspicionless, dog-accompanied drug sweeps of parked cars along sidewalks and in parking lots."

25. See, e.g., *Hearn v. Board of Public Education*, 191 F.3d 1329, 1332–33 (11th Cir. 1999), upholding a warrantless canine drug-detection sweep of a school's parking lot as establishing probable cause to search a faculty member's vehicle; *Horton v. Goose Creek Independent School District*, 690 F.2d 470, 477 (5th Cir. 1982), holding that a warrantless canine drug-detection sniff of the students' lockers and vehicles parked in the school's parking lot was not a "search"; *Hill v. Sharber*, 544 F. Supp. 2d 670, 679 (M.D. Tenn. 2008), upholding a warrantless canine drug-detection sniff of students' vehicles while those vehicles were parked in the school's parking lot.

26. The Court has recognized that schools have a special interest in providing a safe environment for their students—an obligation that includes maintaining drug-free campuses. See *Board of Education of Independent School District No. 92 v. Earles*, 536 U.S. 822, 830 (2002): "A student's privacy interest is limited in a public school environment where the State is responsible for maintaining discipline, health, and safety."; *Vernonia School District 47J v. Acton*, 515 U.S. 646, 656 (1995), upholding the suspicionless drug testing of student athletes; noting that, while students had Fourth Amendment rights, their reasonable expectation of privacy must be weighed against "the schools' custodial and tutelary responsibility for [the] children."; *New Jersey v. T.L.O.*, 469 U.S. 325, 340, 342 (1985), balancing the students' expectation of privacy against the schools' need to "maintain order."

27. *Rodriguez v. U.S.*, 135 S. Ct. 1609, 191 L. Ed. 2d 492 (2015); *Florida v. Jardines*, 133 S. Ct. 1409 (2013); *Florida v. Harris*, 133 S. Ct. 1050 (2013).

28. Although the patrol officer was, himself, a canine handler and had his detection dog with him at the time of the traffic stop, the officer was working alone that night, without a human partner. The officer therefore waited to deploy his detection dog until a backup officer had arrived. In fact, the district court described the patrol officer's decision to wait for backup before conducting the sniff as a reasonable, safety-based decision. See *U.S. v. Rodriguez*, No. 8:12CR170, 2012 WL 5458427 (D. Neb. Aug. 30, 2012), *aff'd*, 741 F.3d 905 (8th Cir.), *cert. granted*, 125 S. Ct. 43 (U.S. Oct. 2, 2014) (No. 13-9972).

29. Brief for Petitioner 7, *U.S. v. Rodriguez*, 741 F.3d 905 (8th Cir.), *cert. granted*, *Rodriguez v. U.S.*, 125 S. Ct. 43 (U.S. Oct. 2, 2014) (No. 13-9972): "[The magistrate judge] also agreed that [the investigating officer] had nothing but a 'big hunch' that Mr. Rodriguez was hiding something in the vehicle and no reasonable suspicion existed to independently support the detention." To be clear, *Rodriguez* involved a *suspicionless* extension of a completed traffic stop in order to perform a canine sniff. In contrast, if a patrol officer develops reasonable suspicion during the traffic stop to believe that contraband is being transported in the vehicle, the traffic stop is properly extended on *that* basis to perform the canine sniff. See, e.g., *U.S. v. Winters*, 782 F.3d 289, 292 (6th Cir.), *cert. denied*, 136 S. Ct. 170 (2015).

30. *Rodriguez*, 2012 WL 5458427, at *2: "Likewise, this court agrees with the magistrate judge that the dog search was constitutional, based on the facts as set forth in the transcript …."

31. *Rodriguez*, 741 F.3d at 908.

32. See Rodriguez Petitioner's Brief, above, at i.

33. *Rodriguez*, 2015 WL 1780927, at *3, quoting *Caballes*, 543 U.S. at 407.

34. *Rodriquez*, at *5, citing *Arizona v. Johnson*, 555 U.S. 323, 327–28 (2009) (questioning during a lawful traffic stop); *Caballes*, 543 U.S. at 406, 408 (canine sniff during a lawful traffic stop).

35. *Rodriguez*, at *6–7. In contrast, a canine sniff of a vehicle is aimed at "detect[ing] evidence of ordinary criminal wrongdoing," quoting *Indianapolis v. Edmond*, 531 U.S. 32, 40–41 (2000).

36. *Rodriguez*, at *7 (internal quotation marks omitted). The case was remanded to the Eighth Circuit, which upheld Rodriguez's conviction on the basis of *Davis v. U.S.*, 131 S. Ct. 2419 (2011), discussed below in notes 70–72. On the *Rodriguez* remand, the Eighth Circuit explained that, at the time the magistrate and trial judge ruled on Rodriguez's suppression motion, a de minimis extension of a traffic stop to perform a canine sniff "was lawful under our then-binding precedent." *U.S. v. Rodriguez*, 799 F.3d 1222, 1224 (8th Cir.), *petition for cert. filed*, __ U.S.L.W. __ (U.S. Nov. 25, 2015) (No.15-7126). Based on *Davis*, the exclusionary rule did not apply (meaning that the contraband found in the physical search of Rodriguez's vehicle was properly admitted) because the vehicle search "was conducted in objectively reasonable reliance on our precedent." *Id.* For now, Rodriguez has both won the battle (regarding suspicionless extensions of traffic stops to perform a canine sniff) but lost the war (because the evidence was nevertheless admissible under *Davis*). Rodriguez's recent petition for certiorari seeking review of the Eighth Circuit's remand decision could mean there are more battles ahead, however.

37. *Caballes*, 543 U.S. at 409, holding that a canine sniff of a vehicle's exterior during a lawful traffic stop did not "implicate legitimate privacy interests."

38. See, e.g., *U.S. v. Willingham*, 140 F.3d 1328, 1331 (10th Cir. 1998), finding a Fourth Amendment violation where the officers opened the doors of a van, took the detection dog off its leash near the open door, and allowed the dog to jump into the van through the open door and sniff the van's interior.

39. See *U.S. v. Vazquez*, 555 F.3d 923, 930 (10th Cir. 2009) (emphasis added); see also *U.S. v. Sharpe*, 689 F.3d 616, 618–20 (6th Cir.) (holding that the detection dog's physical entry into a vehicle through an open window did not violate the Fourth Amendment—even though the dog had a known habit of jumping through vehicles' open windows—because there was no evidence that police had trained the dog to jump into vehicles or had "d[one] something to encourage or facilitate the jump."), *cert. denied*, 133 S. Ct. 777 (2012).

40. See, e.g., *Sharpe*, 689 F.3d at 619–20: "It is a Fourth Amendment violation for a narcotics detection dog to jump into a car because of something the police did, like training the dog to jump into cars as part of the search or facilitating or encouraging the jump[,] but no violation occurs as long as the canine enters the vehicle on its own initiative and is neither encouraged nor placed into the vehicle by law enforcement" (citations and internal quotation marks omitted).

41. See, e.g., *Felders* ex rel. *Smedley v. Malcom*, 755 F.3d 870, 880 (10th Cir. 2014): "But where there is evidence that it is not the driver but the officers who have created the opportunity for a drug dog to go where the officer himself cannot go, the Fourth Amendment protects the driver's right to privacy to the interior compartment until the dog alert from the exterior of the car" (citation and internal quotation marks omitted), *cert. denied*, 135 S. Ct. 975 (2015).

42. *Felders*, at 877, 880, noting, in a Section 1983 action, that the drug-detection dog had not alerted while sniffing the vehicle's exterior but, after entering the vehicle, had alerted on the vehicle's center console—which was found to contain "two bags of jerky" and no contraband.

43. 133 S. Ct. 1409 (2013).

44. 133 S. Ct. 1050 (2013).

45. "Curtilage" is the area around the home that is "intimately linked to the home, both physically and psychologically, and is where privacy expectations are most heightened." *Jardines,* 133 S. Ct. at 1415 (internal quotation marks omitted). The Court treats a home's curtilage as "part of the home itself for Fourth Amendment purposes." *Id.* at 1414, quoting *Oliver v. U.S.*, 466 U.S. 170, 180 (1984).

46. See *Jardines*, 133 S. Ct. at 1415–16.

47. See *Katz v. U.S.*, 389 U.S. 347, 360 (1967) (Harlan, J., concurring), explaining that a Fourth Amendment violation occurs when government officers violate a person's "reasonable expectation of privacy." The *Katz* test—i.e., determining whether an individual has a legitimate expectation of privacy—is thought to have two requirements: "[F]irst that a person ha[s] exhibited an actual (subjective) expectation of privacy and, second, that the expectation be one that society is prepared to recognize as 'reasonable.'"

48. See *Jardines*, 133 S. Ct. at 1417: "The *Katz* reasonable-expectations text has been *added to*, not *substituted for*, the traditional property-based understanding of the Fourth Amendment, and so is unnecessary to consider when the government gains evidence by physically intruding on constitutionally protected areas" (internal quotation marks omitted).

49. See *Jones*, 132 S. Ct. 945, 950 (2012): "*Jones's* Fourth Amendment rights do not rise or fall with the *Katz* formulation. At bottom, we must assure preservation of that degree of privacy against government that existed when the Fourth Amendment was adopted" (internal quotation marks and brackets omitted).

50. See *Jardines*, 133 S. Ct. at 1415: "[Because] the detectives had all four of their feet and all four of their [detection-dog] companion's firmly planted on the constitutionally protected extension of Jardines's home, the only question is whether he had given his leave (even implicitly) for them to do so. He had not."

51. See *Jardines*, at 1416: "But introducing a trained police dog to explore the area around the home in hopes of discovering incriminating evidence is [different from a police knock and talk]." See *id.* at 1423 (Alito, J., dissenting): "[P]olice officers do not engage in a search when they approach the front door of a residence and seek to engage in what is termed a 'knock and talk' ...."

52. See *Jardines*, at 1416 (majority opinion): "Here, the background social norms that invite a visitor to the front door do not invite him there to conduct a search."

53. See *Jardines*, at 1420 (Kagan, J., concurring): "With these further thoughts, suggesting that a focus on Jardines's privacy interests would make an "easy case easy" twice over, I join the Court's opinion in full" (citation and brackets omitted).

54. 533 U.S. 27 (2001). Based on *Katz*, *Kyllo* invalidated the warrantless police use of a thermal-imaging device to perform a thermal scan of Kyllo's home. The thermal-imaging device in *Kyllo* revealed that excessive heat was emanating from portions of Kyllo's roof—heat that was consistent with an indoor marijuana-growing operation—but, importantly, the device *lacked* the capability of providing "through-the-wall surveillance" of the interior of Kyllo's home. And, even though the thermal scan had been performed while the officers were located on a public street—i.e., without the officers' physical trespass onto Kyllo's property—*Kyllo* held that a search warrant was required to use a thermal-imaging device to scan a home. Based on *Katz*'s reasonable-expectation-of-privacy analysis, *Kyllo* concluded that a *search* occurs when police direct a sense-enhancing device—one that is not in general public use—at a person's home to gain information about the home's interior that would not otherwise have been detected without physical entry into the home. See *Kyllo*, at 40: "Where ... the Government uses a device that is not in general public use[] to explore details of the home that would previously have been unknowable without physical intrusion, the surveillance is a 'search' ...."

55. See *Jardines*, 133 S. Ct. at 1419.

56. See *Jardines*, at 1419. Justice Kagan argued that law enforcement performed a search by using a "device not in general use (a trained drug-detection dog) to explore details of the home (the presence of certain substances) that they would not otherwise have discovered without entering the premises" (ellipsis omitted).

57. Compare *Jardines*, at 1417–18 (majority opinion), with *Jardines*, at 1418 (Kagan, J., concurring).

58. See *Jardines*, at 1417–18 (majority opinion).

59. In fact, Justice Alito, writing in dissent, used the likely outcome difference in warrantless apartment sniffs to illustrate one of the problems that he believed the *Jardines's* majority and concurring opinions would produce, complaining that "[t]he concurrence's *Kyllo*-based approach would have a much wider reach" than the majority's property-rights approach. Because *Kyllo* required a warrant to use a thermal

imager on a home—even though the officers in *Kyllo* performed the thermal scan while standing on a public street, Justice Alito argued that a Fourth Amendment search would likewise occur "if a dog alerted while on a public sidewalk or in the corridor of an apartment building." See *Jardines*, 133 S. Ct. at 1426 (Alito, J., dissenting).

60. Compare *North Dakota v. Nguyen*, 841 N.W.2d 676, 681–82 (N.D. 2013), upholding a warrantless canine sniff of the defendant's apartment—performed in a common hallway of the defendant's locked building—because the defendant both lacked a legitimate expectation of privacy in the common hallway of his building and "the common hallway is not an area within the curtilage of [the defendant's] apartment.", *cert. denied*, 135 S. Ct. 2888 (2015), with *Illinois v. Burns*, 25 N.E.3d 1244, 1254 (Ill. App. Ct.), applying *Jardines* to invalidate a warrantless middle-of-the-night canine sniff performed outside the defendant's apartment door in a locked common hallway, *appeal allowed*, 32 N.E.3d 675 (Ill. 2015).

61. See generally *Nguyen*, 841 N.W.2d at 680–82, omitting citation or reference to Justice Kagan's *Jardines* concurrence in holding that the defendant, an apartment dweller, lacked a reasonable expectation of privacy in the information revealed by a canine sniff of his apartment.

62. See *Jardines*, 133 S. Ct. at 1419 (Kagan, J., concurring): "As *Kyllo* made clear, the sense-enhancing tool at issue may be crude or sophisticated, may be old or new (drug-detection dogs actually go back not 12,000 years or centuries, but only a few decades), may be either smaller or bigger than a breadbox; still, at least where (as here) the device is not in general public use, training it on a home violates our minimal expectation of privacy ..." (citation and internal quotation marks omitted).

63. See generally *Jardines*, at 1418–20, arguing that a warrantless canine sniff of a residence violated *Kyllo*. Prior to *Jardines*, some courts upheld warrantless canine sniffs of apartments based on *Place* and, additionally, on *Jacobsen*'s reasoning that individuals lack a legitimate privacy expectation in contraband possession. See, e.g., *U.S. v. Scott*, 610 F.3d 1009, 1016 (8th Cir. 2010), upholding a warrantless canine sniff of the defendant's apartment—performed from the apartment's common hallway—because a canine sniff is not a *search* for Fourth Amendment purposes.

64. Cf. *Jardines*, 133 S. Ct. at 1422 (Alito, J., dissenting), arguing the unsuitability of the majority's trespass-based approach involving "categories of visitors"—observing that "the law of trespass has not attempted such a difficult taxonomy."

65. See *Illinois v. Burns*, 25 N.E.3d 1244 (Ill. App. Ct. 2015).

66. See *id.* at 1254: "[T]he police not only approached defendant's front door with a drug-detection dog to engage in an investigation of her home, they did so in the middle of the night. As *Jardines* makes clear, there is no implicit invitation for the police to do this ...." In fact, even a warrantless nighttime sniff of curtilage by *human* officers was recently found to violate the Fourth Amendment. See *Kelley v. Alaska*, 347 P.3d 1012, 1016 (Alaska Ct. App. 2015), rejecting, based on *Jardines*, a warrantless after-midnight sniff of the suspect's curtilage performed by human officers, even though no drug-detection dog was present.

67. In *Jardines*, all nine Justices agreed that a nighttime sniff of a residence's curtilage would require a warrant. See *Jardines*, 133 S. Ct. at 1416 n.3 (majority opinion), describing the dissent's opposition to nighttime canine sniffs as a "no-night-visits rule" and agreeing with it; *id.* at 1422 (Alito, J., dissenting): "Nor, as a general matter, may a visitor come to the front door in the middle of the night without an express invitation."

68. Compare, e.g., *Nguyen*, 841 N.W.2d at 682, upholding a warrantless canine sniff of the defendant's apartment because the sniff was performed in the common hallway outside of the defendant's apartment—even though the apartment building was locked and secured against public access—because an apartment's curtilage does not extend beyond the resident's own apartment, with e.g., *McClintock v. Texas*, 405 S.W.3d 277, 284 (Tex. App. Ct. 2013) (requiring a warrant to perform a canine sniff of the defendant's apartment because the sniff was performed on the second-floor apartment's "landing"—despite the fact that the landing was unsecured and open to public access—because the stairway leading to the landing was not a "common" area), *rev'd on other grounds*, 444 S.W.3d 15 (Tex. Crim. App. 2014).

69. The good faith exception to the exclusionary rule applies when a police officer acts in objectively reasonable reliance on a search warrant issued by a detached and neutral magistrate. *U.S. v. Leon*, 468 U.S. 897, 913 (1984).

70. See *Davis v. U.S.*, 131 S. Ct. 2419, 2428–29 (2011). The officers in *Davis* had performed a particular type of warrantless automobile search—a *Belton* search—in reliance on the Court's then-decided precedent. See *id.* at 2425, explaining that the officers had relied on *Belton* in performing an incident search of the passenger compartment of Davis's vehicle, citing *New York v. Belton*, 452 U.S. 454, 459–60 (1981). While Davis's case was still on appeal, the Court substantially narrowed the circumstances under which a *Belton* search could be performed. See *Arizona v. Gant*, 556 U.S. 332, 351 (2009), holding that a *Belton* search of the arrestee's vehicle was proper only if, at the time of the search, the arrestee had

not been adequately secured. Even though *Gant* meant that the officers in *Davis* violated the Fourth Amendment in searching Davis's vehicle (because Davis had been secured in the squad car at the time of the search), *Davis* refused to suppress the evidence found during the vehicle search. See *Davis*, 131 S. Ct. at 2429. Instead, because the officers had "conduct[ed] a search in reliance on binding appellate precedent," the good faith exception to the exclusionary rule was applicable.

71. See *Davis*, at 2428: "The question … is whether to apply the exclusionary rule when the police conduct a search in objectively reasonable reliance on binding judicial precedent."

72. Cf. *Davis*, at 2429: "[W]hen binding appellate precedent specifically *authorizes* a particular police practice, well-trained officers will and should use that tool to fulfill their crime-detection and public-safety responsibilities."

73. Compare, e.g., *U.S. v. Givens*, 763 F.3d 987, 992 (8th Cir. 2014), finding that the good faith exception applied in upholding the admissibility of a warrantless canine sniff of the defendant's apartment because binding pre-*Jardines* Eighth Circuit precedent authorized warrantless canine apartment sniffs, *cert. denied*, 135 S. Ct. 1520 (2015), with, e.g., *Illinois v. Burns*, 25 N.E.3d 1244, 1256 (Ill. App. Ct. 2015), refusing to apply the good faith exception because there was "no *binding* appellate precedent specifically authorizing the officers' conduct [in performing a warrantless canine sniff of the defendant's apartment]." See also *Wisconsin v. Scull*, Wisconsin v. Scull, 862 N.W.2d 562, 572 (Wis. 2015), upholding a warrantless canine sniff of the defendant's apartment based on *U.S. v. Leon*, 468 U.S. 897 (1984). *Leon* addresses evidence uncovered in a search authorized by a search warrant and holds that the good faith exception to the exclusionary rule applies unless "a reasonably well trained officer would have known that the search was illegal despite the magistrate's authorization." See *Leon*, 468 U.S. at 922 n.23. Based on *Leon*, the court in *Scull* concluded that, in searching the defendant's apartment, the officers reasonably relied on a search warrant based, in part, on a now-unlawful warrantless canine sniff. See *Scull*, 862 N.W.2d at 568, holding that the officers reasonably relied on the search warrant and noting, additionally, that "[t]he [magistrate]'s decision to grant the warrant was a reasonable application of the unsettled state of the law at the time the warrant issued."

74. See *Minnesota v. Eichers*, 853 N.W.2d 114, 125 (Minn. 2014), upholding a warrantless canine sniff of a parcel performed at a private property location—a UPS mail facility, *cert. denied*, 135 S. Ct. 1557 (2015).

75. See Shoebotham (2012), at 253. For instance, private vendors such as the United States Police Canine Association (UWPCA), National Narcotic Detector Dog Association (NNDDA), and the American Working Dog Association (AWDA) certify detection canines in a variety of fields, including narcotics and explosives detection. See United States Police Canine Assn., http://www.uspcak9.com/; Nat'l Narcotic Detector Dog Assn., http://www.nndda.org; American Working Dog Assn., and http://www.americanworkingdog.com/.

76. See Bird (1996), at 410–415, describing the training and certification of drug-detection dogs by federal and state law enforcement agencies.

77. See Shoebotham (2009), at 836; see also Ensminger (2012), at 121–122, describing the certification requirements for various organizations; Robb (2002), quoting the executive director of the United States Police Canine Association ("USPCA") as saying, "no standards are generally accepted for certifying a dog for police work. In many cases, he said, qualifications are so minimal that they lack credibility."

78. For example, some private vendors, such as the USPCA, require only a 70% accuracy rate in order to certify a drug-detection dog. See Furton and Heller (2005). In contrast, the U.S. Customs Service requires 100% accuracy before it certifies a drug-detection dog for use in the field. In addition to accuracy, other important differences exist. The AWDA trains drug-detection dogs to search vehicles, buildings, and parcels for marijuana, cocaine, heroin, and methamphetamines. See American Working Dog Association, *Certification Standards*, http://nebula.wsimg.com/f252ffa4007497b4c8cd75c1e4e04263 ?AccessKeyId=4DA52325FBE71554A208&disposition=0&alloworigin=1. The detection dog is tested on each of the four drugs for which certification is sought. Each *hide* contains at least 5 g of the tested substance. ("All of the tests hides will be at least 5 grams in weight, to any amount. Preferably some large amounts should be used.") The NNDDA's Narcotic Detection Standard includes, at a minimum, the detection of cocaine and marijuana, with the option to obtain additional certification for the detection of heroin, methamphetamines, and opium. See National Narcotic Detector Dog Association, *Training and Certification Documents*, http://www.nndda.org/officialdocs. The minimum amount that may be stashed is 10 g of cocaine and one-fourth ounce of marijuana. For the USPCA, canines are tested on four substances, which can include marijuana, hashish, cocaine, heroin, methamphetamine, or any certified derivative of these narcotics. See United States Police Canine Association, Inc., *Certification Rules and Regulations* (2007), http://www.uspca1.com/USPCA_Rulebook.pdf.

79. About Us, http://swgdog.fiu.edu/about-us/.
80. SWGDOG Update March 2010, at 2–7. http://swgdog.fiu.edu/about-us/history__ goals_of_swgdog.pdf.
81. See Steffen and Candelaria (2003), at 78: "The team should conduct daily training in the environments in which they will be deployed .... A minimum of 4 hours of weekly training should be conducted with the canine team."
82. *Id.*
83. See, e.g., Ensminger (2012), at 122, describing that certification is in fact for the detection dog and handler together as a *team*, and that certification remains "valid for 12 months."
84. See, e.g., *U.S. v. Ludwig*, 641 F.3d 1243, 1251 n.3 (10th Cir. 2011), stating that an uncertified drug-detection dog's reliability could be established, "at least in theory," by the dog's training history and record of reliability.
85. See Medema (1995), at 7: "Each time the drug canine is called upon to screen vehicles, luggage, packages, or currency, the time, manner, place, and circumstances involving each instance where the canine alerted should be thoroughly documented by the canine handler."
86. See *id.*; see also Ensminger (2012): "Police should keep accurate records, including both training and field records, and police administrators should see that this is being done."
87. See, e.g., *U.S. v. Olivera-Mendez*, 484 F.3d 505, 512 (8th Cir. 2007): "We have held that to establish a dog's reliability ... the affidavit need only state the dog has been trained and certified to detect drugs, and a detailed account of the dog's track record or education is unnecessary."; *South Dakota v. Nguyen*, 726 N.W.2d 871, 878 (S.D. 2007): "With the training being conducted in controlled circumstances, a dog's ability to find and signal the presence of drugs can be accurately measured. In the field, one simply cannot know whether the dog picked up the odor of an old drug scent or whether it mistakenly indicated where there was no drug scent." See also Ensminger (2012), at 126: "[D]epending on the court and the corroborating evidence, a failure to keep complete records may be overcome."
88. 133 S. Ct. 1050 (2013). *Harris* was argued on the same day as *Florida v. Jardines*, 133 S. Ct. 1409 (2013).
89. *Harris*, 133 S. Ct. at 1054. *Harris* assumed that to be the case—that a canine alert, by itself, establishes probable cause—and limited its analysis to how courts should determine whether a detection dog's alert is reliable.
90. See *Caballes*, 543 U.S. 405 (2005).
91. See *Harris*, 133 S. Ct. at 1053. Harris's truck was stopped because of an expired tag.
92. *Harris*, at 1054 (internal quotation marks omitted).
93. *Id.* (citations to record omitted).
94. See *Florida v. Harris*, 71 So. 3d 756, 771 (Fla. 2011): "[T]he State should keep and present records of the dog's performance in the field, including the dog's successes (alerts where contraband that the dog was trained to detect was found) and failures ('unverified' alerts where no contraband that the dog was trained to detect was found)." The Florida Supreme Court also required the State to produce an explanation of the detection dog's training and certification as well as evidence of the canine-handler's training and experience.
95. *Harris*, 133 S. Ct. at 1055.
96. *Harris*, at 1055–56: "The test for probable cause is not reducible to precise definition or quantification" (internal quotation marks omitted).
97. *Harris*, at 1056: "No matter how much other proof the State offers of the dog's reliability, the absent field performance records will preclude a finding of probable cause. That is the antithesis of a totality-of-the-circumstances analysis."
98. *Harris*, at 1057: "If a bona fide organization has certified a dog after testing his reliability in a controlled setting, a court can presume ... that the dog's alert provides probable cause to search. The same is true, even in the absence of formal certification, if the dog has recently and successfully completed a training program ...."
99. Those incentives were described as avoiding "unnecessary risks"—because false positive alerts lead to baseless searches that expose officers in the field to danger—and "wasting limited [law enforcement] time and resources." But see Shoebotham (2012), at 252, arguing that "clear incentives exist for law enforcement to use unreliable drug-detection dogs (or dogs with only marginal reliability) in the field: (1) financial self-interest, based on civil forfeiture statutes ..., and (2) targeting of certain groups, such as racial or ethnic minorities, for police investigation."
100. *Harris*, 133 S. Ct. at 1056: "Making matters worse, the decision below treats records of a dog's field performance as the gold standard in evidence, when in most cases they have relatively limited import."
101. *Harris*, at 1056–57.

102. See *Harris*, at 1057: "[E]ven assuming a dog is generally reliable, circumstances surrounding a particular alert may undermine the case for probable cause—if, say, the officer cued the dog (consciously or not), or if the team was working under unfamiliar conditions."

103. *Harris*, at 1057, quoting the Solicitor General's acknowledgement at oral argument that the trial court could "give [the handler's] answer whatever weight is appropriate."

104. *Harris*, at 1058: "The court should allow the parties to make their best case, consistent with the usual rules of criminal procedure."

105. *Harris*, at 1058: "If the State has produced proof from controlled settings that a dog performs reliably in detecting drugs, and the defendant has not contested that showing, then the court should find probable cause."

106. *Id.*: "And the court should then evaluate the proffered evidence to decide what all the circumstances demonstrate."

107. See, e.g., *U.S. v. Gadson*, 763 F.3d 1189, 1201, 1203 (9th Cir. 2014), upholding the district court's finding of canine reliability based on the canine handler's extensive pretrial testimony and testimony before the jury, as well as the defendant's failure to offer evidence that contradicted the handler, *cert. denied*, 135 S. Ct. 2350 (2015); *U.S. v. Patton*, 517 F. Appx. 400, 403 (6th Cir. 2013): "The [*Harris*] Court held that if the government has produced proof from controlled settings that the dog has performed reliably, the defendant should have an opportunity to challenge the evidence through cross-examination or introducing its own fact or expert witnesses to contest the training or testing standards as flawed or too lax."; *U.S. v. Trejo*, 551 F. Appx. 565, 567 (11th Cir. 2014), noting that the government presented evidence "to support the reliability of the field alerts," and that the defendant then challenged the government's offer of proof with the detection dog's field performance records.

108. See, e.g., *U.S. v. Green*, 740 F.3d 275, 283 (4th Cir.), finding that the drug-detection dog was reliable despite the dog's 25.88% field-performance success rate, *cert. denied*, 135 S. Ct. 207 (2014). See also *Trejo*, 551 F. Appx. at 576.

109. See *Patton*, 517 F. Appx. at 403; see also *Trejo*, 551 F. Appx. at 567, finding that consideration of the drug-detection dog's field performance records had failed to undermine the dog's reliability.

110. See *U.S. v. Thompson*, 540 F. Appx. 445, 447–48 (5th Cir. 2013).

111. See *U.S. v. Rodriguez*, 702 F.3d 206, 210 (5th Cir. 2012), explaining that "a showing of the dog's training and reliability is not required if probable cause is developed on site as a result of a dog sniff of a vehicle," *cert. denied*, 133 S. Ct. 1615 (2013).

112. See *Harris*, 133 S. Ct. at 1057.

113. Compare *id.*, stating that a defendant "must have an opportunity to challenge such evidence of a dog's reliability, whether by cross-examining the testifying officer or by introducing his own fact or expert witnesses," with *Thompson*, 540 F. Appx. at 447–48: "We do not hold that, after *Harris*, a defendant may never obtain an evidentiary hearing based on a claim that a drug-detection dog was manipulated into an alert; rather, we hold only that the bare assertion of manipulation here, with no supporting details or facts, is insufficient to show that the district court abused its discretion by not conducting a hearing."

114. *Thompson*, 540 F. Appx. at 447.

115. See *Harris*, 133 S. Ct. at 1056, reversing the Florida Supreme Court's requirement of "a strict evidentiary checklist, whose every item the State must tick off" in determining canine reliability.

116. See *Harris*, at 1057, explaining that the defendant could cross-examine the canine handler about the detection dog's field accuracy; contest the adequacy of the detection dog's training program; and question the detection dog's performance during the sniff at issue.

117. See *Harris*, at 1058.

118. See *Green*, 740 F.3d at 283, finding reliable a canine sniff performed by a drug-detection dog that had completed a 13-week drug-detection course at the Virginia State Police training academy. See also *U.S. v. Gunnell*, 775 F.3d 1079, 1085 (8th Cir. 2015), finding reliable a canine sniff performed by a drug-detection dog in which the dog and canine handler had completed a 13-week training program, *cert. denied*, 2016 U.S. LEXIS 145 (U.S. Jan. 11, 2016).

119. See *Green*, 740 F.3d at 283, noting that the drug-detection dog passed a certification test after undergoing a 13-week training course; *U.S. v. Holleman*, 743 F.3d 1152, 1157 (8th Cir.), noting that the drug-detection dog and canine handler "were first certified by Northern Michigan K-9 as a narcotics detection team," *cert. denied*, 134 S. Ct. 2890 (2014); *U.S. v. Trejo*, 551 F. Appx. 565, 570 (11th Cir. 2014), discussing certification by a "bona fide" organization, but refusing to require the government to specifically assert that the certifying organization was "bona fide"; *U.S. v. Patton*, 517 F. Appx. 400, 402–03 (6th Cir. 2013), upholding a probable-cause determination based on the government's introduction of "the dog's training, certification and accuracy rate of 'over 90%.'"

120. See *Green*, 740 F.3d at 283, noting that the drug-detection dog and canine handler performed 4 h of training each week and 20 h of in-service training each month. See also *U.S. v. Gunnell*, 775 F.3d 1079, 1085 (8th Cir.), noting that the drug-detection dog and canine handler completed weekly training sessions.

121. See *Green*, 740 F.3d at 283, noting that the drug-detection dog and canine handler had undergone annual recertification as a narcotics-detection team; *Holleman*, 743 F.3d at 1157, noting that the drug-detection dog and canine handler had undergone annual recertification from the time of the team's initial certification to the date of the defendant's vehicle-sniff.

122. See *Green*, 740 F.3d at 283, upholding the government's use of a canine police trainer to give an expert opinion regarding the drug-detection dog's reliability.

123. *Harris*, 133 S. Ct. at 1057. See *Holleman*, 743 F.3d at 1157–58, applying a totality-of-the-circumstances analysis that included, in addition to the detection dog's alert, the officer's suspicions—based on the officer's observations at the traffic stop—that the defendant was transporting drugs in this vehicle.

124. See *U.S. v. Gadson*, 763 F.3d 1189, 1203 (9th Cir. 2014), finding that the canine handler's extensive testimony regarding both his and the drug-detection dog's training and certification supported the district court's probable-cause determination, *cert. denied*, 135 S. Ct. 2350 (2015); *U.S. v. Dimas*, 532 F. Appx. 746, 748 (9th Cir. 2013), noting the canine handler's attendance at dog-handler conferences and classes.

125. See *Gadson*, 763 F.3d at 1202–03, holding that a "full-fledged *Daubert* hearing" was not required; instead, both the state and the defendant were permitted to proffer evidence relating to the detection dog's reliability.

126. *Harris*, 133 S. Ct. at 1057.

127. *Green*, 740 F.3d at 283, upholding the district court's finding of canine reliability based on the drug-detection dog's training and certification records, notwithstanding the defendant's argument that the dog's field accuracy was only 25.88%. Interestingly enough, after *Harris*, courts have also used field-performance success rates to *uphold* a detection dog's reliability. See, e.g., *Holleman*, 743 F.3d at 1157, upholding, as reliable, a 57% "in-field" accuracy rate; *U.S. v. Donnelly*, 475 F.3d 946, 955 (8th Cir. 2007), upholding, as reliable, a 54% "in-field" accuracy rate.

128. *Harris*, 133 S. Ct. at 1057.

129. *Harris*, at 1057–58.

130. *U.S. v. Funds in the Amount of One Hundred Thousand One Hundred and Twenty Dollars ($100,120)*, 730 F.3d 711, 724 (7th Cir. 2013), holding that the claimant "may offer evidence of a drug dog's inadequate training to challenge evidence of the drug dog's field or training performance" evidence. See also *Harris*, 133 S. Ct. at 1057, noting that formal certification is not required if the drug-detection dog has completed a training program that evaluated the dog's proficiency in locating drugs. But see *U.S. v. Burrows*, 564 F. Appx. 486, 492 (11th Cir. 2014), rejecting the defendant's complaints that "the government could not produce logs of the dog's training" in light of *Harris*'s refusal to apply a "strict evidentiary checklist."

131. See *$100,120*, 730 F.3d at 724–25, questioning whether the drug-detection dog was trained to alert to tainted or untainted currency; whether the dog was trained with illicit street cocaine or pseudo-cocaine odors; whether the dog was trained to distinguish cocaine from "cutting" agents, like baking soda or vitamin B-12; and whether the dog was trained in-house by law enforcement or instead at a third-party outside agency. See also *U.S. v. Thomas*, 726 F.3d 1086, 1096 (9th Cir. 2013), holding "that when a defendant requests dog-history discovery to pursue a motion to suppress, Federal Rule of Criminal Procedure 16 compels the government to disclose the 'handler's log,' as well as 'training records and score sheets, certification records, and training standards and manuals' pertaining to the dog," citing *U.S. v. Cedano-Arellano*, 332 F.3d 568, 570–571 (9th Cir. 2003).

132. Compare *$100,120*, 730 F.3d at 725, noting that a certified drug-dog training and behavior expert's statement that "it is an industry standard to certify drug dogs through an *outside agency*" (emphasis added), with *Trejo*, 551 F. Appx. at 570, noting that the drug-detection dog was originally certified by the Florida Highway Patrol before having been recertified by a private company.

133. See, e.g., *Louisiana v. Smith*, 152 So. 3d 218, 222 (La. App. 2 Cir. 2014) ("As to the search of the defendant's vehicle, the trial court noted that it had reviewed the entire dashcam video of the arrest and the K-9 search of the car."), *writ denied*, 2015 La. LEXIS 2453 (La., Oct. 23, 2015). See also *Felders ex rel. Smedley v. Malcolm*, 755 F.3d 870, 880 (10th Cir. 2014): "But it is equally well-established that officers cannot rely on a dog's alert to establish probable cause if the officers open part of the vehicle so the dog may enter the vehicle or otherwise facilitate its entry.", *cert. denied*, 135 S. Ct. 975 (2015).

134. Although field performance records are of "relatively limited import," see *Harris*, 133 S. Ct. at 1056–57, the evidence may nonetheless be relevant in a totality-of-the-circumstances inquiry. Courts determine the relevancy of the field performance records by comparing them to the drug-detection dog's training and certification records. See, e.g., *Green*, 740 F.3d at 283, comparing poor field-performance success rates to exemplary controlled environment success rates, and ultimately determining that the government had established the drug-detection dog's reliability. But see *U.S. v Salgado*, 761 F.3d 861, 867 (8th Cir. 2014), reasoning that the district court had not erred by denying the defendant's access to "minimally probative field-performance records for the purpose of cross-examining" the detection dog's handler.

135. See *Thomas*, 726 F.3d at 1098: "Because the government's failure to turn over a full complement of dog-history discovery was an error that was not harmless, we reverse the district court's denial of the motion to suppress and vacate Thomas's conviction."

136. See Van Smith (2014).

137. See *Harris*, 133 S. Ct. at 1057.

138. Alexander (2015), at 306: "This can occur through pointing, eye gaze, or body positioning. Extensive research performed by Brian Hare at the Duke Canine Cognition Center has concluded that dogs do read and act upon human pointing gestures." See also Lit et al. (2011), at 392: "Cues may also include more subtle unintentional cues given by handlers such as differences in handler proximity to the dog according to scent location, gaze and gesture cues, and postural cues."

139. See Alexander (2015): "Canine handlers have been aware for many decades that handler gestures and body language can hinder canine performance in inadvertent cueing."

140. See Lit et al. (2011): "[T]hese findings confirm that handler beliefs affect working dog outcomes, and human indication of scent location affects distribution of alerts more than dog interest in a particular location." In the Lit study, canine handlers were falsely told that target scents had been placed at marked locations in the search area when, in fact, *no* target scent was present. ("In the current study, there was no target scent present, so that any alert identified by handlers was considered a false alert.") The purpose of the study was to determine whether the canine handler's belief that the target scent was present in the search area affected whether the drug-detection dog would alert. Despite the absence of any target scent, handlers "called an alert" when their detection dogs responded at the locations where handlers believed scents were placed. The Lit study found that the "overwhelming number of incorrect alerts" confirmed that handler beliefs affected detection dog deployment outcomes.

141. This behavioral phenomenon is known as the "Clever Hans" effect and is based on an early twentieth century horse, named Clever Hans, that was believed to be capable of counting and performing other tasks requiring cognition. A psychologist of the era, Oskar Pfungst, studied the horse and found that Clever Hans was actually "recognizing and responding to minute, unintentional postural and facial cues of his trainer or individuals in the crowd" (citation to study omitted). As the Lit study explained: "The Clever Hans effect has become a widely accepted example not only of the involuntary nature of cues provided by onlookers in possession of knowledge unavailable to others, but of the ability of animals to recognize and respond to subtle cues provided by those around them."

142. And, as the Clever Hans effect has shown, the canine handler's cueing may be subtle—unintentional postural and facial signals that the drug-detection dog recognizes as the handler's *expectation* that the dog will alert. See also *$100,120*, 730 F.3d at 722–23 & 722 n.14, noting, in a civil forfeiture case, that the claimant's expert, Dr. Larry Myers, had stated that the government's apparent failure to use "blind testing,"—i.e., testing where neither the canine handler nor the person administering the test is aware of the target scent's location—in training a drug-detection dog could result in the dog being cued to alert. Cf. *U.S. v. Thompson*, 540 F. Appx. 445, 446–47 (5th Cir. 2013), rejecting the defendant's claim that the canine handler had "actively manipulated an alert" because the defendant's conclusory allegation "gave no supporting detail or explanation of the dog's alert in this case … ." *Thompson* contains no mention of the existence of video evidence regarding the two canine sniffs of Thompson's vehicle, however.

143. See *Harris*, 133 S. Ct. at 1057.

144. See *$100,120*, 730 F.3d at 724–25, questioning whether the drug-detection dog was trained to alert to tainted or untainted currency; whether the dog was trained with illicit street cocaine or pseudo-cocaine odors; whether the dog was trained to distinguish cocaine from "cutting" agents, like baking soda or vitamin B-12; and whether the dog was trained in-house by law enforcement or instead at a third-party outside agency.

145. See *Daubert v. Merrell Dow Pharmaceuticals, Inc.*, 509 U.S. 579, 597 (1993), explaining that the trial judge has a "gatekeeping role"; that the Federal Rules of Evidence "assign to the trial judge the task of ensuring that an expert's testimony both rests on a reliable foundation and is relevant to the task at hand."

146. See, e.g., 21 U.S.C. § 881(a)(6), providing for forfeiture of funds that were "furnished or intended to be furnished ... in exchange for a controlled substance, ... proceeds traceable to such an exchange, and all moneys ... used or intended to be used to facilitate [a drug crime]." In addition to the seizure of cash, Section 881(a) also provides for forfeiture of any conveyance—such as a vehicle—as well as real property, used or intended to be used, in a drug crime. See 21 U.S.C. § 881(a)(4), § 881(a)(7). The currency is properly seized if probable cause exists to believe that the funds are connected to a drug crime. To recover the currency, the burden then shifts to the claimant (the money's owner) to establish, in a judicial forfeiture proceeding, that the currency was derived from a lawful source. See, e.g., *U.S. v. $22,474 in U.S. Currency*, 246 F.3d 1212, 1215, 1217 (9th Cir. 2010).

147. See, e.g., *U.S. v. $506,231 in U.S. Currency*, 125 F.3d 442, 453 (7th Cir. 1997); *U.S. v. $30,060 in U.S. Currency*, 39 F.3d 1039, 1043 (9th Cir. 1994).

148. See, e.g., *$506,231*, 125 F.3d at 453; *$30,060*, 39 F.3d at 1043.

149. See, e.g., *U.S. v. Funds in the Amount of Thirty Thousand Six Hundred Seventy Dollars ($30,670)*, 403 F.3d 448, 458 (7th Cir. 2005) (citing Furton et al. 1997b).

150. Relying on Dr. Furton's research, the Seventh Circuit explained that drug-detection dogs do not actually alert to cocaine itself because the drug is a topical anesthetic that "deadens olfactory senses." Again, relying on Dr. Furton's research, the court concluded that methyl benzoate was the only cocaine byproduct-molecule to which drug-detection dogs alert. ("[T]he research indicates that dogs do not alert to byproducts other than methyl benzoate and would not alert to synthetic 'pure' cocaine unless methyl benzoate was added."). See *$30,670*, F.3d at 457-59.

151. See *$30,670*, 403 F.3d at 457–58.

152. See *$100,120*, 730 F.3d at 721.

153. Angelos relied on a different published scientific study, which he testified undermined Dr. Furton's conclusion that drug-detection dogs alert only to the molecule, methyl benzoate, rather than alerting to the cocaine itself or a "potentially longer lasting byproduct". See *id.* at 720-21 (citing Waggoner et al. 1997, at 224).

154. See *$100,120*, challenging the claim that the methyl benzoate generated by cocaine residue on currency quickly drops below detectable levels because the molecule evaporates quickly. Angelos asserted that as long as cocaine remained present on the currency, the cocaine would continue to generate methyl benzoate "and thereby replenish the methyl benzoate lost to evaporation." Angelos supported this assertion by pointing to studies that showed that American currency contained a substantially higher level of cocaine than the Canadian currency that Dr. Furton used in his 1997 study. See *id.* at 721 n.10 (citing Furton et al. 1997b).

155. See *$100,120*, citing inconsistent detection thresholds relied on in Furton et al. (1997b), above, and a study performed in 1999 (Furton et al. 1999).

156. See *$100,120*, at 727. But see *U.S. v. Gadson*, 763 F.3d 1189, 1203 (9th Cir. 2014), rejecting Gadson's request for a *Daubert* hearing to determine the scientific reliability of a canine sniff of the currency found on Gadson's person and in his home—a sniff that the government used to establish that the money had recently been in contact with contraband, *cert. denied*, 135 S. Ct. 2350 (2015). In the Ninth Circuit's view, "*Harris* did not suggest that a district court had to perform a full-fledged *Daubert* hearing to determine whether the dog sniff testimony was sufficiently reliable to establish probable cause." Unlike the claimant in *$100,120*, however, Gadson and his codefendant offered only bare assertions derived from "various studies and reports" concerning the unreliability of currency sniffs and did not introduce any expert testimony on the issue to support their argument that "dog sniff evidence is inherently unreliable and based on junk science." Although some may conclude that *Gadson* categorically prohibits *Daubert* hearings on the scientific reliability of currency sniffs, the decision is likely closely tied to its facts— that Gadson and his codefendant had failed to make the necessary showing to obtain a *Daubert* hearing because they introduced no expert testimony on the issue. See *id.*, finding that the district court's probable-cause determination was adequately supported by the canine handler's extensive testimony regarding both his and the drug-detection dog's training and certification and because "the defendants did not proffer evidence to the contrary."

157. See *U.S. v. Funds in the Amount of One Hundred Thousand and One Hundred Twenty Dollars ($100,120)*, No. 03-C-3644, at 5 (N.D. Ill. Feb. 11, 2015), ECF No. 261 (Order denying *Daubert* as moot). [hereinafter *$100,120 Remand*].

158. The "Furton theory" posits that drug-detection dogs alert to methyl benzoate and not cocaine per se; that methyl benzoate evaporates quickly from the surface of currency; and that drug-detection dogs could only detect methyl benzoate evaporating from currency if the currency had been recently exposed to the methyl benzoate—and, hence, to cocaine. See *$100,120 Remand*, at 3 (quoting *$100,120*, 730 F.3d at 719).

159. See *$100,120 Remand*, at 5–6: "Whatever the propriety of the appellate fact finding conducted in *$30,670*, nothing in that opinion (or any other, to this Court's knowledge) authorizes a party to present expert opinion testimony by reference to publicly available materials in lieu of the testimony of any expert qualified to offer opinion testimony under the requirements of Rule 702 and *Daubert*."

160. See *$100,120 Remand*, at 5, likening the government's insistence that the "law of the case" doctrine barred a *Daubert* hearing—despite the Seventh Circuit's remand in *$100,120* in order for the district court to perform a *Daubert* hearing—to "spitting into the wind."

161. *$100,120 Remand*, at 6, noting that, instead of introducing expert evidence, the government simply relied on the studies discussed in *$30,670* and a prior Seventh Circuit case; "Rather than fight the battle that is required by the Seventh Circuit's rationale ... the government has steadfastly insisted that it need only rely on evidence of the drug dog's performance in training."

162. *$100,120 Remand*, at 6–7 (noting repeatedly the government's "misplaced reliance" on *Harris*).

163. See Kase (2015).

164. See, e.g., Washington's Sniffer Dogs Re-Trained to Ignore Pot and Focus on Hard Drugs. *The Guardian*, May 31, 2013, http://www.theguardian.com/world/2013/may/31/washington-sniffer-dogs-marijuana: "Police say that having a K-9 unit that doesn't alert to pot will lessen challenges to obtaining search warrants because the dog won't be pointing out possible legal amounts of the drug."

165. See Kase (2015): "Most jurisdictions [in the state of Washington] simply won't get new dogs trained to marijuana so they will eventually switch over through attrition, but in the meantime, Seattle police and others in the state are providing extinction training to their dogs."; Washington's Sniffer Dogs, above: "Police departments in Bremerton, Bellevue and Seattle, as well as the Washington state patrol, have either put the dogs through pot desensitization training or plan not to train them for marijuana detection."

166. Cf. Bouton (2004), at 485, undertaking "a selective[] review [of] results and theory from the behavioral literature"—studies involving responses in rats and rabbits—"in an effort to understand what is learned in extinction and what causes the organism to learn it."

167. See *Massachusetts v. Ramos*, 894 N.E.2d 611, 613 (Mass. App. Ct. 2008): "[Drug-detection dogs'] highly developed sense of smell may alert falsely to the stale remnants or traces of drugs already removed from the scene under investigation. So called 'extinction training' can teach the dogs to ignore such trace or 'dead' scents."

168. See *Massachusetts v. Santiago*, 30 Mass. L. Rptr. 81, 2012 WL 2913495, *12 (Mass. Sup. Ct. May 22, 2012): "Extinction training conditions dogs to alert only to [drugs that are actually present rather than residual odors of contraband], which provides yet another reason why training records must be included in a search warrant affidavit."

169. See *U.S. v. Patty*, 96 F. Supp. 2d 703, 709 & n.10 (E.D. Mich. 2000), discussing testimony from the defendant's expert that the detection dog's handler "had not properly implemented 'extinction training'".

170. See, e.g., K9 Working Dogs International, LLC, *Guarantee* (2015), k9wdi.com/company-information/guarantee.html: "K9 Working Dogs International, LLC guarantees that, upon graduation from any K9 Working Dogs Training Program each dog will retain his/her training knowledge and training level for LIFE."

171. Bouton (2004), at 492: "Extinction is a highly complex phenomenon, even when analyzed at a purely behavioral level. It is worth noting that it is probably multiply determined."

172. See generally Bouton (2004), at 492–494, listing studies reviewed.

173. See Bouton (2004), at 485: "[Several extinction phenomena exist that] suggest that extinction does not destroy the original learning but instead involves new learning that is at least partly modulated by the context" (citation to studies omitted).

174. See Bouton (2004): "Extinction is just one example of a retroactive inhibition phenomenon in which new learning inhibits old ...."

175. Bouton (2004) (emphasis added): "In each of [the experimental manipulations conducted after extinction], the extinguished response returns to performance. All of them therefore indicate that extinction is not the same as unlearning, and because all of them can be seen as context effects, they also support the idea that performance after extinction is context-dependent" (citation to studies omitted).

176. Bouton (2004): "Perhaps the most fundamental of these [context-dependent] effects is the renewal effect. In this phenomenon, a change of context after extinction can cause a robust return of conditioned responding .... Several facts about the renewal effect are worth noting. First, it has been observed in virtually every conditioning preparation in which it has been investigated. Second, it can occur after very extensive extinction training" (citation to studies omitted).

177. Bouton (2004), at 486: "The passage of time might also bring about changes in internal and external stimulation that provide a gradually-changing context. Pavlov (1927) first observed another well-known extinction effect. In spontaneous recovery, if time is allowed to pass following extinction, the extinguished response can recover."

178. Bouton (2004): "A third effect further indicates that conditioning is not destroyed in extinction. In rapid reacquisition, when new CS-US [conditional stimulus-unconditional stimulus] pairings are introduced after extinction, the reacquisition of responding can be more rapid than is acquisition with a novel CS [conditional stimulus], indicating that the original learning has been 'saved' through extinction" (citation to studies omitted).

179. Bouton (2004), at 487: "A fourth context-dependent extinction phenomenon is reinstatement. In this effect, the extinguished response returns after extinction if the animal is merely reexposed to the U.S. [unconditional stimulus] alone" (citation to studies omitted).

180. Cf. Washington's Sniffer Dogs, above, reporting a dog-training expert's explanation that extinction training of a drug-detection dog requires "about an initial 30 days [of training] plus *every day reinforcements* to modify the dog's behavior" (emphasis added).

181. See *Daubert*, 509 U.S. at 597: "The scientific project is advanced by broad and wide-ranging consideration of a multitude of hypotheses, for those that are incorrect will eventually be shown to be so, and that in itself is an advance. Conjectures that are probably wrong are of little use, however, in the project of reaching a quick, final, and binding legal judgment …."

182. See *Harris*, 133 S. Ct. at 1057.

183. Cf. *B.C. v. Plumas Unified School District*, 192 F.3d 1260, 1266 (9th Cir. 1999): "The Ninth Circuit has recognized … that the level of intrusiveness is greater when the dog is permitted to sniff a person than when a dog sniffs unattended luggage."

184. See *U.S. v. Kelly*, 302 F.3d 291, 292–93 (5th Cir. 2002), upholding a canine sniff—performed on an international walkway bridge between the United States and Mexico—in which the drug-detection dog "touched her snout to [the defendant's] groin area and alerted." In upholding the sniff, the Fifth Circuit explained: "Certainly, a canine sniff, even one involving some bodily contact, is no more intrusive than a frisk or a pat-down, both of which clearly qualify as routine border searches."

185. See *Horton v. Goose Creek Independent School District.*, 690 F.2d 470, 479 (5th Cir. 1982): "Intentional close proximity sniffing of the person is offensive whether the sniffer be canine or human."

186. See *Horton*, at 478–479, noting that the dogs selected for detecting contraband are often large, intimidating breeds.

187. See *B.C.*, 192 F.3d at 1267: "[T]he district court found that the dog sniff was highly intrusive [because] the body and its odors are highly personal [and the] dogs often engender[ed] irrational fear …." (internal quotation marks omitted). But see *Doe v. Renfrow*, 631 F.2d 91, 92 (7th Cir. 1980), refusing to find the suspicionless, close-proximity sniff of a schoolchild to be a *search*.

188. See *Horton*, 192 F.2d at 477–78. See also Katz and Golembiewski (2007), at 782.

189. See *Jones v. Texas*, __ S.W.3d __, 2015 WL 730845, at *3 (Tex. Ct. App. Feb. 19, 2015), noting that "the noncontact sniff of appellant in this case was 'only minimally intrusive' because it did not involve physical contact."; *U.S. v. Reyes*, 349 F.3d 219, 224 (5th Cir. 2003), upholding the canine sniff of a person where the drug-detection dog spontaneously alerted from a distance of "four to five feet away" and the canine handler had not instructed the dog to sniff for contraband.

190. *Jones*, 2015 WL 730845, at *5 (internal quotation marks omitted).

191. Cf. Shoebotham (2009), at 882–83: "[M]any Muslims view dogs as unclean and that contact with dogs, especially canine saliva, is so offensive that it necessitates a purification ritual." In addition to the offensiveness of dogs to some cultures and religions, drug-detection dogs are oftentimes intimidating animals. See, e.g., *Jones*, 2015 WL 730845, at *5: "Appellant also argues that he was only 'an arm's length' away from [the drug-detection dog] as she was attempting to bite, scratch, and jump on him."; see also *Illinois v. Caballes*, 543 U.S. 405, 421 (2005) (Ginsburg, J., dissenting): "A drug-detection dog is an intimidating animal."

16 Cadaver Detection in Forensic Anthropology and Criminology
An Overview with Personal Notes

Keith P. Jacobi

Dogs find things. We all know that. We also know that dogs like to be helpful and please their owners (Gell 1988, p. 7, describing dogs as "biddable"). In 1998, members of a sheriff's office came to the Laboratory for Human Osteology at the University of Alabama with bone gathered from the grounds surrounding a house that had caught on fire in a rural area of the county and subsequently burned to the ground. I identified the bone as human, and the police asked if I could accompany them to the site of the house fire. As we drove to the site, the investigators indicated that they did not think that I would find any bones, because the fire was too hot and the structure had collapsed and burned pretty completely. I told them that the bones they had brought to me were smoked and burnt but in relatively good shape.

At the site, two pet dogs were playing in the yard. I grabbed one of the vertebrae out of the bag of bones the police had brought me and got out of the car. The two dogs ran up to me. I scratched the smallest dog on the head and held the vertebra to his nose. The dog with stubby legs took off into the brush surrounding the house. In no time, it came back with a human rib. We played the game a few times, with the dog bringing back more bone. The hard part was getting the bone from the mouth of the dog. After a period of this "play," the dog lost interest, and a policeman went to search the brambles for more skeletal material. None was found. The bone the dog brought was heat altered. So, a deceased human was in the house.

The firemen and the police took me into the house, which had no walls or roof, and into the "living room," where another rib had been found by investigators. The person must have fallen asleep on the sofa and burned in the fire, the police and fire investigator said. I looked around and pointed to an area of the destroyed house off to the left of the living room. "What was that room?" "That was the kitchen," a fire investigator said. Now I recognized a stove amid the burnt debris. "Your body will be in the kitchen," I said. "The bone was out here," the fire investigator said. "Dogs find things, but the flies are in there," I replied.

HISTORY BEHIND FORENSIC ANTHROPOLOGY AND CADAVER DOGS

The origins of forensic anthropology come out of the scientific endeavors of individuals who studied and practiced anatomy, chemistry, and medicine. Some of those individuals were on the fringe of archeology, assisting in the analysis of skeletal remains of prehistoric Native Americans. For example, Joseph Jones, a doctor, analyzed skeletal remains from stone box graves in Tennessee, providing data on cranial measurements, cultural modifications to the cranium, and pathological diagnoses on the skeletons (Jones 1876). He even did thin sections to analyze the microstructure of bone. George Dorsey (1868–1931) was probably the first forensic anthropologist. Being a curator of physical anthropology at the Field Museum in Chicago, a professor of comparative anatomy at

Northwestern University, and a professor of anthropology at the University of Chicago, his career was marked by a dissertation on mummies from Peru. His claim to fame was being the first anthropologist ever to testify in an American criminal trial, and it happened to have been in the famous murder trial of Adolph Luetgert, a Chicago sausage factory owner who was thought to have killed his wife in 1897 and made her into sausage. Dorsey was an expert witness for the prosecution, and his testimony was controversial but resulted in Luetgert being convicted. It also resulted in a backlash toward Dorsey, primarily from experts for the defense, that ended in his resignation from the museum and universities he was associated with and resulted in his pursuing other interests besides osteology and anthropology (Klepinger 2006, pp. 9–11).

During the early part of the twentieth century, an anatomist, T. Wingate Todd, continuing the work of Carl August Hamann, helped create a collection of human skeletons derived from modern cadavers that were documented with sex, age, stature, and ethnicity, as well as data on birth, occupation in life, and cause of death (Byers 2011). Early development of forensic anthropology during the 1930s and 1940s involved physical anthropologists attached to museums or working for salvage projects associated with the New Deal programs set up by Franklin D. Roosevelt. Physical anthropologists analyzed the skeletons salvaged from excavation of archeological sites that were endangered, practicing their skills at skeletal analysis, but for the most part, they did not involve themselves in criminal cases. In 1939, Wilton M. Krogman again put physical anthropologists on the radar for criminal investigation. Krogman had an article published in the *FBI Law Enforcement Bulletin* (Krogman 1939) that alerted law enforcement to the skills of physical anthropologists. Krogman eventually wrote the first textbook for forensic anthropology (Krogman 1962).

World War II, the Korean War, and the Vietnam War promoted the use of physical anthropologists and thus furthered the amassing of knowledge that would later be used in the developed field of forensic anthropology (Nafte 2000). Dr. Charles Snow and Dr. Mildred Trotter worked at identifying war dead and developing better ways to analyze human remains at the U.S. Army's Central Identification Laboratory established in 1947 in Hawaii. Korean War dead were identified by physical anthropologists such as T. Dale Stewart, Thomas McKern, Ellis Kerley, and Charles Warren. The work by McKern and Stewart resulted in the publications of *Skeletal Age Changes in Young American Males* (1957) and *Personal Identification in Mass Disasters* (Stewart 1970), which became standard works that have paved the way for further developments in research on and determination of sex, age, and ethnicity in the skeleton (Pickering and Bachman 1997).

In 1979, forensic anthropology became defined as "the applied branch of physical anthropology that deals with the identification of more or less skeletonized human remains for legal purposes" (Stewart 1979, p. 169). The phrase "mass disaster" in the title of Stewart's 1970 publication would develop a wider definition in the latter half of the twentieth century and the beginnings of the twenty-first century, and forensic anthropologists began assisting with plane crashes, space shuttle explosions, terrorist activities, and war and genocide atrocities with accompanying mass graves. Forensic anthropologists, since 1993, have been active participants in the Disaster Mortuary Operational Response Team (D-MORT) in the U.S. Department of Health and Human Services (Kennedy 2010).

Those individuals practicing forensic anthropology today apply standard physical anthropological methods and techniques to identify human remains in order to aid the legal process and to verify human rights violations. In Italy, there is a recent appeal for "a geo-archaeological protocol" for handling a crime scene (Barone et al. 2015). This standardization of protocol, while not always regimented in its procedural order in the United States, approaches a crime scene and the identification of human remains with a multiplicity of disciplines that involve not only forensic anthropologists but also the expertise of geophysical scientists, forensic pathologists, forensic odontologists, entomologists, and homicide investigators. All have the goal of understanding the evidence presented by human remains and the crime scene in order to determine the manner of death, whether by foul play, accident, or natural causes. Concomitant with this combined effort of detection comes the increased involvement by the forensic anthropologist in the recovery of not only skeletonized remains but also various states of decomposing human remains (Komar and Buikstra 2008).

This interest in the decomposition of human remains by forensic anthropologists has had a long evolutionary history and involves paleoanthropologists, paleontologists, and archeologists (Vass 2001). Archeologists, when confronted with a human skeleton in a burial pit, invariably want to know if all of the remains are present. So do paleontologists when they find animal fossils and paleoanthropologists when they find early hominid remains. In some cases, the remains are not all present, and the question is why they are not. The study that pertains to the laws of burial is called taphonomy. What forces move and alter the original position of the body where it was originally deposited at death? Early studies examined movement of bone by water, wind, animals, man, plants, gravity, freezing, heat, and even seismic activity (Chapman and Anderson 1955; Wood and Johnson 1982, Figure 31, for seismic effect).

Seminal studies of taphonomy and fossil death assemblages (Behrensmeyer and Hill 1980; Binford 1981; Brain 1981; Shipman 1981) paved the way for studies on human forensic taphonomy that continue to this day (Haglund and Sorg 1997, 2002a; Pokines and Symes 2014). These more modern studies of taphonomy involve soil effects, plant and animal movement, and alteration of bone (e.g., Alexander et al. 2015; Pokines 2014; Pokines and Baker 2014); movement by water (e.g., Brooks and Brooks 1997; Evans 2014; Haglund and Sorg 2002b; Nawrocki et al. 1997); effects of heating, cooling, freezing, and thawing (e.g., Junod and Pokines 2014; Symes et al. 2014); and cultural alterations to bone and movement by man (e.g., Congram 2014; Paolello and Klales 2014).

Many forensic anthropologists have training in archeology and are versed in the recovery and documentation of items (skeletal remains) deposited on the ground surface or buried subsurface. It is at this juncture that the forensic anthropologist meets the cadaver dog.

SEARCH FOR REMAINS AND RELIABILITY OF CADAVER DOGS

Early search methods for human cadavers (as suggested by Boyd 1979; Morse et al. 1983; Skinner and Lazenby 1983) included the use of infrared aerial photography, the visual search of an area by investigators, and the use of a probe along with a methane gas detector (Killam 1990, p. 235). Killam (1990) suggested that three other methods be added to the search methods for detection of human remains: air-scenting dogs, ground-penetrating radar (GPR), and "electromagnetic (sling-ram) profiling." With the onset of decomposition of a cadaver, Killam recommended the use of air-scenting dogs and suggested that the use of a dog-and-handler team, as opposed to human searchers alone, would lead to faster recovery of the remains. The dog–handler team also would do the least amount of damage to the crime scene and were an option "certainly more economical and manageable than a host of pedestrian searchers." Today, GPR and cadaver dogs are commonly used in concert, with the cadaver dogs being a "minimally invasive search technique" (Ruffell et al. 2014, p. 144). Ruffell notes that in one recent case, dogs helped provide "additional evidence that satisfied the police," which led to the removal of the concrete in a basement floor, which yielded, after excavation, the remains of a missing person.

In the late 1990s, I was called out on a case that involved heavy-equipment grading of the top of a hill at a suspected neo-Nazi camp in the woods. A body was believed to be buried on this hill. Search dogs had been brought out previously and had shown some interest in areas on the hill. So, a full search by authorities was undertaken, and my anthropology graduate students and I came along to offer assistance if human remains were found and to help locate the limits of a possible burial pit. Dogs were brought out again before the bulldozer went to work. The dogs indicated on one specific area. The area did look disturbed and irregular, with stained soil on the ground surface. We methodically started to excavate. What we uncovered was a burnt tree stump. The dogs had indicated on a buried burnt decomposing tree. And after excavation, there was no possibility of a body being at that location. The bulldozer took over, taking soil off the top of the hill in small measured increments in order to provide a clean surface for us to examine for evidence of a pit that would yield a body. There was no pit or body found that day. The police started to bad-mouth the dogs and the handler. This had happened at two other searches that I had attended prior to this particular search.

I knew the dogs could find things but questioned how reliable dogs could be at finding human remains and how reliable the handlers were at recognizing the indications made by the dogs. I had queried a few handlers at the time and asked them about the materials that they used to train their dogs. I was told they used anything from cast-off teeth from dentists and toenail clippings to blood-soaked cloth provided to them by medical examiners.

Enter an inquisitive undergraduate student named Alanna Lasseter, who wanted to do a forensic anthropology project with me. I asked her if she wanted to test the reliability of cadaver dog-and-handler teams, and that is what we set out to do. I searched and found, 20 mi. from the University of Alabama, a trainer of cadaver, search-and-rescue, and drug and explosive detection dogs. The trainer runs the Alabama Canine Law Enforcement Officer's Training Center (ACLEOTC). The facility includes over 150 ac. of land, about 68 ac. of which is used for training. The trainer, Rick Farley, was amenable to the idea of testing the reliability of dogs and handlers because he knew that the dogs could in fact detect cadaver scent. Any problem was most likely in the training of the dog to detect the correct scent and in the training of the handler to understand when the dog was indicating on the scent. We all felt that dogs and their handlers working in the humid southeast would face wholly different problems in detection from dogs and handlers based in other regions of the United States.

At the time, there was one other forensic anthropologist I knew of who had actually tested cadaver dog abilities, and that was Debra Komar (Komar 1999). A chapter by France et al. (1997) entitled "NecroSearch Revisited: Further Multidisciplinary Approaches to the Detection of Clandestine Graves" in an important book on forensic taphonomy by Haglund and Sorg (1997), alludes to the fact that a decomposition dog's success is tied to weather conditions. With temperatures in excess of 85°F (30°C), a dog will be in discomfort and less able to detect a scent and will generally need to be within a meter of a buried source to locate it (France et al. 1997, p. 506). Conversely, lower temperatures also make it difficult for a dog to locate a scent at a distance, "especially if the source is buried" (France et al. 1997, p. 506). It was Komar (1999) who first tried to test the detection of cadaver scent by dogs in colder temperatures, finding that dogs could indeed locate human bone on the ground surface in colder temperatures.

In 2001, fresh human and animal remains, along with animal and human skeletal samples, were buried in May by Lasseter et al. (2003). With support from the medical examiner at the Alabama Department of Forensic Sciences, fresh human remains in the form of gauze that had been soaked by placement inside a cadaver's open autopsy, and fresh animal remains from a meat department of a local grocery store, were obtained. Skeletal remains consisted of forensic material donated for the purpose of scientific study. Both the fresh and skeletal materials were buried in five field areas, each measuring some 50 × 100 yd. One field was an open grassy area ringed by woods, a second field was on the edge of some woods, and the other three "fields" were areas that were deep in the woods. Each field was separated by close to a quarter mile. The fresh and skeletal portions were buried approximately 1–2 ft. deep. Out of 20 dog-and-handler teams contacted, four teams agreed to search the areas, and the search took place during the months of July and August. Various dog breeds were used (two German shepherds, a rottweiler, and a Labrador), aged from 1 year 8 months to 10 years, not all certified, trained on pseudo and real materials, with years of training ranging from "sporadic" to 8 weeks to 7 years. One team had no case experience in the field, while another team had 100 cases of field experience. Three of the teams had worked with the state police and the Federal Bureau of Investigation (FBI). Temperatures for the search ranged from the low 80s to the low 90s (°F), and the humidity ranged from 50% to close to 75%. During the search, the teams were videotaped to document handler-and-dog interaction.

One important finding of the Lasseter et al. (2003) study was the fact that the "dogs were consistent in finding dry human bone." All of the dogs were able to narrow the search or give an alert, but one dog provided an alert that went unrecognized by the handler (which some would call a "miss"), for the areas that contained skeletal remains at some point throughout the trials. The dogs were more readily able to discover buried skeletal remains as opposed to buried fresh remains (15% versus 10% of tests respectively). One dog team found a small skeletonized human cervical vertebra that was buried 2 ft. deep in a heavily wooded search area. This was 2 months after burial. In addition, the study found, through the examination of the videotapes, that dog handlers sometimes failed to understand what the dog was telling them. Thus, alerts sometimes went unrecognized by the handler. A dog might give an indication but not the indication it was taught to give. A dog might be pulled away from a search area when the dog had not finished searching. One dog lay down on the exact spot where something was buried, and the handler took it as a sign that the dog wanted water when in fact, the dog appeared to have been indicating that it had found something. The 2003 study indicated that standardized training was needed for all dog-and-handler teams and that skeletonized bone could be found and needed to be added to the training materials for the cadaver dog (Lasseter et al. 2003). Recently, Riezzo et al. (2014) examined cadaver dogs' ability to detect low concentrations of human cadaveric blood among confounding substance odors. Dogs that were well trained were able to discriminate between the confounding odors (e.g., food remnants, dog menstrual blood, synthetic detergent, swine blood, urine contaminated by blood) and the human cadaver blood even in low concentrations, which indicates "high levels of olfactory sensitivity." The well-trained dog can "identify traces of blood that cannot be perceived by the human eye" (Riezzo et al. 2014).[1]

LOCATING ANTIQUATED BURIED HUMAN BONE

One of the problems that bioarcheologists face when they are actually trying to locate prehistoric and historic graves with their included skeletal remains is the fact that they are dealing with the extreme end-stage decomposition of the human body, the presence of primarily bone. Even in modern forensic cases where police are trying to locate buried human remains that have been subsurface, or on the ground surface, those fresh remains can become bone at a very fast rate. This depends on geographical, environmental, and taphonomic conditions. A carcass in the southeastern United States can become skeletonized extremely fast. In one unscientific test case using two newly dead goats (not sacrificed for this study) placed on the ground surface in Moundville, Alabama (near Tuscaloosa), during the summer (July: average high temperature 93°F, average low temperature 72°F, average precipitation in inches 5.12, per U.S. Climate Data 2015), the goats had fully decomposed to bone within 2 weeks. Temperatures were high, and maggot masses were extremely large and very active on these remains, as could be expected. Of course, a buried body decomposes at a different rate from an exposed body, and that also is dictated by geographical, environmental, and taphonomic conditions (Galloway 1997; Manhein 1997; Micozzi 1997; Pokines and Baker 2014; Rodriguez 1997; Vass 2001, 2012). It is the skeletonized buried body that some bioarcheologists have become interested in finding with cadaver dogs.

Martin et al. (2012) tested the ability of cadaver dogs to locate historic human burials that have been buried for over 70 years. The burials were located in a family cemetery in Tuckaseegee, North Carolina. The graves included modern marked graves and unmarked graves with limited documentation as to their actual location. Some of these graves were upward of 200 years old. First, GPR, a proven technique for locating historic graves (Conyers 2006; Dupras et al. 2006), was used, and this helped locate the coffins and grave shafts. Then six cadaver dogs and four handlers were deployed to search the same area. It was found that GPR was most successful with detecting more modern graves, where remnants of the coffins and the actual burial pits could be discerned. GPR was not as reliable for the older, more historic burials. Conversely, the cadaver dogs had success with detecting the older historic burials "where remains were likely in advanced states of decomposition due to minimal embalming and coffining" (Martin et al. 2012). The authors indicate that both GPR and cadaver dogs should be used together to maximize detection of graves, just as Killam (1990) had previously done.

In a similar examination of a historic home and accompanying cemetery, the Office of Archaeological Research at the University of Alabama was contacted to do a remote sensing analysis of the Weissinger home site. The main impetus behind the project was to locate possible cultural deposits and to attempt to detect the presence of a cemetery. Archeological investigations of certain areas were undertaken by members of the 36th Expedition run by the Alabama Museum of Natural History. GPR was employed to "determine the horizontal and vertical extent of cultural bearing deposits with primary focus on identifying the location of the cemetery, any structural remains and associated features of the house structure (e.g., foundation piers, wells, possible privies, refuse deposits, and other aspects of the landscape at the time of the original occupation)" (Thompson and Gordon 2014). In January of 1822, George Weissinger had purchased land in Perry County, Alabama, to develop into a plantation. He would die in 1837 and be buried on the property, and other family members would be buried in the family cemetery as well. The plantation home would have different owners and burn in a fire in 1918. Grave markers were recognizable into the 1930s. Then, gravestones that marked the place of six individuals were removed, which, according to Charles Weissinger, a descendant, was done to facilitate plowing (Thompson and Gordon 2014, p. 3). A gradiometer investigation of the property by Haley (2011) uncovered a scatter of debris and brick located subsurface that was associated with the house, but he did not succeed in locating a cemetery. A GPR survey (Jones 2010) offered potential areas for location of a cemetery. In 2012, four human remains detection (HRD)-certified dogs and handlers from the Institute for Canine Forensics were brought in to conduct a search of the area for a cemetery and its human remains. The dogs had previously been successful in locating many buried human remains: one instance included discovery of remains from the Donner party (from the mid-nineteenth century) located in the California mountains (Grebenkemper et al. 2012; Thompson and Gordon 2014). The dog-and-handler teams searched areas of the plantation labeled A through H and an associated ravine. The dogs did alert in various of the lettered areas, and those alerts varied in quality from 1 through 3 (1, scent alert = undecided on exact location, possibly disturbed/scattered; 2, committed = holds alert, took time to locate main source of scent; and 3, strongly committed = committed to a specific location, will repeat alert on same location; terms of the Institute for Canine Forensics, 2012, http://www.hhrdd .org/). Numerous red ant hills were alerted on. It is known that ants can feed on corpses and are more likely, as predators, to feed on the other insect species that are helping to decompose the corpse (Anderson 2001; Goff and Catts 1990; Wells and Greenberg 1994). In addition, ants move all sorts of things, bone and tissue included.

The dogs and handlers found that one area, area E, had a high probability of including human remains subsurface, and E was noted as an "area of interest." Jones (2011) followed up by examining the area of interest and other areas with further GPR surveys, which yielded negative results. A backhoe was brought in, area E was dug to 6 ft. below ground surface, and no evidence of burial pits or human remains was located. Archeological investigations of the noted subsurface features thought to be associated with the house found through GPR and gradiometer did uncover those structural elements that were part of the house. Test trench excavations in areas other than area E failed to uncover evidence of the Weissinger cemetery.

One aspect of current research that could help with the detection of older graves and end-stage decomposition of a set of human remains is further training of dogs. When a dog searches an area with known buried skeletal remains and fails to detect the remains, then further training of the dog to detect a fainter and fainter scent of the skeletal remains might prove beneficial. In 2005, fresh and decayed human parts (donated) and animal materials were buried in a field belonging to Rick Farley at the Alabama Canine Law Enforcement Officer's Training Center facility near Samantha, Alabama. The location (coordinates) of these remains was documented. Our intent was to bring out dog-and-handler teams to the field after an extended period of time to determine the reliability of those teams in the detection of decomposed human and animal cadaver material. Originally, we planned to have teams search the field close to a year after the material had been buried. That did not happen. It is now 2015, some 10 years after the burial of the items, and dog-and-handler teams are being invited to search the field. While search of the field by teams is in its introductory phases, it is expected that while there may be success from some dog-and-handler teams, there will also be failure by some teams to detect the material. That is where proper training of the dogs to detect smaller and smaller amounts of the tail end of the process of decomposition (which includes primarily skeletal remains) may in fact help create future successful outcomes in detection by cadaver dogs, especially with buried remains.

Because the remains have been buried at the Alabama Canine Law Enforcement Officer's Training Center for 10 years (since 2005), the ability of dogs to detect residual human cadaver scent off of the buried skeletal remains is problematic with the current training by dog-and-handler teams that uses synthetic canine training aids. Odors emitted through decomposition change, as indicated by insect studies showing that cadaver odor becomes more attractive to certain species of insects at one stage of decomposition and more attractive to other species at another stage of decomposition (Anderson 2001, p. 144). It was with this change-in-odor problem in mind that we tried to assess the effectiveness of the commercially available pseudo corpse scent produced by Sigma-Aldrich Co. The intent was not to demean the product for its attempt to assist in the training of cadaver dogs, but it was felt that the product did not truly cover the entire spectrum of human remains' decomposition odor, falling short on the spectrum end that includes skeletonization. Pseudo scent formulations 1 and 2 were newly obtained in order to identify the primary chemical components using gas chromatography and mass spectrometry. Formulation 1 is used for early detection and in environments below 0°C. Formulation 2 is for postputrefactive detection. The results of the analysis detected "GABA, 2-pyrrolidone, and DBU" in formulation 1 and gamma-aminobutyric acid (GABA), 2-pyrrolidone and DBU, and "putrescine or 1,5-diaminopentane" in formulation 2 (Foyle 2014). These findings corresponded well with a more detailed study by Stadler et al. (2012) even though the experiment "was only conducted in 1-D GC/MS, yielding a much lower resolution" (Foyle 2014). It was determined that even though the compounds that were isolated in the pseudo scent are some of the elements that make up decomposition odor, they may not be the primary components that are necessary to accurately mimic the odor of human decomposition and may not reflect all of the spectrum of human decomposition. (For further discussion of the chemistry of human decomposition, see Chapter 9 herein.) Stadler et al. (2012) found that the pseudo scents were "oversimplifications of the decomposition odour and do not contain compounds that have been previously reported within the headspace of decomposition." And like the Foyle (2014) study, Stadler et al. (2012) feel that a pseudo created with a "larger variety of compounds that represent the variation seen during decomposition would be beneficial" and make a "more effective canine training aid." Vass (2012, p. 240) indicates that the accurate prediction of which compounds will exist at any specific decompositional event is difficult because "the mechanisms of compound formation and the taphonomic influences are not yet fully understood." But Vass's list of odor mortis compounds and taphonomic variables provides a basis for what compounds should be present at a decompositional event (see Table 2 in Vass 2012).

Forensic anthropologists have often been privy to conversations both praising and criticizing dog-and-handler teams brought in to search a site in question. *In the past*, the negatives have come from the underlying beliefs that while it is known that dogs can sniff out drugs, explosives, and living people, it is harder for them to detect residual cadaver odor because accelerated dehydration of human remains makes the odor decrease (Galloway 1997). In addition, part of this difficulty in detecting residual cadaver odor is also due to the fact that it is hard for volunteers to access actual human remains to train their dogs. Sometimes, the human remains can be hazardous to both the dog and the handler. So those who train dogs occasionally resort to using pseudo scents. Pseudo scents are chemical concoctions that artificially recreate a scent that is supposed to resemble the odor of human decomposition. It is difficult to develop a scent or series of scents to mimic the stages of decomposition.

Forensic anthropologists such as Bill Bass, with his Body Farm, and subsequent faculty members and students at the University of Tennessee, as well as other universities, have worked for many years examining the decomposition of the human body in various situations and climates (Bass 1997; Galloway 1997; Gill-King 1997; Rebmann et al. 2000; Rodriguez and Bass 1983; Ross and Cunningham 2011; Stejskal 2013). There are basic stages to decomposition of the human body:

1. Three stages when the body is in a putrid phase
2. Three stages when it is in a bloating phase
3. Four stages of a body destruction and decay phase (Rebmann et al. 2000; Stejskal 2013)

Galloway (1997) notes five phases:

1. Fresh
2. Early decomposition
3. Advanced decomposition
4. Skeletonization
5. Extreme decomposition

Whatever the process through the spectrum of decomposition, future efforts need to be made to train dogs on actual decomposition materials that reflect this entire spectrum, from a freshly deceased body to dry bone skeleton, and/or to develop not only pseudo scents that cover the early stages of decomposition, which they currently do, but also fainter scents that mimic the dwindling decomposition scents found in skeletal material.

CADAVER DOG AND SCENT OF BURNED OR CREMATED HUMAN BONE

While cadaver dogs can detect the varying stages of decomposition, including skeletal remains, if the dogs are trained properly, they also can detect human cremated bone. Fairgrieve (2008, p. 64) found that a dog trained correctly can detect cremated human bone even when it is largely devoid of its organic components (heavily calcined). The detection of cremated remains hinges on the availability of the scent in the air. If the scent is locked into the soil, i.e., buried subsurface, successful detection lessens. (See Chapter 8 herein regarding the aerodynamics of odor.) So, Fairgrieve (2008) suggests that at a fire scene, a soil auger 1 in. in diameter be used to probe soil disturbances to help potentially release human remains cremation scent and increase the availability of that scent into the air, and the turning of the soil exposes scented soil.

In addition, dogs are able to find where cremated human remains had been. A fire pit was indicated by an informant as the location of some missing people. Two separate cadaver dogs "indicated on a series of large stones used as part of the boundary of the pit" (Fairgrieve 2008, pp. 65–66). These stones, when analyzed, were found to have charred bits of human flesh. The pit, when examined, had only a portion of a human hand. The question remained, where were the rest of the remains of the missing individuals? The dogs continued to search the area and indicated on the joists of a small wooden bridge built over a creek. Cremated human material had gotten stuck in the bridge joists. Subsequently, after a search near the bridge of the creek floor some 3.5 ft. in depth, some cremains were found. An accomplice indicated that after the burning, they had dumped the cremated remains off the bridge and buried the rest in a pit on the property.

POSITIVE AND NEGATIVE: JUDICIAL CASES WITH CADAVER DOGS

Some recent court cases are worth discussing as to issues that are arising for scientists, including the author, who are involved in cadaver dog testimony.

WISCONSIN V. EUGENE J. ZAPATA

In 2007, I was asked to evaluate documentary materials on two dog-and-handler teams that were going to be involved in the case of *State of Wisconsin v. Eugene J. Zapata* (2006CF001996). I would serve as a witness evaluating the dog-and-handler teams. The case involved a wife named Jeanette Zapata who was missing from her home in Madison, Wisconsin, since 1976. The thought was that her husband, Eugene Zapata, may have killed her. There was no body. Dogs were brought in to search the properties where Eugene Zapata was known to have visited: his home on Indian Trace, a storage locker in Sun Prairie, and his car, among others areas. Carren Corcoran and her dogs, Cleo and Norse, and Theresa Christ and her dog Sammie were the dog-and-handler teams involved. The documentation I was supplied included information on each dog's training as it related to searching for living and dead humans. The information included discussion on the conditioning and agility exercises as well as obedience training required for the dogs to become cadaver dogs and search-and-rescue dogs. Documentation was provided showing the training of the handlers as well. The handlers noted the body language the dogs provide when they come in contact with the odor of human remains, actual deceased human remains, and distractions. The distractions included animal bone, actual living people, other dogs and animals, a child's toys, sardines, rabbit and squirrel hair, and dead mice.

Corcoran's dog Cleo had been trained on various aids to detect human remains during sessions from 2000 to 2006. The aids included animal bone (turkey, turtle, and deer, for example); animal tissue (dead mice); animal blood (pig); body wipe from a human cadaver; cadaver water; human teeth (dry and bloody); burned human teeth; human skeletal remains (modern fresh and dry); historic skeletal remains (Cleo indicated on buried human remains in a historic cemetery that was used from 1878 through 1914); historic and prehistoric Native American human skeletal remains (whole and fragmented remains); burned human bone; human tissue; human brain matter; a mummified finger (1–2 years old); one-half of a human cadaver; decompositional materials from a human cadaver; a human scalp portion that had been decomposing for 2 years; grave dirt, dry; grave dirt, wet; adipocere; placenta (also frozen placenta); umbilical cord; foreskins; human hair; and burned human hair.

Corcoran also trained Cleo to detect smaller amounts of human material. She started with a general search and then progressed to a more detailed and specific search, which allows the dog to pinpoint smaller human body materials. For example, Cleo was able to detect a small amount of human hair placed under a brick in a hallway (documented 1/26/02). Cleo also indicated on a trace of brain matter in a puddle of water (documented 5/16/02). At times, Corcoran made a *handler error*, which she was able to sort out and correct. Cleo indicated on a small toy, and Corcoran said "no," but in reality, the dog was correct (documented 1/14/03). In actuality, there were two human teeth with the toy. So, Corcoran subsequently rewarded the dog, indicating that the dog was in fact correct.

Theresa Christ trained Sammie to be able to detect human remains by using the following aids during training sessions during the years 1999 through 2007: animal tissue, animal bone (including fresh pork bone), body wipe from a human cadaver, cadaver-scented tennis balls, Native American skeletal remains (both historic and prehistoric), baby teeth, adult teeth (dry and with blood), human blood, pig blood, modern human bone (complete bone and bone fragment), nail clippings, human brain matter, placenta, baby umbilical cords, methane, baby hair, adult hair, burnt bone, burnt teeth, grave dirt, adipocere, calf tissue, decompositional materials from human cadavers, and cadaver brick. The wide variety of actual human body material used in the training of these three dogs is important in that it made these dogs very good at discerning human cadaver residue.

Five videotapes taken of the dog-and-handler teams in the act of searching areas relevant to the Eugene Zapata case were offered for examination and evaluation. The tapes were provided to me without sound, which was frustrating, as I was supposed to evaluate the video for indications made by the dogs in question. This lack of sound was critical because an important part of an indication/alert by the three dogs was a bark, which of course could not be heard on any of the videos. So, as an evaluator working with only the silent movements of the dog and handler on the tape, I had to focus more intently on the face and body language of the dogs in order to pick up when I thought the dogs were indicating. And, of course, I could see the bark action. The lack of sound prevented me from hearing any discussion about what areas the handlers had cleared and any discussion by the handlers and police about the search areas. Even with those restrictions, I could see that the dogs did provide clear indications that human cadaver residue was present at the search areas. I was advised that Corcoran and one of her dogs searched the self-storage facility in February 2007. The dog indicated at a specific storage unit door multiple times (both outside with the door closed and, with the door open, inside the same unit) during a comprehensive search in which the dog did not indicate at other storage units. In a search of a car in question, two dogs indicated on the trunk of the car.

While cadaver residual odor was present, detected by dog-and-handler teams, recorded by video, and witnessed by an evaluator by visual inspection of silent videos, the circuit court judge for the Zapata case denied the admission of the cadaver dog evidence. The judge relied on *Brooks v. Colorado.*[2] The judge found that the canine-produced evidence was relevant and the witness concerning that evidence qualified, but determined that the admission of the evidence would not assist the trier of fact (the jury). The judge also, citing *Brooks,* said that the dogs were of a breed characterized by an acute power of scent and had been trained to detect human remains, but determined that the dogs had not been found by experience to be reliable in detecting or alerting to human scent remains. He made no decision on the question of whether the dogs were "placed on the trail where the person being tracked was known to have been," an issue primarily for tracking dogs. As to the question of whether the dogs detected the odor of human remains within a reasonable time frame, the court said it did not have to reach that issue. The court believed that a cautionary jury instruction would be insufficient to overcome the possibility that the canine evidence could be more prejudicial than probative because people, because of legend, rumor, or experience, would give the canine evidence more credence than the statistics would support. The judge indicated that to establish the dog's reliability might have required further investigation of the areas searched.

The Zapata trial ended with a deadlocked jury. In October 2007, less than a month after the mistrial, prosecutors requested a retrial. With the retrial looming, Eugene Zapata admitted that he killed his wife with a draftsman paperweight, strangled her, and wrapped a cord around her neck. The body was placed in a poplin tent placed in a car and taken to a farm field. Later, the remains were moved to a storage locker in Sun Prairie and then disposed of in the Juneau County landfill (Treleven 2008). So based on the statement by Zapata, the dog-and-handler search teams that searched the car and storage locker facility very likely did detect residual cadaver odor.

California v. Lyle Herring

Other courts have admitted evidence of a cadaver dog to establish the presence of a body. In a recent California case, *California v. Herring,*[3] the defendant, Lyle Herring, also was found guilty of murdering his wife without the presence of a body as evidence. Herring appealed the guilty verdict, saying the cadaver dog evidence was improperly admitted. This appeal was rejected and the judgment affirmed. The crux of the appeal involved the attempt to exclude the cadaver dog evidence because it "lacked foundation and corroboration" under the California Evidence Code. *California v. Malgren*[4] sets requirements for admitting dog-tracking evidence:

> 1. The dog's handler was qualified by training and experience to use the dog; 2. The dog was adequately trained in tracking humans; 3. The dog has been found to be reliable in tracking humans; 4. The dog was placed on the track where circumstances indicated the guilty party to have been; and 5. The trail had not become stale or contaminated.[5]

In a quick synopsis, Lesley Herring and Lyle Herring were having marital difficulties. On or around February 9, 2009, Lesley went missing. A neighbor, after walking his dog, saw Lyle when the elevator door opened at the first floor. Lyle had a 6 ft. tall × 2 ft. wide dolly with a large 5–6 ft. × 10–12 ft. rug. Lyle looked crazed. Later, around midnight, Lyle was seen pushing an empty dolly. Lesley never showed up to work and did not call anyone. After the disappearance, Lyle gave his son his Cadillac, and his son installed subwoofers in the back of the car. Lyle tried to enter Mexico supposedly to look for Lesley because he and his wife had planned to spend vacation time in that country. He was detained. Later, an investigator inquired in Mexico if Lyle ever asked about his wife when he went to Mexico. He had not.

A cadaver dog named Indiana Bones (Indy for short) was used in searches by Karina Peck, who operates out of the Los Angeles County Coroner's Department. Indy and Peck had trained for over 690 h together. The dog had located 752 training aids with only 3 false alerts, which makes the dog's "training reliability…99 percent." On February 19, 2009, Indy searched Lesley's condo and related areas, such as the carport where she parked her car, Lyle's parking space, a walkway behind the condo, and a storage unit in Burbank, and none of these places made Indy alert. Indy did alert on the "base of the garbage trash shoot in the complex, although he did not alert to the trash access point near Lesley's condo."

The next day (February 20), Indy searched a tow yard where both Lyle's and Lesley's cars were being held along with another car. Peck let Indy go with no prompting, and Indy went to the rear of a Mitsubishi and "alerted to an area of the rear of the vehicle where the floor carpeting meets…the plastic trim of the edge of the rear compartment." This area was removed, and Indy did not alert in this area again. At a later date (February 25), Peck and Indy returned to the same facility to search Lyle's Cadillac. Indy alerted in four areas: the driver's-side floor mat, the backseat floor where there happened to be some speaker wires, a hole where speaker wires exited, and trunk mats. Peck and Indy also alerted on two dirt piles near a merry-go-round in Griffith Park, an area where Lyle had been seen after Lesley's disappearance.

The court, on appeal, addressed Herring's contention that the cadaver dog evidence was inadmissible, stating that even though the trial court did not "discuss each *Malgren* factor," it had "clearly considered those factors, because the court had read the parties' papers, which discussed *Malgren*." Then each factor was addressed, showing that under *Malgren*, there was "sufficient foundation to admit the cadaver dog evidence…" Peck and Indy were adequately trained and had extensive experience, with Peck certified as a handler (factor 1). It was found since that the job cadaver dogs do is "analogous to what tracking dogs do, the foundational element was therefore satisfied" (factors 2, 3, and 4). Evidence pointed to the possibility that Lesley's body may have been placed in "one or more of Herring's cars: on the night Lesley disappeared, witnesses saw Herring pushing a dolly and a large rug to the garage." As to the fifth factor involving staleness or contamination of a trail, "if say a blood swatch or an entire decedent was completely contained and not touching directly, the fact that it was placed in a vehicle, the scent emanating from that would be collected in that vehicle and as it remains closed especially that odor will permeate [and] be retained." These residual scents will be picked up by canines. Finally, the court of appeals found that other evidence indicating that Lesley was dead corroborated the evidence furnished by the cadaver dog.

U.S. v. EDISON BURGOS-MONTES

Other courts have seen limits to cadaver dog evidence but have found that its admission was not sufficiently prejudicial to overturn a conviction. In the recently decided First Circuit case, *U.S. v. Burgos-Montes*,[6] Edison Burgos-Montes, who had been convicted of killing an informant (Madelin Semidey-Morales, called *Semidey*) in order to either prevent the informant from testifying or as retribution for the informant giving evidence to the government, appealed his conviction on various grounds. Included in the appeal was a challenge to the testimony of cadaver dog handlers. At the trial, testimony was introduced that a cadaver dog had alerted when "led by an area on Burgos' property where one of the officers had identified a possible grave site approximately six months before." No bodies were found. The testimony was used to "suggest that, because the dog alerted, the jury could conclude that the location had, at one point, concealed a human cadaver." Burgos objected to the testimony, questioning whether a "cadaver dog could reliably locate a spot in which human remains had been buried…and that the government had failed to lay a proper basis for its reliability under *Daubert v. Merrell Dow Pharmaceuticals, Inc.*, 509 U.S. 579, 113 S. Ct. 2786, 125 L. Ed. 2d. 469 (1993)." The testimony was allowed by the district court, and Burgos-Montes challenged the testimony on appeal. The United States Court of Appeals reviewed the objection and agreed with Burgos that the government did not lay out much of a case that a dog could reliably identify a spot in which there had been (presumably months earlier) a human cadaver, as opposed to simply responding to animal remains or to the leash-holding handler's conscious or unconscious cues. It is one thing to use a dog to identify a place in which one might look to see if human remains are present. It is quite another to use a dog to identify dirt that was once exposed to a human cadaver. The prosecution witnesses offered virtually no evidence that the scientific reliability of such a use had been established, or that their investigation protocols were generally accepted for such a use. Burgos' experts…offered much common sense, noting, for example, that the officer using the dog on a leash that alerted…was the officer who had previously identified the suspected spot.

While the court agreed with Burgos on this objection, there was more than enough evidence to support the previous verdict of conviction of Burgos for murdering Semidey, so the admission of the canine evidence was declared harmless error, and no retrial was required.

CADAVER DOGS AND DETECTION OF HUMAN REMAINS IN WATER

In the 1960s, air-scent dogs that were part of the navy's waterdog program were used in Vietnam to prevent attack by surface snorkelers and submerged divers swimming at important facilities such as bridges and docks along rivers and coastal shoreline. The use of air-scent dogs around water continued sporadically into the beginning of the 1980s to help search for missing persons who may have drowned (Osterkamp 2011).

Dogs are commonly used now in water searches for possible submerged bodies. Studies to date have focused on fine-tuning our understanding of how scent-bearing materials that separate from a submerged body are transmitted through the water and into the air to be detected by air-scent dogs (Osterkamp 2011). Recently, Healy (2010), while realizing dogs are a valuable source in detecting submerged remains, proceeded with an alternative detection method, side-scan sonar, to detect pig cadavers in submerged environments of Central Florida. Normally, a dog is placed in the bow of the boat or on an attached platform in front of the boat. The boat is low in the water, and the air-scent dog sniffs the air just above the water. Upon an indication made by the dog, a buoy is placed in the water, marking the area. (For the use of dogs on bows of boats to detect whale scat, see Chapter 23 herein.)

There are variables that can affect a dog's ability to detect an odor, such as the temperature of the air and the movement of air between the scent and the dog, as well as the experience of the dog and handler (Healy 2010; Rebmann 2000). Healy's (2010) side-scan sonar was successful in detecting submerged bodies in clear terrain in shallow lakes and ponds. Small bodies were better detected using a side-scan sonar of 1,800 kHz, 20 m swath width, while medium to large-sized bodies were better detected using a side-scan sonar of 900 kHz, 20 m swath width. However, Healy feels that with vegetation in the waterway that is involved with the terrain subsurface, divers, GPR, and water-search dogs are more appropriate for detecting a submerged body in these conditions (Healy 2010, p. 81).

FUTURE DIRECTIONS

The forensic anthropologist/bioarcheologist is intimately involved in the locating, excavation, and analysis of human remains. The laws of burial, taphonomy, and the process of decomposition are a primary focus of the bioarcheologist because that information dictates how mortuary interment behavior of prehistoric individuals is evaluated. Because of this interest, especially with skeletal remains, the forensic anthropologist can work in concert with cadaver dog-and-handler teams by increasing the effectiveness of recovery of surface and subsurface remains through ongoing training of teams that are trying to increase their expertise with the fainter odors associated with end-stage decomposition.

Cadaver dogs are often helpful during investigations and are often credited with finding bodies, after which other evidence is developed to conduct a prosecution. Cadaver dog evidence may be critical in the prosecution if a body is never found but the alerts of a dog corroborate other evidence indicating that there was a body at a location relevant to the prosecution's theory of the crime. Forensic anthropologists can help set protocols for the use of cadaver dogs because their taphonomic research can help describe aspects of the location where the body may have been buried or hidden for a time. Forensic anthropologists also can be involved in the training exercises and certification tests of cadaver dog-and-handler teams and help refine the search techniques of the teams. Better development of the detection of end-stage decomposition will help not only in locating the recently deceased but also in the pinpointing of historic graves in cemeteries with missing grave markers. Dogs find things. We all know that.

ENDNOTES

1. A program at Western Carolina University headed by Paul Martin and Professor Cheryl Johnston specializes in workshops helping cadaver dog handlers.
2. 975 P.2d 1105, 81 ALR 5th 779 (Colo. 1999).
3. No.B249468, 2015 Cal. App. Unpub. LEXIS 2787 (Ct. App. 2015).
4. 139 Cal.App.3d 234, 188 Cal.Rptr. 569 (1983).
5. See also *California v. Craig*, 86 Cal.App.3d 905, 150 Cal.Rptr. 676 (Ct. App. 1978).
6. 786 F.3d 92 (1st Cir. 2015).

17 Detection of Cocaine on Currency

Thomas H. Jourdan

Under consideration in the federal government's Ninth Circuit Court of Appeals in *United States v. $30,060 in U.S. Currency*,[1] in January of 1994, was the future of narcotics detection canine alerts as an investigative tool of law enforcement in instances where a large sum of currency is encountered in transit and pursuit of the forfeiture process is undertaken. The foundation for the circuit court's ruling would be based upon its 1988 ruling in *United States v. Dickerson*.[2] *Dickerson* had held that with cases of the interdiction of large sums of currency, the transition from mere suspicion to probable cause requires demonstration that the money was involved in drug trafficking.

U.S. v. $30,060

Albert Joseph Alexander had been stopped by Los Angeles County Sheriff's deputies on April 24, 1990, after running a stop sign. Approaching the vehicle, deputies noted on the front passenger seat a plastic bag filled with U.S. currency, configured in $1,000 stacks of a variety of denominations, which Mr. Alexander confirmed was his. While still at the scene, the deputies requested a narcotics detection canine, which subsequently alerted on the bag of money. A follow-on search of Mr. Alexander and his vehicle for drugs or drug paraphernalia was negative.

After having been read his rights, Alexander was questioned about how he came into possession of the approximately $30,000 in the bag. As he was unable to offer a credible explanation, he was taken into custody and the currency seized as the deputies concluded that there was probable cause to believe that it was involved in drug trafficking. Eventually, all local charges against him were dropped, after which the Federal Bureau of Investigation (FBI) adopted the seizure and attempted to forfeit the money under 21 U.S.C. 881(a)(6).

The district court granted summary judgment in favor of Alexander, finding insufficient facts to establish probable cause that the money was connected to drugs since during the associated proceedings, a forensic toxicologist testified that on the order of 75% of the banknotes in the Los Angeles area were contaminated by nanogram-to-milligram (from billionths of a gram up to thousandths of a gram) quantities of cocaine. The Ninth Circuit Court of Appeals provided final clarification, stating that a narcotics detection canine alert constitutes "strong evidence" of probable cause but does not itself establish probable cause, in particular because of the apparent wide-scale cocaine contamination of currency in general circulation.

U.S. v. $215,300

By the mid-1990s, in the Ninth Circuit, the legal burden in instances of the interdiction of large amounts of currency had become that probable cause for forfeiture was created only when an aggregate of facts, or alternatively stated, the totality of the circumstances, linked the currency in question to drug trafficking. Aside from the obvious situation in which the interdiction of a large amount of currency also nets drugs or drug paraphernalia, there have been two notable instances in which the aggregate-of-facts requirement has been satisfied. In one case, the suspect had two prior convictions in addition to a prior arrest for drug possession.[3] On the second occasion, a suspect detained at an airport was found to have concealed and strapped in excess of $200,000 to his body, lied about how he came into possession of the money, had an airline ticket issued through a Miami travel agency that had issued tickets for 20–30 other travelers from whom currency thought to have been related to narcotics trafficking had been seized, and was on a flight to a known drug-source city.[4]

The year 2000 saw the passage of the Civil Asset Forfeiture Reform Act,[5] which provided a uniform standard across all federal district courts as well as all federal appellate courts in civil forfeitures. The government's burden of proof in civil forfeiture cases henceforth would be preponderance of the evidence. In *United States v. $62,552 in U.S. Currency*,[6] on January 23, 2003, claimant Delia J. Baez was processing through security to board a flight to the Dominican Republic and asked for a form on which she could declare that she was taking currency out of the country. During the process of verifying the amount of currency to be declared, she was questioned by law enforcement, after which the currency in question was seized, although Baez was allowed to continue her journey. Civil forfeiture was undertaken after a narcotics detection canine alerted to an envelope containing Baez's currency presented along with three other envelopes containing shredded currency from a Federal Reserve Bank. Ultimately, the government was not able to prove by a preponderance of the evidence a substantial connection between the currency and a narcotics violation, and final judgment was entered for the claimant.

COCAINE ON CURRENCY

By the late 1980s, articles had appeared in the scientific literature alerting the community to the cocaine contamination of U.S., UK, and Canadian currency in general circulation (Aaron and Lewis 1987; Hudson 1989). It was generally recognized that the illicit trafficking of cocaine from South America to the U.S., in particular, is tallied by the Drug Enforcement Administration (DEA) in units of tons, and its subsequent distribution and sale is undertaken on a cash basis. It seemed reasonable that those handling the drug would transfer minute amounts to the involved currency during transactions. The next logical step was the supposition that higher levels of contamination would be associated with banknotes having more recently been involved in a drug transaction. It then followed that over time, in subsequent contact with noncomplicit banknotes in the currency circulation process, those with higher levels would shed residue levels of the drug to less contaminated bills. Such redistribution would result in the "ambient" portion of contaminated bills in the money supply, per toxicologist Jay B. Williams' testimony in *United States v. $30,060* as well as the findings of other researchers in the United States (Jenkins 2001; Oyler et al. 1996; Zuo et al. 2008), United Kingdom (Dixon et al. 2006), and European Union (Esteve-Turrillas et al. 2005).

A recent study of over 4,000 U.S. banknotes drawn from general circulation in 66 cities in 43 states noted measurable levels of cocaine on 97% of the bills encountered (Jourdan et al. 2013). Postulating that it seemed unreasonable to assume that such a large amount of the currency in circulation in the United States could have participated in cocaine trafficking, Jourdan et al. (2013), after encountering several contaminated currency counters in financial institutions, provided one possible explanation. If 1% of a 100 mg "line" of cocaine remains on a rolled-up banknote used to facilitate nasal insufflation (snorting) and that same banknote is then placed in a currency counter, ostensibly on the order of 400,000 banknotes could be contaminated to the level of the national average of about 2.5 ng per banknote observed in that study. What was being argued is that the mechanical currency counters employed in financial institutions, as well as in general commerce, are in effect homogenizing the currency supply with respect to trace contamination by cocaine.

COCAINE "ON" CURRENCY

Developing an understanding of the mechanism by which residue levels of cocaine are retained on banknotes is integral to taking this discussion to the next level, moving on from a drug dog alert on a large sum of money to being able to associate that money with drug trafficking in the absence of other tangible evidence.

Several processes have been proposed for the retention of controlled substances on banknotes. One possibility is that the green ink on U.S. banknotes never fully solidifies. This can be demonstrated by rubbing an old banknote on a white piece of paper and noting the resulting transfer of green pigment to the white surface. This "sticky" surface allows for the adherence of various oils (e.g., from human sebaceous glands) and miscellaneous environmental dirt and grime (including residue amounts of drugs of abuse) during the course of currency circulation. Also postulated as a mechanism accounting for the retention of controlled substances on currency is that, after being in circulation for a time, the fiber matrix of paper money develops interstices, which may facilitate inclusion of small particles (Sleeman et al. 2000).

Additionally involved in this discussion is the strength of the attraction between cocaine particles and the banknote matrix. It has been observed that a typical banknote can be sampled using a household-type canister vacuum outfitted with a collection device to retrieve cocaine residue in the nanogram-per-bill range (Jourdan et al. 2013), and that the same banknote later extracted with methanol realizes cocaine residue levels in the microgram-per-bill range (Jourdan, T., unpublished data). It has been posited that at least two types of interactions are involved. Further postulated is that the lightly bound residue recoverable by the just-mentioned vacuuming process is subject to oscillations in concentration during drug transactions and currency circulation, while the more tightly bound particles, once adhered to the banknote matrix, do not migrate under conditions less invasive than a solvent extraction.

INTERPRETATION OF THE LEVEL OF DRUGS ON CURRENCY

Can banknotes associated with illicit drug trafficking be differentiated from (presumed innocent) banknotes in general circulation? The approach recently taken in the United States in this effort has been to derive the mathematical likelihood of encountering banknotes in general circulation that are more highly contaminated with cocaine than the background level.

Mentioned earlier was a U.S. study in which over 4,000 bills drawn from general circulation in 66 cities in 43 states were examined (Jourdan et al. 2013). Data from this study, presented in Table 17.1, which contains a tabulation by denomination, revealed that the average banknote in circulation over the 1993–2009 time frame was contaminated with 2.34 ng of cocaine. The frequency distribution of the data summarized in Table 17.1 is found in Figure 17.1 and provides the foundation for a mathematical model developed in order to ascertain if a random bill drawn from circulation or

TABLE 17.1

Cocaine Contamination of U.S. Currency as a Function of Denomination

Denomination	Average Contamination, ng per Banknote (±SEM)	Number of Banknotes Sampled ($\Sigma = 4,174$)
$1	2.15 (±0.47)	630
$5	3.62 (±1.54)	628
$10	3.18 (±0.75)	678
$20	1.61 (±0.25)	870
$50	2.26 (±0.62)	688
$100	1.49 (±0.40)	680

Note: SEM, standard error of the mean.

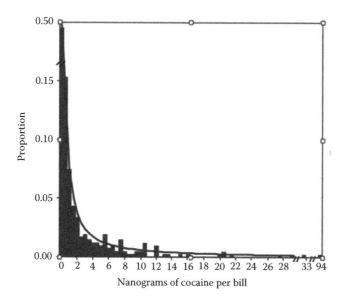

FIGURE 17.1 Frequency distribution and associated power curve for 4,174 currency samples drawn from general circulation. (Courtesy of *Journal of Forensic Sciences*.)

of some other origin could be determined to be contaminated at a level statistically different from (higher than) the background range of cocaine on currency in general circulation. The data tabulated in Table 17.1 and displayed in Figure 17.1 were fitted with a power curve.

$$y = 0.0994(x + 0.0199)^{-1.2191} \tag{17.1}$$

Using this equation, probabilities can be computed for the likelihood of encountering currency in general circulation contaminated in particular concentration ranges. For example:

$$\int_{160}^{180} 0.0994(x + 0.0199)^{-1.2191}\, dx = 0.0038$$

$$\int_{155}^{165} 0.0994(x + 0.0199)^{-1.2191}\, dx = 0.0020$$

$$\int_{159.5}^{160.5} 0.0994(x + 0.0199)^{-1.2191}\, dx = 0.0002$$

for instances of banknotes contaminated by cocaine in the ranges of 160–180 ng, 155–165 ng, or 159.5–160.5 ng, respectively, leading to the data provided in Table 17.2, which lists the probability of drawing a random banknote from circulation at specific concentrations. It is suggested that this information has utility in determining the likelihood that a banknote contaminated by cocaine at a particular level could be drawn at random from general circulation and is clearly useful to the forensic scientist assessing seized currency.

TABLE 17.2
Probabilities of Particular Ranges of Cocaine
Contamination on Banknotes Drawn from
General Circulation by the Proposed Model

Amount	Probability
Less than 1 ng per bill	.6185
Less than 5 ng per bill	.7516
Less than 10 ng per bill	.7964
Less than 20 ng per bill	.8349
40 ± 5 ng per bill	.0111
60 ± 5 ng per bill	.0068
80 ± 5 ng per bill	.0048
150 ± 5 ng per bill	.0022
200 ± 5 ng per bill	.0016
250 ± 5 ng per bill	.0012
300 ± 5 ng per bill	.0009

In Table 17.2, contamination ranges are listed. This approach is adopted as being a more conservative approach than listing or projecting the likelihood of a particular singular value.

SUMMARY

It is assumed that narcotics detection canine alerts will continue to be integral to investigations involving controlled substances. Per the now-applicable Civil Asset Forfeiture Reform Act of 2000, forfeiture of a large sum of money as being related to drug trafficking is based upon a preponderance of the evidence in the case. In currency cases involving a narcotics detection canine alert in which no other tangible evidence is located, it may be possible to satisfy the preponderance-of-the-evidence requirement by assessing the level of cocaine contamination of the currency in question.

ENDNOTES

1. *U.S. v. $30,060 in U.S. Currency*, 39 F.3d 1039 (9th Cir. 1994).
2. *U.S. v. Dickerson*, 873 F.2d 1181 (9th Cir. 1988).
3. *U.S. v. $83,310.78 in U.S. Currency*, 851 F.2d 1231 (9th Cir. 1988).
4. *U.S. v. $215,300 in U.S. Currency*, 882 F.2d 417 (9th Cir. 1989).
5. Civil Asset Forfeiture Reform Act of 2000 ("CAFRA"), PL 106-185, 114 Stat. 202 (2000).
6. *U.S. v. $62,552 in U.S. Currency*, No. 03-10153-RBC, 2015 WL 251242 (DC Mass., January 20, 2015).

18 Narcotic and Explosive Odors
Volatile Organic Compounds as Training Aids for Olfactory Detection

L.E. Papet

"Trained canines represent one of the most widely used and time proven methods of detection" (Parmeter et al. 2000) and provide a wealth of benefit to man. Even though we still do not know exactly what it is the dog is alerting to, "[c]anines are widely regarded as the 'gold standard' in chemical vapor detection" (Johnston and Williams 1999; Fisher et al. 2004). The traditional use of this biological detector has been in law enforcement for illicit drugs and explosives (Joshi et al. 2009), although olfactory disciplines are not limited to drugs or explosives (Lorenzo et al. 2003), and with research and the general appeal of dogs, olfaction disciplines are expanding at a rapid rate.

Training a detection dog to reliably locate and signal acquisition of a desired target requires use of detection *training aids* (Sinn et al. 2010), which are often referred to as *hides* (Furton et al. 2010, p. 19). These terms are used to delineate "between target and non-target odours" (Porritt et al. 2014) that may be encountered by the dog. Training aids are tools composed of source material, which deposit volatile organic compounds (VOCs) in the headspace. Studies have determined that it is this odor being located by the dog and not the actual substance (Lorenzo et al. 2003; Macias et al. 2008), and few studies attempt to identify the exact VOC to which the dog responds (Hoffman et al. 2009).

TYPES OF MATERIALS

While opinions may vary, there are currently three uniquely different types or categories of training aids commonly used for training a detector dog. Each type of aid has advantages and disadvantages, and thus, considerable thought should be used when choosing among them. An overview of these aids provides a quick summary for understanding.

The first type of aid is authentic or parent materials and best described as the exact source material the dog is trained to locate. In other words, a narcotic dog would use marijuana, heroin, cocaine, methamphetamine, and possibly others, while an explosive detection dog would use Composition C-4, dynamite, Semtex, Detasheet, Pyrodex, etc. Although these aids present many challenges and difficulties, they are still the most widely accepted type of training aid in use today. Most field disciplines such as narcotics, explosives, cadaver, accelerant, and many others use authentic material training aids. Some source odor materials present issues that complicate use such as licensing, transportation, storage, security, handling, ethics, etc. Each type of authentic odor material has its own unique challenges that must be considered. Due to the nature of the materials, explosive odor sources create a special level of concern (Furton 2011). Even though authentic materials are expensive to acquire and difficult to obtain, possess, and use, many certification organizations require a parent substance to serve as the training aid for certifications (Furton et al. 2010, p. 19). Creation of alternative training aids is a result of these issues and others.

The second type is an alternative training aid designed to provide an equivalent scent delivery mechanism to that of authentic material without many of the drawbacks associated with the use of real material (Harper et al. 2005). This is accomplished by using a portion of real material as an odor source that has been processed and incorporated into or onto a nonenergetic and nonhazardous delivery mechanism such as silica, petrolatum, or cotton. Sometimes, these are called simulate or mimic aids. Simulates have been developed to replace the high-risk explosive training aids (for dogs and machines) by reducing or eliminating the potential downside of using actual explosive materials. Studies have shown that even though some simulates may use real materials as the odor-producing component, the odor signature varies from the actual material (Kury et al. 1995; Hunter [Lawrence Livermore National Laboratory] 1997; Harper et al. 2005). These products are commercially available and carry very few of the typical safety, storage, handling, or transporting issues associated with actual materials. However, the odor signature produced on simulates can vary based on manufacturer (Kranz et al. 2014b). Unfortunately, canine trials produce mixed results using simulates (Kranz et al. 2014a,b; Strobel et al. 2001).

The third type of aid is pseudo training material that differs significantly from actual, simulate, or mimic aids. Pseudo aids do not use the parent material as the odor-generating portion of the training aid but, rather, attempt to replicate the headspace odor by synthetic or natural means. "The use of synthetic trainings [sic] aids is highly debated" (Stadler et al. 2012). Pseudo aids generally use proprietary formulations of powder or liquid chemicals that attempt to replicate the odor signature of real materials' VOCs. While not requiring the same level of scrutiny as real materials, pseudo material can often be hazardous and may require some of the same precautions as real materials. This is exampled in pseudo cadaver materials. "Putrescine and cadaverine are particularly odorous compounds formed during the decomposition process and are commonly found in pseudo scent mixtures. While pseudo compounds may be easier to obtain, they are hazardous chemicals that must be handled with care" (DeGreeff 2010).

While synthetic pseudo is common with cadaver odor (Orlowski et al. 2001), it is also prevalent in narcotic and explosive aids as well. Some pseudo materials are actually natural in origin, as discussed by Orlowski et al. (1999) with the use of pork in place of human cadaver as a training aid. Certain United States agencies also use pseudo narcotic materials for training (Vu 2001). "At the U.S. Customs and Border Protection's Canine Enforcement Training Center (CETC), pseudo ecstasy, heroin, methamphetamine, and cocaine are prepared four times a year by storage specialists" (Dowell 2004). Even though some pseudo materials have been around for many decades, actual use outside government agencies is still limited.

PURITY

Regardless of which type of aid is used, purity of the substance or item is of paramount concern for it will present the closest and most focused odor upon which a dog can be trained. The amount of pure material may not be important in predicting headspace concentrations (Lotspeich et al. 2012). One study has used the most pure substance available to serve as the training aid (Williams and Johnston 2002). There is a suggestion to use only pure material as the odor source (Furton et al. 2010, p. 119). Once acquired, maintaining material purity is a daily challenge—while handling, storing, transporting, and using. It seems packaging might also play a role in protecting purity as a method of allowing or restricting odor permeation, described in a patented training aid system (Furton and Harper 2008). Permeation should be prevented by storing in separate containers that are impermeable (Scientific Working Group on Dog and Orthogonal detector Guidelines [SWGDOG] SC8 2007).

The typical narcotic training aid material supplied to law enforcement is generally not pure, and at one time, it appears to have been used as a barometer for training aid purity (Furton and Heller 2005). These substances come from U.S. Drug Enforcement Administration (DEA), crime lab, or elsewhere, and are generally street drugs, some of which may not have been lab-tested. Additionally, some of these materials have been stored in property rooms, sometimes for many months or years. In this type of environment, substances may be exposed to confounding odors, which may cause contamination of the initial substance. An example could be the storage of cocaine in the same area as marijuana, causing cross-contamination of both substances. Some drugs may also contain cutting agents such as baking soda, boric acid, caffeine, cornstarch, flour, baby formula, talc, or any number of other odorous material constituting a sizeable portion of the substance supplied. These impurities complicate the odor signature upon which the dogs are being trained due to confounders being present. Each contaminate must be known and used as a distractor to ensure the dog is alerting to only the parent material. One other confounding issue is that most handlers have a limited number of aids, so they train with the same aids most of the time. Without pure materials, the dog may be learning to detect the combination of materials in the aid and not the parent material. This may only become evident when training or testing is done with unfamiliar aids.

Explosive aids are a slightly different matter. While most explosive training aids are real explosives, the United States Bureau of Alcohol, Tobacco, Firearms and Explosives (BATFE or, shortened, ATF) approaches the use of explosive aids differently by using a what is referred to as the family theory.

> For explosive detection canines, there are five main compound classes of odor and dozens of compounds which are potential training aids (positive controls) for bomb dogs with common examples as follows. Aliphatic nitro: nitromethane, hydrazine; aromatic nitro ($C-NO_2$): nitrobenzene (NB); nitrotoluene (NT); dinitrobenzene (DNB); dinitrotoluene (DNT); trinitrobenzene (TNB); 2,4,6-trinitrotoluene (TNT); picric acid. nitrate ester ($C-O-NO_2$): methyl nitrate; nitroglycerin (NG); ethylene glycol dinitrate (EGDN); diethylene glycol dinitrate (DEGN); pentaerythritol tetranitrate (PETN); nitrocellulose; nitroguanidine. nitramines ($C-N-NO_2$): methylamine nitrate; tetranitro-N-methylaniline (Tetryl); trinitrotriazacyclohexane (cyclonite or RDX); tetranitrotetrazacylooctane (Octogen or HMX); hexanitroisowurztitane (CL20). acid salts $\left(NH_4^+, NO_3^- \right)$: ammonium nitrate; ammonium perchlorate; potassium nitrate (in black powder). (Lorenzo et al. 2003)

Each of the five categories contains multiple chemicals from which a suitable aid could be chosen (Harper and Furton 2007, p. 425), which enables the dogs to locate some 19,000 explosives. The hypothesis is that by training on one chemical in each category, the dog will be able to detect all of the other chemicals within the category. There is extremely limited use of this theory.

CURRENT STATE OF ACCESS

The ability to access source materials used for training aids can be extremely difficult. A myriad of local, state, federal, and even international laws often dictate licensing requirements for the ability to acquire these substances. Licensing often mandates background checks, interviews, and documentation that can sometimes span borders and may mandate specific facility requirements for storage and use, such as restricted access, monitored security and fire protection, sprinkler systems, theft detection, biohazard protection, and much more. This type of issue infiltrates areas of many disciplines of detection beyond the obvious illegal drugs and explosives.

> Access to appropriate training aids is a common issue among human remains detection (HRD) canine handlers due to overly legal restrictions, difficulty in access and storage, and the potential biological hazards stemming from the use of actual human remains as training aids. (DeGreeff et al. 2012)

Once materials are accessible, many of the same problems still exist. Acquisition is controlled through specific channels, increasing acquisition costs. Transportation of these items often requires special considerations and permits, furthering the difficulty. Handling these materials for any reason requires specialized access, knowledge, procedures, equipment, and training for each person involved. The mere presence of these substances can require copious paperwork.

For drug dog training aids, the U.S. military may place hides that could consist of either cocaine, marijuana, methylenedioxymethamphetamine, heroin, or methamphetamine, while explosive detection dogs will be presented with aids consisting of one or more materials such as ammonia dynamite, ammonium nitrate, trinitrotoluene, Composition C-4, potassium chlorate, sodium chlorate, water gel, detonation cord, single-base smokeless powder, and sometimes Semtex (U.S. Air Force 2015) for explosive detection dogs. All of these materials have very strict controls and access limited to the kennel master (KM). "The KM team is also responsible for military working dog (MWD) team proficiency training. This team supervises the storage and accountability of the narcotic and explosive training aids as well as all assigned equipment" (U.S. Army 2005). Civilian and law enforcement training aid documentation should be kept according to required standards outlined by licensing, and the aids should be clearly marked (SWGDOG SC2 2009). These many factors weigh heavily on trainers, handlers, agencies, and departments, affecting not only the transportation, storage, and access to training materials but also their use in training.

SAFETY

Once source substance acquisition is permitted, even more issues arise. One of paramount concern is safety to protect persons, animals, and property from potential hazards. Personal protective equipment (PPE) such as disposable latex or nitrile gloves (Willis et al. 2004), breathing masks, and vision and clothing protection are generally needed but seldom used. Other specialized equipment, such as air-handling equipment, wood-lined storage boxes or antistatic mats, and training aid source material containment devices, may be required to ensure safety for the trainer, handler, or dog (Dowell 2004). Appropriate training and protocols should be in place instructing the persons handling these materials on safety procedures.

STORAGE VESSELS

Proper storage is a complex and critical aspect of training aids and materials. This is so important that some agencies have a storage specialist dedicated to maintaining the aids and materials (Dowell 2004). While some training aids are designed with special packaging to restrict permeation (Furton and Harper 2008), other storage vessels could allow permeation into the container, possibly causing issues with false alerts (Walczak et al. 2012). It has also been shown "that for the majority of cases, the vapor concentration of a pure substance in a sealed container is constant and predictable based on the vapor pressure of the compound and the temperature" (Lotspeich et al. 2012). Improper storage could allow contamination of source and associated material, thereby rendering the target odor mostly useless, possibly causing the trainer or handler to believe that the dog is being trained on a specific target odor when, in fact, it is being trained on the contaminant odor. Additionally, some target odors overwhelm and contaminate other materials in close proximity.

> [There is] the potential serious problem of cross-contamination of training explosives with volatile artifacts (including EGDN and DNT) from other explosives stored nearby, thus resulting in the possibility of dogs trained to alert to two or three of the most volatile explosive odorants rather than the nine parent explosives used in training. (Furton and Myers 2001)

This may be negated to a degree through selection of storage vessels that prohibit the permeation of odor (SWGDOG SC8 2007). A proper storage container prevents permeation of odor either into or out of a storage vessel. Restricting the flow of odor into a storage container is of primary concern to maintain as consistent and pure an odor source as possible. To further ensure the integrity of the odor source, "[s]eparate storage containers should be used for marijuana and the other drugs to minimize possible cross contamination issues with the strongest odor aids" (IFRI 2003; Furton and Heller 2005).

Permeation of the source odor out of the storage vessel is a problem as it can contaminate everything in the vicinity of the storage container.

> Methyl benzoate was detected in the headspace of two samples of ecstasy.... Methyl benzoate is known to exist in great abundance in the headspace of cocaine, and as a result is used for training purposes with detection canines.... Prior to sampling, the ecstasy was stored in close proximity to several large samples of cocaine which may have led to cross contamination. (Macias 2009)

One critical aspect of a storage container is that it will not impart odor from nor absorb odor into the construction material of the receptacle. Stainless steel and glass are commonly used in scientific studies as training aid carriers of odor since they absorb very little or no detectable odor amount, as demonstrated in a study on triacetone triperoxide (TATP) explosives.

> The explosive material (in this case, 5 mg of batch A–type TATP) was put into a glass jar and covered with a grid. Stainless steel tubes or pieces of Kings Cotton were placed on top of the grid, and the jar was closed. After 4–7 days they were removed from the glass jar containing the TATP and put into clean glass jars with twist-off lids. These aids were subsequently used for training, usually within a few days but occasionally after a longer period (up to 21 days). After use, the training aids were discarded. (Tubes were cleaned and used again. The Kings Cotton was discarded.) (Schoon et al. 2006)

With this in mind, a best practice might include storing each odor in a separate impermeable container (SWGDOG SC8 2007), of stainless steel or glass, possibly utilizing a lid with a labyrinth or other type seal preventing an exchange of air and to also prevent the absorption or leaching of odor from the stored materials or the container itself.

CONTAMINATION TYPES AND CAUSES

Contamination is one of the most serious issues confronting training aids (see generally Furton et al. 2010). Even a basic understanding of the exchange principle indicates that many possible avenues of contamination are routinely present. This can start with the manufacturer, distributor, dealer, or warehousing of source material. Many explosive dealers or manufacturers have various types of explosives stored in close proximity. Shipping an order means all the explosives are generally placed in the same container and shipped in the same vehicle, packaged just as they were by the manufacturer with no special precaution taken for contamination. After receipt, the environment in which a training aid is stored or created may introduce extraneous odor into the material used for creating the aid. Storage vessels and materials used in packaging can be contaminated via placement in close proximity to secondary odors such as medications or dog training equipment.

Basic handling of the training aid often generates a contamination rarely checked. Human body odor easily transfers to the training aid, becoming part of the aid. Human-associated odor such as cigarette smoke or hand lotion can contaminate as well. Another contamination possibility could happen in placement of a training aid. One of the easiest to spot would be a hide placed in the engine compartment or fuel tank of a vehicle. High-vapor-pressure hydrocarbon-based materials in these areas transfer odor easily. An accidental contamination could place unwanted odor on a training aid when a dog contacts the aid or places its mouth on the hide, leaving saliva (Lit et al. 2011). It is also possible for a handler to pet his dog and then decide to place the hide.

INVERSE CONTAMINATION

A training aid may contaminate the surrounding environment, also causing great problems. Whether properly packaged or not, a training aid can sometimes transfer material or odor into undesirable areas. One common example might be a narcotic training aid being placed in a cabinet. Police often allow an odor or aid to "soak" for a half hour or more after placement (Furton and Heller 2005), permitting equilibrium and presenting the maximum odor available to the dog. Police routinely use the same training locations so placement of these aids over time can easily contaminate the hide area. Another good example might be a training environment such as an aircraft. Leaving a training aid in position for an extended period of time can transfer the odor of the aid to items in close proximity such as a soft, porous seat cover, or even an overhead luggage compartment.

Extended placement is generally unwarranted and should be used with extreme caution. When placing aids, there is a risk of transferring "particulate, microscopic particles of solid material that adhere (contaminate) to surfaces" (David and Lewis 2008). It should also be noted that "particulate contamination is easily transferred from one surface to another" (Parmeter et al. 2000). This should be a consideration when aids are being placed in any area, especially in high-risk areas, where separators such as wax paper or sterile cotton should be used to preclude unnecessary physical contact and to keep the environment as sterile as possible. An often-overlooked portion of this is the hand that carried the aid. Once the aid has been handled, whether gloved or not, the possibility that particulate transfer has occurred must be considered, and care should be taken not to touch anything else until the hand has been washed or the material used to protect the hand has been properly disposed of outside of the training area.

Cross-Contamination

Aids can also contaminate other training aids. Improper storage, handling, or placement can create this problem. Multiple aids placed in close proximity can actually cross-contaminate each other so that none produce the same odor as their primary source materials. It has been shown that some odors, specifically ethylene glycol dinitrate (EGDN) and dinitrotoluene (DNT), can overwhelm others stored nearby, thus creating cross-contamination and perhaps resulting in dogs being trained on two odors instead of the full contingent of nine (Lorenzo et al. 2003). While not recommended for storage, this type of close placement in training is sometimes necessary but should be utilized with caution.

The Unknown

Other issues may add to the difficulty when using training aids. While research has endeavored to explore these issues, many questions still persist (SWGDOG SC7 2010). Selecting a training aid requires knowing the desired target odor. With all the difficulties surrounding the possession and use of narcotic and explosive materials necessary to make training aids, a tremendous amount of research is being performed on replacing these typical substances used to train dogs. However, the single most interesting question is focused directly on the dog. It is difficult to design a replacement aid without knowing the exact odor upon which the dog is indicating (Harper and Furton 2007, p. 400). Some work suggests that while a dog can detect many odors, it usually detects a few (Johnston 1999). Does this mean, however, that the dog will detect one single odor, or is it actually a bouquet of odors? Do the odors have to be in correct relationship to others? Do all dogs detect the same odor for the same substance? At what level must the odor be present for the dog to detect? A surprising lack of knowledge of exactly which odor the dog is detecting or at what levels it is detecting this odor (or these odors) in field conditions makes the correct choice somewhat problematic. Many laboratory experiments have shed light on these issues, but far more questions exist than have been answered.

Another question is the generalization of odor by the canine. Evidence suggests that "it is clearly inappropriate to assume that training dogs on one or two variants of a target substance is sufficient to assure operational levels of detection of all other variants" (Johnston 1999). This finding alone would question an attempt to use any single odor as a primary source for any training aid.

ODOR CONCENTRATION, AVAILABILITY, AND ATTRIBUTES

A laboratory experiment can set very specific limits as to odors, concentrations, and availability of these to the experimental animal. Unfortunately, in the training and field deployment arena, this is extremely difficult, if not next to impossible, to do with current technology and devices. It is common to speak of a training aid in relation to the weight of the material used in the hide (Johnston 1999). Grams, ounces, pounds, and kilos are often the terms used when discussing training aids. While weight may be a gauge of the parent material present in a training aid, it does not reflect a true predictable picture of the odor concentration present or available to the dog. Odor availability is neither easily measured nor imagined and thus is often forgotten in favor of weight measurement.

It is a common misconception that the amount of explosive is the chief contributor to the quantity of vapor that is available to trained canines. In fact, this quantity (known as odor availability) depends on not only the amount of explosive material, but also the container volume, explosive vapor pressure and temperature. (Lotspeich et al. 2012)

Each of these components of odor availability should be considered individually as well as together to produce the correct hide for the scenario. Each training aid is dependent upon several factors to produce the amount of odor available to the dog.

Among these contributing factors is vapor pressure. Each target odor material has a specific vapor pressure that determines the ability to produce odor. Vapor pressure (for a given temperature) is a key element of odor availability. With low vapor pressure, odor may not be available or may be overwhelmed by other VOCs that are present. Alternatively, high vapor pressure could overwhelm all other VOCs present. Some explosive compounds present interesting results.

Relatively volatile explosives such as ethylene glycol dinitrate (EGDN), NG, or TNT have vapor pressures at 25°C of 4.8×10^{-2} torr, 2.3×10^{-4} torr and 4.5×10^{-6} torr, respectively, making them available in air for direct detection by a chemical and biological detector. Other organic explosives of security interest such as RDX, HMX, and PETN have very low vapor pressures, 1.1×10^{-9} torr, 1.6×10^{13} torr, 3.8×10^{-10} torr, respectively, and are not available in the headspace. This essentially makes vapor sampling impossible, yet trained dogs can easily detect these explosives because they utilize volatile chemical signatures of explosive mixtures to reliably located [sic] them under difficult field conditions. (Almirall et al. 2012)

Added to the vapor pressure is packaging, which can weigh heavily on the odor availability by either permitting or restricting odor flow (Kranz and Goodpaster 2015). Claims of "odor-proof" containers exist, although research has yet to establish these claims in the realm of canine olfactory use. An aid may be packaged in many different ways, but unfortunately, there exists no single hide construction that is perfect for all scenarios. Packaging is a way to restrict surface area of the material exposed to produce odor and hence also dictates the amount of odor present at any point in time. Target odor material with ready access to open air permits free exchange of odor with the surrounding areas. The same target odor material placed inside a nonpermeable, sealable aluminum bag may be virtually undetectable. Obviously, a balance should be exercised so as to allow odor permeation and availability without permitting access to the material by the dog.

Some of the more common packaging materials include duck, nylon, or plastic bags; cellophane wrap; sterile cotton or gauze; cotton string or towels; polyvinyl chloride (PVC) pipe or fittings; glass jars or aluminum tins with perforated lids; metal key holders; rubber, metal, or plastic tubes or boxes; hosiery; various Tupperware; wire mesh baskets; stainless vessels; paper, rubber, or plastic toys; jute; etc.

The construction of a narcotic hide, in theory, is quite simple. Often, the parent material such as marijuana will be placed on a sheet of paper, cellophane, or cotton, and wrapped before being placed inside a separate container such as a duck cloth bag, sometimes referred to as a "narc" bag. Over time, the odor of the marijuana will penetrate the inner wrapping to saturate the outside package of duck material. As the hide is used, the duck cloth will be exposed to extraneous odors from various placements. Periodically the outer-shell bag will be replaced with a new or clean version of the same bag. Unfortunately, this does not guarantee against contamination as the storage vessel in which the bag is stored is probably contaminated as well. Additionally, it is also possible for the parent material to have absorbed odor from the packaging materials or environment in which it was used.

An explosive hide may be constructed in a similar fashion or sometimes may not be packaged at all. A common packaging device for explosive aids will sometimes include the use of a small aluminum tin and lid with perforated holes. Parent material such as RDX may be placed inside this container, which is closed with the perforated lid. This configuration is much more impervious to extraneous contamination odor while also presenting use challenges. The perforated holes in the lid are designed to limit egress of material while allowing odor to permeate via the small openings. Unfortunately, these openings are so small that they sometimes become the limiting factor when attempting to reach placement equilibrium in larger areas. "However, once this volume threshold has been reached, the amount of odor escaping from the tin and available to the canine is governed completely by the diffusion of vapor through the perforations in the lid" (Kranz and Goodpaster 2015).

Although not necessarily advisable, parent material may also be placed as a training aid without additional packaging. An example might be a stick of water gel or Deta Gel (distributed by Omni Explosives, K9-WG; Tripwire, K9-WG), which comes from the manufacturer wrapped in a plastic sleeve, approximately 1.5 in. in diameter by 8 in. long, which can become oily due to permeation by the substance. Two main issues arise from using this type of placement. First is a safety issue for both the dog and the handler via contact or ingestion. Second is possible cross-contamination of either the environment or the hide due to the training aid not being protected on the exterior.

Yet another method of increasing or decreasing odor availability is through the use of saturated or soaked materials. This entails using sterile cotton towels, pads, gauze, or similar items along with parent material, although some may perform this with simulates or pseudo materials. Preparing the parent material requires wrapping the substance to prevent any small particulate from escaping the package while simultaneously permitting the material to expel the odor of the substance. Once successfully wrapped, secure the package in a soaking container, preferably on the bottom. Arrange the unscented items in the soaking container to expose the entire surface area of the material without coming in contact with the wrapped explosive or narcotic substance. Cover with a lid to prevent permeation of odor either into or out of the soaking container. Allow these materials time to saturate with odor from the original material, which may take from hours to weeks or even months, depending upon many factors.

Use of this method allows for consistent and relatively predictable odor availability. By varying the surface area size of a given material, different amounts of odor may be available for a given amount of time. Material in a 1 in. square will generally retain far less odor than the same material in a 1 ft. square. The same is true for different types of material. A more coarse and voluminous weave on the sterile item creates more surface area on which odor can be absorbed or released. Combining these things permits a certain odor availability scaling sometimes difficult to achieve otherwise. For a given type of material, odor availability can be easily increased or decreased based upon the material size and count. The surface area of the material available to disperse odor into the environment is key. Any material beyond that which is used to reach environment equilibrium simply becomes excess. For any given hide, the larger the area in which the hide is placed, the longer the time it takes for that environment to reach equilibrium. Hides are used for relatively short periods of time before being collected and should not be allowed to sit for extended periods as it will contaminate the item or area in which it is placed.

The advantages of using this type of mimic hide are many: low cost, ease of preparation, repeatability, and predictable comparability of odor availability are just a few. The items are easily disposable and replaceable. The main disadvantages are the extremely short lifespan, generally in tens of minutes; and this only works well with original materials and the difficulty they bring. This is somewhat offset by reduced handling and possible contamination of the parent material, thereby providing a more pure odor source and longevity of use.

Hide placement also greatly affects odor availability. Two phrases routinely used in relation to training aid placement are *deep hide* and *shallow hide*. It is commonly thought that a deep hide is more difficult than a shallow hide. This is really a misunderstanding and should be realized as a factor of odor availability versus time. A deep hide might be a training aid placed inside a semisealed container, which is then placed inside a car. This placement will need much more time to produce an available odor than does the same nonsealed hide placed inside the vehicle and located in the driver door pocket. This is a factor of the time it takes for an acceptable amount of odor to reach a point where it can be detected by the dog. Deep hides are generally placed in such a way to reduce the immediate odor availability to the dog, thereby making them theoretically more difficult.

VOLATILE ORGANIC COMPOUNDS

Measuring VOCs for investigation involving canine olfaction is commonly performed using gas chromatography–mass spectrometry (GC/MS; discussed in detail in Chapter 7 herein), which not only identifies but also quantifies the VOCs present in a given sample. This is critical for attempting to understand exactly what odor the dog is detecting. While this is still unknown, progress is being made in understanding the complexity of odor detection by dogs.

VOCs are the cornerstone of detection dog deployment as a properly trained canine will locate and indicate upon the target odor with extreme precision. One difficulty is that target odor is not the only odor present and available to the dog.

> The main chemical compound in a substance is not always the dominant volatile compound due to the low vapor pressure or limited olfactory receptor response. In addition, it has been shown that only specific odors are used by canines to detect the various forms of contraband. (Macias et al. 2008)

Each environment offers unique challenges by presenting many odors that the dog must discriminate in order to locate the desired target. A solid command of VOCs is a requirement for any exploration employing the canine olfactory system.

Narcotic detection presents some of the most unusual challenges in the industry. Aside from issues discussed previously, the headspace odor of some substances in this category has been thoroughly investigated. Studies have revealed that illicit drugs sometimes contain a wide array of VOCs, with results that may prove inconsistent.

> The headspace above marijuana has been repeatedly sampled and shown to possess a complex array of organic compounds. This list includes α-pinene; β-pinene; myrcene; limonene; and, in many cases, β-caryophyllene. These compounds have been shown to dominate the headspace of marijuana samples (upwards of 85% …). In a similar manner, it has been conjectured that acetic acid is the dominant odor compound in heroin samples. (Macias et al. 2008)

In some parts of the world, "methamphetamine (MA) is the most common drug of abuse" (Inoue et al. 2008). Due to the chemical synthesis necessary to manufacture this drug, headspace analysis reveals a wide array of VOCs.

> The headspace profiles of 11 methamphetamine (MA) samples were analyzed using solid-phase microextraction/gas chromatography–mass spectrometry (SPME/GC-MS). Eighty-seven different compounds were identified from all samples. Only seven occurred consistently in all seizure samples that were: acetic acid, benzaldehyde, acetophenone, P2P, 1-phenyl 1-1, 2-propanedione (P12P), 3-phenyl-3-buten-2-one, and 1-chloro-1-phenyl-2-propanone. When the reference methamphetamine and P2P samples were included, only two compounds were common to all samples, and these were benzaldehyde and P2P. (Inoue et al. 2008)

This makes understanding exactly what odor a dog might be alerting to even more difficult. Not all drugs tested have such multidimensional headspace. Knowledge of the aroma of cocaine has been longstanding, as outlined in 1981 U.S. Patent 4,260,517. Specifically, methyl benzoate is the chemical substance that is responsible for the aroma of pure cocaine (Woodford 1981).

Further study later confirmed these findings. "The conclusions from this study support the U.S. patent 'Available Odor of Cocaine,' which is described as 'a method and product for providing the aroma of cocaine to the olfactory senses by volatilizing methyl benzoate...'" (Furton et al. 2002) (see Chapter 9 herein for current questions regarding this issue).

Explosive detection training aids present an even more difficult challenge. This was evidenced by experimental results obtained in a scientific project by Jezierski et al. (2012) where drug detection dogs recruited and trained at the same police training center demonstrated better detection performance in terms of shorter searching time, higher percentage of correct indications, and lower percentage of false alerts, compared to explosive detection dogs.

> In general, the odor generated by an explosive can be characterized as "simple" or "complex." Simple odors consist of a single chemical compound. An example of such an odor is nitromethane, an energetic liquid used in binary high explosives that is both volatile and stable. Nitromethane has significant vapor pressure at room temperature, and as such, the explosive itself can be assumed the likely cause of a canine alert. Complex odors, conversely, consist of multiple chemical compounds that might originate from multiple species within the sample, or from the degradation products of a single species, or from a combination of the two. Most explosive formulations fall into the "complex" category. (Kranz et al. 2014a)

One of the most investigated explosives, C-4, appears to challenge conventional thinking.

> The specific example of odor chemicals from the high explosive composition C-4 studied by solid phase microextraction indicates that the volatile odor chemicals 2-ethyl-1-hexanol and cyclohexanone are available in the headspace; whereas, the active chemical cyclo-1,3,5-trimethylene-2,4,6-trinitramine (RDX) is not. (Furton and Myers 2001)

When using parent material aids, one study suggests that significant confusion may exist. It concluded that even the choice of which target odor materials to use might not be as ideal as once thought. Some explosives such as cast explosives and TNT appear to share similar headspace VOCs as do plasticized Composition 4 (C-4) and Detasheet, while differences in the headspace VOCs of smokeless powders produced by different manufacturers are dissimilar, resulting in a need to use several different smokeless powders for training aids (Harper et al. 2005).

Most investigations of current nonhazardous surrogate or simulate training aids have produced inconsistent results or present potential problematic issues.

> Non-Hazardous Explosives for Security Training and Testing (NESTT) aids yielded inconsistent results with most of the deployed bomb dogs tested in a double-blind study with most dogs not alerting to these materials under field operational conditions. These results also show that NESTT aids have potentially undesirable matrix effects with a large hydrocarbon background observed for the petrolatum based aids and dusting with the silica based aids. (Harper et al. 2005)

The reason for this may lie in the fact that when the NESTT TNT vapor concentrations and ratios were compared to military TNT vapor, significant differences were found (Edge et al. 1998).

Other investigations reveal even more issues when attempting to replace real explosives with pseudo materials.

> The two brands of training aids examined here take a different approach to the problem of engineering an effective pseudo explosive. Chemical analysis of product A aids shows that they typically incorporate a bouquet of different odors, seeking to include as many of the compounds cited as being responsible

for causing canines to alert as possible. Chemical analysis of product B aids shows that they emphasize a single odor—typically, the most abundant odor available in the headspace of the explosive they seek to emulate. (Kranz et al. 2014b)

This string of investigation has seen in-depth studies on the implications of

the development of new canine training aids that mimic the scent of an explosive yet contain inert ingredients such as 2E1H, cyclohexanone, or DMNB (so called "pseudo-explosives"). In particular, chemical analysis following our canine trials has shown that 2E1H is linked to common plasticizers like bis(2-ethylhexyl)adipate, bis(2-ethylhexylsebacate) and bis(2-ethylhexyl)phthalate. In addition, PVC based items containing these plasticizers emit 2E1H. This raises red flags about the use of unadulterated 2E1H as a training aid as it may lead to alerts on common, everyday items that happen to bear plasticizers with this particular structural characteristic. However, it is also known that canines can be "trained off" of materials that could be false positives. (Kranz et al. 2014a)

This is important in raising questions for future investigation. While some express a diametrical perspective (Sanchez et al. 2015) to the findings of Kranz et al., it should be pointed out that Sanchez used a patented delivery system, which is called a *Controlled Odor Mimic Permeation System* (Furton and Harper 2008), designed specifically for the controlled delivery of odor in training aids.

In the last response available in the discussion of 2E1H as a possible replacement for C-4 explosives, it seems many questions still exist.

In the end, our results have helped form our view that no single compound makes an effective mimic for Composition C-4. We demonstrated at a 95% confidence level that the response of the canines to these compounds was not positively associated with the canine response to C-4. As stated in our conclusion: "There is a possibility that none of these compounds, by themselves, are responsible for triggering a positive response in canines, and that only the combination of all three compounds in proper proportions will elicit recognition." We think this is an interesting possibility that merits further study. (Kranz and Goodpaster 2015)

One additional concern with some aids might be anosmia or the overwhelming of the canine olfactory ability due to oversaturation with odor (Sanchez et al. 2015).

ODOR AID USAGE IN TRAINING AND DEPLOYMENT

When making a hide, very little thought is typically given outside documenting the aid, the weight of material contained therein, and following some sequence of packaging that has been around for millennia. Rarely will a new container, wrap, or the occasional idea spark some interest to reconsider training aid construction or use. All training aid planning and use should be a process requiring extensive thought on odor availability as circumstances and scenarios change.

Training aids must be constructed with varying amounts of odor availability. In the initial and basic stages of training, extremely large amounts of odor should be available for the dog, allowing the green or naïve dog to acquire odor more easily. A side benefit is this allows the trainer to read dog behavior milestones much more quickly as the dog may react differently as odor availability changes. As training progresses, the amount of odor available can slowly decrease as experience increases, thereby working to decrease the detection threshold to which the dog should routinely react.

Placing a hide seems a rather simple act, but considerable thought should be given before placement. Is this a no-fail training scenario for a green dog or an advanced improvement training session for an experienced dog? What is the relative vapor pressure of the material in the aid? How much odor will be available for the dog to detect? How long will the odor be allowed to saturate, or will it reach equilibrium? Is the dog expected to locate the hide, or is it testing the outer limits of the dog's detection capability? As with most experiments, a hide should be placed only after a hypothesis is developed, scenario designed, and outcomes projected. This is true of both the novice and the experienced dog. Continuous experimentation, changing only one component at a time, using different hide construction or materials will provide instantaneous feedback needed for improvement or expansion of training regimens.

Most trainers, handlers, and other observers automatically presume the hide to be stationary, such as in a drawer, bag, box, or even a vehicle. However, some training aid placement requires the item to assume a kinetic position where a dog must attempt to locate the moving target. These aids are concealed using purses, luggage, backpacks, or even people. The uniqueness of this capability is *nonexistent* as the dog has a natural ability to follow odor and only needs conditioning to the threshold and moving placeholder, just as they do for any other location. However, some minor consideration should take place when deploying this type of aid placement. Training can take place anywhere, but deployments are routinely performed at airports and other major areas of concern worldwide to attempt tracking of the moving odor of explosives using what some call Vapor Wake detection. In the training and testing validation process for this type of training, it is common for these hides to be concealed on a person, sometimes for prolonged periods. Consideration of aid contamination becomes a major concern due to this extended contact. For this reason, barriers are used to wrap the aid to thwart human contamination. In 2013, the U.S. Government Accountability Office (GAO) issued a report to Congress outlining a study noting specifically that some passenger-screening canine (PSC) teams failed to detect explosive odor and some alerted to individuals who were decoys in trials but who were not carrying explosives (GAO 2013).

Life Span

All training aids should be rotated through a life span from acquisition through to destruction. Opinions differ greatly on the useful life of training aids and associated material. Some programs tout replacing materials and all aids annually, while others claim replacement every 2 or 3 years or more. Cases do exist where training aid materials have been kept for much longer periods. While extremely rare, a planned life span is a crucial part of training aid use.

This type of practice is crucial for any field-deployed detection program (Griffin-Valade et al. 2010). It readily supplies a pristine odor available to foundationally support the ability of the dog to alert on the most pure target odor possible. Next, it sets in motion a use pattern to maintain training aid integrity by knowing how a hide is used. By providing a guideline of use for different categories of hides, the aged hide still has value up to the time of destruction. Additionally, this scheduled obsolescence allows exposure to aids of different ages on a routine schedule. It also reduces chances of contamination of other aids, their storage containers, etc. In design, the schedule can be adapted to any philosophy. It is not rigidly structured to any particular age allowance, rotation schedule, or use structure and allows flexibility to alter as needs change.

A best practice might include a staggered system of material and aid management by providing time and type of use stages that each hide will go through as it ages prior to destruction (Figure 18.1). This can be easily calculated to provide the number of equal portions into which the material should be segregated, how frequently each portion should move into the next category, and finally, the time when each portion should be rotated out of service for destruction.

The different stages used can delineate how each stage should be used. An example might be that the first-category material, being the most pristine, could be used for hides in double-blind testing and making odor-saturated simulates. A second category could be set aside for limited use in semipristine environments where the hide is not likely to be contaminated. The third category could be used in normal maintenance training routines. Group four could be used in specific areas that contain extremely dirty or dusty environments. Hiding these aids under vehicles where they will not come in contact with grease or oil or around heavy equipment might be warranted. Group five is for intense ambient odor or such as a hospital or possibly for dry-masking training. The last category

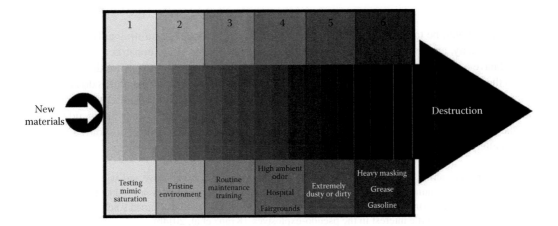

FIGURE 18.1 Cycle of training aid.

could be used to assemble hides for placement in extremely contaminated areas such as next to gasoline, wrapped with grease, inside oil cans or used in wet-masking situations, where the parent material will become saturated with extraneous odor. After heavy use, the last category of material is soon rotated out of service for destruction. It is at this time that a new group of material will arrive and relegate each group to progress in order until each category is supplied with material from the group prior. In total, the additional benefits of keeping relatively new and old materials available for training use and progressing materials through varied uses to permit maximum utilization while maintaining odor integrity in all stages make the management worthwhile.

BOUQUETS

A bouquet of odor is simply the presence of more than one odor. When discussing training aids, bouquets can mean two slightly different things. First, virtually every training aid is made from a material that actually contains many different VOCs, which could be considered a bouquet. Most single-material training aids are comprised of a bouquet of odor. This is highlighted with methamphetamine, which contains many different VOCs that comprise a bouquet of odor for one particular substance. Unfortunately, though, for any given substance, we still do not know which specific odor the dog is detecting (Lorenzo et al. 2003). Bouquets of this nature can also be found in pseudo and simulate materials as well. As discussed by Kranz et al. (2014b) when investigating pseudo materials, this type of hide will "typically incorporate a bouquet of different odors, seeking to include as many of the compounds commonly cited as being responsible for causing canines to alert as possible."

Secondly, the type of bouquet most often discussed in training aids refers to the act of combining two or more different material substances to create an amalgamation of odor, or bouquet. An example of this theory would be the combining of marijuana, heroin, cocaine, and methamphetamine into a single package that, in turn, creates the bouquet of odor to be used as a training aid. Using this type of aid incorporates no change from the standard training normally performed. However, this type of aid is quite controversial and rarely used.

The single most positive aspect of using this type of training aid is a claim of sizable reduction in the amount of time necessary to train the dog. However, testing of the dog to confirm reliability of detection of each odor contained within the bouquet must be demonstrated and thus may severely outweigh any potential benefit. An additional difficulty is that low vapor pressure on any one component could make it succumb to another VOC in the headspace, or stated differently, one particular VOC may be so dominant as to overwhelm all others (Furton and Myers 2001; Lorenzo et al. 2003).

SUMMARY

Great care should be taken when dealing with each and every aspect of training aids to ensure the integrity, purity, and availability of odor. Each component used to store, construct, and use a hide should have a pristine counterpart that can be used for distractor training to ensure the dog is alerting to the parent material and not the associated materials. Ironically, some standards do not include odor detection or training aid requirements (ASTM 2014), while the opposite is true with other standards (generally SWGDOG). Each possible contaminate contained within training aid material should be placed as a distractor odor to ensure reliability of the canine. On the use of real material versus alternative aids, one group makes a compelling statement:

> However, our canine trials confirmed that neither brand of pseudo-explosive aid was an effective replacement for genuine explosives. Canines trained solely on either product A or product B performed poorly across the board when faced with authentic explosives, and canines trained solely on authentic explosives showed little interest in the pseudo-explosives. (Kranz et al. 2014b)

From this and other studies, it would seem wise to err on the side of caution by using actual materials until conclusive evidence argues otherwise (Tipple et al. 2014).

19 Scent Lineups
Variables in Procedures and Statistical Verification

Tadeusz Jezierski

The use of sniffer dogs by law enforcement forces has a centuries-long history, most notably the use of dogs for tracking prison escapees or criminal suspects. Despite its long history, this method was not well documented and therefore suffered from a lack of scientific credibility. Opinions on accuracy and reliability of tracking dogs were mostly a matter of popular belief, sometimes distorted and exaggerated by mass media. According to Prada et al. (2015), the first experimental studies on the ability of canines to discriminate individual human odor were conducted in 1887 by George Romanes, and the usefulness of suspect discrimination by dogs for practical police work was first demonstrated by Inspector Bussenius in 1903 in Germany (Schoon and Haak 2002).

Scent identification lineups have been known since the beginning of the twentieth century (Schoon and Massop 1995). A general rule that has seen little change from the beginning of the application of this method is that scent collected from the scene of a crime was presented to the dog prior to sniffing the lineup, with the dog instructed to find a matching scent in the lineup. Details of this method gradually changed and improved. The first scent lineups consisted of real people: one suspect and several decoys. A drawback of the lineup of real people, which was applied in Poland into the early 1960s, was that the dog could interact with people in the lineup, which could lead to problems with the interpretation of the dog's reactions. Since police patrol dogs were generally used, dogs sometimes became aggressive when the suspects were standing, so lineups began to have suspects lie down. Therefore, lineups consisting of persons were replaced with those consisting of scented objects belonging to the persons being tested. In a further development, the scented objects in the lineup were progressively made more uniform in terms of material, size, shape, and color.

In the 1960s and 1970s, the use of scent lineups in law enforcement for identifying suspects increased, perhaps because law enforcement personnel and judges shared the common perception of dog owners that dogs can recognize individual humans by scent and should therefore be able to retrieve objects scented by a person from a number of otherwise identical objects. Collecting scent samples from the scene of a crime and matching them to scent samples taken from suspects during the investigation is obviously a useful method of producing forensic evidence, because it is difficult for people to avoid leaving scent molecules on objects touched or in places where they were present, even if a human as the source of the scent did not directly touch the object but was above it (Vyplelova et al. 2014). Canine identification became officially acknowledged as a forensic method in some European countries, including Russia, Hungary, Poland, Lithuania, Denmark, the Netherlands, Germany (Bednarek 2008), and, to some extent, the United States (Ensminger 2012, Chapter 7). The reliability of canine identification was often taken for granted, unfortunately without sufficient supporting evidence from formal scientific experiments.

As long as canine identification of suspects in lineups remained an investigative tool, there was little controversy. In the 1980s and 1990s, however, results of canine identification lineups were increasingly presented in courts as evidence of a suspect's presence at the crime scene, sometimes becoming a major factor in a conviction. Due to its simplicity and putative reliability, scent identification came to be regarded, during the period of its peak use from 1996 to 1999, as a "queen

TABLE 19.1

Problems That Can Occur in Processing Olfactory Signals

Stage of Scent Perception	Problems That May Cause Errors in Identification of Scent
Scent molecules in nasal cavity	Molecules cannot reach the receptor
Reaction of scent molecules with receptors	No proper receptor available for certain kinds of molecules
Chemical reaction in sensory neuron	Sensory neuron does not react
Conduction of impulse through nerve	Nerve does not react
Processing of the impulse in the brain	Brain interprets information incorrectly

Source: Schoon, G.A.A., Scent Perception, Theory and Application for Training Search Dogs, Typewritten syllabus, 1999.

of evidences" (Bednarek 2000, 2003, 2008). During this period in Poland, from 1600 to 1800, "osmological expert witnesses" were provided to criminal courts by 36 police canine laboratories deploying 117 certified police scent identification dogs.

The branch of forensic science and practice dealing with canine identification lineups in some countries is called osmology or odorology. The high reputation of this evidence was crafted principally by lawyers during trials, rather than from experimental data based on scientific and statistically sound research. Instead of experimental tests assessing false alerts or the probability of a correct identification in a lineup occurring by chance, the value of canine identification was extrapolated by lawyers from conviction rates and anecdotal accounts introduced into evidence in specific prosecutions. As a consequence, a survey of 41 Polish judges presiding over criminal trials found that only 22% regarded canine scent lineup evidence as sufficiently "scientific" to convict and sentence a defendant in cases where scent lineup results were the only available evidence (Wojcikiewicz 1999; see Ensminger, id., re corroboration requirements in U.S. courts).

In Western Europe, courts have been particularly skeptical of the results of canine scent lineup identifications. For example, in the Netherlands a series of studies, including a PhD dissertation, were conducted by Schoon (1996, 1997a, 1998) using certified police dogs from the Dutch police canine unit to assess the reliability of canine identification for forensic purposes and its evidentiary reliability in courts. Although the canine unit of the Dutch police employed 15 full-time ID dog handlers and 15 certified Belgian Malinois specially trained for working scent lineups, both police and forensic personnel were generally more skeptical than was true at the time in Poland.

The canine lineup method has been deemed by many lawyers as not meeting judicial scientific criteria (e.g., Taslitz 1990; Jaworski 1999; Widacki 1999, 2000). Strictly speaking, average identification accuracy has been estimated in several scientific publications, though in experiments that had different setups, so results could not be compared (e.g., Brisbin and Austad 1991; Sommerville et al. 1993; Schoon and De Bruin 1994; Settle et al. 1994; Schoon 1996, 1998).

Judicial attitude as to the validity of canine identification has been increasingly skeptical, with the approach increasingly perceived as a "black-box technology," with the factors explaining correct versus incorrect responses by a dog often being unknown (Frijters 2006) (see Chapter 20 herein). An attempt to outline problems that can occur at various stages of the olfactory process and might lead to incorrect responses by a dog was undertaken by Schoon (1999) (Table 19.1).

INDIVIDUAL ODOR THEORY

There is scientific evidence that dogs can distinguish individual humans by odor (e.g., Kalmus 1955; Hepper 1988; Sommerville et al. 1990; Schoon and De Bruin 1994; Settle et al. 1994; Schoon 1996;

DeGreeff et al. 2011). Individually and gender distinct and reproducible gas chromatograph–mass spectrometry fingerprints in human axillary sweat were reported by Penn et al. (2007; see Agapiou et al. 2015, for a recent survey).

Some studies looked at a possible genetic component of individual human scent by having dogs attempt to distinguish between identical twins (recently, see Pinc et al. 2011). Kalmus (1955) found dogs able to discriminate between odors of identical twins in a tracking task. Hepper (1988) showed that dogs could discriminate scents of identical twins provided that the twins differed in environmental factors. Experiments conducted by Harvey et al. (2006) demonstrated that trailing and differentiating between monozygotic twins, compared with pairs of related and unrelated humans, is problematic for bloodhounds. In this study, dogs were given the scent of one twin and had no hesitancy in selecting a handkerchief scented by the second monozygotic twin from among a group of handkerchiefs. If handkerchiefs of both twins were placed in an array, however, the dog would select whichever handkerchief it came to first. The lessons from the study of Harvey et al. (2006) are that (1) the more genetically related two people are, the more difficult it is for a dog to distinguish them, and (2) the discriminatory capabilities of dogs seem to depend substantially upon a person's genetically derived odor type, also called the osmological phenotype. To differentiate between twins, environmental factors that furnish odor cues play a role for dogs.

RATIONALE FOR IDENTIFICATION BY SCENT LINEUP FOR FORENSIC PURPOSES

In scent lineup research, it is assumed that individual humans leave scent molecules on objects that have been touched or have had contact with the person (Brisbin and Austad 1991; Schoon 1996). Several assumptions underlie a reliable canine identification:

- Each person has a unique odor.
- This unique odor is unchangeable, not removable, and reproducible over time.
- A trained dog can differentiate between individual odors of different people.
- Each person is identified by dogs on the basis of odor with the same accuracy.
- Identification of the odor of one person in the lineup does not influence the identification of other persons.
- A lineup can be conducted in a fair, methodologically correct, and objective manner.

In order to make the forensic application of canine identification more plausible, a theoretical model of a human scent sample has been proposed. According to this model, a scent sample is composed of four possible components (Jezierski et al. 2002):

- An individual human odor component, probably genetically determined, unchangeable, unremovable, and unique to each individual.
- A metabolic odor component, related to each individual's diet, metabolic disorders, disease, medications, and possibly transitory emotions, like fear (Ackerl et al. 2002).
- An external component, related to each individual's cosmetics and substances used for body care, personal hygiene, etc., which can vary given changes in the individual's hygiene habits.
- An external environmental odor component related to the material used for odor sampling (tubes, cloths) and the location where odor samples were collected.

Ideally, scent identification dogs should focus on the individual genetic component and disregard all other components. In order to avoid confusing dogs when working in a lineup, other components of scent samples placed in the lineup should be uniform, even, to the extent possible, as to personal care products used and foods eaten by participants.

FIGURE 19.1   Indication by a dog of target odor in lineup.

DIFFERENT SCENT FOR DIFFERENT BODY PARTS

Dogs may also have problems identifying the same person on the basis of scent samples taken from different body parts. Dogs used by Brisbin and Austad (1991) distinguished, in 75.7% of trials, the scent of their handler's hand from the scent from hands of strangers but were not able to distinguish their handler's scent samples taken from the crook of arm from scent samples from the hands of other persons (57.9% responses correct, not significantly above chance). These authors suggested that either an individual human odor does not exist, or dogs must be trained using scents taken from different body parts.

Body part–specific odors may be due to variations in conditions for bacterial activity in local scent glands, which differ in particular regions of the human body. Variations in the body part–specific odor component may confuse dogs trained using scents from only one body part. Settle et al. (1994), using seven dogs to match pieces of cloth worn by six persons, achieved 80% correct responses against 17% correct responses by chance. Three dogs had to compare the scent collected from different body parts with that collected from hands on steel tubes. In this case, on average, 85% correct indications were obtained but with a large variation between dogs on consecutive test days (70–100%).

The results of both Brisbin and Austad (1991) and Harvey et al. (2006) show that environmental factors influencing the scent presented to a dog should be taken into consideration as a possible confusing factor. In the lineup method, dogs point out matching odor by performing an operant reaction, mostly sitting or lying down in front of the target odor sample (Figure 19.1). Failure to give an operant response during a trial does not necessarily mean the dog could not discriminate a scent sample with its sense of smell. For example, the best result of Brisbin and Austad (1991) was that dogs distinguished objects scented by their handler's hand from objects with no human scent 93% of the time. It seems implausible that those dogs were not able to sniff out the difference between no human scent and the scent of their handler. Alternate explanations could be that this difference was not interesting to the dogs, that the dogs did not associate the handler's scent with the reward, were not motivated to earn the reward during a particular test, or were simply not adequately trained.

EVALUATION OF INDICATIONS AND VALIDITY OF CANINE IDENTIFICATION

As summarized in Table 19.2, there are essential differences between odor detection, such as with drugs or explosives, and scent or odor identification, as in scent lineups. Training dogs to identify individual human scent in a lineup is one of the most difficult tasks in canine training. The dog

TABLE 19.2
Differences between Odor Detection and Odor Identification

Item for Comparison	Odor Detection (Searching/Finding)	Odor Identification (Comparing/Choosing)
Number of odors trained	Generally no more than 6–8 (e.g., drugs, explosives)	Many (e.g., individual humans)
Odor differences	Big/stable	Small/variable
Environment	Different locations	Fixed location (sniffing room, lineup)
Working method	Mutual interaction and giving cues between handler and dog	Dog has to work and decide on its own

has to find a matching scent while disregarding varying odor concentrations and without being distracted or confused by a number of other odor components. During tests, the dog has to correctly distinguish subtle differences between scents of people previously unknown to it.

Although conducting scent identification tests using a lineup may seem simple, analysis of the results requires a sound logical approach. A scheme for assessing correct versus wrong responses, depending on the kind of trial, is provided in Table 19.3. When assessing the reliability of scent lineups, one must be aware that forensic reality has to be distinguished from the experimental reality. Contrary to experimental situations, in forensic reality, it is not possible to ascertain whether an indication of the target sample is false positive or true positive, nor whether a nonindication is a false negative (a miss) or a true negative indication.

A fundamental issue concerns how to record observations for statistical analysis. During an active trial, when the scent presented to the dog at the starting point is also placed as the target sample in the lineup, four different responses are possible:

1. Dog indicates the target sample by a trained reaction (sitting or lying down) with no hesitation (correct reaction).
2. Dog does not indicate to the target sample (miss).
3. Dog indicates falsely to a control decoy (false alert).
4. Dog demonstrates hesitation or an incomplete reaction.

There are two possible ways of assessing success or failure by a dog, which can be taken as single observation units for statistical calculations:

1. *Choosing target sample exclusively from all samples in the lineup.* This means that a dog should choose only the target sample, generally only one out of all stations. The probability of a success can be estimated by this approach:

$$P = 1/\text{number of stands actually sniffed} \tag{19.1}$$

Any false alert or hesitation at a stand with a decoy sample results in classifying the trial as a mistake. Although dogs are trained during the initial phase of the training to sniff all the stands in the lineup, some dogs may develop a habit of sniffing samples irregularly (not in order of the arrangement in the sniffing room), of skipping some stands, or of not sniffing remaining stands in the lineup after they have successfully indicated to the correct stand.

Usually, there is one target odor sample in the lineup to be indicated. To encourage the dog to sniff all samples in the lineup, more than one target sample can be put in the lineup to give the dog the chance to earn more than one reward. With more target samples in the

TABLE 19.3

Ways of Concluding Correctness or Falsity of Alert in Lineups during Control Trials and Test Trials, and in Forensically Conducted Scent Lineups

Scent Sample Provided to Dog before Lineup	Comparative Scent Samples in Lineup	Dog's Indications of Comparative Scents in Lineup			
		Scent of Suspect	Scent of Decoys	Scent of Control Person X	No Indication during Lineup
		Control Trials to Check Dog's Ability			
Control person X	Control person X, suspect, decoys	Alert would be false and dog disqualified (attraction of suspect's scent)	Alert would be false; dog could be disqualified or decoy exchanged before a new trial	Alert would be correct; failure to alert would be a miss	Miss (per prior column)
Control person X not in lineup (zero trial)	Suspect, decoy	(Same)	(Same)	n/a	No indication would be only correct response
		Test Trials in Experimental Reality			
Evidential scent of suspect	Suspect, decoys	Alert would be correct	Alert would be false; dog could be disqualified or decoy changed	n/a	No indication would mean a miss
Evidential scent of individual not in lineup (zero trial)	(Same)	Alert would be false; dog should be disqualified	Alert would be false; dog could be disqualified or decoy changed	n/a	No indication would be correct response
		Forensic Reality			
Scent from crime scene (perpetrator = suspect?)	Suspect, decoys	Alert to suspect's scent not known to be correct or false	Alert would be false; dog could be disqualified or decoy changed	n/a	Not known if correct or a miss

Source: Modified from Schoon, G.A.A., *J. Forensic Sci.*, 43, 1, 70–75, 1998.

lineup, however, the probability of correct indication by chance increases, and there is the risk that a dog will begin to indicate to all samples in turn in an effort to get a reward.

Trials are generally conducted over a test day with several dogs. The sniffed material (scented steel tubes or cloths in jars) should be exchanged after each trial to avoid the target sample being marked with saliva left by the dog during sniffing or with scent from a pad while pawing a scent container. Provided that such marking of the target sample has been prevented, when trials are repeated several times with several dogs, the probability of correct indication of the target sample by chance can be calculated using a formula given by Koziol and Sutowski (1998), as follows:

$$P = \left(\frac{k!(n-k)!}{n!} \right)^{lm}$$

(19.2)

where
$P =$ probability of correct indication by chance in repeating trials several times with several dogs
$k =$ number of target samples in the lineup
$n =$ number of stands in the lineup
$! =$ factorial (thus, if $n = 6$, $6! = 6 \times 5 \times 4 \times 3 \times 2 \times 1 = 720$)
$l =$ number of dogs used
$m =$ number of trials conducted

Thus, if there is one target sample in the lineup but six stands in the lineup, three dogs are used (with three trials conducted for each dog—total of nine trials), and all dogs indicated to the same station with the target sample, the probability of this occurring by chance would be

$$[1 \; (5 \times 4 \times 3 \times 2 \times 1)/(6 \times 5 \times 4 \times 3 \times 2 \times 1)]^{3 \times 3}$$
$$= [120/720]^9$$
$$= 1.6666666^9$$
$$= 0.000000099$$

As indicated by this example, repeating trials several times with several dogs that achieve the same result gives an extremely low probability of a correct indication of the target sample having been made by chance. However, this formula does not take into account that dogs, after one or more trials, may learn which sample is the target sample; thus, the consecutive trials may not be fully independent.

2. *Reaction yes/no toward each sample in the lineup that was actually sniffed.* This means that the reaction toward each sniffed sample during a trial is considered separately, and a dog in one trial (run) makes as many comparisons with a pattern odor recalled from its olfactory memory as odor samples it actually sniffs in the lineup. The samples that are not sniffed (omitted) are not taken into consideration. The probability of the correct indication by chance is 0.5 independently of how many samples are sniffed by the dog. During the same trial, the dog may have both correct and false alerts.

VALIDITY OF SCENT LINEUPS

Since scent lineup identifications began to be proffered in courts as evidence, a favorite question asked by attorneys concerned the reliability and validity of the method. Parameters for comparing canine identification of perpetrators with other forensic methods have been proposed by Schoon (1998). For a practical assessment of the identification reliability, this author calculated a "diagnostic ratio" of a positive identification as follows:

$$\text{Diagnostic ratio of positive ID} = \frac{\% \text{ correct ID in suspect} = \text{perpetrator cases}}{\% \text{ false ID in suspect} = \text{perpetrator cases}} \quad (19.3)$$

As indicated in Table 19.3, where the suspect *is* the perpetrator in forensic reality, the evidential scent will also be the suspect's scent in the lineup. When the suspect *is not* the perpetrator in forensic reality, the evidential scent will not be present in the lineup. Taking into account disqualifications of dogs in control trials and all factors that could negatively bias the identification, Schoon (1998) estimated that the diagnostic ratio of a positive identification was 13.6 (though this was determined with an assumption regarding the frequency with which an error would be repeated). This would mean that out of every 13–14 alerts, 1 would likely be false. Schoon calculated the diagnostic ratio for a negative identification as follows:

$$\text{Diagnostic ratio of negative ID} = \frac{\% \text{ correct reactions (misses) in suspect} \neq \text{perpetrator cases}}{\% \text{ misses in suspect} = \text{perpetrator cases}} \quad (19.4)$$

The diagnostic ratio of negative identification was calculated by Schoon (1998) as 2.6, so that, based on her experiments, out of every two to three negative identifications by dogs, one is likely to be a false negative, i.e., a miss where, in forensic reality, an actual perpetrator is not identified. The asymmetry of positive and negative ID diagnostic ratios shows that a positive identification is more reliable than a negative one.

Another way of evaluating results of odor lineups can be taken from medical diagnostics, applying the terms of test sensitivity and specificity, as well as positive and negative predictive values, to provide the ratios specified in Table 19.4. An ideal test should have both high sensitivity and high specificity (either 1 or approaching 1). However, some tests are characterized by high sensitivity and lower specificity. Such tests rarely give false negative results and are appropriate if a positive detection rate is the primary goal and false alerts have no serious consequences. Tests characterized by a high specificity may be more appropriate if certainty in identification is particularly important, e.g., in identification of perpetrators in forensic investigations and in presenting identification results to

TABLE 19.4

Scheme for Calculation of Test Sensitivity, Specificity, and Positive and Negative Values

Test Results with Dogs	Actual Identity of Two Scents (Number of Cases)	
	Scents Identical	Scents Different
ID trial result positive	True positive	False positive
ID trial result negative	False negative	True negative

Note:

Test sensitivity = true positive/(true positive + false negative).

Test specificity = true negative/(true negative + false positive).

Positive predictive value (PPV) = true positive/(true positive + false positive).

PPV estimates the probability that a positive test result actually means the detection of the scent.

Negative predictive value (NPV) = true negative/(true negative + false negative).

NPV estimates the probability that a negative test result actually means the nondetection of the scent.

courts as evidence. For the predictive values of the test, both sensitivity and specificity, as well as the number of cases of identical and nonidentical scents, play a role.

PREFERRED SCENTED ITEMS FOR LINEUPS

In human odor lineups, depending on the local methodology, two kinds of scented objects are used for tests:

- Parallelepiped steel tubes about 7 cm long and 1.5 cm wide, fixed to small platforms on the floor. See Figure 19.2 for the type of steel tubes used by the Dutch police.
- Cotton cloths placed in jars, used, e.g., in Hungary, Poland and Russia, as shown in Figure 19.3.

Steel tubes are preferable for dogs that passionately retrieve objects since such tubes become, for them, both scented objects to sniff and a reward to retrieve. The tubes can be scented by holding them. Some dogs, however, may be reluctant to retrieve hard metallic objects. Using an electromagnetic device, only the target steel tube in the lineup can be released for the dog to pick up and play

FIGURE 19.2 Collecting individual scent on a steel tube.

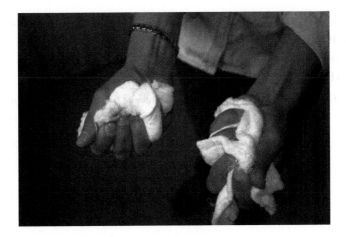

FIGURE 19.3 Collecting individual scent on cotton cloths.

with. Retrieving steel tubes can be self-rewarding for a dog, and the influence of dog–handler interactions during sniffing and rewarding can be excluded. Scented steel tubes, after being retrieved, cannot be repeatedly used, because saliva left on the tube may cue the dog during a subsequent trial in the lineup. Ideally, after each trial, scented steel tubes should be washed and sterilized.

Cotton cloths as scented objects are suitable for dogs that are more motivated for a treat as a reward. Cloths are placed in jars to prevent them from being touched by a dog's nose or tongue. Cloths can be cut into smaller pieces or reused if not salivated upon.

ATTRACTIVENESS

For an identification method to be reliable, all individuals of a human population should be identified by dogs with the same accuracy. In police practice, it was found that dogs would give more false alerts to odor samples of particular persons, suggesting that the odor of some persons is more "attractive" to dogs. If a person whose odor attracts dogs is a suspect, such an individual may have an increased likelihood of being indicated falsely by dogs.

Control trials have been introduced into scent lineup protocols for two main reasons. First, the scent attractiveness of a suspect should be assessed by using this scent as a decoy in two or three trials prior to the actual test (discussed below in text concerning Table 19.6). If the suspect's scent is indicated by dogs as false alerts in control trials, this scent is regarded as attractive to the dogs and could be indicated by the dog whether the suspect is the perpetrator or not. Exclusions of suspects with attractive scents from a scent lineup could arguably improve identification validity (Bednarek and Sutowski 1999). This does not seem proper, however, since the attractiveness may be a variable or unpredictable trait. Attractiveness might, for instance, not be found in control trials but may appear in actual forensic tests. Jezierski et al. (2003) estimated scent attractiveness of 186 persons on the basis of the percentage of false alarms toward these persons when their scents were used in 30–100 trials as decoys. Of the persons examined, 19.3% had a nonattractive scent to dogs (i.e., produced 0% false alerts); 142 of 186 persons (76.3%) had a scent that was of low attractiveness to dogs (>0–25% of false alerts); and only 1.1% of persons were of higher attractiveness to dogs (50–75% false alerts) (Table 19.5). The experimental results suggest that scent attractiveness is not a binary trait but, rather, is a continuous trait. Therefore, attractiveness should be regarded as a false alert (Jezierski et al. 2003). It is not known what makes the scent of a person attractive to dogs. Gawkowski (2001) speculated that scent attractiveness may be related to the interference of the scent memory from a scent perceived by dogs as pleasant or unpleasant.

TABLE 19.5

Distribution of Persons with Different Degrees of Attractiveness for Dogs (186 Persons Investigated)

Degree of Attractiveness	% False Alerts	Number of Persons	% Persons Investigated
None	0	36	19.3
Low	>0–25	142	76.3
Medium	25–50	6	3.2
High	50–75	2	1.1
Extreme	>75	0	0

FAMILIARITY AND GENDER

Dogs identify the scent of persons known to them better than that of unknown persons. Schoon and De Bruin (1994) found that dogs responded correctly in 75% of trials to scent samples of people well known to them, 67% for people whose scents were frequently used in tests, and only 25% for people completely unknown to them. These results were achieved using only three dogs, so no certain conclusions can be drawn.

There is some evidence that the scent of individual women is more readily distinguishable to dogs than that of individual men (Jezierski et al. 2012). Analysis of 3675 trials with lineups consisting of exclusively male scents (2523 trials) or exclusively female scents (1152 trials) showed that dogs made significantly ($P < .05$) more correct choices (66.8%) when they had to find in a lineup a matching female scent sample than when they had to find a matching male scent sample (63.4%). Additionally, the dogs made nonsignificantly fewer false alarms toward female scents than toward male scents and significantly ($P < .05$) fewer misses in relation to female scents. In 1997, however, Schoon (1997a) found no evidence that dogs use information on gender of the scent donor. It should be mentioned that forensic lineup methodology generally requires that scents in a lineup not differ as to sex, age, odor sample collection condition, storage time, etc. to avoid additional factors that may play a role in identification.

TIME FACTOR IN SCENT RECOGNITION

Forensic analysis sometimes seeks to determine which place in a car was occupied by a suspect and which by other persons at the time of the crime. In such a small space as a car cabin, individual human odors can disperse and be found throughout due to rough sedimentation, without contact with the substratum. Gawkowski (2000) showed that if two persons were sitting in a car for 30 min and the scent samples were taken from the seats within 60 min, it is possible for a dog to ascertain which seat was occupied by the suspect. When the time elapsed from the passengers leaving the car to the collection of scent samples exceeded 60 min, however, the identification of the seat occupied by the suspect is less certain, and after 2 h, identification of the suspect's location becomes impossible. On the other hand, Krawczyk and Wesolowski (1998) found that it is impossible to detect odor molecules of specific individuals from 1 to 12 h after they had been in a room where those individuals had neither touched nor had direct body contact with objects in the room. Thus, sedimentation alone was insufficient to leave an odor detectable by canines.

COSMETICS AND SMOKING

Gawkowski (2000) found that the external component of human odor related to cosmetics does not impede canine identification on the basis of individual scent. Dogs, during identification trials, were not confused by a common odor component related to the same cosmetics used by the scent donors. This was proven by a very low percentage of false alerts (1.92%) toward people wearing the same cosmetics. According to Schoon (1997a) and Misiewicz (2000), smoking of cigarettes by scent donors did not influence the correctness of identifications.

CONTROL TRIALS

As noted initially, lineup procedures have changed over the years. Originally, control trials were never or seldom performed to check dogs' ability to work properly, taking into account possible variation in motivation, mood, and other factors, as well as to assess the attractiveness of the suspect's scent. Forensic and judicial aspects of canine lineup identification prompted more detailed studies on the influence of experimental setup on the diagnostic value of this method (Schoon 1996,

1998; Gawkowski 2000; Jezierski et al. 2003). To increase reliability, various protocols involving control trials were introduced. Control trials are used before real trials to check the ability of the dog to work properly on a test day and to check whether the suspect's scent would not be indicated falsely due to attractiveness.

NUMBER OF STATIONS AND TARGET SAMPLES

There are no standards for how many stations and target samples should be in a scent lineup. Polish police most typically use five stations, one of which contains a target, as indicated in Table 19.6 (see Gawkowski 2000). Dutch police usually employ two parallel scent lineups of six or seven stations (Schoon 1996, 1998). Whatever the number of stations, a dog should sniff all stations in a lineup since omitting stations increases the probability that the sample is indicated correctly by chance (Jezierski et al. 2003).

Although dogs are trained to sniff and systematically compare several scents (stands) in the lineup during a trial, some dogs may omit or not sniff some samples. Taking this into account, Schoon (1997b) proposed a new experimental design using an odd–even paradigm. In this proposed paradigm, dogs sniffed only two stations, one randomly chosen to contain the target sample and the other blank. Schoon concluded that the level of matching even scents was comparable but the level of nonmatching in odd comparison was substantially higher in the new design. Although scent identification with this odd–even paradigm seemed more reliable than the customary design, Schoon acknowledged that introducing the new design would require significant changes in attitude and working conditions by the police, and it was never implemented in practice.

TABLE 19.6
Scheme of Identification Test Including Control Trials, Zero Trials, and Corpus Delicti Trials

Odor Sample Presented to Dogs before Start	Stations in Lineup				
	1	2	3	4	5
Control trial, sample C1	A	B	X	C1	D
Control trial, sample C1	B	X	A	D	C1
Zero trial, sample C1	B	D	E	A	X
Control trial, sample C2	X	C2	B	E	A
Actual trial, corpus delicti odor	E	A	D	X	B
Actual trial, corpus delicti odor	D	A	X	B	E
Encouraging trial, sample C3	E	D	B	A	C3

Note:

A, B, D, E: decoys (odor samples from donors not related to the forensic investigation).

C1, C2, C3: control odor samples (from donors not related to the forensic investigation).

X: odor sample from suspect.

Corpus delicti: odor sample from crime scene.

CONTROL AND "ZERO" TRIALS

One of the most common approaches to improve reliability of canine lineups has been to implement different systems of control trials in combination with "zero" trials where no matching scent to that presented to the dog directly before the trial is placed in the lineup. It was claimed (e.g., Schoon 2002) that assessing dogs' performance in control trials would improve their reliability in real trials conducted in forensic reality. Examples of lineup protocols used in the Netherlands and their impact on identification results are summarized in Table 19.7.

Weighted averages per Schoon 2002. Scent to be matched is in bold in description of lineup. Different dogs were used for trials with steel tubes and cloth. In protocols 7.1 and 7.2, order of lineups varied by trial; in protocol 7.3, lineup 2 was used if the dog successfully identified the control scent in lineup 1.

Using steel tubes as scented items in the lineup generally produces a higher percentage of correct indications (Table 19.7, protocols 7.1., 7.2, and 7.3) but also a higher percentage of false positive indications (false alerts), compared to scented cloths. When using cloth odor samples, a higher percentage of misses was characteristic. It must be mentioned, however, that direct comparison of steel tubes and cloths, as presented in Table 19.7, may be biased since different dogs were used for tests with steel tubes and with cloths.

Introduction of zero trials in protocol 7.2 (Table 19.7) resulted in an increase in the percentage of false positive identifications and a decrease in the percentage of correct identifications compared

---

TABLE 19.7
Identification Results Using Three Different Protocols and Two Kinds of Scent Material

Experimental Protocol	Scented Material in the Lineup					
	Steel Tubes to Be Retrieved			Cloth, Lying-Down Response		
Protocol 7.1						
Lineup 1: **suspect** + 5 decoys						
Lineup 2: **suspect** + 5 decoys						
Final outcome:	% Correct	% Miss	% False	% Correct	% Miss	% False
	49.6	8.2	44.9	18.5	48.2	33.3
Protocol 7.2						
Lineup 1: **suspect** + 5 decoys						
Lineup 2: 6 decoys (zero trial)						
Final outcome:	% Correct	% Miss	% False	% Correct	% Miss	% False
	31.2	8.4	60.4	14.8	40.0	44.4
Protocol 7.3						
Lineup 1: **control scent** + suspect + 5 decoys						
Lineup 2: **suspect** + 5 decoys						
Final outcome:	% Correct	% Miss	% False	% Correct	% Miss	% False
	57.9	21.0	21.1	41.7	41.6	18.6

to protocol 7.1. Applying a control trial and disqualification for failure to indicate a control scent (protocol 7.3.) reduced the percentage of false positive identifications almost by half and increased the percentage of correct identifications.

Comparing several of her experiments, Schoon (2002) demonstrated that introducing two control trials in which dogs have to identify the same control scent in two lineups, and disqualification for failure even in one of these two trials, was very effective, since only 1.2% of identifications proved to be false (Table 19.8, protocol 8.1).

TABLE 19.8
Identification Results Using Three Different Protocols with Different Rates of Disqualification in Control Trials

Protocol 8.1

Lineup 1: **control scent** + suspect + 5 decoys

Lineup 2: **control scent** + suspect + 5 decoys

11% disqualification for not identifying control scent in lineups 1 and 2

Lineup 3: **suspect** + 5 decoys

Lineup 4: **suspect** + 5 decoys

Final outcome:	% Correct	% Miss	% False
	92.0	6.8	1.2

Protocol 8.2

Lineup 1: **control scent A** + control scent B + suspect + 5 decoys

Lineup 2: **control scent B** + suspect + 5 decoys

25.6% disqualification for not identifying control scents A and B

Lineup 3: 6 decoys (zero trial)

Lineup 4: **suspect** + 5 decoys

Final outcome:	% Correct	% Miss	% False
	79.9	9.5	10.7

Protocol 8.3

Lineup 1: **control scent** + suspect + 6 decoys

Lineup 2: 6 decoys (zero trial)

19.4% disqualification for not identifying control scent and/or mistake
  in zero trial

Lineup 3: **suspect** + 6 decoys

Final outcome:	% Correct	% Miss	% False
	88.7	0	16.3

Note: Weighted averages per Schoon 2002. In lineup descriptions, **bold** = scent to be matched. Results of final outcome were for dogs that made correct identifications in lineups 1 and 2.

Applying two control trials with two different control scents to be matched not only resulted in increasing the percentage of disqualifications but also increased the percentage of false alerts (protocol 8.2). The lesson learned from Schoon (2002) is that through control trials, the rate of dogs' disqualifications was higher, but the impact of control trials on the rate of false identification was ambiguous. In comparing Tables 19.7 and 19.8, it can be said that in most cases, the control trials reduced the rate of false identifications, but this is not always the case. Generally, it could be stated that through strengthening the criteria of dogs' qualifications in the control and zero trials, the percentage of false identifications can be, to an extent, reduced, but the number of dogs that pass the control trials and are allowed to perform actual trials is also decreased. It sometimes happens that no dogs pass control trials, making actual identification tests impossible under such a protocol.

EFFECT OF INCREASING THE NUMBER OF DOGS USED

Another approach intended to increase the reliability of identifications, focusing particularly on the number of dogs qualified in control and zero trials and therefore available for actual trials, was examined by Jezierski et al. (2002). The rationale of this approach was that the more dogs that qualified in control trials, and the more that indicate unanimously in real trials, the more reliable is the final identification. Six trained dogs identifying 34 scents (persons) were used for this analysis. From a general database, results were selected in which three to four control trials and a zero trial were performed prior to actual identification trials. This approach used control trials, test trials, and forensic reality, the steps shown in Table 19.3. When control trials were not taken into account for disqualification of dogs, there were a total of 34% of false positive results in the actual trials. In 295 actual trials that followed after all control trials had been correctly performed, false positive indications were reduced to 21%. This meant that disqualification for not performing correctly in control trials resulted in 13% false positives.

Disqualifying dogs for one mistake in control trials may, however, eliminate most of them, so that few or no dogs remain to perform real trials. Second, fewer dogs used in real trials may mean that if they do not agree, there are no results that can be relied upon. These factors should be taken into consideration in choosing variant protocols, four of which are described in Table 19.9.

Variant A. In this protocol, a milder variant of dog qualification from control and zero trials was assumed since a single mistake in a control trial did not disqualify a dog if the majority of control trials were correctly performed. In this variant, it was decided that at least one dog should be available for real trials after it positively passed control trials and, for a positive ultimate scent identification, indication of this single dog would suffice. It could, however, happen that more than one dog qualified in control trials but their indications in real trials were inconsistent, so that the indications of a majority of dogs in real trials would be accepted. If two dogs qualified but there is a discrepancy between them in the real trials, the final identification is considered inconclusive. If more than two dogs qualified, at least one dog more should indicate positively compared to dogs showing negative indications. This means that if three dogs qualified, at least two would have to indicate positively, though one could indicate negatively for an identification to be accepted.

Using variant A for testing 34 scents, in experimental reality when evidentiary scent = comparative scent, 47% of identifications were correct, while 8.8% of identifications were false positive, producing a diagnostic ratio of 5.3 (47/8.8). Of the ultimate identifications, 44.2% were inconclusive.

Variant B. This protocol assumes that at least two dogs must be positively qualified after control and zero trials and both should indicate positively in real trials. If more than three dogs qualified, more than two had to indicate positively. If more than three dogs qualified in control trials, for a positive ultimate identification, at least two had to indicate positively. Using this protocol, 38.2% of positive ultimate identifications were correct, and 5.9% were

TABLE 19.9

Identification Results Using Four Different Variants Depending on the Number of Dogs Qualified in Control Trials

Variants of Dogs' Disqualifications in Control Trials	% of Final Identifications			Diagnostic Ratio (a/b)
	Correct (a)	False (b)	Inconclusive	
Variant A: Minimum 1 dog must qualify and indicate positively; if >2 dogs qualify, 1 dog more must indicate positively to accept identification	47.0	8.8	44.2	5.3
Variant B: Minimum 2 dogs qualify and all indicate positively; if >3 dogs qualified, >2 dogs must indicate positively to accept identification	38.2	5.9	55.9	6.5
Variant C: Minimum 2 dogs qualify, and all must indicate positively; if >4 dogs qualify, >3 dogs indicate positively to accept identification	35.3	2.9	61.8	12.2
Variant D: Minimum 3 dogs qualify, and all must indicate positively; if >5 dogs qualified, >4 must indicate positively to accept identification	23.5	0	76.5	Diagnostic ration could not be calculated because denominator is 0. 100% certainty for correctness of 23.5% positive identifications.

Source: Jezierski, T. et al., Ethological Analysis of Mistakes Made During Identification of Humans on the Basis of Scent by Police Special Dogs (in Polish), Final Report on grant no. TOOA 02618, of the Polish State Committee for Scientific Research, 2002.

false. The remaining 55.9% of identifications were inconclusive. The diagnostic ratio of positive identification was calculated as 38.2/5.9 = 6.5.

Variant C. The only difference between variants B and C was that in the latter, where more than four dogs qualified for real trials, for a positive final identification, the number of dogs indicating positively should be more than three compared to those indicating negatively.

Variant D. At least three dogs have to qualify, and all indicate positively. If more than five dogs qualify, more than four have to indicate positively. Under this protocol, only 23.5% of positive ultimate identifications were correct, but there were no false ultimate identifications. Thus, the calculation of the diagnostic ratio of positive identification was not possible (division by 0). However, 76.5% of ultimate identifications were inconclusive, which makes this protocol less practical.

Comparing these four variants, it is evident that increasing qualification criteria in control and real trials decreases the rate of false ultimate identification but also decreases the rate of correct ultimate identification and thus increases the rate of inconclusive final outcomes. Schoon (2002) stated that differences in experimental protocols lead to differences in dogs' performance, which in turn will affect the reliability of a given protocol. Schoon indicates that in the Netherlands, more fixed protocols were used when scent lineups were still possible. It was believed that fixed protocols allowed better measurement of a dog's performance and improved the reliability of ultimate identification. On the other hand, in police practice in Poland, the protocols were more variable as determined by osmology experts conducting investigations (Bednarek and Sutowski), meaning estimation of the reliability could vary.

The lack of expected efficacy of control trials for elimination of false ultimate identifications can be explained by a random distribution of dogs' mistakes in consecutive controls and real trials within a test day. In other words, if no mistakes were committed by a dog in control trials, there is no guarantee that the following actual trials will be faultless. Although through control trials, the best dogs are selected for the actual trials, the mistakes in real trials cannot be eliminated using control trials. The most convincing methods for assessing the validity of canine work in the lineup are double-blind trials in which the actual status of the tested scent sample (matching versus nonmatching to the evidential scent sample) is only known to the assistant, who is absent during the trials, and neither the dog handler nor the experimenter knows the status of the sample, which should assess only on the basis of dogs' indications.

CLEVER HANS EFFECT

One of the reasons to conduct double-blind trials where the dog handler and the experimenter are blind to the position of the target sample in the lineup is the Clever Hans effect (Ensminger 2012). This effect concerns the possibility of unconscious and slight cues or signals being given to the dog by the handler, and perhaps by a participant in an experiment that might be visible to the dog. Dogs are exceptionally responsive to human pointing gestures when finding food or a toy at a place indicated by a human (Soproni et al. 2002; Miklosi et al. 2005).

Gawkowski (2000) conducted an experiment on the Clever Hans effect during the last phase of dog scent lineup training and during certification procedures for police identification dogs. He evaluated responses of 83 handler–dog pairs in the zero trials only. The experimenter deliberately suggested to the dog handler that this was not a zero trial but an active trial, and he informed the handler about the position of the target sample in the lineup. In 54.5% of trials, the dogs worked correctly, not indicating any of the samples, as it was in a zero trial. In 13.1% of trials, however, the dogs worked correctly but clearly demonstrated some uncertainty and/or fear of being wrong. In 22.2% of trials, dogs made false alerts but toward other samples than the suggested matching sample, and in 10.2% of trials, dogs gave false alerts exactly to the sample that was suggested as matching. Unfortunately, the author gives no precise statistical analysis of the results. Nevertheless, on the basis of his experiments, Gawkowski concluded that the Clever Hans effect exists in the case of a strong and long-lasting emotional bond between the handler and the dog. See also Lit et al. (2011).

This effect can appear not only between handler and dog but also between other experiment participants and the dog. Osmology experts are generally aware of this effect, at least as to the handler, who thus is not made aware of the position of the target sample in the lineup. The experimenter often observes the dog work in the lineup via monitor or behind the one-way mirror. Double-blind trials seem to be a good way to eliminate the Clever Hans effect, but since dogs are usually not rewarded in double-blind trials, this may be discouraging or frustrating to the dogs if such trials are conducted too often.

LOCATION OF TARGET SAMPLES IN LINEUPS

Since the trials are usually repeated several times a day, location of the target sample in a particular station in the lineup should be changed quasi-randomly to prevent conditioning a dog to indicate more often at one particular station. Jezierski et al. (2002) found that more false alerts are made by dogs at the first and the second stands in a lineup (Figure 19.4). If, due to full randomization, target samples are placed several times repeatedly at the same stand, which has already been preferred by the dog, the existing habit of the dog would be reinforced. During training, the location of the

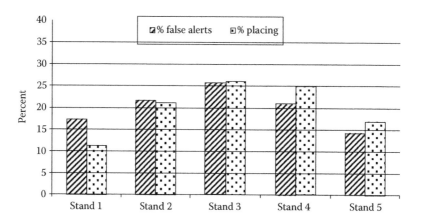

FIGURE 19.4 Stands in the lineup.

target sample in each trial should be carefully chosen by the experimenter, applying a quasi-random location.

Searching in a lineup involves resolving the problem of a hidden object. The dog may also use spatial information where the target sample was hidden during the previous trial. Studies by Fiset et al. (2000) have shown that the processes used by dogs to encode the spatial position of a hidden object are highly flexible. These processes in dogs are primarily based on egocentric spatial information (under the animal's own spatial coordinates), but if the experimental situation precludes a successful use of egocentric spatial information, dogs can encode allocentric spatial information (referring to the relationships between the target position and the objects surrounding it).

ABILITIES OF INDIVIDUAL DOGS

In 4100 experimental trials conducted by Jezierski et al. (2002), using six dogs that had completed all training stages, compared with eight certified police identification dogs in 590 tests, without applying any disqualification system, marked individual differences between dogs were found, both in percentage of correctly performed trials (success unit 1) and percentage of trials with false alerts. The best dog performed correctly in 72.7% of trials, whereas the worst one, in 32.1% of trials. The percentage of false alerts for the best dog was 15.6% and for the worst one, 52.8%. These results were calculated without prior control trials to check the dogs' working ability on the day when the tests were conducted. Schoon (1996), applying scent collected on steel tubes and using eight certified service dogs of the Dutch police, obtained similar results. The best dog achieved 65% correct indications, and the worst, 26%. As for false alerts, the best dog gave 22% false alerts, and the worst, 59%.

Brisbin et al. (2000) point out that in strictly controlled experiments, certified police dogs achieved generally worse results than expected by police dog handlers and experts. Taking into account all dogs and all tests, the dogs performed between 10% and 20% of trials erroneously. A relatively wide range between the best and the worst dogs suggests both genetic variability as to olfactory acuity and different ability to perform well after operant conditioning (training methods) and environmental variability. The appropriate genetic variability could be used for successful genetic selection toward scent detection ability. Such systematic selection has not been used to date in police dog populations. The certification systems for identification dogs have not taken individual genetic differences between dogs into consideration, but with increasing knowledge of genetic factors in olfactory ability, this may change.

Studies on information-seeking behavior of dogs during match-to-sample training in the lineup were conducted by Jezierski et al. (2008). These authors found significant individual differences in dogs' performance in operant conditioning during match-to-sample trials. The style of sniffing, the searching time, and the number of sniffed stations in the lineup were found to influence the percentage of false positive and false negative indications. For example, a relatively high and significant correlation was found between the time of sniffing the target sample before a trial and the score for sniffing style ($r = -0.98$; $P < .001$), and the mean searching time for the target sample in the lineup in trials with correct indications was significantly shorter (13.4 ± 12.1 s) than in trials with false alerts (28.9 ± 20.0 s) or in trials with misses (23.2 ± 17.1 s).

Individual variability of dogs' performance at scent identification brings up a number of problematic issues that have an impact on identification reliability and deserve further studies. Those potential problems involve the following:

- Varying physiological ability to perceive the scent differences by the dog as affected, e.g., by subclinical sickness, hormonal states of the dog, environmental factors, etc.
- Varying motivation of dogs to resolve the problem, i.e., to indicate the matching scent in the lineup by performing a learned response to earn the reward (e.g., from mood disorders).
- Systematic canine work in the lineup, i.e., sniffing all stands with no preference for indication of particular stands and no omitting of others.
- Scent attractiveness of some people and aversion to the scent of others so that all humans should be identified by dogs with the same accuracy.
- Experimental setup should exclude effect of dog–handler interactions on detection accuracy, in particular due to the Clever Hans effect.
- Rewarding should not distract dogs from work and should positively influence the dog's performance.
- Ability of dogs to inhibit learned reaction (go/no-go paradigm) when no matching scent is available in the lineup.
- Quasi-randomness of positioning of the target sample in the lineup and of conducting zero versus active trials. Conducting trials according to a rigid scheme or full randomness may be less favorable as it can produce a learned schematic response.
- Contamination of scent molecules between samples.
- Exclusion of marking the target sample by the dog during trials, e.g., by nosing or pawing on them.
- Controlling or exclusion of using modalities and cues other than olfaction by dogs (visual, acoustic) during trials.

It is to be hoped that these issues will be addressed by the research teams working in this area.

OTHER USES OF CANINE LINEUPS

In this chapter, only canine identification of individual humans using scent lineups has been considered. However, the scent lineup method can be potentially used for the identification of any type of odor, especially if the direct sniffing of objects or materials by dogs is not possible or desirable. For example, lineups were used for canine detection of odor markers of cancer diseases in humans (e.g., McCulloch et al. 2006) or for land mine detection using filters (Remote Explosive Search Training [Fjellanger et al. 2002]), although strictly speaking, in the latter method, a circular multiple-choice apparatus with 6–12 arms instead of a true lineup was applied. See Chapter 24 herein for more on cancer detection.

CONCLUSION

Canine training in scent lineup using operant conditioning involves not only the canine sense of smell but also an ability to produce a firm association between target odor and response, reinforced by a reward. The odor lineup is a useful and relatively simple method of identification of odor samples especially when direct sniffing of materials/individuals is not possible. Trained dogs are able to identify an individual human on the basis of a scent sample at a rate that is statistically better than chance. Statistical criteria typical for biological experiments that are fulfilled by dogs identifying humans on the basis of scent are not sufficient for forensic purposes as evidence to be presented in courts, where near 100% certainty is sought. An extensive and variable system of control trials before actual identification trials does not always improve the validity and reliability of canine identification.

20 How U.S. Courts Deal with the "Black Box" of Canine Scent Identification

John Ensminger

Scientists called to review and testify regarding canine evidence must understand why their knowledge is being sought inside the judicial system. Trial lawyers are not peer reviewers, and judges and juries are not editors of scientific journals, yet they all can be as critical in their own ways as the system that scientists regularly encounter in trying to get their work published. As a witness in a criminal case, the scientist wants his or her expertise acknowledged and opinions accepted, yet the lawyer for the other side is likely to hammer repetitively at weaknesses that might be trivial in the peer-reviewing system of a journal. Some understanding of the use of science in trials will therefore be helpful to scientists whose perspectives are sought by the judicial system. This chapter will examine how scientific research on the ability of dogs to match scents of suspects to odors left at crime scenes has been taken into account during criminal trials.

Handlers have often been the only expert witnesses in tracking and scent lineup cases (though not all courts have deemed them experts), and battles of experts in such cases are often battles between the handler of the dog in the case and a handler called by the other side. That is beginning to change as more defense lawyers see the need to fault the work of a police handler by placing it alongside the procedures used by scientists in highly controlled experiments. If the trends described here continue, the use of scientific witnesses to question the validity of the practices of handlers will increase. Unfortunately, scent identification is not a heavily researched area, particularly in the United States, so finding a scientist willing to be subjected to the withering fire from an attorney for the other side may not be easy. In any case, handlers should familiarize themselves with the developing research on scent identification and should also be aware of how that research may be used to undermine their claims as to the operation of their dogs.

Tracking is a discipline where the dog is trained to track, sometimes footstep to footstep, the path a person takes. The track may be started with an article believed to have been touched or otherwise been in contact with an unknown suspect. Other times, the dog may range across an area in an attempt to pick up the track or scent of an individual who left the scene of a crime.[1] Scent identification, on the other hand, uses a methodology that more closely follows scent discrimination disciplines such as those involving narcotics or explosives canines. First a process of gathering and storing odor is performed by collecting scent, perhaps on a sterile pad, and storing in nonpermeable containers. Next, items from a person of interest (or suspect) are placed in a lineup. Lastly, the dog is prescented to the stored odor and asked to locate that same odor in the lineup. Some variations and hybrids of these procedures have been developed by certain police departments, such as station identifications where a dog is prescented odor at one location, perhaps outside a police station, and asked to find a matching individual inside the station.

DEVELOPMENT OF FOUNDATIONAL REQUIREMENTS
FOR TRACKING EVIDENCE

Tracking law in the United States grew out of the experience of using dogs to track humans, beginning most unfortunately with their use to track runaway slaves before and during the Civil War, but soon adapted to catch escaped convicts and perpetrators of crimes where scent was presumed to be available in sufficient abundance at the scene of a crime.[2] The ability of certain dogs, particularly bloodhounds, to follow the trail after a crime needed no detailed explanation as it was "common knowledge that dogs may be trained to follow the tracks of a human being with considerable certainty and accuracy."[3]

Early tracking cases often involved dogs following a trail to a suspect or to a location where a suspect was found. In 1921, in the case of *West Virginia v. McKinney*, dogs trailed to a house in which a suspect was sleeping. The suspect was aroused and taken 75–100 yd. from house. Dogs were put on his trail outside the house and "went to him and gave manifestations of their identity of him as the person they had been trailing."[4] A 1979 Vermont case describes a tracking dog finding a man hiding in tall grass whom the police handcuffed. The dog then went up to the man, as he was standing between the officers, "and placed her paws on his chest, indicating that she had found the person for whom she was searching."[5] Canine identification has been accepted as occurring even when dogs were taken off the trail but later encountered a suspect in a patrol car or a police station.[6] "Station identifications" have even become something of a formal procedure with some California police departments.[7]

Through much of American judicial history, tracking evidence was admitted and considered without the benefit of scientific experts or citation of scientific publications, though as early as 1903 in *Brott v. Nebraska*, the Supreme Court of Nebraska found weakness in the common-knowledge argument and rejected the idea that any set of foundational requirements could overcome this weakness. That court responded to the effort of the prosecutor to introduce tracking evidence with the following analysis:

> It is a commonly accepted notion that [a bloodhound] will start from the place where a crime has been committed, follow for miles the track upon which he has been set, find the culprit, confront him, and *mirabile dictu*, by accusing bay and mien declare, "Thou art the man." This strange misbelief is with some people apparently incorrigible. It is a delusion which abundant actual experience has failed to dissipate.... But it is nevertheless a delusion—an evident and obvious delusion. The sleuthhound of fiction is a marvelous dog, but we find nothing quite like him in real life. We repudiate utterly the suggestion that there is any common knowledge of the bloodhound's capacity for trailing which would justify us in accepting his conclusions as trustworthy under circumstances like those disclosed by the present record.... To get a nearer and clearer view of the nature of the evidence erroneously admitted, let us consider closely what trailing is. The path of every human being through the world, at every step, from the cradle to the grave, is strewn with the putrescent excretions of his body.[8] This waste matter is in process of decomposition. It is being resolved into its constituent elements, and its power to make an impression on the olfactory nerves of a dog or other animal becomes fainter and fainter with lapse of time. Under favorable conditions, such as free exposure to air and sun, every compound particle is rapidly separated into its original parts, and when the dissolution is complete its characteristic scent is gone. The bloodhound is endowed with a remarkably keen scent. He has great ability for differentiating smells. His method of trailing is simple and well understood. Particles of waste matter given off by a particular individual fall to the ground, and while undergoing chemical change come in contact with the olfactory nerves of the dog, and produce an impression which he is able to recognize, as distinct and different from all other impressions. Hence for a short time a man may be easily trailed in the woods or in the open country by the effluvia in his wake. But in a city, and after the lapse of considerable time, the trailing is obviously more difficult, and often manifestly impossible. But difficulties do not deter the bloodhound from pursuing his business. He trails as best he can. He always follows some scent, and he goes somewhere. Undoubtedly nice and delicate questions are time and again presented to him for decision. But the considerations that induced him in a particular case to adopt one conclusion rather

than another cannot go to the jury.... In attempting to separate one smell from ten, twenty, fifty, or a hundred similar smells with which it is intermixed and commingled, it is highly probable, if not quite certain, that the bloodhound undertakes a task altogether beyond his capacity. Like other dogs, he has his limitations, and they must be recognized in courts of justice, if not elsewhere. That the conclusions of the bloodhound are generally too unreliable to be accepted as evidence in either civil or criminal cases is, we believe, the teaching of that common knowledge and ordinary experience which we may rightfully bring to the examination of this subject. If such evidence were held to be legal evidence, it would, standing alone, sustain a conviction; and courts, in this golden age of enlightenment, would now and again be under the humiliating necessity of adjudging that some citizen be deprived of his property, his liberty, or his life, because, forsooth, within 24 or 40 hours after the commission of a crime, a certain dog indicated by his conduct that he believed the scent of some microscopic particles supposed to have been dropped by the perpetrator of the crime was identical with, or closely resembled, the scent of the person who had been accused and put upon trial. There are, we know, some cases in this country which hold that this kind of evidence is competent, but it seems the judicial history of the civilized world is against them. The bloodhound is, we admit, frequently right in his conclusions, but that he is frequently wrong is a fact well attested by experience. What he does in trailing may be regarded as the declaration of a disinterested party, but, so regarded, the authorities are opposed to its admission. It is unsafe evidence, and both reason and instinct condemn it.[9]

Despite the Nebraska Supreme Court's declaration that "the judicial history of the civilized world" was against those cases that had accepted tracking evidence, by far the majority of states had already or later accepted tracking evidence as long as certain foundational elements could be established.[10]

In 1968, the Court of Special Appeals of Maryland considered that, in deciding which way to take Maryland on the issue of the admissibility of tracking evidence, a detailed summary of the treatment of such evidence in other jurisdictions was appropriate.[11] This court observed that states that rejected tracking evidence tended to say that such evidence made the dog into a witness, whereas states that accepted the evidence were inclined to see the handler as a valid, even expert, interpreter of the dog's behavior. The court felt that "[o]nce the proper foundation has been laid the evidence may be used to identify the accused as the perpetrator or for some other reason as long as the evidence is corroborated."[12] Nowhere in this court's analysis does *science* or *scientific* appear.

Courts occasionally had to consider objections to the admission of tracking evidence based on a lack of scientific support. In a 1978 case, *California v. Craig*, a dog was scented on the interior of a vehicle and followed a path from the vehicle to the point where the detention occurred.[13] The defendants objected that the canine evidence did not meet scientific requirements.[14] The court rejected the argument, saying that cases dealing with "inanimate scientific techniques" did not apply, because such cases did not deal with the "specific recognition of one animal's ability to utilize a subjective, innate capability," and elaborated:

When dealing with animate objects, however, we must assume each and every unit is an individual and is different from all others. Within one breed of dog, or even with two dogs of the same parentage, it cannot be said each dog will have the same exact characteristics and abilities. Therefore, while the reliability of a machine can be duplicated and passed down the assembly line with relative ease, the abilities and reliability of each dog desired to be used in court must be shown on an individual basis before evidence of that dog's efforts is admissible. We simply cannot say all dogs can trail a human, or even that all dogs of specific breeds can do so.

The court said that a dog's ability to trail a human was a fact that could be proven by expert testimony from a person "sufficiently acquainted with the dog, his training, ability and past record of reliability."

A 1997 New York case that involved dog tracking concluded that "no scientific principle or procedure was at issue," because the dog's work was "an investigative rather than a scientific procedure." Again, all that was required for admission of the tracking evidence was a proper foundation.[15]

In a 2004 California case, however, 6 days after an incident, a suspect was arrested, and a scent sample was taken by rubbing the palm and back of both hands with a sterile gauze pad. The dog was scented to this odor and then trailed from the location of the shootings involved to a location where the suspect may have gotten into a car. Dr. Lawrence Myers, according to the court, testified for the defense "that dog scent tracking has scientific components, but it is not a science. There were no scientific studies concluding what human scent is or how it dissipates or degrades." The trailing in the case took place 5 days after the crime, and Myers indicated that, according to the court, "a scent trail more than three days old is less reliable than a more recent one."

> Myers testified that the method used here was not scientifically appropriate because the detective who had prepared the scent pads had been at the crime scene and had walked the trail at least twice before [the handler] was called in.

The California appellate court was particularly concerned with the fact that the dog was not deployed until 6 days after the crime but stated more broadly the following:

> In the absence of an adequate foundation from scientific or academic sources as to how long the scent would remain at the location, whether every person has a unique scent such as to permit an accurate basis for scent identification, the powers of the dog as to scent and discrimination, and the adequacy of the certification procedures for scent identifications…, the evidence was erroneously admitted in this case.[16]

It was not clear that deployment of the dog closer to the time of the crime would have resulted in evidence concerning a trail being rejected.

SCENT LINEUPS

In a case considered by the Sixth Circuit in 1982,[17] a dog was scented to a sandal left by a perpetrator fleeing a bank robbery and picked the defendant from a lineup by placing his head on the defendant's lap. The dog's prior experience, according to a concurring opinion, had consisted primarily of being scented to an individual and matching that person's scent to an object in a row of objects. The majority opinion discussed tracking criteria but accepted the evidence as admissible, though not to be given undue weight. The concurrence noted the following:

> No foundation was laid which would allow the trial court or a reviewing court to conclude that the use of tracking dogs in lineup identifications is reliable nor was there evidence that the lineup procedure is generally accepted as reliable either by those who train and handle dogs or law enforcement agencies.

Again, however, there was no discussion, even in this hesitant concurrence, of any scientific requirement for tracking or scent identification.

In 1983, a New York federal district court made minimal reference to science where a dog had been scented to a sock worn by a suspect and given an array of tools, including bolt cutters used in a break-in of a post office. The prosecution wanted to use the object lineup as evidence that the defendant had touched the bolt cutters, but the defense argued that it had not been established that individuals have unique odors. The district court, in *U.S. v. McNiece*,[18] stated the following:

> [I]t must be noted that defendant does not dispute the fact that the relevant scientific data support the conclusion that a well-trained dog is able to distinguish among the "odors" of specific individuals and is able to detect the "odor" of a particular individual on a particular object [Citing Davis 1974; Hafez 1969[19]; Kalmus 1955]. In fact, defendant's own olfaction expert, Dr. Robert E. Henkin, unqualifiedly admitted on cross examination at the pretrial hearing that dogs possess these capabilities.

The court acknowledged that it had not been conclusively established that individuals have unique odors but again focused on the fact that a dog is an animate object, to be distinguished from a scientific instrument.

[A]lthough we have, to this point, evaluated the dog as though it is an "instrument," and therefore for the purposes of our analysis equivalent to the spectograph [sic, spectrograph], the nonmechanical, animate nature of the dog distinguishes the evidence it produces from the evidence produced by a mechanical, inanimate instrument. Unlike a precise, mechanical instrument such as the spectograph [sic, id.], which jurors may view as incapable of error, a dog may be seen as more "human-like" and therefore subject to lapses in judgment and perception. Thus, because of the lesser potential prejudicial impact that evidence resulting from a dog's identification may have on the jury, courts need not apply as strict a standard when considering the admissibility of such evidence as they are required to apply when considering the admissibility of the seemingly flawless evidence produced by a mechanical instrument.

The court felt that jury instructions and a substantial amount of other evidence of guilt could overcome any weakness in the canine evidence.

[T]he jury will be instructed that it may not convict defendant on the basis of the dog's identification alone; rather, it may use such evidence to convict defendant only if it first finds that all the other evidence in the case establishes defendant's guilt by at least clear and convincing evidence. Thus, unlike the case of the spectograph [sic], in which the nonlikelihood that two persons could produce identical spectograms [sic, spectrograms] has been established and the evidence of which, even when standing alone, may be sufficient to convict a defendant, evidence of a dog's identification, under this instruction, could only be used by the jury to convict in cases where a substantial amount of other evidence is present.

The court thus flirted with the fact that there were scientific aspects of the evidence but remained within the traditional experiential analysis of tracking cases.

In a 1984 Arizona case, *Arizona v. Roscoe*,[20] a trained dog made a series of scent matches between items and locations the victim and defendant may have touched or been present at with scent samples from each individual, to which the defense objected that there was no general acceptance of the procedures. The court stated the following:

It was not the theories of Newton, Einstein or Freud which gave the evidence weight; if so, the *Frye* test should have been applied. It was, rather, Preston's knowledge, experience and integrity which would give the evidence weight and it was Preston who was available for cross-examination. His credentials, his experience, his motives and his integrity were effectively probed and tested. Determination of these issues does not depend on science; it is the exclusive province of the jury.

A footnote referred to "some support for this in the scientific data," citing a training manual (Davis 1974) and a 1955 article in the *British Journal of Animal Behaviour* (Kalmus 1955), but emphasized that "scientific data was not, however, the basis of the foundation for the evidence nor for its presentation to the jury." The court saw the scenting of the dog to both the victim and the defendant and its use in multiple contexts as evidence of its consistency, rather than considering that the multiple scents and trials may have effectively meant the dog was matching nothing at all.

In 1986, the Florida Supreme Court was sufficiently disturbed by the differences between tracking and a scent lineup to insist that more than a tracking foundation was necessary:

We do not rule out the use of dog scent-discrimination lineup evidence as a method of proof, but find that before it may be admitted it must be established that (1) this type of lineup evidence is reliable; (2) the specific lineup is conducted in a fair, objective manner; and (3) the dog used has been properly trained and found by experience to be reliable in this type of identification. In the instant case, the reliability of this type of lineup was not established, nor was the test conducted in a fair manner.

We conclude, therefore, that the admission of this particular lineup evidence was prejudicial error. Accordingly, we reverse appellant's conviction and remand for a new trial.[21]

There was, however, no discussion as to what kind of testimony would be needed to establish the specific evidentiary requirements.

In a 1999 Colorado case, a rather spontaneous scent lineup was conducted in a garage with a hand-cuffed defendant and some police officers who happened to be present.[22] The Colorado Supreme Court held that no scientific inquiry under *Daubert*[23] or *Frye*[24] was necessary. The court found that tracking was an "experience-based specialized knowledge which is not dependent on scientific explanation." The court did not distinguish the lineup from tracking, stating only that "the reliability of scent track-ing evidence is not dependent on the scientific explanation of canine olfaction." In 2002, a Texas appel-late court also found "little distinction between a scent lineup and a situation where a dog is required to track an individual's scent over an area traversed by multiple persons."[25]

In 2003, a California appellate court could not "ascertain why dog scent-discrimination evidence is distinguishable from dog scent-tracking evidence...."[26] The court said that the defendant had the opportunity to cast doubt on the scent match performed during the investigation, and had been able to do so with the aid of Dr. I. Lehr Brisbin. The court held that there was no error in admitting the evidence, as it was corroborated. Substantial noncanine evidence allowed another California appel-late court to say the following:

> While we acknowledge the issue of dog scent identification lineups is academically interesting, we conclude their efficacy need not be decided in this case because the dog evidence was not crucial to the prosecution's case. Even without Reilly, there was overwhelming circumstantial evidence that Hackett was the person who killed Hollis and ransacked the house.[27]

Thus, any error in admitting the evidence was harmless because the scent evidence was not crucial.

SCENT TRANSFER UNITS

The introduction of the scent transfer unit (STU), a suction device used to collect odor on a gauze pad (not too inaccurately described as a "modified dust buster"[28]), added a complication that the courts saw as having a scientific element, though not always requiring a hearing on its scientific validity. In a 2002 California case, a dog was scented to pads that had been inside an STU-100 when it was passed over seats in a van. Testimony indicated that the dog trailed in a police station to the separate cells of four suspects, providing evidence against four suspects. Concerning the STU, the court stated the following:

> The scent transfer unit is simply a device used to implement the obvious principle that scent travels in air. There is no novel scientific principle behind the use of suction to move air and the scent contained in it; it is the same principle at work in air filters in every home. *Kelly/Frye* does not require a founda-tional hearing on this principle in order to support the admission of testimony involving the use of the scent transfer unit.[29]

The court said that even if the admission of the station identifications or the evidence produced from the STU were to be deemed error, it was harmless given the weight of other evidence.[30]

Within a year, however, in *California v. Mitchell*,[31] an appellate found it "far from obvious that, assuming a vacuum device would transfer scent to a gauze pad under the protocol used in this case, that scent would not degrade or become contaminated." The court noted that certain bloodhound organizations might not be on board with use of the device:

> As reported in *The Baltimore Sun* in an article regarding California bloodhounds brought to the East Coast to investigate the anthrax incidents of 2001, the Law Enforcement Bloodhound Association and

the National Police Bloodhound Association have not endorsed the scent transfer unit, saying "it offers little advantage over using a gauze pad alone and in fact might confound matters."[32]

The court found that the STU was a novel device and that a hearing should have been held on the admissibility of evidence produced from its use:

> Difficulty in understanding the precise nature and parameters of a dog's ability to discriminate scents does not take this phenomenon out of the realm of science. The feats attributed to Reilly, both in training and in the scent lineup conducted in this case, are truly extraordinary. An object may have many scents. The scent on an object touched by a target person will include the scent of any other person who touched the object. Here, the prosecution asserted that at least two persons had touched the murder victim's shirt (Mitchell and the victim himself), and it may be that more than one person touched the bullets that were fired at the scene. Thus, to make a match, Reilly was required to compare the scent of every person who had touched the shirt with not only the scent of every person who touched the bullets, but also the scent of every person who had touched the detectives' chairs.

Yet this court also stated that "even if *Kelly* were not deemed to apply to scent identification evidence in general, a greater foundation than the one provided here is needed for its admission." Thus, an adjustment to the foundation requirements might be all that would be required to admit a scent identification procedure.

In 2004, a California appellate court determined that dog trailing is different from scent recognition, and as to the STU, stated the following:

> The dog handler who testified for the prosecution is not a scientist or an engineer; therefore, he is not qualified to testify about the characteristics of the STU or the unit's acceptance in the scientific community. There was also no proof that the dog handler used correct scientific procedures while employing the STU.[33]

The court said that the prosecution could not rely on anecdotes regarding the dog's capabilities.

> Instead, a foundation must be laid from academic or scientific sources regarding (a) how long scent remains on an object or at a location; (b) whether every person has a scent that is so unique that it provides an accurate basis for scent identification, such that it can be analogized to human DNA; (c) whether a particular breed of dog is characterized by acute powers of scent and discrimination; and (d) the adequacy of the certification procedures for scent identifications.... None of these foundational requirements were met in this case.

The defectiveness of the scent identification did not lead to a reversal, however, as the court concluded that it was not reasonably probable the jury would have reached a different result had the dog scent evidence been excluded. The conviction was affirmed.[34]

CALIFORNIA v. SALCIDO

Finally, in 2005, a full-scale evidentiary hearing was held on "whether human scent is unique; how long scent will remain at a location; how long captured scent will remain on a gauze pad; whether, as a breed, bloodhounds have acute powers of scent and scent discrimination; whether dogs can be trained to discriminate between scents, such as in a scent lineup...."[35] As to the STU, the trial court said that it had to be determined "(1) whether the STU [was] generally accepted as reliable in the relevant scientific community; (2) whether the witnesses testifying about the STU [were] properly qualified experts on the subject; and (3) whether the person performing the test in this case used correct scientific procedures."

The dog in the case was scented on gauze pads that, with the help of an STU, held odor from (1) the sill of a window where the perpetrator was thought to have gained entry to the house where the victim was stabbed and (2) the knife used in the crime. With these items for scenting, the dog tracked from the scene of the crime to a location where the defendant had been and also performed a station identification, where the dog led the handler to the suspect in a locked room and jumped on him.

Dr. Kenneth Furton testified for the prosecution regarding the use of an STU. He indicated that he thought it should be cleaned between uses, that there should be blank trials, and that it should be operated under specific protocols. He was apparently asked about the fact that some bloodhound associations had not approved use of the device. The court summarized his testimony as follows:

> Dr. Furton believes that for a technique to be scientifically reliable there must be a protocol and it must be established that the protocol works. A blank run between cases would help insure no contamination. Maintenance of the STU-100 requires only cleaning and storage. The unit is essentially a dust buster with a motor. There is little mechanical maintenance. Either it works or it doesn't. Dr. Furton listened to the testimony of FBI Agent Rex Stockham and in his opinion, the controls used by the FBI satisfy Dr. Furton's maintenance requirements. What Dr. Furton has read as well as what he has heard in Court satisfies him that a protocol has been set and testing has been done to show no carryover. This is consistent with his belief that a vigorous cleaning with alcohol would be sufficient to ensure no discernable carryover. He would be most comfortable if blanks were run between every test. His opinion regarding the STU is not affected by the fact that not every dog handlers' association had endorsed its use. Groups are resistant when one tries to raise their level of training.

It is to be noted that Dr. Furton subsequently published research on the STU (DeGreeff et al. 2011) examining the effectiveness of several sorbent materials and suggesting a cleaning protocol that could serve as a model for field operations.[36]

Dr. Brian Eckenrode also testified in *Salcido* regarding the STU and ran his own tests on the device. He specifically referred to the gauze pads used in the STU:

> In Dr. Eckenrode's opinion, the cotton gauze pads that agencies currently use in the United States with the scent transfer unit work for the purpose of absorbing scent. He believes that a cleaning protocol is good practice analytically even though he is not convinced that it is necessary because he is not convinced that there is carryover.

A Federal Bureau of Investigation (FBI) agent, Rex Stockham, testified that the STU is used nationally by the FBI. Stockham specifically called into question the testimony of a defense witness, Dr. Lawrence Myers:

> [Stockham] is familiar with Dr. Larry Meyers' [sic] claim that because the housing unit of the STU is porous, scent can transfer from one pad to another and contaminate the pad. Agent Stockham testified that there is no evidence to support this claim, and that Dr. Meyers has not tested the STU-I00. The housing unit is powder coated metal, not plastic. Only a small part of the unit is plastic. The scent of the plastic is a background smell that will not mask the freshest scent. The plastic part does not negatively affect the STU's reliability. Dogs can differentiate between multiple smells. A scent article with multiple scents is not "contaminated." Scent discrimination dogs and trailing dogs are trained to follow the freshest scent. There are no articles that have just one human scent on them. That is what is referred to as layering or "layered scent." For example, if four people contributed scent to a crime scene—one victim, one assailant, one police officer and one crime technician, a dog handler is trained to have the victim, the police officer and the technician at the start of the trail and the dog is trained to follow the "missing member." Using proper protocol, the operator relies on the dog to see if the STU is "contaminated." The dogs are trained to say "yes" or "no." If a blank pad with no scent article is put through the STU and there is no detectible carryover, the handler should get a negative response from the dog. In Agent Stockham's opinion, the STU is a reliable tool for field work. It has proven reliable in case studies and empirical studies. In Agent Stockham's opinion, the STU is forensically the best method for scent collection. He believes that this is the consensus of the relevant scientific community. Protocol, proficiency of the dog and use of the actual scent article are critical to the reliability of the method.[37]

Dr. Lawrence Myers, the defense expert, disparaged by Stockham, argued that the reliability of the STU was untested.

> The basis of [Myers'] opinion is as follows: 1. He is critical of the materials used in its construction, metal and plastic, because plastic is porous. 2. He prefers supercritical carbon dioxide, dry ice, as a cleaning material to alcohol. 3. Even if you improve the materials and the cleaning methods, you cannot trust that the STU will work properly due to contamination. You need regular chemical evaluations of the level of contamination. If you are going to use the instrument with dogs, you have to do tests with dogs. This evaluation would consist of obtaining odor with the STU, presenting the odor to the dogs, and having the scent match tested in a double blind situation. Neither the handler, dog, nor observer would know if there were any match present. He would also want to see a duplication of the test by an independent investigator.

Myers observed that one of Stockham's articles about the STU was peer-reviewed by the device's creator, William Tolhurst. He testified that he was "not happy" with the cleaning method used for the device. Although expressing confidence in the experts for the prosecution, "[h]e believes that there is always carryover because you cannot ever get anything clean, even in a laboratory." Nevertheless, Myers apparently acknowledged that an object can be cleaned sufficiently that carryover scents will not be detectible by dogs.

> His concern is that the cumulative contamination is never measured and he does not know how much contamination a dog can work through. Dr. Myers has not done any research to demonstrate that the cleaning protocols presently in place for the STU are inadequate to effectively clean the machine for forensic application in the field.

Stockham testified concerning how long scent remained at a location. Furton testified as to how long it will remain on a gauze pad. Furton described his own research relevant to the issue of the uniqueness of human scent. Stockham cited the research of Adee Schoon in the Netherlands on scent lineups, as did Myers on cross-examination.[38] Myers's evidence on this issue was summarized by the court as follows:

> "Canine detection" deals with the use of dogs and dog handler teams to identify a variety of chemicals, and includes the chemistry of scent. Scent is a series of chemicals detectible by sense of smell. Although the volatile compounds and particulates that comprise human scent have not all been identified, he believes that humans have an "odor signature" meaning certain chemicals are associated with the person. He believes that at least some of what dogs detect comes from both direct emissions of odor and skin rafts, which are portions of dead cells that are dropped off human bodies and that contain some scent compounds.

Nevertheless, the court said that Myers "does not agree with Dr. Furton's opinion that, to a reasonable certainty, human scent is unique." Myers described his own involvement with the research of Brisbin and Austad.

> Dr. Myers is familiar from before this case with the 1990 study by Lehr Brisbin and Steven Austad, *Testing the Individual Odour Theory of Canine Olfaction.*[39] Brisban [sic] performed experiments with three dogs and suggested in his article that his results called into question the use of dogs in human scent identification.... Dr. Myers peer reviewed the article. It almost wasn't published because Dr. Myers said he overstated the conclusion based upon limited samples. Brisban [sic] has not published any studies in the last approximately 10 years in the area of human scent discrimination, but Dr. Myers still considers him an individual to be included in the relevant scientific community. It would not surprise him to learn that Adee Schoon, in her 2002 book,[40] discussed how flawed Brisbin's results were.[41]

In addition to the testimony, Judge Rosenblatt stated that she had read 42 articles submitted by the prosecution. She concluded that the STU "is generally accepted as reliable in the scientific community"; that the experts had "established to a reasonable scientific certainty, human scent is unique"[42]; that "scent can remain on an object for days, months and even years, through bomb blasts, under water and in the elements"; that a human scent pattern, once on a gauze pad, remains despite dissipation over several months; that pulling "scent from an object using the STU does not degrade the scent"; and that experts had established "that dogs can be trained to accurately discriminate between human scents, such as in a scent lineup." Judge Rosenblatt's extensive analysis of the scientific issues in a scent lineup was entered into the record by the prosecution in a 2011 case, even though that case involved a station identification and not a scent lineup.[43]

Myers was also a defense witness in a 2009 California case, *California v. White*,[44] whose reservations were taken by the trial court as suggestions for improvement, not as going to the admissibility of the procedure. Here, Myers had raised the possibility of cueing by third parties, but the court was satisfied that this was not an issue as long as the handler did not know where the defendant's scent was placed.

COURTS BEGIN TO QUESTION VALIDITY OF SCENT LINEUPS

In a 2011 Texas case,[45] a handler ran lineups with three dogs against six paint cans, one of which had a gauze pad with the scent of the suspect and five of which had foils. The handler did not know the location of the suspect's scent pad among the cans, though other officers watching the procedure did know. The location of the scent pad was changed between the lineups with the three dogs. Dr. Kenneth Furton testified that the handler's methodology was reliable, though he expressed some qualms about the storage of the samples used in the lineup and acknowledged that from videos of prior cases, he could not always confirm the handler's determination that a dog was alerting. Furton said that the handler alone must decide when to call an alert.

In the same case, the defense called Dr. I. Lehr Brisbin, who testified in contrast that the methodology in the scent lineups was unreliable because (1) the handler used a leash during the lineups and could have cued the dogs; (2) the lineups were not double-blind, as the officer placing the gauze pads remained present, which could cue the handler or the dog as to the location of that pad; (3) the dogs after the first dog could have alerted at the same point as the first dog (presumably because the can with the target scent might now contain saliva or some other indicator from the first dog); (4) there were no blank trials in the lineups; (5) no "outside auditor" evaluated the handler's results; (6) the handler's records were not consistent with what Brisbin observed of the lineup ("Brisbin stated that the records indicated that the dog successfully alerted by baying, but contrary to the recorded observations, he saw the dog baying at every can."); and (7) the handler claimed to have an almost perfect record, indicating to Brisbin that the handler did not understand what he was observing.

Further criticism of the lineup might also have mentioned (1) reuse during trials of paint cans holding scent; (2) nonstatistical randomization of the placement of the can containing the odor in the lineup; (3) no preliminary trials to determine if any of the dogs used was working effectively at the time of the trials; (4) failure to determine if the suspect's odor was "attractive" to any of the dogs, reducing or eliminating the significance of some alerts (see Chapter 19 herein); and (5) no requirement that the handler call each alert (which may be identical with Brisbin's outside-auditor criticism).

The trial court concluded the following:

> Canine scent identification is not junk science, but it has not yet been developed to the point that it is accurate, repeatable, verifiable and reliable to the extent that it should be used as evidence in court.

The Texas appellate court determined that the record supported this finding as well as the trial court's suppression of the scent lineup evidence.

In a Texas murder case that involved a number of defendants prosecuted separately, and for whom appeals were taken over a number of years, a 2010 decision noted that scent lineups were the primary reason for convicting Richard Lynn Winfrey.[46] The other evidence consisted primarily of the defendant's own belief that he was the prime suspect. The court noted that even if the defendant's scent was at the crime scene, an article by Rex Stockham emphasized that this did not of itself establish complicity or a "direct or indirect relationship to the scene."[47] The appellate court entered a judgment of acquittal for the defendant.[48]

Scent lineups were not admitted into evidence in a Texas case that reached an appellate level in 2011.[49] The trial court made a number of findings of fact regarding the proffered scent lineup evidence, including that blank lineups without the defendant's scent were not run, that no validation testing was conducted, that there was no clearly accepted method for conducting scent lineups, that no literature was offered by the prosecution in support of the manner the scent lineups were conducted in the case, that the prosecution did not make available other experts regarding the procedures used in the case, and that it was unclear if the results could be duplicated by others following the same methods. The trial court also referred to defense evidence that the handler could have cued the dogs ("intentionally or unintentionally influenced") given the way the lineup was set up and performed.

The prosecution argued that the trial court had effectively applied Texas case law regarding scientific validation to the scent lineup evidence, rather than considering the use of the technique as one of experience, as with tracking. The Texas appellate court noted that "hard science methods of validation, such as assessing the potential rate of error or subjecting a theory to peer review," might be appropriate "for testing the reliability of fields of expertise outside of hard science in appropriate cases." This is one of the most important observations of any court in this area, given that many courts, once having decided to require the foundational elements for tracking, never considered whether scientific results might inform those elements beyond their historical roots or find additional complexity that could make them more than simplistic threshold questions. The appellate court said that a "trial court should not admit expert testimony that is connected to existing data only by the expert's own assertions." Therefore, the trial court did not abuse its discretion in excluding the scent lineup evidence.[50]

The U.S. experience with scent lineups may be leading to a decrease in the faith that courts give to this procedure, but the Netherlands, where much of the best research on scent lineups was conducted, has completely rejected the use of scent lineups to produce evidence in criminal trials.[51] (See Box 20.1.)

DUTCH SCENT IDENTIFICATION: WHAT WENT WRONG?—DANIELLE BES

BOX 20.1

During a period of about a century, canine scent identification in the Netherlands began, improved, and then came to an end. Why? It was due neither to failures of the dogs nor to a lack of interest in scent identification, but rather, to the only weak point in the whole method: the human factor.

In 1919, in a crime of breaking and entering in the region of Alkmaar, Netherlands, a police officer decided to use his search dog to identify a corpus delicti with a suspect. His idea was that if a dog can follow the scent of a human in a trail, he will be able to identify a suspect in a lineup. So he placed the suspect in a lineup with other police officers, brought his dog in, let the dog get the scent of the corpus delicti, and watched the dog do his work. Because of the fact that the dog went straight to the suspect, the police officer brought this evidence to court. The judge decided this method was a validated method and declared the suspect guilty of breaking and entering.[52]

Over time, the method evolved. The first change was not to put the suspect in the open but to hide the suspect behind a screen. This was to make sure the dog was making an identification based on scent and not on any human reaction. This approach continued for years.

One day in 1985 at Schiphol airport, Netherlands, a new approach changed the way scent identification was performed in the Netherlands. An incoming flight from Nicaragua had a passenger, Gonzalez, who was carrying a suitcase with drugs. A second passenger, Colombo, was suspected of being in control of the drug operation. Officers gave both men, as well as the other people on the plane, steel tubes and directed that they put the tubes in their pants for 10 min. The officers then put the scented tubes on the ground 50 cm (about 20 in.) apart. The scent dog was allowed to sniff the suitcase with the drugs. The dog went to the tube that had been scented by Colombo. This procedure was repeated to see if the dog was correct. Later on, the evidence was used in court.

Improvements continued to be made on the use of steel tubes for scent identification. In 1989, new guidelines for police procedures were issued under which a suspect and foils had to hold tubes in their hands for 10 min after washing their hands with perfume-free soap. The tubes were to be placed in jars and kept inside the jars for at least 15 min.[53]

More improvements continued to be made until 1997, when forensic technical procedures (Forensisch-Technische Norm) were established.[54] The Kluger-Hans (Clever Hans) effect was taken into account at this time. The dog and the handler had to remain unaware of the scent of the suspect (or suspects) in the lineup. Two dice were rolled to determine the order in which the tubes were placed in the lineup (with 36 possible options).[55] These procedures continued to be updated until 2006. (See discussion in Chapter 19 on the work of Adee Schoon and others regarding Dutch and European procedures.)

In 2007 (July 18), Dr. J.E.R. Frijters wrote to the Procureurs-Generaal (prosecutors general, the highest Dutch judges) that he suspected there were irregularities in how the procedure was being performed by the police. He had, for a long period, been serving as an expert witness in cases involving scent lineups and, along with another expert, J. Boksem, had concluded that there were problems with the scent lineup methodology. Some of their concerns had been voiced in a paper published in 2004 (Frijters and Boksem 2004). In analyzing the papers of Dr. Schoon, Dr. Frijters was familiar with her results indicating that dogs generally performed with an 8% error rate. He advertised in a law journal to get information from lawyers who had handled scent lineup cases and collected 114 reports from lawyers and experts who had been involved in such cases. He was, however, blocked from getting police reports, even anonymous reports, because of Dutch law prohibiting publication of such reports.[56]

In a 2004 article, Frijters and Boksem had referred to results of the Dutch police dog service (Dienst Levende Have Politie [DLHP]).[57] In those results, 44.6% of the tests resulted in identifications, 3.5% were disqualified, and 48.4% resulted in no identification. Frijters and Boksem focused on the 44.6% positive results, though of course, false negatives could occur when there is no identification (meaning that a guilty person was not identified). They argued that from 4% to 8% of the results could be false positives, though they acknowledged that with a second trial, the percentage of false positives might be reduced to less than 1%. Although the 114 reports were not a statistically reliable sample (only from lawyers with convicted suspects), he published his analysis, questioning the validity of the scent lineup technique. The Procureurs-Generaal found his arguments troubling enough to begin their own investigation.[58]

After a conversation with a police official (when the scent lineup was active), the judges began a statistical investigation of the results of scent identification. Two researchers[59] of the University of Delft, Netherlands, analyzed the results of the handlers statistically and reported to the judges on May 21, 2010.[60] The investigation focused on the dog–handler–helper teams that had performed over 180 tests, and raised statistical discrepancies regarding

8 of 12 handlers. Unfortunately, the actual statistics are not available and will not be for nearly 100 years under Dutch law.

This resulted in a major investigation of all the handlers, almost all of whom were interrogated, even those whose results were not put into question by the report of the Delft University researchers.[61] On April 6, 2011, the College van Procureurs-Generaal (College of Prosecutors-General) elected to discontinue the use of scent identification as evidence admissible in court. The possibility of false positives was a major concern of the judges.[62]

After the investigation, four handlers were found guilty of improperly performing the procedure by knowing where the scent of the suspect was in lineups. In other words, the procedure was not being performed in a double-blind manner. Three handlers were found not guilty because specific instances of misconduct could not be established with regard to them.[63]

With proper safeguards, scent identification procedures should be allowed in police investigations. The lawyer of the suspect as well as the prosecutor should have the chance to be at the scent lineup and verify that protocols are being followed by those performing the procedure. Scent lineup evidence should only be admitted in court, however, when there is additional evidence available.

HOW DO COURTS DEAL WITH THE "BLACK BOX"?

The "black box" description of canine-produced evidence is a scientific concept, or a distillation of one, but it would be simplistic, indeed inaccurate, to say courts ignore it. As far back as *Brott* in 1903, U.S. courts have been concerned with allowing the behavior of dogs to provide evidence of identification. Saying that it was not the dog that was testifying but the handler familiar with the dog's behavior gave some comfort to courts that wanted to acknowledge the repeatedly successful social experience of dogs tracking from crime scenes to a place where a perpetrator was found. Even here, there was a requirement that there be additional evidence, corroboration, of what the dog's actions were being taken as indicating.

When dogs began to be used not to trail an odor but to distinguish the odor of one human from others, and to indicate that such an odor left at a crime scene was identical to an odor on a gauze pad or steel tube, some courts initially accepted the arguments of handlers that the process was nearly identical with what happens when a dog on a track loses it for a few minutes and then casts about and finds it again. In tracking, courts had been concerned that a dog could focus on human scent and that dogs with the propensity to leave the track of the perpetrator and follow that of a deer that crossed the path had always been considered unsuitable for the work, that is, unreliable. Dogs that were reliable in tracking were often automatically considered reliable in scent lineups, without any scientific evidence for such a conclusion. When the scent from the crime scene began to be obtained with a piece of equipment that was patented in 1998, the STU-100, courts began to insist that there be evidence that the introduction of this instrument had not somehow corrupted the process, and being generally satisfied that it had not, they blessed its use by police canine handlers.

Because scent lineups involved comparison of scents of different individuals, courts began to be concerned with the question that scientists had been asking for some time, whether each individual has an odor that dogs could distinguish from that of all other people. After all, what if the odor of the perpetrator from the crime scene was similar but not identical to that of a suspect? Was the dog making a specific identification or just indicating that two individuals might smell alike because of genetic and environmental similarities in their backgrounds and lives? Such questions began to be asked, and the testimony of scientists who had published research in the area began to be deemed essential to answer such questions. Answering such general questions, however, was often deemed enough to allow in the description of the handler how he had gathered scent at the crime scene, how he had gathered scent from the suspect, and under what circumstances he had created a situation in which the dog could behave in such a way as to match these two items of scent.

What was not asked by courts often enough, and far too often was not even raised by defense counsel, was what sort of error rates even the best of dogs in the most ideal experimental conditions could have in matching scents.[64] Reliability in much of American case law on scent identification lacks any statistical aspect. There was also too little investigation as to what sorts of errors, such as cueing, might make the results of a dog in a field procedure, such as a station identification, appear much better than would be the case in a laboratory environment, where variables can be identified and controlled. This has been and continues to be the major failure across a number of American courts and their decisions when it comes to the evaluation of scent identification evidence.

Finally, and only in the new century, some courts began to recognize that scent lineups had been themselves the subject of intense research and that there are error rates of false identification even in sophisticated procedures involving sterile environments, multiple scent stations, double-blind environments in which no one in the presence of the dog knows where the scent of the suspect is, repetitive cleaning of the scent stations and even the floors on which the dogs walked, and multiple dogs. Comparison of these laboratory testing environments with those used by individual police dog handlers with paint cans and STU-100s finally began to disturb some judges.

As discussed in detail in Chapter 19 herein, one line of research indicates that in order to eliminate false identifications in the scent lineups examined in one research project, at least three dogs had to be used, with various types of preliminary trials that might easily preclude a final test for identification from being conducted at all. This number of dogs and handlers is generally not practical, yet it raises the question of whether scent lineups, with fewer dogs and fewer controls and greater risk of false identifications, should be accepted by courts at all.[65]

ENDNOTES

1. Dogs have sometimes been trained solely to recognize the presence of a human, without any specific individual being sought. Lloyd (1948) records that in the Second World War, dogs trained to accompany reconnaissance patrols in no-man's land were trained "to recognize human scent (body odor) in precisely the same manner that a gundog recognizes game scent; on recognizing the prey the dog 'froze' on point like a Pointer or Setter."

2. In *Bob (a slave) v. Alabama*, 32 Ala. 560, 1858 WL 538 (1858), a pre-Civil War case heard by the Alabama Supreme Court, "negro dogs" were used to track from the location at which a man was shot. The dogs tracked in the direction that the shooting victim had come from, which was presumed to be where the shooter had gone. When shoe tracks were found at a point the dogs led the search party to, it was presumed they were the tracks of the perpetrator. A slave with the same shoe size was arrested, tried, and convicted, but the Alabama Supreme Court reversed, finding that certain confessions should not have been admitted. For the early history of tracking in the American South by a judge who lived through some of it, see McWhorter (1920). For a detailed analysis of this history, see Ensminger (2012), Chapter 3: History and Judicial Acceptance of Tracking and Trailing Evidence.

3. *Hodge v. Alabama*, 98 Ala. 10, 13, 13 So. 385 (1893).

4. *West Virginia v. McKinney*, 88 W.Va. 400, 106 S.E. 894, 895 (Sup. Ct. 1921).

5. *Vermont v. Bourassa*, 137 Vt. 62, 65, 399 A. 2d 507, 510 (Sup. Ct. 1979).

6. *O'Quinn v. Georgia*, 153 Ga. App. 467, 265 S.E. 2d 824 (Ct. App. 1980).

7. *California v. Chavez*, B166473, 2004 WL 1173075 (Cal. App. 2 Dist. 2004). For extensive analysis of station identifications, see Ensminger et al. (2010).

8. In 2009, a North Carolina appellate court referred to the testimony of a canine handler that "the tracking dog could follow the scent of a person based on 'riffs,' or dead skin cell put off during high adrenaline situations." *North Carolina v. Cross*, 2009 WL 2177766 (2009). This is similar to the description given by a famous handler, William Syrotuck, who in his book, *Scent and the Scenting Dog*, originally published in 1972, described "airborne rafts coming to rest on the ground," left by a person walking.

9. *Brott v. Nebraska*, 70 Neb. 395, 97 NW 593 (1903). The Illinois Supreme Court reached the same conclusion, with nearly identical reasoning, 11 years later. *Illinois v. Pfanschmidt*, 262 Ill. 411, 104 N.E. 804 (1914).

10. For lists of states accepting and rejecting tracking evidence, see Ensminger (2012), pp. 27–28.

11. *Terrell v. Maryland*, 3 Md. App. 340, 239 A. 2d 128 (Ct. Spec. Appeals 1968).

12. In *Connecticut v. Kelly*, No. CR0661742, 2009 WL 323481 (Superior Court of Conn., January 8, 2009), for instance, the court said that "to the extent the state demonstrates to the jury that the defendant was, in fact, the man seated in the driver seat of the parked car that Daro jumped up on, and was also one of the men being questioned inside the house where Daro subsequently jumped up on its back door, then a jury can reasonably infer that Daro identified the defendant."

13. *California v. Craig*, 86 Cal. App. 3d 905, 150 Cal. Rptr. 676 (Ct. App. 1978).

14. The defendants cited *California v. Kelly*, 17 Cal. 3d 24, 130 Cal. Rptr. 144, 549 P. 2d 1240 (1976), describing California's history of application of the federal test from *Frye v. U.S.*, 293 F. 1013 (D.C. Cir. 1923).

15. *New York v. Roraback*, 242 A.D. 2d 400, 662 N.Y.S. 2d 327 (App. Div.1997).

16. *California v. Gutierrez*, B163632, 2004 WL 723161 (Cal. App. 2Dist. 2004) Myers' assertion that there are no scientific studies on what makes up human scent could now be challenged. See Meadow et al. (2015).

17. *U.S. v. Gates*, 680 F. 2d 1117 (6th Cir. 1982).

18. 558 F. Supp. 612 (ED N.Y. 1983).

19. M.W. Fox and M. Bekoff, who wrote the chapter on dog behavior in Hafez's book, described the research of Konrad Most from the 1920s, where a wheel suspended by a pulley system was used to demonstrate that dogs were able to track by smelling (1) earth odor from compression of soil where a person stepped; (2) plant odor from stepping on vegetation, such as grass; (3) odor traces from shoes and shoe polish; (4) odor traces from decaying animal or other organic matter; and (5) body odor that was specific to a particular person. Yet if a dog was following tracks of one person, which connected with identical tracks of another person who was also stepping on soil and grass, the dog would continue to follow the second person. This might indicate that factors other than individual odor were important in tracking, and arguably in identification. Humphrey and Warner (1934), writing 6 years after Most's 1928 paper, noted that Most's work called into question whether a dog will always continue to follow a human's trail when that trail has been overlaid by others. For pictures of Most's device, see Gerritsen and Haak (2010), pp. 100–101.

20. 145 Ariz. 212, 700 P. 2d 1312 (1984).

21. *Ramos v. Florida*, 496 So. 2d 121 (1986).

22. *Colorado v. Brooks*, 975 P. 2d 1105, 81 A.L.R. 5th 779 (Colo. Sup. Ct., 1999).

23. *Daubert v. Merrell Dow Pharmaceuticals, Inc.*, 509 U.S. 579, 113 S. Ct. 2786, 125 L.Ed. 2d 469 (1993).

24. *Frye v. U.S.*, 54 App. D.C. 46, 293 F. 1013 (1923).

25. *Winston v. Texas*, 78 S.W. 3d 522 (Ct. App. 2002). See also *Michigan v. Giles*, No. 275207, 2008 WL 2436529 (Ct. App. 2008), 769 N.W. 2d 683 (2009) (order denying leave to appeal) (court was "not persuaded" evidence from scent lineups "was of such a 'scientific' nature as to necessitate application of *Daubert* to the scent lineup").

26. *California v. Demirdjian*, No. B157230, 2003 WL 1963204, *affirmed* 144 Cal. App. 4th 10, 50 Cal. Rptr. 3d 154 (2006).

27. *California v. Hackett*, B154152, 2003 WL 463976 (Cal. App. 2d Dist. 2003). The harmless-error argument shows up repeatedly in scent identification decisions.

28. *California v. Mitchell*, 110 Cal. App. 4th 772, 2 Cal. Rptr. 3d 49 (Ct. App. 2003).

29. *California v. Sandoval*, B154152, 2002 WL 519848 (Cal. App. 2d Dist. 2002). Eckenrode et al. (2006) found that the device "has a significant trapping efficiency at ambient temperature." The parameters of operating an STU have not been defined beyond basic instructions of the manufacturer, and the amount of time the device should operate, how close it should be to the source, and how large an area it should cover may vary considerably from operator to operator.

30. Station identifications, particularly popular in California, may be an attempt to avoid using scent lineups and the lines of research that have indicated that only very carefully controlled trials can produce scientifically significant results. Courts have too readily admitted such procedures conceived by handlers in the field. Because some period of tracking or trailing is involved, courts have accepted the procedures as substantially identical to a bloodhound's following a perpetrator from a crime scene, failing to appreciate that an identification is implicit in the results of the procedure and the choices available to the dog are often very different than applies in a tracking situation. See *California v. Oudin*, G050682, 2015 WL 3645861 (Ct. App. 2015). The fact that a dog might track correctly but not identify the correct individual at the end of the tracking has also received too little attention. See Curran et al. (2010).

31. *California v. Mitchell*, 110 Cal. App. 4th 772, 2 Cal. Rptr. 3d 49 (Ct. App. 2003).

32. Citing Shane, S., FBI's Use of Bloodhounds in Anthrax Probe Disputed, *The Baltimore Sun*, October 29, 2002.

33. *California v. Willis*, 115 Cal. App. 4th 379, 9 Cal. Rptr. 3d 235 (Ct. App. 2004).

34. For a discussion of improvements being made on the STU-100, see Prada et al. (2015), at 56–57.

35. *California v. Salcido*, GA052057 (March 10, 2005).

36. See also DeGreeff et al. (2012).

37. Many of the same arguments were made by Furton and Stockham in *California v. Elias*, B224372, 2011 WL 3949808 (Ct. App. 2011).

38. There was no discussion as to how the procedures used in the case before the court would compare to the protocols developed by Schoon.

39. Brisbin and Austad (1991). A version in advance of publication was presumably made available in 1990.

40. Schoon and Haak (2002).

41. Testimony in a 2013 California case was to the effect that the handler had discussed his methods with Dr. Schoon and that she had "approved his procedures." The handler used only four stations in his line-ups, fewer than what Schoon standardly recommended. *California v. Childs*, No. B236982, 2013 WL 4034206 (Ct. App. 2013).

42. More recent research has tended to confirm that each human has a specific odor. Xu et al. (2007) sought to determine whether "individual chemical fingerprints" could be found in human sweat samples using gas chromatography/mass spectrometry (GC/MS). This team expected "the individual chemical signature to be multivariate in nature, even if in part or in whole of genetic origins, and so no one compound is likely to be uniquely and universally characteristic of a specific individual." Agapiou et al. (2015), looking at volatile organic compounds (VOCs) that might be emitted by victims at disaster sites, and therefore be detectable by chemical sensors being developed, discussed odor coming from sweat, urine, breath, and other sources. They noted that breath and skin are major sources of human VOCs (see also Martinez-Lozano et al. 2013; Statheropoulos et al. 2014). Skin, accounting for almost 15% of a human's body weight, emits VOCs continuously, though "glandular secretion and skin bacteria may differ considerably between individuals, giving rise to highly disparate VOC profiles." Additional variation is added by diet, disease, and other factors. Nevertheless, "the chemical nature and the identities of the human markers perceived by dogs remain unknown, as does the true sensitivity and selectivity data." The fact that chemical sensors may establish that individual humans have unique odor patterns, however, does not establish that dogs recognize the same patterns as are detected with such equipment and procedures. Meadow et al. (2015) used high-throughput sequencing to characterize the "airborne bacterial contribution" of individuals in sanitized climate chambers and found that individual "[b]acterial clouds" from individuals were statistically distinct, demonstrating that "individuals release their own personalized microbial cloud."

43. *California v. Watts*, B214517, 2011 WL 2150147 (Ct. App. 2011).

44. No. B204494, 2009 WL 3111677 (Super. Ct. 2009).

45. *Texas v. Dominguez*, 425 S.W. 3d 411 (Ct. App. 2011).

46. *Winfrey v. Texas*, 323 S.W. 3d 875, (Tex. Crim. App. 2010), reversing 291 SW3d 68 (Tex. App. 2009); motion for sufficiency review denied, 2011 WL 130492 (Ct. App. 2011).

47. Stockham et al. (2004). The court also cited Andrew Taslitz (1990), who had discussed the differences between a dog's function in drug detection and in a scent lineup.

48. Citing *Winfrey*, Professor Jennifer Lauren (2013) of the University of Texas School of Law noted that "dog scent experts have a curious habit of intervening late in cases in which other forensic evidence has proved unsuccessful in linking identified suspects to crimes."

49. *Texas v. Smith*, 335 S.W. 3d 706 (Ct. App. 2011).

50. In a separate suit by Richard Lynn Winfrey against the dog handler, the Fifth Circuit reversed the trial court's grant of summary judgment for the defendants on grounds of qualified immunity. The Fifth Circuit concluded that sufficient evidence had been presented that the handler had cued his dog that summary judgment was inappropriate. The evidence of cueing was the testimony of another handler, but there was no additional discussion of scientific research or testimony provided by any researcher concerning cueing. *Winfrey v. San Jacinto County*, No. 11-20555, 481 Fed. Appx. 969, 2012 WL 3062159 (5th Cir. 2012).

51. For discussion of procedures in Argentina and Finland, see Prada et al. (2015), at 88–90.

52. Weekblad van het Recht, W9022.

53. Crombag, Van Koppen, Wagenaar, Dubieuze zaken p. 220–228, 2006, 6ᵉ druk, Olympus.

54. Forensisch-technische norm 325.01 and Forenisch-technische norm 326.01.

55. Frijters, Dobbelen en positievoorkeuren bij canine geuridentificatieproeven, Expertise en recht, 2008-1.

56. Broeders, De kwalijke reuk van de geuridentificatieproef, Expertise en Recht, 2008.
57. Dienst Levende Have Politie (in English, "Police Livestock Service"), which deploys horses as well as dogs.
58. Unfortunately, the investigation of the judges will not, under Dutch law, be opened for public inspection until 100 years after the criminal proceedings closed.
59. Professor Geurt Jongbloed and Dr. F.H. van der Meulen.
60. Letter to Mr. Frijters van Het college van procureurs-generaal, 2011.
61. Mr. Dick Evegaars gave this information to the author in a telephone call, but the facts were never published.
62. Letter to Mr. Frijters van Het college van procureurs-generaal, 2011.
63. Broeders, De kwalijke reuk van de geuridentificatieproef, Expertise en recht, 2008-1.
64. In *Texas v. Dominguez*, 425 S.W.3 411 (Ct. App. 2011), the handler claimed 100% success in the tests involved in the case, which Dr. Furton "conceded … was uncommon." The fact that no research has claimed such perfection should have received greater attention.
65. This is functionally the same result as argued for by Taslitz (1990), though in theory, a sufficiently large program could be established to conduct admissible evidence from scent lineups. As argued by Danielle Bes in the box in this chapter, the use of scent lineups during investigations, but not to produce evidence to be used at trial, is not to be discouraged.

Section V

Uses in Conservation and Remediation

Dogs can eat, and have been used to hunt, many types of animals, so using them to survey endangered and threatened species is a logical extension of their capabilities. An ancient Buddhist text, *The Jataka* (Cowell 1895, p. 303), describes a hunter who used dogs to find iguanas in their burrows. Although insects are not a common part of the human diet, a South American canid, the hoary fox (*Pseudalopex vetulus*), subsists predominantly on insects, particularly termites and dung beetles (Courtenay et al. 2006). Charles Hamilton Smith (1839), visiting South America in the first half of the nineteenth century and writing about a variety of now rare or extinct canids, such as the crab-eating aguara dog (classified by him as *Dusicyon canescens*), described them as eating "fish, crabs, limpets, lizards, toads, serpents, and insects." It is thus no surprise that any animal's lair, scat, trail, or food source can provide an odor that can be used in surveying population levels or, in the case of invasive species, finding and eliminating a pest.

FINDING SCAT

Finding scat, a frequent responsibility of dogs used in conservation detection, continues an ancient function of tracking and hunting dogs. Late medieval hunters developed different names for the scat of the animals they hunted. A book written in the early 15th century (Edward, Second Duke of York, *The Master of the Game*) states that the excrement of hart was called *fumes*; that of buck and roebuck the same or *croteys*, wild boar, bears, and wolves *lesses* (*laisses* in French); hare and conies *croties*; fox *the wagging* or *fiantes*; badger *the wardrobe*; and otter *spraintes* (the latter being found by water dogs). The lymer (or limer, a dog responsible for tracking but not generally used in bringing down the game, for which greyhounds were employed) was rewarded for finding droppings, which would often be displayed on a plate for the lord for whose pleasure the hunt was being held. The experienced huntsman was expected to be able to tell the age of a hart, how recently the droppings were left, whether the animal was in a rut, whether it was diseased, and other particulars on which he would advise whether it was worth hunting. The accuracy of his predictions determined the favors the chief huntsman would receive from a king or lord. (Hunting with dogs continues to be vital in certain cultures. See Koster and Takersley 2012; Lupo 2011.)

Training and using dogs for conservation and eradication purposes on the basis of finding scat requires that the dogs discriminate the species-specific odor of scat and ignore scat from other species. This is a more natural behavior for dogs than working in a scent lineup, and conservation work often involves searching rugged terrain and negotiating woodland, thick brush, water, changes in wind direction, and weather extremes. The target odor of scat and other means of identifying target species for conservation dogs, such as lairs and trails, involve training on more natural odors than those detected by drug and bomb dogs (as noted in the chapters in this section and the chapter on training conservation dogs in the behavior section of this book). Thus, in some ways, this section has a closer connection to the long history of canine service to the hunter than any other part of this book, and some of this discussion will even be of interest to older traditions of canine work.

FINDING INSECTS

As discussed in the first chapter (Chapter 21) in this section, dogs are commonly used in detecting insects, a field that has received attention in the popular press with stories about bedbug beagles. The chapter following describes the author's experience in using dogs on islands in the South Pacific where invasive species need to be controlled and eliminated if species native to the islands are to survive. Unfortunately, this work comes too late for certain species and many islands, but a great effort is now being made to preserve what can be preserved. The third chapter in the section looks at conservation survey work with dogs, which now occurs in a wide range of environments, including the oceans with whales and ice fields with seals. The use of dogs for surveys has been so successful that government agencies now mandate this approach for certain endangered and threatened species.

CONSERVATION SURVEYS

Using dogs for conservation surveys and eradicating pests and invasive species may be the fastest-growing area for detection dogs in the early twenty-first century. Both aspects of this function involve adaptation of the hunting skills of dogs, though in conservation, the idea is to prevent the dog from going in for the kill or getting too close too fast, so that the species being surveyed and its habitat remain as undisturbed as possible. As noted in the second chapter in the behavior and training section of this book, training dogs for conservation functions is different from training dogs for other detection functions. The dog, for instance, may be taught to alert some feet away from the animal that is the source of the target odor. Dogs used for eradicating invasive species, such as on islands, may have to be able to point to or kill one species while remaining uninterested in or perhaps even friendly towards other potential prey species. This was long ago prefigured in the use of hawks and other hunting birds with dogs who have to work together, perhaps to find another type of bird such as the partridge (Michell 1900).

ENVIRONMENTAL WORK

Detection dogs are becoming ever more useful in environmental research and remediation, but even here, there is early precedent. Lloyd (1948) describes a Labrador that was taught, before World War II, to find leaks in the tubing of an underground cable at a BBC receiving station. The dog was trained to recognize "a particular pungent stink," which was pumped under pressure into the tubing. The smell "ascended to the surface where leakages occurred," though apparently not at a level where humans could detect the odor.

> Leading the dog along the line where the cable had been sunk several feet in the marshes, this dog in two days' work, accomplished the astounding performance of discovering every leak, thus saving the expense and trouble of unearthing some four miles of cable.

In 2002, Kauhanen et al. trained dogs to detect mold and decay damage in buildings, while Schoon et al. (2014) trained dogs to detect corrosion under insulation, which they argue could become part of a plant maintenance system. Van De Werfhorst et al. (2014) trained two dogs to respond to the scent of municipal wastewater as a means of surveying human fecal contamination. As discussed in the final chapter of this section, dogs have been used not only to survey wildlife (sometimes even including plants) but also to detect poisons being used illegally to harm wildlife. The trend toward finding new areas where canine detection may be useful will undoubtedly continue.

John Ensminger, Tadeusz Jezierski, and L.E. Papet

21 Trained Dogs in Insect Detection

Margie P. Lehnert and Emma N.I. Weeks

Insects can be both beneficial and harmful, and a myriad of reasons exist for human beings to utilize a surveillance system for both types of insects. Detecting insects by more traditional methods (i.e., visual detection, trap monitoring) can be difficult, and using canines trained to detect insects is often a more efficient and cost-effective method. However, a specific set of challenges are associated with training canines to detect insects.

BENEFICIAL INSECTS

Insects, though seemingly small and insignificant, impact our lives in substantial ways. In many aspects, they are beneficial to the human population, and our continued existence is dependent upon their everyday actions. The economic impact of the ecosystem services provided by wild insects in the United States through dung burial, pollination, pest control, and wildlife nutrition is estimated to be $57 billion (Losey and Vaughn 2006). Pollination, the movement of pollen from the male to the female parts of a flower to enable the fertilization and reproduction of the plant, is vitally important to both our natural ecosystems and crop production. Thirty-five percent of the world's crops rely on pollinators for production (Klein et al. 2007), and insects are the most common pollinators, with bees, wasps, moths, butterflies, flies, and beetles providing the most assistance to plants. Insects not only enable the production of crops, but they also can be a direct food source for many animals (Losey and Vaughn 2006). Human entomophagy, the consumption of insects by human beings, was widespread in the hunter/gatherer communities of Africa, Asia, and the Americas before crops and domesticated animals were introduced from the Middle East (DeFoliart 1999). Although insects still remain a large part of the diet in many cultures today, consumption in westernized countries and urbanized areas is rare (DeFoliart 1999; van Huis et al. 2013). Recently, entomophagy is being reintroduced into cultures that have ceased its practice, because it is a sustainable alternative to large livestock farming (van Huis 2013). Insects also produce nonfood materials, such as silk (silk moth), beeswax (bees), and dyes (beetles and scales), and are often farmed for these purposes (Irwin and Kampmeier 2002).

Insects are also valuable to the medical profession. They often are used in the early stages of medical research to establish potential treatments for diseases and to test novel pharmaceutical drugs. *Drosophila melanogaster* Meigen, a species of fruit fly, is used by scientists to improve understanding of biological systems and human disease processes without the need for vertebrate animal models. The use of insects or insect products for medicine has a long history (Ratcliffe et al. 2011) but, like eating insects, has died out in many cultures. Only the use of honey and other bee products still remains widespread. The antimicrobial properties of these bee products have been shown to be effective against potentially infectious agents in laboratory studies (Ratcliffe et al. 2011). Maggot therapy, i.e., the use of maggots to clean wounds, was introduced in the United States after World War II. Although it went out of favor after the invention of antibiotics, maggot therapy is now being increasingly used to treat antibiotic-resistant bacterial infections. The fly species whose larvae are used, the greenbottle (*Lucilia sericata* Meigen), prefers to feed on dead tissue and is highly effective at cleaning out wounds. In addition to removing dead tissue, the maggots disinfect the wound through the production of antimicrobial peptides, and accelerate wound healing (Sherman et al. 2000).

HARMFUL INSECTS

While the positive effects of insects on the lives of human beings far outweigh the negative impacts, insects also can be harmful to us. Insects affect the health of human beings and animals in several ways. Some insects, such as mosquitoes, feed on the blood of their host. The bites can be merely a nuisance or can lead to allergies, secondary infections, or the transmission of pathogens. Diseases caused by pathogens transmitted by insects include malaria and dengue fever, which are transmitted by mosquito species. In sub-Saharan Africa, mosquito-transmitted malaria causes between 1 and 3 million deaths per year (Breman 2001). Unlike malaria, dengue represents a direct risk to the United States, with frequent introductions as well as some locally acquired cases in Florida. For example, in 2014, there were six locally acquired cases of dengue fever in Miami-Dade County in Florida, as well as 80 travel-associated cases (Florida Department of Health 2014). Some blood-feeding insects do not contribute toward the spread of diseases yet still manage to cause great distress in afflicted individuals, as occurs with bed bugs. Others may be parasitic and live more closely with the host, an example of which would be the head louse. Some insects do not feed on human beings but may cause harm due to the defensive strategies of stinging or biting when disturbed or threatened, e.g., wasps and ants.

Currently, over 6 billion human beings populate the Earth, with a projected 9.6–12.3 billion worldwide population by the year 2100 (Gerland et al. 2014). As the human population increases, feeding the people of the Earth will become increasingly difficult. According to the Food and Agriculture Organization, herbivorous insects destroy 20% of the world's crop production every year (Sallam 1999). Insect pests not only eat the crops while they are growing in the fields but also attack stored crops postharvest. Battling insects and the damage they cause to crops is crucial to the survival of the future human population.

Most insects are not easily classified into one category and can be both beneficial and harmful at the same time. For example, termites are ecologically important because of their ability to decompose dead plant material but also are harmful due to the damage they can cause to homes and other wooden structures. Termite damage can be severe if not noticed early and will have a negative impact on the value of a property (Su and Scheffrahn 1990).

DIFFICULTIES WITH DETECTING INSECTS

Whether beneficial or harmful, insects in general have some common characteristics. Visually locating a specific species of insect can be very difficult because millions of species exist, and the natural history of most species is not well known. Even locating a pest species, in which the preferred habitat might be well documented, can be troublesome because of the small size of the insect in comparison to the large size of the habitat. For example, locating corn pests on farms that have many fields of monoculture corn crop would be difficult to accomplish through visual inspection. Some species, such as bed bugs, are nocturnal and cryptic in their behavior, hiding in cracks and crevices during the day and only exposing themselves at night during host searching and feeding (Usinger 1966). Endangered insects generally have very low population densities; that, coupled with our limited knowledge of their preferred habitat, makes it so that observations of less than 20 individuals per 6-week period is not uncommon (Lehnert 2008). While any human being almost anywhere on Earth could take a walk outside and see tens or hundreds of insects in a relatively short time, locating a specific species of insect can be next to impossible.

Insects are generally small and consequently typically hard to find and difficult to identify by species. Knowing the species of an insect is crucial because even closely related insects often have different food sources and preferred habitats. The members of the insect family

Reduviidae are all terrestrial predators. However, while the subfamily Triatominae contains the blood-feeding kissing bugs, a pest and vector of human disease-causing pathogens (Rolon et al. 2011), the other subfamilies are comprised of insect predators that often provide natural biological control by feeding on insect pests and are, therefore, considered to be beneficial to humans (Sahayaraj 2014). Therefore, not all species of the same family or even genera are of concern to human beings. Closely related pest species can cause significantly different damage and live in different areas, and thus require completely different management strategies. For example, the German cockroach, *Blattella germanica* L., prefers areas of high humidity and temperature, such as around the piping under a kitchen sink. The oriental cockroach, *Blatta orientalis* L., prefers cooler areas of high moisture, such as around basements, in drains, or under porch slabs. Following correct identification of an insect, monitoring is crucial to enable the development of an appropriate management plan. Depending upon the technique used, monitoring or surveillance enables detection of the insect (i.e., presence/absence), an understanding of temporal and spatial distribution, an estimation of population density, and an evaluation of management choices (Madeiros et al. 2013). Monitoring techniques that are often used include visual inspection and trapping. When used correctly, both methods may provide accurate monitoring of pest species, which will reduce the cost of control efforts (Cohnstaedt et al. 2012). However, the difficulties with species identification of insects can make visual inspection for a particular species time-consuming and often impractical.

Pheromone traps, which are designed to attract and contain individuals of a particular species, can be useful in such instances. Pheromones are chemicals used for communication between individuals of the same species. A pheromone is secreted by an individual and influences the behavior of another individual of the same species, an example of which would be a female moth releasing a pheromone to attract a male for reproductive purposes. However, identifying the chemical composition of pheromones is not easy, as the odors emitted are often highly complex and released at low rates (Wallner and Ellis 1976). Furthermore, researchers often take many years to determine the correct chemicals, concentrations, and ratios before the chemicals can be implemented in a trap for monitoring. The use of canines to detect insect target odors for location of insect species allows us to bypass the chemical identification step and to use the dog's highly sensitive olfactory system coupled with its ability to learn to establish an efficient monitoring system for a particular species or closely related group of insects. Canine insect scent detection, or the use of trained dogs to locate insects, has been investigated and incorporated over the past 40 years for surveillance of many different insects, including forest (Schlyter and Johansson 2010; Wallner and Ellis 1976), structural (Brooks et al. 2003), household (Lin et al. 2011), blood-feeding (Pfiester et al. 2008; Rolon et al. 2011), livestock (Welch 1990), and crop pests (Lee et al. 2014; Nakash et al. 2000), as well as beneficial and endangered insects (Waters et al. 2011).

ADVANTAGES OF CANINE INSECT SCENT DETECTION

Canine insect scent detection is particularly useful in situations where the insect is cryptic, either due to camouflage or because it hides away in hard-to-inspect areas (Johnson 1976). For example, bed bugs hide away in the cracks and crevices of structures and furniture and are hard to locate by visual inspection (Pfiester et al. 2008). This can be extremely frustrating to the occupants of the infested home, given the proximity and obvious presence of bed bugs. Trained dogs could be used to identify the refuges of bed bugs and nests of other insects that are cryptic, such as the brown marmorated stink bug (*Halyomorpha halys* Stal), an invasive agricultural pest in the United States that is native to China, Japan, and Taiwan. This would allow for economic resources to be focused on treatment of infested areas, with fewer resources allotted to scouting or visual pest inspection. Similarly, social insects that make nests, such as ants and bees, can provide a challenge for management if the nests are hard to locate. Visual observation and trapping will typically only record the presence of foraging insects, which does not enable an accurate estimation of population size.

Furthermore, protection or management of the nest, depending on the situation, only becomes a viable option once its location has been determined. Using canines to locate the nest can allow for a more accurate estimation of the target insect population size in a significantly shorter period of time than would occur if human visual location were the only available tool.

Insects that are present at low numbers, which often occurs in areas where a species is threatened, endangered, or in the early stages of a pest infestation, provide another situation where canine insect scent detection could be highly valuable. For example, forest pests invading new territory may only infest one tree out of many, and visual inspection of all trees would be impossible (Coulston et al. 2008). Additionally, sampling trees for a pest insect is often a destructive process, either partially or completely incapacitating the sampled organism. Surveillance in these areas is essential, so in the absence of an effective baited trap, a trained canine would be a valuable addition to provide early warning of invasion, and allow for a more selective sampling process with minimal destruction. Similarly, in a large crop field, a trained canine could be used to determine the presence of a pest as well as identify hot spots where management is necessary, saving time and economic resources that might otherwise have been used to treat the entire crop. Insects in need of conservation are often present in low numbers (Datt et al. 2006). Although beneficial, threatened, and endangered insects do not have a negative impact on human beings, it is still important to monitor them to determine population health (Madeiros et al. 2013). As protection of the species is the goal, surveillance through trapping is not ideal, and a nondestructive method such as canine insect scent detection could be useful. Often, insects that are present in low numbers are also cryptic and hard to locate, once again reiterating that a sensitive detector such as a trained canine might prove invaluable in these situations.

EARLY HISTORY OF CANINE INSECT SCENT DETECTION

Canines have been used to detect insects for many years. Observing the sensitivity of canines being used to detect other concealed objects such as drugs, firearms, and explosives, the technique was soon implemented for pest insect detection. For example, pest management professionals have been using dogs to assist in termite detection since the mid-1970s (Lewis et al. 1997). However, the first experimental study of the use of canines to detect insects was completed by Wallner and Ellis in 1976. These scientists were working on the gypsy moth, (*Lymantria dispar* L.), a devastating pest of many tree species. Trained dogs were able to pinpoint the egg masses of the gypsy moth, thereby identifying infested trees and areas at risk of tree damage (Wallner and Ellis 1976).

After the gypsy moth in 1976, several other insects were targeted for detection by canines, including screwworms (*Cochliomyia* spp.) (Welch 1990), red palm weevils (*Rhynchophorus ferrugineus* Olivier) (Nakash et al. 2000; Soroker et al. 2013; Suma et al. 2014), termites of many species (Brooks 2001; Brooks et al. 2003), bed bugs (*Cimex lectularius* L.) (Cooper et al. 2014; Pfiester et al. 2008), Asian and citrus longhorn beetles (*Anoplophora* spp.) (Hoyer-Tomiczek and Sauseng 2012), bumble bees (*Bombus* spp.) (Waters et al. 2011), triatomine bugs (*Triatoma* spp.) (Rolon et al. 2011), red imported fire ants (*Solenopsis invicta* Buren) (Lin et al. 2011), spruce bark beetles, (*Ips typographus* L.) (Kelley 2013; Schlyter et al. 2010), and brown marmorated stink bugs (Lee et al. 2014).

EFFICACY OF CANINE DETECTION FOR INSECT SURVEILLANCE

To date, there have been several published reports on the efficacy of the technique of canine detection for insect surveillance. The majority of these reports have been for the detection of pest species, including insects that are considered by human beings to have a negative impact on their lives. Overall, data have demonstrated that detector canines can be trained to locate insects with a high level of accuracy (Table 21.1). Reported positive indication rates, in which dogs positively and correctly indicated that the target insect was present, ranged from 78% to 100%.

FOREST PESTS

One of the most devastating forest pest insects, the gypsy moth, was the first target for canine insect scent detection. In the late 1960s, the moth was imported as a potential source for silk and then accidentally released into the United States. It became established and has since wreaked havoc with its destructive impact on the U.S. forestry industry (Holmes et al. 2009; McManus et al. 1989). In the 1980s, 13 million acres of deciduous forest were defoliated, which means that 50% or more of the forest canopy leaves were eaten by the gypsy moth (McManus et al. 1989). Defoliation can kill trees because the leaves provide the mechanics for collecting sunlight to produce food during photosynthesis; no leaves means no food for the trees. Foliage also provides protection from predators for native bird species' nestlings, which can decline in number during gypsy moth outbreaks (Thurber et al. 1994).

Wallner and Ellis (1976) wanted to detect gypsy moth eggs in order to provide a reliable population estimate. Gypsy moth eggs are laid in the leaf litter or under flaps in tree bark, so human detection, especially in areas where populations are sparse, is almost impossible (Campbell et al. 1975). The detection of egg masses using canines would be highly beneficial for early detection at the advancing border of the gypsy moth territory, where control strategies can be implemented to prevent the spread of the invasive species (United States Department of Agriculture 2010).

A second study has investigated the use of canines for detection of another forest pest, the spruce bark beetle, which has caused tree death across 1.2 million acres of forest in Alaska (Kelley 2013; Schlyter et al. 2010). As with gypsy moths, canines provide a way to quickly scan a forest for infested trees, a process that would be unfeasible by visual inspection. Asian longhorn beetles and citrus longhorn beetles also cause damage to forests, but the latter also damage crop trees. Canines were successfully trained to locate both Asian longhorn beetles and citrus longhorn beetles (Hoyer-Tomiczek and Sauseng 2012). The trained dogs were able to detect the beetles in wooden materials, potted plants, and established trees (Hoyer-Tomiczek and Sauseng 2012), so they could be useful at border control as well as at detecting infested plants in parks and plant nurseries.

CROP PESTS

Canine insect scent detection also has been tested for the detection of crop pests. Date palms are an important fruit crop in the Middle East and often become infested with red palm weevils. Detection of infestations at an early stage permits plant rescue through various treatments, but red palm weevil damage, which occurs inside the tree, is not readily visible. Palms infested with red palm weevils were successfully detected by canines trained to locate either the live insect or the damage caused by the insect (Nakash et al. 2000; Soroker et al. 2013; Suma et al. 2014). The brown marmorated stink bug is an invasive species in the United States that causes high economic losses for crops and is a nuisance for household ornamentals. Detection of the stink bug during its overwintering stage enables estimation of population density and risk of plant damage in the following year. Trained canines were able to detect overwintering stink bugs in both laboratory experiments and field trials (Lee et al. 2014).

VETERINARY PESTS

The primary screwworm, *Cochliomyia hominivorax* (Coquerel), was eradicated from the United States in 1983. However, there is much concern about the risk of reintroduction from infested areas, as several instances of importation of infested animals resulted in reintroduction of the species, which had to be managed each time at great expense to the government and taxpayers. As a result of these repeated reintroductions, detection of infested animals at the port of arrival was deemed to be necessary, and efficient methods were sought. A study by Welch (1990) found that canines were able to detect screwworm larvae and pupae and so could be a valuable addition to a quarantine and inspection program.

TABLE 21.1

Summary of Results of Studies That Trained Canines to Detect Insects

Target Insect (Common Name)	Number of Dogs Tested	Training Material	Type of Experiment[a]	% False Positives[b,c]	Material Instigating False Positives[d]	% Missed Indication[e]	% Positive Indication[f]	Citation
Gypsy moth	2	Pheromone (disparlure), eggs	Lab. experiment, field trials	NR	Plant material, soil, etc. where eggs can be laid	NR	24 initially, increased to 95	Wallner and Ellis 1976
Screwworm	1	Live insects, natural scent (exudate from infested wounds)	Field simulation	NR	NR	NR	100	Welch 1990
Red palm weevil (RPW)	2	Natural scent (tree "ooze" caused by RPW)	Field simulation, field trials	NR	NR	NR	100	Nakash et al. 2000
RPW	3	Live insects	Field simulations	13	NR	NR	78	Suma et al. 2014
Termite	6	Live insects, natural scent (solvent wash of termites)	Lab. experiment	3	Termite-damaged wood	0	96–97	Brooks et al. 2003
Bed bug	6	Live insects	Lab. experiment, field simulation	3	Feces	0 on bed bugs, 10 on eggs	97	Pfiester et al. 2008

(Continued)

TABLE 21.1 (CONTINUED)
Summary of Results of Studies That Trained Canines to Detect Insects

Target Insect (Common Name)	Number of Dogs Tested	Training Material	Type of Experiment[a]	% False Positives[b,c]	Material Instigating False Positives[d]	% Missed Indication[e]	% Positive Indication[f]	Citation
Asian and citrus long-horned beetles	4	NR	Field trials	NR	NR	NR	NR	Hoyer-Tomiczek 2009
Bumble bees	1	Nests	Field simulation, field trials	0	NA	0	100	Waters et al. 2010
Triatomine bug	1	Live insects	Field simulation, field trials	NR	NR	NR	NR	Rolon et al. 2011
Red imported fire ant	3	Live and dead insects	Field simulation, field trials	4	Empty insect holder, other ant species	NR	98	Lin et al. 2011
Spruce bark beetle	NR	Pheromone	Field trials	NR	NR	NR	NR	Schlyter and Johansson 2012
Brown marmorated stink bug	2	Live insects	Field simulation, lab. experiment, field trials	8	Empty insect holder	NR	93	Lee et al. 2014

[a] Laboratory (Lab.) experiments were conducted inside in a controlled environment. Field simulation experiments were conducted in areas similar to the habitat of the target insect. Field trials indicates use of the dogs in the service for which they were trained. If field trials were conducted, the trained dogs successfully located previously unknown individuals of the target insect.

[b] A false-positive indication was defined as the dog positively indicating the target as present when the target was not present.

[c] NR means not reported in citation.

[d] NA means not applicable because no false-positive indications had occurred in the study.

[e] A missed indication was defined as the dog not indicating the target as present when the target was present.

[f] A positive indication was defined as the dog positively indicating the target as present when the target was present.

HOUSEHOLD PESTS

Blood-feeding insects that reside in human residences, such as bed bugs (Cooper et al. 2014; Pfiester et al. 2008) and triatomine bugs (Rolon et al. 2011), that are cryptic in nature and therefore hard to locate also have been targeted with canine insect scent detection. Bed bugs are not known to transmit diseases, but bites often lead to allergic reactions or secondary infections and psychological issues that can even lead to suicide of the affected individual (Burrows et al. 2013; Usinger 1966). Many triatomine bug species are capable of transmitting the protozoan *Trypanasoma cruzi* Chagas, which causes Chagas disease in human beings. These two blood-feeding insects hide in cracks and crevices of the infested area, causing visual inspection to be time-consuming. Canine detection was successful in detecting infested areas in both cases.

Other household pests also have received attention, and canines were able to detect termites and fire ants (Brooks 2001; Brooks et al. 2003; Lin et al. 2011; Zahid et al. 2012). Termite and fire ant management, monitoring, and control is hindered by the difficulty in locating nest sites. To confirm the presence of termites in a structure, it is necessary to open up the walls, which is highly destructive and usually undesirable for the owners of the structure (Brooks 2001). Monitoring is typically achieved through bait stations, but these capture foraging individuals and give no information about nest site location or size. Canines were able to identify the location of nests and allow for accurate population estimations and treatment applications for control of termites without the destruction of the potentially infested structure. Although dogs were unable to locate small numbers (i.e., 5–10 individuals) of termites artificially inoculated into a wooden block (Zahid et al. 2012), as social insects, termites are typically found in nests with much higher numbers than 10 individuals.

BENEFICIAL INSECTS (BEES)

Several studies have investigated the use of trained canines to detect an insect that is considered more beneficial than harmful, the bumble bee (O'Connor et al. 2012; Waters et al. 2011). Bees are crucially important for the ecological services they provide in the form of plant pollination. The decline of commercial honey bee hives has caused an increased interest in conservation of native bumble bees to provide pollination services to crops and garden plants. Location of bumble bee nests is difficult as the nests are often underground or in dense vegetation, yet they are important for accurate population estimates, which are vital to ensure that the species is conserved (Madeiros et al. 2013). Trained dogs were able to detect *Bombus* species nests in laboratory and field trials. However, it might not be cost-effective to train canines to locate bumble bee nests, as they did not locate any more nests when compared to visual inspection, and the nests located were not located more quickly than they were by human beings (O'Connor et al. 2012).

FALSE-POSITIVE INDICATIONS

Most studies did not report the false-positive indication percentage, in which a dog indicates that the target odor is present when it is not. A high number of false-positive indications is often the result of using training materials that were contaminated with a nontarget odor (Hallowell et al. 1997). The studies that did report this occurrence showed that canines would falsely indicate the presence of the target odor when materials related to the dog's training were present, such as plant materials on which gypsy moth eggs might be laid (Wallner and Ellis 1976) or damaged wood that had once contained termites (Brooks et al. 2003). Essentially, false positives occur when canines are inadvertently trained on multiple scents. For example, during bed bug–detection trials, with the first canine trained on the bed bug target odor, false positives occurred in response to bed bug feces (Pfiester et al. 2008). The bugs used for training purposes were fed and kept inside plastic vials with a paper harborage. The vials and their contents were then used to provide the target odor to the dogs. Bed bugs condense their blood meals, defecating nonessential fluids quickly, with half of the weight of the blood meal eliminated within the first few hours (Usinger 1966). Therefore, as training progressed, more and more fecal stains were accruing within the training vials of live bed bugs. When the target odor was presented to the canines, they were trained on the live bed bug scent as well as the feces. Once the error was recognized, the problem was resolved by only using unfed bed bugs for training, and with this improvement, no more false-positive indications occurred on bed bug feces (Pfiester et al. 2008).

Eliminating false-positive responses from the behavior of canines trained to detect insects is crucial to the success of many pest control programs utilizing canine insect scent detection. Although difficult to locate, insects often leave evidence of their inhabitance in an area. Termites, red palm weevils, and spruce bark beetles build a complex tunnel system within wood; gypsy moths lay eggs on a variety of different plants; and bed bugs deposit feces almost anywhere within an infested area. When a pest species is involved, the evidence of the pest (e.g., fecal stains) often remains even when a control treatment is successful and elimination of the insects has occurred. Training canines to indicate only on live insects and not on insect-related materials, such as feces, ensures that false positives do not occur due to a previously eliminated infestation. This provides fair economic treatment of the pest control customer while helping to eliminate nonessential insecticide applications. The training of dogs exclusively on live insect target odors also allows for insect-detecting canines to be used as a follow-up tool for measuring the success of a pest control treatment, i.e., determining whether an infestation has been successfully eliminated (Pfiester et al. 2008). In these situations, pest evidence almost certainly will be present, and it is important that the canine does not falsely indicate when the infestation has been removed and the management was successful.

TRAINING DOGS WITH LIVE INSECTS

To date, most studies of canine insect scent detection efficacy used live insects for training purposes. However, once a dog has been trained to locate an insect, that training must be maintained daily. This requires the canine handler to have a constant supply of live insects. During the gypsy moth training and trials, the target insect was an invasive pest species that did not occur in the geographical region where the training was performed. Training on live insects may therefore be difficult when bringing live insects into an unaffected geographical region is illegal without a permit from the United States Department of Agriculture Animal and Plant Health Inspection Service (USDA APHIS; 7 CFR 330.200). The illegality of this action stems from the unbelievable destructive power of some of these insect pests, especially if they do not naturally occur in the affected area. For example, the gypsy moth is able to feed on the foliage of many different species of trees and often occurs in large groups. As an invasive species, it has few predators in North America to prevent populations from growing large and causing damage. As a result, a group of gypsy moths can wipe out an entire forest in a season, and movement of the pest species is highly regulated by government organizations, such as the USDA. The USDA APHIS releases domestic quarantine notices for destructive invasive pest species, such as the pink bollworm, emerald ash borer, and red imported fire ant, which quarantine infested states and prohibit interstate movement of potentially infested materials (7 CFR Part 301). For example, there are 20 states that are quarantined due to gypsy moth infestation (7 CFR 301.45); this federal regulation prohibits the movement of potentially affected materials, such as firewood, out of quarantined states (United States Department of Agriculture 2010).

Maintaining colonies of live insects is not an easy task and is often unwelcome, especially in situations when the target species is not looked upon favorably, as with bed bugs. Dead bed bugs and fecal materials must be constantly removed from training vials to ensure that cross-training on nontarget scents is not occurring. This requires handlers to open the vials and remove dead bed bugs or change paper harborages with live bed bugs still contained in the vials. Opening the vials exposes handlers, usually not trained entomologists, to potential bites and the possibility of a bed bug infestation. Bed bugs require regular blood meals in order to reproduce, but providing a food source for blood-feeding insects often requires additional paperwork and permissions. Some insects have a life cycle that takes 2–3 years to complete, as with the red palm weevil, making proliferation of the colony a slow process that could be thwarted if even low numbers of insect deaths occur. The difficulties with maintaining colonies of insects might force canine handlers to either regularly purchase insects from an entomological supply company or frequently search for their own live insects.

ALTERNATIVES TO LIVE INSECTS FOR TRAINING

While the use of live insects for training of insect scent detection canines is preferred, it is not always possible. An alternative to the use of live insects for training is the use of natural scents (i.e., insect-derived odor) or pseudoscents. Training aids, such as pseudoscents, have been used more frequently in other areas of canine scent detection (Stadler et al. 2012). Natural scents may be an extract of the insect collected by maceration of the insect or washing of the insect in a solvent. Pseudoscents are synthetic mixtures created by mixing known chemicals associated with the odor of the organism to be detected. A few studies have experimented with alternatives to live insects, including synthetic pheromones, a type of pseudoscent (Rolon et al. 2011; Schlyter et al. 2010; Wallner and Ellis 1976), and natural scents including insect extracts (Brooks 2001; Pfiester et al. 2008) and insect-associated odors (Nakash et al. 2000; Welch 1990). The problem with designing pseudoscents for training canines is that we often do not know what the dog is using to differentiate between target and nontarget odor (Brooks 2001). This "detection odor signature" that the dogs are using may be an individual chemical or a complex blend of multiple chemicals at different ratios.

PHEROMONES

As already described, pheromones are chemicals used for communication between individuals of the same species. Chemical communication involves an emitter and a receiver. The emitter produces the pheromone and secretes the chemical into the environment. A receiver, an insect of the same species, uses specialized organs (e.g., antennae) to detect the pheromone in the environment, and physiological or behavioral responses occur as a result. Although pheromones are designed for communication between individuals of the same species, "eavesdropping" often occurs. In this instance, a receiver individual that is of a different species detects the pheromone and uses it to its advantage. For example, a predator may detect the presence of a sex or aggregation pheromone of its prey for location. Similarly, trained dogs for insect detection are likely to be detecting the presence of their target insect using pheromones along with other associated odors.

In order to train a dog on a pseudoscent of insect pheromone, the target insect pheromone must be known and available. Three studies have used insect pheromones as the target odor for training dogs to detect: gypsy moth, triatomine bug, and spruce bark beetle (Rolon et al. 2011; Schlyter et al 2010; Wallner and Ellis 1976). The first ever use of canines for insect scent detection, for gypsy moth management, also assessed the ability of dogs to detect pheromone-treated material (Wallner and Ellis 1976). Disparlure (2-methyl-7R,8S-epoxy-octadecane), a synthetic version of the female gypsy moth-produced sex pheromone (Bierl et al. 1970), was applied to wood, metal, and plastic, and the ability of canines to detect the treated materials was determined in the laboratory (Wallner and Ellis 1976). Disparlure-treated wood resulted in the greatest number of positive indications (>82%) compared to metal (>70%) or plastic (>50%) (Wallner and Ellis 1976). Wood is much more absorbent than metal and plastic and might have resulted in a decreased release rate of the pheromone over a longer period of time. Although this study trained dogs to detect a pheromone, it did not test the ability of those trained dogs to detect live insects in the field.

Another study that targeted forest pests, particularly the spruce bark beetle, also used a synthetic pheromone for dog training (Kelly 2013; Schlyter et al. 2010). The alarm pheromone produced by triatomine bugs, isobutyric acid (Manrique et al. 2006; Vitta et al. 2009), was used to test canines that had been trained for detection of triatomine-infested areas with live triatomines (Rolon et al. 2011). Although the canines were able to detect the pheromone-treated vial, the dogs did not clearly indicate target odor presence like they did for a live triatomine bug. The odor of live insects is complex, and pheromones are just one component of that odor, which is the risk of training dogs to detect insects using synthetic pheromones or other pseudoscents; the odor of the insects may be determined by the dog to be different from the pheromone and, therefore, not result in a positive indication.

INSECT EXTRACTS

Extracts of insects, or natural scents, could be an alternative. Two studies have experimented with the use of insect extracts for training canines for insect scent detection. The first study of the use of natural scents for canine insect detection was completed by Brooks (2001). Dogs were trained on live insects and a pentane rinse of termites (*Reticulitermes flavipes* Kollar) and were instructed to locate live insects or a natural scent-treated object. Dogs trained on the scent were able to detect the insects and the scent (97% positive indications). Likewise, dogs trained on live insects were able to detect the scent and live insects (95% positive indications) (Brooks 2001). A later study, by Pfiester et al. (2008), trained canines to detect bed bugs using live insects and tested their ability to detect a natural scent. The pentane extract of 50 live adult mixed-sex bed bugs resulted in 100% positive indication from canines trained to locate live bed bugs (Pfiester et al. 2008). The benefit of using a natural scent over a pheromone or pseudoscent is that the multiple steps of chemical identification can be bypassed, and a greater number of the chemicals comprising the insect odor are captured. This increases the chance that the detection odor signature that the dog is using to locate the target is captured. A disadvantage is that extraction may be inconsistent or unsuccessful or result in an unrealistic composition either qualitatively or quantitatively. For example, Pfiester et al. (2008) found that, out of four extracts with different solvents (i.e., pentane, methanol, acetone, and water), only the pentane extract produced positive indications. Therefore, the choice of solvent could be crucial, and the best choice will likely change depending upon the chemicals that are essential for dog detection.

INSECT-ASSOCIATED MATERIALS

In some cases, the target insect is extremely cryptic, or its natural habitat is a contained area such as a tree, and thus, releasing odors at high concentrations into the environment is unlikely. In these situations, insect-associated odors may be more useful odor targets for training. There have been two studies that trained canines to detect odors associated with insect damage (Nakash et al. 2000; Welch 1990). In both cases, the insects were hidden from the environment, and so insect-produced volatiles might have been overwhelmed by the background of the host. For example, red palm weevils develop inside palms and are hard to detect, especially by visual inspection. Palms infested by the red palm weevil produce an "ooze" that is composed of chewed rotting plant material from the insect entry wounds. Canines were successfully trained to detect the plant damage odor (Nakash et al. 2000), but experiments were not completed to test the ability of those canines to detect infested palms (Soroker et al. 2013). Similarly, screwworm-infested animals are difficult to identify as the fly larvae are hidden within the host. Canines that were trained to detect the exudate from wounds infested with screwworms were successful in locating an exudate-treated ball or rope toy (Welch 1990). The dogs were also able to detect infested animals after training with infested animal odors (Welch 1990).

EFFICACY OF ALTERNATIVES TO LIVE INSECTS FOR TRAINING PURPOSES

Pseudoscents used as training aids for detector canines are generally considered to be overly simplistic (Stadler et al. 2012). Studies that have tested the use of training aids have found that although dogs trained on pseudoscents were able to locate the target organism, the opposite was not always true, i.e., dogs trained to detect a target organism were not able to locate a pseudoscent-treated object (Stadler et al. 2012). This inconsistency between training and practice has resulted in suspicion and a tendency to avoid the use of such training tools. Few studies have tested the use of an alternative scent to live insects as a training tool for detection of live insects in the field, to remove the necessity of maintaining an insect colony. A study that tested the ability of canines trained to detect live triatomine bugs to instead detect a synthetic pheromone indeed found that, although the dogs were able to locate the pheromone, they did not indicate on it (Rolon et al. 2011). Similar responses have been observed in narcotics detection, with dogs that were trained on real materials and then asked to find a pseudoscent-treated object; the dogs are able to detect and locate the pseudoscent-treated object, but they do not indicate, as the object is missing some chemicals present in the real material.

In canine insect scent detection, several investigators have completed similar experiments but with natural scents comprised of solvent washes of the target insect (Brooks 2001; Pfiester 2008). Canines trained to indicate on live termites or bed bugs were able to detect, locate, and indicate on the natural scent. Furthermore, canines trained to indicate on termite scent were able to detect, locate, and indicate on the live termites. It is possible that the added complexity of the scent, due to its natural origin, provided a more realistic odor profile for the dogs, and so they were satisfied that they had located the correct item. Further work is needed to determine the ability of natural scents and pseudoscents to replace live insects in canine insect scent detection training. However, it seems that natural scents, such as insect extracts, hold greater promise. Each system will need to be carefully evaluated before these scents are incorporated. Training a dog solely on a scent and then testing if that dog can locate the live insect needs to be completed before assessing scents as a viable replacement for training insect-detecting canines.

APPLIED CANINE INSECT SCENT DETECTION

Many studies have documented the fact that training canines to locate target odors of a variety of insect species is possible, and the studies document the training process along with the obstacles the trainers and handlers encountered. However, studies also have been conducted in which the authors were not associated with the training process and the handlers were from the pest control industry. In these studies, the canines were less accurate in locating the target odor, especially without the occurrence of false-positive indications. For example, the average accuracy of four termite-detecting canines was revealed to be approximately 85% with a 28% false-positive indication rate after experimental evaluation (Lewis et al. 1997), lower than the 96% accuracy rate and higher than the 3% false-positive rate reported from a study in which a known experienced dog trainer was used to train and handle the tested canines (Brooks et al. 2003). The lower accuracy rate was likely due in part to the low number of termites ($n = 5$) used, resulting in the highest amount of missed identification of the target odor.

In a similar situation, bed bug–detecting canines that were trained and handled by known experienced dog handlers had an average accuracy of 97% in locating bed bugs, with a 3% false-positive rate (Pfiester et al. 2008). However, a study evaluating 11 working bed bug–detecting canine/handler teams showed only a 44% accuracy rate, with a 15% false-positive rate (Cooper et al. 2014). This study went a step further and determined that a canine/handler team that used an experienced dog handler was not more accurate in locating the target odor than a canine/handler team that used novice dog handlers. However, the dogs had different initial trainers, and training was maintained differently (as indicated by the certifications of canine/handler teams, if any). Proper daily maintenance of canine training is crucial to success of the team. High false-positive rates combined with low accuracy rates could result from cross-training of canines on bed bugs and bed bug–related materials (e.g., feces, dead bed bugs, cast skins) or a lack of available live bed bugs for target odor maintenance for the canine.

CONCLUSION

Canines can be trained to accurately detect the target odor of insects, and the technique can be useful in many ways. Using canines makes locating small population levels of insects easier, especially if a large habitat needs to be searched. Locating cryptic insect species, as well as species that cause internal damage to trees and structures, is also easier with trained canines. Canine detection is usually a better economic option because it is quicker, and pest management strategies can be targeted to the infested areas. Training and maintaining insect-detecting canines can be difficult because training with live insects is preferred, but methods using insect-related materials for training also have been successful. However, a discrepancy seems to exist between the performance of canines trained for research studies and those trained and used as applied tools in pest control, with the former performing with a higher level of accuracy and a lower false-positive rate. Reasons as to why this discrepancy exists and how to improve efficacy and motivation of commercial dog/handler teams need to be explored in more detail.

22 Detection Dogs in Strategies for Eradicating Pest Species from Natural Environments

Keith Springer

Dogs have been assisting humans with hunting for centuries, but only relatively recently has this aspect of canine assistance been fine-tuned to enhance conservation actions, by assisting in the removal of invasive species from natural environments. The development of detection dogs to assist in the removal of pest species is partly the convergence of two canine functions: firstly, the use of dogs trained to detect rare and protected species (often birds or mammals), and secondly, the use of dogs to assist hunters with locating game animals.

The field of conservation detection dogs has developed in parallel but more or less independently in numerous places around the world, with a degree of cross-fertilization of ideas and training methods. Agencies, individuals, or companies operating conservation detection dogs are found in the United States, the United Kingdom, Australia, New Zealand, and many African nations, among others. The species targeted for detection vary by region and country but typically reflect the list of some of the world's worst mammal invasive species, including feral cats, European rabbits, mustelids, rodents, goats, pigs, and some deer species. As well as detecting invasive animal and plant species, other detection dogs work in the wider conservation field, including tracking wildlife for species management and survey purposes (e.g., Paula et al. 2011), and detecting poaching and illegal trade in wildlife. See Chapter 23 herein.

In the pest detection discipline, countries with large numbers of introduced invasive species (and consequent impacts on natural ecosystems) typically find themselves with relatively higher use of canines trained to detect a wider range of species. New Zealand, for example, had no native mammals apart from two species of bat before human arrival around 1000 AD. Maori colonizers introduced the dog and Pacific or Polynesian rat (*Rattus exulans*), and European settlers from the 1800s introduced a wide range of mammalian herbivores and predators, usually deliberately. With virtually no native mammals, New Zealand had evolved a wide and diverse avifauna, none of which had needed to cope—and mostly proved unable to cope—with mammalian predators or competitors. Extinctions of bird species on a large scale ensued from soon after colonization by Maori and accelerated after the arrival of the Europeans. Currently, New Zealand has many threatened native bird species unable to coexist with introduced mammal predators. In response, conservation agencies in New Zealand could only put remnant native bird populations on islands to avoid losing more species but first had to clear those islands of introduced predators. This work has been ongoing since 1960, with the pace accelerating from the 1990s as new technology and methodology improved outcomes and increased capacity.

The New Zealand Department of Conservation (DOC) now has access to staff and contractors with dogs trained to detect the primary bird predators: stoats (*Mustela erminea*); rodents (*Rattus norvegicus*, *Rattus rattus*, *Rattus exulans*, and *Mus musculus*); feral cats (*Felis catus*); possums (*Trichosurus vulpecula*); and hedgehogs (*Erinaceus europaeus*). These dogs and their handlers are used both to monitor pest-free island sanctuaries to ensure no incursions have occurred, and to assist in detection of individual pests when an island pest eradication is in progress.

This chapter describes the approach taken to using detection dogs for invasive species removal, primarily using Australian case studies, and also outlines the international collaboration that enhances the development of training systems.

MACQUARIE ISLAND

Macquarie Island is a sub-Antarctic island lying at S 54°30', E 158°57', with an area of 12,785 ha (31,800 ac.). A part of the Australian state of Tasmania, it lies 1,500 km (930 mi.) from the Tasmanian capital of Hobart, in a latitudinal band renowned for near-constant gales and cloud, with snowfall frequent in winter but possible year-round (Figure 22.1). It was discovered by sealers in July 1810. Fur seals (*Arctocephalus* sp.) were harvested to near-total annihilation within 15 years. Elephant seals, royal penguins (*Eudyptes schlegeli*), and king penguins (*Aptenodytes patagonica*) were then harvested for oil from the 1870s until 1919 (Cumpston 1968; Jenkin et al. 1981). During this period, several mammal species were introduced to the island and established feral populations.

VERTEBRATE PESTS ON MACQUARIE ISLAND

Rodents (mice, *Mus musculus*, and ship rats, *Rattus rattus*) came ashore accidentally, and cats (*Felis catus*) and dogs (*Canis familiaris*), probably deliberately by 1815, while rabbits (*Oryctolagus cuniculus*) and weka (*Gallirallus australis*—a flightless rail from New Zealand) were introduced as a food source in the 1880s (Cumpston 1968). Feral dogs died out naturally, but the other species

FIGURE 22.1   Detection work in snow.

mentioned all maintained abundant feral populations. The combination of expanding rabbit populations (Figures 22.2 and 22.3) and feral cats is thought to have resulted in the extinction of the two endemic land birds from Macquarie Island by the mid-1890s—a rail and a parakeet (Taylor 1979). Macquarie is classified as a nature reserve under the Tasmanian National Parks and Reserves Management Act 2002 and was inscribed on the register of World Heritage sites in 1997, establishing the island as having state, national, and international significance for its natural values.

Concern about the impact of rabbits on native vegetation was expressed shortly after the establishment of a scientific station on the island by the Australian Antarctic Division (AAD) in 1948 (Taylor 1955; Costin and Moor 1960), and in the 1970s, a study estimated that feral cats were killing an estimated 60,000 seabirds annually (Jones 1977). Early measures at controlling species relied on poisoning and myxomatosis (rabbits) (Brothers et al. 1982) or shooting (cats and weka, an invasive bird). These methods did successfully eradicate weka by 1988 (Copson 1995). In the mid-1990s, after some 20 years of cat control, a concerted effort was made to eradicate them, and this commenced in 1998. Detection dogs were intended to be an integral part of the eradication effort, and two cat detection dogs[1] were contracted to be trained by a New Zealand trainer. In a twist of

FIGURE 22.2 Rabbit hunting on Macquarie Island.

FIGURE 22.3 Dog with dead rabbits (Bruny Island).

inconvenience, the ship that was to transport the dogs to the island in late 1999 was routed via the resupply of AAD stations on the Antarctic continent, and because of the Madrid Protocol of the Antarctic Treaty, animals cannot be taken south of S 60°, even though the dogs were never intended to leave the ship and were specifically for a conservation program. As a result, the dogs were not deployed to the island until late in 2000, by which time the cat population had been reduced to apparently zero by a combination of trapping and shooting (Robinson and Copson 2014). They still performed an invaluable function, though, as one of the key challenges facing managers of pest eradication programs is how to gain the confidence that the last individual of a population has been removed and that hunting pressure can cease. On large islands with rugged terrain and inhospitable weather conditions such as Macquarie, this is a significant issue because the remote isolated location makes it difficult to maintain staff for long periods of time in sufficient numbers to ascertain that eradication has been successful. As a result, the use of two cat detection dogs was considered vital to increase the confidence that cats had been removed and that the eradication could be declared successful after 2 years of monitoring. With cats removed, birdlife was relieved of one source of predation pressure, and some species began to recover in number or reestablish on the island after decades of absence (Brothers and Bone 2008).

The successful eradication of cats and weka was not sufficient to allow reestablishment or recovery of all native bird species, however, nor of vegetation. With no woody vegetation, all species must nest either on the ground surface or in burrows and, in both locations, were vulnerable to predation by ship rats, especially in the egg or chick phase. With rabbit numbers expanding (Terauds 2009) in the early and mid-2000s and the myxoma virus becoming less effective after 20 years of use (Dowding et al. 2009), an eradication was proposed by the Tasmania Parks and Wildlife Service (PWS) to simultaneously tackle the remaining three feral mammal species on the island, i.e., rabbits, ship rats, and mice.

Early planning toward this goal in 2004 recognized the parallels in the then-recent (2001) Norway rat eradication successfully carried out on 11,300 ha (27,900 ac.) Campbell Island by the DOC, which was a new milestone in terms of the size of island from which rats could successfully be eradicated (Howald et al. 2007). An approach to the DOC resulted in that agency's pool of eradication experience and knowledge being made available as a consultative body to review the eradication planning for Macquarie Island.[2] At this stage, the Macquarie Island project was considered extremely challenging and very ambitious on a global scale, due to the size of the island, the fact that multiple pest species were targeted for eradication, and the remote location of the island, coupled with the challenging and adverse prevailing weather conditions. At that time, the largest island worldwide that had had rabbits successfully eradicated was 800 ha (1970 ac.) Saint-Paul (France), whereas for mice, it was 710 ha (1750 ac.) Enderby Island (New Zealand). This reinforced the scale of the ambitious plans for removing these species from Macquarie Island at 12,785 ha.

Using information about previous rabbit eradications from islands in New Zealand and elsewhere (e.g., Saint-Paul in the southern Indian Ocean [Micol and Jouventin 2002]), it became apparent that poisoning using an anticoagulant was highly effective at killing rabbits (while developed as a rodenticide). In many programs, a kill rate in excess of 99.5% was achieved, but for unknown reasons, a very small number of individual rabbits did not consume bait and thus survived to potentially form the nucleus of a replacement population. It was clear that without planning for follow-up hunting, the eradication of rabbits from Macquarie Island by baiting alone was likely to fail, and equally clear from experience elsewhere that the use of dogs to detect surviving rabbits was a significant and effective tool in the challenge to find and remove rabbits faster than they could find each other and breed.

THE MACQUARIE ISLAND PEST ERADICATION PROJECT

Funding was secured for the Macquarie Island Pest Eradication Project in June 2007, and from that point, planning efforts accelerated. Previous discussions with dog handlers, trainers, and eradication managers had suggested that to train dogs to the level required on Macquarie Island would take up to 2 years. A large part of this time was in nontarget aversion training, as it was vital that native animals—Macquarie Island is home to vast colonies of penguins, seals, and seabirds, including Critically Endangered wandering albatross—not be harmed by dogs trained to hunt rabbits.

The context of the proposed eradication also needed to be reflected in the number of dogs that were required for rabbit detection and which procurement model best secured the project's needs. The eradication project was planned in two main stages: (1) an aerial baiting phase in which bait pellets containing brodifacoum (an anticoagulant toxin) would be broadcast from sowing buckets slung under helicopters, which was designed to eradicate both rodent species and an estimated 99.5% of rabbits, and (2) a hunting phase using dogs, firearms, burrow fumigants, and traps, designed to locate and remove surviving rabbits. Given population estimates of over 150,000 rabbits (Terauds et al. 2014), even a 0.005% survival rate potentially left several hundred rabbits alive post-baiting.

To undertake this follow-up hunting, team size needed to be large enough to maintain hunting pressure on surviving rabbits while spending the majority of time in the field and small enough that it was logistically feasible to support the team in the field. To optimize this work, five field huts (converted plastic water tanks) were installed around the island to supplement five existing field huts maintained by the AAD. With 10 huts plus the main station at the northern end of the island, a team size of 12–14 hunters could be supported on the island in 12-month deployments (as only one resupply/staff changeover voyage is scheduled each year). With the island divided into six hunting blocks, two hunters were scheduled to spend a month in each hunting block, and one of these was a designated dog handler. With the ability to handle up to two dogs each, this suggested that 11 dogs would be required for the 5 years of postbaiting fieldwork. Three years had been scheduled for the removal of all rabbits, anticipating that breeding would occur during the hunting phase and that a considerable time period would be needed to find each individual and remove it. A further 2 years was scheduled as a monitoring period to commence after the last known rabbit was killed, maintaining the search effort at a comparable level to ascertain that eradication was successful. Eleven dogs also made allowance for an expected attrition rate, while hopefully not dropping below one dog per handler.

This context led to considerable discussion within the project team as to the best model to use to ensure the supply of dogs for the project. The first model was to rely on recruiting six dog handlers with their own one or two trained dogs each year for 5 years. This model had the advantage that a more effective canine detection unit would be in place from the outset each year when the new team arrived on the island, as the bond between dog handler and canine was already established and efficiency should be maximized. The second model was based on the PWS owning and maintaining the dogs, which would stay on the island for the full 5 years of the project duration and be matched with handlers who were recruited annually. This was considered to be slightly less efficient as it would take time for a new handler–dog combination to become used to each other and perform as an effective rabbit detection team. It did, however, have the advantage that the department had control over the supply and standards that the canine team was trained to.

In assessing the relative merits of each model, the overall objective of the success of rabbit eradication was paramount. Given that ultimate goal, from a risk management perspective, the decision became straightforward. The model employing staff with their own trained dogs required that each year for 5 years, recruitment would have to be successful not only in selecting six staff who all met the selection criteria for employment on the team and who wanted to spend a year on a remote island in challenging weather conditions, but also in ensuring that they would each have one or two dogs trained to the standards required. Moreover, while New Zealand had a pool of dog handlers used to the DOC standards, Australia did not, suggesting limited recruitment of staff and dogs from Australia under this model. If in any one year, the desired number of handlers and dogs were not recruited, then compromises would need to be made. Either fewer handlers would be deployed to the island, or the quality standards of staff and/or dogs would need to be lowered. The prospect of lowering standards for either handlers or dogs for a challenging posting to a World Heritage-listed nature reserve was not an attractive option. Both scenarios challenged the likelihood of successful rabbit eradication. Given the motivational challenges faced in conducting successful eradication operations, the prospect of finding the right number of the right people with the right dogs at the right time seemed highly unlikely. Going with the model where the department owned and trained the canine team at least reduced the risk of not having the canine section of the team at the required standard, and assured the project of the presence of trained dogs on the island throughout the project, thus removing an entire field of risk.

With the decision made for Tasmania Parks and Wildlife to provide the canine team outright, the next issue was procurement. The PWS could employ staff directly to acquire and train the dogs in-house, but the agency was not set up for that type of facility or work considering the number of dogs required. Alternately, trained dogs could be bought that were trained to the department's specifications by private contractors. Due to the likely expenditure for the trained dogs, government procurement policy required that the training be tendered.

NEW ZEALAND DEPARTMENT OF CONSERVATION PEST DETECTION DOG PROGRAM

At this point, discussions with the DOC resulted in the PWS adopting the DOC Protected Species and Predator Detection Dog training system.[3] This program is based on a bilevel assessment and certification system, which aims to ensure that consistent standards are applied across all dogs in the program and that the dogs in the program are suitable for use on conservation land with high-profile protected species as part of the natural environment.

Here, a little more background on the DOC program is warranted. Historically, New Zealand is considered the first country to have used dogs for conservation purposes (Helton 2009), when Richard Henry used his dog to find kiwi (*Apteryx* sp.) and kakapo (*Strigops habrotilus*) in the 1890s. Working in Fiordland National Park, Henry translocated the captured birds to predator-free islands in Dusky Sound. The New Zealand Wildlife Service (a predecessor of DOC) used dogs to assist in locating threatened bird species (including kakapo and kiwi) during the 1970s and 1980s. Variable performance and discipline amongst the canines nationwide led to DOC developing national standards, commencing with a pilot program in 1998 and following with an established program within DOC from 2000 (Karen Vincent, National Coordinator, Conservation Dogs Program, DOC, personal communication, 2015). Dogs within the program are divided between threatened-species dogs (to detect threatened bird, insect, or reptile species) and pest detection dogs (to detect animal or plant pests).

The training program structure is based on a two-tier system. In the first tier, a (usually) young dog is trained by its handler with training focusing on basic obedience and aptitude for locating target scents. The dog is usually trained to respond to commands by voice, whistle, and hand signals. The training exercises are formalized and nationally consistent, and all dogs are assessed against the training exercises by a national assessor. Those dogs scoring a pass are awarded an *interim certificate* that essentially recognizes that the dog (and handler) has met the requisite skill level for obedience and control and shows sufficient promise to warrant progressing to more in-depth training. After receiving the interim certificate, a dog may be permitted to work on conservation land or in the presence of threatened species, usually in a controlled situation. An interim certificate is valid for 6 months.

The second level is more involved and takes considerable time. The training exercises are more complex and varied. There is a strong focus on the target scent that the canine will be detecting in its working life. In addition, obedience training is maintained. A variety of nontarget scents are introduced, and the dog is trained to ignore them. Depending on the environment the dog may be working in, the dog may be regularly exposed to various distracting environments that replicate conditions it will face while working. Given that many dogs are used on islands with no public access or landing facilities, these scenarios may include traveling in helicopters, light aircraft, or small boats. Steadiness under firearm use is a common training component for pest detection dogs. Others may include aversion to traps and acceptance of muzzles.

Again, each dog is assessed against a specific set of criteria, with a set score required for a pass. If a handler and dog are successful in passing this assessment, the dog is awarded a *full certificate* and is considered fit for conservation work on the target species it was trained for. A full certificate is valid for 3 years. Most dogs take about 18 months from entering training to becoming fully certified. New Zealand currently has about 80 dogs with full certification. Of these, about 55 find threatened species and 25 find pests (including plants). Of the pest detection dog handlers, 9 are DOC staff, and 14 are external contractors. DOC also offers a kiwi aversion course for dog owners amongst the wider community who may take dogs on land that has kiwi populations.[4] Internationally, the training criteria and assessment are considered very rigorous and demanding. This is the background to the system adopted and modified by the Macquarie Island Pest Eradication Project.

BREEDS FOR MACQUARIE ISLAND

There was considerable discussion and debate about the breeds considered suitable for the work on Macquarie Island, as well as the preferred gender. The breeds selected needed to have three key characteristics. Firstly, they needed to demonstrate a strong hunting drive. Most of the dogs submitted for consideration fulfilled this criterion. Secondly, the dogs needed to be able to withstand the harsh climatic conditions found on Macquarie Island, where the summer temperature rarely exceeded 8°C (46°F) and the winter rarely dropped below −10°C (14°F) on the higher parts of the island, but where wind chill from the frequent gales was far lower than that. In addition, the dogs would frequently be working in thick tussock vegetation (which intercepted rainfall) and would make the dogs wet for long periods. They could also be expected to have to swim creeks, lakes, and occasionally coastal sections and would almost inevitably fall into the fetid elephant seal wallows found around the coastal zone, from which extraction would often be difficult. In short, the dog breeds selected needed to be able to sustain wet, cold conditions for long periods. Finally, but critically, the selected breed needed to be adaptable to working for a new handler each year. Dogs that displayed a high degree of loyalty to one handler to the point of not working for a new handler were considered a liability to the successful implementation of the project.

PROCUREMENT OF DOGS FOR MACQUARIE ISLAND

The DOC dog training criteria were expanded and additional exercises drawn up to reflect the specific working environment on Macquarie Island. For instance, large congregations of penguins and seals crowd the coast, often leaving little passing room, an environment very few dogs are ever exposed to. Due to the presence of generally protected wildlife, with some species listed as Threatened, Endangered, or Critically Endangered under Australian legislation, a very high priority was placed on absolute obedience of the dogs, which were initially worked with muzzles.

The tender, when let, included details of all the training criteria and associated assessment exercises. Tenderers were requested to outline their intended training approach and facilities and propose dog breeds for consideration. The then-national assessor for DOC was contracted to fill the role of Dog Training Coordinator for the Macquarie Island project. In this role, he maintained contact with selected dog trainers, hosted workshops, ensured consistency of training methods and commands, and conducted all interim and full certificate assessments. Contract progress payments for each dog were linked to passing the interim and full certificates, with a percentage paid on delivery to the project office in Hobart, Tasmania.

Two other aspects were emphasized in the tender prescription. It was important that the dog-handling team on the island not be distracted from the hunting task by having to deal with pups from accidental pregnancies. One measure to prevent this was to neuter male dogs, but a number of experienced handlers counseled against this due to the possibility of a slightly reduced hunting drive. To remove any possibility of dogs falling pregnant once on the island, it was specified that only entire male dogs would be considered for the project. Once training commenced, one of the handlers was so impressed by the potential of a bitch in training that the project team agreed to take her if she was spayed. The second important consideration was that trainers only acquire pups or young dogs to commence training. With the training period expected to take 2 years and the dogs intended to remain working on the island in harsh weather and terrain conditions for 5 years, even if acquired as pups, the dogs would be nearly 8 years old by the end of the projected time frame and thus considered to be toward the end of their working life. A dog acquired at, say, 3 or 4 years of age would be closer to 11 or 12 years of age by the later years of the project and could not be expected to maintain the necessary level of hunting activity.

Once tenders had been received, the Dog Training Coordinator joined the project manager and assistant project manager (who had prior experience in training goat detection dogs in the Galapagos Islands) to form a selection panel. Three tenders were received from Australia and three from New Zealand (an economic agreement between the two countries makes it straightforward for nationals of either country to participate in tenders or seek employment in the other). All tenderers were visited for discussion and demonstration of their dog training style and dogs.

With risk management again a prime consideration, the selection panel requested three of the six tenderers to supply a total of 11 trained rabbit detection dogs for the project, two in New Zealand each training two Labrador retrievers and one in Australia training seven English springer spaniels. In relation to the criterion that dog breeds must be willing to work for different handlers each year, these breeds were considered very adaptable; put simply, the food ethic of Labrador retrievers suggested they would work for whoever fed them, and the work ethic of the springer spaniels suggested they would work for whoever took them hunting. It was clear to all trainers that they needed to start training more dogs than they were contracted to supply, as the rigorous training criteria convinced them that not all dogs would pass the full certificate, and they needed to have backups for that eventuality.

By selecting three different suppliers, several risks were mitigated. First, if all dogs were trained by one trainer, there was a risk of disease at a kennel reducing the number of dogs under training, possibly at a critical juncture. Second, if all dogs were with one trainer and that trainer's personal, professional, or economic circumstances altered adversely, the project could be exposed to nondelivery of some or all of the contracted dogs. Thirdly, if all dogs were with one trainer and the trainer proved unable to train the required number of dogs to the full certification standard, then there would be insufficient time to source replacement dogs elsewhere. All three considerations exposed the project to risk that the desired number of dogs would not be on the ship to Macquarie Island in time to commence hunting operations immediately after the aerial baiting was completed (delivery of dogs was scheduled for June 2010). Spreading the supply of dogs amongst three trainers reduced all of these risks.

Once tenderers were selected and contracts signed for delivery of the required number of dogs, the project team could switch efforts to planning other aspects of the overall eradication, which was a major logistical exercise for the aerial baiting phase, requiring the procurement and transport of 28 staff, 4 helicopters, 305 tonnes (336 short tons) of rodenticide bait, some 500 drums of helicopter fuel, and various ancillary equipment to the island. As well, some 30 permits or regulatory approvals were required. Most of the day-to-day implementation of the dog training program was left to the trainers and the Dog Training Coordinator, with the assistant project manager providing oversight and liaison with the dog training team, including maintenance of records and the keeping of a file on each dog in the program.

CANINE TRAINING

The training of dogs to the required standard did take about 18–24 months, as expected. While the trainers found the training criteria demanding, and not all of their dogs made it to the final assessment, only 1 of 11 dogs failed the final assessment, and that by a small margin. As that trainer had no backup dogs and the other trainers did, an 11th dog was purchased from one of the other trainers to make up the full number required. The Australian-based trainer was highly experienced and, over a long career, had trained detection dogs for military, police, biosecurity, and border protection/customs functions, yet he rated the training criteria for the Macquarie Island project as the most stringent he had worked with.

The baiting phase of the project was not completed as scheduled in the winter of 2010, due to extended bad weather, so the dogs were not required as planned in June 2010. Accordingly, their trainers' contracts were extended for a further 10 months, and kenneling, upkeep, and training standards continued for that time. In the interim, the project acquired a border terrier from a New Zealand DOC dog handler. The terrier had an interim certificate and had been under training as a rodent detection dog, but "wouldn't stay off rabbit scent." The terrier went to one of the New Zealand-based trainers for further training and was fully certified as a rabbit detection dog before delivery to Tasmania, bringing the total canine team to 12 dogs.

Deployment to Macquarie Island

The dogs were delivered to Tasmania in late April 2011 and traveled to Macquarie Island with the aerial baiting team. This meant some months of inactivity for them while the aerial baiting phase was completed but had the advantage that they were conditioned over the winter and were in place to commence hunting as soon as the baiting was completed. Because there were two dog handlers on the aerial baiting team, they were able to look after the dogs during the winter when they were not needed and use them on occasions when an individual rabbit sign was found as the baiting work concluded.

Prior to the bait drops, the rabbit hemorrhagic disease virus (RHDV) had been released, and this and the bait had removed nearly every rabbit of the 150,000-plus population. Once dogs were deployed in the field, care was needed to ensure they did not ingest baits or scavenge toxic rabbit carcasses, and all dogs wore muzzles initially to manage this risk. The active ingredient in the bait was an anticoagulant (brodifacoum), and plentiful stocks of the antidote (vitamin K) were taken to the island, as well as testing equipment for blood clotting analysis. Not only were the dogs considered a vital asset in detecting surviving rabbits and thus integral to the success of the eradication project; there was also an investment of some AU\$450,000 in the canine team, so they were a valuable asset in financial terms as well as operational.

Commencement of Rabbit Detection

The commencement of the hunting phase was undertaken with significant interest in the abundance and distribution of surviving rabbits. It was already clear from visual observations that RHDV had massively reduced rabbits before baiting (Springer and Carmichael 2012), and after the baiting, rabbit abundance was obviously near zero. Areas where dozens of rabbits had previously been observed simultaneously were now devoid, and to the casual observer, it would appear that all rabbits had been eradicated. Fifteen long-established[5] 2 ha rabbit count areas spread around the island continued to be counted monthly, as they had been for many years, and no rabbits were seen in the count areas after May 2011.

It was at this point that the lessons learned from previous projects proved invaluable, as the project team had the budget, staff, dogs, tools, and infrastructure all set up on the assumption that a miniscule percentage of rabbits would have survived, even if at near-undetectable levels. As the calculated percentages suggested that even with very optimistic kill rates, there were potentially several dozen to several hundred survivors, it was vital to assess the likely remaining population in order to fine-tune the hunting strategy and allocate resources to areas appropriately. The likely behavior of surviving rabbits was unknown. Previously, rabbits were not considered to stray far from their natal warrens, but with the complete disintegration of the social structure of the rabbit population, it was unknown whether survivors would stay in their local area (as there would no longer be any competition for food) or would become more mobile in an effort to find potential mates and social contact.

With the aerial baiting completed, the hunting teams deployed to the hunting blocks, with a dog handler with two dogs allocated to each of the six hunting blocks, along with another hunter. The hunting team stayed in the field for a 4-week roster, taking Sundays off while in the field and returning to the station at the north end of the island at the end of each month for a 4-day break. At each field hut, dogs were kenneled in 209 L (44 gal.) steel drums, each with an access door cut in the lid with a weather flap, a wooden floor with foam insulation beneath, and sacking provided for bedding. The drums sat in wooden cradles to remove them from ground contact. Given the high work demands and cold conditions, dog food containing 30% fat was used in the field and supplemented with meat and vegetable kitchen scraps while on station.

Almost immediately, evidence was found of two rabbits (prints and sighting), and both of these were located within 2–3 days with the assistance of the dog team and dispatched. Another rabbit had been located prior to completion of baiting when seen by a staff member, and this had also been accounted for without canine involvement.

It quickly became apparent that the kill rate from RHDV and baiting had exceeded even highly optimistic predictions. Hunting teams found very few signs of rabbit survivors. The typical work routine was to search areas systematically but focusing on covering the terrain, using the dogs to cover more ground and check warren areas for presence of rabbits. That the dogs were focused on their target scent was clear as they retrieved numerous dead rabbits back to their handlers. Any signs of grazing, paw prints, or droppings were followed up with the dogs.

Over the subsequent months, with the onset of the austral spring, signs were found in widely spaced areas of the island. In some instances, the rabbit was located relatively quickly. One particular rabbit consumed significant time for most of the dog–handler teams. Leaving sporadic signs over a wide area, it was not clear if it was the same rabbit leaving signs or there was more than one. Sometimes, it would be a week between finding new sign evidence. Nor was it clear if the rabbit was remaining in the area or had moved on. The dogs were used extensively in pursuit of this rabbit, but it was not located by any of the dogs, and they showed inconsistent levels of interest over the 4 weeks this rabbit was pursued. It was eventually trapped in an area where an increasing number of traps had been set. However, most rabbits taken, whether by digging out of burrows or taken in traps, were as a result of one of the dogs indicating strongly and tracking scent to a specific burrow.

The value of the input by the olfactory capability of the dogs is reinforced when considering the large areas to be covered in the search for rabbits. With literally tens of thousands of recently occupied rabbit burrows, and thousands of hectares to be searched, there was no way that human searchers could have covered the ground thoroughly enough to determine which burrow might still have a rabbit occupant, especially with the certainty that a dog can bring when indicating. On at least three occasions, dogs picked up the ground scent of a rabbit in the course of general searching and indicated strongly. On each occasion, the ground scent was followed by the dog, on one occasion for some 700 m, to a burrow. The handler was then able to either dig out the burrow or set traps in burrow entrances and capture the rabbit.

The different breeds tended to work quite differently. The Labradors were usually worked fairly close into the handler, within a radius of about 20 m. When traveling in the field (as opposed to hunting), they tended to naturally heel. The springer spaniels had much higher levels of energetic enthusiasm and ranged far wider, often up to 80 m from the handler, typically ranging in a wide figure-eight pattern across the terrain. This could be an advantage as the coastal terrain had many rock stacks, which were favored burrowing habitats for rabbits. The spaniels could be sent out to further-away rock stacks to check for scent, while the Labradors were worked on rock stacks closer in. The terrier was a particular asset as many of the rock stacks were steep and often inaccessible, and the terrier was light and nimble enough to be passed up onto the rock stack to cover areas humans could not safely access.

In the final analysis, there were 12 rabbits taken after the completion of the aerial baiting, all of them in the first 4 months after baiting. Of these, 10 were found with the direct involvement of a detection dog. Of the surviving 12 rabbits, only 8 were adults, of which two were female. One of the females was lactating, and this initiated a more intensive search in the vicinity, resulting in the location of burrows containing four recently weaned runners. The value of the dogs was thus amply illustrated.

While unknown at the time hunting commenced, the surviving adult rabbit population post-baiting was in single figures, spread over 12,875 ha: a rate of one rabbit per 1,600 ha (3,950 ac.). It would have been nearly impossible for humans to locate and remove these eight adults from such an area within the same time frame without canine assistance. While human hunting methods should eventually have found sufficient signs to remove these rabbits, it is likely that it would have taken far longer to achieve, thus increasing the chances that further breeding would occur and increasing the number of offspring that could survive undetected until they were of breeding age. In that situation, the risk was that the rabbit population may breed faster than individuals could be located and removed, although given the small number of survivors, the hunting team should still have been able to remove them, but it would certainly have taken much longer.

Monitoring for Rabbit Absence

Hunting teams remained on the island for a further 2.5 years continuing the search for rabbits. Of this period, 2 years was the designated monitoring period commencing after it was felt that there were no surviving rabbits, a point reached by April 2012. Although by December 2011, there were at least four areas where clear rabbit signs had been found but the rabbit leaving it had not knowingly been accounted for, after a further 4 months of searching these areas intensively, it was unlikely that any rabbits had survived. They were still vulnerable to predatory skua and the RHD virus or may have been old enough to be near the end of their natural life.

The emphasis on nontarget species aversion during the training period meant that very few incidents of adverse wildlife encounters were experienced, and of course, during the period that the dogs spent working, they were constantly exposed on a daily basis to native wildlife. Some individual dogs did show more interest in burrowing petrels than others, especially as rabbits became harder to find and motivation levels dropped off, and handlers did need to be ready to correct dogs when they showed too much interest. The dogs showed little interest in penguins or seals and generally looked uncomfortable in close proximity to these animals. Despite the initial training and ongoing training/correction work on the island, dogs did kill a small number of burrowing seabirds, usually when they were sniffing at a burrow and a bird (mostly Antarctic prions, *Pachyptila desolata*) emerged.

Canine Health Issues

Dogs were groomed daily, as a major irritant was the abundant seeds of the native buzzy (*Aceana magellanica*), a prostrate burnet with seed heads covered in a round ball of hooked spikes (Figure 22.4). These would attach to the dogs' coats in large numbers and were extremely difficult to remove, requiring sometimes hours each day of painstaking grooming by the handler. Trimming the coats and feathers, especially of the longer-haired spaniels, reduced the extent of this problem to a degree. Seeds from other grass species were prone to embedding in the dogs' feet, gums, or jowls and often were very difficult to detect. Some developed into large abscesses and required surgery to remove and drain. Surgery and other dog treatments were usually conducted by the station doctor, although on one occasion, a visiting tourist ship had three veterinarians on board who agreed to treat two dogs that had abscesses at the time of their visit. Veterinary advice was provided by

FIGURE 22.4   Dogs with buzzies.

e-mail/phone by a vet in Australia, who also made the round trip on the annual resupply voyage to check the dogs physically and follow up on any outstanding health issues. Apart from the issues caused by grass seeds, one springer spaniel developed a skin condition after nearly 3 years on the island that resulted in large areas of the scrotum, pads, and muzzle flaking off skin and leaving raw unhealed areas. This was thought to be a progressive cold-related injury.

Four of the 12 dogs were retired early from the program. One springer spaniel displayed lameness soon after hunting commenced, once sustained work demands came into play. While absolutely keen, the dog was unable to perform consistently due to knee problems and was unable to take further part in hunting work. He returned to Hobart after 4 months (December 2011) and subsequently had knee surgery. A second springer spaniel developed severe arthritis in both hind knees after several months' work on the island and was returned to Hobart in April 2012, where corrective surgery to both knees improved his mobility significantly. A third springer spaniel twice landed awkwardly when twisting midair when descending from steep rock stacks. These incidents cumulatively appear to have caused a spinal injury, which made any leaping or climbing painful, although no untoward symptoms were evident on flat ground. Given the arduous nature of the fieldwork, it was difficult to maintain the dog only for flat-country work, so this dog was retired in April 2013. The border terrier, already about 9 years old when acquired by the program, became more reluctant to work on the higher, colder parts of the island as time went on. He was eventually returned to Hobart in April 2013 and subsequently retrained on rodents, and was then used at the AAD cargo and biosecurity facility to check cargo and facilities for rodent egress prior to voyages departing for Macquarie Island.

Two of the Labrador dogs sustained potentially fatal falls over steep faces while working on the island. One surprised his handler by not being dead after tumbling 150 m down a steep rocky gully. He had been knocked off his feet by a springer spaniel returning to heel rather more enthusiastically than the precarious location on a steep spur warranted. He sustained grazing and bruising but, after 2 days off work, appeared none the worse for this substantial tumble. The second Labrador fell down a steep bank into a pool of water at the top of a waterfall, from which there was no escape either up or down. A rope was retrieved from a hut and, with a loop in the end, was thrown 10 m down to the dog, who took the loop in his mouth and tried to hang on while being pulled up the face, only to have to let go partway up each time. Eventually, the loop was changed to a noose, and with the dog taking it in his mouth once more, the noose tightened around the lower jaw, and after several trying hours, he was dragged up the face to safety.

Motivational Challenges

With the last rabbit found in November 2011 but the dogs staying on the island for a further 3 years, motivation of dogs (and handlers) when not finding their target scent was a real concern. Anticipating this, 50 rabbits were shot prior to the commencement of baiting and frozen on station, to be used to refresh the dogs to the target scent after wild rabbits could not be located. Once these were all used, about 40 rabbits were shot annually in Tasmania and sent to the island frozen. At the end of each month, while on station for a break, the dog handlers and dogs would all spend a day undertaking training exercises before deploying to the field for the next 4-week roster. This was overseen by the assistant eradication team leader, a person with responsibility for on-island training and coordination of the dogs and handlers. Usually once a month, this person would circulate around all the hunting blocks on the island to spend a day with each handler and ensure that consistency of commands and working methods was being maintained.

The handlers had all participated in a 2-day training course prior to deployment to the island, using as demonstration dogs the two springer spaniels that had been retired early in the project. The monthly on-island training would include using drags of thawed rabbits, plus use of the "scent-o-matic"—a locally made training device consisting of sheets of ply with 100 mm (4 in.) polyvinyl chloride (PVC) drainage pipe inserts that were accessed from the back of the board and in which various target and nontarget objects (such as bird and rabbit carcasses) could be placed. Dead rabbit drags were also conducted in the field in areas unknown to the handlers.

Rodent Detection Dogs

The project operational plan called for a rodent detection dog to spend 12 months on the island 2 years after aerial baiting. The 2-year period is a relatively arbitrary figure but is designed to allow any remnant rodent survivors from a bait drop to build up to more readily detectable numbers. If the monitoring effort is thorough after a 2-year period and no rodents are found, eradication success is usually declared. Rodent detection dogs have proven successful at locating rats at extremely low densities on islands in New Zealand (Shapira et al. 2011).

For the rodent detection dogs, as only one was required, the decision was made to recruit a person with a fully certified rodent dog rather than have the PWS train and own the dog as with the rabbit detection teams. There was a high chance of finding an appropriately experienced person and dog for the 1-year deployment. At the recruitment stage, two candidates showed high suitability and, between them, had three DOC-certified rodent detection dogs. As the confidence in rodent eradication success was commensurate with the level of search effort that could be applied, and the budget was available, both handlers were employed (with the three dogs, all border/fox terrier crosses), and both ended up spending a full year on the island, more than doubling the initially intended monitoring capacity.

The rodent dog team initially focused their efforts on the coastal zones as it was winter shortly after arrival, and during winter, many of the penguin and elephant seal colonies emptied out as the animals migrated for the winter; in summer, coastal access is much more difficult due to the number of penguin colonies around the coastline. The coast and escarpment slopes where tussock was the predominant vegetation were prime rat habitat, while rats were almost completely absent from the short grassland and feldmark habitats on the uplifted plateau, where mice were widely distributed. Having covered the coastline during the winter months, the team moved onto the plateau for the summer months. After surveying the island over a 12-month period, no sign of live rodents was encountered. As with the rabbit detection dogs, dead rats and mice were sent to the island to use for target refresher purposes.

Search Coverage

Both rabbit and rodent detection team staff carried GPS units (Garmin Csx 60) to log search areas. Data were downloaded fortnightly by the eradication team leader, who circulated around the hunting blocks during the month-long field roster. Data were collated to look at consistency of areas searched, identify any gaps that needed to be checked, and plan the following month's work. Dogs carried GPS tracking collars (Garmin Astro), but the area covered was not recorded by these units. Cumulatively over the 32 months of fieldwork, the rabbit and rodent hunting teams covered over 92,000 km (57,300 mi.) of search effort, on an island 34 km (21 mi.) long by 4 km (2.5 mi.) wide.

In April 2014, the final team returned home, and the eradication of rabbits, rats, and mice on Macquarie Island was declared successful, an outcome that the canine members of the team had made a significant contribution to. In the case of rabbits, it is possible that eradications on this scale may only be feasible with the use of detection dogs to tip the balance in favor of the hunters who strive to reduce pest numbers faster than they can breed.

The outcomes of the eradication are already evident and will continue in years to come. Vegetation recovery in the absence of grazing rabbits is dramatic and widespread. Some palatable plant species had been heavily grazed to the point of scarcity on the island—several are now making a strong comeback. Since the removal of rats and mice, some seabird species absent from the island for decades have already recolonized the island and established breeding burrows, while others have reestablished on the main island from remnant populations on rat-free offshore rock stacks. Invertebrate fauna is also more abundant. An important outcome is the demonstration that successful eradication of rabbits and mice is feasible on islands far larger than previously attempted, thus encouraging other countries to consider similar projects.

Transfer of Methodology

During the period that the Macquarie Island Pest Eradication Project operated rabbit and rodent detection dogs on the island, other agencies adapted the training methodology for their own situations. Two nearby examples were the use of canines to detect fox scats for the Fox Eradication Branch of the Tasmanian Department of Primary Industries, Parks, Water and Environment. With foxes thought to be established on Tasmania early this century in extremely low densities, there was difficulty in establishing eradication efforts to try and prevent statewide establishment. Fox scat detection dogs were trained to cover the landscape and identify scats from the red fox (*Vulpes vulpes*) to identify areas for following up with poisoning. Scats were sent to a laboratory for DNA analysis.

On Phillip Island, a 10,000 ha (24,700 ac.) island off the coast of Victoria in southeastern Australia, foxes have been established for over 100 years and had been subject to either control or eradication attempts for nearly all of that time. As well as causing pastoral losses, foxes also impacted native wildlife, including significant mortality to resident fairy penguins (*Eudyptula minor*), which formed a major economic resource for the island by means of commercial penguin-watching opportunities. A 2013 review of the fox eradication program implemented by the Phillip Island Nature Parks in 2006 (after decades of control programs) recommended introducing fox detection dogs to aid the program. This was implemented in May 2014 using one of the same trainers who trained the Macquarie Island dogs. The introduction of the olfactory capabilities of the dogs (springer spaniels) has significantly improved the confidence of the two-person fox eradication team that they can now focus on areas where the dogs are indicating recent fox activity.

The training criteria used for the Macquarie Island dogs were also shared with the United States Department of Agriculture (USDA) Wildlife Services managers leading the Chesapeake Bay Nutria Eradication Project, to help inform their training standards for the establishment of a detection dog team to detect nutria (*Myocastor coypus*) scat and assess hair samples from the project area in Chesapeake Bay.

CONCLUSION

Programs to eradicate pest species from islands in Australia and New Zealand have profited from the participation of detection dogs. Although the use of dogs for such purposes fits within the broader category of conservation detection work, there are unique aspects to using dogs for elimination of target species, as opposed to other conservation functions. The dogs may have to be trained, for instance, to work while there may be gunfire, and there must be concern for the dogs' welfare when poisons are used as part of the program to eradicate a pest from an island or other isolated environment. This function is likely to increase as many programs will not be able to verify the success of eradication efforts without using dogs to survey and remove remnants of populations that have largely been eliminated. Key lessons exist not only in the critical importance of dogs to the success of the program but also in the importance of careful planning of how dogs will be procured, used, trained, and provided for when undertaking this type of work.

ENDNOTES

1. A curly-coated retriever and a dalmatian–German shorthaired pointer cross.
2. The Island Eradication Advisory Group (IEAG).
3. Now known as the New Zealand Conservation Dogs Program.
4. Information at http://www.doc.govt.nz/parks-and-recreation/know-before-you-go/dog-access/conservation-dog-programme/.
5. Half of the rabbit count areas had been established in 1974 and the rest in 2004–2005 and were counted monthly.

23 Canine Biodetection in Conservation, Eradication, and Border Protection
A Regulatory Perspective

John Ensminger

Surveying and sampling animal and even plant species and populations in danger, eradicating pests, determining the impact of human activities and environmental change on species and populations, and preventing import or export of pests or rare species all increasingly involve dogs trained as biodetectors. This may be the fastest-growing profession for detection dogs and handlers as this use does not face the legal barriers of narcotics, explosives, cadaver, or other canine work for law enforcement, nor is it limited by the clinical standards of medical screening, meaning that there is generally less inherent resistance to deployment of dogs with conservation functions.[1]

Many of the studies undertaken with dogs trained to recognize the presence of certain species by finding live animals or carcasses, scat or trails, or their presence in cargo shipments, consider such deployments effective if the resulting data are more accurate than has been obtained by other means, such as human visual or vocal observation, cameras triggered by sensors, trapping, hair snares, or scent stations. Previously captured animals can be followed by GPS collars or surveyed by tags.[2] Success rates are sometimes a limiting factor in using biodetection dogs for nonresearch purposes, such as finding bedbugs, where customers appropriately demand that the pests be correctly identified before undertaking expensive eradication measures, and this area has already been marked by certain allegations of fraud (Buckley 2010). (See Chapter 21 herein regarding insect detection.) Table 23.1 lists target species in studies that involved the use of detection dogs, many of which are discussed in the various sections below.

CONSERVATION

Biodetection dogs have been particularly useful in surveying populations of species of animals that are declining to the point where extinction is a possibility, if not a probability. Legal protections, both in the United States and in many countries around the world, require that such species and populations be regularly surveyed to see if preservation and recovery programs are necessary or effective. In the United States, the Endangered Species Act and other legislative and regulatory initiatives are implemented by a number of federal and state agencies, which may have different survey requirements. Global awareness of the need for protecting endangered species is increasing, and dogs have an important role to play in preservation efforts.[3]

ENDANGERED SPECIES ACT

Under the Endangered Species Act of 1973,[4] Congress acknowledged that various species were extinct "as a consequence of economic growth and development untempered by adequate concern and conservation," while "other species of fish, wildlife, and plants have been so depleted in numbers that they are in danger of or threatened with extinction."[5] The act was intended "to provide a

TABLE 23.1

Summary of Target Species and Key Factors in Major Research Studies Using Biodetection Dogs

Target Species (Common Name/Scientific Name)	Legal Status (FWS[a]/IUCN[b])	Description of Dogs/Teams	Environment Where Dogs Deployed	Means of Surveying/Identification with Dogs	Additional/Compared Survey Methods
Mammals: Gorilla (*Gorilla gorilla diehli*)	Endangered/critically endangered	3 dogs trained to identify gorilla feces; training completed at Kagwene Gorilla Sanctuary[c]	African tropical forest between Nigeria and Cameroon	Loop transects and straight walks in certain grids; also searches based on experience	Fecal samples collected for genetic analysis
Black bear, *Ursus americanus*	Threatened in certain areas/least concern	Crossbreeds of redbone and Walker hounds[d]	Forest	Air scenting from hood of vehicle	Tracks, radio collars placed on bears
Polar bear, *Ursus maritimus*	Threatened/vulnerable; 18 CFR 18.117, 18.128 (offshore exploration requirements)	Karelian bear dogs,[e] identifying lairs under ice	Arctic, ice-covered	Dogs rode in vehicle on tundra	Cameras set up where dogs indicated
Cougar, *Puma concolor*	Threatened/least concern	Unspecified working dogs[f]; dogs trained	Forest, grazing range, developed agriculture	Scat detection to determine home range of cougars; also location of kill sites, and tracking cougars[g]	GPS collars, human observers
Fisher, *Martes pennanti*	Proposed threatened[b]/least concern	Dogs were trained in a manner that involved detection as well as something similar to search and rescue	Survey sites throughout Vermont[i]	Transect search by scat detection dog, handler, and "orienteer," who was responsible for navigating and keeping team on transect	DNA analysis, but only for select scats

(Continued)

TABLE 23.1 (CONTINUED)

Summary of Target Species and Key Factors in Major Research Studies Using Biodetection Dogs

Target Species (Common Name/*Scientific Name*)	Legal Status (FWS[a]/*IUCN*[b])	Description of Dogs/Teams	Environment Where Dogs Deployed	Means of Surveying/ Identification with Dogs	Additional/Compared Survey Methods
Feral cat, *Felis catus*	Pest species on islands	Survey describes no specific approaches	Islands in Australia, the Channel Islands off California	Dogs found to cover large areas quickly	Trapping, poison bating, shooting, and recovering carcasses
Bobcat, *Lynx rufus*	Not listed, but Mexican bobcat is endangered/*least concern*	Id.; also Harrison (2006)	Id.; Harrison surveyed woodlands in New Mexico	Id.; Harrison used dogs unleashed but kept near handler	Id.; Harrison compared hair snares, cameras, and scent stations; DNA tested from scat; for capture–recapture, see Ruell et al. (2009)
Kit fox, *Vulpes macrotis*	*V. macrotis* spp. *mutica* in California endangered/*least concern*	Dog initially taught to recognize scat of kit fox, then red and gray fox	San Joaquin Valley, CA	Transect routes in surveyed areas walked by dog–handler team and navigator	DNA analysis of scat
Franklin's ground squirrel, *Poliocitellus franklinii*	Not listed (except by Illinois)/*least concern*	Dogs had to distinguish this particular squirrel from similar species	Midwestern States, dense grassland vegetation	Surveys consisted of dog and handler walking along two 90 m trapping transects twice	Livetrapping surveys took much more time
Black-footed ferret, *Mustela nigripes*	Endangered/*endangered*	Scat detection; dogs trained to ignore barking of prairie dogs; cacti required fitting dogs with protective boots	Wildlife refuge in Montana	Searches of colonies of prairie dogs the ferret depends upon for food	Spotlight surveys at night

(Continued)

TABLE 23.1 (CONTINUED)
Summary of Target Species and Key Factors in Major Research Studies Using Biodetection Dogs

Target Species (Common Name/Scientific Name)	Legal Status (FWS[a]/IUCN[b])	Description of Dogs/Teams	Environment Where Dogs Deployed	Means of Surveying/Identification with Dogs	Additional/Compared Survey Methods
Brocket species, South American deer, *Mazama*, spp. (*M. americana*, *M. gouazoubira*, *M. bororo*)	Not listed/*M. americana* (unknown), *M. gouazoubira* (least concern), *M. bororo* (vulnerable)	Female mixed-breed dog trained as narcotics detection dog	Dense Brazilian forest	Effective perpendicular distance from search line was 7.2 m	Observers visually searching did not find fecal samples but found tracks
Bush dog, *Speothos venaticus*	Near threatened and decreasing	Detection dog	Upper Parana Atlantic Forest, Misiones, Argentina	Dog located 11 bush dog areas, 4 of which were confirmed	Largely reported by opportunistic sightings; camera traps with taped calls and conspecific urine
Giant armadillo, *Priodontes maximus*; giant anteater, *Myrmecophaga tridactyla*	Endangered/vulnerable and decreasing; vulnerable and decreasing	Dogs trained to recognize scat of 2 species of xenarthrans[j]	Central Brazilian jungle around Emas National Park	Dogs identified localities of animals as indicated by scat	Scat samples used for DNA and diet, hormone, and disease analysis
Ringed seal, *Phoca hispida*	Threatened[k]/least concern; 50 CFR 217.144, 217.146 (trained dog survey requirement)	Dogs trained to locate breathing holes and subnivean lairs by odor of ringed seals[l]	Ice, northern Alaska	Dogs ran ahead of snow machine, indicated seal odor by digging in snow above[m]	Use of dogs required by federal regulations; radio transmitters attached to seals' hind flippers

(Continued)

TABLE 23.1 (CONTINUED)

Summary of Target Species and Key Factors in Major Research Studies Using Biodetection Dogs

Target Species (Common Name/Scientific Name)	Legal Status (FWS[a]/IUCN[b])	Description of Dogs/Teams	Environment Where Dogs Deployed	Means of Surveying/Identification with Dogs	Additional/Compared Survey Methods
Right whale, Eubalaena glacialis	Endangered/endangered	Dogs had to have good physical stability and persistence in locating scat, and be calm	Training off Lubec, Maine; surveys in Bay of Fundy, Canada	Dogs positioned on bow; boat transects were conducted perpendicular to wind direction at 5–7 knots; helmsman steered toward direction indicated by dog	Dogs more than 4× more effective than opportunistic collection of scat; individual whales have been identified by DNA
Siberian tiger, Panthera tigris altaica	Endangered (species-wide)/endangered	Dogs trained to recognize individual tigers by scat[n]	Laboratory identification using glass jars	Procedures similar to scent lineups under Dutch protocols	Track size measurements, camera traps, genetic analysis of hair and scat
Hoary bat, Lasiurus cinereus (and other bats, particularly migratory foliage-roosting species)[o]	Endangered/least concern	2-year-old German shepherd[p]	Various wind energy facilities have used dogs in surveys of bird and bat mortality	Dogs trained to point and bark in presence of carcass[q]	Dogs located 73% of bats, humans only 20%[r]; another study had between 70% and 80% for dogs, 14% to 42% for humans[s]
Koala bear, Phascolarctos cinereus	Threatened/least concern/designated vulnerable species by Australia	Dogs searched for koala scats	Australian Eucalypt woodlands	Handler moved with dog off leash and redirected dog when it moved from established transect	Human-only surveys using government employees
Birds: Mexican spotted owl, Strix occidntalis ludica; northern spotted owl, Strix occidntalis caurina	Both threatened (ranges overlap)/near threatened	Dogs searched for accumulated Strix owl pellets; teams included an orienteer using a GPS to keep team in survey areas (polygons)	Northern California forest	Dogs walked 5–6 km/h, sat on target pellets to indicate	mtDNA in pellets analyzed; vocalization surveys compared

(Continued)

TABLE 23.1 (CONTINUED)

Summary of Target Species and Key Factors in Major Research Studies Using Biodetection Dogs

Target Species (Common Name/Scientific Name)	Legal Status (FWS[a]/IUCN[b])	Description of Dogs/Teams	Environment Where Dogs Deployed	Means of Surveying/Identification with Dogs	Additional/Compared Survey Methods
House sparrow, *Passer domesticus*	Not listed/*least concern but decreasing*	Hunting dogs, but no special training for searches; humans active searchers with dogs[t]	Low, rolling moraines in North and South Dakota	Searches of marked areas of specified size	Human searchers found 45% of placed carcasses, while dogs found 92%
Reptiles: Desert tortoise, *Gopherus agassizii*	Threatened/*vulnerable*	Working-breed dogs, used off leash guided by voice commands[u]; "combination of hunt and play drives is most desirable in a wildlife detection dog"[v]	North-central Mojave Desert, desert scrub vegetation	Dog teams employed zigzag or contour search strategy; detection distance ranged up to 62.8 m	Canine teams slightly more effective than human surveyors, but dogs somewhat better in vegetation;[w] tortoises also tracked with radio telemetry and water-soluble paint on carapace
Eastern indigo snake, *Drymarchon corais couperi*	Threatened/*least concern but decreasing*	Labrador mix used to locate shed skins and live snakes in tortoise burrows	Sandhill sites in Georgia and Florida	Defined survey areas indicated by aerial photographs	Dog more effective in detecting shed skins than live snakes below ground, but highly effective in both cases
Brown tree snake, *Boiga irregularis*	Pest species	Jack Russell terriers and beagles, trained to recognize snake but also for other agricultural inspections	Cargo searches	Protocols established by U.S. Department of Agriculture	Difficulties result from typhoons etc.[x]

(Continued)

TABLE 23.1 (CONTINUED)
Summary of Target Species and Key Factors in Major Research Studies Using Biodetection Dogs

Target Species (Common Name/Scientific Name)	Legal Status (FWS[a]/IUCN[b])	Description of Dogs/Teams	Environment Where Dogs Deployed	Means of Surveying/Identification with Dogs	Additional/Compared Survey Methods
Insects: Bumblebee (Bombus spp.)	Some bumblebee species, such as Bombus franklini, are endangered	English springer spaniel	Dog searched transects in four different environments	Scotland, Island of Tiree	Human encounters with underground nests are generally only by chance
Gypsy moth (Porthetria dispar)	Pest species	German shepherds[y]	Detection in stone, woods, and bark	Dogs could detect up to 2 m away	Actual field density estimates could be established
Stinkbug, Halyomorpha halys	Pest species	3-year-old Labrador retrievers, previously trained in mollusk detection	Woodlands in Maryland and West Virginia	Dogs took an average of 6.2 min to survey a 500 m squared transect with about 15 dead trees; >84% accuracy in laboratory and semifield trials	Human surveyors "destructively sampled" dead trees, also leaf litter
Sarcoptic mange, Sarcoptes scabiei	Parasite of over 100 mammals, including chamois	Bavarian Mountain hounds	Dolomite Alps	Dogs and handlers walked on mountain paths, with dogs on zigzag pattern; free-ranging dogs were used to find live mangy animals	Parasitologists noted smell of infected animals
Red fire ants, Solenopsis invicta	Pest species	Beagles previously used in customs detection work	Grassland in Taiwan that had previously been treated with pesticides and baits	Dogs trained to sit by targets but not so close as to be attacked by ants	Visual inspection, pitfall traps, and bait traps; satellite and aerial imagery indicate mound distributions

(Continued)

TABLE 23.1 (CONTINUED)
Summary of Target Species and Key Factors in Major Research Studies Using Biodetection Dogs

[a] Fish & Wildlife Service (FWS); 50 CFR 17.11(h).

[b] International Union for Conservation of Nature (IUCN) Red List of Threatened Species (http://www.iucnredlist.org/search), one of several databases maintained by IUCN.

[c] Arandjelovic et al. (2015).

[d] Akenson et al. (2001, 2013). See also Long et al. (2007), surveying fishers and bobcats as well.

[e] Kirschhoffer (2013).

[f] Clark (2014).

[g] Clark (2014); Davidson et al. (2014).

[h] Department of the Interior, FWS, proposed rule: Threatened Species Status for West Coast Distinct Population Segment of Fisher, 79 Fed. Reg. 60419 (October 7, 2014) (also see entry on Environmental Conservation Online System: http://ecos.fws.gov/speciesProfile/profile/speciesProfile.action?spcode=A0HS).

[i] Long et al. (2007).

[j] Vynne et al. (2009).

[k] Various subspecies are listed as threatened and endangered by the Fish & Wildlife Service, 50 CFR 17.11(h).

[l] Kelly et al. (2010).

[m] Kelly et al. (1986).

[n] Kerley (2010); Kerley and Salkina (2007).

[o] Dogs have also been used to measure bird mortality at wind farms. Paula et al. (2011) trained dogs on 17 bird species, including the Eurasian skylark (*Alauda arvensis*, not listed); the common swift (*Apus apus*, not listed); Eurasian buzzard (*Buteo buteo*, not listed); common woodpigeon (*Columba palumbus*, not listed, though some pigeons are endangered in the United States); common quail (*Coturnix coturnix*, not listed but decreasing); corn bunting (*Emberiza calandra*, not listed); common kestrel (*Falco tinnunculus*, not listed, though some falcons are); red-rumped swallow (*Hirundo daurica*, least concern); common nightingale (*Luscinia megarhynchos*, least concern); white wagtail (*Motacilla alba*, least concern); house sparrow (*Passer domesticus*, least concern); warblers (*Pylloscopus*, various species, generally least concern but some vulnerable); pipistrelle (various species, generally least concern); common stonechat (*Saxicola torquatus*, least concern); blackcap (*Sylvia atricapilla*, least concern); Eurasian blackbird (*Turdus merula*, least concern); and common barn owl (*Tyto alba*, least concern).

[p] Paula et al. (2011).

[q] Bernardino et al. (2012)

[r] Mathews et al. (2013).

[s] Arnett (2006).

[t] Homan et al. (2001).

[u] Nussear et al. (2008).

[v] Cablk and Heaton (2006).

[w] Nussear et al. (2008). Cablk and Heaton (2006) had better results with canine teams.

[x] Engeman et al. (2002).

[y] Wallner and Ellis (1976).

means whereby the ecosystems upon which endangered species and threatened species depend may be conserved, to provide a program for the conservation of such endangered species and threatened species," and to honor treaties and conventions and work with other countries as necessary.

The act more specifically defines an endangered species as

> [A]ny species which is in danger of extinction throughout all or a significant portion of its range other than a species of the Class Insecta determined by the Secretary to constitute a pest whose protection... would present an overwhelming and overriding risk to man.

A threatened species is "any species which is likely to become an endangered species within the foreseeable future throughout all or a significant portion of its range."[6]

The Secretary of the Interior is to publish lists of endangered and threatened species, specifying over what portion of the range of the species it is endangered or threatened, and issue "such regulations as he deems necessary and advisable to provide for the conservation of such species."[7] The Secretary is to develop and implement recovery plans for the conservation and survival of listed species. Such plans are to have "objective measurable criteria which, when met, would result in a determination...that the species be removed from the list."[8] Thus, measurement of the population that is endangered is inherent in the federal law applicable to the activities of the U.S. Fish & Wildlife Service (and other federal agencies, such as the Department of Commerce).

Recovery plans issued by the Fish & Wildlife Service "do not create a legal obligation beyond existing legal requirements." Such plans are intended to "delineate reasonable actions for the conservation and survival of listed species, based upon the best scientific and commercial data available."[9] Fish & Wildlife Service uses a ranking system for categorizing the degree of threat and recovery potential (Table 23.2).

TABLE 23.2

U.S. Government Ranking System for Threat Levels to Listed Species

Degree of Threat	Recovery Potential	Taxonomy	Priority	Conflict
High	High	Monotypic genus	1	1C
		Species	2	2C
		Subspecies/DPS	3	3C
	Low	Monotypic genus	4	4C
		Species	5	5C
		Subspecies/DPS	6	6C
Moderate	High	Monotypic genus	7	7C
		Species	8	8C
		Subspecies/DPS	9	9C
	Low	Monotypic genus	10	10C
		Species	11	11C
		Subspecies/DPS	12	12C
Low	High	Monotypic genus	13	13C
		Species	14	14C
		Subspecies/DPS	14	15C
	Low	Monotypic genus	16	16C
		Species	17	17C
		Subspecies/DPS	18	18C

Note: DPS, distinct population segment.

By monitoring population progress, surveys may detect whether conservation efforts are working and whether they are working within or beyond designated conservation areas.[10] Verification of the effectiveness of recovery plans has involved, for instance, dog teams working on black-footed ferrets[11] and desert tortoises.[12]

OCEAN AND RIVER ENVIRONMENTS

Marine mammals are protected under the Marine Mammal Protection Act of 1972.[13] Congress states that marine mammal "species and population stocks should not be permitted to diminish beyond the point at which they cease to be a significant functioning element in the ecosystem of which they are a part, and, consistent with this major objective, they should not be permitted to diminish below their optimum sustainable population." This act describes a species or population stock as "depleted" if it is listed as endangered or threatened under the Endangered Species Act of 1973. *Conservation* is defined as

> the collection and application of biological information for the purposes of increasing and maintaining the number of animals within species and populations of marine mammals at their optimum sustainable population. Such terms include the entire scope of activities that constitute a modern scientific resource program, including, but not limited to, research, census, law enforcement, and habitat acquisition and improvement. Also included within these terms, when and where appropriate, is the periodic or total protection of species or populations as well as regulated taking.[14]

The act contemplates that marine mammals may be taken accidentally in fishing, oil exploration, and other operations. When a species is endangered or threatened, incidental taking levels are to be limited, and a recovery plan and a monitoring program are to be in place.[15] Federal financial assistance may be provided to states "with agencies which have entered into a cooperative agreement to assist in the preservation of threatened and endangered species."[16]

The National Estuarine Research Reserve System regulations state in 15 CFR 921.1(d) the following:

> Habitat manipulation for resource management purposes is prohibited except as specifically approved by NOAA [National Oceanic and Atmospheric Administration] as…an activity necessary for the protection of public health or the preservation of other sensitive resources which have been listed or are eligible for protection under relevant Federal or state authority (e.g., threatened/endangered species or significant historical or cultural resources)….

The National Oceanic and Atmospheric Administration is an agency in the Department of Commerce.

USE OF DETECTION DOGS

Finding scat is a common function of detection dogs in conservation, and scat sampling has proven particularly effective in detecting wildlife presence and movements but has also been used in analyzing diet and disease and hormone status of target species.[17] Reed et al. (2011) state that dogs have been used in wildlife surveys for more than a century but that "recent applications have expanded both the scope and sophistication of their contributions, particularly through scent detection and discrimination work." This team notes that dogs have been used to recover carcasses, locate invasive or endangered species, detect scent trails, and identify burrows.

> Scats collected in detection dog surveys can be combined with recent advancements in laboratory techniques to generate a wealth of information about wildlife populations, including species- and individual-level identification, diet, disease, reproductive status, and physiological condition.

Dogs often allow for surveying longer trails and larger areas. Reed et al. (2011) further state the following:

> As recent contributions to the literature suggest, surveys using conservation detection dogs will become increasingly common in wildlife research and management. Because the influence of environmental conditions is likely to vary substantially by study environment and individual dog, it is important for researchers to quantify the factors affecting detection rates and minimize potential biases. At a minimum, we recommend that researchers report the conditions under which wildlife detection surveys took place and analyze whether detection rates vary as a function of temperature, humidity, wind, precipitation, and other locally important environmental factors.

Arandjelovic et al. (2015) found that dogs used to survey the Cross River gorilla in an African tropical forest were impeded by dense vines but noted that the "mobility of the dog handlers was generally the limiting factor in all searches with dogs." DeMatteo et al. (2009) used dogs effectively to find bush dog scat and dens in the Upper Parana Atlantic forest of Brazil.

Thompson et al. (2012) note, however, that dog surveys come with their own problems:

> Detector dog surveys are unique among non-invasive survey techniques in that sampling does not follow a spatially structured survey design based on fixed trap locations, transects, quadrats, or other spatial units. Despite researchers' best intentions regarding transects or survey grids, scent travels with air currents and dogs must be given some amount of leeway to track down the source. Although this greatly increases survey efficiency and subsequent sample size, it biases the sampling design resulting in violations of traditional CMR [capture–mark–recapture/resight] assumptions. Consequently, precise delineation of where sampling occurs is difficult. Coverage of an area can also vary greatly depending on climatic and topographic conditions, the individual dog used, and population density of the species being studied. Detector dog surveys therefore do not produce well-defined spatial encounter histories.

To deal with such problems, Thompson et al. (2012) developed an approach where a spatial structure was imposed on the survey area after the survey was completed, which they believe facilitates estimation of population density.

Some researchers have acknowledged that canine teams are not always operated as objectively as might be desired. Veseley (2008) described the training of conservation detection dogs to locate Kincaid's lupine (*Lupinus sulphureus kincaidi*), a plant listed as threatened by the U.S. Fish & Wildlife Service,[18] in prairie habitats:

> Observations during the trials suggest that target plants missed on plots and false alerts resulted from transitory miscommunications between dog and handler, manipulative behaviors by the dog to solicit a reward, or failure of the handler to direct the dog to completely search the transect.

Critescu et al. (2015) used a detection dog in experimental and field-based trials to find koala bear (*Phascolarctos cinereus*) scat. The dog had a 97% success rate, but off leash, a 100% success rate. The use of the leash in the environment often meant that the handler's movement restrictions became the dog's, and the leash could become entangled and "waste time or break the search."

In law enforcement uses of detection dogs, an alert where no drugs are found is sometimes attributed to the odor being residual, i.e., that drugs were present at one time but are no longer at the location. Stevenson et al. (2010), surveying the eastern indigo snake (*Drymarchon corais couperi*, or *D. couperi*), note that dogs may have alerted to tortoise burrows used by snakes but that the presence of a snake could not always be verified. The researchers stated that they "strongly suspect that the dog would have performed better with additional training with live snakes prior to these trials."

COMPARISON OF CANINE EFFECTIVENESS WITH OTHER SURVEY METHODS

Numerous studies involving dogs in surveying target species either compare the success rates of dogs with prior studies or involve the use of several types of survey techniques that are compared as a principal subject of the paper.

Wasser et al. (2012), studying the Mexican spotted owl (*Strix occidentalis ludica*) in the southwest and the northern spotted owl (*Strix occidentalis caurina*) along the west coast into British Columbia, state that the use of detection dogs "to locate DNA-confirmable wildlife sign can provide a useful complementary survey strategy that is largely independent of the target species' behavioral response or physiological status." Behavioral response detection can involve wildlife entering a trap and walking past a location, and vocalization in response to simulated calls. Dogs have the advantage of being able "to cover large landscapes over difficult terrain, with a consistently high probability of detecting sign from a wide variety of target species across habitat types...." In this study, dogs "located owl roosts by searching for accumulated *Strix* owl pellets, subsequently confirmed for species identities by restriction fragment-length polymorphism (RFLP) analysis of mtDNA [mitochondrial DNA] extracted from the swabs of each pellet...." DNA analysis identified which species of owl was involved, but the researchers note that confirmation "of sex and individual identities from nuclear DNA analysis may be possible on a portion of collected pellets."

In a survey of the two owl species in the Shasta-Trinity National Forest in northern California, two dogs were used by a canine survey team, whose results were to be compared with a vocalization survey team, both teams looking in the same areas but independently of each other. Some areas could not be searched as much as desired because they were deemed dangerous because of illegal marijuana farming. Comparing the two types of surveys, the researchers found that "there were three DNA-confirmed dog detections of spotted owl that were not detected by vocal surveys..., whereas only one vocal detection could not be DNA-confirmed from the dog-detected pellets...." Overall,

> Dog surveys had significantly higher detection probabilities for northern spotted owls than did vocalization surveys, and this difference increased with the number of surveys conducted per polygon. Dog surveys had cumulative detection probabilities of DNA confirmed northern spotted owls of 29% after session 1, 62% after session 2, and 87% after session 3. Cumulative detection probability of northern spotted owls by vocalization surveys was 25% after session 1, and increased to 59% by session 6....

For barred owls, which there were much fewer of, mean detection probability was 20.1% by dog surveys and 7.3% by vocal surveys. Separate dog teams "were not significantly different from one another, nor were vocalization teams." As to the possibility that the dogs might disturb the owls, the researchers note that they "were trained not to chase or otherwise harass wildlife."

Darren Clark (2014), in a thesis studying cougars in northeast Oregon, stated the following:

> Detection dogs were able to locate kill sites of cougars on average 11.6 minutes faster than human observers and were able to search non-kill sites on average 21.4 minutes faster than human observers.... During the course of the cougar predation study, 3365 potential predation sites were searched, of which prey remains were located at 1172 and were not located at 2193. Given the average difference in search times between detection dogs and human observers, if detection dogs would have been utilized during the entire study a total of 1008 hours of search time (126 days of labor assuming 8 hour days) could have been saved.

Dogs could locate kill sites during winter, even under a foot or two of snow, whereas human observers would have to wait until snow had melted. Clark cautions, however, that the "long-term nature of predation studies will likely make it cost prohibitive to use detection dogs to locate kill sites of large carnivores."

Harrison (2006) compared automatic cameras, hair snares, scent stations, and a detector dog trained to find bobcat (*Lynx rufus*) scats. Comparing these approaches as to detection rate, cost, and time required, he found that the "detector dog produced nearly 10 times the number of bobcat detections as the other methods combined." Nevertheless,

> The detector dog was the most expensive method and, depending upon weather and number of scats required, required more field time than the other methods. However, use of detector dogs requires only one visit to each survey site. Hair-snares and scent stations were the cheapest methods but produced the least detections. Field time for hair-snares, cameras, and scent stations was similar. Use of detector dogs has the potential to consistently achieve sufficient detection rates to provide useful indices for population monitoring of bobcats.

Arandjelovic et al. (2015) found using dogs initially trained in the United States to survey Cross River gorilla populations in Cameroon to be very expensive, particularly with handlers also from the United States. They recommended that local dogs be used instead, which would also be less susceptible to disease in the area of operation, and that a handler program be developed in central or west Africa. Teaching the dogs to detect more than one target species could also reduce costs.

Ralls et al. (2010) noted that a dog used in a series of studies was more successful at finding kit fox (*Vulpes macrotis*) scat than human observers and "was consistently accurate at finding only kit fox scats (and ignoring those of other species such as coyotes [*Canis latrans*])...." They also noted that "dogs locate many old scats that contain DNA that is too degraded for successful polymerase chain reaction (PCR) amplification of the zinc finger protein genes used for determining sex...." Smith et al. (2003) also determined that trained dogs could distinguish kit fox scat from scat of other foxes, noting that "DNA tests of 1298 scats showed that all dogs were 100% accurate at distinguishing kit fox scats under our field conditions.... Four dogs were 100% accurate at choosing a kit fox scat when red fox scats were present (*n* = 64 trials), but were less accurate at ignoring red fox scats in trials where a kit fox scat was absent." In conjunction with DNA testing, Smith et al. (2003) note the cost savings:

> The cost of extracting DNA from scats and conducting species identification analysis is ~$50.00 per scat sample. Hence, in our case, pre-screening of the scats by detection dogs would have generated a savings of approximately $6,000 ($50 × 120 red fox scats ignored by the dogs which would otherwise have been sent to the lab for species identification).[19]

Human observers may, according to Sanchez et al. (2004), be unable to distinguish scat of one canid from another (e.g., coyote from feral dog).

Duggan (2011) found that surveys of sites by two dog teams of prairies inhabited by the Franklin's ground squirrel (*Poliocitellus franklinii*) resulted in detection rates much faster than livetrapping surveys (less than 1 h for the dogs compared to 2 days of trapping) with only a moderate increase in cost. Her thesis recommended a two-stage strategy for this and similar cryptic species "whereby livetrapping is conducted only at sites where detection dog surveys indicate presence."

Reindl-Thompson et al. (2006) compared the use of two detection dogs for finding black-footed ferrets against flashlight surveys in the Buffalo Gap National Grasslands in South Dakota. Ferrets were released in the area from 1996 to 1999, producing a growing population estimated at about 300 in 2003.

> [F]irst-time searches of test colonies by dog teams resulted in correctly determining ferret presence in 86% of colonies and absence in 88% of colonies.... Second-time searches of the same test colonies yielded a correct assessment of ferret presence in 79% of occasions and ferret absence in 88% of occasions.

The researchers reported that the dogs never falsely indicated the presence of ferrets. Dogs were found to be faster than spotlight surveyors at searching the colonies. Dogs were also able to find ferrets where spotlight surveyors could not:

A United States Forest Service crew…conducted spotlight surveys on the colonies for 2 nights, but did not observe ferrets. In an effort to confirm ferret presence as indicated by the dogs, we set traps where one of the dogs indicated ferret presence and an adult male ferret was trapped there that night. This anecdotal information further indicates that dogs can provide a useful auxiliary method for determining the presence of ferrets.

The team provided some cost estimates and concluded that "using scent-detection dogs is economically comparable to the most common ferret monitoring method." Prairie dogs sometimes "distracted the detection dogs with their frequent barking and movement when the dogs were in close proximity…." Cacti may sometimes require that the dogs be fitted with protective boots.

Rolland et al. (2006) measured fecal sample collection rates for right whales (*Eubalaena glacialis*) using detection dogs and a GPS chart plotter to mark the location of track lines and positions where dogs detected scent from right whale scat. The team concluded that detection dogs working from boats were more than four times more effective than opportunistic collection methods in finding whale scat.[20]

For desert tortoises (*Gopherus agassizii*), Nussear et al. (2008) noted that surveys of desert tortoises "are labor intensive and, therefore, can be costly." They found "statistically and functionally no difference between human and dog team detection of tortoises." Specifically,

Detectability of tortoises was not statistically different for either team, and was estimated to be approximately 70% (SE = 5%). Dogs found a greater proportion of tortoises located in vegetation than did humans. The dog teams finished surveys 2.5 hours faster than the humans on average each day. The human team cost was approximately $3,000 less per square kilometer sampled. Dog teams provided a quick and effective method for surveying for adult Desert Tortoises; however, we were unable to determine their effectiveness at locating smaller size classes.

They elaborated on the cost:

Our estimated cost to survey two passes on 1 km² of Desert Tortoise habitat by the human team was US$4,658 and the cost for the dog teams for the same survey was US$7,872. Therefore, the cost of the human team was 60% that of the dog teams. Each search team ultimately required the same number of personnel (12); however, the cost discrepancy was largely due to the costs of dog handlers, which were more expensive (by US$120 per day) than even the senior personnel on the human team, and twice as many were required.

Surveys of bird and bat mortalities at wind turbine farms have shown that dogs are often far better than human surveyors.[21] Paula et al. (2011), training dogs to identify 17 target species, found that "while dogs detected 96% of carcasses placed, human searches only found 9%." The accuracy of the dogs was "independent of vegetation density and the effects of carcass decomposition state, distances to the carcass and weather conditions…." Mathews et al. (2013) found that dogs "located 73% (46/63) of bats, whereas humans found 20% (12/60)." The dogs also took less time to complete a survey, about 25% less than humans, which this team considered as sufficient to mean that the two approaches cost about the same given that setup costs for the dog teams were higher. Even earlier, Arnett (2006) determined that dogs found 71% of bats at one site and 81% at another, compared to 42% and 14% for human searchers, respectively.

Homan et al. (2001) sought to determine if an avicide intended to kill overabundant blackbird populations was killing too many house sparrows. Sparrow carcasses are particularly difficult to find in dense vegetation.

We placed carcasses of house sparrows (*Passer domesticus*) in dense cover of residual and newly grown vegetation and compared searching efficiency of humans and canines. Dogs received no special training in searching for passerine carcasses. In 36 trials conducted in 5 × 40–m plots, human searchers found 45% (SD = 19) of the carcasses compared to 92% (SD = 13) for dogs (P = 0.005).

Marcio de Oliveira et al. (2012), studying deer (*Mazama americana*, *Mazama gouazoubira*, and *Mazama bororo*) in dense Brazilian jungles, found that a dog could survey larger areas than human observers and found scat while human observers only reliably found tracks. They noted that herbivore feces have a weaker odor compared with carnivores, which may reduce success compared to studies on carnivores such as foxes. They concluded that "scat-detection dogs remain an under exploited resource by Neotropical researchers."

Further research is needed concerning the training of dogs for conservation surveys. Kelly (2009) notes that "inexperienced dogs tend to overshoot the scent plume and, once they are beyond the plume, they lack clues of which direction to travel."

REGULATORY REQUIREMENTS FOR ARCTIC SURVEYS

The use of dogs is usually a choice of environmental agencies and groups, and of researchers attempting to survey certain populations. With certain arctic species, whales and seals, supervisory agencies have introduced strong suggestions, and in the case of ringed seals, requirements, for the use of dogs in surveys. Polar bear (*Ursus maritimus*) dens may be affected by drilling and construction activities in Alaska, and this species is listed as threatened throughout their entire range.[22] Under 50 CFR 18.117(a)(5)(iii)(A) and 18.128(a)(2)(ii), oil companies carrying out onshore exploration activities in known or suspected polar bear denning habitats "must make efforts to locate occupied polar bear dens within and near proposed areas of operation, utilizing appropriate tools, such as forward looking infrared (FLIR) imagery and/or *polar bear scent–trained dogs*."[23]

In 2009, BP (formerly British Petroleum) requested regulations to authorize the incidental taking of marine mammals for drilling operations in the Beaufort Sea from January 2014 to January 2019.[24] BP sought authorization to take six mammal species incidental to operation of the Northstar development in the Beaufort Sea for 5 years. Northstar Island, a man-made facility created for drilling operations, was completed in 2001. From 2014 through 2019, BP intends to continue drilling operations, though not on the scale conducted in earlier years. These operations will have both acoustic and nonacoustic effects on marine mammals in the area resulting from "vehicles operating on the ice, vessels, aircraft, generators, production machinery, gas flaring, and camp operations." Animals that will be affected are bowhead whales (*Balaena mysticetus*), gray whales (*Eschrichtius robustus*), beluga whales (*Delphinapterus leucas*), ringed seals (*Phoca hispida*), bearded seals (*Erignathus barbatus*), spotted seals (*Phoca largha*), polar bears (*Ursus maritimus*), and Pacific walruses (*Odobenus rosmarus divergens*). BP estimated that it would take about five ringed seals annually by injury or mortality. The other species will be "harassed" but less affected than the ringed seals. Walruses and polar bears are managed by the Fish & Wildlife Service (Department of the Interior), so they were not considered in the rules of the Department of Commerce.

Ringed seals build subnivean lairs under the snowpack in the Beaufort Sea in the spring months, which can be located by dogs (Kelly et al. 2010a,b). Specifically as to how seals might be injured, the preamble states the following:

> Potential non-acoustic effects could result from the physical presence of personnel, structures and equipment, construction or maintenance activities, and the occurrence of oil spills. In winter, during ice road construction, and in spring, flooding on the sea ice may displace some ringed seals along the ice road corridor. There is a small chance that a seal pup might be injured or killed by on-ice construction or transportation activities. A major oil spill is unlikely and, if it occurred, its effects are difficult to predict.

Ringed seals give birth in late March and April, and at that time of year, young pups may get close to BP facilities. BP is to notify the National Marine Fisheries Service (NMFS) within 24 h if more than five ringed seals are killed annually by BP's activities. The regulations state that "to reduce the taking of ringed seals to the lowest level practicable, BP must begin winter construction activities, principally ice roads, as soon as possible once weather and ice conditions permit such activity."[25] The regulations require the use of detection dogs:

> Any ice roads or other construction activities that are initiated after March 1, in previously undisturbed areas in waters deeper than 10 ft (3 m), *must be surveyed, using trained dogs* in order to identify and avoid ringed seal structures by a minimum of 492 ft (150 m).[26]

> * * *

> After March 1, trained dogs must be used to detect seal lairs in previously undisturbed areas that may be potentially affected by on-ice construction activity, if any. Surveys for seal structures should be conducted to a minimum distance of 492 ft (150 m) from the outer edges of any disturbance.[27]

As to road construction, the preamble to the regulations explains how the use of dogs becomes important:

> In order to reduce impacts to ringed seal construction of birth lairs, BP must begin winter construction activities (e.g., ice road construction) on the sea ice as early as possible once weather and ice conditions permit such activities. Any ice road or other construction activities that are initiated after March 1 in previously undisturbed areas in waters deeper than 10 ft (3 m) must be surveyed, *using trained dogs*, in order to identify and avoid ringed seal structures by a minimum of 492 ft (150 m). *If dog surveys are conducted, trained dogs shall search all floating sea ice for any ringed seal structures.* Those surveys shall be done prior to the new proposed activity on the floating sea ice to provide information needed to prevent injury or mortality of young seals. Additionally, after March 1 of each year, activities should avoid, to the greatest extent practicable, disturbance of any located seal structure.

> * * *

> If BP initiates significant on-ice activities (e.g., construction of new ice roads, trenching for pipeline repair, or projects of similar magnitude) in previously undisturbed areas after March 1, *trained dogs, or a comparable method*, will be used to search for seal structures.... If specific mitigation and monitoring are required for activities on the sea ice initiated after March 1 (*requiring searches with dogs for lairs*), during the operation of strong sound sources (requiring visual observations and shutdown procedures), or for the use of new sound sources that have not previously been measured, then a preliminary summary of the activity, method of monitoring, and preliminary results will be submitted within 90 days after the cessation of that activity.

The second paragraph includes the only reference to a "comparable method." Other references to dogs make their use mandatory by BP.

HABITAT FRAGMENTATION

In addition to helping in surveys of populations, dogs have been helpful in research regarding the effects of habitat fragmentation and in supporting measures to assure connections between isolated groups of animals. Vynne et al. (2009), for instance, used scat detection dogs to find locations of giant armadillos (*Priodontes maximus*) and giant anteaters (*Myrmecophaga tridactyla*) in jungles in central Brazil. Verifying locations of the species persuaded the researchers that requirements that landowners set aside some of their property as protected were helping these species survive.

IDENTIFICATION OF INDIVIDUAL TIGERS

Like drug dogs or cadaver dogs, conservation detection dogs are generally trained to recognize a general scent, in this case, one that belongs to all members of a target species. An exception involves dogs that are being used to monitor the status of the Amur, or Siberian, tiger (*Panthera tigris altaica*), found in the Russian Far East (Kerley and Salkina 2007; Kerley 2010). This involves training dogs under procedures similar to those used for scent lineups in criminal investigations where the dog is asked if there is a match to a scent from the crime in a lineup of scents from foils and a suspect in the crime. Monitoring tigers has involved track size measurements, camera traps, and genetic analysis of hair and scat. Genetic analysis has been largely ineffective because of the low genetic variability of the remaining Amur tiger population. Camera traps often malfunction in cold temperatures, though winter may be the best time to survey these animals.[28]

DETECTION OF DISEASE IN WILDLIFE

Alasaad et al. (2012) trained dogs not to detect any particular species of wildlife, but to detect sarcoptic mange *on* wildlife. The ectoparasite *Sarcoptes scabiei* infects more than 100 species of mammals, both wild and domestic. Infected animals have a "foul aromatic odour" that is "unique and distinguishable," so this team believed that disease detector dogs could be trained for work with chamois (*Rupicapra rupicapra*) populations in the Dolomite Alps of Italy. At least three-quarters of the population had died from the results of mange, as had significant numbers of other animals such as the alpine ibex (*Capra ibex*). In addition to finding carcasses, two trained dogs could recognize sick living animals, on which euthanasia (humane shooting) was used. Alasaad et al. state that "in no case did the *Sarcoptes*-detector dogs misdiagnose mange infection." The dogs "identified more mangy females than males," but this "was not a sex-biased difference in sensitivity to scabies or a greater accuracy of dogs in detecting females" but, rather, due to "a female-biased sex ratio in the affected chamois population...."[29]

VULTURES, POISONS, AND POLLUTANTS

Dogs may also be used to detect poisons that are being used illegally against wildlife. Ogada et al. (2011) note the following:

> Spain has taken an innovative approach to tackling this problem by training dogs to detect specific poisons (baits and carcasses of poisoned animals) that are most commonly used against wildlife. Dogs detected 70% more poisoned baits than did specialized (human) detection teams. Funded by the regional government, the canine unit assists in the discovery of offenders as well as in dissuading poisoning through routine inspections in known hotspots.

In Asia, *Gyps* vultures have declined more than 95% due to poisoning by the veterinary drug diclofenac, though this has now been banned. Dogs have been used to find scat of river otters, not for survey purposes but so that the scat can be tested for certain pharmaceutical contamination of waterways (Richards et al. 2014).

ERADICATION

Eliminating pest species is something of the opposite of conservation work, at least as to the pests, as discussed in Chapter 22 herein. Here also, dogs may have more than one function, such as hunting the pest as well as surveying to determine the success of eradication programs.[30] Feral cats have become predators and competitors of native species on many islands, and therefore the subjects of eradication efforts in certain countries. Parkes et al. (2014) state that eradication efforts have involved "aerial and ground-based poison baiting, fumigation in rabbit burrows used by cats, cage and leghold trapping, day and night shooting, and hunting with dogs." Eradication has been successful on 83 islands.

Importation of the brown tree snake (*Boiga irregularis*) is prohibited under federal regulations regarding importation of live reptiles or their eggs.[31] The brown tree snake is also mentioned in federal regulations in connection with the U.S. territory of Guam, where the snake is identified as having destroyed the primary range of the Guam rail, a flightless bird, leading to the bird's extirpation on Guam.[32]

Wildlife Services, a section of the U.S. Department of Agriculture, employs handlers with trained dogs (specifically Jack Russell terriers) to search cargo leaving Guam in an effort to prevent the spread of the reptile.[33] Engeman et al. (2002) report that three beagle teams have been used in Hawaii to inspect inbound cargo to that island for brown tree snakes. The dogs are cross-trained for agricultural inspections. Engeman et al. (2002) found that dogs failed to alert more than twice as often as handlers failed to follow protocols on search patterns. The dogs had an overall efficacy rate of 62% in 1998 and 1999, a figure that Vice et al. (2009) indicate has remained consistent since.[34] Tree snake discoveries in cargo are not consistent over time, as events such as typhoons may destroy tree snake habitats and increase their dispersal, including into cargo loading areas. See Vice and Engeman (2000).

As early as 1976, Wallner and Ellis used three German shepherds to locate egg masses of the gypsy moth (*Porthetria dispar*), noting that the dogs could alert up to 2 m away from a mass, suggesting they could "be used for quarantine inspection of vehicles or to detect suspect infestations of *P. dispar*."

The stinkbug (*Halyomorpha halys*) is an invasive species from Asia affecting agricultural production in the U.S. mid-Atlantic region, as well as being a nuisance in urban and suburban areas because the adults attempt to overwinter in protected environments. Lee et al. (2014) used trained canines to locate overwintering sites of the stinkbug in natural landscapes, finding that they can often be found in dry crevices in dead but standing trees.

Lin et al. (2011), following research of Huang et al. (2007), used beagles to detect red imported fire ants (*Solenopsis invicta*) and their nests. Overuse of a fire ant pesticide, diazinon, "produced massive amounts of waste and water pollutants that failed to pass the state and federal discharge standards in the United States." See Drees (2003). This meant that "an accurate assessment of the level of red imported fire ant infestation is needed before more precise insecticide treatments can be applied as to reduce both the environmental and economical costs associated with chemical control." Lin et al. found that dogs could be taught to discriminate fire ants from other ant species and could find small nests in a pretreated outdoor area, allowing for specific actions to be taken. The dogs had an overall positive indication rate of greater than 98%.[35]

In a paper published in *Invasive Plant Science and Management*, Goodwin et al. (2010) compared accuracy and detection distances of dogs and humans in locating spotted knapweed (*Centaurea stoebe*) invasions. Dog accuracy was similar to humans for large-size invasions but improved as invasions got smaller. Dogs were much more effective when further away from target plants.[36]

SUMMARY

Detection dogs have proven more effective in finding many target species than other approaches, but their deployment comes with risks and costs that may sometimes mean they either cannot be used or can only be used in particular environments, seasons, or situations. In some research programs, hunting or tracking dogs are used to locate target individuals for tagging or radio-collaring, while other dogs may be used for surveys. Dogs can also be used to find disease in wildlife or find poisons used illegally to kill wildlife. Preventing pest species from leaving islands or reducing illegal trade in endangered species is also a common function of dogs at borders. Because of the generally consistent effectiveness of dogs in surveys, this application will continue to grow.

ACKNOWLEDGMENT

The author thanks Dr. Brian Kelly for comments on an earlier draft of this chapter.

ENDNOTES

1. Dogs have also been used in protection work for endangered species. In Australia, dogs have been trained in the manner of livestock-guarding dogs to protect endangered birds on islands close to the mainland shore, where foxes and dingoes can cross over during low tide and eat the protected species. See van Bommel (2010).

2. Dogs are sometimes used to capture animals for tagging or radio-collaring and thus are a component of a separate survey or identification process. See, e.g., Akenson et al. (2001, 2013), where different dogs fulfilled capturing and surveying functions. Use of dogs to capture animals for tagging or radio-collaring may sometimes run afoul of antihunting legislation unless there is a mechanism to grant an exception for nonlethal hunting for conservation purposes. Surveys may specifically be conducted to determine whether areas where hunting with dogs is illegal show higher populations than areas where it remains legal. See Clark (2014).

3. Data from around the world on endangered species is collected and posted by the International Union for Conservation of Nature, or IUCN, which has a useful website (http://www.iucnredlist.org) listing thousands of species and their status from extinct to "least concern."

4. PL 93-2015, as revised in 1979 and 1982 by PL 97-304 and PL 100-478, respectively.

5. 16 U.S.C. 1531(a)(1), (2).

6. 16 U.S.C. 1532(6), (20).

7. 16 U.S.C. 1533(c), (d).

8. 16 U.S.C. 1533(f).

9. Black-footed Ferret Recovery Plan (2013).

10. See Vynne et al. (2009). It is to be noted that scat surveys may be conducted by other agencies in the Department of the Interior besides the U.S. Fish & Wildlife Service. In March 2014, the U.S. Geological Survey sought to give the University of Washington a noncompetitive award for a "trained canine scent detection team" to survey badgers near San Diego (G14PS00221).

11. USFWS (2013); see Reindl-Thompson et al. (2006).

12. USFWS (2011); see Cablk et al. (2006). Dogs have been used to survey the tuatara (*Sphenodon punctatus*), the Marlborough green gecko (*Naultinus manukanus*), and the forest gecko (*Hoplodactylus granulatus*) on New Zealand (Browne et al. 2015). The Hawaii Wildlife Fund has indicated its intention to use a turtle nest detector dog on several islands. 80 Fed. Reg. 51830 (August 26, 2015).

13. 16 U.S.C. 1361–1389.

14. 16 U.S.C. 1362.

15. 16 U.S.C. 1371(a)(5)(E)(i).

16. 15 CFR subtitle A, Part 8, Appendix A, National Oceanic and Atmospheric Administration (NOAA), 3. NOAA may revoke permits under the Marine Mammal Protection Act for violations of conditions and may subsequently deny an application under the Endangered Species Act. 15 CFR 904.301(b)(2). Under 15 CFR 904.509, "Loans may be made to responsible agencies of foreign governments in accordance with the Convention on International Trade in Endangered Species of Wild Fauna and Flora." This refers to loans of forfeited property approved for disposal.

17. Chromatrograms have been used to distinguish scat of five canid species with a misclassification rate of 17.6%, which Burnham et al. (2008) considered "low given the close genetic relationships among the canid species...."

18. 75 Fed. Reg. 37460 (June 29, 2010). Kincaid's lupine is one of five species included in the Recovery Plan for the Prairie Species of Western Oregon and Southwestern Washington signed by the director of Region 1, Portland Oregon (May 20, 2010), http://ecos.fws.gov/docs/recovery_plan/100629.pdf.

19. See Harrington et al. (2010) recommending use of dogs to reduce costs of DNA analysis to verify presence of American mink (*Neovison vison*) in Scotland.

20. See also Hunt et al. (2013).

21. Surveys initially focused primarily on birds but, in the last decade, have included research on bat fatalities. See Baerwald et al. (2009).

22. 50 CFR 17.11(h).

23. See Smith et al. (2007) and Kirschhoffer (2013) for polar bear studies using dogs.

24. Department of Commerce, 78 Fed. Reg. 75488 (December 12, 2013).

25. 50 CFR 217.144(a)(1).

26. 50 CFR 217.144(a)(1)(ii). Here and elsewhere in this chapter, italics added for emphasis by author.

27. 50 CFR 217.146(c)(1).

28. See also Wasser et al. (2009), discussed in Chapter 11 herein, regarding individual animal detection.

29. Dogs have been used to detect parasites on domestic animals. See Richards et al. (2008). Welch (1990) used a German wirehaired pointer to locate screwworm (*Cochliomyia hominivorax*) pupae as well as animals infected with screwworms.

30. Dogs themselves may be an invasive species, as has been indicated for the Mariana Islands. Manor and Saltz (2010) (noting similarity in effects of predators on fragmented population areas to alien species on islands); 80 Fed. Reg. 59453 (October 1, 2015). Feral and loose dogs are, of course, regularly identified as predators of endangered and threatened species. 80 Fed. Reg. 60483 (October 6, 2015) concerning the black pine snake, a threatened species in Alabama, Louisiana, and Mississippi; 80 Fed. Reg. 60327 (October 6, 2015) concerning desert tortoises; 80 Fed. Reg. 60996 (October 8, 2015), concerning the Sierra Nevada red fox.

31. 50 CFR 16.15. Four other snake species are listed in the same regulation, three of which are species of pythons, as well as the yellow anaconda. Other live reptiles can be imported "without a permit, for scientific, medical, educational, exhibitional or propagating purposes, but no such live reptiles or any progeny or eggs thereof may be released into the wild except by the State wildlife conservation agency having jurisdiction over the area of release or by persons having prior written permission for release from such agency." 50 CFR 16.15(b).

32. There is now an experimental population of the Guam rail on Rota in the Commonwealth of the Northern Mariana Islands, which is protected from the snakes by 50 km of ocean. 50 CFR 17.84(f)(7). Concern has been expressed that the snake could colonize other islands in the Pacific. See Shwiff et al. (2010). Kahl et al. (2012) argue that the snake could be a potential invasive species in the U.S. mainland. They note the logistical difficulties of expanding the canine program to U.S. ports.

33. USDA/Wildlife Services Factsheet (January 2011). Brown Tree Snake: An Invasive Reptile. http://www .aphis.usda.gov/publications/wildlife_damage/content/printable_version/fs_brown_tree_snake_2011 .pdf. Also see No Escape from Guam: Stopping the Spread of the Brown Tree Snake. Program Aid No. 1636. http://www.aphis.usda.gov/wildlife_damage/nwrc/downloads/no_escape_from_guam.pdf.

34. Initial success rates were higher. See Engeman et al. (1998).

35. See Waters et al. (2011) on use of a dog to find bumblebee (*Bombus terrestris*) nests in four different habitats on the Scottish island of Tiree.

36. The U.S. Fish & Wildlife Service discusses spotted knapweed in a web page devoted to invasive species management, http://www.fws.gov/refuge/Seney/what_we_do/Exotic_Species_Management.html.

Section VI

Uses in Detection of Diseases and Medical Conditions

Due to its companionship and loyalty, the dog is called man's best friend. This description, often attributed to Frederic II, King of Prussia, is perhaps due to continuing innovations in our coexistence, even more accurate now than when it was first expressed. One of those innovations, particularly in recent decades, is the expansion of roles played by dogs in human health care.

GUIDE DOGS AFTER WORLD WAR I

In the First World War, Red Cross dogs were taught to help wounded soldiers off the battlefield and bring them to safety (Jager 1917). When the soldier's wound was too great for him to move himself, the dog had a bringsel on its collar, which the soldier could put in the dog's mouth, or the dog could do this, so that upon the dog's return behind the lines, a medic would understand that it had found a wounded soldier (von Stephanitz 1923). Presumably, these ambulance dogs relied in part on their sense of smell to lead a stretcher team to the wounded soldier. (For a discussion of the bringsel in modern training techniques, see Chapter 14 herein.)

Guide dog programs began after the First World War for soldiers blinded on the battlefields, with some dogs being trained by the same German dog clubs that had trained dogs for war duty. Other types of service dogs began to be trained in the 1960s and later. Although guide dogs are not touted for their olfactory ability, there can be little doubt that dogs used by blind people from antiquity even into modern times in some cultures often followed fixed paths so that their masters could find food and survive. As argued by Montaigne in an essay written over four centuries ago (*An Apology for Raymond Sebond*), dogs could lead blind men to doors where they were accustomed to receive alms. Indeed, a fresco from first-century Pompeii was thought by Otto Keller, in *Die Antike Tierwelt* (1909), to show a blind beggar being led by a little dog, quite likely following a fixed route to a market. These dog servants would have needed all their senses, including perhaps following their own markings, on the daily journey they took with their masters.

THE CANCER SNIFFERS

Another possible role of dogs in health care emerged when dogs were found to be able to detect cancer. The first case report of a pet dog detecting melanoma on the body of its master—and trying to bite it off—was published in *The Lancet* in 1989, but serious research on whether this phenomenon could be generalized in such a way that dogs could be trained to reliably recognize melanomas and other cancers began with the new century. This skill of dogs has been sensationalized by the mass media and is sometimes described as a dog doctor giving a diagnosis, though from a medical viewpoint, the phenomenon is not a diagnosis but may in fact be a potential screening method. As described in the first chapter in this section (Chapter 24), the ultimate value of this approach in a clinical setting may depend on whether alternative screening methods are more invasive and less accurate. Some cancers already have early screening methods that are highly effective and minimally invasive, but others do not. If the dog's indications can be shown to be sufficiently reliable, then canine detection may in fact become a step in justifying more invasive procedures to determine if certain cancers are present.

Chapter 24 summarizes most of the peer-reviewed literature on cancer detection dogs. These studies vary by the type of cancer, how odor samples were obtained, breeds of dogs chosen, training and testing methods used in developing and selecting dogs for this kind of work, experimental setups in which trials with the dogs were conducted, and the results obtained. Studies conducted so far suffer from two major weaknesses. The first is a lack of standardization of materials and methods. A full standardization in this respect seems to be difficult to obtain agreement on, since it must first be demonstrated (repeatedly) that a proposed standardization outperforms other possible approaches in reliability and validity. The second weakness, from an oncologist's perspective, is that all studies published so far show that dogs are more or less able to discriminate odor samples taken from patients with histopathologically diagnosed cancers from those of healthy individuals. The results, however, ranged from 100% sensitivity and specificity to no better than chance. To make the use of dogs in cancer detection clinical, it will need to be demonstrated that they can identify cancers very early, in preclinical stages. This has not been reported so far, though it must be acknowledged that this research area is in its infancy.

MEDICAL ALERTING

The second chapter of this section (Chapter 25) deals with canine signaling of seizures, glycemic changes, and migraines. This work differs considerably from cancer detection in that this involves patient–dog dyads. Here, it is not clear how much dogs are relying on odor and how much they may be relying on slight changes in a patient's movements or behavior before or at the early stages of a disease episode. The dog may in fact be using odor cues along with visual and acoustic cues, another example of the "black box" phenomenon discussed in a number of contexts in this book. Training dogs for this kind of work is also difficult in that for practical and ethical reasons, experimentally inducing seizures or hypoglycemia in patients is not possible. A high proportion of the studies involve surveys filled out by individuals, many of whom firmly insist that they receive advance warnings from their dogs. The chapter shows that there are still many open questions as to the reliability of dogs alerting to seizures and medical conditions, and notes that certain legal issues regarding the status of such dogs as service animals have yet to be conclusively resolved.

There is a need for more research as to both these types of medical functions for dogs. In cancer screening, research should continue as to the types of cancer that dogs may recognize, at what stage the cancer must be for the dog to recognize it, and what sampling procedures will provide the greatest chance that deploying the dogs will be useful and practical to patients and affordable by the health care system. With medical alerting dogs, research should also continue as to what diseases, conditions, and episodes can be recognized by dogs; how much in advance and how reliable this recognition may be; and what sorts of responses are most useful for the dogs to give when alerting the user or owner to take action because of an imminent threat to his or her health. Efforts to obtain video evidence of advance alerting, mentioned in some research, should continue, provided ethical hurdles can be crossed.

We believe there may be promise here, and like most topics discussed in this book, the area is hardly static. These are new horizons for our best friend, and for us.

Tadeusz Jezierski, John Ensminger, and L.E. Papet

24 Detection of Human Cancer by Dogs

Tadeusz Jezierski

In the last 20 years, one more mission that could be fulfilled by canines has been reported and discussed, namely, the ability of dogs to sniff out cancer in humans. Cancer is a leading cause of death worldwide, accounting for 8.2 million deaths in 2012 (World Health Organization 2015), and often comes with symptoms that may be unspecific, overlooked, or ignored. Early diagnosis in curable or operable stages is crucial for successful therapy as it may allow for more efficient treatments with lower toxicity and result in longer survival (e.g., Negm et al. 2002; Ganti and Mulshine 2006). Therefore, noninvasive, low-cost, safe, and effective screening methods for detection of early cancer stages, including nonconventional ones, are desirable.

An ability to distinguish sick individuals from healthy ones by emitted odors is one of the intriguing abilities of animals, not only of canines. For example, the ability of mice to distinguish sick and healthy individuals of their own species by odor has been documented in literature concerning, e.g., infection with parasites (Kavaliers and Colwell 1995; Ehman and Scott 2001, 2002; Kavaliers et al. 2003), influenza (Penn et al. 1996), mouse mammary tumor virus (Yamazaki et al. 2002), and inflammatory processes (Arakawa et al. 2010).

Frequent spontaneous smelling and licking of their own wounds by canines has been considered self-therapy. In humans, histatin-5, a low-molecular-weight salivary protein, appears to have antifungal and antibacterial properties and may accelerate healing of injuries (Xu and Oppenheim 1993; Gusman et al. 2001). Mice have been shown capable of distinguishing urinary odor of conspecifics with and without cancer with accuracy of 94–100% (Matsumura et al. 2010).

In human medicine, it has been known since the time of Hippocrates that detectable changes in human odor (e.g., breath odor) may be symptoms of particular diseases (McCulloch et al. 2012; Bijland et al. 2013; Dent et al. 2013). For example, a sweet-fruity acetone-like breath odor suggests uncontrolled diabetes, a fishy reek is associated with a liver disease, and urine-like odor suggests kidney dysfunction (Phillips 1992). The role of odor in disease diagnosis was basic to traditional Chinese medicine but largely neglected in scientific medicine. More recently, however, the possibility of using odor analyses for human disease detection or diagnosis was picked up by chemists (Amann et al. 2014).

Williams and Pembroke (1989) reported in *The Lancet* the first case of a pet dog that evidently made its owner aware of a lesion on the owner's thigh that was thereafter diagnosed as malignant melanoma. The authors hypothesized that dogs are able to detect cancer in humans through an odor signature of the disease. This first short case report was largely ignored for more than 10 years until a similar case with malignant melanoma was described by Church and Williams (2001). The pet dogs described in both reports demonstrated a constant interest in lesions by sniffing, licking, and trying to bite the lesions, even through clothing. After the carcinoma lesions had been excised, the dogs showed no further interest in the sites.

In 2003, Dr. John Church initiated a conference in Saunderton (United Kingdom) attended by people interested in training and using dogs for cancer detection. This conference gave rise to more systematic experimental studies on cancer detecting dogs, resulting over the next 10 years in at least 14 peer-reviewed publications in medical and behavioral scientific journals, presenting experimental results of cancer detection by trained dogs (Pickel et al. 2004; Willis et al. 2004; McCulloch et al. 2006; Gordon et al. 2008; Horvath et al. 2008, 2010, 2013; Cornu et al. 2011; Sonoda et al. 2011; Ehmann et al. 2012; Walczak et al. 2012; Amundsen et al. 2014; Elliker et al. 2014; Taverna et al. 2014). Some articles reviewed developments in the area (Moser and McCulloch 2010; Bhadra 2011; Lippi

TABLE 24.1

Methods for Calculating Detection Sensitivity and Specificity

		Actual Presence or Absence of Cancer	
		Present	**Absent**
Test outcome with dogs	Positive indication	True positive (TP)	False positive (FP)
	Negative	False negative (FN)	True negative (TN)

Note: Sensitivity = TP/(TP + FN); *Specificity* = TN/(TN + FP).

and Cervellin 2011; Boedeker et al. 2012; McCulloch et al. 2012) or evaluated hypotheses that might explain the phenomenon of canine cancer detection (Balseiro and Correia 2006).

Effectiveness and availability of current medical screening methods vary for the different types of cancer, making canine detection of different value depending on other approaches that might be preferable or easier to implement. This chapter will discuss methods and results of experimental training of canines to detect different types of cancer. As parameters of detection accuracy, sensitivity, and specificity will be compared, the calculation methods for sensitivity and specificity are given in Table 24.1.

MALIGNANT MELANOMA

Currently, about 132,000 melanoma cases occur globally per year. Although melanoma accounts for only about 2% of all cancer cases, making it one of the least common cancers, it is the most deadly skin cancer, frequently metastasizing to other organs. Moreover, the global incidence of melanoma continues to increase, probably due to depletion of ozone levels as the atmosphere loses its protective function against solar UV radiation as well as from increasing exposure of many people to the sun and sunburn. As melanoma lesions typically occur on the body surface, it seems to be logical that odors produced by these lesions are easily accessible to pet dogs without special collecting techniques. This supposition could be supported by the first two case reports, already discussed, of spontaneous detection of melanoma by untrained dogs on the bodies of their owners.

To prove not only that cases of spontaneous detection of melanoma on a patient's body by dogs would occur but also that dogs could be specially trained to detect melanoma under experimental conditions, Pickel et al. (2004) trained two dogs to identify melanoma tissue samples hidden in a lineup of boxes or placed on the skin of healthy volunteers. Although the number of dogs, samples, and trials was small, the authors reported that the dogs demonstrated reliable localization of melanoma tissue on the skin of actual patients. One of the dogs identified lesions in five out of seven patients that were subsequently confirmed by histopathological examination. Melanoma indicated by the dog in a sixth patient was negative in an initial pathological examination despite clinical suspicion but was confirmed as a melanoma in a fraction of cells in a second, more thorough, examination. In a seventh patient, the dog failed to indicate a melanoma that was confirmed histopathologically. The responses of the second dog used by Pickel et al. (2004) agreed in four of seven patients sniffed by the first dog.

Walczak (2009) used breath samples in lineups and trained three dogs to distinguish not only patients with melanoma from healthy volunteers but also patients with breast and lung cancer. The detection sensitivity for melanoma was lower as compared to breast and lung cancer and ranged from 32.2% to 66.3% for the three fully trained dogs and from 58.6% to 80.2%, with probability of correct indication by chance of 20% and 50%, respectively.

Using trained dogs as screening tools for melanoma does not seem to have good prospects, because this type of neoplastic disease is not frequent and an early diagnosis does not present a big problem for an experienced dermatologist. The two statistical canine studies are compared in Table 24.2.

TABLE 24.2

Detection of Melanoma by Trained Canines

Authors	Odor Samples	Number of Dogs per Breed	Odor Lineup or Circle, Number of Samples	Detection Sensitivity	Detection Specificity	Probability of Correct Indication by Chance
Pickel et al. (2004)	Tissue scraps put on bodies of volunteers	1 schnauzer, 1 golden retriever	I. Lineup of 10	100%		$10^{-8.99}$ $10^{-7.26}$
		1 schnauzer, 1 golden retriever	II. Tissue scraps on the body of volunteers	100%		$10^{-5.04}$ $10^{-5.12}$
Walczak (2009)	Breath	3 crossbreeds	Lineup of 5: 1 cancer + 4 controls	66–80% 32–58%	77–87% –	50% 20%

LUNG CANCER

Lung cancer is the most commonly diagnosed cancer worldwide (1.8 million, 13% of all cancer cases) and the most common cause of cancer death (1.6 million, 19.4% of the total). Although computer tomography (CT) is considered more accurate than traditional chest x-rays (Chien and Chen 2008), Ravenel et al. (2008) note that so far no screening method is noninvasive, accurate, safe, painless, and sure to reduce mortality rates. CT and positron emission tomography (PET) scans can detect lesions as small as 1 mm in diameter and thus are more sensitive than chest x-rays and/or sputum cytology, which have a high false negative rate at early cancer stages, but systematic screening of broader human populations using these methods is problematic because of cost, limited accessibility, and concerns about safety of frequently applied radiation (Perneger et al. 2010; Smith-Bindman 2010). The specificity of lung cancer detection using CT varies between 49% and 89% (Manser 2004). Lung cancer, therefore, is a good candidate for a new screening method, and trained canines have good prospects as unconventional lung cancer screeners.

Four of the 12 experimental studies on experimental training of canines to detect cancer have focused on lung cancer, summarized in Table 24.3. McCulloch et al. (2006), using five dogs and samples of exhaled air, achieved very high lung cancer detection sensitivity of 99% and specificity of 99%. This high detection accuracy for pattern samples was obtained under double-blind conditions. Walczak (2009), with three trained dogs and breath samples collected into the same type of sampling tubes as used by McCulloch et al. (2006), achieved detection sensitivity of 53–58% in tests where there was a 20% probability of being correct by chance, and 83–84% in tests where there was a 50% probability of being correct by chance. Ehmann et al. (2012), using breath samples and four dogs, reported 71% sensitivity and 93% specificity with lung cancer detection independent of chronic obstructive pulmonary disease (COPD), tobacco smoking, or food odors. Two drugs were, however, determined to be potential confounders. These authors concluded that exhaled breath analysis could be a promising method of noninvasive lung cancer screening even in early-stage lung cancer, though they acknowledged that the sampling was limited and concluded that it is too early to determine that sniffer dogs may be employed as reliable lung cancer screeners.

Less optimistic results were obtained by Amundsen et al. (2014), in whose work detection dogs failed to meet the level of specificity needed for clinical application. Using four dogs to detect non-small-cell lung cancer (NSCLC), in the first group of 46 patients, the dogs achieved a sensitivity of 70% but a relatively low specificity of 8.3% for breath samples. Small-cell lung cancer (SCLC) was detected with 55.6% sensitivity and, again, 8.3% specificity. After additional intensive training, in the second group of patients, for NSCLC, sensitivity decreased to 60%, and specificity increased

TABLE 24.3

Detection of Lung Cancer by Trained Canines

Authors	Odor Samples	Number of Dogs per Breed	Odor Lineup or Circle, Number of Samples	Detection Sensitivity	Detection Specificity	Probability of Correct Indication by Chance
McCulloch et al. (2006)	Breath	3 Labrador retrievers, 2 Portuguese water dogs	Lineup of 5: 1 cancer + 4 controls	99%	99%	50%
Walczak (2009)	Breath	3 crossbreeds	Lineup of 5: 1 cancer + 4 controls	83–84% 53–58%	78–81% –	50% 20%
Ehmann et al. (2012) (lung cancer and COPD)	Breath	2 German shepherds, 1 Australian shepherd, 1 Labrador retriever	Circle of 5: 1 cancer + 4 controls	71%	93%	(Not indicated)
Amundsen et al. (2014)	Breath, urine	1 Belgian shepherd, 1 border collie, 1 dachshund, 1 rottweiler	Circle of 6: 0–6 cancer + 6–0 controls	56–64% 64–74%	8–33% 25–29%	(Not indicated)

to 33.3%. After the additional training, for SCLC, the sensitivity increased to 100%, and specificity increased to 33.3%, as in the case of NSCLC. Slightly better detection specificity was obtained using urine samples. The olfactory test of urine samples produced for the first group of patients a sensitivity for NSCLC of 65.7% and 25% specificity, and for SCLC, a sensitivity of 90% and 25% specificity, respectively. Additional intensive training resulted in a decrease of sensitivity to 60% and 80% for NSCLC and SCLC, respectively, and in a slight improvement of detection specificity to 29.2% both for NSCLC and SCLC. Despite the disappointing results, Amundsen et al. (2014) concluded that canine olfactory testing holds promise for early-stage cancer detection.

BREAST CANCER

It was estimated that more than 1.7 million new cases of breast cancer occurred among women worldwide in 2012 (11.9% of all cancers). Breast cancer is the most common cause of cancer death worldwide for women and the fifth most common cancer overall, with around 522,000 deaths in 2012 (15% of female deaths and 6% of the total). Although there is evidence that mammography screening reduces breast cancer mortality (Shen and Zelen 2001), there is still uncertainty as to this procedure due to the variable quality of the studies (Gotzsche and Olsen 2000) and inconsistencies in results across studies (Freeman et al. 2004).

Computer-aided mammography shows about 90% sensitivity (Kim et al. 2008) but, in approximately 8% of tests, detects noncancerous lesions, giving false alarms and leading to additional testing and anxiety (Elmore et al. 2005). CT and mammography are being systematically improved, but complementary methods based on the detection of cancer biomarkers, e.g., in blood, exhaled air, urine, feces, etc., which may help in early detection, are worth investigating. Thus, there is still room for unconventional low-cost and simple tests for breast cancer screening, such as trained canines, especially as mammography is not sufficiently accessible in poorer countries.

TABLE 24.4

Detection of Breast Cancer by Trained Canines

Authors	Odor Samples	Number of Dogs per Breed	Odor Lineup or Circle, Number of Samples	Detection Sensitivity	Detection Specificity	Probability of Correct Indication by Chance
McCulloch et al. (2006)	Breath	3 Labrador retrievers, 2 Portuguese water dogs	Lineup of 5: 1 cancer + 4 controls	88%	98%	50%
Walczak (2009)	Breath	3 crossbreeds	Lineup of 5: 1 cancer + 4 controls	89–90% 66–68%	84–88%	50% 20%
Gordon et al. (2008)	Urine	1 cocker mix, 1 collie mix, 1 German shepherd, 1 Rhodesian ridgeback, 1 boxer, 1 Italian greyhound	Lineup of 7: 1 cancer + 6 controls	22% No dogs better than chance	2 out of 6 dogs better than chance	(Not indicated)

Canines were trained to detect breast cancer in exhaled breath odor in three studies, summarized in Table 24.4. McCulloch et al. (2006) obtained a mean sensitivity of 88% and specificity of 98% for breast cancer detection using the same five dogs trained to detect lung cancer. These authors found detection sensitivity for breast cancer to be 10% lower than for lung cancer. Walczak (2009) also trained three dogs for both lung and breast cancer detection. In contrast to McCulloch et al. (2006), this author found a higher detection sensitivity for breast cancer than for lung cancer.

Gordon et al. (2008) trained six dogs to detect breast cancer using urine samples but failed to demonstrate that dogs could discriminate urine samples from breast cancer patients versus healthy volunteers. None of the six dogs achieved detection sensitivity better than chance (mean sensitivity 22%, best individual 28%) and only two of six dogs showed specificity better than chance. Despite of this lack of success, the authors allowed that further studies might establish the ability of dogs to detect cancer, perhaps with better management of urine samples and more stringent training protocols.

PROSTATE CANCER

Prostate cancer, with more than 1.1 million cases worldwide in 2012, accounts for around 8% of all new cancer cases and 15% in men. A dramatic increase of age-adjusted incidence rates of prostate cancer is largely due to increased availability of screening for prostate-specific antigen (PSA) in men without symptoms of the disease. This test leads to detection of many prostate cancers that are small or might otherwise remain unrecognized and which may or may not advance to higher stages. Wide variation exists internationally for prostate cancer rates due to differences in detection practices, treatment, and lifestyle and genetic factors. The PSA blood test remains the most widely used method for prostate cancer detection, and efforts continue to overcome its unsatisfactory specificity. Alternative biomarkers in urine or blood have been proposed, but none of them is currently widely used (see material cited in Cornu et al. 2011).

Four peer-reviewed publications on prostate cancer detection by trained canines have been published in the last decade, summarized in Table 24.5. In these studies, urine samples were used. Gordon et al. (2008) trained four dogs from breeds not commonly used as sniffer dogs

TABLE 24.5

Detection of Prostate Cancer by Trained Canines

Authors	Odor Samples	Number of Dogs per Breed	Odor Lineup or Circle, Number of Samples	Detection Sensitivity	Detection Specificity	Probability of Correct Indication by Chance
Gordon et al. (2008)	Urine	1 Chihuahua mix, 1 goldendoodle, 1 Welsh corgi, 1 border collie	Lineup of 7: 1 cancer + 6 controls	18% No dogs better than chance	2 out of 4 dogs better than chance	(Not indicated)
Cornu et al. (2011)	Urine	1 Belgian Malinois	Lineup of 6: 1 cancer + 5 controls	91%	91%	(Not indicated)
Elliker et al. (2014)	Urine	1 Labrador retriever, 1 border collie selected out of 10 dogs	Lineup of 4: 1 cancer + 3 controls or blanks	Labrador: 13%, border: 25%, none better than chance	Labrador: 71%, border: 75%	(Not indicated)
Taverna et al. (2014)	Urine	2 dogs	(Not indicated)	99%	97%	(Not indicated)

(Chihuahua mix, miniature goldendoodle, Pembroke Welsh corgi, and border collie). This may be a cause of unsatisfactory results since of the four, only two performed better than chance in specificity and none in sensitivity. The combined sensitivity for all dogs was 18%, and for the best individual, 28%. The authors did not indicate clearly the probability of correct indication by chance, but from the information that there were seven samples in each run (one cancer and six controls), it can be deduced that this probability was approximately 14%. The dog training in this study was based on operant conditioning using a clicker and food treats as rewards for alerting to the cancer urine samples. The authors did not require specific training methods but left this to professional dog trainers. Despite not producing a desired outcome, Gordon et al. (2008) noted that the literature supports a potential to use canines for human cancer detection. These authors believe that a better management of urine samples and a more stringent training protocol than that used in their study may have provided new evidence as to the feasibility of using dogs for cancer detection.

Interesting results concerning prostate cancer detection by a trained Belgian Malinois were achieved by Cornu et al. (2011). Investigating 33 patients with prostate cancer and 33 controls presenting negative biopsies, the dog showed detection sensitivity and specificity of 91% in correctly indicating the prostate cancer samples in 30 of 33 cases. Three samples were wrongly classified by the dog as cancer, though one sample was rebiopsied and prostate cancer was diagnosed, confirming the dog's indication. This may be regarded as relatively rare proof that dogs may be complementary to medical screening methods.

Taverna et al. (2014) investigated a relatively large group of prostate cancer patients ($n = 320$), ranging from very-low-risk to metastatic prostate cancer, and a control group of 357, including a heterogeneous cohort of healthy subjects or patients affected by nonneoplastic diseases or nonprostate tumors. These authors, using two highly trained dogs, achieved a hardly thinkable detection accuracy of 98.1% with sensitivity of 99.2% and specificity of 97.1%, excluding any possible olfactory interference. In their short communiqué, they gave no details on the training and testing methods for the dogs. They concluded that a real clinical opportunity exists for cancer detecting dogs.

In their follow-up study on detection of prostate cancer by dogs, Taverna et al. (2015) gave more details on dogs and dog training and had recruited more study participants (a total of 902). The authors did not indicate if they used the same two dogs as in their first short report but informed in the latter publication that they used two 3-year old German Shepherd females previously trained as explosive detection dogs. The authors added important information, e.g., that operant conditioning using a clicker was applied and the training was a full-time job for the handler–dog team. To exclude effects of memorization of odors, a total of 200 urine samples from prostate cancer patients and 230 samples from the control group analyzed during the training phase were not reused during the evaluation phase. In order to identify confounding factors, Taverna et al. (2015) divided the group of 362 prostate cancer patients into several subgroups: (1) those who had been treated with open or robotic radical prostatectomy surgery (180 patients), (2) those with increased serum PSA (>2.5 ng/mL) or abnormal digital rectal examination and after prostate biopsy had a histological diagnosis of prostate cancer (120 patients), (3) those in whom prostate cancer was detected incidentally at transurethral prostate resection (22 patients), (4) those who had metastatic prostate cancer or were receiving hormonal therapy for biochemical relapse (29 patients), and (5) those with synchronous primary prostate cancer and another different tumor (11 patients). The control group that comprised 540 donors was heterogenic in Taverna et al. (2015). There were 50 healthy nonpregnant younger and older women; 72 women with nonneoplastic conditions such as urinary infection, urolithiasis, neurological or metabolic disorders, or even cancer (bladder, breast, kidney, ovary, vulva, uterus, stomach, colon, liver, skin, blood, or pancreas); 60 healthy young men with a family history negative for prostate cancer; 240 older men with a negative family history for prostate cancer, negative digital rectal examination, serum PSA < 1 ng/mL or < 2.5 ng/mL but stable with time, and urological or systemic disease; 40 men with PSA < 2.5 ng/mL stable with time but who had urinary obstruction treated with transurethral prostate resection for benign prostate hyperplasia; and 78 men with PSA < 2.5 ng/mL stable with time who had a family history negative for prostate cancer and negative digital rectal examination, but had nonprostatic cancer.

Unique in the study of Taverna et al. (2015) was that dogs in the first phase of the training were confronted with urine samples of men with prostate cancer and urine samples from women as controls. In this way, the authors wanted to be certain that no specific prostate VOCs could confuse the dogs. Similarly to the experimental setup used by Amundsen et al. (2014), in Taverna et al. (2015), among six samples tested during a run, there were variable numbers of cancer urine samples (0–6) and control samples (6–0), respectively. No criterion was given to be fulfilled to complete the training phase. Their results confirmed the very high detection accuracy in their earlier paper. The first dog achieved 100% sensitivity and 98.7% specificity, and for the second dog, the sensitivity and specificity were 98.6% and 97.6%, respectively. Interestingly, they found no consistent pattern in distribution of false alerts among participant demographics or tumor characteristics. Despite the extremely high detection accuracy, they recommend further studies to investigate the potential predictive value of detection of prostate cancer by dogs using urine samples.

Elliker et al. (2014) used double-blind trials on urine samples, but out of 10 dogs that began the training, only 2 learned to discriminate prostate cancer samples from controls. These two dogs, however, were unable to discriminate new samples of urine from prostate cancer patients that had not been used during the training. The sensitivity of these two dogs was low (13–25%), though specificity was relatively high (71–75%). As a reason for this disappointing result, the authors cited poor generalization of dogs on prostate cancer odor and exposure to a large number of individual cancer odors during training. Despite the disappointing results, these authors considered that dogs might be trained to detect prostate cancer odor with rigorous double-blind methods and the avoidance of confounding effects.

BLADDER CANCER

Bladder cancer is the ninth most common cancer in the world, with 430,000 new cases diagnosed in 2012. It is three times more common in men than women. Smoking is a major cause of bladder

TABLE 24.6

Detection of Bladder Cancer by Trained Canines

Author	Odor Samples	Number of Dogs per Breed	Odor Lineup or Circle, Number of Samples	Detection Sensitivity	Detection Specificity	Probability of Correct Indication by Chance
Willis et al. (2004)	Urine	6 dogs: 1 mongrel, 1 Labrador retriever, 3 cocker spaniels, 1 papillon	Lineup of 7: 1 cancer + 6 controls	41%	(Not indicated)	14%

cancer. Infection with schistosomes (particularly *Schistosoma haematobium*) is a cause of this cancer, especially in middle- and low-income countries. Another cause is exposure to industrial chemicals, such as aromatic amines.

Screening tests for bladder cancer look for different substances or cancer cells in the urine. No major professional organizations recommend routine screening of the general public for bladder cancer at this time. The U.S. Preventive Services Task Force (August 2011) states that the current evidence is insufficient to assess the balance of benefits and harms of screening for bladder cancer in asymptomatic adults. This is because no screening test has been shown to lower the risk of dying from bladder cancer in people who are at average risk. If bladder cancer is suspected, noninvasive urinary cytology (voided or bladder wash) will be performed initially. This test has high specificity in high-grade tumors but moderate sensitivity. Urine biomarkers are being evaluated extensively, but to date, there is no consensus regarding their use for the diagnosis of bladder cancer. It may be concluded that room exists for using dogs for bladder cancer screening.

Only one team has been studying using dogs for bladder cancer detection, as indicated in Table 24.6. Six dogs of varying breeds and ages were trained over 7 months by Willis et al. (2004) to identify people with bladder cancer on the basis of urine odor samples from 54 donors. In a lineup of seven urine odor samples (one donor with bladder cancer and six healthy controls), the dogs as a group correctly selected the cancer sample on 41% of occasions, with a 95% confidence interval of 23–58%. This result was statistically better than the 14% that would have been expected by chance alone in a lineup of seven samples.

OVARIAN CANCER

Ovarian cancer is the 7th most common cancer in women worldwide (18th most common cancer overall), with 239,000 new cases diagnosed in 2012. The mean relative 5-year survival rate (44.2%) is much lower than other cancers that affect women and varies greatly depending on the stage of diagnosis. Women diagnosed at an early stage, before the cancer has spread, have a much higher 5-year survival rate than those diagnosed at a later stage. Only about 15% of ovarian cancer patients are diagnosed with early-stage disease. Recent studies have shown, however, that women with ovarian cancer often have some symptoms or signs even if the cancer is in an early stage. Currently, there are no acceptable screening techniques available for ovarian cancer (Horvath et al. 2010).

Only one research team has so far studied the use of dogs for ovarian cancer detection, as indicated in Table 24.7. A dog trained by Horvath et al. (2008) to distinguish samples of different histopathological types and grades of ovarian carcinoma tumors, from samples (3 mm scraps) of abdominal fat and muscle, in double-blind tests achieved 100% detection sensitivity and 97.5% specificity. The practical usefulness of using tumor tissue for ovarian cancer screening is questionable, since the odor samples (tumor, abdominal fat, and muscle) were obtained using highly invasive methods. Since a full histopathological diagnosis can be done on such samples, there is no need

TABLE 24.7

Detection of Ovarian Cancer by Trained Canines

Authors	Odor Samples	Number of Dogs per Breed	Odor Lineup or Circle, Number of Samples	Detection Sensitivity	Detection Specificity	Probability of Correct Indication by Chance
Horvath et al. (2008)	Ovarian tumor tissue	1 giant schnauzer	Lineup of 5: 1 cancer + 4 controls; lineup of 10: 2 cancers + 8 controls	100%	97.5%	(Not indicated)
Horvath et al. (2010)	Tissue, blood	2 giant schnauzers	Circle of 6: 1 cancer + 5 controls	100% 100%	95% 98%	(Not indicated)
Horvath et al. (2013)	Tissue, blood	2 giant schnauzers	Lineup of 4–10: 1–3 cancer + 9–7 controls	97% 97% (cancer recurrence detection in 3 of 10 patients)	99% 99%	(Not indicated)

to confirm it by dogs. Horvath et al. (2008) supposed that the most common ovarian carcinoma is characterized by a single specific odor and this odor differs from those of other gynecological malignances, such as cervical, endometrial, and vulvar carcinomas, but this hypothesis is not supported by chemical analyses.

In a follow-up study on ovarian cancer, Horvath et al. (2010) used blood plasma samples as an odor source for dog training and testing a giant schnauzer that had been previously trained to indicate ovarian tumor samples, while another giant schnauzer was trained on blood plasma samples only. The dogs discriminated blood plasma samples from patients with ovarian cancer and from patients with cervical, vulvar, and endometrial carcinomas, as well as from healthy controls, with sensitivity of 100% and specificity of 98%, which was practically identical to the accuracy achieved with tissue samples. These authors concluded that a trained dog could discriminate different histopathological types and grades of ovarian carcinoma tissues, including borderline tumors, from healthy control samples, some of which came from postmenopausal women. Moreover, the dog was able to discriminate ovarian carcinoma tissue from all other gynecological malignancies. The same team (Horvath et al. 2010), using the same dogs, conducted a retrospective study of detection by dogs of patients during treatment and 3 and 6 months after treatment. Again, the two dogs showed very high detection sensitivity (97%) and specificity (99%), both for viable cancer cells and molecular cancer markers in blood plasma. Interestingly, the dogs indicated 3 patients who had recurrences out of 10 patients investigated at both the 3- and 6-month follow-ups. Thus, the dogs demonstrated an ability to detect recurrences of this cancer.

COLORECTAL CANCER

Colorectal cancer is the third most common type of nonskin cancer in both men (after prostate cancer and lung cancer) and women (after breast cancer and lung cancer). It is the second leading cause of cancer death in the United States after lung cancer. Worldwide, 1.4 million new cases of colorectal cancer (9.7% of all cancers) are recorded annually.

Several screening tests have been developed to find colorectal cancer early, when it may be more treatable. Some tests that detect adenomas and polyps can actually prevent the development of

TABLE 24.8
Detection of Colorectal Cancer by Trained Canines

Author	Odor Samples	Number of Dogs per Breed	Odor Lineup or Circle, Number of Samples	Detection Sensitivity	Detection Specificity	Probability of Correct Indication by Chance
Sonoda et al. (2011)	Breath, feces	1 Labrador retriever	Lineup of 5: 1 cancer + 4 controls	91% 97%	99% 99%	(Not indicated)

cancer because these tests allow growths that might otherwise become cancer to be removed. Thus, colorectal cancer screening may be a form of cancer prevention, not just early detection. Expert medical groups, including the U.S. Preventive Services Task Force, generally recommend that people at average risk of colorectal cancer get screened at regular intervals with high-sensitivity fecal occult blood tests (FOBTs), sigmoidoscopy, or colonoscopy, beginning at age 50. The most economical and noninvasive screening method for colorectal cancer is FOBT; however, FOBT shows a positive predictive value of approximately 10%, and many patients with positive FOBT results must subsequently undergo a total colonoscopy. Thus, there is room for development of a new screening method for colorectal cancer that is more effective but at least as economical and noninvasive as FOBT. Such a method could be based on analyzing cancer-specific volatile compounds.

As of this writing, only one peer-reviewed publication on colorectal cancer screening with odor material by canine scent detection has been published, as indicated in Table 24.8. Sonoda et al. (2011) trained a female Labrador retriever to discriminate breath samples and watery stool samples from patients with colorectal cancer and from healthy controls. A five-station lineup was used, with one cancer sample and four controls. The sensitivity of canine scent detection of breath samples was 91% at 99% specificity, while for watery stool samples, sensitivity and specificity were, respectively, 97% and 99%. More importantly, detection accuracy was even higher for early-stage cancers and was not confounded by current smoking, benign colorectal disease, inflammatory disease, or the presence of hemoglobin or transferrin. This team concluded that a specific cancer scent exists. Although the study did not identify cancer-specific volatile organic compounds (VOCs), the authors believe odor detection may become an effective tool for colorectal cancer screening.

STATE OF RESEARCH AND PROSPECTS FOR CLINICAL APPLICATION

Even if some studies failed to show dogs capable of discriminating cancer odor samples at better than chance, none of the authors excluded the possibility of using canines for practical cancer screening. There is, however, skepticism among oncologists about the validity and reliability of a broad use of canines as a screening method. Some oncologists acknowledge that, even if a method is not yet ideal, if dogs can save human lives, they might be worth deploying in clinical contexts. Dog training centers have begun to train cancer detection dogs.[1] Nevertheless, a canine method is still a "black-box technology" because the stimuli the dogs are reacting to are not known. Some authors have hypothesized that the pattern of VOCs found in the exhaled breath of lung and breast cancers may be identified by using gas chromatography and mass spectrometry (GC/MS) (Phillips et al. 1999, 2003a,b, 2007) or an "electronic nose" (D'Amico et al. 2010; Peng et al. 2010; Bikov et al. 2014). For a discussion of the development of GC/MS, see Chapter 7 herein.

Neither GC/MS analysis nor tests with trained canines have established whether different types of cancer have a common odor signature or each type of cancer has its own odor signature. If a common cancer odor signature does exist, training of dogs on several types of cancer would facilitate amassing samples of different cancers for training (Elliker et al. 2014) and would make dogs more versatile detectors. If, however, a common odor signature does not exist, multicancer training could induce dogs to generalize on the odor of a particular type of cancer, while missing others (Jezierski et al. 2015).

The main problem with using GC/MS for cancer screening in practice is not only the sampling procedure but also the interpretation of results. Since more than 30 VOCs may be identified in the breath of cancer patients and healthy controls, and the VOCs may be present in different combinations and quantities (Phillips et al. 2007; Buszewski et al. 2012a,b), employing a single VOC as a cancer marker is likely impossible. Multivariate analysis of several markers in different combinations could better predict disease, so sophisticated methods such as fuzzy logic have been used for results obtained from GC/MS (Phillips et al. 2007). Canine indications in a scent lineup are mostly binary (with yes/no responses), making interpretation of results easier.

To establish cancer detection dogs as something more than a black-box technology, VOCs responsible for canine indications will have to be identified. Buszewski et al. (2012a) attempted to correlate analyses of breath of cancer patients and healthy donors using GC/MS with results obtained by parallel testing of breath samples from the same patients using trained dogs. They identified no single VOC or any defined combination of VOCs that constituted a fixed cancer odor signature. Using statistical methods, this team found that dogs' indications showed the highest positive correlations in the presence of 2-pentanone and ethyl acetate ($r = 0.97$ and $r = 0.85$ respectively), meaning that breath samples containing higher amounts of these two compounds led to better results from dogs. On the other hand, the content of 1-propanol and propanal in breath samples was negatively correlated with dogs' indications ($r = -0.98$ and $r = -0.87$ respectively), i.e., the percentage of correct indications by dogs tended to decrease when these two compounds in breath samples were higher.

One of the problems in using canines may be inconsistent and noncomparable results. Jezierski et al. (2015) noted that the variability of results of experimental studies on cancer detection by trained canines published to date could be partly due to a lack of methodological standardization. No direct comparison of dog breeds trained for cancer detection has so far been conducted, and this issue should receive additional attention. It may be that the most suitable candidates for cancer detection training may be found among typical working breeds, e.g., German shepherds or Labrador retrievers, rather than among pet breeds. The greater potential of the two mentioned breeds as sniffer dogs has been also suggested based on genetic diversity of olfactory receptors (Robin et al. 2009; Lippi and Cervillin 2011). Elliker et al. (2014) opined that dogs might be bred specifically for cancer detection.

METHODOLOGY ISSUES

No standards exist as to odor sampling methods. Taking into account the importance of noninvasiveness in methods, the most suitable materials to use seems to be exhaled breath and urine. For exhaled breath, sampling researchers have adopted different types of tubes originally used for other purposes, e.g., for land mine detection or respiratory and anesthesia procedures. Sampling tubes should be simple and handy to use without special training. Breath sampling tubes (see Figure 24.1) should absorb different types of VOCs without reacting with them or changing odor properties and should be impermeable for odors. They should also be structured so as to be employed without the dog touching the tube with its nose or saliva (Jezierski et al. 2015).

Storing odor samples after collecting and before testing with dogs may be important for logistical reasons. With GC/MS procedures, analysis is recommended within hours of sample collection. No detailed studies have been done on the influence of sample storage time on the accuracy of dogs' indications, and storage time has varied considerably in published studies. Willis et al. (2004) stored frozen urine samples up to 5 months before testing with dogs for bladder cancer. McCulloch et al. (2006) stored breath samples at room temperature no longer than 60 days before trials. Gordon et al. (2008) tested urine samples stored at $-20°C$ for 1 week to 5 months, thawing the samples before tests for breast and prostate cancers.

Odor lineups or circles in identification procedures should ideally be standardized for future studies and before clinical implementation. To compare results obtained by different authors, the probability of correct indication by chance should be estimated. Too many samples in a lineup cannot be recommended, because dogs may not sniff all samples, meaning the response to some samples would be unknown and the probability of a correct indication by chance would vary depending on how many

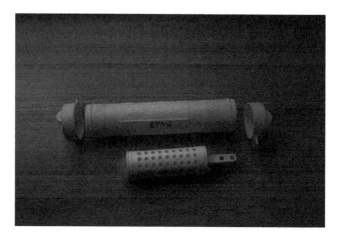

FIGURE 24.1   Breath sampling tubes.

samples were actually sniffed. Two different criteria could be used for recording correct indication during a trial in a lineup, which may have consequences for the magnitude of results reported by authors:

- *Criterion I.* Yes/no response to each sniffed sample in the lineup. In this approach, a dog could, in a single trial, provide both a correct indication toward the target sample and false alert(s) toward controls. The probability of a correct response by chance to the target sample is 50% and does not depend on the number of scent samples presented or sniffed by the dog. This calculation method yields a higher percentage of correct responses, as indicated in Table 24.9 (Walczak 2009).
- *Criterion II.* The dog is only permitted to choose one target sample (or more if more than one target sample is included in the lineup) out of all sniffed samples without any false alerts or hesitations for the test to be scored a correct positive response. For example, if five samples in the lineup have been sniffed, the probability of correct indication in one trial is 20%. In this approach, the number of odor samples in the lineup or circle plays a role for the probability of correct indications by chance, i.e., the more samples sniffed before indication, the lower the probability of correct indication by chance alone. The same trials evaluated according to this approach give a lower percentage of success, also indicated in Table 24.9.

TABLE 24.9

Comparison of Detection Sensitivity in % for Three Types of Cancer by the Same Trained Dogs, Depending on Probability of Correct Indication by Chance

Dogs (Names)	Melanoma		Breast Cancer		Lung Cancer	
	20% Correct by Chance	50% Correct by Chance	20% Correct by Chance	50% Correct by Chance	20% Correct by Chance	50% Correct by Chance
Court	32.2%	66.3%	66.9%	89.2%	53.4%	83.6%
Cygun	58.6%	80.2%	67.7%	89.5%	58.2%	84.5%
Gromit	39.7%	67.1%	67.8%	90.5%	54.0%	83.4%

Source: Walczak, M., Operant Conditioning of Dogs for Detection of Odor Markers of Cancer Diseases (PhD thesis in Polish), Institute of Genetics and Animal Breeding of the Polish Academy of Sciences, Jastrzębiec, Poland, 2009.

Horvath et al. (2008) calculated that the probability of a dog correctly indicating two target samples in each of a series of 10 tests with 10 samples in each is extraordinarily small, i.e., 1.02×10^{-7}. The tests in each series must be independent, as repeating the same target sample in consecutive trials may involve a learning process resulting in progressively more correct indications. See Figure 24.2, from Walczak et al. (2012).

Another problem mentioned by Elliker et al. (2014) is a risk of dogs memorizing particular odor samples during training and thereby developing poor generalization capability as to any characteristic cancer odor signature. It is not clear, however, if dogs really demonstrate a poor ability to generalize on a cancer odor signature or if individual variability in composition, proportion, and concentration of VOCs in cancer patients and healthy controls makes for a cancer odor signature that is too variable to be generalized by dogs. That dogs may show some ability to generalize odor components could be concluded from Walczak et al. (2012), as the dogs used in this study probably generalized from typical hospital odors, given that breath sampling occurred mostly in hospitals. These dogs falsely alerted to control (healthy) samples taken inside hospitals significantly more often than to controls taken outside hospital rooms. Moreover, the dogs falsely alerted to the samples of ambient air collected in hospital rooms, at the same rate (approximately 30%) as to the samples of control persons.

Elliker et al. (2014) recommend that repeated presentation of samples from the same donors should be minimized. This decreases the likelihood of memorization of individual odor samples but could also decrease the reliability of results since there will be fewer repetitions of the trials on the same samples.

Generally, a double-blind protocol is to be recommended for testing odor samples with dogs, which means that the experimenter and the handler should be blind to the location of the target sample (cancer pattern odor) in the lineup to prevent unconscious signaling to the dog of which sample the it is expected to indicate (the so-called Clever Hans effect). However, to avoid extinction of the reaction learnt by operant conditioning, the dog's correct indications of the target sample in a lineup must be reinforced by a reward that follows a correct response. Practically, this means that either a person, who knows the status of the target sample and confirms that the dog's response is correct by giving a signal (acoustic or visual) to the handler to reward the dog, is totally isolated visually and acoustically from the site of the test, or the dog is not rewarded during double-blind trials, because it is not known if the response was correct or false. Although different forms of reinforcement schedules can be derived from the animal learning theory, e.g., delayed reinforcement or variable reinforcement schedule (rewarding only for a proportion of correct indications), dogs, upon not being rewarded several times in turn, may change their strategy in double-blind trials, as suggested by Elliker et al. (2014). Depending on the temperament and learning ability, if one strategy

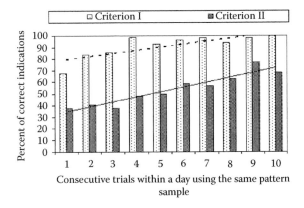

FIGURE 24.2   Percentage of correct indications in consecutive trials within a day using the same pattern sample.

proves unrewarding, some dogs may indicate any sample in the lineup in expectation that one of them will lead to a reward. Thus, more false alerts may be made in double-blind trials. This should be trained and tested prior to trial, so a baseline from which to work should be assessed.

Elliker et al. (2014) suggested an alternative to training and testing by habituation–dishabituation rather than by search-based discrimination tasks as have been used so far. The superiority of such a training and testing method has not yet been proven experimentally. While it may have advantages, it is extremely difficult to produce consistently with trainers and dogs.

CONCLUSIONS

Trained canines can discriminate odor samples, mostly exhaled breath and urine from patients with diagnosed skin (melanoma), lung, breast, colorectal, prostate, and ovarian cancers from odor samples of healthy people. Detection sensitivity and specificity varied across studies from no better than chance to close to 100% accuracy. Studies conducted to date generally do not demonstrate that dogs are actually able to detect very early or preclinical stages of cancer before medical diagnosis. Therefore, using dogs for practical cancer screening remains largely experimental, though clinical implementation is worth considering in environments where alternative tests are unavailable or too expensive.

ENDNOTE

1. See, e.g., InSitu Foundation, http://www.dogsdetectcancer.org.

25 Medical Alerting to Seizures, Glycemic Changes, and Migraines
Significance of Untrained Behaviors in Service Dogs

John Ensminger

Canine alerting to oncoming seizures, hypoglycemic episodes, and migraines has been a subject of articles in the popular press and scientific journals for decades in the case of epilepsy, almost as long in the case of diabetes, and more recently in the case of migraines. Advance alerting has sometimes been reported by sufferers of other conditions.[1] Chemical phenomena have been linked with such conditions, and it has often been suggested that the dogs are using their olfactory skills to recognize changes in the way that the humans smell, though behavioral changes in the humans have also been postulated, and it is possible that dogs are assembling a number of different types of cues in reacting to these episodic conditions.

As with cancer detection by dogs, initial reports of alerts to episodic conditions were anecdotal, and much of the research remains effectively self-reported in articles based on surveys or records and diaries kept by participants.[2] Nevertheless, direct observation, particularly by videotaping, has also been used, though this kind of research has been limited by cost limitations and privacy issues. There appear to be dogs that can detect certain kinds of episodes before their masters are aware, but how much in advance this is possible remains uncertain, as do the exact nature of the episodes that can be detected and the chemical or behavioral mechanisms of canine detection.[3] Whether dogs with this skill are to be defined as service animals, however, involves a number of considerations, including whether the condition alerted to qualifies as a disability and whether the dog itself meets the requirements for being considered a service animal. The latter issue is in turn complicated by the fact that there is no single definition of what constitutes a service animal.

AMERICANS WITH DISABILITIES ACT

Under the Americans with Disabilities Act (ADA), as passed by Congress in 1990,[4] a disability includes a physical or mental impairment that substantially limits one or more of the major life activities of such individual. It was not initially clear, however, whether a condition had to be permanent and continuous to be a disability, and prior to 2008, a number of American courts had held that episodic conditions were not disabilities under the ADA. Thus, a Texas federal district court determined that an individual's epilepsy, which involved seizures during which the victim could not speak, was not sufficiently limiting to qualify as a disability under the ADA, because the seizures occurred only occasionally.[5] In 2008, however, in the ADA Amendments Act of 2008,[6] Congress amended the definition of disability in 42 U.S.C. 12102 to provide that an "impairment that is episodic or in remission is a disability if it would substantially limit a major life activity when active." The legislative history to the 2008 Act stated that Congress expected that individuals with impairments that are episodic or in remission (e.g., epilepsy, multiple sclerosis, cancer) will be able to establish coverage if, when active, the impairment or the manner in which it manifests (e.g., seizures) substantially limits a major life activity.[7]

Congress disapproved of the judicial reasoning in cases declaring that victims of epilepsy or posttraumatic stress disorder could not have disabilities. In issuing regulations under the ADA that took into account the change in the law, the Equal Employment Opportunity Commission said that other examples of episodic conditions that could be disabilities included, but were not limited to, "hypertension, diabetes, asthma, major depressive disorder, bipolar disorder, and schizophrenia."[8] This agency elaborated:

> The fact that the periods during which an episodic impairment is active and substantially limits a major life activity may be brief or occur infrequently is no longer relevant to determining whether the impairment substantially limits a major life activity. For example, a person with post-traumatic stress disorder who experiences intermittent flashbacks to traumatic events is substantially limited in brain function and thinking.[9]

The definitional section of Department of Justice (DOJ) regulations, 28 CFR 36.104, that defines *service animal*, also states that a physical or mental impairment includes epilepsy and diabetes, along with mental retardation, emotional illness, specific learning disabilities, and HIV disease. Migraines are not mentioned, and a 2011 Tenth Circuit decision held that a claim that migraines compelled an employee to go to sleep in the evenings instead of caring for herself "was insufficiently developed and insufficiently supported" to establish an ADA-level disability.[10] With additional facts, however, a case might have been made (Morris 2014). A Washington State appellate court accepted that migraines could be sufficiently debilitating to qualify as a disability but found that the dog in the case before it was not trained and was, therefore, not a service dog.[11]

The service dog industry has taken note of medical alerting, and dogs are being trained and sold to individuals who expect that they will be notified in advance that an episode is about to begin. The more responsible training organizations generally do not provide guarantees that the dogs will alert, since the present state of research indicates that not all dogs have the capability to detect such events in advance, or at least do not have the ability to notify the individual with the condition in advance. Training organizations generally focus on teaching dogs to respond at the beginning of an episode in such a way as to provide assistance to the individual with the condition, or to bring others who will be able to provide assistance. Thus, the industry has developed useful "response" animals that can be functional service animals even if they do not consistently or ever alert in advance. In any case, providing advance warning of such episodic events is important for those who suffer from certain conditions and improves the quality of their lives, whatever explains the phenomenon. The significance of spontaneous alerting in dogs not otherwise trained to be service dogs will be discussed at the end of this chapter.

SEIZURE ALERTING

Dr. Elizabeth Rudy, a veterinarian, stated in a short note in 1995 that dogs might be alerting in advance to seizures by perceiving "slight changes in a person's body language or behavior" or "very subtle changes in a person's body odor prior to a seizure." She mentioned a report indicating that this could happen even hours before an episode:

> Dogs have been observed to lick owner's hands, bark at the owner's face, or act restless and pace prior to the person's seizure. The amount of time from when the dog alerts to the actual onset of the seizure varies from dog to dog. One dog would consistently gather all his toys and dump them in front of the owner several hours prior to a seizure. Identifying consistent alerting behavior in a dog that alerts long before a seizure requires an astute and careful observer due to the lapse of time between the alert and

the event. Some dogs alert only for their owners. Other dogs, given time and exposure to other people with seizures, can develop the ability to alert for more than one person. At least one puppy has apparently learned to alert from an older dog.

Most subsequent studies have narrowed the time frame of advance recognition considerably.[12] Also, few of the studies discussed here have mentioned the possibility that dogs would alert to individuals other than their masters, though the nature of training for advance alerting might involve the dogs learning off of other individuals before being assigned as service dogs to specific individuals with the relevant disability. If the dogs were trained on human actors pretending to have seizures, odor recognition would not be involved in the training, which does not prove that it could not be part of the dog's ultimate recognition arsenal.

RISK TO DOGS RECOGNIZING SEIZURES

Strong and Brown (1999, 2000) reviewed 36 cases documented by a charitable service dog organization of dogs spontaneously reacting to seizures and found that in a number of cases, the dogs became highly agitated and aggressive, and sometimes even died. One assistance dog was described as "attacking owner during seizures and aggressive towards paramedics." Another assistance dog was described as "showing escape behaviour and avoidance towards owner during seizure. Dog also required reassurance from family members." In eight cases, the length of time before the dog developed a conspicuous reacting behavior to human seizures, which varied from 3 to 15 weeks, was noted. Despite the reports about the two assistance dogs, the authors stated the following:

> There is evidence that dogs can be specially trained to recognize specific changes preceding a seizure and give an overt signal enabling the dog to warn his/her significant human. SUPPORT DOGS, a registered charity in Britain, which trains dogs to assist disabled people, has successfully trained a number of Seizure Alert Dogs™. The dogs are able to provide overt signals to their owners within time periods varying from 15–45 minutes prior to a seizure occurring. Each dog has an accurate and constant prediction time.

They also noted that no dog trained by the group to which the lead author belonged "exhibited a fearful or avoidance response." They said that individuals with dogs from this group reported decreased seizure frequency. Because of the risk to untrained dogs, they argued that future research should not use control groups of such dogs, which they acknowledged raised methodological issues. Strong and Brown (2000) argued for "only using dogs that have been selected for their suitability and have received appropriate structured training from a behavioural specialist for this work." They stated that without such training, "the health and welfare of the dog may be compromised and the safety of the person with epilepsy and the general public may be jeopardized." Aggressive and fearful reactions to seizures have not been mentioned in a number of separate studies.

Strong and Brown, joined by two additional coauthors (Strong et al. 2002), specifically considered tonic–clonic seizure frequency in a paper published 2 years after their initial study. They concluded that dogs could be trained to provide a useful warning of a seizure "based on canine sensitivity to what are often subtle behavioural changes in humans." In this study, "[a]ll subjects had a diagnosis of epilepsy with tonic–clonic seizures uncomplicated by non-epileptic attack disorder, as confirmed by their referring neurologist." Tonic–clonic seizures were included because "these are relatively easy to count and it was felt that such counting would be reliable." Diaries were kept by subjects.

> Monthly tonic–clonic seizure frequency recorded during baseline varied between subjects from 6.3 to 45.6 with a mean of 13.8. This changed during the 12 week training period to a mean of 9.7 (1.7–37) and dropped further to 8.8 (1.7–30) and 8.5 (2–30) during the first and second 12 week periods of follow up, respectively.... At the end of the study overall seizure frequency had reduced by 43%, with 9/10 subjects showing a reduction of 34% or more.

The team acknowledged that one individual was not helped by having the dog.

Dalziel et al. (2003) argued that "research to verify the innate seizure-alerting abilities of dogs has been inconclusive," noting that "some service dog trainers believe the patient is unknowingly providing a behavioral cue." They acknowledged that this would not explain cases of alerting by dogs that could not see their handlers at the time of the alert. Thus, "one has to consider the possibility of a scent, auditory cue or some other signal independent of visual cues." They also thought that a combination of several senses could be involved. They sent out a questionnaire that was completed by 93 subjects, 9 of whom had dogs that responded to a seizure and 3 of whom had dogs that alerted to an impending seizure.

> Although not statistically significant, subjects with alerting/responding dogs were more inclined to have complex partial seizures, migraines, and reported a range of auras that could potentially offer the dog visual, auditory, and or scent cues to an impending seizure. The type of medication, dose or frequency of use did not appear to be a factor in the dogs' alerting/responding ability.

Those whose dogs alerted in advance were thereby able to take medication and get to a safe place or position. "The alerting behavior was described as attention-getting behavior that included whining, pacing in front of or around the patient, anxious barking or intent staring at the patient." Elsewhere in the article, the researchers also listed pawing as an alerting behavior. Once alerting behavior was identified, the researchers reported that some trainers begin to reinforce that behavior. The authors expressed concern that "some entrepreneurs may take advantage of this phenomena and sell 'seizure-alert dogs' to epilepsy patients." Combining the references to training in the 2000 and 2002 papers in which Strong and Brown participated, it appears that they would argue that seizure alerting could be trained but that many unscrupulous trainers and even some assistance dog trainers might not develop sufficiently effective training programs to achieve the desired result.[13]

Kirton et al. (2004) gathered data from a survey indicating that 42% of families with dogs reported that the animals had seizure-related behaviors, which were evident about a month from when the dog was acquired.

> The most common response behavior was licking, often of the face, observed in 13 of 22 SRDs (59%). Other common responses included decreased motor activity (55%), "protective" behavior without aggression (50%), and whimpering (36%).

Nine seizure-response dogs also had alerting behavior, amounting to 20% of all families living with such a dog.

> Female dogs comprised approximately 80% of the SAD [seizure-alert dog] subgroup.... The median anticipation time was 2.5 (0.9, 15.0) minutes with a range from 10 seconds to 5 hours. The accuracy of alerting behaviors was high, with a median sensitivity estimate of 80% (66, 92). Anticipatory behaviors were never demonstrated without a subsequent seizure. The majority of families (6/10) believed the anticipation abilities existed with the first seizure, whereas the rest reported it developing within 1 month.

Alerting behaviors were, according to this team, often protective, with no instances of overt aggression being reported, unlike what Strong and Brown had found. "Six of the nine SAD families felt the mechanism of anticipation was a unique sensory ability outside of the traditional five senses. Two others felt it was likely related to smell."

Kirton et al. (2008) found that spontaneous alerting behavior developed in 59% of seizure-response dogs.

> Onset was often within 4 weeks (46%), the remainder evolving over months. Anticipation behaviors were varied and distinct from response behaviors. Intense staring was most common (6/13, 46%) but never reported as response behavior. Other alerting behaviors included close attachment (5), sniffing (3), barking/whimpering (3), jumping (3), and licking (2). Five (38%) alerting animals physically prevented their owners from leaving the house prior to seizures. Anticipation was reported to occur

an average of 31 minutes (range: 0.5–180) prior to clinical seizure onset. The anticipation interval increased over time in 6 of 13 participants (42%). Anticipation behaviors were reported as reliable in both character and timing, and most reported no missed events (11/13, 85%). Alerting abilities directly influenced 8 (62%) patients' management of their epilepsy, including notification of family/caregivers, assumption of safe positions/locations, and, in one case, taking abortive anticonvulsant medication.

This argues that the service dog industry should focus on seizure-response training since seizure alerting has a certain likelihood of developing once a dog is with a patient for a short time.

STUDIES WITH VIDEOTAPING

Ortiz and Liporace (2005) were able to videotape two patients with seizure-alert dogs who had been admitted to the epilepsy care unit of a Philadelphia hospital. As to one patient with frontal lobe epilepsy, the researchers said the following:

> Patient 1 had eight complex partial seizures during his 4-day stay in the hospital. Four seizures occurred while awake and four seizures during sleep. The EEG revealed a left frontal lobe seizure onset. The seizure-alert dog alerted the patient prior to one of the seizures by quickly standing up from a sitting position and staring at the patient for 2 seconds prior to the seizure. For seven of the eight seizures, the dog was sleeping and did not alert the patient. The dog did wake up a few seconds after the patient's seizure began and alerted family members by barking and/or by constantly walking around the bed. There were no false detections by the dog.

As to the second patient, the researchers stated the following:

> Patient 2 had five of her typical seizures during her stay in the ECU [Epilepsy Care Unit]. Her seizure-alert dog was present during only one of her seizures. The dog alerted her, and 7 minutes later, the patient had her seizure. There was no EEG change with the seizure and the patient was diagnosed with nonepileptic seizures.

The researchers concluded that the alert of the dogs before seizures was poor for Patient 1. They also believed that "the seizure-alert dog of patient 2 contributed to her nonepileptic seizures by alerting and increasing the frequency of her events." They concluded that in their "limited but objective experience, 'seizure dogs,' were not as effective as previously thought in predicting seizure activity." They acknowledged that the epilepsy care unit might not be an ideal location to test a dog's ability as the dog might be "distracted by other people having seizures in nearby rooms." As to the reason dogs can anticipate seizures, this paper stated the following:

> Visual cueing on subtle early seizure behaviors has been suggested as the mechanism for seizure anticipation, whereas olfactory sensation seems less likely. Alternatively, being able to sense behavior would confer a significant survival advantage to a dog and be perpetuated through natural selection.... Intriguing new and controversial research has begun to explore the abilities of animals to sense human brain activities. Simple experiments with SADs could solve the mystery.

The final sentence of this quotation appears to have been overly optimistic. The focus to date has been more on whether dogs can detect seizures (or other episodic medical events) in advance, rather than the specific mechanism of how they do so.

Di Vito et al. (2010) described a dog that reacted to a child's seizures at onset:

> At the very beginning of the seizure, the dog would alert the patient's parents by running to them barking and then going back to the patient. After this phase, as shown in the videos, the dog developed "protective" behaviour during the seizure which involved barking and not allowing anybody to touch the patient, jumping on her legs and stopping her from standing up. The dog tried to stimulate the patient

by gently biting her feet or licking her feet or ears…. The dog remained close to the patient during the seizure and afterwards usually calmed down and often fell asleep close to its owner. When present, the dog behaved consistently during all of the patient's seizures, without exception, showing the same response in all cases and also during both types of seizures.

The dog was not trained for assistance work. The dog "was able to recognize the seizure at onset but *never developed an alerting behaviour.*" The patient exhibited a decrease in seizure frequency and intensity after the dog's arrival, but "this benefit cannot be attributed solely to the dog as some therapeutic adjustments were also made during recent years."

Pseudoseizure Dogs

Skepticism as to whether dogs were recognizing all types of seizures became evident in two papers published in 2007. Krauss et al. (2007) looked at patients who had acquired seizure-response dogs and who claimed that the dogs were alerting them to the onsets of their seizures. The team determined that the four patients had psychogenic nonepileptic seizures (PNESs). The researchers conceded that the patient with epilepsy had a dog that alerted prior to her seizures by pacing. They argued that individuals with primarily psychiatric conditions might benefit from the emotional support of seizure-response dogs but that they did not need epileptic seizure dogs.[14]

Doherty and Haltiner (2007) described a case study of a patient whose seizures were determined by a multidisciplinary team to be psychogenic nonepileptiform events (PNES). Those events "included anterior-to-posterior plane pelvic bucking, head-bobbling movements, psychomotor unresponsiveness, and postevent flaccidity." The patient's husband also had seizures, and the couple's dog, a blue heeler, was said to predict both of their seizures. In the wife's case, the dog would lie across her chest prior to and during convulsions.[15] The researchers noted that "[s]elf-reported and even performance-based neuropsychological profiles measured in patients with PNES often do not correlate with independent objective measurements."[16] These researchers raised a number of important questions:

> If dogs can predict PNES, could events be viewed as conditioned responses to stereotyped dog behaviors? If teddy bears present during adult VEEG telemetry correlate with PNES, might SADs [seizure-alert dogs] similarly prove red flags for potential patients with PNES? Do the dogs perceive a stimulus, perhaps an audible frequency or a peculiar odor, that represents seizure (or pseudoseizure) onset? Are dogs detecting early ictus, and are the families or patients under the impression this is preseizure? Given the costs of training SAD dogs, should patients inquiring about SADs be specifically screened with VEEG for PNES? Do SADs change the frequency of PNES?

Doherty and Haltiner (2007) thus raised the possibility that PNES patients might have seizures in response to certain canine behaviors, and that having a seizure-alert dog might actually indicate that the patient's seizures are psychogenic. On the other hand, they acknowledged that dogs might be reacting to a peculiar odor or an auditory stimulus.

How Do Dogs Recognize Seizure Onsets?

How dogs might recognize the onset of a seizure was considered by Brown and Goldstein (2011). They speculated that seizure-alert dogs "probably alert to subtle pre-ictal human behaviour changes, but may also be sensitive to heart rate or olfactory cues."

> Clinicians specialising in epilepsy will be familiar with carers and relatives of people with epilepsy occasionally making a claim that they can detect changes in the person's appearance, presentation or behaviour that are premonitory to seizure activity even before the person is aware of the situation. Further discussion sometimes also reveals a claim that the family pet (usually, but not always a dog) may display specific behaviours prior to the person having a seizure, where no warning signs have been noticed by the person or their human carers or family.[17]

They cite earlier researchers as having "felt that in these cases (both in trained dogs and in those who learn spontaneously) the mechanism is probably based on canine sensitivity to what are often subtle behavioural changes in humans."

> It is perfectly possible that some relevant human behaviours might not be obvious to humans themselves but are noted by dogs because they signify anticipation of reward. It is not currently possible to state whether dogs are sensitive to subtle changes in human respiratory rate, or whether their acute hearing may enable sensitivity to human heart rate changes, or whether some olfactory phenomenon may play a part. It is possible that more than one mechanism may be relevant.

They elaborated on the last sentence of this quote by noting that "[b]earing in mind the variable length of warning before seizures that is described, it would seem reasonable to allow for several mechanisms to be relevant, with different ones applying in different situations and possibly corresponding to different seizure types." They argued "for more tightly controlled prospective studies of SADs' alerting abilities, especially if such alerting abilities are thought to occur in response to pre-ictal changes in the person with epilepsy."

The paper described training dogs with reward-based operant conditioning to display seizure-alerting behavior. The authors found that by training the dogs in this manner, "there was a 43% mean reduction in seizure frequency ($p = 0.002$), with a mean monthly seizure frequency at baseline of 13.8 (range 6.3–45.6) falling to 8.5 (range 2–30) during the last 12 weeks of follow-up." The decrease in seizure frequency "was an unexpected finding and had not originally been regarded as an outcome." They state that "no specific breed or gender seems to be preferred; successful training is felt to depend on the person–dog bonding, which is very individual."

As to reports that dogs initiate alert behavior out of sight of the patient, they stated the following:

> [R]eview of video evidence from the home placement phase of training described above shows that a dog situated in another room in the house typically enters the room and appears to check the human every 15 min or so, and therefore shows alert behaviour as a result of their regular checking and observation of the human, rather than entering the room because they are displaying alert behaviour. Likewise, video scrutiny shows that the sleeping pattern of SADs seems to include waking regularly and looking at the human. (Strong, pers. comm.)

These observations place the burden of arguing that there is a significant olfactory element in the advance detection of seizures upon those who would argue for such an explanation. Clearly, as of this writing, many issues remain open (Ramgopal et al. 2014).[18] Another area needing investigation may be the degree to which dogs, who themselves can have epileptic seizures (Thomas and Dewey 2003), may react to oncoming seizures in conspecifics.[19]

HYPERGLYCEMIA AND HYPOGLYCEMIA ALERTING

Chen et al. (2000a) described dogs that, according to their owners, were able to detect hypoglycemic symptoms. A woman with type 2 diabetes noticed "unusual stereotyped behaviour displayed by Candy, her 9 year old mongrel bitch, which occurs only before hypoglycaemic episodes. Candy jumps up, runs out of the room, and hides under a chair in the hallway…, and reemerges only when the patient has taken carbohydrate." This occurred before the patient was aware of any hypoglycemic symptoms. Two similar cases were described in the paper and summarized:

> [E]ach dog showed her specific behaviours only when the patient had documented hypoglycaemia. Susie and Natt deserve special mention because they were able to detect nocturnal episodes in their owners and then undertook further corrective action by waking them to eat—thus going further than any available glucose sensor.

As to the mechanism by which the dogs detect the condition, the paper stated the following:

The physiological basis is uncertain, but direct contact with the diabetic patient was not required in any of these cases. Possible clues include olfactory changes (possibly related to sweating), muscle tremor, or behavioural alterations such as the patient's failure to respond to her dog in her usual way. We are attracted by the notion of the "sixth sense" with which dogs are commonly credited, but acknowledge that this will need to be substantiated by further research.

Wells et al. (2008) found the following:

Thirty-six percent of the sample [of 212 dog owners] believed that their dogs reacted most of the times they went "low"; 33.6% indicated that their pets reacted before they themselves were aware they were hypoglycemic. Dogs' behavioral responses to their owners' hypoglycemic episodes varied. Most animals behaved in a manner suggestive of attracting their owners' attention, for example, vocalizing (61.5%), licking them (49.2%), nuzzling them (40.6%), jumping on top of them (30.4%), and/or staring intently at their faces (41.3%). A smaller proportion showed behavioral responses suggestive of fear, including trembling (7.2%), running away from the owner (5.1%), and/or hyperventilating (2.2%).

One reason for understanding the mechanism of how dogs detect a hypoglycemic episode would be to "develop noninvasive electronic sensor systems to perform the same task." The authors primarily surveyed people with type 1 diabetes but noted that "a few people with type 2 diabetes" also indicated "that their dogs reliably showed 'alert' behavior." They stated the following:

Increases in sweating have been repeatedly noted in hypoglycemic individuals. As in the case of cancer, it is possible that dogs can detect changes in the chemical composition of their owners' sweat, using their acute sense of smell. However, it cannot be ignored that dogs may respond to other cues besides olfactory ones, including, for example, subtle changes in their owner's mood (with people often becoming more irritable as their sugar levels drop) or visual signals related to their owner's behavior (with some people trembling, becoming disorientated, losing consciousness, or having seizures). The possibility that individual animals employ multiple signals, or that different dogs use entirely different cues equally cannot be dismissed.

Chemical changes involving volatile organic compounds may also be detectable by dogs from breath, as has been indicated by studies involving gas chromatography–mass spectrometry.[20] One patient did not find that her dog could alert in advance while she was asleep.

Although not eligible for participation in this investigation, a female owner of a trained hypoglycemia alert dog, reported an inability of the animal to detect decreases in her sugar levels while she slept, presumably because the animal had only been trained to alert to subtle visual changes in behavior associated with her sugar level's dropping; in this case rubbing of her hands over her face was the visual cue.

This might suggest that training with actors simulating behaviors could interfere with olfactory detection of physiological changes. These researchers argued that their study and others present "convincing evidence for a proportion of dogs being able to spontaneously detect hypoglycemia-related cues in their owners." Wells et al. favored odor as a principal factor:

Although it was not the goal of this project to explore how dogs detect hypoglycemia, the results hint at an odor cue, although other signals (e.g., changes in owner behavior due to impaired cognitive functioning) cannot be dismissed.

O'Connor et al. (2008) described a dog alerting to an individual's hypoglycemic episodes. The wife of a man admitted to an emergency ward said that she was alerted to a change in her husband's condition by their pet dog, "who was barking, running in and out of the bedroom, and generally acting strangely." The patient was not diabetic but was hypoglycemic on admission. This happened again 6 months later, and again the couple's pet King Charles spaniel had been acting strange and agitated. The authors observed that Dr. Frederick Banting had "discovered the therapeutic use of insulin to treat type 1 diabetes in depancreatectomized dogs." This team stated the following:

> The exact method by which dogs can detect hypoglycaemia is unclear but postulated theories include direct olfactory changes related to sweating, detection of muscle tremor or behavioural alterations, and a link between the vomero-nasal organ and the sense of smell, but direct contact between the dog and patient does not appear to be necessary for detection. One other possibility may be the dogs' detection, of energy wave changes in a person's electrical and/or magnetic fields during a hypoglycaemic episode.

O'Connor et al. describe the dog's hypoglycemia detection abilities as a potential "non-invasive companion based alarm system for hypoglycemia."

A study of patients with type 1 diabetes by Rooney et al. (2013) involved dogs trained by Medical Detection Dogs, a UK organization. The subjects found that the dogs alerted them "with significant, though variable, accuracy at times of low and high blood sugar." The study depended on self-reporting of the patients, who "reported reduced unconscious episodes and paramedic call outs...." The researchers noted the following:

> [F]or 80% of the clients providing sufficient data, when their dog was recorded to perform an alerting behaviour their blood was significantly more likely to be out of target range than it was during routine samples. In addition, comparison of owner's routine test records from before and after obtaining their dog, showed highly significant overall change: all but one client being more likely to be within target range post-dog; five out of nine clients experienced a significantly reduced incidence of low blood sugars, and three of the remaining four showed a significant reduction in high blood sugars, suggesting improved glycaemic control in most clients. The two clients who showed no significant increase in percentage within target (1 and 5), had dogs which were unqualified and the clients reported to be experiencing training problems, which were subsequently resolved.

Study subjects had lived with a hypoglycemia alert dog for as short as 4 months and as long as 7 years. The subjects provided detailed information about how having an alert dog had changed their lives, including the estimated frequency of low blood sugar predog and with the dog, of episodes of losing consciousness, and of paramedic calls. All subjects reported a decrease in at least one of these categories after obtaining a trained dog. Eight people who reported having episodes of unconsciousness before getting a dog said they did not have such episodes after getting one. Three people reported having made paramedic calls before getting a dog but not after. Almost all subjects (15) trusted their dogs to alert to low blood sugar levels, while 13 trusted them to alert to high blood sugar levels. The scientists explained this discrepancy with the fact that alerting to high blood sugar "is a secondary task, trained subsequent to a strong alert to low blood sugar."

In the second phase of the study, subjects were asked to record their dog's alerting behavior and to provide blood test results. The study found that blood tests for 8 of 10 subjects showed that a sample taken after a dog's alert was significantly more likely to be out of target range than was a routine sample. One dog was apparently alerting at random. The study stated that for "the best performing dog, the odds of an alert being when bloods were out of range were 10,000 times higher than that of routine tests." Eight subjects who recorded nocturnal lows predog had fewer nocturnal lows postdog, though two had an increase postdog.

As to what the dogs are actually alerting to, these scientists argued that odor cues are the most plausible explanation, particularly given that when this occurs when owners are asleep, behavioral cues would presumably be few, "although changes in breathing rate may occur." Also, some owners reported the dogs alerting when they were in another room. Thus, it "is likely that dogs detect changes in the chemical composition of their owners' sweat, or breath (including products of ketosis)...."

TABLE 25.1

Results of Each Dog and All Dogs in Hypoglycemia Study

	Dog 1	Dog 2	Dog 3
Percent correct, each	54.2	58.3	50.0
Percent correct, all dogs	54.2		
Sensitivity, each	50.0	58.3	58.3
Sensitivity, all dogs	55.5		
Specificity, each	58.3	58.3	41.7
Specificity, all dogs	52.8		

Source: Adapted from Dehlinger, K. et al., *Diabetes Care, 36,* e-98–e-99, 2013.

The value of diabetic alert dogs was indicated by another survey study in 2013. The survey, by Gonder-Frederick et al. (2013), asked how often respondents experienced hypoglycemia with no corresponding alert from their service dog. More than a third (36.1%) reported no such occurrences, 27.8% reported fewer than one event per week, and 36.1% reported more than one per week. Respondents reported significant decreases of severe and moderate hypoglycemia since getting a dog. Respondents also reported decreased worry about hypoglycemia and hyperglycemia, and increased participation in physical activities. The authors concluded that their preliminary results justify additional research.

Study Using Swabs from Patients' Skin

A study by Dehlinger et al. (2013) that did not use self-reporting had less impressive results than the survey studies. The three dogs in this study were trained to push a bell after sniffing a container containing a swab of an owner taken during a hypoglycemic period, but not during a normal glycemic period. The owners, who had type 1 diabetes, and the trainer believed that the dogs were consistently able to detect hypoglycemia. Each dog was tested with 24 samples by being presented with each sample for 30 to 45 seconds. The overall results for each dog, and combined, are contained in Table 25.1.

The researchers did not provide an explanation as to why dogs trained to alert to hypoglycemic swabs (and believed by the owners and the trainer to do so consistently in the home) could not do so in their experimental setting. The researchers concluded that "trained dogs were largely unable to identify skin swabs obtained from hypoglycemic T1D subjects." They indicated that future studies should factor in behavioral effects and should perhaps look at swabs taken only from the usual human companions of the dogs.

MIGRAINE ALERTING

Migraine alerting became a serious study with the work of Dawn Marcus. In 2012, Marcus listed behaviors of pet dogs occurring before the onset of migraine symptoms.

> Similar to hypoglycemia, migraine is an episodic disorder with attacks often preceded by subtle changes called the migraine prodrome…. Similar to the report by Wells et al. [2008] for hypoglycemia-alerting dogs, the migraine-alerting behaviors likewise involved behaviors designed to attract the attention of the migraine sufferer in the very early stages of a migraine before painful symptoms occurred…. A wide range of breeds was included, with most female dogs (bitches). Interestingly, new alerting behaviors were recognized in puppies as well as adult dogs, typically within months of the dog first starting to live with the migraine sufferer.

On completion of the survey, Marcus and Bhowmick (2013) reported the following:

The survey was completed by 1029 adult migraineurs (94.9% women), with migraines typically occurring ≤8 days per month in 63.4% of participants. A recognized change in the dog's behavior prior to or during the initial phase of migraine was endorsed by 552 participants (53.7%), most commonly unusual attentiveness to the owner (39.9%). Among the 466 participants providing details about their dog's behavior with their migraines, 57.3% were able to identify dog alerting behavior before symptoms of a migraine attack would typically begin, with changes usually noticed within 2 hours before the onset of initial migraine symptoms. The dog's behavior was considered to be often or usually linked with the development of a migraine for 59.2% of migraineurs, and 35.8% of migraineurs endorsed beginning migraine treatments after the dog's behavior was recognized and before migraine symptoms had started.

The researchers concluded that about one in four migraineurs believe that they recognize a change in their companion dogs' behavior before themselves recognizing initial symptoms of a migraine attack. The most common behavior reported was "the dog refusing to leave the migraineur." Table 25.2 describes the different types of alerting behaviors reported, and the time before initial migraine symptoms.

Some participants only reported one behavior in the dog, but others reported more, some more than four behaviors. Over a third of participants who noticed changes in a dog's behavior regularly began treatment for the migraine as a result of the dog's alert.

Although over half of participants endorsed that the change in the dog's behavior was often or usually linked with the subsequent development of a migraine, the retrospective nature of reporting in this study prohibited confirmation of consistency between the dog's behavior and migraine development.

This area deserves more attention in the future.[21]

TABLE 25.2
Migraine-Alerting Behaviors

Alerting Behavior	Number (%)
Staring at migraineur	126 (27%)
Barking at migraineur	15 (3.2%)
Sitting on migraineur	103 (22.1%)
Refusing to leave migraineur's side	364 (78.1%)
Whining	56 (12%)
Pawing at migraineur	101 (21.7%)
Other (e.g., licking, restricting usual activity level, herding migraineur to couch or bed)	130 (27.9%)
Duration between alerting behavior and initial migraine symptoms	
0–15 min	52 (11.2%)
16–30 min	70 (15%)
31–60 min	65 (13.9%)
1–2 h	60 (12.9%)
More than 2 h before migraine	20 (4.3%)
Total identifying alerting behavior before symptoms of migraine attack began	**267 (57.3%)**
Migraine symptoms usually begin before noticing dog's behavior	199 (42.7%)

Source: Adapted from Marcus and Bhowmick, 2013.

LEGAL STATUS OF SPONTANEOUSLY ALERTING DOGS

Most of the types of detection dogs described in this book are used in governmental and institutional endeavors, e.g., forensics and conservation work, and do not have functions specific to the medical or psychological conditions of their handlers. (The first dogs to recognize melanoma were owned by individuals, as noted in Chapter 24, but most cancer detection research involves dogs working in laboratory settings.) Dogs that alert to medical conditions or episodes of their owners, as noted at the beginning of this chapter, raise questions regarding their access to locations where pets are excluded because the functions they perform may relate to disabilities of a handler or user. Under American disability law, these dogs may be classified as service animals or assistance animals, terms that are defined somewhat differently depending on which agency or court is providing the definition.

A dog that alerts in advance of a seizure or glycemic episode may be doing so spontaneously. Regulations issued by the DOJ, which apply to places of public accommodation, such as restaurants and hotels, define a service animal as "any dog that is individually trained to do work or perform tasks for the benefit of an individual with a disability, including a physical, sensory, psychiatric, intellectual, or other mental disability."[22] A dog that alerts spontaneously does not appear to satisfy the "individually trained" requirement. In the 2008 release accompanying this regulation, the department noted that a service animal can provide "minimal protection" by doing such things as "alerting and protecting a person who is having a seizure." The release also refers to "protecting the handler from injury resulting from seizures or unconsciousness."[23] If alerting in advance allows the victim to take action to avoid injury or limit the effects of a seizure, then arguably, a dog that spontaneously alerts in advance, but does nothing else, could be considered a service animal. The issue remains unclear.[24]

The Department of Transportation, on the other hand, allows that a service animal, under its rules for air carrier access, does not always have to be individually trained:

> Generally, a service animal is individually trained to perform functions to assist the passenger who is a qualified individual with a disability. In a few extremely limited situations, an animal such as a seizure alert animal may be capable of performing functions to assist a qualified person with a disability without individualized training. Also, an animal used for emotional support need not have specific training for that function. Similar to an animal that has been individually trained, the definition of a service animal includes: An animal that has been shown to have the innate ability to assist a person with a disability; or an emotional support animal.[25]

The Centers for Disease Control has, at least for some purposes, defined *assistance dog* fairly broadly to include, among many others, "seizure alert dogs, seizure response dogs, [and] diabetic alert dogs."[26]

Whether the more restrictive perspective of the DOJ will prevail in places of public accommodation may ultimately have to be settled by courts.[27] A Washington State appeals court reversed a lower court holding concerning a dog that alerted to the severe migraines of its owner, which occurred about three times a week, allowing her to take a nasal spray that sometimes prevented a migraine. An administrative judge and a lower court had accepted the dog as a service dog, finding that not much training was required in this situation:

> When Spicey was seven to nine months old, she began responding to Candida's migraines. If Candida had a migraine, Spicey found Scott or another person nearby and would "freak out" by running, jumping, barking, scratching on a door, or pulling at their leg to alert them.... The person alerted would then assist Candida. While Candida receives assistance, Spicey stands quietly and watches. After Candida receives assistance, Spicey is told she is a "good girl" and may be given a treat.[28]

A neurologist had provided the dog's owner with a letter stating that, according to the appellate court, it was reasonable for the patient to have the dog as a service animal to alert others when the patient was ill. The appellate court determined that "there must be some evidence of individual training to set the service animal apart from the ordinary pet." This court concluded that the dog was not a service animal and said the administrative judge's "reasoning that Spicey's training consisted of getting what she wanted—attention from Candida—would make any family pet into a service animal."[29]

NEED FOR FURTHER RESEARCH

The advantages of dogs to people with seizure conditions are, of course, much broader than alerting functions (Terra et al. 2012). All three of the types of advance alerting to episodic medical conditions described here are in their infancy as far as research attention and conclusions are concerned. The fact that researchers on epilepsy might prefer behavioral explanations of alerting, while researchers on glycemic conditions might prefer olfactory explanations, may say no more than that much research on epilepsy involves electroencephalograms (EEGs), while much on diabetes involves blood sugar analysis. Establishing chemical profiles that a dog could detect in the ambient air near a patient will be difficult to work into a research design given issues of privacy and practicality. Nevertheless, this is an important area, and it must be hoped that additional answers will begin to appear.

ENDNOTES

1. Marcus (2012), mentioning service dogs trained to alert to low cortisol levels for individuals with Addison's disease. The author of this chapter received an email from an individual who said his dog could detect serious drops in his blood pressure, and inquiries to several scientists indicated that the phenomenon was not unknown.
2. Litt and Krieger (2007) note the tendency of studies suggesting that dogs can predict seizures to "rely upon patient and family reports of dog and patient behavior."
3. In addition to the conditions discussed in this chapter, chemical biomarkers, which conceivably could be detected and identified by dogs, have been found in the breath of patients with asthma (Kostikas et al. 2003; Montuschi et al. 1999; Smolinska et al. 2014), chronic obstructive pulmonary disease (COPD) (Kostikas et al. 2005; Montuschi et al. 2000), and even schizophrenia (Phillips 1992; Smith and Sines 1960).
4. PL 101-336; 42 U.S.C. 12102.
5. *Todd v. Academy Corp.*, 57 F. Supp. 2d 448 (SD Tex. 1999).
6. PL 110-325.
7. Committee on the Judiciary Report together with Additional Views (to accompany H.R. 3195), H.R. Rep. No. 110–730 part 2, 110th Cong., 2d Sess. (June 23, 2008).
8. 58 Fed. Reg. 16978, 17010 (March 25, 2011).
9. 58 Fed. Reg. 17011.
10. *Allen v. Southcrest Hospital*, 455 Fed. Appx. 827, 2011 U.S. App. LEXIS 25488 (10th Cir. 2011).
11. *Timberlane Mobile Home Park v. Washington State Human Rights Commission*, 122 Wash. App. 896, 95 P.3 1288 (Ct. App. 2004). The administrative law judge, whose decision on the matter was reversed, had concluded that not much training is required for an alert dog, and had also noted that the dog had a "propensity" to alert others to the master's needs. Migraines were found "disabling" in conjunction with polycystic ovary syndrome in *Dickinson v. University of North Carolina*, 91 F.Supp. 3d 755 (MD N.C. 2015).
12. Where seizure-alert dogs have been involved in legal disputes, courts have generally not delved into the question of whether advance alerting can be verified. See, e.g., *Alboniga v. School Board of Broward County, Florida*, 87 F.Supp. 3d 1319 (SD Fla. 2015), stating, "Stevie alerts Plaintiff approximately thirty to forty minutes prior to the seizure, and during the seizure, performs the 'cover' task to assist."
13. The New York attorney general, Eric T. Schneiderman, announced in May 2013 that his office had taken action to shut down Seizure Alert Dogs for Life, Inc. Press Release: "A.G. Schneidermann Shuts Down North Country Sham 'Seizure Alert Dog' Business," May 23, 2013 (http://www.ag.ny.gov/press-release /ag-schneiderman-shuts-down-north-country-sham-seizure-alert-dog-business-0).
14. Litt and Krieger (2007) also noted the potential therapeutic effect of owning seizure-alert dogs but said that "the benefit is more likely to be psychological than neurologic." See also Spencer (2007), putting the issues in terms for patients without scientific backgrounds.

15. A letter by Peter Flegg to the editor of *Neurology* (Flegg 2008) raised the possibility that some of the alerting behavior described by Kirton et al., such as sitting on a child's chest, might have actually induced seizures rather than predicting them.

16. Doherty and Haltiner cite Binder et al. (1998) for this observation. Binder's team found results consistent with previous studies suggesting that "neuropsychologic abnormalities are not pathognomonic of brain dysfunction in this population," i.e., for patients with nonepileptic seizures.

17. Brown and Goldstein cite Pinikahana and Dono (2009), who had found that among persons with epilepsy and their caregivers, 63.6% and 51.3%, "respectively, indicated that they can tell when a seizure is about to occur, and 26.7% and 15.4%, respectively, indicated that they felt they could stop a seizure."

18. Chemical components to seizures continue to be discussed in the literature. See Katzel et al. (2014). For earlier discussion of chemistry and epilepsy, see Natelson et al. (1979) and De Deyn et al. (1992).

19. The author of this chapter has been advised by a researcher on epilepsy in dogs that owners have reported that other dogs than one that is epileptic "show strange behavior before the seizure starts ('heavy' aura)...before the ictus starts." Another scientist said that a service dog was chosen from a shelter to be trained as an alert/response dog because it was observed reacting in advance to seizures occasionally suffered by a cat in a nearby cage.

20. Novak et al. (2007) described exhaled methyl nitrate as a noninvasive marker of hyperglycemia in type 1 diabetes. Yadav and Jayanand (2014) have described a method of using exhaled breath for diabetes monitoring. See Shirasu and Touhara (2011), noting that acetone is found in the breath and urine of patients with diabetes.

21. Service dogs working with migraine sufferers often perform tasks such as mobility assistance, retrieval of medications, going for help, etc.

22. 28 CFR 36.104.

23. 75 Fed. Reg. 56266 (September 15, 2010).

24. Dogs with seizure-alerting capabilities are often trained to perform multiple functions. In "Investigation of Gates-Chili Central School District, DJ No. 204-53-128," the DOJ determined that a dog performing a number of functions, including alerting in advance to seizures, was a service dog under the agency's rules (http://www.ada.gov/briefs/gates-chili_lof.pdf).

25. 77 Fed. Reg. 39804 (July 5, 2012). Under regulations for transportation services for individuals with disabilities, the Department of Transportation defines a service animal as an animal "individually trained to work or perform tasks for an individual with a disability, including, but not limited to...alerting individuals with impaired hearing to intruders or sounds, providing minimal protection or rescue work, ... or fetching dropped items." 49 CFR 37.3.

26. Returning Our Veterans to Employment and Reintegration (ROVER): National Surveys of Assistance Dog Providers and Veterans: Request for Office of Management and Budget Review and Approval for Federally Sponsored Data Collection. Full document posted on West Virginia University website of ROVER program (http://rover.wvu.edu/survey-of-assistance-dog-providers), definition on document page 17 of 21; summary information at 79 Fed. Reg. 63402 (October 23, 2014).

27. *Alboniga v. School Board of Broward County, Florida*, 87 F.Supp. 3d 1319 (SD Fla. 2015), involved a dog that alerted "30 to 45 minutes in advance of a seizure" and performed a task called "Cover" to keep a child's head up "to prevent airway distraction or choking on saliva during a seizure episode." This occurred regularly at night but had not been seen by any staff of the school the child attended. Neither the school nor the court questioned the assertion, or sought further evidence, of the unusually long interval between alert and episode. In any case, the dog qualified as a service animal under Department of Justice standards because, in addition to alerting, it performed the "Cover" task and was trained in other ways to deal with the child's disabilities.

28. *Timberlane Mobile Home Park v. Washington State Human Rights Commission*, 122 Wash. App. 896, 95 P.3d 1288 (2004). In a later case, however, this appellate court found that beginning and intermediate obedience training was sufficient on the issue of service animal status to survive a directed verdict, reversing the trial court. *Storms v. Fred Meyer Stores*, 129 Wn. App. 820, 120 P.3d 126 (2005).

29. Id. Under the facts as presented by the appellate court, rewarding the dog for summoning help may have made this behavior more consistent and arguably could qualify as training.

U.S. Legal Decisions and Orders by Jurisdiction

FEDERAL CASES

U.S. Supreme Court

Arizona v. Gant, 556 U.S. 332 (2009)

Arizona v. Johnson, 555 U.S. 323 (2009)

Board of Education of Independent School District No. 92 v. Earles, 536 U.S. 822 (2002)

Brigham City v. Stuart, 547 U.S. 398 (2006)

California v. Carney, 471 U.S. 386 (1985)

Daubert v. Merrell Dow Pharmaceuticals, Inc., 509 U.S. 579 (1993)

Davis v. U.S., 131 S. Ct. 2419 (2011)

Florida v. Harris, 133 S. Ct. 1050 (2013), *reversing Florida v. Harris*, 71 So. 3d 756 (Fla. 2011)

Florida v. Jardines, 133 S. Ct. 1409 (2013)

Florida v. Royer, 460 U.S. 491 (1983)

Illinois v. Caballes, 543 U.S. 405 (2005)

Illinois v. Gates, 462 U.S. 213 (1983)

Indianapolis v. Edmond, 531 U.S. 32 (2000)

Katz v. U.S., 389 U.S. 347 (1967)

Kyllo v. U.S., 533 U.S. 27 (2001)

Maryland v. Dyson, 527 U.S. 465 (1999)

New Jersey v. T.L.O., 469 U.S. 325 (1985)

New York v. Belton, 452 U.S. 454 (1981)

Oliver v. U.S., 466 U.S. 170 (1984)

Riley v. California, 134 S. Ct. 2473 (2014)

Rodriguez v. U.S., 135 S. Ct. 1609 (2015), *vacating and remanding* 741 F.3d 905 (8th Cir. 2014); on remand, 799 F.3d 1222 (8th Cir. 2015)

Terry v. Ohio, 392 U.S. 1 (1968)

U.S. v. Jacobsen, 466 U.S. 109 (1984)

U.S. v. Jones, 132 S. Ct. 945 (2012)

U.S. v. Leon, 468 U.S. 897 (1984)

U.S. v. Place, 462 U.S. 696 (1983)

Vernonia School District 47J v. Acton, 515 U.S. 646 (1995)

First Circuit (Districts of Maine, Massachusetts, New Hampshire, Puerto Rico, and Rhode Island)

U.S. v. $62,552 in U.S. Currency, No. 03-10153-RBC, 2015 WL 251242, 2015 U.S. Dist. LEXIS 6280 (D. Mass. January 20, 2015)

U.S. v. Burgos-Montes, 741 F.3d 905 (1st Cir. 2015)

Second Circuit (Districts of Connecticut, New York, and Vermont)

U.S. v. McNiece, 558 F. Supp. 612 (ED N.Y. 1983)

Fourth Circuit (Districts of Maryland, North Carolina, South Carolina, Virginia, and West Virginia)

Dickinson v. University of North Carolina, 91 F. Supp. 3d 755 (MD N.C. 2015)
U.S. v. Green, 740 F.3d 275 (4th Cir.), *cert. denied*, 135 S. Ct. 207 (2014)

Fifth Circuit (Districts of Louisiana, Mississippi, and Texas)

Horton v. Goose Creek Independent School District, 690 F.2d 470 (5th Cir. 1982)
Jennings v. Joshua Independent School District, 877 F.2d 313 (5th. Cir. 1989)
Todd v. Academy Corp., 57 F. Supp. 2d 448 (SD Tex. 1999)
U.S. v. Kelly, 302 F.3d 291 (5th Cir. 2002)
U.S. v. Reyes, 349 F.3d 219 (5th Cir. 2003)
U.S. v. Rodriguez, 702 F.3d 206 (5th Cir. 2012), cert. denied, 133 S.Ct. 1615 (2013)
U.S. v. Thompson, 540 F. Appx. 445 (5th Cir. 2013)
Winfrey v. San Jacinto County, No. 11-20555, 481 Fed. Appx. 969, 2012 WL 3062159 (5th Cir. 2012)

Sixth Circuit (Districts of Kentucky, Michigan, Ohio, and Tennessee)

Hill v. Sharber, 544 F. Supp. 2d 670 (MD Tenn. 2008)
Jones v. U.S. Drug Enforcement Administration, 819 F. Supp. 698 (MD Tenn. 1993)
U.S. v. $53,082, 773 F. Supp. 26 (ED Mich. 1991), 985 F.2d 245 (6th Cir. 1993)
U.S. v. Gates, 680 F.2d 1117 (6th Cir. 1982)
U.S. v. Patton, 517 F. Appx. 400 (6th Cir. 2013)
U.S. v. Patty, 96 F. Supp. 2d 703 (ED Mich. 2000)
U.S. v. Sharpe, 689 F.3d 616 (6th Cir.), *cert. denied* 133 S. Ct. 777 (2012)
U.S. v. Winters, 782 F.3d 289 (2015)

Seventh Circuit (Districts of Illinois, Indiana, and Wisconsin)

Doe v. Renfrow, 631 F.2d 91 (7th Cir. 1980)
Huff v. Reichert, 744 F.3d 999 (7th Cir. 2014)
U.S. v. $30,670, 403 F.3d 448 (7th Cir. 2005)
U.S. v. $100,120, 730 F.3d 711 (7th Cir. 2013), *on remand* No. 03-C-3644, 2015 U.S. Dist. LEXIS 120816 (N.D. Ill. February 11, 2015), ECF No. 261
U.S. v. $506,231, 125 F.3d 442 (7th Cir. 1997)

Eighth Circuit (Districts of Arkansas, Iowa, Minnesota, Missouri, Nebraska, and North Dakota)

Muhammed v. DEA, Asset Forfeiture Unit, 92 F.3d 653 (8th Cir. 1996)
U.S. v. Bowman, 660 F.3d 338 (8th Cir. 2011)
U.S. v. Donnelly, 475 F.3d 946 (8th Cir. 2007)
U.S. v. Givens, 763 F.3d 987 (8th Cir. 2014)
U.S. v. Gunnell, 775 F.3d 1079 (8th Cir. 2015)

U.S. v. Holleman, 743 F.3d 1152 (8th Cir. 2014), cert. denied, 134 S. Ct. 2890 (2014)

U.S. v. Johnson, 2008 U.S. Dist. LEXIS 118503, adopted by 2008 U.S. Dist. LEXIS 23151 (D. Neb. 2008)

U.S. v. Olivera-Mendez, 484 F.3d 505 (8th Cir. 2007)

U.S. v. Scott, 610 F.3d 1009 (8th Cir. 2010)

U.S. v. Sundby, 186 F.3d 873 (8th Cir. 1999)

Ninth Circuit (Districts of Alaska, Arizona, California, Hawaii, Idaho, Montana, Nevada, Oregon, and Washington)

B.C. v. Plumas Unified School District, 192 F.3d 1260 (9th Cir. 1999)

U.S. v. $215,300 in U.S. Currency, 882 F.2d 417 (9th Cir. 1989)

U.S. v. $22,474.00 in U.S. Currency, 246 F.3d 1212 (9th Cir. 2010)

U.S. v. $30,060 in U.S. Currency, 39 F.3d 1039 (9th Cir. 1994)

U.S. v. $83,310.78, 851 F.2d 1231 (9th Cir. 1988)

U.S. v. Cedano-Arellano, 332 F.3d 568 (9th Cir. 2003)

U.S. v. Dickerson, 873 F.2d 1181 (9th Cir. 1988)

U.S. v. Dimas, 532 F. Appx. 746 (9th Cir. 2013)

U.S. v. Gadson, 763 F.3d 1189 (9th Cir. 2014), *cert. denied*, 135 S. Ct. 2350 (2015)

U.S. v. Thomas, 726 F.3d 1086 (9th Cir. 2013)

Tenth Circuit (Districts of Colorado, Kansas, New Mexico, Oklahoma, Utah, and Wyoming)

Allen v. Southcrest Hospital, 455 Fed. Appx. 827, 2011 U.S. App. LEXIS 25488 (10th Cir. 2011)

Felders ex rel. Smedley v. Malcolm, 755 F.3d 870 (10th Cir. 2014), cert. denied, 135 S. Ct. 975 (2015)

U.S. v. Ludwig, 10 F.3d 1523 (10th Cir. 1993)

U.S. v. Ludwig, 641 F.3d 1243 (10th Cir. 2011)

U.S. v. Parada, 577 F.3d 1275 (10th Cir. 2009)

U.S. v. Vazquez, 555 F.3d 923 (10th Cir. 2009)

U.S. v. Willingham, 140 F.3d 1328 (10th Cir. 1998)

Eleventh Circuit (Districts of Alabama, Florida, and Georgia)

Alboniga v. School Board of Broward County, 87 F. Supp. 3d 1319 (SD Fla. 2015)

Hearn v. Board of Public Education, 191 F.3d 1329 (11th Cir. 1999)

U.S. v. $242,484, 389 F.3d 1149 (11th Cir. 2004)

U.S. v. Burrows, 564 F. Appx. 486 (11th Cir. 2014)

U.S. v. Trejo, 551 F. Appx. 565 (11th Cir. 2014)

District of Columbia Circuit

Frye v. U.S., 54 App. D.C. 46, 293 F. 1013 (DC Cir. 1923)

U.S. v. $639,558, 955 F.2d 712 (DC Cir. 1992)

STATE CASES

Alabama

Bob (a slave) v. Alabama, 32 Ala. 560, 1858 WL 538 1858 Ala. LEXIS 151 (1858)
Hodge v. Alabama, 98 Ala. 10, 13 So. 385 (1893)

Alaska

Kelley v. Alaska, 347 P. 3d 1012 (Alaska Ct. App. 2015)

Arizona

Arizona v. Roscoe, 145 Ariz. 212, 700 P. 2d 1312 (1984)

Arkansas

Farm Bureau Mutual Insurance Co. of Arkansas, Inc. v. Foote, 341 Ark. 105, 14 S.W. 3d
    512 (2000)

California

California v. Adams, H030529, 2008 WL 2115357, 2008 Cal. App. Unpub. LEXIS 4091
    (Ct. App. 2008)
California v. Chavez, B166473, 2004 WL 1173075, 2004 Cal. App. Unpub. LEXIS 5070
    (Cal. App. 2 Dist. 2004)
California v. Childs, B236982, 2013 WL 4034206, 2013 Cal. App. Unpub. LEXIS 5609
    (Ct. App. 2013)
California v. Craig, 86 Cal. App. 3d 905, 150 Cal. Rptr. 676 (Ct. App. 1978)
California v. Demirdjian, B157230, 2003 WL 1963204, 2003 Cal. LEXIS 4589, affirmed
    144 Cal. App. 4th 10, 50 Cal. Rptr. 3d 154 (2006); habeas denied, 2009 WL 2767673,
    2009 U.S. Dist. LEXIS 77347 (CD Cal. 2009)
California v. Elias, B224372, 2011 WL 3949808 2011 Cal. App. Unpub. LEXIS 6802
    (Ct. App. 2011)
California v. Gutierrez, B163632, 2004 WL 723161, 2004 Cal. App. Unpub. LEXIS 3064
    (Cal. App. 2Dist. 2004)
California v. Hackett, B154152, 2003 WL 463976, 2003 Cal. App. Unpub. LEXIS 1778
    (Ct. App. 2003)
California v. Herring, B249468, 2015 WL 1862799, 2015 Cal. App. Unpub. LEXIS 2787
    (Ct. App. 2015)
California v. Kelly, 17 Cal. 3d 24, 130 Cal. Rptr. 144, 549 P. 2d 1240 (1976)
California v. Malgren, 139 Cal. App. 3d 234, 188 Cal. Rptr. 569 (1983)
California v. Mitchell, 110 Cal. App. 4th 772, 2 Cal. Rptr. 3d 49 (Ct. App. 2003)
California v. Oudin, G050682, 2015 WL 3645861, 2015 Cal. App. Unpub. LEXIS 4147
    (Ct. App. 2015)
California v. Salcido, GA052057 (Los Angeles Super. Ct. March 10, 2005)
California v. Sandoval, B147718, 2002 WL 519848, 2002 Cal. App. Unpub. LEXIS 2291
    (Ct. App. 2002)
California v. Sommer, 12 Cal. App. 4th 1642, 16 Cal. Rptr. 2d 165 (Ct. App. 1993)
California v. Watts, B214517, 2011 WL 2150147, 2011 Cal. App. LEXIS 876 (Ct. App. 2011)

California v. White, No. B204494, 2009 WL 3111677, 2009 Cal. LEXIS 13593 (Super. Ct. 2009)
California v. Willis, 115 Cal. App. 4th 379, 9 Cal. Rptr. 3d 235 (Ct. App. 2004) Colorado
Colorado v. Brooks, 975 P. 2d 1105, 81 A.L.R. 5th 779 (1999)

Connecticut

Connecticut v. Kelly, No. CR0661742, 2009 WL 323481, 2009 Conn. Super. LEXIS 98 (Superior Court of Conn. January 8, 2009)

Florida

Berry v. CSX Trans., Inc., 709 So. 2d 552 (Fla. Ct. App. 1998)
Florida v. Harris, 71 So.3d 756 (Fla. 2011), rev'd 133 S.Ct. 1050 (2013)
Florida v. Sercey, 825 So. 2d 959 (Ct. App. 2002)

Georgia

O'Quinn v. Georgia, 153 Ga. App. 467, 265 S.E. 2d 824 (Ct. App. 1980)

Illinois

Illinois v. Burns, 25 N.E. 3d 1244 (Ct. App. 2015)
Illinois v. Pfanschmidt, 262 Ill. 411, 104 N.E. 804 (1914)

Louisiana

Louisiana v. Smith, 152 So. 3d 218 (Ct. App. 2014)

Maryland

Terrell v. Maryland, 3 Md. App. 340, 239 A. 2d 128 (Ct. Spec. Appeals 1968)

Massachusetts

Massachusetts v. Ramos, 894 N.E. 2d 611 (Mass. App. Ct. 2008)
Massachusetts v. Santiago, 30 Mass. L. Rptr. 81, 2012 WL 2913495, 2012 Mass. Super. LEXIS 136 (Mass. Sup. Ct. May 22, 2012)

Michigan

Michigan v. Giles, No. 275207, 2008 WL 2436529, 2008 Mich. App. LEXIS 1256 (Ct. App. 2008), leave to appeal denied, 484 Mich. 863, 769 N.W. 2d 683 (2009)

Minnesota

Minnesota v. Eichers, 853 N.W. 2d 114 (Minn. 2014), *cert. denied* 135 S. Ct. 1557 (2015)

Nebraska

Brott v. Nebraska, 70 Neb. 395, 97 N.W. 593 (1903)

New York

New York v. Roraback, 242 A.D. 2d 400, 662 N.Y.S. 2d 327 (App. Div. 1997)

North Carolina

North Carolina v. Cross, COAO8-1474, 2009 WL 2177766 2009 N.C. App. LEXIS 1226
   (Ct. App. 2009)

North Dakota

North Dakota v. Nguyen, 841 N.W. 2d 676 (N.D. 2013), cert. denied, 135 S. Ct. 2888 (2015)

South Dakota

South Dakota v. Lockstedt, 695 N.W. 2d 718 (2005)
South Dakota v. Nguyen, 726 N.W. 2d 871 (S.D. 2007)

Texas

Jones v. Texas, 2015 WL 730845, 2015 Tex. App. LEXIS 1554 (Tex. Ct. App. February
   19, 2015)
McClintock v. Texas, 405 S.W. 3d 277 (Tex. App. Ct. 2013)
Texas v. Dominguez, 425 S.W. 3d 411 (Ct. App. 2011)
Texas v. Smith, 335 S.W. 3d 706 (Ct. App. 2011)
Winfrey v. Texas, 323 S.W. 3d 875, (Tex. Crim. App. 2010), *reversing* 291 S.W. 3d 68 (Tex.
   App. 2009); *motion for sufficiency review denied* 2011 WL 130492, 2010 Tex.Crim.
   App. LEXIS 1507 (Ct. App. 2011)
Winston v. Texas, 78 S.W. 3d 522 (Ct. App. 2002)

Vermont

Vermont v. Bourassa, 137 Vt. 62, 399 A. 2d 507 (Sup. Ct. 1979)

Virginia

Hetmeyer v. Virginia, 19 Va. App. 103, 448 S.E. 2d 894 (Ct. App. 1994)

Washington

Timberlane Mobile Home Park v. Washington State Human Rights Commission, 122
   Wash. App. 896, 95 P. 3 1288 (Ct. App. 2004)

West Virginia

West Virginia v. McKinney, 88 W. Va. 400, 106 S.E. 894 (1921)

Wisconsin

Wisconsin v. Eugene J. Zapata (2006CF001996) (search of Westlaw Next produced 7 non-
   decisional documents)
Wisconsin v. Scull, 361 Wisc. 2d 288, 862 N.W. 2d 561 (2015)

References

Aaron, R., and Lewis, P. (1987). Technical Article: Cocaine Residues on Money. *Crime Laboratory Digest, 14(1)*, 18.

Ackerl, K., Atzmueller, M., and Grammer, K. (2002). The Scent of Fear. *Neuroendocrinology Letters, 23(2)*, 79–84.

Ackerman, B.H., and Kasbekar, N. (1997). Disturbances of Taste and Smell Induced by Drugs. *Pharmacotherapy, 17(3)*, 482–496.

Adamkiewicz, E., Jezierski, T., Walczak, M., Gorecka-Bruzda, A., Sobczynska, M., Prokopczyk, M., and Ensminger, J. (2013). Traits of Drug and Explosives Detection Dogs of Two Breeds as Evaluated by Their Handlers and Trainers. *Animal Science Papers and Reports, 31(3)*, 205–218.

Adams, D.R., and Wiekamp, M.D. (1984). The Canine Vomeronasal Organ. *Journal of Anatomy, 138(Pt 4)*, 771–787.

Agapiou, A., Amann, A., Mochalski, P., Statheropoulos, M., and Thomas, C.L.P. (2015). Trace Detection of Endogenous Human Volatile Organic Compounds for Search, Rescue and Emergency Applications. *Trends in Analytical Chemistry, 66*, 158–175.

Agapiou, A., Mikedi, K., Karma, S., Giotaki, Z.K., Kostoumbis, D., Papgeorgiou, C., Zorba, E., Spiliopoulou, C., Amann, A., and Statheropoulos, M. (2013b). Physiology and Biochemistry of Human Subjects during Entrapment. *Journal of Breath Research, 7(1)*, 016004.

Agapiou, A., Mochalski, P., Schmid, A., and Amann, A. (2013a). Potential Applications of Volatile Organic Compounds in Safety and Security, pp. 515–558, in *Volatile Biomarkers: Non-Invasive Diagnosis in Physiology and Medicine* (Amann, A., and Smith, D., eds.). Oxford, UK: Elsevier.

Aguayo, A.J., David, S., and Bray, G.M. (1981). Influences of the Glial Environment on the Elongation of Axons after Injury: Transplantation Studies in Adult Rodents. *Journal of Experimental Biology, 95*, 231–240.

Akenson, J.J., Henjum, M.G., Wertz, T.L., and Craddock, T.J. (2001). Use of Dogs and Mark-Recapture Techniques to Estimate American Black Bear Density in Northeastern Oregon. *Ursus, 12*, 203–209.

Akenson, J.J., Wertz, T.L., Henjum, M.G., and Johnson, B.K. (2013). Population Ecology of Black Bears in Starkey Wildlife Management Unit of Northeastern Oregon, 1993–2000. *Wildlife Technical Report 002-2013.*

Akos, Z., Beck, R., Nagy, M., Vicsek, T., and Kubinyi, E. (2014). Leadership and Path Characteristics during Walks Are Linked to Dominance Order and Individual Traits in Dogs. *PLoS Computational Biology, 10(1)*, e1003446.

Alasaad, S., Permunian, R., Gakuya, F., Mutinda, M., Soriguer, R.C., and Rossi, L. (2012). Sarcoptic-Mange Detector Dogs Used to Identify Infected Animals during Outbreaks in Wildlife. *BMC Veterinary Research, 8*, 110.

Alexander, M.B., Friend, T., and Haug, L. (2011). Obedience Training Effects on Search Dog Performance. *Applied Animal Behaviour Science, 132(3–4)*, 152–159.

Alexander, M.B., Hodges, T.K., Bytheway, J., and Aitkenhead-Peterson, J.A. (2015). Application of Soil in Forensic Science: Residual Odor and HRD Dogs. *Forensic Science International, 249*, 304–313.

Alioto, T.S., and Ngai, J. (2005). The Odorant Receptor of Teleost Fish. *BMC Genomics, 6*, 173.

Almirall, J., Diaz-Guerra, P., Holness, H., and Furton, K. (2012). *Field Detection of Drugs and Explosives by SPME-IMS*: Final Technical Report to U.S. Department of Justice. Award No. 2006-DN-BX-K027. Available at https://www.ncjrs.gov/pdffiles1/nij/grants/237837.pdf.

Altman, J. (1969). Autoradiographic and Histological Studies of Postnatal Neurogenesis. Cell Proliferation and Migration in the Anterior Forebrain, with Special Reference to Persisting Neurogenesis in the Olfactory Bulb. *Journal of Comparative Neurology, 137(4)*, 433–457.

Altom, E.K., Davenport, G.M., Myers, L.J., and Cummins, K.A. (2003). Effect of Dietary Fat Source and Exercise on Odorant-Detecting Ability of Canine Athletes. *Research in Veterinary Science, 75*, 149–155.

Amann, A., Ligor, M., Ligor, T., Bajtarevic, A., Ager, C., Pienz, M., Denz, H. et al. (2010). Analysis of Exhaled Breath for Screening. *Magazine of European Medical Oncology, 3(3)*, 106–112.

Amann, A., Miekisch, W., Schubert, J., Buszewski, B., Ligor, T., Jezierski, T., Pleil, J., and Risby, T. (2014). Analysis of Exhaled Breath for Disease Detection. *Annual Review of Analytical Chemistry, 7*, 455–482.

Amundsen, T., Sundstrøm, S., Buvik, T., Gederaas, O.A., and Haarverstad R. (2014). Can Dogs Smell Lung Cancer? First Study Using Exhaled Breath and Urine Screening in Unselected Patients with Suspected Lung Cancer. *Acta Oncologica, 53*, 307–315.

Anderson, G.S. (2001). Insect Succession on Carrion and its Relationship to Determining Time of Death, pp. 143–175, in *Forensic Entomology: The Utility of Arthropods in Legal Investigations* (Byrd, J.H., and Castner, J.L. eds.). Boca Raton: Taylor & Francis/CRC Press.

Anderson, W.L., Parsons, B.M., and Rennie, D. (2001). Daubert's Backwash: Litigation-Generated Science. *University of Michigan Journal of Law Reform, 34*, 619–682.

Andress, M., and Goodnight, M.E. (2013). Heatstroke in a Military Working Dog. *U.S. Army Medical Department Journal* (Jan–Mar 2013), 34–37.

Anfora, G., Frasnelli, E., Maccagnani, B., Rogers, L.J., and Vallortigara, G. (2010). Behavioural and Electrophysiological Lateralization in a Social (*Apis mellifera*) and in a Non-Social (*Osmia cornuta*) Species of Bee. *Behavioural Brain Research, 206*, 236–239.

Angle, C.T., Wakshlag, J.J., Gillette, R.L., Steury, T., Haney, P., Barrett, J., and Fisher, T. (2014). The Effects of Exercise and Diet on Olfactory Capability in Detection Dogs. *Journal of Nutritional Science, 3*, e44.

Anselm von Feuerbach, P.J. (1808). *Wertwurdige Criminal Rechtsfalle* (Important Criminal Cases). Giessen: Ben Lasche and Muller.

Antonitis, J.J. (1951). Response Variability in the White Rat during Condition, Extinction, and Reconditioning. *Journal of Experimental Psychology, 42(4)*, 273–281.

April, L.B., Bruce, K., and Galizio, M. (2013). The Magic Number 70 (Plus or Minus 20): Variables Determining Performance in the Rodent Odor Span Task. *Learning and Motivation, 44(3)*, 143–158.

Arakawa, H., Arakawa, K., and Deak T. (2010). Sickness-Related Odor Communication Signals as Determinants of Social Behavior in Rat: A Role for Inflammatory Processes. *Hormones and Behavior, 57(3)*, 330–341.

Arandjelovic, M., Bergl, R.A., Ikfuingei, R., Jameson, C., Parker, M., and Vigilant, L. (2015). Detection Dog Efficacy for Collecting Faecal Samples from the Critically Endangered Cross River Gorilla (*Gorilla gorilla diehli*) for Genetic Censusing. *Royal Society Open Science, 2(2)*, 140423.

Arnett, E.B. (2006). A Preliminary Evaluation on the Use of Dogs to Recover Bat Fatalities at Wind Energy Facilities. *Wildlife Society Bulletin, 34(5)*, 1440–1445.

Arnold, C.D. (1979). Possible Evidence of Domestic Dog in a Paleoeskimo Context. *Arctic, 32(3)*, 263–265.

Asa, C.S., Mech, L.D., Seal, U.S., and Plotka, E.D. (1990). The Influence of Social and Endocrine Factors on Urine-Marking by Captive Wolves (*Canis lupus*). *Hormones and Behavior, 24(4)*, 497–509.

Asa, C.S., Seal, U.S., Plotka, E.D., Letellier, M.A., and Mech, L.D. (1986). Effect of Anosmia on Reproduction in Male and Female Wolves (*Canis lupus*). *Behavioral and Neural Biology, 46(3)*, 272–284.

Asan, E., and Drenckhahn, D. (2005). Immunocytochemical Characterization of Two Types of Microvillar Cells in Rodent Olfactory Epithelium. *Histochemistry and Cell Biology, 123(2)*, 157–168.

Astic, L., and Saucier, D. (2001). Neuronal Plasticity and Regeneration in the Olfactory System of Mammals: Morphological and Functional Recovery Following Olfactory Bulb Differentiation. *Cellular and Molecular Life Sciences, 58(4)*, 538–545.

ASTM (2014). Standard Designation: F1847–14, Standard Guide for Minimum Training of Search Dog Crews or Teams, ASTM International, West Conshohocken, PA, 2003, doi: 10.1520/C0033-03, http://www.astm.org.

Au, E., and Roskams, A.J. (2003). Olfactory Ensheathing Cells of the Lamina Propria in Vivo and in Vitro. *Glia, 41*, 224–236.

Au, W.W., Treloar, H.B., and Greer, C.A. (2002). Sublaminar Organization of the Mouse Olfactory Bulb Layer. *Journal of Comparative Neurology, 446(1)*, 68–80.

Ayres, K.L., Booth, R.K., Hempelmann, J.A., Koski, K.L., Emmons, C.K., Baird, R.W., Balcomb-Bartok, K., Hanson, M.B., Ford, M.J., and Wasser, S.K. (2012). Distinguishing the Impacts of Inadequate Prey and Vessel Traffic on an Endangered Killer Whale (*Orcinus orca*) Population. *PLoS/ONE, 7(6)*, e36842.

Azzouzi, N., Barloy-Hubler, F., and Galibert, F. (2014). Inventory of the Cichlid Olfactory Receptor Gene Repertoires: Identification of Olfactory Genes with More than One Coding Exon. *BMC Genomics, 15*, 586.

Baars, B.J. (2013). Multiple Sources of Conscious Odor Integration and Propagation in Olfactory Cortex. *Frontiers in Psychology, 4*, 930.

Baars, B.J., Franklin, S., and Ramsoy, T.Z. (2013). Global Workspace Dynamics: Cortical "Binding and Propagation" Enables Conscious Contents. *Frontiers in Psychology, 4*, 200.

Baerwald, E.F., Edworthy, J., Holder, M., and Barclay, R.M.R. (2009). A Large-Scale Mitigation Experiment to Reduce Bat Fatalities at Wind Energy Facilities. *The Journal of Wildlife Management, 73(7)*, 1077–1081.

Bainbridge, D.R.J. (2008). *Beyond the Zonules of Zinn*. Cambridge, Massachusetts: Harvard University Press.

Bajtarevic, A., Ager, C., Pienz, M., Klieber, M., Schwarz, K., Ligor, M., Ligor, T. et al. (2009). Noninvasive Detection of Lung Cancer by Analysis of Exhaled Breath. *BMC Cancer, 9(348)*, 1–16.

Balseiro, S.C., and Correia, H.R. (2006). Is Olfactory Detection of Human Cancer by Dogs Based on Major Histocompatibility Complex-Dependent Odour Components?—A Possible Cure and a Precocious Diagnosis of Cancer. *Medical Hypotheses, 66*, 270–272.

Barber, P.C., and Raisman, G. (1978). Cell Division in the Vomeronasal Organ of the Adult Mouse. *Brain Research, 141*, 57–66.

Barela, P.B. (1999). Theoretical Mechanisms Underlying the Trial-Spacing Effect in Pavlovian Fear Conditioning. *Journal of Experimental Psychology: Animal Behavior Processes, 25(2)*, 177–193.

Barja, I., de Miguel, F.J., and Barcena, F. (2004). The Importance of Crossroads in Faecal Marking Behaviour of the Wolves (*Canis lupus*). *Naturwissenschaften, 91(10)*, 489–492.

Barnett, S.C., and Chang, L. (2004). Olfactory Ensheathing Cells and CNS Repair: Going Solo or in Need of a Friend? *Trends in Neurosciences, 27(1)*, 54–60.

Barnett, S.C., and Franceschini, I.A. (1999). Adhesion Molecule Expression and Phenotype of Glial Cells in the Olfactory Tract. *Advances in Experimental Medicine and Biology, 468*, 297–307.

Barnett, S.C., and Riddell, J.S. (2007). Olfactory Ensheathing Cell Transplantation as a Strategy for Spinal Cord Repair—What Can It Achieve? *Nature Clinical Practice Neurology, 3(3)*, 152–161.

Barone, P.M., Di Maggio, R.M., and Ferrara, C. (2015). Forensic Geo-Archaeology in Italy: Materials for a Standardisation. *International Journal of Archaeology, 3(1–1)*, 45–56.

Barraud, P., Seferiadis, A.A., Tyson, L.D., Zwart, M.F., Szabo-Rogers, H.L., Ruhrberg, C., Liu, K.J., and Baker, C.V.H. (2010). Neural Crest Origin of Olfactory Ensheathing Glia. *Proceedings of the National Academy of Sciences (USA), 107(49)*, 21040–21045.

Barraud, P., St John, J.A., Stolt, C.C., Wegner, M., and Baker, C.V.H. (2013). Olfactory Ensheathing Glia Are Required for Embryonic Olfactory Axon Targeting and the Migration of Gonadotropin-Releasing Hormone Neurons. *Biology Open 2*, 750–759.

Barrios, A.W., Sánchez-Quinteiro, P., and Salazar, I. (2014). Dog and Mouse: Toward a Balanced View of the Mammalian Olfactory System. *Frontiers in Neuroanatomy, 8*, Article 106, 1–7.

Barton, R.A. (2012). Embodied Cognitive Evolution and the Cerebellum. *Philosophical Transactions of the Royal Society B, 367(1599)*, 2097–2107.

Bass, W.M. (1997). Outdoor Decomposition Rates in Tennessee, pp. 181–186, in *Forensic Taphonomy: The Postmortem Fate of Human Remains*. (Haglund, W.D., and Sorg, M.H. eds.). Boca Raton: Taylor & Francis/CRC Press.

Beckmann, J.P. (2006). Carnivore Conservation and Search Dogs: The Value of a Novel, Non-Invasive Technique in the Greater Yellowstone Ecosystem, pp. 20–26 in *Greater Yellowstone Public Lands: A Century of Discovery, Hard Lessons, and Bright Prospects* (Wondrak Biel, ed.). Wyoming, USA Proceedings of the 8th Biennial Scientific Conference on the Greater Yellowstone Ecosystem, Yellowstone Center for Resources Yellowstone National Park.

Bednarek, T. (2000). Randomness, Certainty or Doubts. More Remarks on Overall Image of Scent Examination (in Polish). *Problemy Kryminalistyki 227*, 64–69.

Bednarek, T. (2003). Some Remarks on the Validity of Osmological Investigations (in Polish). *Problemy Współczesnej Kryminalistyki* (Gruza, E., Tomaszewski, T., and Goc, M., eds.), *Vol. VII(2)*, 217–225. Polish Forensic Society, University of Warsaw, Faculty of Law & Administration, Department of Forensic Science.

Bednarek, T. (2008). Dowod osmologiczny. Aspekty kryminalistyczne i procesowe (in Polish) (Osmological Evidence. Forensic and Legal Aspects). Wydawnictwo Centralnego Laboratorium Kryminalistycznego KGP, Warszawa, Poland, ISBN 978-83-919144-8-9.

Bednarek, T., and Sutowski, G. (1999). Scheme of Expertise of Forensic Scent Trace Examination (in Polish). *Problemy Kryminalistyki, 224*, 5–11.

Beerda, B., Schilder, M.B., van Hooff, J.A., and de Vries, H.W. (1997). Manifestations of Chronic and Acute Stress in Dogs. *Applied Animal Behaviour Science, 52(3)*, 307–319.

Behrensmeyer, A.K., and Hill, A.P. (1980). *Fossils in the Making: Vertebrate Taphonomy and Paleoecology*. Chicago: The University of Chicago Press.

Ben-Arie, N., Lancet, D., Taylor, C., Khen, M., Walker, N., Ledbetter, D.H., Carrozzo, R. et al. (1994). Olfactory Receptor Gene Cluster on Human Chromosome 17: Possible Duplication of an Ancestral Receptor Repertoire. *Human Molecular Genetics, 3(2)*, 229–135.

Benbernou, N., Robin, S., Tacher, S., Rimbault, M., Rakotomanga, M., and Galibert, F. (2011). cAMP and IP3 Signaling Pathways in HEK_{293} Cells Transfected with Canine Olfactory Receptor Genes. *Journal of Heredity, 102(Suppl. 1),* S47–S61.

Benbernou, N., Tacher, S., Robin, S., Rakotomanga, M., Senger, F., and Galibert, F. (2007). Functional Analysis of a Subset of Canine Olfactory Receptor Genes. *Journal of Heredity, 98(5),* 500–505.

Bennett, M.R., and Hacker, P.M.S. (2005). Emotion and Corticol–Subcorticol Function: Conceptual Developments. *Progress in Neurobiology, 75,* 29–52.

Bentosela, M., Barrera, G., Jakovecevic, A., Elgier, A.M., and Mustaca, A.E. (2008). Effect of Reinforcement, Reinforcer Omission and Extinction on a Communicative Response in Domestic Dogs (*Canis familiaris*). *Behavioural Processes, 78,* 464–469.

Bernardino, J., Bispo, R., Mascarenhas, M., and Costa, H. (2012). Are We Properly Assessing Bird and Bat Mortality at Onshore Wind Farms? Proceedings of the 32nd Annual Meeting of the International Association of Impact Assessment (May 21–June 1, 2012). Centro de Congresso da Alfandega. Porto, Portugal.

Bernhardson, B.M., Tishelman, C., and Rutqvist, L.E. (2009). Olfactory Changes among Patients Receiving Chemotherapy. *European Journal of Oncology Nursing, 13(1),* 9–15.

Bernier, U.R., Booth, M.M., and Yost, R.A. (1999). Analysis of Skin Emanations by Gas Chromatography/Mass Spectrometry. 1. Thermal Desorption of Attractants for the Yellow Fever Mosquito (*Aedes aegypti*) from Handled Glass Beads. *Analytical Chemistry, 71(1),* 1–7.

Berns, G.S., Brooks, A.M., and Spivak, M. (2012). Functional MRI in Awake Unrestrained Dogs. *PLoS/ONE, 7(5),* e38027.

Berns, G.S., Brooks, A.M., and Spivak, M. (2013). Replicability and Heterogeneity of Awake Unrestrained Canine fMRI Responses. *PLoS/ONE, 8,* e81698.

Berns, G.S., Brooks, A.M., and Spivak, M. (2015). Scent of the Familiar: An fMRI Study of Canine Brain Responses to Familiar and Unfamiliar Human and Dog Odors. *Behavioural Processes, 110,* 37–46.

Berridge, K.C. (2004). Motivation Concepts in Behavioural Neuroscience. *Physiology & Behavior, 81,* 179–209.

Berridge, T.E., and Robinson, T.E. (1998). What Is the Role of Dopamine in Reward: Hedonic Impact, Reward Learning, or Incentive Salience? *Brain Research Reviews, 28,* 309–369.

Berridge, K.C., Robinson, T.E., and Aldridge, J.W. (2009). Dissecting Components of Reward: "Liking", "Wanting", and Learning. *Current Opinion in Pharmacology, 9(1),* 65–73.

Bhadra, A. (2011). Woof! Smells Like Cancer. *Current Science, 101(4),* 480–483.

Bhagavan, S., and Smith, B.H. (1997). Olfactory Conditioning in the Honey Bee, *Apis mellifera*: Effects of Odor Intensity. *Physiology and Behavior, 61(1),* 107–117.

Bhalla, P., Sally, Pippa, and Williams, G. (2001). An Inexpensive and Edible Aid for the Diagnosis of Puberty in the Male: Multispecies Evaluation of an Alternative Orchidometer. *BMJ Clinical Research, 323(7327),* 1486.

Bhattacharjee, Y. (2005). Citizen Scientists Supplement Work of Cornell Researchers. *Science, 308,* 1403.

Bielicka-Daszkiewicz, K., Milczewska, K., and Voelhel, A. (2005). Zastosowania metod chromatograficznych (English: *Application of Chromatographic Methods*). Poznan: Wydawnictwo Politechniki Poznanskiej.

Bierl, B.A., Beroza, M., and Collier, C.W. (1970). Potent Sex Attractant of the Gypsy Moth: Its Isolation, Identification and Synthesis. *Science, 170,* 87–89.

Bijland, L.R., Bomers, M.K., and Smulders, Y.M. (2013). Smelling the Diagnosis: A Review on the Use of Scent in Diagnosing Disease. *The Netherlands Journal of Medicine, 71(6),* 300–307.

Bikov, A., Hernadi, M., Korosi, B.Z., Kunos, L., Zsamboki, G., Sutto, Z., Tarnoki, A.D., Tarnoki, D.L., Losonczy, G., and Horvath, I. (2014). Expiratory Flow Rate, Breath Hold and Anatomic Dead Space Influence Electronic Nose Ability to Detect Lung Cancer. *BMC Pulmonary Medicine, 14,* 202.

Bilheux, H.Z., Cekanova, M., Vass, A.A., Nichols, T.L., Bilheux, J.C., Donnell, R.L., and Finochiarro, V. (2015). A Novel Approach to Determine Post Mortem Interval Using Neutron Radiography. *Forensic Science International, 251,* 11–21.

Bilheux, H.Z., Cekanova, M., Vass, A.A., Nichols, T.L., Bilheux, J.C., Legendre, A., and Donnell, R.L. (2014). Investigation of a Novel Approach to Forensic Analysis Using Neutron Imaging Techniques. Award No. 2010-93071-TN-DN. Oak Ridge National Laboratory. National Criminal Justice Reference Service. Available at https://www.ncjrs.gov/pdffiles1/nij/grants/248454.pdf.

Binder, L.M., Kindermann, S.S., Heaton, R.K., and Salinsky, M.C. (1998). Neuropsychologic Impairment in Patients with Nonepileptic Seizures. *Archives for Clinical Neuropsychology, 13,* 513–522.

Binford, L.R. (1981). *Bones: Ancient Men and Modern Myths.* New York: Academic Press.

Bird, D.J., Amirkhanian, A., Pang, B., and Van Valkenburgh, B. (2014). Quantifying the Cribriform Plate: Influences of Allometry, Function, and Phylogeny in Carnivora. *Anatomical Record, 297(11)*, 2080–2092.

Bird, R.C. (1996). An Examination of the Training and Reliability of the Narcotics Detection Dog. *Kentucky Law Journal, 85*, 405.

Bixby, J.L., Lielien, J., and Reichardt, L.F. (1988). Identification of the Major Proteins that Promote Neuronal Process Outgrowth on Schwann Cells in Vitro. *Journal of Cell Biology, 107(1)*, 353–361.

Blair, C.A.J., Blundell, P., Galtress, T., Hall, G., and Killcross, S. (2003). Discrimination between Outcomes in Instrumental Learning: Effects of Preexposure to the Reinforcers. *The Quarterly Journal of Experimental Psychology: Section B, 56(3)*, 253–265.

Blatt, C.M., Taylor, C.R., and Habal, M.B. (1972). Thermal Panting in Dogs: The Laternal Nasal Gland, a Source of Water for Evaporative Cooling. *Science, 177(4051)*, 804–805.

Bleasel, A.F., McLeod, J.G., and Lane-Brown, M. (1990). Anosmia after Doxycycline Use. *Medical Journal of Australia, 152(8)*, 440.

Blumstein, D.T. (2000). Understanding Antipredator Behavior in Conservation. *Open Country, 1(2)*, 37–44.

Blumstein, D.T. (2002). Moving to Suburbia: Ontogenetic and Evolutionary Consequences of Life on Predator-Free Island. *Journal of Biogeography, 29*, 685–692.

Bock, P., Beineke, A., Techangamsuwan, S., Baumgärtner, W., and Wewetzer, K. (2007). Differential Expression of HNK-1 and p75^{NTR} in Adult Canine Schwann Cells and Olfactory Ensheathing Cells in Situ but Not in Vitro. *The Journal of Comparative Neurology, 505*, 572–585.

Bock, P., Rohn, K., Beineke, A., Baumgärtner, W., and Wewetzer, K. (2009). Site-Specific Population Dynamics and Variable Olfactory Marker Protein Expression in the Postnatal Canine Olfactory Epithelium. *Journal of Anatomy, 215(5)*, 522–535.

Boedeker, E., Friedel, G., and Walles, T. (2012). Sniffer Dogs as Part of a Bimodal Bionic Research Approach to Develop a Lung Cancer Screening. *Interactive CardioVascular and Thoracic Surgery, 14*, 511–515.

Boghdadi, M.S., and Henning, R.J. (1997). Cocaine: Pathophysiology and Clinical Toxicology. *Heart Lung, 26(6)*, 484–485.

Bomers, M.K., van Agtmael, M.A., Luik, H., van Veen, M.C., Vandenbroucke-Grauls, C.M.J.E., and Smulders, Y.M. (2012). Using a Dog's Superior Olfactory Sensitivity to Identify *Clostridium difficile* in Stools and Patients: Proof of Principle Study. *BMJ, 345*, e7396.

Boumba, V.A., Ziavrou, K.S., and Vougiouklakis, T. (2008). Biochemical Pathways Generating Post-Mortem Volatile Compounds Codetected during Forensic Ethanol Analyses. *Forensic Science International, 174(2–3)*, 133–151.

Bouton, M.E. (2004). Context and Behavioral Processes in Extinction. *Learning and Memory, 11(5)*, 485–494.

Bowerbank, C.R., Wirth, T.C., Lee, E.D., and Later, D.W. (2009). Rapid Field Detection of Chemical Warfare Agents, Simulants, By-Products, and Precursors Using Solid Phase Microextraction and Portable GC-TMS. LC-GC North America: *The Application Notebook*, 61. Available at http://connection.ebsco host.com/c/articles/42842782/rapid-field-detection-chemical-warfare-agents-simulants-by-products -precursors-using-solid-phase-microextraction-portable-gc-tms.

Boxall, J., Heath, S., Bate, S., and Brautigam, J. (2004). Modern Concepts of Socialisation for Dogs: Implications for their Behaviour, Welfare and Use in Scientific Procedures. ATLA: *Alternatives to Laboratory Animals, 32(Suppl. 2)*, 81–93.

Boyd, R.M. (1979). Buried Body Cases. *F.B.I. Law Enforcement Bulletin, 48(2)*, 1–7.

Boyett-Anderson, J., Lyons, D., Reiss, A., Schatzberg, A., and Menon, V. (2003). Functional Brain Imaging of Olfactory Processing in Monkeys. *Neuroimage, 20(1)*, 257–264.

Braem, M.D., and Mills, D.S. (2010). Factors Affecting Response of Dogs to Obedience Instruction: A Field and Experimental Study. *Applied Animal Behaviour Science, 125(1–2)*, 47–55.

Brain, C.K. (1981). *The Hunters or the Hunted? An Introduction to African Cave Taphonomy*. Chicago: University of Chicago Press.

Bramerson, A., Johansson, L., Ek, L., Nordin, S., and Bende, M. (2004). Prevalence of Olfactory Dysfunction: The Skövde Population-Based Study. *Laryngoscope, 114(4)*, 733–737.

Brandes, G., Khayami, M., Peck, C.-T., Baumgartner, W., Bugday, H., and Wewetzer, K. (2011). Cell Surface Expression of 27C7 by Neonatal Rat Olfactory Ensheathing Cells In Situ and In Vitro Is Independent of Axonal Contact. *Histochemistry and Cell Biology, 135(4)*, 397–408.

Brann, J.H., and Firestein, S.J. (2014). A Lifetime of Neurogenesis in the Olfactory System. *Frontiers in Neuroscience, 8*, Article 182, 1–11.

Branson, N., Cobb, M., and McGreevy, P. (2012). Australian Working Dog Industry Action Plan 2012. Available at http://www.workingdogalliance.com.au/wp-content/uploads/2013/05/AWDIAP_2012 _BransonCobbMcGreevy.pdf.

Brasseur, C., Dekeirsschieter, J., Schotsmans, E.M.J., de Koning, S., Wilson, A.S., Haubruge, E., and Focant, J.-F. (2012). Comprehensive Two-Dimensional Gas Chromatography-Time-of-Flight Mass Spectrometry for the Forensic Study of Cadaveric Volatile Organic Compounds Released in Soil by Buried Decaying Pig Carcasses. *Journal of Chromatography A, 1255*, 163–170.

Bray, G.M., Villegas-Perez, M.P., Vidal-Sanz, M., and Aguayo, A.J. (1987). The Use of Peripheral Nerve Grafts to Enhance Neuronal Survival, Promote Growth and Permit Terminal Reconnections in the Central Nervous System of Adult Rats. *Journal of Experimental Biology, 132*, 5–19.

Breer, H., Fleischer, J., and Strotmann, J. (2006). The Sense of Smell: Multiple Olfactory Subsystems. *Cellular and Molecular Life Sciences, 63*, 1465–1475.

Breman, J.G. (2001). The Ears of the Hippopotamus: Manifestations, Determinants, and Estimates of the Malaria Burden. *American Journal of Tropical Medicine and Hygiene, 64(Suppl. 1–2)*, 1–11.

Brisbin, I.L., and Austad, S.N. (1991). Testing the Individual Odour Theory of Canine Olfaction. *Animal Behaviour, 42*, 63–69.

Brisbin, I.L., Austad, S., and Jacobson, S.K. (2000). Canine Detectives: The Nose Knows—Or Does It? *Science, 290(5494)*, 1093.

Brixhe, J. (1996). *Levriers, Chiens de Chass, de Travail et de Compagnie dans l'Egypte Ancienne.* Memores de la Section d'Histoire et Philologie Orientales, Universite Liege, 110–111 ("l'action est censée se situer aux confins de la Palestine").

Brooks, S., and Brooks, R.H. (1997). The Taphonomic Effects of Flood Waters on Bone, pp. 553–565, in *Forensic Taphonomy: The Postmortem Fate of Human Remains* (Haglund, W.H., and Sorg, M.H., eds.). Boca Raton: Taylor & Francis/CRC Press.

Brooks, S.E. (2001). *Canine Termite Detection.* University of Florida, Master of Science thesis.

Brooks, S.E., Oi, F.M., and Koehler, P.G. (2003). Ability of Canine Termite Detectors to Locate Live Termites and Discriminate Them from Non-Termite Material. *Journal of Economic Entomology, 96*, 1259–1266.

Brothers, N., and Bone, C. (2008). The Response of Burrow-Nesting Petrels and Other Vulnerable Bird Species to Vertebrate Pest Management and Climate Change on Sub-Antarctic Macquarie Island. *Papers and Proceedings of the Royal Society of Tasmania, 142(1)*, 123–148.

Brothers, N.P., Eberhard, I.E., Copson, G.R., and Skira, I.J. (1982). Control of Rabbits *Oryctolagus cuniculus* on Macquarie Island by Myxomatosis. *Australian Wildlife Research, 9(3)*, 477–485.

Brown, S.W., and Goldstein, L.H. (2011). Can Seizure-Alert Dogs Predict Seizures? *Epilepsy Research, 97*, 236–242.

Browne, C., Stafford, K., and Fordham, R. (2006). The Use of Scent-Detection Dogs. *Irish Veterinary Journal, 59(2)*, 97–103.

Browne, C.M. (2005). *The Use of Dogs to Detect New Zealand Reptile Scents* (MS thesis). Massey University. Available at http://mro.massey.ac.nz/handle/10179/5093.

Browne, C.M., Stafford, K.J., and Fordham, R.A. (2015). The Detection and Identification of Tuatara and Gecko Scents by Dogs. *Journal of Veterinary Behavior: Clinical Applications and Research, 10(6)*, 496–503.

Brunjes, P.C. (1994). Unilateral Naris Closure and Olfactory System Development. *Brain Research Reviews, 19(1)*, 146–160.

Buck, L., and Axel, R. (1991). A Novel Multigene Family May Encode Odorant Receptors: A Molecular Basis for Odor Recognition. *Cell, 65*, 175–187.

Buck, L.B., and Bargmann, C.I. (2013). Smell and Taste: The Chemical Senses, pp. 712–735, in *Principles of Neural Science* (Kandel, E.R., Schwartz, J.H., Jessell, T.M., Siegelbaum, S.A., and Hudspeth, A.J., eds., 5th edition). New York: McGraw Hill.

Buckley, C. (2010). Doubts Rise on Bedbug-Sniffing Dogs. *New York Times*, November 11, 2010. Available at http://www.nytimes.com/2010/11/12/nyregion/12bedbugs.html?pagewanted=all&_r=0.

Burch, M.R., and Pickel, D. (1990). A Toast to Most: Konrad Most, a 1910 Pioneer in Animal Training. *Journal of Applied Behavior Analysis, 23(2)*, 263.

Burghardt, W.F. (2003). Behavioral Considerations in the Management of Working Dogs. *The Veterinary Clinics of North America: Small Animal Practice, 33(2)*, 417–446.

Burne, T.H., and Rogers, L.J. (2002). Chemosensory Input and Lateralization of Brain Function in the Domestic Chick. *Behavioural Brain Research, 133(2)*, 293–300.

Burnham, E., Bender, L.C., Eiceman, G.A., Pierce, K.M., and Prasad, S. (2008). Use of Volatile Organic Components in Scat to Identify Canid Species. *Journal of Wildlife Management, 72(3)*, 792–797.

Burrows, S., Perron, S., and Susser, S. (2013). Suicide Following an Infestation of Bed Bugs. *The American Journal of Case Reports, 14*, 176–178.

Buszewski, B., Kęsy, M., Ligor, T., and Amann, A. (2007). Human Exhaled Air Analytics: Biomarkers of Diseases. *Biomedical Chromatography, 21(6)*, 553–566.

Buszewski, B., Ligor, T., Jezierski, T., Wenda-Piesik, A., Walczak, M., and Rudnicka, J. (2012a). Identification of Volatile Lung Cancer Markers by Gas Chromatography-Mass Spectrometry: Comparison with Discrimination by Canines. *Analytical and Bioanalytical Chemistry, 404*, 141–146.

Buszewski, B., Rudnicka, J., Ligor, T., Walczak, M., and Jezierski, T. (2012b). Analytical and Unconventional Methods of Cancer Detection Using Odor. *Trends in Analytical Chemistry, 38*, 1–12.

Buytendijk, F.J.J. (1936). *The Mind of the Dog.* Boston: Houghton Mifflin Co.

Byers, S.N. (2011). *Introduction to Forensic Anthropology* (4th ed.). Upper Saddle River, NJ: Pearson.

Cablk, M., and Harmon, R. (2011). *Validation and Development of a Certification Program for Using K9s to Survey Desert Tortoises.* Final Report. ESTCP Project RC-200609. Available at https://www.serdp-estcp.org/Program-Areas/Resource-Conservation-and-Climate-Change/Natural-Resources/Arid-Lands-Ecology-and-Management/RC-200609.

Cablk, M.E., and Heaton, J.S. (2006). Accuracy and Reliability of Dogs in Surveying for Desert Tortoise (*Gopherus agassizii*). *Ecological Applications, 16(5)*, 1926–1935.

Cablk, M.E., Sagebiel, J.C., Heaton, J.S., and Valentin, C. (2008). Olfaction-Based Detection Distance: A Quantitative Analysis of How Far Away Dogs Recognize Tortoise Odor and Follow It to Source. *Sensors, 8(4)*, 2208–2222.

Cablk, M.E., Szelagowski, E.E., and Sagebiel, J.C. (2012). Characterization of the Volatile Organic Compounds Present in the Headspace of Decomposing Animal Remains, and Compared with Human Remains. *Forensic Science International, 220(1–3)*, 118–125.

Cain, W.S. (1982). Odor Identification by Males and Females: Predictions vs. Performance. *Chemical Senses, 7(2)*, 129–142.

Calderon-Garciduenas, L., Maronpot, R.R., Torres-Jardon, R., Henríquez-Roldan, C., Schoonhoven, R., Acuna-Ayala, H., Villarreal-Calderon, A. et al. (2003). DNA Damage in Nasal and Brain Tissues of Canines Exposed to Air Pollutants Associated with Evidence of Chronic Brain Inflammation and Neurodegeneration. *Toxicologic Pathology, 31(5)*, 524–538.

Calof, A.L., Hagiwara, N., Holcomb, J.D., Mumm, J.S., and Shou, J. (1996). Neurogenesis and Cell Death in Olfactory Epithelium. *Journal of Neurobiology, 30*, 67–81.

Campbell, L.F., Farmery, L., George, S.M.C., and Farrant, P.B.J. (2013). Canine Olfactory Detection of Malignant Melanoma. BMJ Case Reports, 2013. Available at http://casereports.bmj.com/content/2013/bcr-2013-008566.abstract.

Campbell, R.W., Hubbard, D.L., and Sloan, R.J. (1975). Location of Gypsy Moth Pupae and Subsequent Pupal Survival in Sparse, Stable Populations. *Environmental Entomology, 4*, 597–600.

Caraballo, N.I. (2014). Identification of Characteristic Volatile Organic Compounds Released During the Decomposition Process of Human Remains and Analogues. Ph.D. dissertation, Florida International University. Available at http://digitalcommons.fiu.edu/etd/1391/.

Caroni, P., and Schwab, M.E. (1993). Oligodendrocyte- and Myelin-Associated Inhibitors of Neurite Growth in the Adult Nervous System. *Advances in Neurology, 61*, 175–179.

Cassidy, B., McCoy, D.G.L., and Harmer, M. (2000). The Sweet Smell of Success. *Anaesthesia, 55(8)*, 823.

Catania, A.C. (2007). *Learning* (4th ed.) U.S.: Sloan Publishing.

Cerreta, M.M., and Furton, K.G. (2015). An Assessment of Detection Canine Alerts Using Flowers that Release Methyl Benzoate, the Cocaine Odorant, and an Evaluation of Their Behavior in Terms of the VOCs Produce. *Forensic Science International, 251*, 107–114.

Chaaban, M.R., and Pinto, J.M. (2012). Olfactory Disorders. *Otorinolaringologia, 62(1)*, 47–61.

Chapman, C.H., and Anderson, L.O. (1955). The Campbell Site: A Late Mississippi Town Site and Cemetery in Southeast Missouri. *Missouri Archaeologist, 17(2–3)*, 10–139.

Chehrehasa, F., St John, J., and Key, B. (2005). The Sorting Behaviour of Olfactory and Vomeronasal Axons during Regeneration. *Journal of Molecular Histology, 36*, 427–436.

Chen, D., and Haviland-Jones, J. (2000). Human Olfactory Communication of Emotion. *Perceptual and Motor Skills, 91*, 771–781.

Chen, M., Daly, M., Natt, Susie, Candy, and Williams, G. (2000a). Non-Invasive Detection of Hypoglycaemia Using a Novel, Fully Biocompatible and Patient Friendly Alarm System. *BMJ, 321*, 1565–1566.

Chen, M.S., Huber, A.B., van der Haar, M.E., Frank, M., Schnell, L., Spillmann, A.A., Christ, F., and Schwab, M.E. (2000b). Nogo-A Is a Myelin Associated Neurite Outgrowth Inhibitor and an Antigen for Monoclonal Antibody IN-1. *Nature, 403(6768)*, 434–439.

Chen, R., Irwin, D.M., and Zhang, Y.-P. (2012). Differences in Selection Drive Olfactory Receptor Genes in Different Directions in Dogs and Wolf. *Molecular Biology and Evolution, 29(11)*, 3475–3484.

Chen, W.-K., Swartz, J.D., Rush, L.J., and Alvarez, C.E. (2009). Mapping DNA Structural Variation in Dogs. *Genome Research, 19(3)*, 500–509.

Chien, C.R., and Chen, T.H. (2008). Mean Sojourn Time and Effectiveness of Mortality Reduction for Lung Cancer Screening with Computed Tomography. *International Journal of Cancer, 122(11)*, 2594–2599.

Church, J., and Williams, H. (2001). Another Sniffer Dog for the Clinic? *The Lancet, 358(9285)*, 930.

Clark, D.A. (2014). *Implications of Cougar Prey Selection and Demography on Population Dynamics of Elk in Northeast Oregon*. Doctoral thesis: Oregon State University. Available for download at http://www.academia.edu/7196998/Implications_of_cougar_prey_selection_and_demography_on _population_dynamics_of_elk_in_northeast_Oregon.

Cleland, T.A., Narla, V.A., and Boudadi, K. (2009). Multiple Learning Parameters Differentially Regulate Olfactory Generalization. *Behavioral Neuroscience, 123(1)*, 26–35.

Cohnstaedt, L.W., Rochon, K., Duehl, A.J., Anderson, J.F., Barrera, R., Su, N.-Y., Gerry, A.C. et al. (2012). Arthropod Surveillance Programs: Basic Components, Strategies, and Analysis. *Annals of the Entomological Society of America, 105*, 135–149.

Concha, A., Mills, D.S., Feugier, A., Zulch, H., Guest, C., Harris, R., and Pike, T.W. (2014). Using Sniffing Behavior to Differentiate True Negative from False Negative Responses in Trained Scent-Detection Dogs. *Chemical Senses, 39*, 749–754.

Congram, D. (2014). Deposition and Dispersal of Human Remains as a Result of Criminal Acts: *Homo sapiens sapiens* as a Taphonomic Agent, pp. 249–285, in *Manual of Forensic Taphonomy* (Pokines, J.T., and Symes, S.A., eds.). Boca Raton: Taylor & Francis/CRC Press.

Contreras, J.A., Murray, J.A., Tolley, S.E., Oliphant, J.L., Tolley, H.D., Lammert, S.A., Lee, E.D., Later, D.W., and Lee, M.L. (2008). Hand-Portable Gas Chromatograph-Toroidal Ion Trap Mass Spectrometer (GC-TMS) for Detection of Hazardous Compounds. *Journal of the American Society for Mass Spectrometry, 19(10)*, 1425–1434.

Conyers, L.B. (2006). Ground-Penetrating Radar Techniques to Discover and Map Historic Graves. *Historic Archaeology, 40(3)*, 64–73.

Cook, P.F., Spivak, M., and Berns, G.S. (2014). One Pair of Hands Is Not Like Another: Caudate BOLD Response in Dogs Depends on Signal Source and Canine Temperament. *PeerJ, 2*, e596.

Cooper, G.M. (1998). An Unexpected Benefit of Anaesthesia. *Anaesthesia, 53(8)*, 830.

Cooper, J.C., Ashton, C., Bishop, S., West, R., Mills, D.S., and Young, R.J. (2003). Clever Hounds: Social Cognition in the Domestic Dog (*Canis familiaris*). *Applied Animal Behaviour Science, 81(3)*, 229–244.

Cooper, R., Wang, C., and Singh, N. (2014). Accuracy of Trained Canines for Detecting Bed Bugs (Hemiptera: Cimicidae). *Journal of Economic Entomology, 107(6)*, 2171–2181.

Cooper, W.E., and Burghardt, G.M. (1990). Vomerolfaction and Vomodor. *Journal of Chemical Ecology 16(1)*, 103–105.

Coppinger, R. (2014). Why Do Breeds of Dogs Behave Differently? 2014 Conference of the Society for the Promotion of Applied Research in Canine Science (SPARCS). Video available at http://caninescience .info/sparcs-videos/breeds-dogs-behave-differently-2014/.

Coppinger, R., and Coppinger, L. (2001). *Dogs: A New Understanding of Canine Origin, Behavior and Evolution*. New York: Scribner.

Coppinger, R., Coppinger, L., and Skillings, E. (1998). Observations on Assistance Dog Training and Use. *Journal of Applied Animal Welfare Science, 1*, 133–144.

Coppola, C.L., Grandin, T., and Enns, R.M. (2006). Human Interaction and Cortisol: Can Human Contact Reduce Stress for Shelter Dogs? *Physiology & Behavior, 87(3)*, 537–541.

Copson, G.R. (1995). An Integrated Vertebrate Pest Strategy for Subantarctic Macquarie Island, pp. 29–33, in *Proceedings of the 10th Vertebrate Pest Control Conference*. Hobart, Tasmania May 1995.

Copson, G.R., and Whinam, J. (2001). Review of Ecological Restoration Programme on Subantarctic Macquarie Island: Pest Management Progress and Future Directions. *Ecological Management and Restoration, 2(2)*, 129–138.

Cormier, S., Fobes, J.L., Hallowell, S.F., and Barrientos, J.M. (1995). Systems Analysis of the Federal Aviation Administration's K-9 Program. DOT/FAA/AR-95/123 (prepared for the U.S. Department of Transportation, Federal Aviation Administration under Contract No. DTFA03-92-C-00035). Atlantic City, NJ: FAA Technical Center. Available at http://www.tc.faa.gov/its/worldpac/techrpt/ar95123.pdf.

Cornu, J.-N., Cancel-Tassin, G., Ondet, V., Girardet, C., and Cussenot, O. (2011). Olfactory Detection of Prostate Cancer by Dogs Sniffing Urine: A Step Forward in Early Diagnosis. *European Urology, 59*, 197–201.

Costin, A.B., and Moore, D.M. (1960). The Effects of Rabbit Grazing on the Grasslands of Macquarie Island. *Journal of Ecology, 48(3)*, 729–732.

Coulston, J.W., Koch, F.H., Smith, W.D., and Sapio, F.J. (2008). Invasive Forest Pest Surveillance: Survey Development and Reliability. *Canadian Journal of Forest Research, 38*, 2422–2433.

Courtenay, O., Macdonald, D.W., Giolingham, S., Almeida, G., and Dias, R. (2006). First Observations on South America's Largely Insectovorous Canid: The Hoary Fox (*Pseudalopex vetulus*). *Journal of Zoology, 268(1)*, 45–54 (January).

Courtiol, E., and Wilson, D.A. (2014). Thalamic Olfaction: Characterizing Odor Processing in the Mediodorsal Thalamus of the Rat. *Journal of Neurophysiology, 111(6)*, 1274–1285.

Cowell, E.B. (1895). *The Jataka or Stories of the Buddha's Former Births, Vol. I.* Cambridge: Cambridge University Press.

Cracknell, N.R., Mills, D.S., and Kaulfuss, P. (2008). Can Stimulus Enhancement Explain the Apparent Success of the Model-Rival Technique in the Domestic Dog (*Canis familiaris*)? *Applied Animal Behaviour Science, 114(3)*, 461–472.

Craig, A.D. (2005). Forebrain Emotional Asymmetry: A Neuroanatomical Basis? *Trends in Cognitive Sciences, 9(12)*, 566–571.

Craven, B.A., Neuberger, T., Paterson, E.G., Webb, A.G., Josephson, E.M., Morrison, E.E., and Settles, G.S. (2007). Reconstruction and Morphometric Analysis of the Nasal Airway of the Dog (*Canis familiaris*) and Implications Regarding Olfactory Airflow. *The Anatomical Record, 290(11)*, 1325–1340.

Craven, B.A., Paterson, E.G., and Settles, G.S. (2009). The Fluid Dynamics of Canine Olfaction: Unique Nasal Airflow Patterns as an Explanation of Macrosmia. *Journal of the Royal Society Interface, 7(47)*, 933–943.

Crimaldi, J.P., Wiley, M.B., and Koseff, J.R. (2002). The Relationship between Mean and Instantaneous Structure in Turbulent Passive Scalar Plumes. *Journal of Turbulence, 3(1)*, 1–24.

Critescu, R.H., Foley, E., Markula, A., Jackson, G., Jones, D., and Frere, C. (2015). Accuracy and Efficiency of Detection Dogs: A Powerful New Tool for Koala Conservation and Management. *Scientific Reports, 5*, Article 8349.

Cummings, D.M., and Belluscio, L. (2008). Charting Plasticity in the Regenerating Maps of the Mammalian Olfactory Bulb. *Neuroscientist, 14(3)*, 251–263.

Cummings, D.M., Snyder, J.S., Brewer, M., Cameron, H.A., and Belluscio, L. (2014). Adult Neurogenesis Is Necessary to Refine and Maintain Circuit Specificity. *The Journal of Neuroscience, 34(41)*, 13801–13810.

Cumpston, J.S. (1968). *Macquarie Island.* ANARE Scientific Reports, Series A (1): ANARE Publication No. 93. Antarctic Division, Department of External Affairs, Melbourne.

Curran, A.M., Prada, P.A., and Furton, K.G. (2010). Canine Human Scent Identifications with Post-Blast Debris Collected from Improvised Explosive Devices. *Forensic Science International, 199(1–3)*, 103–108.

Curtis, M.A., Kam, M., Nannmark, U., Anderson, M.F., Axell, M.Z., Wikkelso, C., Holtas, S. et al. (2007). Human Neuroblasts Migrate to the Olfactory Bulb via a Lateral Ventricular Extension. *Science, 315(5816)*, 1243–1249.

Custance, D., and Mayer, J. (2012). Empathic-Like Responding by Domestic Dogs (*Canis familiaris*) to Distress in Humans: An Exploratory Study. *Animal Cognition, 15(5)*, 851–859.

da Matta Chasin, A.A., and Midio, A.F. (2000). Validation of an Ion-Trap Gas Chromatographic-Mass Spectrometric Method for the Determination of Cocaine and Metabolites and Cocaethylene in Post-Mortem Blood. *Forensic Science International, 109*, 1–13.

Dagley, K., and Perkins, J. (2005). The Canine Behaviour Type Index. *Current Issues and Research in Veterinary Behavioral Medicine 2005*, pp. 63–65 in Papers Presented at the Fifth Veterinary Behavior Meeting. Posted at http://espace.library.uq.edu.au/view/UQ:8522/CBTIminnesota.pdf.

Dahlgren, D.K., Elmore, R.D., Smith, D.A., Hurt, A., Arnett, E.B., and Connelly, J.W. (2012). Use of Dogs in Wildlife Research and Management, pp. 140–153, in *Wildlife Techniques Manual: Research, Vol. 1* (Silvy, N.J., ed.). Baltimore: John Hopkins University Press.

Dalton, P., and Wysocki, C.J. (1996). The Nature and Duration of Adaptation Following Long-Term Odor Exposure. *Perception and Psychophysics, 58(5)*, 781–792.

Dalziel, D.J., Uthman, B.M., McGorray, S.P., & Reep, R.L. (2003). Seizure-Alert Dogs: A Review and Preliminary Study. *Seizure, 12*, 115–120.

D'Amico, A., Pennazza, G., Santonico, M., Martinelli, E., Roscioni, C., Galluccio, G., Paolesse, R., and Di Natale, C. (2010). An Investigation on Electronic Nose Diagnosis of Lung Cancer. *Lung Cancer, 68(2)*, 170–176.

Darimont, C.T., Reimchen, T.E., and Paquet, P.C. (2003). Foraging Behaviour by Gray Wolves on Salmon Streams in Coastal British Columbia. *Canadian Journal of Zoology, 81(2)*, 349–353.

Darwin, C. (1873). *The Expression of the Emotions in Man and Animals.* New York: D. Appleton & Co.

Datt, B., Apan, A., and Kelly, R. (2006). *Early Detection of Exotic Pests and Diseases in Asian Vegetables by Imaging Spectroscopy.* Rural Industries Research and Development Corporation, Australia, RIRDC Publication No 05/170.

David, J., and Lewis, A.M. (2008). Explosive Detection Equipment and Technology for Border Security. Joint Research Centre, Institute for the Protection and Security of the Citizen. Luxembourg: Office for Official Publications of the European Communities Scientific and Technical Research Series, ISSN 1018-5593.

Davidson, G.A., Clark, D.A., Johnson, B.K., Waits, L.P., and Adams, J.R. (2014). Estimating Cougar Densities in Northeast Oregon using Conservation Detection Dogs. *Journal of Wildlife Management, 78(6),* 1104–1114.

Davis, L.W. (1974). *Go Find! Training Your Dog to Track.* New York: Howell Book House.

Davis, S.J.M., and Valla, F.R. (1978). Evidence for Domestication of the Dog 12,000 Years Ago in the Natufian of Israel. *Nature, 276,* 608–610.

Daw, N.D., Gershman, S.J., Seymour, B., Dayan, P., and Dolan, R.J. (2011). Model-Based Influences on Humans' Choices and Striatal Prediction Errors. *Neuron, 69,* 1204–1215.

de Beer, G.R. (1937). *The Development of the Vertebrate Skull.* London: Oxford University Press.

De Deyn, P.P., D'Hooge, R., Marescau, B., and Pei, Y.-Q. (1992). Chemical Models of Epilepsy with Some Reference to Their Applicability in the Development of Anticonvulsants. *Epilepsy Research, 12,* 87–110.

de Groot, J.H., Semin, G.R., and Smeets, M.A. (2014). I Can See, Hear, and Smell Your Fear: Comparing Olfactory and Audiovisual Media in Fear Communication. *Journal of Experimental Psychology: General, 143(2),* 825–834.

de Oliveira, M.L., Norris, D., Ramirez, J.F.M., Peres, P.H. de F., Galetti, M., and Duarte, J.M.B. (2012). Dogs Can Detect Scat Samples More Efficiently Than Humans: An Experiment in a Continuous Atlantic Forest Remnant. *Zoologia, 29(2),* 183–186.

de Waegh, S., and Brady, S.T. (1990). Altered Slow Axonal Transport and Regeneration in a Myelin-Deficient Mutant Mouse: The Trembler as an in vivo Model for Schwann Cell-Axon Interactions. *The Journal of Neuroscience, 10(6),* 1855–1865.

de Waegh, S.M., Lee, V.M., and Brady, S.T. (1992). Local Modulation of Neurofilament Phosphorylation, Axonal Caliber, and Slow Axonal Transport by Myelinating Schwann Cells. *Cell, 68(3),* 451–463.

Dean, E.E. (1972). *Training Dogs for Narcotic Detection.* San Antonio, Texas: Southwest Research Institute.

DeFoliart, G.R. (1999). Insects as Food: Why the Western Attitude Is Important. *Annual Review of Entomology, 44,* 21–50.

DeGreeff, L.E. (2010). Development of a Dynamic Headspace Concentration Technique for the Non-Contact Sample of Human Odor Samples and the Creation of Canine Training Aids. Ph.D. dissertation, Florida International University, Department of Chemistry and Biochemistry. Available at http://digitalcommons .fiu.edu/cgi/viewcontent.cgi?article=1382&context=etd.

DeGreeff, L.E., Curran, A.M., and Furton, K.G. (2011). Evaluation of Selected Sorbent Materials for the Collection of Volatile Organic Compounds Related to Human Scent Using Non-Contact Sampling Mode. *Forensic Science International, 209(1–3),* 133–142.

DeGreeff, L.E., and Furton, K.G. (2011). Collection and Identification of Human Remains Volatiles by Non-Contact, Dynamic Airflow Sampling and SPME-GC/MS Using Various Sorbent Materials. *Analytical and Bioanalytical Chemistry, 401,* 1295–1307.

DeGreeff, L.E., Weakley-Jones, B., and Furton, K.G. (2012). Creation of Training Aids for Human Remains Detection Canines Utilizing a Non-Contact, Dynamic Airflow Volatile Concentration Technique. *Forensic Science International, 217(1–3),* 32–38.

Dehlinger, K., Tarnowski, K., House, J.L., Los, E., Hanavan, K., Bustamante, B., Ahmann, A.J., and Ward, W.K. (2013). Can Trained Dogs Detect a Hypoglycemic Scent in Patients with Type 1 Diabetes? *Diabetes Care, 36,* e-98-9.

Deisig, N., Sandoz, J.-C., Giurfa, M., and Lachnit, H. (2007). The Trial-Spacing Effect in Olfactory Patterning Discrimination in Honeybees. *Behavioural Brain Research, 176(2),* 314–322.

Dejarme, L.E., Gooding, R.E., Lawhon, S.J., Ray, P., and Kuhlman, M.R. (1997). Formation of Methyl Benzoate from Cocaine Hydrochloride under Different Temperatures and Humidities, pp. 19–25 in *Chemistry- and Biology-Based Technologies for Contraband Detection* (Pilon, P., and Burmeister, S., eds.), *SPIE, 2937*: Washington, DC.

Dekeirsschieter, J., Stefanuto, P.-H., Brasseur, C., Haubruge, E., and Focant, J.-F. (2012). Enhanced Characterization of the Smell of Death by Comprehensive Two-Dimensional Gas Chromatography-Time-of-Flight Mass Spectrometry (GCxBC-TOFMS). *PLoS/ONE, 7(6),* e39005.

Deldalle, S., and Gaunet, F. (2014). Effects of 2 Training Methods on Stress-Related Behaviors of the Dog (*Canis familiaris*) and on the Dog-Ownership Relationship. *Journal of Veterinary Behavior: Clinical Applications and Research, 9(2),* 58–65.

DeMatteo, K.E., Rinas, M.A., Sede, M.M., Davenport, B., Arguelles, C.F., Lovett, K., and Parker, P.G. (2009). Detection Dogs: An Effective Technique for Bush Dog Surveys. *Journal of Wildlife Management, 73(8),* 1436–1440.

Deng, C., Zhang, J., Xiaofeng, Y., Zhang, W., and Zhang, X. (2004). Determination of Acetone in Human Breath by Gas Chromatography-Mass Spectrometry and Solid-Phase Microextraction with On-Fiber Derivatization. *Journal of Chromatography B, 810(2),* 269–275.

Dennis, J.C., Allgier, J.G., Desouza, L.S., Eward, W.C., and Morrison, E.E. (2003). Immunohistochemistry of the Canine Vomeronasal Organ. *Journal of Anatomy, 203(3),* 329–338.

Denny, M.W. (1993). *Air and Water: The Biology and Physics of Life's Media.* Princeton, NJ: Princeton University Press.

Dent, A.G., Sutedja, T.G., and Zimmerman, P.V. (2013). Exhaled Breath Analysis for Lung Cancer. *Journal of Thoracic Disease, 5(Supp. 5),* S540–S550.

Dent, B., Forbes, S., and Stuart, B. (2004). Review of Human Decomposition Processes in Soil. *Environmental Geology, 45(4),* 576–585.

Department of Commerce: National Oceanic and Atmospheric Administration (2013). *Taking and Importing Marine Mammals; Taking Marine Mammals Incidental to Operation of Offshore Oil and Gas Facilities in the U.S. Beaufort Sea.* RIN 0648-AY63, 78 Fed. Reg. 75488 (December 12, 2013).

Department of Justice (2015, April 13). Investigation of Gates-Chili Central School District, DJ No. 204-53-128. Letter of Rebecca Bond, Chief, Disability Rights Section, to David Oakes. Posted by DOJ at http://www.ada.gov/briefs/gates-chili_lof.pdf.

Dery III, G.M. (2006). Who Let the Dogs Out? The Supreme Court Did in Illinois v. Caballes by Placing Absolute Faith in Canine Sniffs. *Rutgers Law Review, 58,* 377.

Detje, C.N., Meyer, T., Schmidt, H., Kreuz, D., Rose, J.K., Bechmann, I., Prinz, M., and Kalinke, U. (2009). Local Type I IFN Receptor Signaling Protects Against Virus Spread within the Central Nervous System. *Journal of Immunology, 182(4),* 2297–2304.

di Francesco, F., Fuoco, R., Trivella, M., and Ceccarini, A. (2005). Breath Analysis: Trends in Techniques and Clinical Applications. *Microchemical Journal, 79(102),* 405–410.

Di Vito, L., Naldi, I., Mostacci, B., Licchetta, L., Bisulli, F., and Tinuper, P. (2010). A Seizure Response Dog: Video Recording of Reacting Behaviour during Repetitive Prolonged Seizures. *Epileptic Disorders, 12(2),* 142–145.

Dielenberg, R.A., and McGregor, I.S. (2001). Defensive Behavior in Rats towards Predatory Odors: A Review. *Neuroscience and Biobehavior Reviews, 25(7–8),* 597–609.

Dixon, S.J., Brereton, R.G., Carter, J.F., and Sleeman, R. (2006). Determination of Cocaine Contamination on Banknotes Using Tandem Mass Spectrometry and Pattern Recognition. *Analytica Chimica Acta, 559(1),* 54–63.

Doherty, M.J., and Haltiner, A.M. (2007). Wag the Dog: Skepticism on Seizure Alert Canines. *Neurology, 68,* 309.

Doty, R.L., and Bromley, S.M. (2004). Effects of Drugs on Olfaction and Taste. *Otolaryngologic Clinics of North America, 37(6),* 1229–1254.

Doty, R.L., and Cameron, E.L. (2009). Sex Differences and Reproductive Hormone Influences on Human Odor Perception. *Physiology and Behavior, 97(2),* 213–228.

Doty, R.L., and Kamath, V. (2014). The Influences of Age on Olfaction: A Review. *Frontiers in Psychology, 5,* 20.

Doucette, R. (1990). Glial Influences on Axonal Growth in the Primary Olfactory System. *Glia, 3(6),* 433–449.

Doucette, R. (1991). PNS-CNS Transitional Zone of the First Cranial Nerve. *Journal of Comparative Neurology, 312,* 451–466.

Doucette, R. (1993). Glial Cells in the Nerve Fiber Layer of the Main Olfactory Bulb of Embryonic and Adult Mammals. *Microscopy Research and Technique, 24(2),* 113–130.

Doucette, W., Milder, J., and Restrepo, D. (2007). Adrenergic Modulation of Olfactory Bulb Circuitry Affects Odor Discrimination. *Learning & Memory, 14(8),* 539–547.

Doving, K.B., and Trotier, D. (1998). Structure and Function of the Vomeronasal Organ. *The Journal of Experimental Biology, 201(21),* 2913–2925.

Dow, S.W., LeCouteur, R.A., Poss, M.L., and Beadleston, D. (1989). Central Nervous System Toxicosis Associated with Metronidazole Treatment of Dogs: Five Cases (1984–1987). *Journal of the American Veterinary Medical Association, 195(3),* 365–368.

Dowding, J.E., Murphy, E.C., Springer, K., Peacock, A.J., and Krebs, C.J. (2009). Cats, Rabbits *Myxoma* Virus, and Vegetation on Macquarie Island: A Comment on Bergstrom et al. (2009). *Journal of Applied Ecology, 46(5),* 1129–1132.

Dowell, C.H. (2004). NIOSH Health Hazard Evaluation Report 2004-0012-2948, U.S. Customs and Border Protection Canine Enforcement Training Center, Front Royal, Virginia. Available at http://www.cdc.gov/niosh/hhe/reports/pdfs/2004-0012-2948.pdf.

Dray, A., Perez, P., Moore, D., Dietze, P., Bammer, G., Jenkinson, R., Siokou, C., Green, R., Hudson, S.L., and Maher, L. (2012). Are Drug Detection Dogs and Mass-Media Campaigns Likely to Be Effective Policy Responses to Psychostimulant Use and Related Harm? Results from an Agent-Based Stimulation Model. *International Journal of Drug Policy, 23*, 148–153.

Drea, C.M., Vignieri, S.N., Cunningham, S.B., and Glickman, S.E. (2002). Responses to Olfactory Stimuli in Spotted Hyenas (*Crocuta crocuta*): I. Investigation of Environmental Odors and the Function of Rolling. *Journal of Comparative Psychology, 116(4)*, 331–341.

Drees, B.M. (2003). Estimated Amount of Insecticide Ingredients Used for Imported Fire Ant Control Using Various Treatment Approaches. Fire Ant Plan Fact Sheet 042, Texas Imported Fire Ant Research and Management Project, College Station, Texas. Available at http://fireant.tamu.edu/materials/factsheets_pubs/pdf/042_jun03.pdf.

Drickamer, L.C., Vessey, S.H., and Jakob, E. (2008). *Animal Behavior: Mechanisms, Ecology, Evolution* (5th ed.). New York: McGraw-Hill Publishing Co.

Dudareva, N., Murfitt, L.M., Mann, C.J., Gorenstein, N., Kolosova, N., Kish, C.M., Bonham, C., and Wood, K. (2000). Developmental Regulation of Methyl Benzoate Biosynthesis and Emission in Snapdragon Flowers. *The Plant Cell, 12(6)*, 949–961.

Duggan, J.M. (2011). Occupancy Dynamics, Personality, and Behavior of Franklin's Ground Squirrel in Agricultural Landscapes. Ph.D. Thesis, University of Illinois at Urbana-Champaign.

Duggan, J.M., Heske, E.J., Schooley, R.L., Hurt, A., and Whitelaw, A. (2011). Comparing Detection Dog and Livetrapping Surveys for a Cryptic Rodent. *Journal of Wildlife Management, 75(5)*, 1209–1217.

Dulac, C., and Axel, R. (1995). A Novel Family of Genes Encoding Putative Pheromone Receptors in Mammals. *Cell, 83(2)*, 195–206.

Dunn, M., and Degenhardt, L. (2009). The Use of Drug Detection Dogs in Sydney, Australia. *Drug and Alcohol Review, 28(6)*, 658–662.

Dupras, T.L., Schultz, J.J., Wheeler, S.M., and Williams, L.J. (2006). *Forensic Recovery of Human Remains: Archaeological Approaches*. Boca Raton: Taylor & Francis/CRC Press.

Eckenrode, B.A., Ramsey, S.A., Stockham, R.A., Van Berkel, G.J., Asano, K.G., and Wolf, D.A. (2006). Performance Evaluation of the Scent Transfer Unit™ (STU-100) for Organic Compound Collection and Release. *Journal of Forensic Sciences, 51(4)*, 780–789.

Eden, R.S. (1985). *Dog Training for Law Enforcement*. Calgary: Detselig Enterprises.

Edge, C.C., Gibb, J.M., and Wasserzug, L.S. (1998). Comparative Analysis of the Vapor Headspace of Military-Grade TNT versus NESTT™ TNT Under Dynamic and Static Conditions, pp. 502–509, in *Detection and Remediation Technologies for Mines and Minelike Targets III* (Dubey, A.C., Harvey, J.F., and Broach, J.T., eds.), *SPIE, 3392*: Washington, DC.

Edward, Second Duke of York (1909 reprint). *The Master of the Game by Edward, Second Duke of York: The Oldest English Book on Hunting* (Wm. A. and F. Baillie-Grohman, eds., forward by Theodore Roosevelt). London: Chatto & Windus.

Ehman, K.D., and Scott, M.E. (2001). Urinary Odour Preferences of MHC Congenic Female Mic, *Mus domesticus*: Implications for Kin Recognition and Detection of Parasitized Males. *Animal Behaviour, 62(4)*, 781–789.

Ehman, K.D., and Scott, M.E. (2002). Female Mice Mate Preferentially with Non-Parasitized Males. *Parasitology, 125(5)*, 461–466.

Ehmann, R., Boedeker, E., Friedrich, U., Sagert, J., Dippon, J., Friedel, G., and Walles, T. (2012). Canine Scent Detection in the Diagnosis of Lung Cancer: Revisiting a Puzzling Phenomenon. *European Respiratory Journal, 39(3)*, 669–676.

El-Aneed, A., Cohen, A., and Banoub, J. (2009). Mass Spectrometry: Review of the Basics: Electrospray, MALDI, and Commonly Used Mass Analyzers. *Applied Spectroscopy Reviews, 44(3)*, 210–230.

Elliker, K., Sommerville, B.A., Broom, D.M., Neal, D.E., Armstrong, S., and Williams, H.C. (2014). Key Considerations for the Experimental Training and Evaluation of Cancer Odour Detection Dogs: Lessons Learnt from a Double-Blind, Controlled Trial of Prostate Cancer Detection. *BMC Urology, 14*, 22–30.

Elmore, J.G., Armstrong, K., Lehman, C.D., and Fletcher, S.W. (2005). Screening for Breast Cancer. *The Journal of the American Medical Association, 293(10)*, 1245–1256.

Elterman, K.G., Mallampati, S.R., Kaye, A.D., and Urman, R.D. (2014). Postoperative Alterations in Taste and Smell. *Anesthesiology and Pain Medicine, 4(4)*, 1–4.

Engeman, R.M., Vice, D.S., Rodriguez, D.V., Gruver, K.S., Santos, W.W., and Pitzler, M.E. (1998). Effectiveness of the Detector Dogs Use for Deterring the Dispersal of Brown Tree Snakes. *Pacific Conservation Biology, 4*, 256–260.

Engeman, R.M., Vice, D.S., York, D., and Gruver, K.S. (2002). Sustained Evaluation of the Effectiveness of Detector Dogs for Locating Brown Tree Snakes in Cargo Outbound from Guam. *International Biodeterioration & Biodegradation, 49(2–3)*, 101–106.

Ensminger, J.J. (2012). *Police and Military Dogs.* Boca Raton, FL: Taylor & Francis/CRC Press.

Ensminger, J.J., Jezierski, T., and McCulloch, M. (2010). Scent Identification in Criminal Investigations and Prosecutions: New Protocol Designs Improve Forensic Reliability. Posted on SSRN at http://dx.doi.org/10.2139/ssrn.1664766.

Ensminger, J., and Papet, L.E. (2011a, updated periodically). Cueing and Probable Cause: Research May Increase Defense Attacks on and Judicial Skepticism of Detection Dog Evidence. Michigan State University Animal Legal & Historical Center, online article. Available at https://www.animallaw.info/article/cueing-and-probable-cause-research-may-increase-defense-attacks-and-judicial-skepticism.

Ensminger, J., and Papet, L.E. (2011b). How to Prevent Cueing Arguments from Getting Canine Evidence Thrown Out in Court. *Deputy and Court Officer, 3(2)*, 36–38.

Ensminger, J., and Papet, L.E. (2014). Walking Search Warrants: Canine Forensics and Police Culture after Florida v. Harris. *Journal of Animal & Natural Resource Law, 10*, 1–40.

Erdohegyi, A., Topal, J., Viranyi, Z., and Miklosi, A. (2007). Dog-Logic: Inferential Reasoning in a Two-Way Choice Task and Its Restricted Use. *Animal Behaviour, 74(4)*, 725–737.

Ericsson, K.A. (2008). Deliberate Practice and Acquisition of Expert Performance: A General Overview. *Academic Emergency Medicine, 15*, 988–994.

Escanilla, O., Mandairon, N., and Linster, C. (2008). Odor-Reward Learning and Enrichment Have Similar Effects on Odor Perception. *Physiology and Behavior, 94(4)*, 621–626.

Esteve-Turrillas, F.A., Armenta, S., Moros, J., Garrigues, S., Pastor, A., and de la Guardia, M. (2005). Validated, Non-Destructive and Environmentally Friendly Determination of Cocaine on Euro Bank Notes. *Journal of Chromatography A, 1065(2)*, 321–325.

Evans, H.E. (1993). *Anatomy of the Dog.* Philadelphia: Saunders.

Evans, T. (2014). Fluvial Taphonomy, pp. 115–141, in *Manual of Forensic Taphonomy.* (Pokines, J.T., and Symes, S.A., eds.). Boca Raton: Taylor & Francis/CRC Press.

Ezeh, P.I., Myers, L.J., Hanrahan, L.A., Kemppainen, R.J., and Cummins, K.A. (1992). Effects of Steroids on the Olfactory Function of the Dog. *Physiology and Behavior, 51(6)*, 1183–1187.

Fairgrieve, S.I. (2008). *Forensic Cremation: Recovery and Analysis.* Boca Raton: Taylor & Francis/CRC Press.

Farbman, A.I., Brunjes, P.C., Rentfro, L., Michas, J., and Ritz, S. (1988). The Effect of Unilateral Naris Occlusion on Cell Dynamics in the Developing Rat Olfactory Epithelium. *The Journal of Neuroscience, 8(9)*, 3290–3295.

Farrell, J.A., Murlis, J., Long, X., Li, W., and Carde, R.T. (2002). Filament-Based Atmospheric Dispersion Model to Achieve Short Time-Scale Structure of Odor Plumes. *Environmental Fluid Mechanics, 2(1–2)*, 143–169.

Felder, R.M., and Silverman, L.K. (1988). Learning and Teaching Styles in Engineering Education. *Engineering Education, 78(7)*, 674–681.

Feldmesser, E., Olender, T., Khen, M., Yanai, I., Ophir, R., and Lancet, D. (2006). Widespread Ectopic Expression of Olfactory Receptor Genes. *BMC Genomics, 7*, 121.

Feller, D.A. (2005). *Heir of the Dog: Canine Influences on Charles Darwin's Theories of Natural Selection.* Thesis: University of Hawaii.

Feller, D.A. (2009). Dog Fight: Darwin as Animal Advocate in the Antivivisection Controversy of 1875. *Studies in History and Philosophy of Science Part C: Studies in History and Philosophy of Biological and Biomedical Sciences, 40(4)*, 265–271.

Fernandez-Valle, C., Bunge, R.P., and Bunge, M.B. (1995). Schwann Cells Degrade Myelin and Proliferate in the Absence of Macrophages: Evidence from *in vitro* Studies of Wallerian Degeneration. *Journal of Neurocytology, 24*, 667–679.

Ferster, C.B., and Skinner, B.F. (1957). *Schedules of Reinforcement.* East Norwalk, Conn.: Appleton-Century-Crofts. Available at http://psycnet.apa.org/psycinfo/2004-21805-000.

Ferworn, A., Sadeghian, A., Barnum, K., Rahnama, H., Pham, H., Erickson, C., Ostrom, D., and Dell'Agnese, L. (2006). Urban Search and Rescue with Canine Augmentation Technology. *Proceedings of the 2006 IEEE/SMC International Conference on System of Systems Engineering.*

Feuerbacher, E.N., and Wynne, C.D.L. (2012). Relative Efficacy of Human Social Interaction and Food as Reinforcers for Domestic Dogs and Hand-Reared Wolves. *Journal of the Experimental Analysis of Behavior, 98(1)*, 105–129.

Feuerbacher, E.N., and Wynne, C.D.L. (2014). Most Domestic Dogs (*Canis lupus familiaris*) Prefer Food to Petting: Population, Context, and Schedule Effects in Concurrent Choice. *Journal of the Experimental Analysis of Behavior, 101(3)*, 385–405.

Feuerbacher, E.N., and Wynne, C.D.L. (2015). Shut Up and Pet Me! Domestic Dogs (*Canis lupus familiaris*) Prefer Petting to Vocal Praise in Concurrent and Single-Alternative Choice Procedures. *Behavioural Processes, 110*, 47–59.

Field, P., Li, Y., and Raisman, G. (2003). Ensheathment of the Olfactory Nerves in the Adult Rat. *Journal of Neurocytology, 32*, 317–324.

Figueres-Onate, M., Gutierrez, Y., and Lopez-Mascaraque, L. (2014). Unraveling Cajal's View of the Olfactory System. *Frontiers in Neuroanatomy, 8*, Article 55, 1–12.

Finelli, M.J., Wong, J.K., and Zou, H. (2013). Epigenetic Regulation of Sensory Axon Regeneration after Spinal Cord Injury. *The Journal of Neuroscience, 33(50)*, 19664–19676.

Fischer-Tenhagen, C., Tenhagen, B.-A., and Heuwieser, W. (2013). Short Communication: Ability of Dogs to Detect Cows in Estrus from Sniffing Saliva Samples. *Journal of Dairy Science, 96*, 1081–1084.

Fiset, S., Gagnon, S., and Beaulieu, C. (2000). Spacial Encoding of Hidden Objects in Dogs (*Canis familiaris*). *Journal of Comparative Psychology, 114(4)*, 315–324.

Fiset, S., and LeBlanc, V. (2007). Invisible Displacement Understanding in Domestic Dogs (*Canis familiaris*): The Role of Visual Cues in Search Behavior. *Animal Cognition, 10(2)*, 211–224.

Fisher, M., Sikes, J., and Prather, M. (2004). Explosive Detection Using High-Volume Vapor Sampling and Analysis by Trained Canines and Ultra-Trace Detection Equipment, pp. 409–417, Proceedings SPIE (International Society of Optical Engineering) 5403, *Sensors, and Command, Control, Communications, and Intelligence (C3I) Technologies for Homeland Security and Homeland Defense III* (15 September 2004).

Fitzgerald, K.T. (2012). Metronidazole, pp. 653–658, in *Small Animal Toxicology* (3rd ed., Talcott, P., and Peterson, M., eds.). St. Louis, Missouri: Elsevier Saunders.

Fjellanger, R., Andersen, E.K., and McLean, I.G. (2002). A Training Program for Filter-Search Mine Detection Dogs. *International Journal of Comparative Psychology, 15*, 277–286.

Flegg, P. (2008). Letter to the Editor: (Comment on Kirton et al. (2004), Seizure-alerting and -response behaviors in dogs living with epileptic children). *Neurology, 64(3)*, 581.

Fleischer, J., Breer, H., and Strotmann, J. (2009). Mammalian Olfactory Receptors. *Frontiers in Cellular Neuroscience, 3*, Article 9, 1–10.

Fleischer, J., Schwarzenbacher, K., Besser, S., Hass, N., and Breer, H. (2006). Olfactory Receptors and Signalling Elements in the Grueneberg Ganglion. *Journal of Neurochemistry, 98(2)*, 543–554.

Fleischer, J., Schwarzenbacher, K., and Breer, H. (2007). Expression of Trace-Amine Associated Receptors in Gruneberg Ganglion. *Chemical Senses, 32(6)*, 623–631.

Flohr, E.L.R., Arshamian, A., Wieser, M.J., Hummel, C., Larsson, M., Mühlberger, A., and Hummel, T. (2014). The Fate of the Inner Nose: Odor Imagery in Patients with Olfactory Loss. *Neuroscience, 30(268)*, 118–127.

Florida Department of Health. (2014). Florida Arbovirus Surveillance: Week 52: December 21–27, 2014. Florida Arbovirus Surveillance Report, Florida Department of Health. Accessed April 6, 2015. Available at http://www.floridahealth.gov/diseases-and-conditions/mosquito-borne-diseases/_documents /2014/week52arbovirusreport-12-27-14.pdf.

Fogle, B. (1992). *The Dog's Mind*. London: Pelham Editions.

Fonteyn, S., Huart, C., Deggouj, N., Collet, S., Eloy, P., and Rombaux, P. (2014). Non-Sinonasal-Related Olfactory Dysfunction: A Cohort of 496 Patients. *European Annals of Otorhinolaryngology, Head and Neck Diseases, 131(2)*, 87–91.

Forbes, S.L., and Perrault, K.A. (2014). Decomposition Odour Profiling in the Air and Soil Surrounding Vertebrate Carrion. *PLoS/ONE, 9(4)*, e95107.

Forbes, S.L., Perrault, K.A., Stefanuto, P.-H., Nizio, K.D., and Focant, J.-F. (2014). Comparison of the Decomposition VOC Profile during Winter and Summer in a Moist, Mid-Latitude (Cfb) Climate. *PLoS/ONE, 9(11)*, e113681.

Forni, P.E., and Wray, S. (2012). Neural Crest and Olfactory System: New Prospective. *Molecular Neurobiology, 46*, 349–360.

Forster, E.S. (1941). Dogs in Ancient Warfare. *Greece & Rome, 10(3)*, 114–117.

Fox, M. (1971). *Behaviour of Wolves, Dogs and Related Canids*. New York: Harper & Row.

Fox, M.W., and Bekoff, M. (1969). The Behaviour of Dogs, pp. 370–409, in *The Behavior of Domestic Animals* (Hafez, E.S.E., ed.). London: Bailliere-Tindall.

Fox, P.R., Puschner, B., and Ebel, J.G. (2008). Assessment of Acute Injuries, Exposure to Environmental Toxins, and Five-Year Health Surveillance of New York Police Department Working Dogs Following the September 11, 2001, World Trade Center Terrorist Attack. *Journal of the American Veterinary Medical Association, 233(1)*, 48–59.

Foyle, S.D. (2014). *G/MS Analysis of Synthetic Cadaver Dog Training Scents.* Unpublished Manuscript on file at the Laboratory for Human Osteology. University of Alabama, Tuscaloosa.

France, D.L., Griffin, T.J., Swanburg, J.G., Lindemann, J.W., Davenport, G.C., Trammell, V., Travis, C.T. et al. (1997). NecroSearch Revisited: Further Multidisciplinary Approaches to the Detection of Clandestine Graves, pp. 497–509, in *Forensic Taphonomy: The Postmortem Fate of Human Remains* (Haglund, W.D., and Sorg, M.H., eds.). Boca Raton: Taylor & Francis/CRC Press.

Franceschini, I.A., and Barnett, S.C. (1996). Low-Affinity NGF-Receptor and E-N-CAM Expression Define Two Types of Olfactory Nerve Ensheathing Cells that Share a Common Lineage. *Developmental Biology, 173(1)*, 327–343.

Franklin, R.J., and Barnett, S.C. (1997). Do Olfactory Glia Have Advantages over Schwann Cells for CNS Repair? *Journal of Neuroscience Research, 50(5)*, 665–672.

Franklin, R.J., and Barnett, S.C. (2000). Olfactory Ensheathing Cells and CNS Regeneration: The Sweet Smell of Success? *Neuron 28(1)*, 15–18.

Fransen, E. (2005). Functional Role of Entorhinal Cortex in Working Memory Processing. *Neural Networks, 18(9)*, 1141–1149.

Franssen, E.F., de Bree, F.M., Essing, A.H.W., Ramon-Cueto, A., and Verhaagen, J. (2008). Comparative Gene Expression Profiling of Olfactory Ensheathing Glia and Schwann Cells Indicate Distinct Tissue Repair Characteristics of Olfactory Ensheathing Glia. *Glia, 56(12)*, 1285–1298.

Freeman, D.A., Petitti, D.B., and Robins, J.M. (2004). On the Efficacy of Screening for Breast Cancer. *International Journal of Epidemiology, 33*, 43–55.

Freitag, J., Krieger, J., Strotmann, J., and Breer, H. (1995). Two Classes of Olfactory Receptors in *Xenopus laevis. Neuron, 15(6)*, 1383–1392.

Freitag, J., Ludwig, G., Andreini, I., Rossler, P., and Breer, H. (1998). Olfactory Receptors in Aquatic and Terrestrial Vertebrates. *Journal of Comparative Physiology A, 183(5)*, 635–650.

Frijters, J.E.R. (2006). De Geuridentificatieproef in het Licht van het Falsificatiebeginsel [The Dog Scent Lineup in the Light of the Falsification Principle]. *NJB [Nederlands Juristenblad], 714*, 945–948.

Frijters, J.E.R., and Boksem, J. (2004). Een positieve geuridentificatieproef dient vrijwel altijd in een tegenonderzoek te worden herhaald (A Positive Odor Identification Test Almost Always Needs to Be Repeated in a Counter-Investigation). *NJB, 14*, 729–734.

Frysinger, G.S., and Gaines, R.B. (2002). Forensic Analysis of Ignitable Liquids in Fire Debris by Comprehensive Two-Dimensional Gas Chromatography. *Journal of Forensic Sciences, 47*, 471–482.

Fu, S.Y., and Gordon, T. (1997). The Cellular and Molecular Basis of Peripheral Nerve Regeneration. *Molecular Neurobiology, 14(1–2)*, 67–116.

Fuchs, P., Loeseken, C., Schubert, J.K., and Miekisch, W. (2010). Breath Gas Aldehydes as Biomarkers of Lung Cancer. *International Journal of Cancer, 126(11)*, 2663–2670.

Fugazza, C., and Miklosi, A. (2014). Should Old Dog Trainers Learn New Tricks? The Efficiency of the Do as I Do Method and Shaping/Clicker Training Method to Train Dogs. *Applied Animal Behaviour Science, 153*, 53–61.

Fukuda, N., Yomogida, K., Okabe, M., and Touhara, K. (2004). Functional Characterization of a Mouse Testicular Receptor and Its Role in Chemosensing and in Regulation of Sperm Mobility. *Journal of Cell Science, 117*, 5835–5845.

Fukuzawa, M., and Hayashi, N. (2013). Comparison of 3 Different Reinforcements of Learning in Dogs (*Canis familiaris*). *Journal of Veterinary Behavior: Clinical Applications and Research, 8(4)*, 221–224.

Furton, K. (2011). Improving Canine Consistency by Employing Field Calibrants and International Best Practices. 2011 Penn Vet (9) International Working Dog Conference. Handout and posted at http://pennvetwdc.org/wp-content/uploads/2011/09/3-Furton1.pdf.

Furton, K.G., Caraballo, N.I., Cerreta, M.N., and Holness (2015). Advances in the Use of Odour as Forensic Evidence through Optimizing and Standardizing Instruments and Canines. *Philosophical Transactions B, 370(1674)*.

Furton, K., Greb, J., and Holness, H. (2010). *The Scientific Working Group on Dog and Orthogonal detector Guidelines (SWGDOG).* Award No. 2005-IJ-CX-K031. Rockville, Maryland: National Criminal Justice Reference Service, U.S. Department of Justice. Available at https://www.ncjrs.gov/pdffiles1/nij /grants/231952.pdf.

Furton, K., and Harper, R.J. (2008). "Controlled Odor Mimic Permeation System." U.S. Patent US20080295783 A1.

Furton, K.G., and Heller, D.P. (2005). Advances in Reliable Location of Forensic Specimens through Research and Consensus: Best Practice Guidelines for Dog and Orthogonal Instrumental Detectors. *Canadian Journal of Police and Security Services, 3(2)*, 97–107.

Furton, K.G., Hong, Y.-C., Hsu, Y.-L., Luo, T., Rose, S., and Walton, J. (2002). Identification of Odor Signature Chemicals in Cocaine Using Solid-Phase Microextraction-Gas Chromatography and Detector-Dog Response to Isolated Compounds Spiked on U.S. Paper Currency. *Journal of Chromatographic Science, 40*, 147–155.

Furton, K.G., Hsu, Y.-L., Luo, T.-Y., Alvarez, N., and Lagos, P. (1997a). Novel Sample Preparation Methods and Field Testing Procedures Used to Determine the Chemical Basis of Cocaine Detection by Canines, pp. 56–62, in *Forensic Evidence Analysis and Crime Scene Investigations* (Hicks, J., DeForest, P.R., and Baylor, V.M., eds.). *SPIE Proceedings, 2941*: Washington, DC.

Furton, K.G., Hsu, Y.-L., Luo, T., Norelus, A., and Rose, S. (1999). Field and Laboratory Comparison of the Sensitivity and Reliability of Cocaine Detection on Currency Using Chemical Sensors, Humans, K-9s and SPME/GC/MS/MS Analysis, pp. 41–46, in *Investigation and Forensic Science Technologies* (Higgins, K., ed.), *SPIE Proceedings, 3576*: Washington, DC.

Furton, K.G., Hsu, Y.-L., Luo, T.-Y., Wang, J., and Rose, S. (1997b). Odor Signature of Cocaine Analyzed by GC/MS and Threshold Levels of Detection for Drug Detection Canines, *Current Topics in Forensic Sciences. Proceedings of the International Association of Forensic Sciences, 14(2)*, 329–332.

Furton, K.G., and Myers, L.J. (2001). The Scientific Foundation and Efficacy of the Use of Canines as Chemical Detectors for Explosives. *Talanta, 54*, 487–500.

Gadbois, S., and Reeve, C. (2014). Canine Olfaction: Scent, Sign, and Situation, pp. 3–29, in *Domestic Dog Cognition and Behavior* (Horowitz, A., ed.). Berlin: Springer.

Gaines, A. (2013). Olfactory Disorders. *American Journal of Rhinology and Allergy, 27(Suppl. 1)*, S45–S47.

Gallagher, G., Wysocki, C.J., Leyden, J.J., Spielman, A.I., Sun, X., and Preti, G. (2008). Analyses of Volatile Organic Compounds from Human Skin. *British Journal of Dermatology, 159(4)*, 780–791.

Gallistel, C., and Gibbon, J. (2000). Time, Rate and Conditioning. *Psychological Review, 107(2)*, 289–344.

Galloway, A. (1997). The Process of Decomposition: A Model from the Arizona-Sonoran Desert, pp. 139–150, in *Forensic Taphonomy: The Postmortem Fate of Human Remains* (Haglund, W.D., and Sorg, M.H., eds.). Boca Raton: Taylor & Francis/CRC Press.

Gamper, E., Zabernigg, A., Wintner, L.M., Giesinger, J.M., Oberguggenberger, A., Kemmler, G., Sperner-Unterweger, B., and Holzner, B. (2012). Coming to Your Senses: Detecting Taste and Smell Alterations in Chemotherapy Patients. A Systematic Review. *Journal of Pain and Symptom Management, 44(6)*, 880–895.

Ganti, A.K., and Mulshine, J.L. (2006). Lung Cancer Screening. *The Oncologist 11(5)*, 481–487.

Garcia-Lopez, P., Garcia-Marin, V., and Freire, M. (2010). The Histological Slides and Drawings of Cajal. *Frontiers in Neuroanatomy, 4*, Article 9, 1–16.

Garner, K.J., Busbee, L., Cornwell, P., Edmonds, J., Mullins, K., Radar, K., Johnston, J.M., and Williams, J.M. (2001). Duty Cycle of the Detector Dog: A Baseline Study. Report prepared for the U.S. Government by the Institute for Biological Sciences, Auburn University (FAA Grant # 97-G-020).

Gaspar, E.M., Lucena, A.F., Duro da Costa, J., and Chaves das Neves, H. (2009). Organic Metabolites in Exhaled Human Breath—A Multivariate Approach for Identification of Biomarkers in Lung Disorders. *Journal of Chromatography A, 1216(14)*, 2749–2756.

Gawkowski, M. (2000). Identification of Humans on the Basis of Scent Samples (in Polish). Legionowo Poland: Edition Police Training Center.

Gawkowski, M. (2001). Odor Memory and Effectiveness of the Canine Lineups in Osmological Forensic Investigations (in Polish) *Problemy Kryminalistyki, 233*, 52–56.

Gazit, I., Goldblatt, A., and Terkel, J. (2005a). Formation of an Olfactory Search Image for Explosives Odours in Sniffer Dogs. *Ethology, 111(7)*, 669–680.

Gazit, I., Goldblatt, A., and Terkel, J. (2005b). The Role of Context Specificity in Learning: The Effects of Training Context on Explosives Detection Dogs. *Animal Cognition, 8(3)*, 143–150.

Gazit, I., Lavner, Y., Bloch, G., Azulai, O., Goldblatt, A., and Terkel, J. (2003). A Simple System for the Remote Detection and Analysis of Sniffing in Explosives Detection Dogs. *Behaviour Research Methods, Instruments, & Computers, 35*, 82–89.

Gazit, I., and Terkel, J. (2003a). Domination of Olfaction over Vision in Explosives Detection by Dogs. *Applied Animal Behaviour Science, 82(1)*, 65–73.

Gazit, I., and Terkel, J. (2003b). Explosives Detection by Sniffer Dogs Following Strenuous Physical Activity. *Applied Animal Behaviour Science, 81*, 149–161.

Gell, A. (1988). Technology and Magic. *Anthropology Today, 4(2),* 6–9.

Geneva International Centre for Humanitarian Demining (GICHD) (2003). *Mine Detection Dogs: Training, Operations, and Odour Detection.* Geneva: International Centre for Humanitarian Demining.

Gerber, B., and Ullrich, J. (1999). No Evidence for Olfactory Blocking in Honeybee Classical Conditioning. *Journal of Experimental Biology, 202(13),* 1839–1854.

Gerland, P., Raftery, A.E., Sevcikova, H., Li, N., Gu, D., Spoorenberg, T., Alkema, L. et al. (2014). World Population Stabilization Unlikely This Century. *Science, 346,* 234–237.

Gerritsen, R., and Haak, R. (2010). *K9 Fraud! Fraudulent Handling of Police Search Dogs.* Calgary, Canada: Detselig Enterprises.

Ghanizadeh, A. (2009). Loss of Taste and Smell during Treatment with Topiramate. *Eating and Weight Disorders, 14(2–3),* e137–e138.

Gheusi, G., Cremer, H., McLean, H., Chazal, G., Vincent, J.-D., and Lledo, P.-M. (2000). Importance of Newly Generated Neurons in the Adult Olfactory Bulb for Odor Discrimination. *Proceedings of the National Academy of Sciences USA, 97(4),* 1823–1828.

Gheusi, G., and Lledo, P.M. (2014). Adult Neurogenesis in the Olfactory System Shapes Odor Memory and Perception. *Progress in Brain Research, 208,* 157–175.

Ghirlanda, S., and Enquist, M. (2003). A Century of Generalization. *Animal Behaviour, 66(1),* 15–36.

Gilad, Y., and Lancet, D. (2003). Population Differences in the Human Functional Olfactory Repertoire. *Molecular Biology and Evolution, 20(3),* 307–314.

Gilad, Y., Segre, D., Skorecki, K., Nachman, M.W., Lancet, D., and Sharon, D. (2000). Dichotomy of Single-Nucleotide Polymorphism Haplotypes in Olfactory Receptor Genes and Pseudogenes. *Nature Genetics, 26,* 221–224.

Gillette. (1999). Performance of the Caine Athlete—Advanced. Animal Health & Performance Program, Auburn University, AL, 445–448. Posted at https://apdt.com/docs/apdt/conference/2014/handouts/robert-l-gillette-b8734-performance-of-the-canine-athlete—basic.pdf.

Gill-King, H. (1997). Chemical and Ultrastructural Aspects of Decomposition, pp. 93–108, in *Forensic Taphonomy: The Postmortem Fate of Human Remains* (Haglund, W.D., and Sorg, M.H., eds.). Boca Raton: Taylor & Francis/CRC Press.

Gloriam, D.E.I., Bjarnadottir, T.K., Yan, Y.-L., Postlethwait, J.H., Schioth, H.B., and Fredriksson, R. (2005). The Repertoire of Trace Amine G-Protein-Coupled Receptors: Large Expansion in Zebrafish. *Molecular Phylogenetics and Evolution, 36(2),* 470–482.

Glusman, G., Yanai, I., Rubin, I., and Lancet, D. (2001). The Complete Human Olfactory Subgenome. *Genome Research, 11,* 685–702.

Gobba, F. (2006). Olfactory Toxicity: Long-Term Effects of Occupational Exposures. *International Archives of Occupational and Environmental Health, 79(4),* 322–331.

Gobba, F., and Abbacchini, C. (2012). Anosmia after Exposure to a Pyrethrin-Based Insecticide: A Case Report. *International Journal of Medicine and Environmental Health, 25(4),* 506–512.

Goff, M.L., and Catts, E.P. (1990). Arthropod Basics-Structure and Biology, pp. 38–71, in *Entomology and Death: A Procedural Guide* (Catts, E.P., and Haskell, N.H., eds). Clemson: Joyce's Print Shop, Inc.

Goldberg, M.B., Langman, V.A., and Taylor, C.R. (1981). Panting in Dogs: Paths of Air Flow in Response to Heat and Exercise. *Respiration Physiology, 43(3),* 327–338.

Gonder-Frederick, L., Rice, P., Warren, D., Vajda, K., and Shepard, J. (2013). Diabetic Alert Dogs: A Preliminary Survey of Current Users. *Diabetes Care, 36,* e47.

Gong, Q., Bailey, M.S., Pixley, S.K., Ennis, M., Liu, W., and Shipley, M.T. (1994). Localization and Regulation of Low Affinity Nerve Growth Factor Receptor Expression in the Rat Olfactory System during Development and Regeneration. *The Journal of Comparative Neurology, 344(3),* 336–348.

Goodman, P. (1978). *Scent Rolling in Wolves (Canis lupus).* M.A. thesis, Purdue University, Lafayette, Indiana.

Goodwin, K.M., Engel, R.E., and Weaver, D.K. (2010). Trained Dogs Outperform Human Surveyors in the Detection of Rare Spotted Kapweed (*Cenaurea stoebe*). *Invasive Plant Science and Management, 3(2),* 113–121.

Gorder, K.A., and Dettenmaier, E.M. (2011). Portable GC/MS Methods to Evaluate Sources of cVOC Contamination in Indoor Air. *Ground Water Monitoring & Remediation, 31(4),* 113–119.

Gordon, A.S., Moran, D.T., Jafek, B.W., Eller, P.M., and Strahan, R.C. (1990). The Effect of Chronic Cocaine Abuse on Human Olfaction. *Archives of Otolaryngology—Head and Neck Surgery, 116(2),* 1415–1418.

Gordon, R.T., Schatz, C.B., Myers, L.J., Kosty, M., Gonczy, C., Kroener, J., Tran, M. et al. (2008). The Use of Canines in the Detection of Human Cancers. *Journal of Alternative and Complementary Medicine, 14(1),* 61–67.

Goth, A., McLean, I.G., and Trevelyan, J. (2003). Odour Detection: The Theory and Practice, Part 1: How Do Dogs Detect Landmines? pp. 195–208 (Chapter 5, Part 1), in *Mine Detection Dogs: Training, Operations and Odour Detection*. Geneva: Geneva International Centre for Humanitarian Demining.

Gotzsche, P.C., and Olsen, O. (2000). Is Screening for Breast Cancer with Mammography Justifiable? *The Lancet, 355,* 129–134.

Government Accountability Office (GAO) (2002). Endangered Species: Research Strategy and Long-Term Monitoring Needed for the Mojave Desert Tortoise Recovery Program, GAO-03-23.

Government Accountability Office (GAO) (2013). TSA Explosives Detection Canine Program: Actions Needed to Analyze Data and Ensure Canine Teams Are Effectively Utilized. GAO-13-239.

Graham, D.W. (2015). Heraclitus, in *The Stanford Encyclopedia of Philosophy* (Zalta, E.N., ed.). Available at http://plato.stanford.edu/entries/heraclitus/.

GrandPre, T., Nakamura, F., Vartanian, T., and Strittmatter, S.M. (2000). Identification of the Nogo Inhibitor of Axon Regeneration as a Reticulon Protein. *Nature, 403(6768),* 439–444.

Granger, N., Blamires, H., Franklin, R.J., and Jeffery, N.D. (2012). Autologous Olfactory Mucosal Cell Transplants in Clinical Spinal Cord Injury: A Randomized Double-Blinded Trial in a Canine Translational Model. *Brain, 135(11),* 3227–3237.

Graziadei, P.P., Levine, R.R., and Graziadei, G.A. (1978). Regeneration of Olfactory Axons and Synapse Formation in the Forebrain after Bulbectomy in Neonatal Mice. *Proceedings of the National Academy of Sciences USA, 75(10),* 5230–5234.

Graziadei, P.P., and Graziadei, G.A. (1979). Neurogenesis and Neuron Regeneration in the Olfactory System of Mammals. I. Morphological Aspects of Differentiation and Structural Organization of the Olfactory Sensory Neurons. *Journal of Neurocytology, 8,* 1–18.

Graziadei, P.P., and Monti Graziadei, G.A. (1985). Neurogenesis and Plasticity of the Olfactory Sensory Neurons. *Annals of the New York Academy of Sciences, 457,* 127–142.

Graziadei, P.P., and Samanen, D.W. (1980). Ectopic Glomerular Structures in the Olfactory Bulb of Neonatal and Adult Mice. *Brain Research, 187(2),* 467–472.

Grebenkemper, J., Johnson, K., and Morris, A. (2012). Locating the Grave of John Snyder: Field Research on a Donner Party Death. *Overland Journal, 30(3),* 92–108.

Green, P.A., Van Valkenburgh, B., Pang, B., Bird, D., Rowe, T., and Curtis, A. (2012). Respiratory and Olfactory Turbinal Size in Canid and Arctoid Carnivorans. *Journal of Anatomy, 221(6),* 609–671.

Griffin-Valade, L., Kahn, D., Adams-Wannberg, K., and MacKay, B. (2010). Portland Police Bureau: Drug Training and Procedures Strengthened; Recently Improved Practices Should Continue. Report #391, Chapter 18. Available at http://webcache.googleusercontent.com/search?q=cache:_Ih9ksrzzmUJ:www.portlandonline.com/auditor/index.cfm%3Fa%3D301483%26c%3D51639+&cd=15&hl=en&ct=clnk&gl=us.

Grothe, C., Meisinger, C., Hertenstein, A., Kurz, H., and Wewetzer, K. (1997). Expression of Fibroblast Growth Factor-2 and Fibroblast Growth Factor Receptor 1 Messenger RNAs in Spinal Ganglia and Sciatic Nerve: Regulation after Peripheral Nerve Lesion. *Neuroscience, 76(1),* 123–135.

Grothe, C., and Wewetzer, K. (1996). Fibroblast Growth Factor and Its Implications for Developing and Regenerating Neurons. *International Journal of Developmental Biology, 40,* 403–410.

Gruneberg, H. (1973). A Ganglion Probably Belonging to the N. terminalis System in the Nasal Mucosa of the Mouse. *Zeitschrift fur Anatomir und Entwicklungsgeschichte, 140,* 39–52.

Grus, W.E., Shi, P., Zhang, Y., and Zhang, J. (2005). Dramatic Variation of the Vomeronasal Pheromone Receptor Gene Repertoire among Five Orders of Placental and Marsupial Mammals. *Proceedings of the National Academy of Sciences USA, 102(16),* 5767–5772.

Gudziol, V., Hoenck, I., Landis, B., Podlesek, D., Bayn, M., and Hummel, T. (2014). The Impact and Prospect of Traumatic Brain Injury on Olfactory Function: A Cross-Sectional and Prospective Study. *European Archives of Oto-Rhino-Laryngology, 271(6),* 1533–1540.

Guerrieri, F., Lachnit, H., Gerber, B., and Giurfa, M. (2005). Olfactory Blocking and Odorant Similarity in the Honeybee. *Learning and Memory, 12(2),* 86–95.

Gusman, H., Travis, J., Helmerhorst, E.J., Potempa, J., Troxler, R.F., and Oppenheim, F.G. (2001). Salivary Histatin 5 Is an Inhibitor of Both Host and Bacterial Enzymes Implicated in Periodontal Disease. *Infection and Immunity, 69(3),* 1402–1408.

Guthrie, E.R. (1935). *The Psychology of Learning.* New York: Harper.

Gutzwiller, K.J. (1990). Minimizing Dog-Induced Biases in Game Bird Research. *Wildlife Society Bulletin, 18,* 351–356.

Haberly, L.B. (2001). Parallel-Distributed Processing in Olfactory Cortex: New Insights from Morphological and Physiological Analysis of Neuronal Circuitry. *Chemical Senses, 26(5),* 551–576.

Hafez, E.S.E. (1969). *The Behavior of Domestic Animals.* London: Bailliere-Tindall.

Haglund, W.D., and Sorg, M.H. (1997). *Forensic Taphonomy: The Postmortem Fate of Human Remains*. Boca Raton: Taylor & Francis/CRC Press.

Haglund, W.D., and Sorg, M.H. (2002a). *Advances in Forensic Taphonomy: Method, Theory, and Archaeological Perspectives*. Boca Raton: Taylor & Francis/CRC Press.

Haglund, W.D., and Sorg, M.H. (2002b). Human Remains in Water Environments, pp. 201–218, in *Advances in Forensic Taphonomy: Method, Theory, and Archaeological Perspectives*. (Haglud, W.D., and Sorg, M.H., eds.). Boca Raton, FL: Taylor & Francis/CRC Press.

Hahn, C.G., Han, L.Y., Rawson, N.E., Mirza, N., Borgmann-Winter, K., Lenox, R.H., and Arnold, S.E. (2005). In Vivo and in Vitro Neurogenesis in Human Olfactory Epithelium. *Journal of Comparative Neurology, 483(2)*, 154–163.

Hakim, M., Broza, Y.Y., Barash, O., Peled, N., Phillips, M., Amann, A., and Haick, H. (2012). Volatile Organic Compounds of Lung Cancer and Possible Biochemical Pathways. *Chemical Reviews, 112(11)*, 5949–5966.

Haley, B.S. (2011). *A Search for an Historic Structure and Cemetery in Perry County, Alabama: Magnetic Gradiometer Survey Results*. Report submitted to Office of Archaeological Research, Moundville.

Hall, N.J., Smith, D.W., and Wynne, C.D. (2013). Training Domestic Dogs (*Canis lupus familiaris*) on a Novel Discrete Trials Odor-Detection Task. *Learning and Motivation, 44(4)*, 218–228.

Hall, N.J., Smith, D.W., and Wynne, C.D.L. (2014). Effect of Odor Preexposure on Acquisition of an Odor Discrimination in Dogs. *Learning and Behavior, 42(2)*, 144–152.

Hall, N.J., Smith, D.W., and Wynne, C.D.L. (2015). Pavlovian Conditioning Enhances Resistance to Disruption of Dogs Performing an Odor Discrimination. *Journal of the Experimental Analysis of Behavior, 103(3)*, 484–497.

Hallowell, S.F., Fischer, D.S., Brasher, J.D., Malone, R.L., Gresham, G.L., and Rae, C. (1997). Effectiveness of Quality Control Aids in Verifying K-9 Team Explosive Detection Performance. *SPIE Proceedings, 2937*, 227–234.

Handy, W.F., Harrington, M., and Pittman, D.J. (1961). The K-9 Corps: The Use of Dogs in Police Work. *The Journal of Criminal Law, Criminology, and Police Science, 52*, 328–337.

Harberts, E., Yao, K., Wohler, J.E., Maric, D., Ohayon, J., Henkin, R., and Jacobson, S. (2011). Human Herpesvirus-6 Entry into the Central Nervous System through the Olfactory Pathway. *Proceedings of the National Academy of Sciences USA, 108(33)*, 13734–13739.

Hare, B., Brown, M., Williamson, C., and Tomasello, M. (2002). The Domestication of Social Cognition in Dogs. *Science, 298(5598)*, 1634–1636.

Hare, B., Rosati, A., Kaminski, J., Brauer, J., Call, J., and Tomasello, M. (2010). The Domestication Hypothesis for Dogs' Skills with Human Communication: A Response to Udell et al. (2008) and Wynne et al. (2008). *Animal Behaviour, 79(2)*, e1–e6.

Hare, B., and Tomasello, M. (2005). Human-Like Social Skills in Dogs? *Trends in Cognitive Sciences, 9(9)*, 439–444.

Harper, R.J., Almirall, J.R., and Furton, K.G. (2004). Improving the Scientific Reliability of Biological Detection of Explosives by *Canis familiaris* Through Active Odour Signatures and Their Implications. Proceedings of the 8th International Symposium on the Analysis and Detection of Explosives (ISADE), Ottawa, Canada.

Harper, R.J., Almirall, J., and Furton, K. (2005). Identification of Dominant Odor Chemicals Emanating from Explosives for Use in Developing Optimal Training and Combinations and Mimics for Canine Detection. *Talanta, 67(2)*, 313–327.

Harper, R.J., and Furton, K.G. (2007). Biological Detection of Explosives, pp. 395–431, in *Counterterrorist Detection Techniques of Explosives* (Yinon, J., ed.) Amsterdam: Elsevier.

Harrington, F., and Asa, C.S. (2003). Wolf Communication, pp. 66–103, in *Wolves: Behavior, Ecology and Conservation* (Mech, L.D., and Boitani, L., eds.). Chicago: University of Chicago Press.

Harrington, L.A., Harrington, A.L., Hughes, J., Stirling, D., and Macdonald, D.W. (2010). The Accuracy of Scat Identification in Distribution Surveys: American Mink, *Neovison vison*, in the Northern Highlands of Scotland. *European Journal of Wildlife Research, 56*, 377–384.

Harris, J.A., West, A.K., and Chuah, M.I. (2009). Olfactory Ensheathing Cells: Nitric Oxide Production and Innate Immunity. *Glia, 57(16)*, 1848–1857.

Harrison, R.L. (2006). From the Field: A Comparison of Survey Methods for Detecting Bobcats. *Wildlife Society Bulletin, 34(2)*, 548–552.

Harvey, L.M., and Harvey, J.W. (2003). The Reliability of Bloodhounds in Criminal Investigations. *Journal of Forensic Sciences, 48(4)*, 811–816.

Harvey, L.M., Harvey, S.J., Hom, M.M., Perna, A., and Salib, J. (2006). The Use of Bloodhounds in Determining the Impact of Genetics and the Environment on the Expression of Human Odortype. *Journal of Forensic Sciences, 51(5)*, 1109–1114.

Hashiguchi, Y., and Nishida, M. (2005). Evolution of Vomeronasal-Type Odorant Receptor Genes in the Zebrafish Genome. *Gene, 362*, 19–28.

Hashiguchi, Y., and Nishida, M. (2007). Evolution of Trace Amine Associated Receptor (TAAR) Gene Family in Vertebrates: Lineage-Specific Expansions and Degradations of a Second Class of Vertebrate Chemosensory Receptors Express in the Olfactory Epithelium. *Molecular Biology and Evolution, 24(9)*, 2099–2107.

Hasin, Y., Olender, T., Khen, M., Gonzaga-Jauregui, C., Kim, P.M., Urban, A.E., Snyder, M., Gerstein, M.B., Lancet, D., and Korbel, J.O. (2008). High-Resolution Copy-Number Variation Map Reflects Human Olfactory Receptor Diversity and Evolution. *PLoS Genetics, 4(11)*, e1000249.

Hasselmo, M.E., Hay, J., Ilyn, M., and Gorchetchnikov, A. (2002). Neuromodulation, Theta Rhythm and Rat Special Navigation. *Neural Networks, 15(4–6)*, 689–707.

Hauser, M.D., Comins, J.A., Pytka, L.M., Cahill, D.P., and Velez-Calderon, S. (2010). What Experimental Experience Affects Dogs' Comprehension of Human Communicative Actions? *Behavioural Processes, 86(1)*, 7–20.

Haverbeke, A., Laporte, B., Depiereux, E., Giffroy, J.-M., and Diederich, C. (2008). Training Methods of Military Dog Handlers and Their Effects on the Team's Performances. *Applied Animal Behaviour Science, 113(1–3)*, 110–122.

Hayes, J.E., and Jinks, A.L. (2012). Evaluation of Smoking on Olfactory Thresholds of Phenyl Ethyl Alcohol and n-Butanol. *Physiology and Behavior, 107(2)*, 177–180.

Hayter, D. (2003). Training Dogs to Detect Tripwires, pp. 109–138 (Chapter 13), in *Mine Detection Dogs: Training, Operations and Odour.* Geneva: International Centre for Humanitarian Demining.

Head, E. (2011). Neurobiology of the Aging Dog. *Age, 33(3)*, 485–496.

Head, E. (2013). A Canine Model of Human Aging and Alzheimer's Disease. *Biochimica et Biophysica Acta—Molecular Basis of Disease, 1832(9)*, 1384–1389.

Head, E., Mehta, R., Hartley, J., Kameka, M., Cummings, B.J., Cotman, C.W., and Milgram, N.W. (1995). Spatial Learning and Memory as a Function of Age in the Dog. *Behavioral Neuroscience, 109(5)*, 851.

Healy, C.A. (2010). *Detecting Submerged Remains: Controlled Research Using Side-Scan Sonar to Detect Proxy Cadavers.* MA Thesis. Department of Anthropology. University of Central Florida, Orlando.

Hecht, J., and Rice, E.S. (2015). Citizen Science: A New Direction in Canine Behavior Research. *Behavioural Processes, 110*, 125–132.

Heilmann, S., Huettenbrink, K.B., and Hummel, T. (2004). Local and Systemic Administration of Corticosteroids in the Treatment of Olfactory Loss. *American Journal of Rhinology, 18(1)*, 29–33.

Helton, W.S. (ed.) (2009). *Canine Ergonomics. The Science of Working Dogs.* New York: Taylor and Francis.

Henkin, R.I. (1994). Drug-Induced Taste and Smell Disorders. Incidence, Mechanisms and Management Related Primarily to Treatment of Sensory Receptor Dysfunction. *Drug Safety, 11(5)*, 318–377.

Henkin, R.I., Levy, L.M., and Fordyce, A. (2013). Taste and Smell Function in Chronic Disease: A Review of Clinical and Biochemical Evaluations of Taste and Smell Dysfunction in Over 5000 Patients at the Taste and Smell Clinic in Washington, DC. *American Journal of Otolaryngology, 34(5)*, 477–489.

Hennessy, M.B., Davis, H.N., Williams, M.T., Mellott, C., and Douglas, C.W. (1997). Plasma Cortisol Levels of Dogs at a County Animal Shelter. *Physiology & Behavior, 62(3)*, 485–490.

Hepper, P.G. (1988). The Discrimination of Human Odour by the Dog. *Perception, 17*, 549–554.

Hepper, P.G., and Wells, D.L. (2005). How Many Footsteps Do Dogs Need to Determine the Direction of an Odour Trail? *Chemical Senses, 30(4)*, 291–298.

Herrada, G., and Dulac, C. (1997). A Novel Family of Putative Pheromone Receptors in Mammals with a Topographically Organized and Sexually Dimorphic Distribution. *Cell, 90(2)*, 763–773.

Herstik, M. (2009). Training Detection Dogs. *Police K9 Magazine*, 31–34, May/June 2009.

Herzog, H.A. (2007). Gender Differences in Human–Animal Interactions: A Review. *Anthrozoos, 20(1)*, 7–21.

Hickey, S., McIlwraith, F., Bruno, R., Matthews, A., and Alati, R. (2012). Drug Detection Dogs in Australia: More Bark Than Bite? *Drug and Alcohol Review, 31(6)*, 778–783.

Hilliard, S. (2003). Principles of Animal Learning, pp. 23–42, in *Mine Detection Dogs: Training, Operations and Odour.* Geneva: International Centre for Humanitarian Demining.

Hirai, T.K., Kojima, S., Shimada, A., Umemura, T., Sakai, M., and Itakura, C. (1996). Age-Related Changes in the Olfactory System of Dogs. *Neuropathology and Applied Neurobiology, 22(6)*, 531–539.

Hoffman, E.M., Curran, A.M., Dulgerian, N., Stockham, R.A., and Eckenrode, B.A. (2009). Characterization of the Volatile Organic Compounds Present in the Headspace of Decomposing Human Remains. *Forensic Science International, 186*, 6–13.

Holmes, T.P., Aukema, J.E., Von Holle, B., Liebhold, A., and Sills, E. (2009). The Year in Ecology and Conservation Biology, 2009: Economic Impact of Invasive Species in Forests: Past, Present and Future. *Annals of the New York Academy of Sciences, 1162*, 18–38.

Homan, H.J., Linz, G., and Peer, B.D. (2001). Dogs Increase Recovery of Passerine Carcasses in Dense Vegetation, *Wildlife Society Bulletin, 29(1)*, 292–296.

Horowitz, A. (2009). *Inside of a Dog: What Dogs See, Smell, and Know*. New York: Scribner.

Horvath, G., Andersson, H., and Nemes, S. (2013). Cancer Odor in the Blood of Ovarian Cancer Patients: A Retrospective Study of Detection by Dogs during Treatment, 3 and 6 Months Afterward. *BMC Cancer, 13*, 396–402.

Horvath, G., Andersson, H., and Paulsson, G. (2010). Characteristic Odor in the Blood Reveals Ovarian Carcinoma. *BMC Cancer, 10*, 643–649.

Horvath, G., Järverud, G.K., Järverud, S., and Horvath, I. (2008). Human Ovarian Carcinomas Detected by Specific Odor. *Integrative Cancer Therapy, 7(2)*, 76–80.

Hosler, J.S., and Smith, B.H. (2000). Blocking and the Detection of Odor Components in Blends. *Journal of Experimental Biology, 203(18)*, 2797–2806.

Houpt, K.A., Shepherd, P., and Hintz, H.F. (1978). Two Methods for Producing Peripheral Anosmia in Dogs. *Laboratory Animal Science, 28(2)*, 173–177.

Howald, G., Donlan, C.J., Galvan, J.B., Russell, J.C., Parkes, J., Samaniego, A., Wang, Y. et al. (2007). Invasive Rodent Eradications on Islands. *Conservation Biology, 21(5)*, 1258–1268.

Howell, T., Conduit, R., Toukhsati, S., and Bennett, P. (2011). Development of a Minimally-Invasive Protocol for Recording Mismatch Negativity (MMN) in the Dog (*Canis familiaris*) Using Electroencephalography (EEG). *Journal of Neuroscience Methods, 201(2)*, 377–380.

Hoyer-Tomiczek, U., and Sauseng, G. (2009). Spürhunde erschnüffeln Quarantäneschädlinge ALB und CLB (Detection Dogs Sniff for Quarantine Pests ALB and CLB). *Forstschutz Aktuell, 48*, 2–5.

Hoyer-Tomiczek, U., and Sauseng, G. (2012). Alternative Detection Method for ALB and CLB. *Forstschutz Aktuell, 55*, 43–45.

Huang, E.Y.-F., Lai, P.-Y., Chyi, W.W.-L., Yen, K.T.-B., and Chen, Y.-Y. (2007). Utilization of Odor Sensibility of Dogs in Detecting the Red Imported Fire Ant (*Solenopsis invicta*) in Taiwan. Proceedings, 2007 Annual Imported Fire Ant Conference, April 2007, Gainesville, Florida. Available at http://www.ars .usda.gov/sp2UserFiles/Place/60360510/docs/Proceedings2007IFAConf-withcovers_29Oct07.pdf.

Hudoleev, V. (2014, August 22). Mi sluzhim vmeste [We serve together]. *Krasnaya Zvezda*. Available at http:// www.redstar.ru; http://www.redstar.ru/index.php/daty/item/18129-my-sluzhim-vmeste.

Hudson, J. (1989). Analysis of Currency for Cocaine Contamination. *Canadian Society of Forensic Science Journal, 22(2)*, 203–218.

Humphrey, E., and Warner, L. (1934). *Working Dogs*. Baltimore: The Johns Hopkins Press.

Hunt, K.E., Moore, M.J., Rolland, R.M., Kellar, N.M., Hall, A.J., Kershaw, J., Raverty, S.A. et al. (2013). Overcoming the Challenges of Studying Conservation Physiology in Large Whales: A Review of Available Methods. *Conservation Physiology, 1*. 10.1093/conphys/cot006.

Hunter, J.C., and Riegner, D.E. (2012). Characterization of Solid Phase Microextraction (SPME) Using Field Portable GC-MS for Detection of Explosive Taggants EGDN and DMNB. 243rd American Chemical Society National Meeting and Exposition, San Diego (March 26, 2012). Available at http://acselb-529643017 .us-west-2.elb.amazonaws.com/chem/243nm/program/view.php?pub_num=308&par=CHED.

Hunter, S. (1997). Research Highlight: Taming Explosives for Training, pp. 24–25, in *Science & Technology Review*. Lawrence Livermore National Laboratory.

Huntingford, J.L., Kirn, B.N., Cramer, K., Mann, S., and Wakshlag, J.J. (2014). Evaluation of a Performance Enhancing Supplement in American Foxhounds during Eventing. *Journal of Nutritional Science, 3*, e24.

Hurt, A., and Smith, D.A. (2009). Conservation Dogs, p. 1750194, in *Canine Ergonomics: The Science of Working Dogs* (Helton, W.S., ed.) Boca Raton: Taylor & Francis/CRC Press.

Hussain, A., Saraiva, L.R., and Korsching, S.I. (2009). Positive Darwinian Selection and the Birth of an Olfactory Receptor Clade in Teleosts. *Proceedings of the National Academy of Sciences USA, 106(11)*, 4313–4318.

Hyspler, R., Crhova, S., Gasparic, J., Zadak, Z., Cizkova, M., and Balasova, V. (2000). Determination of Isoprene in Human Expired Breath Using Solid-Phase Microextraction and Gas Chromatography-Mass Spectrometry. *Journal of Chromatography B, 739(1)*, 183–190.

Illig, K.R., and Haberly, L.B. (2003). Odor-Evoked Activity Is Spatially Distributed in Piriform Cortex. *The Journal of Comparative Neurology, 457(4)*, 361–373.

Imayoshi, I., Sakamoto, M., Ohtsuka, T., Takao, K., Miyakawa, T., Yamaguchi, M., Mori, K., Ikeda, T., Itohara, S., and Kageyama, R. (2008). Roles of Continuous Neurogenesis in the Structural and Functional Integrity of the Adult Forebrain. *Nature Neuroscience, 11(10)*, 1153–1161.

Inoue, H., Iwata, Y.T., and Kuwayama, K. (2008). Characterization and Profiling of Methamphetamine Seizures. *Journal of Health Science, 54(6)*, 615–622.

International Forensic Research Institute (IFRI) (2003). *Draft Best Practice Guidelines for Detector Dog Teams*. North Miami Beach, Florida: Third National Detector Dog Conference, May 19–23, 2003. Available at http://landofpuregold.com/the-pdfs/ddogs-best-practices.pdf.

International Union for Conservation of Nature and Natural Resources (IUCN). Red List of Threatened Species. Available at http://www.iucnredlist.org.

Irwin, M.E., and Kampmeier, G.E. (2002). Commercialization of Insects and Their Products, pp. 220–226, in *Encyclopedia of Insects* (Resh, V.H., and Carde, R., eds). San Diego: Academic Press.

Issel-Tarver, L., and Rine, J. (1996). Organization and Expression of Canine Olfactory Receptor Genes. *Proceedings of the National Academy of Sciences USA, 93(20)*, 10897–10902.

Ivanov, A. (2007, October 6). Sobachey predanostyu i volchey hvatkoy obladayut redchayshie zhivotniye—volkosobi [Volkosob—A rare animal that has the loyalty of a dog and the grip of a wolf]. *Perviy Kanal*. Available at https://www.1tv.ru/news/social/85475.

Jackson, M.M., Zeagler, C., Valentin, G., Martin, A., Martin, V., Delawalla, A., Blount, W. et al. (2013, September). FIDO-Facilitated Interactions for Dogs with Occupations: Wearable Dog-Activated Interfaces, pp. 81–88, in *Proceedings of the 2013 International Symposium on Wearable Computers*. ACM. Available at http://dl.acm.org/citation.cfm?id=2494334&dl=ACM&coll=DL&CFID=513351099&CFTOKEN=61485904.

Jacobs, L.F. (2012). From Chemotaxis to the Cognitive Map: The Function of Olfaction. *Proceedings of the National Academy of Sciences USA, 109(Suppl. 1)*, 10693–10700.

Jafek, B.W., Linschoten, M.R., and Murrow, B.W. (2004). Anosmia after Intranasal Zinc Gluconate Use. *American Journal of Rhinology, 18(3)*, 137–141.

Jager, T.F. (1917). *Scout, Red Cross, and Army Dogs*. New York: Arrow Printing Co.

Jain, S.K., Singhai, J., and Jain, S. (2013). Comprehensive Detection of Human Body Odour in Air Matrices. *International Journal of Scientific Research Engineering & Technology, 2(8)*, 464–467.

James, A.T., and Martin, A.J.P. (1952). Gas–Liquid Partition Chromatography: The Separation and Micro-Estimation of Volatile Fatty Acids from Formic Acid to Dodecanoic Acid. *Biochemical Journal, 50*, 679–690.

Jaworski, R. (1999). Identification of Scent or of Emotion (in Polish). *Problemy Kryminalistyki, 224*, 54–57.

Jeffery, N.D., Lakatos, A., and Franklin, R.J. (2005). Autologous Olfactory Glial Cell Transplantation Is Reliable and Safe in Naturally Occurring Canine Spinal Cord Injury. *Journal of Neurotrauma, 22(11)*, 1282–1293.

Jeffery, N.D., Smith, P.M., Lakatos, A., Ibanez, C., Ito, D., and Franklin, R.J. (2006). Clinical Canine Spinal Cord Injury Provides an Opportunity to Examine the Issues in Translating Laboratory Techniques into Practical Therapy. *Spinal Cord, 44(10)*, 584–593.

Jenkin, J.F., Johnstone, G.W., and Copson, G.R. (1981). Introduced Animal and Plant Species on Macquarie Island. Colloque sur les Ecosystems Subantarctiques. Staion Biologique de Paimpont, *Comite National Francais pour les Recherches Antartiques, 52*, 301–313.

Jenkins, A.J. (2001). Drug Contamination of U.S. Paper Currency. *Forensic Science International, 121(3)*, 189–193.

Jenkins, E.K., Lee-Fowler, T.M., Angle, T.C., Behrend, E.N., and Moore, G.E. (2014). The Effects of Oral Metronidazole and Doxycycline Administration on Olfactory Detection Capabilities of Explosive Detection Dogs. *Journal of Veterinary Internal Medicine, 28*, 1091.

Jenkins, H.M., and Moore, B.R. (1973). The Form of the Auto-Shaped Response with Food or Water Reinforcers. *Journal of the Experimental Analysis of Behavior, 20(2)*, 163–181.

Jezierski, T., Adamkiewicz, E., Walczak, M., Sobczyńska, M., Górecka-Bruzda, A., Ensminger, J., and Papet, E. (2014). Efficacy of Drug Detection by Fully-Trained Police Dogs Varies by Breed, Training Level, Type of Drug and Search Environment. *Forensic Science International, 237*, 112–118.

Jezierski, T., Bednarek, T., Gorecka, A., Gebler, E., and Stawicka, A. (2002). Ethological Analysis of Mistakes Made During Identification of Humans on the Basis of Scent by Police Special Dogs (in Polish). Final Report on the grant No. TOOA 02618, of the Polish State Committee for Scientific Research.

Jezierski, T., Bednarek, T., Gorecka, A., Gebler, E., and Stawicka, A. (2003). Factors Influencing the Reliability of Canine Identification of Humans on the Basis of Scent (in Polish). *Problemy Współczesnej Kryminalistyki* (Gruza, E., Tomaszewski, T., and Goc, M., eds.), *Vol. VII(2)*, 207–215. Polish Forensic Society, University of Warsaw, Faculty of Law & Administration, Department of Forensic Science.

Jezierski, T., Gorecka-Bruzda, A., Walczak, M., Swiergiel, A.H., Chruszczewski, M.H., and Pearson, B.L. (2010). Operant Conditioning of Dogs (*Canis familiaris*) for Identification of Humans Using Scent Lineup. *Animal Science Papers and Reports, 28(1)*, 81–93.

Jezierski, T., Sobczynska, M., Walczak, M., Gorecka-Bruzda, A., and Ensminger, J. (2012). Do Trained Dogs Discriminate Individual Body Odor of Women Better Than Those of Men? *Journal of Forensic Science, 57(3)*, 647–653.

Jezierski, T., Walczak, M., and Gorecka, A. (2008). Information-Seeking Behaviour of Sniffer Dogs during Match-to-Sample Training in the Scent Lineup. *Polish Psychological Bulletin, 39(2)*, 71–80.

Jezierski, T., Walczak, M., Ligor, T., Rudnicka, J., and Buszewski, B. (2015). Study of the Art: Canine Olfaction Used for Cancer Detection on the Base of Breath Odor: Perspectives and Limitations. *Journal of Breath Research, 9(2)*, 027001.

Jessen, K.R., and Mirsky, R. (2002). Signals that Determine Schwann Cell Identity. *Journal of Anatomy, 200(4)*, 367–376.

Jessen, K.R., and Mirsky, R. (2005). The Origin and Development of Glial Cells in Peripheral Nerves. *Nature Reviews Neuroscience, 6(9)*, 671–682.

Jia, H., Pustovyy, O.M., Waggoner, P., Beyers, R.J., Schumacher, J., Wildey, C., Barrett, J. et al. (2014). Functional MRI of the Olfactory System in Conscious Dogs. *PLoS/ONE, 9(1)*, e86362.

John, J.S., and Key, B. (2005). A Model for Axon Navigation Based on Glycocodes in the Primary Olfactory System. *Chemical Senses, 30(Suppl. 1)*, i123–i124.

Johnen, D., Heuwieser, W., and Fischer-Tenhagen, C. (2013). Canine Scent Detection—Fact or Fiction? *Applied Animal Behaviour Science, 148(3–4)*, 201–208.

Johnson, G.R. (1976). Gypsy Moth Egg Detection Dogs. *Off-Lead*, 8–11 (October).

Johnston, J. (1999). Canine Detection Capabilities: Operational Implications of Recent R and D Findings. Institute for Biological Detection Systems, Auburn University, 1(7). ms, Auburn University, 1–7. Available at http://barksar.org/K-9_Detection_Capabilities.pdf.

Johnston, J.M., and Williams, M. (1999). Enhanced Canine Explosive Detection: Odor Generalization, Unclassified Final Report for Contract no. DAAD05-96-D-7019, Office of Special Technology.

Johnstone, R.A.W., and Rose, M.E. (1996). *Mass Spectrometry for Chemists and Biochemists*, 2nd. ed. Cambridge, UK: Cambridge University Press.

Jones, A.W., and Holmgren, P. (2001). Uncertainty in Estimating Blood Ethanol Concentrations by Analysis of Vitreous Humour. *Journal of Clinical Pathology, 54*, 699–702.

Jones, A.W., Lagesson, V., and Tagesson, C. (1995). Determination of Isoprene in Human Breath by Thermal Desoprtion Gas Chromatography with Ultraviolet Detection. *Journal of Chromatography, B: Analytical Technology in the Biomedical and Life Sciences, 672(1)*, 1–6.

Jones, E. (1977). Ecology of the Feral Cat *Felis catus (L.)*, (Carnivorus: Felidae) on Macquarie Island. *Australian Wildlife Research, 4(3)*, 249–262.

Jones, J. (1876). Explorations of the Aboriginal Remains of Tennessee. *Smithsonian Contributions to Knowledge, 22*, 1–171. Washington, DC: Smithsonian Institution.

Jones, K.E., Dashfield, K., Downend, A.B., and Otto, C.M. (2004). Disaster Medicine. *Journal of the American Veterinary Medical Association, 225(6)*, 854–860.

Jones, R., and Rog, D. (1998). Olfaction: A Review. *Journal of Laryngology and Otology, 112*, 11–24.

Jones, V.S. (2010). *A Preliminary Report of a Phase I/Remote Sensing and Boundary Delineation Survey of the Weissinger Ancestral Home Site, near Hamburg in Perry County, Alabama. Report submitted to Mr. Charles H. Weissinger by the Office of Archaeological Research, University of Alabama Museums*, Tuscaloosa. (A copy of this publication may be obtained from the Laboratory for Human Osteology at the Alabama Museum of Natural History of the University of Alabama, Moundville, Alabama.)

Jones, V.S. (2011). *Management Summary of Additional Remote Sensing Activities at the Weissinger Ancestral Home Site Near Hamburg in Perry County, Alabama*. Report submitted to Mr. Charles H. Weissinger by the Office of Archaeological Research, University of Alabama Museums, Tuscaloosa. (A copy of this publication may be obtained from the Laboratory for Human Osteology at the Alabama Museum of Natural History of the University of Alabama, Moundville, Alabama.)

Joshi, M., Delgado, Y., Guerra, P., Lai, H., and Almirall, J.R. (2009). Detection of Odor Signatures of Smokeless Powders Using Solid Phase Microextraction Coupled to an Ion Mobility Spectrometer. *Forensic Science International, 188*, 112–118.

Jourdan, T., Veitenheimer, A., Murray, C., and Wagner, J. (2013). The Quantitation of Cocaine on U.S. Currency: Survey and Significance of the Levels of Contamination. *Journal of Forensic Sciences, 58(3)*, 616–624.

Junod, C.A., and Pokines, J.T. (2014). Subaerial Weathering, pp. 287–314, in *Manual of Forensic Taphonomy* (Pokines, J.T., and Symes, S.A., eds.). Boca Raton: Taylor & Francis/CRC Press.

Kafitz, K.W., and Greer, C.A. (1998). The Influence of Ensheathing Cells on Olfactory Receptor Cell Neurite Outgrowth in vitro. *Annals of the New York Academy of Sciences, 855*, 266–269.

Kahl, S.S., Henke, S.E., Hall, M.A., and Britton, D.K. (2012). Brown Treesnakes: A Potential Invasive Species for the United States. *Human–Wildlife Interactions, 6(2)*, 181–203.

Kalinke, U., Bechmann, I., and Detje, C.N. (2011). Host Strategies against Virus Entry via the Olfactory System. *Virulence, 2(4)*, 367–370.

Kalmey, J.K., Thewissen, J.G.M., and Dluzen, D.E. (1998). Age-Related Size Reduction of Foramina in the Cribiform Plate. *Anatomical Record, 251(3)*, 326–329.

Kalmus, H. (1955). The Discrimination by the Nose of the Dog of Individual Human Odours and in Particular the Odours of Twins. *British Journal of Animal Behaviour, 3(1)*, 25–31.

Kaluza, J.F., Gussing, F., Bohm, S., Breer, H., and Strotmann, J. (2004). Olfactory Receptors in the Mouse Septal Organ. *Journal of Neuroscience Research, 76*, 442–452.

Kamin, L.J. (1969). Predictability, Surprise, Attention, and Conditioning, pp. 279–286, in *Punishment and Aversive Behavior* (Campbell, B.A., and Church, R.M. eds.). New York: Appleton-Century Crofts.

Karacic, V., and Skender, L. (2001). Analysis of Drugs of Abuse in Urine by Gas Chromatography/Mass Spectrometry: Experience and Application. *Archives of Industrial Hygiene and Toxicology, 51(4)*, 389–400.

Kardong, K.V. (2002). *Vertebrates: Comparative Anatomy, Function, Evolution*. New York: McGraw-Hill.

Kase, A. (2015, March 15). Teaching Old Dogs New Tricks, Literally: Can Police Dogs Be Un-Trained to Sniff for Cannabis? Reset.me online newsletter. Available at http://reset.me/story/teaching -old-dogs-new-tricks-literally-can-police-dogs-be-un-trained-to-sniff-for-cannabis/.

Kasimov, V.M., Horoshilov, I.A., Dorofeev, V.S., and Tebenkova, O.A. (2005, August 13). Experiment s volchey krovyu [An experiment with wolf blood]. *Vsegda Ryadom*, pp. 18–19. Available at http://perm-dog .narod.ru/vr/index.htm.

Katotomichelakis, M., Balatsouras, D., Tripsianis, G., Davris, S., Maroudias, N., Danielides, V., and Simopoulos, C. (2007). The Effect of Smoking on the Olfactory Function. *Rhinology, 45(4)*, 273–280.

Katz, L.R., and Golembiewski, A.P. (2007). Curbing the Dog: Extending Protection of the Fourth Amendment to Police Drug Dogs. *Nebraska Law Review, 85*, 735–792.

Katz, S.R., and Midkiff, C.R. (1998). Unconfirmed Canine Accelerant Detection: A Reliability Issue in Court. *Journal of Forensic Sciences, 43*, 329–333.

Katzel, D., Nicholson, E., Schorge, S., Walker, M.C., and Kullman, D.M. (2014). Chemical–Genetic Attenuation of Focal Neocortical Seizures. *Nature Communications, 5:3847.*

Kauhanen, E., Harri, M., Nevalainen, A., and Nevalainen, T. (2002). Validity of Detection of Microbial Growth in Buildings by Trained Dogs. *Environment International, 28*, 153–157.

Kavaliers, M., and Colwell, D.D. (1995). Discrimination by Female Mice between the Odours of Parasitized and Non-Parasitized Males. *Proceedings of the Royal Society, B, 282(1804)*, 31–35.

Kavaliers, M., Colwell, D.D., Braun, W.J., and Choleris, E. (2003). Brief Exposure to the Odour of a Parasitized Male Alters the Subsequent Mate Odour Responses of Female Mice. *Animal Behaviour, 65(1)*, 59–68.

Kavoi, B., Makanya, A., Hassanali, J., Carlsson, H.-E., and Kiama, S. (2010). Comparative Functional Structure of the Olfactory Mucosa in the Domestic Dog and Sheep. *Annals of Anatomy, 192*, 329–337.

Kay, L.M., Crk, T., and Thorngate, J. (2005). A Redefinition of Odor Mixture Quality. *Behavioral Neuroscience, 119(3)*, 726–733.

Keller, A., and Vosshall, L. (2008). Better Smelling through Genetics: Mammalian Odor Perception. *Current Opinion in Neurobiology, 18*, 364–369.

Keller, A., Zhuang, H., Chi, Q., Vosshall, L.B., and Matsunami, H. (2007). Genetic Variation in Human Odorant Receptor Alters Odour Perception. *Nature, 449*, 468–472.

Keller, O. (1909). *Die Antike Tierwelt, Vol. I: Saugetiere*. Leipzig: Wilhelm Engelmann.

Kelley, P. (2013). Dogs Detect Pheromone. *Fumigants and Pheromones, 105*, 1–2.

Kelly, B.P. (2009). Studying Seals in Their Sea Ice Habitat: Application of Traditional and Scientific Methods, pp. 301–344, in *Field Techniques for Sea Ice Research* (Eicken, H., and Gradinger, R., eds.). Fairbanks: University of Alaska Press.

Kelly, B.P., Badajos, O.H., Kunnasranta, M., Moran, J.R., Martinez-Bakker, M., Wartzok, D., and Boveng, P. (2010a). Seasonal Home Ranges and Fidelity to Breeding Sites among Ringed Seals. *Publications, Agencies and Staff of the U.S. Department of Commerce*. Paper 168.

Kelly, B.P., Bengtson, J.L., Boveng, P.L., Cameron, M.F., Dahle, S.P., Jansen, J.K., Logerwell, E.A. et al. (2010b). Status Review of the Ringed Seal (*Phoca hispida*), NOAA Technical Memorandum NMFS-AFSC-212, 128.

Kelly, B.P., Quakenbush, L.T., and Rose, J.R. (1986). Ringed Seal Winter Ecology and Effects of Noise Disturbance, Final Report: Outer Continental Shelf Environmental Assessment Program, Research Unit 32.

Kennedy, K.A.R. (2010). Principal Figures in Early 20th-Century Physical Anthropology: With Special Treatment of Forensic Anthropology, pp. 105–125, in *Histories of American Physical Anthropology in the Twentieth Century* (Kennedy, K.A.R., and Little, M.A., eds.). Lanham, Maryland: Lexington Books.

Keno, L.A., and Langston, C.E. (2011). Treatment of Accidental Ethanol Intoxication with Hemodialysis in a Dog. *Journal of Veterinary Emergency and Critical Care, 21(4)*, 363–368.

Kepecs, A., Uchida, N., and Mainen, Z.F. (2006). The Sniff as a Unit of Olfactory Processing. *Chemical Senses, 31(2)*, 167–179.

Kerepesi, A., Jonsson, G.K., Miklosi, A., Topál, J., Csányi, V., and Magnusson, M.S. (2005). Detection of Temporal Patterns in Dog-Human Interaction. *Behavioural Processes, 70(1)*, 69–79.

Kerley, L.L. (2010). Using Dogs for Tiger Conservation and Research. *Integrative Zoology, 5(4)*, 390–396.

Kerley, L.L., and Salkina, G.P. (2007). Using Scent-Matching Dogs to Identify Individual Amur Tigers from Scats. *Journal of Wildlife Management, 71(4)*, 1349–1356.

Killam, E.W. (1990). *The Detection of Human Remains.* Springfield, Illinois: Charles C. Thomas.

Killeen, P.R. (2014). Pavlov + Skinner = Premack. *International Journal of Comparative Psychology, 27(4)*, 544–568.

Kim, S.J., Moon, W.K., Cho, N., Cha, J.H., Kim, S.M., and Im, J.G. (2008). Computer-Aided Detection in Full-Field Digital Mammography: Sensitivity and Reproducibility in Serial Examinations. *Radiology, 246(1)*, 71–80.

Kirschhoffer, B.J. (2013). Den-Sniffing Dogs, on website of Polar Bears International. Posted March 13, 2013. Available at http://www.polarbearsinternational.org/news-room/scientists-and-explorers-blog/den -sniffing-dogs.

Kirton, A., Winter, A., Wirrell, E., and Snead, O.C. (2008). Seizure Response Dogs: Evaluation of a Formal Training Program. *Epilepsy & Behavior, 13*, 499–504.

Kirton, A., Wirrell, E., Zhang, J., and Hamiwka, L. (2004). Seizure-Alerting and -Response Behaviors in Dogs Living with Epileptic Children. *Neurology, 62*, 2303–2305.

Kiviranta, A.M., Laitinen-Vapaavuori, O., Hielm-Björkman, A., and Jokinen, T. (2013). Topiramate as an Add-On Antiepileptic Drug in Treating Refractory Canine Idiopathic Epilepsy. *Journal of Small Animal Practice, 54(10)*, 512–520.

Klein, A-M., Vaissiére, B.E., Cane, J.H., Steffan-Dewenter, I., Cunningham, S.A., Kremen, C., and Tscharntke, T. (2007). Importance of Pollinators in Changing Landscapes for World Crops. *Proceedings of the Royal Society B, 274*, 303–313.

Klepinger, L.L. (2006). *Fundamentals of Forensic Anthropology.* Hoboken, NJ: Wiley-Liss.

Kogan, L.R., Schoenfeld-Tacher, R., and Simon, A.A. (2012). Behavioral Effects of Auditory Stimulation in Kenneled Dogs. *Journal of Veterinary Behavior: Clinical Applications and Research, 7(5)*, 268–275.

Kohn, M.H., and Wayne, R.K. (1997). Facts from Faeces Revisited. *Trends in Ecology & Evolution, 6*, 223–227.

Komar, D. (1999). The Use of Cadaver Air Scent Detection Dogs in Locating Scattered, Scavenged Human Remains: Preliminary Field Test Results. *Journal of Forensic Sciences, 44(2)*, 405–408.

Komar, D.A., and Buikstra, J.E. (2008). *Forensic Anthropology: Contemporary Theory and Practice.* New York: Oxford University Press.

Konig, H.E., and Liebich, H.-G. (2007). *Veterinary Anatomy of Domestic Animals.* Stuttgart: Schattauer.

Kopaliani, N., Shakarshvili, M., Guriedlidze, Z., Qurkhuli, T., and Tarkhnishvili, D. (2014). Gene Flow between Wolf and Shepherd Dog Populations in Georgia (Caucasus). *Journal of Heredity, 105(3)*, 345–353.

Kornack, D.R., and Rakic, P. (2001). The Generation, Migration, and Differentiation of Olfactory Neurons in the Adult Primate Brain. *Proceedings of the National Academy of Sciences USA, 98(8)*, 4752–4757.

Korytin, S.A., and Azbukina, M.D. (1986). Sezonnye izmeneniya ostroty oboyaniya u zhivotnih I vliyanie na neye trenirovki obonyatel'nogo analizatora [Seasonal changes in olfactory acuity in animals and its effect on olfactory training]. In V.E. Sokolov, *Himicheskaja Kommunikaciya Zhivotnik: Teoriya i Praktika [Chemical Signaling in Animals: Theory and Practice].* A. N. Severcov Institute of Evolution, Morphology, and Ecology of Animals: Nauka.

Koster, J.M., and Tankersley, K.B. (2012). Heterogeneity of Hunting Ability and Nutritional Status among Domestic Dogs in Lowland Nicaragua. *Proceedings of the National Academy of Sciences USA, 109(8)*, e463–e470.

Kostikas, K., Gaga, M., Papatheodorou, G., Karamanis, T., Orphanidou, D., and Loukides, S. (2005). Leukotriene B4 in Exhaled Breath Condensate and Sputum Supernatant in Patients with COPD and Asthma. *Chest, 127(5)*, 1553–1559.

Kostikas, K., Papatheodorou, G., Psathakis, K., Panagou, P., and Loukides, S. (2003). Prostaglandin E2 in the Expired Breath Condensate of Patients with Asthma. *European Respiratory Journal, 22(5)*, 743–747.

Kostopanagiotou, G., Kalimeris, K., Kesidis, K., Matsota, P., Dima, C., Economou, M., and Papageorgiou, C. (2011). Sevoflurane Impairs Post-Operative Olfactory Memory but Preserves Olfactory Function. *European Journal of Anaesthesiology, 28(1)*, 63–68.

Kotrschal, K., Schöberl, I., Bauer, B., Thibeaut, A.M., and Wedl, M. (2009). Dyadic Relationships and Operational Performance of Male and Female Owners and Their Male Dogs. *Behavioural Processes, 81(3)*, 383–391.

Koziol, P., and Sutowski, G. (1998). Scent Identification: Chance or Certainty? (in Polish). *Problemy Kryminalistyki, 222*, 37–39.

Kranz, W., and Goodpaster, J. (2015). Author's Response to Sanchez et al. entitled "On the Importance of Training Aids and the Definition of an Explosive Odor Signature: Commentary on Kranz et al." *Forensic Science International, 251*, e20–e21.

Kranz, W., Kitts, K., Strange, N., Cummins, J., Lotspeich, E., and Goodpaster, J. (2014a). On the Smell of Composition C-4. *Forensic Science International, 236*, 157–163.

Kranz, W.D., Strange, N.A., and Goodpaster, J.V. (2014b). "Fooling Fido"—Chemical and Behavioral Studies of Pseudo-Explosive Canine Training Aids. *Analytical and Bioanalytical Chemistry, 406(30)*, 7817–7825.

Krauss, G.L., Choi, J.S., and Lesser, R.P. (2007). Pseudoseizure Dogs. *Neurology, 68*, 308–309.

Krawczyk, A., and Wesolowski, I. (1998). Osmological Experiment with Non-Contact Trace (in Polish). *Problemy Kryminalistyki, 222*, 45–48.

Krogman, W.M. (1939). A Guide to the Identification of Human Skeletal Material. *FBI Law Enforcement Bulletin, 8*, 3–31.

Krogman, W.M. (1962). *The Human Skeleton in Forensic Medicine.* Springfield, IL: Charles C. Thomas.

Krudewig, C., Deschl, U., and Wewetzer, K. (2006). Purification and in vitro Characterization of Adult Canine Olfactory Ensheathing Cells. *Cell and Tissue Research, 326(3)*, 687–696.

Krusemark, E.A., Novak, L.R., Gitelman, D.R., and Li, W. (2013). When the Sense of Smell Meets Emotion: Anxiety-State-Dependent Olfactory Processing and Neural Circuitry Adaptation. *The Journal of Neuroscience, 33(39)*, 15324–15332.

Krushinsky, L.V., and Fless, D.A. (1959). Isskustvennoe usilie oboyaniya u sluzhebnyh sobak [Artificial enhancement of olfactory ability in working dogs]. *Zhurnal Vysshey Nervnoi Deyatel'nosti [Journal of Higher Nervous Activity], 9(2)*, 284–290.

Kury, J.W., Simpson, R.L., and Hallowell, S.F. (1995). Development of Non-Hazardous Explosives for Security Training and Testing (NESTT). Internal report, Lawrence Livermore National Laboratory.

Kurz, M.E., Schultz, S., Griffith, J., Broadus, K., Sparks, J., Dabdoub, G., and Brock, J. (1996). Effect of Background Interference on Accelerant Detection by Canines. *Journal of Forensic Sciences, 41(5)*, 868–873.

Kusano, M., Mendez, E., and Furton, K.G. (2011). Development of Headspace SPME Method for Analysis of Volatile Organic Compounds Present in Human Biological Specimens. *Analytical and Bioanalytical Chemistry, 400(7)*, 1817–1826.

Lakatos, G., Gacsi, M., Topal, J., and Miklosi, A. (2012). Comprehension and Utilisation of Pointing Gestures and Gazing in Dog–Human Communication in Relatively Complex Situations. *Animal Cognition, 15(2)*, 201–213.

Lakatos, A., Smith, P.M., Barnett, S.C., and Franklin, R.J. (2003). Meningeal Cells Enhance Limited CNS Remyelination by Transplanted Olfactory Ensheathing Cells. *Brain 126(Part 3)*, 598–609.

Landis, B.N., Konnerth, C.G., and Hummel, T. (2004). A Study on the Frequency of Olfactory Dysfunction. *Laryngoscope, 114(10)*, 1764–1769.

Larsson, B.T. (1965). Gas Chromatography of Organic Volatiles in Human Breath and Saliva. *Acta Chemica Scandinavica, 19*, 159–164.

Laska, M., Seibt, A., and Weber, A. (2000). "Microsmatic" Primates Revisited: Olfactory Sensitivity in the Squirrel Monkey. *Chemical Senses, 25(1)*, 47–53.

Lasseter, A.E., Jacobi, K.P., Farley, R., and Hensel, L. (2003). Cadaver Dog and Handler Team Capabilities in the Recovery of Human Remains in the Southeastern United States. *Journal of Forensic Sciences, 48(3)*, 617–621.

Lattimore, R. (1975). *The Odyssey of Homer.* New York: Harper Colophon.

Lauren, J. (2013). Remapping the Path Forward: Toward a Systemic View of Forensic Science Reform and Oversight, *Texas Law Review, 91*, 1051.

Lazarini, F., and Lledo, P.M. (2011). Is Adult Neurogenesis Essential for Olfaction? *Trends in Neurosciences, 34(1)*, 20–30.

Lazarowski, L., and Dorman, D.C. (2014). Explosives Detection in Military Working Dogs: Olfactory Generalization from Components to Mixtures. *Applied Animal Behaviour Science, 151*, 84–93.

Leco Corp. (2014). Pegasus 4D GCxGC-TOFMS Brochure. Available at http://www.leco.com/component /edocman/?task=document.viewdoc&id=52&Itemid=0.

Lee, D.-H., Cullum, J.P., Anderson, J.L., Daugherty, J.L., Beckett, L.M., and Leskey, T.C. (2014). Characterization of Overwintering Sites of the Invasive Brown Marmorated Stink Bug in Natural Landscapes Using Human Surveyors and Detector Canines. *PLoS/ONE, 9(4)*, e91575.

Lee, K.E., Nam, S., Cho, E.A., Seong, I., Limb, J.K., Lee, S., and Kim, J. (2008). Identification of Direct Regulatory Targets of the Transcription Factor Sox10 Based on Function and Conservation. *BMC Genomics, 9*, 408.

Lefebvre, D., Giffroy, J.-M., and Diederich, C. (2008). Cortisol and Behavioral Responses to Enrichment in Military Working Dogs. *Journal of Ethology, 27(2)*, 255–265.

Lehnert, M.S. (2008). The Population Biology and Ecology of the Homerus Swallowtail, *Papilio (Pterourus) homerus*, in the Cockpit Country, Jamaica. *Journal of Insect Conservation, 12*, 179–188.

Lesniak, A., Walczak, M., Jezierski, T., Sacharczuk, M., Gawkowski, M., and Jaszczak, K. (2008). Canine Olfactory Receptor Gene Polymorphism and Its Relation to Odor Detection Performance by Sniffer Dogs. *Journal of Heredity, 99(5)*, 518–527.

Leung, C.T., Coulombe, P.A., and Reed, R.R. (2007). Contribution of Olfactory Stem Cells to Tissue Maintenance and Regeneration. *Nature Neuroscience, 10(6)*, 720–726.

Leung, J.Y., Chapman, J.A., Harris, J.A., Hale, D., Chung, R.S., West, A.K., and Chuah, M.I. (2008). Olfactory Ensheathing Cells Are Attracted to, and Can Endocytose, Bacteria. *Cellular & Molecular Life Sciences, 65(17)*, 2732–2739.

Lewin, A.H. (2006). Receptors of Mammalian Trace Amines. *The AAPS Journal, 8(1)*, E138–E145.

Lewis, V.R., Fouche, C.F., and Lemaster, R.L. (1997). Evaluation of Dog-Assisted Searches and Electronic Odor Devices for Detecting the Western Subterranean Termite. *Forest Products Journal, 47(10)*, 79–84.

Li, C., Yousem, D.M., Doty, R.L., and Kennedy, D.W. (1994). Neuroimaging in Patients with Olfactory Dysfunction. *American Journal of Roentgenology, 162(2)*, 411–418.

Li, N., Deng, C., Yao, N., Shen, Z., and Zhang, X. (2005). Determination of Acetone, Hexanal and Heptanal in Blood Samples by Derivatization with Pentafluorobenzyl Hydroxylamine followed by Headspace Single-Drop Microextraction and Gas Chromatography-Mass Spectrometry. *Analytica Chimica Acta, 540(2)*, 317–323.

Li, W., Lopez, L., Osher, J., Howard, J.D., Parrish, T.B., and Gottfried, J.A. (2010). Right Orbitofrontal Cortex Mediates Conscious Olfactory Perception. *Psychological Science, 21(10)*, 1454–1463.

Liberles, S.D., and Buck, L.B. (2006). A Second Class of Chemosensory Receptors in the Olfactory Epithelium. *Nature, 442(7103)*, 645–650.

Lilja, S. (1976). *Dogs in Ancient Greek Poetry*. Commentationes Humanarum Litterarum. Helsinki: Societas Scientiarum Fennica.

Lin, D.-L., Wang, S.-M., Wu, C.-H., Chen, B.-G., and Liu, R.H. (2008). Chemical Derivatization for the Analysis of Drugs by GC-MS—A Conceptual Review. *Journal of Food and Drug Analysis, 16(1)*, 1–10.

Lin, H.-M., Chi, W.-L., Lin, C.-C., Tseng, Y.-C., Chen, W.-T., Kung, Y.-L., Lien, Y.-Y., and Chen, Y.-Y. (2011). Fire Ant-Detecting Canines: A Complementary Method in Detecting Red Imported Fire Ants. *Journal of Economic Entomology, 104(1)*, 225–231.

Lindblad-Toh, K., Wade, C.M., Mikkelsen, T.S., Karlsson, E.K., Jaffe, D.B., Kamal, M., Clamp, M. et al. (2005). Genome Sequence, Comparative Analysis and Haplotype Structure of the Domestic Dog. *Nature, 438(7069)*, 803–819.

Lindemann, L., Ebeling, M., Kratochwil, N.A., Bunzow, J.R., Grandy, D.K., and Hoener, M.C. (2005). Trace Amine-Associated Receptors Form Structurally and Functionally Distinct Subfamilies of Novel G Protein-Coupled Receptors. *Genomics, 85(3)*, 372–385.

Lippi, G., and Cervellin, G. (2011). Canine Olfactory Detection of Cancer versus Laboratory Testing: Myth or Opportunity? *Clinical Chemistry and Laboratory Medicine, 49(10)*, 435–439.

Lit, L., and Crawford, C.A. (2006). Effects of Training Paradigms on Search Dog Performance. *Applied Animal Behaviour Science, 98(3–4)*, 277–292.

Lit, L., Schweitzer, J.B., and Oberbauer, A.M. (2011). Handler Beliefs Affect Scent Detection Dog Outcomes. *Animal Cognition, 14(3)*, 387–394.

Litt, B., and Krieger, A. (2007). Of Seizure Prediction, Statistics, and Dogs: A Cautionary Tail. *Neurology, 68*, 250–251.

Livermore, A., and Laing, D.G. (1996). Influence of Training and Experience on the Perception of Multicomponent Odor Mixtures. *Journal of Experimental Psychology: Human Perception and Performance, 22(2)*, 267–277.

Lloyd, H.S. (1948). The Dog in War, pp. 177–194, in *The Book of the Dog* (Vesey-Fitzgerald, B., ed.). London: Nicholson & Watson.

LoBue, V., and DeLoache, J.S. (2008). Detecting the Snake in the Grass: Attention to Fear Relevant Stimuli by Adults and Young Children. *Psychological Science, 19(3)*, 284–289.

Lochner, A., Weisner, S., Zlatkis, A., and Middleditch, B.S. (1986). Gas Chromatographic–Mass Spectrometric Analysis of Volatile Constituents in Saliva. *Journal of Chromatography, 378(2)*, 267–282.

Lois, C., García-Verdugo, J.M., and Alvarez-Buylla, A. (1996). Chain Migration of Neuronal Precursors. *Science 271(5251)*, 978–981.

Long, R.A., Donovan, T.M., MacKay, P., Zielinski, W.J., and Buzas, J.S. (2007). Effectiveness of Scat Detection Dogs for Detecting Forest Carnivores. *Journal of Wildlife Management, 71(6)*, 2007–2017.

Lopes, B., Alves, J., Santos, A., and Pereira, G.D.G. (2015). Effect of a Stimulating Environment during the Socialization Period on the Performance of Adult Police Working Dogs. *Journal of Veterinary Behavior: Clinical Applications and Research, 10(3)*, 199–203.

Lopez, B.H. (1978). *Of Wolves and Men*. New York: Scribner.

Lorenzo, N., Wan, T.-L., Harper, R.J., Hsu, Y.-L., Chow, M., Rose, S., and Furton, K.G. (2003). Laboratory and Field Experiments Used to Identify *Canis lupus* var. *familiaris* Active Odor Signature Chemicals from Drugs, Explosives, and Humans. *Analytical and Bioanalytical Chemistry, 376(8)*, 1212–1224.

Loseva, E., Yuan, T.F., and Karnup, S. (2009). Neurogliogenesis in the Mature Olfactory System: A Possible Protective Role against Infection and Toxic Dust. *Brain Research Reviews, 59(2)*, 374–387.

Losey, J.E., and Vaughan, M. (2006). The Economic Value of Ecological Services Provided by Insects. *Bioscience, 56(4)*, 311–323.

Lotsch, J., Geisslinger, G., and Hummel, T. (2012). Sniffing Out Pharmacology: Interactions of Drugs with Human Olfaction. *Trends in Pharmacological Sciences, 33(4)*, 193–199.

Lotspeich, E., Kitts, K., and Goodpaster, J. (2012). Headspace Concentrations of Explosive Vapors in Containers Designed for Canine Testing and Training: Theory, Experiment, and Canine Trials. *Forensic Science International, 220(1–3)*, 130–134.

Lubow, R.E. (1973). Latent Inhibition. *Psychological Bulletin, 79(6)*, 398–407.

Lubow, R.E., Kahn, M., and Frommer, R. (1973). Information Processing of Olfactory Stimuli by the Dog: 1. The Acquisition and Retention of Four Odor-Pair Discriminations. *Bulletin of the Psychonomic Society, 1(2)*, 143–145.

Lulina, I. (2014, November 10). Interesnye facty o "Krasnoy Zvezde" [Interesting facts about the "Red Star Kennel"]. *Vse o Sobakah*. Available at http://guard-dog.ru.

Lupo, K.D. (2011). A Dog Is for Hunting, pp. 4–12, in *Ethnozooarchaeology* (Albarella, U., and Trentacoste, A., eds.). Oxford: Oxbow Press.

Luskin, M.B. (1998). Neuroblasts of the Postnatal Mammalian Forebrain: Their Phenotype and Fate. *Journal of Neurobiology, 36(2)*, 221–233.

Luzardo, O.P., Almeida, M., Zumbado, M., and Boada, L.D. (2011). Occurrence of Contamination by Controlled Substances in Euro Banknotes from the Spanish Archipelago of the Canary Islands. *Journal of Forensic Sciences, 56(6)*, 1588–1593.

Lytridis, C., Virk, G.S., Rebour, Y., and Kadar, E.E. (2001). Odor-Based Navigational Strategies for Mobile Agents. *Adaptive Behavior, 9(3–4)*, 171–187.

MacDonald, C.J., Carrow, S., Place, R., and Eichenbaum, H. (2013). Distinct Hippocampal Time Cell Sequences Represent Odor Memories in Immobilized Rats. *The Journal of Neuroscience, 33(36)*, 14607–14616.

Macherey-Nagel (2015). *Gas Chromatography Application Guide/Technical Handbook*. Posted at ftp://ftp .mn-net.com/english/Flyer_Catalogs/Chromatography/GC/GC%20Applis.pdf.

Macias, M.S. (2009). The Development of an Optimized System of Narcotic and Explosive Contraband Mimics for Calibration and Training of Biological Detectors (Ph.D. thesis). FIU Electronic Theses and Dissertations. Available at https://www.researchgate.net/profile/Michael_Macias/publication/48 189468_The_development_of_an_optimized_system_of_narcotic_and_explosive_contraband_mimics _for_calibration_and_training_of_biological_detectors/links/0046353c690c7de659000000.pdf.

Macias, M.S., Guerra-Diaz, P., Almirall, J.R., and Furton, K.G. (2010). Detection of Piperonal Emitted from Polymer Controlled Odor Mimic Permeation Systems Utilizing *Canis familiaris* and Solid Phase Microextraction-Ion Mobility Spectrometry. *Forensic Science International, 195*, 132–138.

Macias, M.S., Harper, R.J., and Furton, K.G. (2008). A Comparison of Real versus Simulated Contraband VOCs for Reliable Detector Dog Training Utilizing SPME-GC-MS. *American Laboratory, 40(1)*, 16–19.

MacKay, P., Smith, D.A., Long, R.A., and Parker, M. (2008). Scat Detection Dogs, pp. 183–222, in *Noninvasive Survey Methods for Carnivores* (Long, R.A., Mackay, P., Zielinski, W.J., and Ray, J.C., eds.). Washington, District of Columbia: Island Press.

Mackay-Sim, A., and Feron, F. (2013). Clinical Trials for the Treatment of Spinal Cord Injury: Not So Simple. *Methods in Molecular Biology, 1059*, 229–237.

Mackay-Sim, A., Feron, F., Cochrane, J., Bassingthwaighte, L., Bayliss, C., Davies, W., Fronek, P. et al. (2008). Autologous Olfactory Ensheathing Cell Transplantation in Human Paraplegia: A 3-Year Clinical Trial. *Brain, 131(9)*, 2376–2386.

Mackay-Sim, A., and St John, J.A. (2011). Olfactory Ensheathing Cells from the Nose: Clinical Application in Human Spinal Cord Injuries. *Experimental Neurology, 229*, 174–180.

MacLean, P.D., Flanigan, S., Flynn, J.P., Kim, C., and Stevens, J.R. (1955). Hippocampal Function: Tentative Correlations of Conditioning, EEG, Drug, and Radioautographic Studies. *The Yale Journal of Biology and Medicine, 28(3–4)*, 380.

MacNeilage, P.F., Rogers, L.J., and Vallortigara, G. (2009). Origins of the Left and Right Brain. *Scientific American, 301*, 60–67.

Madeiros, M.J., Eiben, J.A., Haines, W.P., Kaholoaa, R.L., King, C.B.A., Krushelnycky, P.D., Magnacca, K.N., Rubinoff, D., Starr, F., and Starr, K. (2013). The Importance of Insect Monitoring to Conservation Actions in Hawaii. *Proceedings of the Hawaiian Entomological Society, 45*, 149–166.

Maejima, M., Inoue-Murayama, M., Tonosaki, K., Matsuura, N., Kato, S., Saito, Y., Weiss, A., Murayama, Y., and Ito, S.I. (2007). Traits and Genotypes May Predict the Successful Training of Drug Detection Dogs. *Applied Animal Behaviour Science, 107(3)*, 287–298.

Mahoney, A.M. (2012). Mine Detection Rats: Effects of Repeated Extinction on Detection Rates. Western Michigan University. Available at http://scholarworks.wmich.edu/cgi/viewcontent.cgi?article=1067&context=dissertations.

Mahoney, A., Cox, C., Weetjens, B.J., Tewelde, T., Gilbert, T., Durgin, A., and Poling, A. (2013). Reinforcement for Operational Mine Detection Rates. *The Journal of ERW and Mine Action, 17(3)*, 58–62.

Malik, S.Z., Lewis, M., Isaacs, A., Haskins, M., Van Winkle, T., Vite, C.H., and Watson, D.J. (2012). Identification of the Rostral Migratory Stream in the Canine and Feline Brain. *PLoS/ONE, 7(5)*, e36016.

Malnic, B., Godfrey, P.A., and Buck, L.B. (2004). The Human Olfactory Receptor Gene Family. *Proceedings of the National Academy of Sciences USA, 101(8)*, 2584–2589.

Malnic, B., Hirono, J., Sato, T., and Buck, L.B. (1999). Combinatorial Receptor Codes for Odors. *Cell, 96*, 713–723.

Mandairon, N., Stack, C., Kiselycznyk, C., and Linster, C. (2006). Enrichment to Odors Improves Olfactory Discrimination in Adult Rats. *Behavioral Neuroscience, 120(1)*, 173–179.

Mangalam, M., and Singh, M. (2013). Sex and Physiological State Influence the Rate of Resource Acquisition and Monopolisation in Urban Free-Ranging Dogs, *Canis familiaris*. *Behaviour, 150*, 199–213.

Manhein, M.H. (1997). Decomposition Rates of Deliberate Burials: A Case Study of Preservation, pp. 469–481, in *Forensic Taphonomy: The Postmortem Fate of Human Remains* (Haglund, W.D., and Sorg, M.H., eds.). Boca Raton: Taylor & Francis/CRC Press.

Manor, R., and Saltz, D. (2004). The Impact of Free-Roaming Dogs on Gazelle Kid/Female Ratio in a Fragmented Area. *Biological Conservation, 119(2)*, 231–236.

Manrique, G., Vitta, A.C.R., Ferreira, R.A., Zani, C.L., Unelius, R., Lazzari, C.R., Diotaiuti, L., and Lorenzo, M.G. (2006). Chemical Communication in Chagas Disease Vectors: Source, Identity and Potential Function of Volatiles Released by the Metasternal and Brindley's Glands of *Triatoma infestans* Adults. *Journal of Chemical Ecology, 32(9)*, 2035–2052.

Manser, R. (2004). Screening for Lung Cancer: A Review. *Current Opinion in Pulmonary Medicine 10(4)*, 266–271.

Mar, F.M., Bonni, A., and Sousa, M.M. (2014). Cell Intrinsic Control of Axon Regeneration. *EMBO Reports, 15*, 254–263.

Marchlewska-Koj, A. (2011). Feromony Ssaków ich Rola w Fizjologii i Zachowaniu (Polish, translated: Pheromones in Mammals—Their Role in Physiology and Behavior). Polska Akademia Umiejętności. Rozprawy Wydziału Przyrodniczego, Vol 4. Cracow, Poland.

Marcus, D.A. (February 2012). Canine Responses to Impending Migraines. *Journal of Alternative and Complimentary Medicine, 18(2)*, 106–108.

Marcus, D.A., and Bhowmick, A. (2013). Survey of Migraine Sufferers with Dogs to Evaluate for Canine Migraine-Alerting Behaviors. *The Journal of Alternative and Complementary Medicine, 19(6)*, 501–508.

Marshall, L. (2007, July 16). Elephants "Learn" to Avoid Land Mines in War-Torn Angola. *National Geographic News*. Available at http://news.nationalgeographic.com/news/2007/07/070716-elephants-mines.html.

Marshall-Pescini, S., Passalacqua, C., Barnard, S., Valsecchi, P., and Prato-Previde, E. (2009). Agility and Search and Rescue Training Differently Affects Pet Dogs' Behaviour in Socio-Cognitive Tasks. *Behavioural Processes, 81(3)*, 416–422.

Marshall-Pescini, S., Valsecchi, P., Petak, I., Accorsi, P.A., and Prato Previde, E. (2008). Does Training Make You Smarter? The Effects of Training on Dogs' Performance (*Canis familiaris*) in a Problem Solving Task. *Behavioural Processes, 78(3)*, 449–454.

Marston, L.C., Bennett, P.C., and Coleman, G.J. (2004). What Happens to Shelter Dogs? An Analysis of Data for 1 Year from Three Australian Shelters. *Journal of Applied Animal Welfare Science, 7(1)*, 27–47.

Martin, A.J.P., and Synge, R.L.M. (1941). A New Form of Chromatogram Employing Two Liquid Phases. *Biochemical Journal, 35*, 1358–1368.

Martin, P.S., Tormey, B.R., Reda, K.M., and Nelsen, R.C. (2012). Dog versus Machine: Exploring the Utility of Cadaver Dogs and Ground-Penetrating Radar in Locating Human Burials at Historic Archeological Sites. Abstract of Poster given at 61st Annual Meeting of The Geological Society of America (April 1–2, 2012). Available at https://gsa.confex.com/gsa/2012SE/finalprogram/abstract_202398.htm.

Martinelli, D. (2010). *A Critical Companion to Zoosemiotics: People, Paths, Ideas* (Biosemiotics 5). Heidelberg: Springer Science & Business Media.

Martinez-Lozano Sinues, P., Kohler, M., and Zenobi, R. (2013). Human Breath Analysis May Support the Existence of Individual Metabolic Phenotypes. *PLoS/ONE 8(4)*, e59909.

Mathews, F., Swindells, M., Goodhead, R., August, T.A., Hardman, P., Linton, D.M., and Hosken, D.J. (2013). Effectiveness of Search Dogs Compared with Human Observers in Locating Bat Carcasses at Wind-Turbine Sites: A Blinded Randomized Trial. *Wildlife Society Bulletin, 37(1)*, 34–40.

Matsumura, K., Opiekun, M., Oka, H., Vachani, A., Albelda, S.M., Yamazaki, K., and Beauchamp, G.K. (2010). Urinary Volatile Compounds as Biomarkers for Lung Cancer: A Proof of Principle Study Using Odor Signatures in Mouse Models of Lung Cancer. *PLoS/ONE 5(1)*, e8819.

Matsunami, H., and Buck, L.B. (1997). A Multigene Family Encoding a Diverse Array of Putative Pheromone Receptors in Mammals. *Cell, 90(4)*, 775–784.

Matulionis, D.H. (1974). Ultrastructure of Olfactory Epithelia of Mice after Smoke Exposure. *Annals of Otology, Rhinology and Laryngology, 83(2)*, 192–201.

Matychenko, A.V. (2008). Otbor porod sobak dlya poiska narkotikov po ostrote obonyaniya [The selection of dog breeds for narcotics detection by olfactory acuity] (Doctoral dissertation from the Rossiyskyi Gosudarstvennyi Agrarnyi Zaochnyi Universitet imini K.A. Timiryazeva [Timiryazev Federal Agricultural Academy]). Available at DisserCat accession number 06.02.01, http://www.dissercat.com/content/otbor-porod-sobak-dlya-poiska-narkotikov-po-ostrote-obonyaniya.

Mazur, J.E. (2006). *Learning and Behavior.* Prentice Hall/Pearson Education. Upper Saddle River, NJ: Prentice Hall/Pearson Education.

McAlpine, J.D., and Ruby, M. (2004). Using CFD to Study Air Quality in Urban Microenvironments, pp. 1–24, in *Environmental Sciences and Environmental Computing, Vol. II* (Zannetti, P., ed.). Fremont, CA: The EnviroComp Institute.

McCartney, W. (1968). *Olfaction and Odours: An Osphresiological Essay.* New York: Springer-Verlag.

McCluskey, L.R., and Small, K. (2013). Quantitatively Evaluating the Effectiveness of a Canine Companion Training Curriculum. *Association of Pet Dog Trainers Chronicle of the Dog*; APDT e-learning Certificate Course Syllabus. Available at http://www.moongazer.com/training/docs/ChronicleOfTheDog0213.pdf.

McCulloch, M., Jezierski, T., Broffman, M., Hubbard, A., Turner, K., and Janecki, T. (2006). Diagnostic Accuracy of Canine Scent Detection in Early- and Late-Stage Lung and Breast Cancers. *Integrative Cancer Therapies, 5(6)*, 1–9.

McCulloch, M., Turner, K., and Broffman, M. (2012). Lung Cancer Detection by Canine Scent: Will There Be a Lab in the Lab? *European Respiratory Journal, 39(3)*, 511–512.

McEwen, D.P., Jenkins, P.M., and Martens, J.R. (2008). Olfactory Cilia: Our Direct Neuronal Connection to the External World. *Current Topics in Developmental Biology, 85*, 333–370.

McKern, T.W., and Stewart, T.D. (1957). *Skeletal Age Changes in Young American Males.* Quartermaster Research and Development Center, Environment Protection Research Division, Technical Report EP-45. Natick, MA: Headquarters Quartermaster Research and Development Command.

McKinley, S., and Young, R.J. (2003). The Efficacy of the Model-Rival Method when Compared with Operant Conditioning for Training Domestic Dogs to Perform a Retrieval-Selection Task. *Applied Animal Behaviour Science, 81(4)*, 357–365.

McMahon, S., Macpherson, K., and Roberts, W.A. (2010). Dogs Choose a Human Informant: Metacognition in Canines. *Behavioural Processes, 85(3)*, 293–298.

McManus, M., Schneeberger, N., Reardon, R., and Mason, G. (1989). *Gypsy Moth.* United States Department of Agriculture Forest Service Leaflet 162. Available at http://www.na.fs.fed.us/spfo/pubs/fidls/gypsymoth/gypsy.htm.

McPhail, L.T., Plunet, W.T., Das, P., and Ramer, M.S. (2005). The Astrocytic Barrier to Axonal Regeneration at the Dorsal Root Entry Zone Is Induced by Rhizotomy. *European Journal of Neuroscience, 21(1)*, 267–270.

McWhorter, J.C. (January/February 1920). The Bloodhound as a Witness. *American Law Review, 54*, 109–125.

Meadow, J.F., Altrichter, A.E., Bateman, A.C., Stenson, J., Brown, G.Z., Green, J.L., and Bohannan, B.J.M. (2015). Humans Differ in Their Personal Microbial Cloud. *PeerJ 3*, e31258.

Meagher, R.K., and Mason, G.J. (2012). Environmental Enrichment Reduces Signs of Boredom in Caged Mink. *PLoS/ONE, 7(11)*, e49180.

Medema, R.A. (1995). *Guide to Canine Interdiction: Maximizing the Impact of Drug Scent Evidence.* Springfield, VA: Drug Enforcement Administration, U.S. Department of Justice. Available at https://www.ncjrs.gov/pdffiles1/Photocopy/165673NCJRS.pdf.

Menashe, I., Abaffy, T., Hasin, Y., Goshen, S., Yahalom, V., Luetje, C.W., and Lancet, D. (2007). Genetic Elucidation of Human Hyperosmia to Isolvaleric Acid. *PLoS Biology, 207(5),* e284.

Menashe, I., Man, O., Lancet, D., and Gilad, Y. (2002). Population Differences in Haplotype Structure within a Human Olfactory Receptor Gene Cluster. *Human Molecular Genetics, 11(12),* 1381–1390.

Menzel, R., Manz, G., Menzel, R., and Greggers, U. (2001). Massed and Spaced Learning in Honeybees: The Role of CS, US, the Intertrial Interval, and the Test Interval. *Learning and Memory, 8(4),* 198–208.

Merlen, R.H.A. (1971). *De Canibus.* London: J.A. Allen & Co. Ltd.

Mesloh, C., Henych, M., and Wolf, R. (2002). Sniff Test: Utilization of the Law Enforcement Canine in the Seizure of Paper Currency. *Journal of Forensic Identification, 56(6),* 704–724.

Meunier, L.D. (2006). Selection, Acclimation, Training, and Preparation of Dogs for the Research Setting. *ILAR* [Institute for Laboratory Animal Research] *Journal, 47(4),* 326–347.

Meyer, I., and Ladewig, J. (2008). The Relationship between Number of Training Sessions per Week and Learning in Dogs. *Applied Animal Behaviour Science, 111(3–4),* 311–320.

Meyer, J., Anderson, B., and Carter, D.O. (2013). Seasonal Variation of Carcass Decomposition and Gravesoil Chemistry in a Cold (Dfa) Climate. *Journal of Forensic Sciences, 58(5),* 1175–1182.

Michell, E.B. (1900). *The Art and Practice of Hawking.* London: Methuen & Co.

Micol, T., and Jouventin, P. (2002). Eradication of Rats and Rabbits from Saint-Paul Island, French Southern Territories, pp. 233–239, in *Turning the Tide: The Eradication of Invasive Species* (Veitch, C.R. & Clout, M.N., eds.). Gland, Switzerland: IUCN. Occasional paper of the IUCN Species Survival Commission No. 27.

Micozzi, M.S. (1997). Frozen Environments and Soft Tissue Preservation, pp. 171–180, in *Forensic Taphonomy: The Postmortem Fate of Human Remains* (Haglund, W.D., and Sorg, M.H., eds.). Boca Raton: Taylor & Francis/CRC Press.

Miekisch, W., Schubert, J.K., and Noeldge-Schomburg, G.F. (2004). Diagnostic Potential of Breath Analysis—Focus on Volatile Organic Compounds. *Clinica Chimica Acta, 347(1–2),* 25–39.

Miekisch, W., Schubert, J.K., Vagts, D.A., and Geiger, K. (2001). Analysis of Volatile Disease Markers in Blood. *Clinical Chemistry, 47,* 1053–1060.

Migala, A.F., and Brown, S.E. (2012). Use of Human Remains Detection Dogs for Wide Area Search after Wildfire: A New Experience for Texas Task Force 1 Search and Rescue Resources. *Wildnerness Environmental Medicine, 23,* 337–342.

Miklosi, A. (2007). *Dog Behaviour, Evolution and Cognition.* Oxford: Oxford University Press.

Miklosi, A., Polgardi, R., Topal, J., and Csanyi, V. (1998). Use of Experimenter-Given Cues in Dogs. *Animal Cognition, 1(2),* 113–121.

Miklosi, A., Pongracz, P., Laketos, G., Topal, J., and Csanyi, V. (2005). A Comparative Study of the Use of Visual Communicative Signals in Interactions between Dogs (*Canis familiaris*) and Humans and Cats (*Felis catus*) and Humans. *Journal of Comparative Psychology, 119(2),* 179–186.

Miklosi, A., and Topal, J. (2013). What Does It Take to Become "Best Friends"? Evolutionary Changes in Canine Social Competence. *Trends in Cognitive Sciences, 17(6),* 1–8.

Milakovic, B., and Parker, K.L. (2011). Using Stable Isotopes to Define Diets of Wolves in Northern British Columbia, Canada. *Journal of Mammalogy, 92(2),* 295–304.

Miller, A.K., Hensman, M.C., Hensman, S., Schultz, K, Reid, P., Shore, M., Brown, J., Furton, K.G., and Lee, S. (2015). African Elephants (*Loxodonta Africana*) Can Detect TNT Using Olfaction: Implications for Biosensor Application. *Applied Animal Behavior Science, 171,* 177–183.

Miller, H.C., and Bender, C. (2012). The Breakfast Effect: Dogs (*Canis familiaris*) Search More Accurately When They Are Less Hungry. *Behavioural Processes, 91(3),* 313–317.

Millot, J.L. (1994). Olfactory and Visual Cues in the Interaction Systems between Dogs and Children. *Behavioural Processes, 33(1–2),* 177–188.

Millot, J.L., Filiatre, J.C., Eckerlin, A., Gagnon, A.C., and Montagner, H. (1987). Olfactory Cues in the Relations between Children and Their Pet Dogs. *Applied Animal Behaviour Science, 19(1),* 189–195.

Mills, D. (2005). Management of Noise Fears and Phobias in Pets. *In Practice, 27(5),* 248–255.

Mills, G.A., and Walker, V. (2001). Headspace Solid-Phase Microextraction Profiling of Volatile Compounds in Urine: Application to Megabolic Investigations. *Journal of Chromatography B, 753(2),* 259–268.

Miragall, F., and Dermietzel, R. (1992). Immunocytochemical Localization of Cell Adhesion Molecules in the Developing and Mature Olfactory System. *Microscopic Research and Technique, 23(2),* 157–172.

Miragall, F., Kadmon, G., Husmann, M., and Schachner, M. (1988). Expression of Cell Adhesion Molecules in the Olfactory System of the Adult Mouse: Presence of the Embryonic Form of N-CAM. *Developmental Biology, 129(2)*, 516–531.

Miragall, F., Kadmon, G., and Schachner, M. (1989). Expression of L1 and N-CAM Cell Adhesion Molecules during Development of the Mouse Olfactory System. *Developmental Biology, 135(2)*, 272–286.

Misiewicz, K. (2000). Influence of Nicotine on Performance of Scent Identification Dogs (in Polish). *Problemy Kryminalistyki, 229*, 38–40.

Mitchell, D.S. (1976). *Training and Employment of Land Mine and Booby Trap Detector Dogs. Volume II*. San Antonio, Texas: Southwest Research Institute, Department of Bioengineering.

Mitchell, R.W., and Edmonson, E. (1999). Functions of Repetitive Talk to Dogs during Play: Control, Conversation, or Planning? *Society & Animals, 7(1)*, 55–81.

Mithen, S. (1996). *The Prehistory of the Mind: A Search for the Origins of Art, Religion and Science*. London: Thames & Hudson.

Mochalski, P., Krapf, K., Ager, C., Wiesenhofer, H., Agapiou, A., Statheropoulos, M., Fuchs, D., Ellmerer, E., Buszewski, B., and Amann, A. (2012). Temporal Profiling of Human Urine VOCs and Its Potential Role under the Ruins of Collapsed Buildings. *Toxicology Mechanisms and Methods, 22*, 502–511.

Mombaerts, P. (1996). Targeting Olfaction. *Current Opinion in Neurobiology, 6(4)*, 481–486.

Mombaerts, P. (2001). How Smell Develops. *Nature Neuroscience, 4*, 1192–1198.

Mombaerts, P., Wang, F., Dulac, C., Chao, S.K., Nemes, A., Mendelsohn, M., Edmondson, J., and Axel, R. (1996). *Cell, 87*, 675–686.

Mondello, L., Tranchida, P.Q., Dugo, P., and Dugo, G. (2008). Comprehensive Two-Dimensional Gas Chromatography–Mass Spectrometry: A Review. *Mass Spectrometry Reviews, 27(2)*, 101–124.

Montague, M.J., Li, G., Gandolfi, B., Khan, R., Aken, B.L., Searle, S.M.J., Minx, P. et al. (2014). Comparative Analysis of the Domestic Cat Genome Reveals Genetic Signatures Underlying Feline Biology and Domestication. *Proceedings of the National Academy of Sciences USA, 111(48)*, 17230–17235.

Montuschi, P., Collins, J.V., Cabattoni, G., Lazzeri, N., Corradi, M., Kharitonov, S.A., and Barnes, P.A. (2000). Exhaled 8-Isoprostane as an In Vivo Biomarker of Lung Oxidative Stress in Patients with COPD and Health Smokers. *American Journal of Respiratory and Critical Care Medicine, 162(3, Pt. 1)*, 1175–1177.

Montuschi, P., Corradi, M., Ciabattoni, G., Nightingale, J., Kharitonov, S.A., and Barnes, P.J. (1999). Increased 8-Isoprostane, a Marker of Oxidative Stress, in Exhaled Condensate of Asthma Patients. *American Journal of Respiratory and Critical Care Medicine, 160(1)*, 216–220.

Moody, J.A., Clark, L.A., and Murphy, K.E. (2006). Working Dogs: History and Applications. *Cold Spring Harbor Monograph Archive, 44*, 1–18.

Moore, C.H., Pustovyy, O., Dennis, J.C., Moore, T., Morrison, E.E., and Vodyanoy, V.J. (2012). Olfactory Responses to Explosives Associated Odorants Are Enhanced by Zinc Nanoparticles. *Talanta, 88*, 730–733.

Moore, P., and Crimaldi, J. (2004). Odor Landscapes and Animal Behavior: Tracking Odor Plumes in Different Physical Worlds. *Journal of Marine Systems, 49(1)*, 55–64.

Mori, I., Goshima, F., Imai, Y., Kohsaka, S., Sugiyama, T., Yoshida, T., Yokochi, T., Nishiyama, Y., and Kimura, Y. (2002). Olfactory Receptor Neurons Prevent Dissemination of Neurovirulent Influenza A Virus into the Brain by Undergoing Virus-Induced Apoptosis. *Journal of General Virology, 83(Part 9)*, 2109–2116.

Mori, K., Takahashi, Y., Igarashi, K., and Nagayama, S. (2005). Odor Maps in the Dorsal and Lateral Surfaces of the Rat Olfactory Bulb. *Chemical Senses, 30(Suppl. 1)*, 103–104.

Morris, F.C. (2014). *Selected Developments under the Americans with Disabilities Act*. ALI CLE Course of Study Materials: Advanced Employment Law and Litigation 2014.

Morse, D., Duncan, J., and Stoutamire, J. (1983). *Handbook of Forensic Archaeology and Anthropology*. Tallahassee, FL: Rose Printing Co.

Moser, E., and McCulloch, M. (2010). Canine Scent Detection of Human Cancers: A Review. *Journal of Veterinary Behavior—Clinical Applications and Research, 5*, 145–152.

Most, K. (1928). Neue Versuche uber Spurfahigkeit. Das Problem der Spurenreinheit auf der menschlichen Spur im Lichte der zumal mit der Fahrtenbahn erzielten Versuchsergebnisse. *Der Hund, 18*, 31–35.

Most, K. (1954). 2014. *Training Dogs*. (J. Cleugh, Trans.). London: Popular Dogs Publishing Company. (Original work published 1910 as *Abrichtung des Hundes*).

Moulton, D.G. (1975). Factors Influencing Odor Sensitivity in the Dog: Final report prepared for Air Force Office of Scientific Research, Grant AFOSR-73-2425.

Muller, A. (1955). Quantitative Untersuchungen am Riechepithel des Hundes. *Zeitschrift für Zellforschung und Mikroskopische Anatomie, Bd. 41*, S. 335–350.

Muller, C.A., Schmitt, K., Barber, A.L.A., and Hubert, L. (2015). Dogs Can Discriminate Emotional Expressions of Human Faces. *Current Biology, 25(5)*, 601–605.

Munger, S.D., Leinders-Zufall, T., and Zufall, F. (2009). Subsystem Organization of the Mammalian Sense of Smell. *Annual Review of Physiology, 71*, 115–140.

Murdoch, J.D. (2004). Scent Marking Behaviour of the San Joaquin Kit Fox *(Vulpes macrotis mutica)* (MS thesis). University of Denver, Denver, Colorado.

Murphy, L.A., Gwaltney-Brant, S.M., Albretsen, J.C., and Wismer, T.A. (2003). Toxicologic Agents of Concern for Search-and-Rescue Dogs Responding to Urban Disasters. *Journal of the American Veterinary Medical Association, 222(3)*, 296–304.

Musshoff, F., and Madea, B. (2006). Review of Biologic Matrices (Urine, Blood, Hair) as Indicators of Recent or Ongoing Cannabis Use. *Therapeutic Drug Monitoring, 28(2)*, 155–163.

Mustard, J.A., Edgar, E.A., Mazade, R.E., Wu, C., Lillvis, J.L., and Wright, G.A. (2008). Acute Ethanol Ingestion Impairs Appetitive Olfactory Learning and Odor Discrimination in the Honey Bee. *Neurobiology of Learning and Memory, 90(4)*, 633–643.

Myers, L.J. (1985). Thresholds of the Dog for Detection of Inhaled Eugenol and Benzaldehyde Determined by Electroencephalographic and Behavioral Olfactometry. *American Journal of Veterinary Research, 46(11)*, 2409–2412.

Myers, L.J., Hanrahan, L.A., Swango, L.J., and Nusbaum, K.E. (1988a). Anosmia Associated with Canine Distemper. *American Journal of Veterinary Research, 49(8)*, 1295–1297.

Myers, L.J., Nash, R., and Elledge, H.S. (1984). Electro-Olfactography: A Technique with Potential for Diagnosis of Anosmia in the Dog. *American Journal of Veterinary Research, 45(11)*, 2296–2298.

Myers, L.J., Nusbaum, K.E., Swango, L.J., Hanrahan, L.N., and Sartin, E. (1988b). Dysfunction of Sense of Smell by Canine Parainfluenza Virus Infection in Dogs. *American Journal of Veterinary Research, 49(2)*, 188–190.

Nadi, N.S., Hirsch, J.D., and Margolis, F.L. (1980). Laminar Distribution of Putative Neurotransmitter Amino Acids and Ligand Binding Sites in the Dog's Olfactory Bulb. *Journal of Neurochemistry, 34*, 138–146.

Nafte, M. (2000). *Flesh and Bone: An Introduction to Forensic Anthropology.* Durham: Carolina Academic Press.

Nageris, B., Braverman, I., Hadar, T., Hansen, M.C., and Frenkiel, S. (2001). Effects of Passive Smoking on Odour Identification in Children. *Journal of Otolaryngology, 30(5)*, 263–265.

Nakajima, T., Sakaue, M., Kato, M., Saito, S., Ogawa, K., and Taniguchi, K. (1998). Immunohistochemical and Enzyme-Histochemical Study on the Accessory Olfactory Bulb of the Dog. *The Anatomical Record, 252*, 393–402.

Nakamura, T., and Gold, G.H. (1987). A Cyclic Nucleotide-Gated Conductance in Olfactory Receptor Cilia. *Nature, 325(6103)*, 442–444.

Nakash, J., Osem, Y., and Kehat, M. (2000). A Suggestion to Use Dogs for Detecting Red Palm Weevil *(Rhynchophorus ferrugineus)* Infestation in Date Palms in Israel. *Phytoparasitica, 28*, 153–155.

Natelson, S., Miletich, D.J., Seals, C.F., Visintine, D.J., and Albrecht, R.F. (1979). Clinical Biochemistry of Epilepsy. I. Nature of the Disease and a Review of the Chemical Findings in Epilepsy. *Clinical Chemistry, 25(6)*, 889–897.

Nawrocki, S.P., Pless, J.E., Hawley, D.A., and Wagner, S.A. (1997). Fluvial Transport of Human Crania, pp. 553–565, in *Forensic Taphonomy: The Postmortem Fate of Human Remains.* (Haglund, W.D., and Sorg, M.H., eds.). Boca Raton: Taylor & Francis/CRC Press.

Nazareth, L., Lineburg, K.E., Chuah, M.I., Tello Velasquez, J., Chehrehasa, F., St John, J.A., and Ekberg, J.A. (2015). Olfactory Ensheathing Cells Are the Main Phagocytic Cells that Remove Axon Debris during Early Development of the Olfactory System. *The Journal of Comparative Neurology, 523(3)*, 479–494.

Nedelec, S., Dubacq, C., and Trembleau, A. (2005). Morphological and Molecular Features of the Mammalian Olfactory Sensory Neuron Axons: What Makes These Axons So Special? *Journal of Neurocytology, 34(1–2)*, 49–64.

Negm, R.S., Verma, M., and Srivastava, S. (2002). The Promise of Biomarkers in Cancer Screening and Detection. *Trends in Molecular Medicine, 8(6)*, 288–293.

Negrusz, A., Perry, J.L., and Moore, C.M. (1998). Technical Note: Detection of Cocaine on Various Denominations of United States Currency. *Journal of Forensic Sciences, 43(3)*, 626–629.

Negus, V.E. (1958). *The Comparative Anatomy and Physiology of the Nose and Paranasal Sinuses.* Edinburgh: Livingstone.

Nevin, J.A., and Grace, R.C. (2000). Behavioral Momentum and the Law of Affect. *Behavioral and Brain Sciences, 23(1)*, 73–90.

Nevin, J.A., and Shahan, T.A. (2011). Behavioral Momentum Theory: Equations and Applications. *Journal of Applied Behavior Analysis, 44(4)*, 877–895.

Nguyen, H., and Kemp, C.C. (2008, October). Bio-Inspired Assistive Robotics: Service Dogs as a Model for Human-Robot Interaction and Mobile Manipulation, pp. 542–549, in *Biomedical Robotics and Biomechatronics*, 2008. BioRob 2008. 2nd IEEE RAS & EMBS International Conference.

Nguyen-Khoa, B.A., Goehring Jr., E.L., Vendiola, R.M., Pezzullo, J.C., and Jones, J.K. (2007). Epidemiologic Study of Smell Disturbance in 2 Medical Insurance Claims Populations. *Archives of Otolaryngology—Head and Neck Surgery, 133(8)*, 8, 748–757.

Nicholas, T.J., Cheng, Z., Ventura, M., Mealey, K., Eichler, E.E., and Akey, J.M. (2009). The Genomic Architecture of Segmental Duplications and Associated Number Variants in Dogs. *Genome Research, 19(3)*, 491–499.

Nieto-Sampedro, M. (2003). Central Nervous System Lesions That Can and Those That Cannot Be Repaired with the Help of Olfactory Bulb Ensheathing Cell Transplants. *Neurochemical Research, 28(11)*, 1659–1676.

Novak, B.J., Blake, D.R., Meinardi, S., Rowland, F.S., Pontello, A., Cooper, D.M., and Galassetti, P.R. (2007). Exhaled Methyl Nitrate as a Noninvasive Marker of Hyperglycemia in Type 1 Diabetes. *Proceedings of the National Academy of Sciences USA, 104(40)*, 15613–15618.

Nozawa, M., Kawahara, Y., and Nei, M. (2007). Genomic Drift and Copy Number Variation of Sensory Receptor Genes in Humans. *Proceedings of the National Academy of Sciences USA, 104(51)*, 20421–20426.

Nussear, K.E., Esque, T.C., Heaton, J.S., Cablk, M.E., Drake, K.K., Valentin, C., Yee, J.L., and Medica, P.A. (2008). Are Wildlife Detector Dogs or People Better at Finding Desert Tortoises (*Gopherus agassizii*)? *Herpetelogical Conservation and Biology, 3(1)*, 103–115.

Ochsenbein-Kölble, N., von Mering, R., Zimmermann, R., and Hummel, T. (2007). Changes in Olfactory Function in Pregnancy Postpartum. *International Journal of Gynecology and Obstetrics, 97(1)*, 10–14.

O'Connor, M.B., O'Connor, C., and Walsh, C.H. (2008). A Dog's Detection of Low Blood Sugar: A Case Report. *Irish Journal of Medical Science, 177(2)*, 155–157.

O'Connor, S., Park, K.J., and Goulson, D. (2012). Humans versus Dogs: A Comparison of Methods for the Detection of Bumble Bee Nests. *Journal of Apicultural Research, 51(2)*, 204–211.

Ogada, D.L., Keesing, F., and Virani, M.Z. (2011). Dropping Dead: Causes and Consequence of Vulture Population Declines Worldwide. *Annals of the New York Academy of Sciences, 1249(1)*, 57–71.

Olby, N. (2010). The Pathogenesis and Treatment of Acute Spinal Cord Injuries in Dogs. *Veterinary Clinics: Small Animal Practice, 40(5)*, 791–807.

Olender, T., Fuchs, T., Linhart, C., Shamir, R., Adams, M., Kalush, F., Khen, M., and Lancet, D. (2004). The Canine Olfactory Subgenome. *Genomics, 83*, 361–372.

Omar, M., Bock, P., Kreutzer, R., Ziege, S., Imbschweiler, I., Hansmann, F., Peck, C.-T., Baumgärtner, W., and Wewetzer, K. (2011). Defining the Morphological Phenotype: 2′,3′-Cyclic Nucleotide 3′-Phosphodiesterase (CNPase) Is a Novel Marker for *in situ* Detection of Canine but not Rate Olfactory Ensheathing Cells. *Cell and Tissue Research, 344(3)*, 391–405.

Omar, M., Hansmann, F., Kreutzer, R., Kreutzer, M., Brandes, G., and Wewetzer, K. (2013). Cell Type- and Isotype-Specific Expression and Regulation of β-tubulins in Primary Olfactory Ensheathing Cells and Schwann Cells in vitro. *Neurochemical Research, 38(5)*, 981–988.

Orlowski, T., Jezierski, T., and Bednarek, T. (1999). Efektywność wyszukiwania zapachu zwłok na lądzie przez psy specjalne, w zależności od różnych czynników (translated from Polish to English: Efficacy of Searching for Human Cadaver on Land by Specially Trained Dogs Depending on Factors). *Problemy Kryminalistyki (Problems of Forensics), 225*, 43–48.

Orlowski, T., Jezierski, T., and Bednarek, T. (2001). Efektywność wyszukiwania zapachu zwłok w wodzie przez psy specjalne, w zależności od różnych czynników (translated: Efficacy of Searching for Human Cadaver in Water by Specially Trained Dogs Depending on Different Factors). *Problemy Kryminalistyki (Problems of Forensics), 234*, 45–48.

Ortiz, R., and Liporace, J. (2005). "Seizure-Alert Dogs": Observations from an Inpatient Video/EEG Unit. *Epilepsy & Behavior, 6(4)*, 620–622.

Osterkamp, T. (2011). K9 Water Searches: Scent and Scent Transport Considerations. *Journal of Forensic Sciences, 56(4)*, 907–912.

Osthaus, B., Lea, S.E.G., and Slater, A.M. (2003). Training Influences Problem-Solving Abilities in Dogs (*Canis lupus familiaris*). *Proceedings of the Annual Meeting of British Society of Animal Science, 103*.

Osthaus, B., Lea, S.E.G., and Slater, A.M. (2005). Dogs (*Canis lupus familiaris*) Fail to Show Understanding of Means-End Connections in a String-Pulling Task. *Animal Cognition, 8(1)*, 37–47.

Otto, T., and Eichenbaum, H. (1992). Complementary Roles of Orbital Prefrontal Cortex and the Perirhinal-Entorhinal Cortices in and Odor-Guided Delayed Non-Matching to Sample Task. *Behavioural Neuroscience, 106*, 763–776.

Overall, K.L., and Arnold, S.E. (2007). Olfactory Neuron Biopsies in Dogs: A Feasibility Pilot Study. *Applied Animal Behaviour Science, 105(4)*, 351–357.

Oxley, J.C., and Waggoner, L.P. (2009). Chapter 3—Detection of Explosives by Dogs, pp. 27–40, in *Aspects of Explosives Detection* (Marshall, M., and Oxley, J.C. eds.) Amsterdam: Elsevier. Available at http://www.sciencedirect.com/science/article/pii/B9780123745330000039.

Oyler, J., Darwin, W.D., and Cone, E.J. (1996). Cocaine Contamination of United States Paper Currency. *Journal of Analytical Toxicology, 20(4)*, 213–216.

Ozaki, S., Toida, K., Suzuki, M., Nakamura, Y., Ohno, N., Ohashi, T., Nakayama, M. et al. (2010). Impaired Olfactory Function in Mice with Allergic Rhinitis. *Auris Nasus Larynx, 37(5)*, 575–583.

Pace, U., Hanski, E., Salomon, Y., and Lancet, D. (1985). Odorant-Sensitive Adenylate Cyclase May Mediate Olfactory Reception. *Nature, 316*, 255–258.

Palouzier-Paulignan, B., Lacroix, M., Aimé, P., Baly, C., Caillol, M., Congar, P., Julliard, A.K., Tucker, K., and Fadool, D.A. (2012). Olfaction under Metabolic Influences. *Chemical Senses, 37(9)*, 769–797.

Paolello, J.M., and Klales, A.R. (2014). Contemporary Cultural Alterations to Bone, pp. 181–199, in *Manual of Forensic Taphonomy* (Pokines, J.T., and Symes, S.A., eds.). Boca Raton: Taylor & Francis/CRC Press.

Parkes, J., Fisher, P., Robinson, S., and Aguirre-Munoz, A. (2014). Eradication of Feral Cats from Large Islands: An Assessment of the Effort Required for Success. *New Zealand Journal of Ecology, 38(2)*, 307–314.

Parmeter, J.E., Murray, D.W., and Hannum, D.W. (2000). *Guide for the Selection of Drug Detectors for Law Enforcement*. Albuquerque, New Mexico: Contraband Detection Technologies Department, Sandia National Laboratories.

Parnafes-Gazit, I. (2005). Variables Influencing Behavior and Detection Efficiency in Explosives Detector Dogs. Ph.D. thesis, Tel Aviv University.

Parthasarathy, V. (2011). *What Smells? Using Scentwork as Part of Behavior Modification Protocols. ACVB/AVSAB Scientific Program, St. Louis, Mo.*, p. 48. Portland, Oregon: Synergy Behavior Solutions.

Pasquini, C., Spurgeon, T., and Pasquini, S. (1995). *Anatomy of the Domestic Animals*. Pilot Point: Sudz.

Passe, D.H., and Walker, J.C. (1985). Odor Psychophysics in Vertebrates. *Neuroscience & Biobehavioral Reviews, 9(3)*, 431–467.

Paula, J., Leal, M.C., Silva, M.J., Mascarenhas, R., Costa, H., and Mascarenhas, M. (2011). Dogs as a Tool to Improve Bird-Strike Mortality Estimates at Wind Farms. *Journal of Nature Conservation, 19*, 202–208.

Pavlov, I.P. (1927). *Conditioned Reflexes: An Investigation of the Physiological Activity of the Cerebral Cortex*. London: Oxford University Press.

Pencea, V., Bingaman, K.D., Freedman, L.J., and Luskin, M.B. (2001). Neurogenesis in the Subventricular Zone and Rostral Migratory Stream of the Neonatal and Adult Primate Forebrain. *Experimental Neurology, 172(1)*, 1–16.

Peng, G., Hakim, M., Broza, Y.Y., Billan, S., Abdah-Bortnyak, R., Kuten, A., Tisch, U., and Haick, H. (2010). Detection of Lung, Breast, Colorectal and Prostate Cancers from Exhaled Breath Using an Array of Nanosensors. *British Journal of Cancer, 103(4)*, 542–551.

Penn, D., Schneider, G., White, K., Slev, P., and Potts, W. (1996). Influenza Infection Neutralizes the Attractiveness of Male Odor to Female Mice *(Mus musculus)*. *Ethology, 104*, 685–694.

Penn, D.J., Oberzauer, E., Grammer, K., Fischer, G., Soini, H.A., Wiesler, D., Novotny, M.V., Dixon, S.J., Xu, Y., and Brereton, R. (2007). Individual and Gender Fingerprints in Human Body Odour. *Journal of the Royal Society Interface, 4*, 331–340.

Perneger, T.V., Cullati, S., Schiesari, L., and Charvet-Berard, A. (2010). Impact of Information about Risks and Benefits of Cancer Screening on Intended Participation. *European Journal of Cancer, 46*, 2267–2274.

Perrault, K.A., Stuart, B.H., and Forbes, S.L. (2014). A Longitudinal Study of Decomposition Odour in Soil Using Sorbent Tubes and Solid Phase Microextraction. *Chromatography, 1(3)*, 120–140.

Peters, R., and Mech, D. (1978). Scent Marking in Wolves, pp. 133–147, in *Wolf and Man* (Hall, R.L., and Sharp, H.S., eds.). New York: Academic Press.

Peterson, R.O., and Ciucci, P. (2003). The Wolf as a Carnivore, pp. 104–130, in *Wolves: Behavior, Ecology and Conservation* (Mech, L.D., and Boitani, L., eds.). Chicago: University of Chicago Press.

Pfiester, M., Koehler, P.G., and Pereira, R.M. (2008). Ability of Bed Bug-Detecting Canines to Locate Live Bed Bugs and Viable Bed Bug Eggs. *Journal of Economic Entomology, 101*, 1389–1396.

Pfister, P., and Rodriguez, I. (2005). Olfactory Expression of a Single and Highly Variable V1r Pheromone Receptor-Like Gene in Fish Species. *Proceedings of the National Academy of Sciences USA, 102(15)*, 5489–5494.

Pfungst, O. (1911). *Clever Hans: (The Horse of Mr. Von Osten.): A Contribution to Experimental Animal and Human Psychology*. New York: Henry Holt & Co.

Phillips, A.A., and Willcock, M.M. (1999). *Xenophon and Arrian on Hunting with Hounds*. Warminster, Wilshire, UK: Aris & Phillips, Ltd.

Phillips, M. (1992). Breath Tests in Medicine. *Scientific American, 267(1)*, 74–79.

Phillips, M., Altorki, N., Austin, J.H., Cameron, R.B., Cataneo, R.N., Greenberg, J., Kloss, R. et al. (2007). Prediction of Lung Cancer Using Volatile Biomarkers in Breath. *Cancer Biomarkers, 3(2)*, 95–109.

Phillips, M., Boman, E., Osterman, H., Willhite, D., and Laska, M. (2011). Olfactory and Visuospatial Learning and Memory Performance in Two Strains of Alzheimer's Disease Model Mice—A Longitudinal Study. *PLoS/ONE, 6(5)*, e19567.

Phillips, M., Byrnes, R., Cataneo, N.R., Chaturvedi, A., Kaplan, P.D., Libardoni, M., Mehta, V. et al. (2013a). Detection of Volatile Biomarkers of Therapeutic Radiation in Breath. *Journal of Breath Research, 7(3)*, 1–8.

Phillips, M., Cataneo, R.N., Chaturvedi, A., Kaplan, P.D., Libardoni, M., Mundada, M., Patel, U., and Zhang, X. (2013b). Detection of an Extended Human Volatome with Two-Dimensional Gas Chromatography Time-of-Flight Mass Spectrometry. *PLoS/ONE, 8(9)*, e75274.

Phillips, M., Cataneo, R., Cummin, A., Gagliardi, A.J., Gleeson, K., Greenberg, J., Maxfield, R.A., and Rom, W.M. (2003a). Detection of Lung Cancer with Volatile Markers in the Breath. *Chest 123(6)*, 2115–2123.

Phillips, M., Cataneo, R.N., Ditkoff, B.A., Fisher, P., Greenberg, R., Gunawardena, R., Kwon, C.S., Rahbari-Oskoui, F., and Wong, C. (2003b). Volatile Markers of Breast Cancer in the Breath. *The Breast Journal, 9(3)*, 184–191.

Phillips, M., Gleeson, K., Hughes, J.M.B., Greenberg, J., Cataneo, R.N., Baker, L., and McVay, W.P. (1999). Volatile Organic Compounds in Breath as Markers of Lung Cancer: A Cross-Sectional Study. *The Lancet, 353*, 1930–1933.

Phillips, M., Sabas, M., and Geenberg, J. (1993). Increased Pentane and Carbon Disulfide in the Breath of Patients with Schizophrenia. *Journal of Clinical Pathology, 46(9)*, 861–864.

Phipps, T. (2014). Probable Cause on a Leash. *Boston University Public Interest Law Journal, 23*, 57.

Pickel, D.P., Manucy, G.P., Walker, D.B., Hall, S.B., and Walker, J.C. (2004). Evidence of Canine Olfactory Detection of Melanoma. *Applied Animal Behaviour Science, 89(1–2)*, 107–116.

Pickering, R.B., and Bachman, D.C. (1997). *The Use of Forensic Anthropology*. Boca Raton: Taylor & Francis/CRC Press.

Pierce, W.D., and Cheney, C.D. (2013). *Behavior Analysis and Learning*. New York: Psychology Press.

Pierman, S., Douhard, Q., Balthazart, J., Baum, M.J., and Bakker, J. (2006). Attraction Thresholds and Sex Discrimination of Urinary Odorants in Male and Female Aromatase Knockout (ArKO) Mice. *Hormones and Behavior, 49*, 96–104.

Pilley, J.W., and Reid, A.K. (2011). Border Collie Comprehends Object Names as Verbal Referents. *Behavioural Processes, 86(2)*, 184–195.

Pinc, L., Bartos, L., Reslova, A., and Kotrba, R. (2011). Dogs Discriminate Identical Twins. *PLoS/ONE, 6(6)*, e20704.

Pinikahana, J., and Dono, J. (2009). The Lived Experience of Initial Symptoms of and Factors Triggering Epileptic Seizures. *Epilepsy & Behavior, 15(4)*, 513–520.

Plonsky, M. (1998). Dr. P's Dog Training: Science and Dog Training. Posted online at http://www4.uwsp.edu/psych/dog/LA/DrP1.htm.

Pokines, J.T. (2014). Faunal Dispersal, Reconcentration, and Gnawing Damage to Bone in Terrestrial Environments, pp. 201–248, in *Manual of Forensic Taphonomy* (Pokines, J.T., and Symes, S.A., eds.). Boca Raton: Taylor & Francis/CRC Press.

Pokines, J.T., and Baker, J.E. (2014). Effects of Burial Environment on Osseous Remains, pp. 73–114, in *Manual of Forensic Taphonomy*. (Pokines, J.T., and Symes, S.A., eds.). Boca Raton: Taylor & Francis/CRC Press.

Pokines, J.T., and Symes, S.A. (2014). *Manual of Forensic Taphonomy*. Boca Raton: Taylor & Francis/CRC Press.

Poli, D., Goldoni, M., Corradi, M., Acampa, O., Carbognani, P., Internullo, E., Casalini, A., and Mutti, A. (2010). Determination of Aldehydes in Exhale Breath of Patients with Lung Cancer by Means of On-Fiber-Derivatisation SPME-GC/MS. *Journal of Chromatography B, 878(27)*, 2643–2651.

Poling, A., Weetjens, B., Cox, C., Beyene, N., and Sully, A. (2011a). Using Giant African Pouched Rats (*Cricetomys gambianus*) to Detect Landmines. *The Psychological Record, 60(4)*, 715–728.

Poling, A., Weetjens, B., Cox, C., Beyene, N.W., Bach, H., and Sully, A. (2011b). Using Trained Pouched Rats to Detect Land Mines: Another Victory for Operant Conditioning. *Journal of Applied Behavior Analysis, 44(2)*, 351–355.

Pongracz, P., Miklosi, A., Kubinyi, E., Topal, J., and Csanyi, V. (2003). Interaction between Individual Experience and Social Learning in Dogs. *Animal Behaviour, 65(3)*, 595–603.

Pongracz, P., Vida, V., Banhegyi, P., and Miklosi, A. (2008). How Does Dominance Rank Status Affect Individual and Social Learning Performance in the Dog (*Canis familiaris*)? *Animal Cognition, 11*, 75–82.

Pool, R. (1989). Crime and Chemical Analysis, *Science, 243(4898)*, 1554–1556.

Poole, C. (2012). *Gas Chromatography*. Amsterdam: Elsevier.

Porritt, F., Mansson, R., Berry, A., Cook, N., Sibbald, N., and Nicklin, S. (2014). Validation of a Short Odour Discrimination Test for Working Dogs. *Applied Animal Behaviour Science, 165*, 133–142.

Porritt, F., Shapiro, M., Waggoner, P., Mitchell, E., Thomson, T., Nicklin, S., and Kacelnik, A. (2015). Performance Decline by Search Dogs in Repetitive Tasks, and Mitigation Strategies. *Applied Animal Behaviour Science, 166*, 112–122.

Prada, P.P., Curran, A.M., and Furton, K.G. (2015). *Human Scent Evidence*. Boca Raton: Taylor & Francis/CRC Press.

Premack, D. (1959). Toward Empirical Behavior Laws: I. Positive Reinforcement. *Psychological Review, 66(4)*, 219–233.

Price, E.O. (2008). *Principles and Applications of Domestic Animal Behavior: An Introductory Text*. Oxfordshire, UK: CAB International.

Putnam, R.J. (1984). Facts from Faeces. *Mammal Review, 14(2)*, 79–97.

Quaranta, A., Siniscalchi, M., Albrizio, M., Volpe, S., Buonavoglia, C., and Vallortigara, G. (2008). Influence of Behavioural Lateralisation on Interleukin-2 and Interleukin-6 Gene Expression in Dogs Before and After Immunization with Rabies Vaccine. *Behavioural Brain Research, 186(2)*, 256–260.

Quaranta, A., Siniscalchi, M., Frate, A., and Vallortigara, G. (2004). Paw Preference in Dogs: Relations Between Lateralise Behaviour and Immunity. *Behavioural Brain Research, 153(2)*, 521–525.

Quaranta, A., Siniscalchi, M., and Vallortigara, G. (2007). Asymmetric Tail-Wagging Responses by Dogs to Different Emotive Stimuli. *Current Biology, 17(6)*, R199–R201.

Quignon, P., Giraud, M., Rimbault, M., Lavigne, P., Tacher, S., Morin, E., Retout, E. et al. (2005). The Dog and Rat Olfactory Receptor Repertoires. *Genome Biology, 6*, R83.

Quignon, P., Rimbault, M., Robin, S., and Galibert, F. (2012). Genetics of Canine Olfaction and Receptor Diversity. *Mammalian Genome 23(1–2)*, 132–143.

Quignon, P., Tacher, S., Rimbault, M., and Galibert, F. (2006). The Dog Olfactory and Vomeronasal Receptor Repertoires, pp. 221–231, in *The Dog and Its Genome*. Cold Spring Harbor Monograph Archive.

Radtke, C., and Wewetzer, K. (2009). Translating Basic Research into Clinical Practice or What Else Do We Have to Learn about Olfactory Ensheathing Cells? *Neuroscience Letters, 456(3)*, 133–136.

Raikos, N., Christopoulou, K., Theodoridis, G., Tsoukali, H., and Psaroulis, D. (2003). Determination of Amphetamines in Human Urine by Headspace Solid-Phase Microextraction and Gas Chromatography. *Journal of Chromatography B, 789*, 59–63.

Raisman, G. (1985). Specialized Neuroglial Arrangement May Explain the Capacity of Vomeronasal Axons to Reinnervate Central Neurons. *Neuroscience, 14(1)*, 237–254.

Ralls, K., Sharma, S., Smith, D.A., Bremner-Harrison, S., Cypher, B.L., and Maldonado, J.E. (2010). Changes in Kit Fox Defecation Patterns during the Reproductive Season: Implications for Noninvasive Surveys. *Journal of Wildlife Management, 74(7)*, 1457–1462.

Ralls, K., and Smith, D.A. (2004). Latrine Use by San Joaquin Kit Foxes (*Vulpes macrotis mutica*) and Coyotes (*Canis latrans*). *Western North American Naturalist, 64(4)*, 544–547.

Ramer, M.S., Priestley, J.V., and McMahon, S.B. (2000). Functional Regeneration of Sensory Axons into the Adult Spinal Cord. *Nature, 403*, 312–316.

Ramer, L.M., Richter, M.W., Roskams, A.J., Tetzlaff, W., and Ramer, M.S. (2004). Peripherally-Derived Olfactory Ensheathing Cells Do Not Promote Primary Afferent Regeneration Following Dorsal Root Injury. *Glia, 47(2)*, 189–206.

Ramgopal, S., Thome-Souze, S., Jackson, M., Kadish, N.E., Fernandez, I.S., Klehm, J., Bosl, W., Reinsberger, C., Schachter, S., and Loddenkemper, T. (2014). Seizure Detection, Seizure Prediction, and Closed-Loop Warning Systems in Epilepsy. *Epilepsy & Behavior, 37*, 291–307.

Ramnani, N., and Owen, A. (2004). Anterior Prefrontal Cortex: Insights into Function from Anatomy and Neuroimaging. *Nature Reviews Neuroscience, 5*, 184–194.

Ramon-Cueto, A., and Avila, J. (1998). Olfactory Ensheathing Glia: Properties and Function. Brain Ensheathing Glia: Properties and Function. *Brain Research Bulletin, 46(3)*, 175–187.

Ramon-Cueto, A., Perez, J., and Nieto-Sampedro, M. (1993). In Vitro Enfolding of Olfactory Neurites by p75 NGF Receptor Positive Ensheathing Cells from Adult Rat Olfactory Bulb. *European Journal of Neuroscience, 5(9)*, 1172–1180.

Ramon-Cueto, A., and Valverde, F. (1995). Olfactory Bulb Ensheathing Glia: A Unique Cell Type with Axonal Growth-Promoting Properties. *Glia, 14*, 163–173.

Range, F., Heucke, S.L., Gruber, C., Konz, A., Huber, L., and Viranyi, Z. (2009). The Effect of Ostensive Cues on Dogs' Performance in a Manipulative Social Learning Task. *Applied Animal Behaviour Science, 120(3)*, 170–178.

Ratcliffe, N.A., Mello, C.B., Garcia, E.S., Butt, T.M., and Azumbuja, P. (2011). Insect Natural Products and Processes: New Treatments for Human Disease. *Insect Biochemistry and Molecular Biology, 41(10)*, 747–769.

Ravenel, J.G., Costello, P., and Silvestri, G.A. (2008). Screening for Lung Cancer. *American Journal of Roentgenology, 190(3)*, 755–761.

Raymer, J., Wiesler, D., Novotny, M., Asa, C., Seal, U.S., and Mech, L.D. (1984). Volatile Constituents of Wolf (*Canis lupus*) Urine as Related to Gender and Season. *Experientia, 40(7)*, 707–709.

Raymer, J., Wiesler, D., Novotny, M., Asa, C., Seal, U.S., and Mech, L.D. (1986). Chemical Scent Constituents in Urine of Wolf (*Canis lupus*) and Their Dependence on Reproductive Hormones. *Journal of Chemical Ecology, 12(1)*, 297–314.

Read, E.A. (1908). A Contribution to the Knowledge of the Olfactory Apparatus in Dog, Cat and Man. *American Journal of Anatomy, 8(1)*, 17–42.

Rebmann, A., David, E., and Sorg, M.H. (2000). *Cadaver Dog Handbook: Forensic Training and Tactics for the Recovery of Human Remains.* Boca Raton: Taylor & Francis/CRC Press.

Reed, S.E., Bidlack, A.L., Hurt, A., and Getz, W.M. (2011). Detection Distance and Environmental Factors in Conservation Detection Dog Surveys. *Journal of Wildlife Management, 75(1)*, 243–251.

Reid, A., Dick, F., and Semple, S. (2004). Dog Noise as a Risk Factor for Hearing Loss among Police Dog Handlers. *Occupational Medicine, 54(8)*, 535–539.

Reiger, I. (1979). Scent Rubbing in Carnivores. *Carnivores, 2*, 17–25.

Reindl-Thompson, S.A., Shivik, J.A., Whitelaw, A., Hurt, A., and Higgins, K.F. (2006). Efficacy of Scent Dogs in Detecting Black-Footed Ferrets at a Reintroduction Site in South Dakota. *USDA National Wildlife Research Center—Staff Publications, Paper 438.*

Rennaker, R.L., Chen, C.-F.F., Ruyle, A.M., Sloan, A.M., and Wilson, D.A. (2007). Spatial and Temporal Distribution of Odorant-Evoked Activity in the Piriform Cortex. *The Journal of Neuroscience, 27(7)*, 1534–1542.

Richards, K.M., Cotton, S.J., and Sandeman, R.M. (2008). The Use of Detector Dogs in the Diagnosis of Nematode Infections in Sheep Feces. *Journal of Veterinary Behavior, 3*, 25–31.

Richards, N.L., Hall, S.W., Harrison, N.M., Gautam, L., Scott, K.S., Dowling, G., Zorilla, I., and Fajardo, I. (2014). Merging Wildlife and Environmental Monitoring Approaches with Forensic Principles: Application of Unconventional and Non-Invasive Sampling in Eco-Pharmacovigilance. *Journal of Forensic Research, 5(3)*, 1000228.

Riel, D.V., Verdijk, R., and Kuiken, T. (2014). The Olfactory Nerve: A Shortcut for Influenza and Other Viral Diseases into the Central Nervous System. *Journal of Pathology, 235(2)*, 277–287.

Riezzo, I., Neri, M., Rendine, M., Bellifemina, A., Cantatore, S., Fiore, C., and Turillazzi, E. (2014). Cadaver Dogs: Unscientific Myth or Reliable Biological Devices? *Forensic Science International, 244*, 213–221.

Rimbault, M., Robin, S., Vaysse, A., and Galibert, F. (2009). RNA Profiles of Rat Olfactory Epithelia: Individual and Age Related Variations. *BMC Genomics, 10*, 572.

Robb, J. (2002, June 4). Despite Training for Police Work, Dogs Are Still Dogs. *Omaha World Herald*, p. 1a.

Roberts, W.A. (2002). Are Animals Stuck in Time? *Psychological Bulletin, 128(3)*, 473.

Robin, S., Tacher, S., Rimbault, M., Vaysse, A., Dreano, S., Andre, C., Hitte, C., and Galibert, F. (2009). Genetic Diversity of Canine Olfactory Receptors. *BMC Genomics, 10*, 21.

Robinson, A.M., Conley, D.B., Shinners, M.J., and Kern, R.C. (2002). Apoptosis in the Aging Olfactory Epithelium. *The Laryngoscope, 112(8)*, 1431–1435.

Robinson, S.A., and Copson, G.R. (2014). Eradication of Cats (*Felis catus*) from Sub-Antarctic Macquarie Island. *Ecological Management & Restoration, 15(1)*, 34–40.

Rocznik, D., Sinn, D.L., Thomas, S., and Gosling, S.D. (2015). Criterion Analysis and Content Validity for Standardized Behavioral Tests in a Detector-Dog Breeding Program. *Journal of Forensic Science, 60(Suppl. 1)*, S213–S221.

Rodel, W., and Wolm, G. (1992). *Chromatografia Gazowa* (English: *Gas Chromatography*). Warsaw: Wydawnictwo Naukowe PWN.

Rodriguez, I. (2005). Remarkable Diversity of Mammalian Pheromone Receptor Repertoires. *Proceedings of the National Academy of Sciences USA, 102(19)*, 6639–6640.

Rodriguez, W.C. (1997). Decomposition of Buried and Submerged Bodies, pp. 459–467, in *Forensic Taphonomy: The Postmortem Fate of Human Remains* (Haglund, W.D., and Sorg, M.H., eds.). Boca Raton: Taylor & Francis/CRC Press.

Rodriguez, W.C., and Bass, W.M. (1983). Insect Activity and Its Relationship to Decay Rates of Human Cadavers in East Tennessee. *Journal of Forensic Sciences, 28*, 423–432.

Roet, K.C., Bossers, K., Franssen, E.H., Ruitenberg, M.J., and Verhaagen, J. (2011). A Meta-Analysis of Microarray-Based Gene Expression Studies of Olfactory Bulb-Derived Olfactory Ensheathing Cells. *Experimental Neurology, 229(1)*, 10–45.

Roet, K.C., Franssen, E.H., de Bree, F.M., Essing, A.H., Zijlstra, S.J., Fagoe, N.D., Eggink, H.M. et al. (2013). A Multilevel Screening Strategy Defines a Molecular Fingerprint of Progenerative Olfactory Ensheathing Cells and Identifies SCARB2, a Protein that Improves Regenerative Sprouting of Injured Spinal Axons. *The Journal of Neuroscience, 33(27)*, 11116–11135.

Roet, K.C., and Verhaagen, J. (2014). Understanding the Neural Repair-Promoting Properties of Olfactory Ensheathing Cells. *Experimental Neurology, 261*, 594–609.

Rogers, L.J., and Andrew, R.J. (2002). *Comparative Vertebrate Lateralization.* New York: Cambridge University Press.

Rogers, L.J., Andrew, R.J., and Burne, T.H. (1998). Light Exposure of the Embryo and Development of the Embryo and Development of Behavioral Lateralisation in Chicks, I: Olfactory Responses. *Behavioural Brain Research, 97(1–2)*, 195–200.

Rogers, L.J., Vallortigara, G., and Andrew, R.J. (2013). *Divided Brains. The Biology and Behaviour of Brain Asymmetries.* Cambridge: Cambridge University Press.

Rokni, D., Hemmelder, V., Kapoor, V., and Murthy, V.N. (2014). An Olfactory Cocktail Party: Figure-Ground Segregation of Odorants in Rodents. *Nature Neuroscience, 17(9)*, 1225–1232.

Rolak, R.T. (2000). Use of Police Dog Units in Narcotic Searches of Vehicles. School of Police Staff and Command, Eastern Michigan University. Posted online at http://www.emich.edu/cerns/downloads /papers/PoliceStaff/Unsorted/Use%20of%20Police%20Canine%20Units%20in%20Narcotic%20 Searches%20of%20Vehicles.pdf).

Rolland, R.M., Hamilton, P., Kraus, S.D., Davenport, B., Gillett, R., and Wasser, S.K. (2006). Fecal Sampling Using Detection Dogs to Study Reproduction and Health in North Atlantic Right Whales (*Eubalaena glacialis*). *Journal of Cetacean Research and Management, 8(2)*, 121–125.

Roloff, F., Ziege, S., Baumgartner, W., Wewetzer, K., and Bicker, G. (2013). Schwann Cell-Free Adult Canine Olfactory Ensheathing Cell Preparations from Olfactory Bulb and Mucosa Display Differential Migratory and Neurite Growth-Promoting Properties in vitro. *BMC Neuroscience, 14*, 141.

Rolon, M., Vega, M.C., Roman, F., Gomez, A., and Rojas de Arias, A. (2011). First Report of Colonies of Sylvatic *Triatoma infestans* (Hemiptera: Reduviidae) in the Paraguayan Chaco, Using a Trained Dog. *PLoS Neglected Tropical Diseases, 5*, e1026.

Rooney, N., Gaines, S., and Hiby, E. (2009). A Practitioner's Guide to Working Dog Welfare. *Journal of Veterinary Behavior: Clinical Applications and Research, 4(3)*, 127–134.

Rooney, N.J., and Bradshaw, J.W.S. (2004). Breed and Sex Differences in the Behavioural Attributes of Specialist Search Dogs—A Questionnaire Survey of Trainers and Handlers. *Applied Animal Behaviour Science, 86*, 123–135.

Rooney, N.J., Bradshaw, J.W., and Almey, H. (2004). Attributes of Specialist Search Dogs—A Questionnaire Survey of UK Dog Handlers and Trainers. *Journal of Forensic Sciences, 49(2)*, 300–306.

Rooney, N.J., Bradshaw, J.W.S., and Gaines, S.A. (2005). UK Detection Dog Rearing Project: An Investigation into Factors Affecting Search Ability. Abstract from 6th International Seminar on Detection Dogs. Kincardine, Scotland, UK.

Rooney, N.J., Gaines, S.A., Bradshaw, J.W.S., and Penman, S. (2007a). Validation of a Method for Assessing the Ability of Trainee Specialist Search Dogs. *Applied Animal Behaviour Science, 103*, 90–104.

Rooney, N.J., Gaines, S.A., and Bradshaw, J.W. (2007b). Behavioural and Glucocorticoid Responses of Dogs (*Canis familiaris*) to Kennelling: Investigating Mitigation of Stress by Prior Habituation. *Physiology & Behavior, 92(5)*, 847–854.

Rooney, N.J., Morant, S., and Guest, C. (2013). Investigation into the Value of Trained Glycaemia Alert Dogs to Clients with Type 1 Diabetes. *PLoS/ONE 8(8)*, 369921.

Rosier, E., Loix, S., Develter, W., Van de Voorde, W., Tygat, J., and Cuypers, E. (2015). The Search for a Volatile Human Specific Marker in the Decomposition Process. *PLoS/ONE, 10(9)*, e0137341.

Ross, A.H., and Cunningham, S.L. (2011). Time since Death and Bone Weathering in a Tropical Environment. *Forensic Science International, 204*, 126–133.

Rothman, R.J., and Mech, L.D. (1979). Scent-Marking in Lone Wolves and Newly Formed Pairs. *Animal Behaviour, 27(Part 3)*, 750–760.

Rowe, T.B., Macrini, T.E., and Luo, Z.X. (2011). Fossil Evidence on Origin of the Mammalian Brain. *Science, 332(6032)*, 955–957.

Rowland, J.W., Hawryluk, G.W., Kwon, B., and Fehlings, M.G. (2008). Current Status of Acute Spinal Cord Injury Pathophysiology and Emerging Therapies: Promise on the Horizon. *Neurosurgical Focus, 25(5)*, E2.

Royet, J.P., and Plailly, J. (2004). Lateralization of Olfactory Processes. *Chemical Senses, 29(8)*, 731–745.

Rubio, M.P., Munoz-Quiles, C., and Ramon-Cueto, A. (2008). Adult Olfactory Bulbs from Primates Provide Reliable Ensheathing Glia for Cell Therapy. *Glia, 56(5)*, 539–551.

Rudd, P.A., Bastien-Hamel, L.E., and von Messling, V. (2010). Acute Canine Distemper Encephalitis Is Associated with Rapid Neuronal Loss and Local Immune Activation. *Journal of General Virology, 91(4)*, 980–989.

Rudd, P.A., Cattaneo, R., and von Messling, V. (2006). Canine Distemper Virus Uses Both the Anterograde and the Hematogenous Pathway for Neuroinvasion. *Journal of Virology, 80(19)*, 9361–9370.

Rudnicka, J., Kowalkowski, T., Ligor, T., and Buszewski, B. (2011). Determination of Volatile Organic Compounds as Biomarkers of Lung Cancer by SPME-GC-TOF/MS and Chemometrics. *Journal of Chromatography, B: Analytical Technology in the Biomedical and Life Sciences, 879(30)*, 3360–3366.

Rudnicka, J., Walczak, M., Kowalkowski, T., Jezierski, T., and Buszewski, B. (2014). Determination of Volatile Organic Compounds as Potential Markers of Lung Cancer by Gas Chromatography—Mass Spectrometry versus Trained Dogs. *Sensors and Actuators B, 202*, 615–621.

Rudy, L. (1995). Service Dogs for People with Seizure Disorders. *Alert: National Dog Center Newsletter, 6(4)*.

Ruell, E.W., Riley, S.P.D., Douglas, M.R., Pollinger, J.P., and Crooks, K.R. (2009). Estimating Bobcat Population Sizes and Densities in a Fragmented Urban Landscape Using Noninvasive Capture-Recapture Sampling. *Journal of Mammology, 90(1)*, 129–135.

Ruffell, A., Pringle, J.K., and Forbes, S. (2014). Search Protocols for Hidden Forensic Objects beneath Floors and Within Walls. *Forensic Science International, 237*, 137–145.

Ryba, N.J., and Tirindelli, R. (1997). A New Multigene Family of Putative Pheromone Receptors. *Neuron, 19(2)*, 371–379.

Ryon, J., Fentress, J.C., Harrington, F.H., and Bragdon, S. (1986). Scent Rubbing in Wolves (*Canis lupus*): The Effect of Novelty. *Canadian Journal of Zoology, 64(3)*, 573–577.

Sahayaraj, K. (2014). Reduviids and Their Merits in Biological Control, pp. 195–214, in *Basic and Applied Aspects of Biopesticides* (Sahayaraj, K., ed.). India: Springer.

Sakamoto, M., Ieki, N., Miyoshi, G., Mochimaru, D., Miyachi, H., Imura, T., Yamaguchi, M. et al. (2014). Continuous Postnatal Neurogenesis Contributes to Formation of the Olfactory Bulb Neural Circuits and Flexible Olfactory Associative Learning. *The Journal of Neuroscience, 34(17)*, 5788–5799.

Salazar, I., Barber, P.C., and Cifuentes, J.M. (1992). Anatomical and Immunohistological Demonstration of the Primary Neural Connections of the Vomeronasal Organ in the Dog. *The Anatomical Record, 233(2)*, 309–313.

Salazar, I., Cifuentes, J.M., and Sánchez-Quinteiro, P. (2013). Morphological and Immunohistochemical Features of the Vomeronasal System in Dogs. *Anatomical Record, 296(1)*, 146–155.

Sallam, M.N. (1999). Insect Damage: Damage on Post-Harvest. *In* Insect Damage: Post-Harvest Operations (Mejia, D., ed.). INPho—Post-Harvest Compendium, Food and Agriculture Organization of the United Nations. 37 pp. Available at http://www.fao.org/fileadmin/user_upload/inpho/docs/Post_Harvest _Compendium_-_Pests-Insects.pdf.

Salvin, H.E., McGrath, C., McGreevy, P.D., and Valenzuela, M.J. (2012). Development of a Novel Paradigm for the Measurement of Olfactory Discrimination in Dogs (*Canis familiaris*): A Pilot Study. *Journal of Veterinary Behavior: Clinical Applications and Research, 7(1)*, 3–10.

Sanchez, C.L., Prada, P.A., and Furton, K.G. (2015). On the Importance of Training Aids and the Definition of an Explosive Odor Signature: Commentary on Kranz et al. *Forensic Science International, 251*, e18–e19.

Sanchez, D.M., Krausman, P.R., Livingston, T.R., and Gipson, P.S. (2004). Persistence of Carnivore Scat in the Sonoran Desert. *Wildlife Society Bulletin, 32(2)*, 366–372.

Sanders, C.R. (2006). "The Dog You Deserve" Ambivalence in the K-9 Officer/Patrol Dog Relationship. *Journal of Contemporary Ethnography, 35(2)*, 148–172.

Santos-Benito, F.F., and Ramon-Cueto, A. (2003). Olfactory Ensheathing Glia Transplantation: A Therapy to Promote Repair in the Mammalian Central Nervous System. *Anatomical Record Part B: The New Anatomist, 271B(1)*, 77–85.

Sargisson, R.J., and McLean, I.G. (2010). The Effect of Reinforcement Rate Variations on Hits and False Alarms in Remote Explosive Scent Tracing with Dogs. *The Journal of ERW and Mine Action, 14(3)*. Available at http://www.jmu.edu/cisr/journal/14.3/r_d/sargisson/sargisson.shtml.

Sargolini, F., Fyhn, M., Hafting, T., McNaughton, B.L., Witter, M.P., Moser, M.B., and Moser, E.I. (2006). Conjunctive Representation of Position, Direction, and Velocity in Entorhinal Cortex. *Science, 312(5774)*, 758–762.

Sato, M., Kodama, N., Sasaki, T., and Ohta, M. (1996). Olfactory Evoked Potentials: Experimental and Clinical Studies. *Journal of Neurosurgery, 85(6)*, 1122–1126.

Savic, I. (2005). Brain Imaging Studies of the Functional Organization of Human Olfaction. *Chemical Senses, 30(Suppl. 1)*, i222–i223.

Savidge, J.A., Stanford, J.W., Reed, R.N., Haddock, G.R., and Yackel Adams, A.A. (2011). Canine Detection of Free-Ranging Brown Treesnakes on Guam. *New Zealand Journal of Ecology, 35,* 174–181.

Schilder, M.B.H., and van der Borg, J.A.M. (2004). Training Dogs with Help of the Shock Collar: Short and Long Term Behavioural Effects. *Applied Animal Behaviour Science, 85(3–4),* 319–334.

Schlyter, F., and Johansson, A. (2010). Detection Dogs Recognize Pheromone from Spruce Bark Beetle and Follows It to Source: A New Tool from Chemical Ecology to Forest Protection. International Society of Chemical Ecology 26th Annual Meeting, Tours, France (31 July–4 August 2010).

Schofield, P.W., Moore, T.M., and Gardner, A. (2014). Traumatic Brain Injury and Olfaction: A Systematic Review. *Frontiers in Neurology, 5,* 5.

Schoon, G.A.A. (1996). Scent Identification Lineups by Dogs *(Canis familiaris)*: Experimental Design and Forensic Application. *Applied Animal Behaviour Science, 49,* 257–267.

Schoon, G.A.A. (1997a). The Performance of Dogs in Identifying Humans by Scent (Ph.D. dissertation). University of Leiden, The Netherlands.

Schoon, G.A.A. (1997b). Scent Identification by Dogs *(Canis familiaris)*: A New Experimental Design. *Behaviour, 134,* 531–550.

Schoon, G.A.A. (1998). A First Assessment of the Reliability of an Improved Scent Identification Line-Up. *Journal of Forensic Sciences, 43(1),* 70–75.

Schoon, G.A.A. (1999). Scent Perception. Theory and Application for Training Search Dogs. Typewritten Syllabus.

Schoon, G.A.A. (2002). Influence of Experimental Setup Parameters of Scent Identification Lineups on Their Reliability (in Polish). *Problemy Kryminalistyki, 226,* 43–49.

Schoon, G.A.A., and De Bruin, J.C. (1994). The Ability of Dogs to Recognize and Cross-Match Human Odours. *Forensic Science International, 69,* 111–118.

Schoon, G.A.A., Fjellanger, R., Kjeldsen, M., and Goss, K.-U. (2014). Using Dogs to Detect Hidden Corrosion. *Applied Animal Behaviour Science, 153,* 43–52.

Schoon, A., Gotz, S., Heuven, M., Vogel, M., and Karst, U. (2006). Training and Testing Explosive Detection Dogs in Detecting Tracetone Triperoxide. *Forensic Science Communications, 8(4).* Washington, DC: FBI.

Schoon, G.A.A., and Haak, R. (2002). *K-9 Suspect Discrimination: Training and Practicing Scent Identification Line-Ups.* Calgary, Alberta, Canada: Detselig Enterprises.

Schoon, G.A.A., and Massop A.R.L. (1995). History of Scent Identification Line-Ups by Tracker Dogs in the Netherlands (in Dutch). *Delikt en Delikwent, 25(9),* 964–976.

Schott, M., Klein, B., and Vilcinskas, A. (2015). Detection of Illicit Drugs by Trained Honeybees *(Apis mellifera)*. *PLoS/ONE, 10(6),* e0128528.

Schriever, V.A., Reither, N., Gerber, J., Iannilli, E., and Hummel, T. (2013). Olfactory Bulb Volume in Smokers. *Experimental Brain Research, 225(2),* 153–157.

Schubert, C.R., Cruickshanks, K.J., Klein, B.E.K., Klein, R., and Nondahl, D.M. (2011). Olfactory Impairment in Older Adults: Five-Year Incidence and Risk Factors. *Laryngoscope, 121(4),* 873–878.

Schultz, W., Dayan, P., and Montague, P.R. (1997). A Neural Substrate of Prediction and Reward. *Science, 275(5306),* 1593–1599.

Schwob, J.E. (2002). Neural Regeneration and the Peripheral Olfactory System. *The Anatomical Record, 269(1),* 33–49.

Scientific Working Group on Dog and Orthogonal detector Guidelines (SWGDOG). SWGDOG SC3 (2006). Selection of Serviceable Dogs.

Scientific Working Group on Dog and Orthogonal detector Guidelines (SWGDOG). SWGDOG SC5 (2006). Selection of Handlers.

Scientific Working Group on Dog and Orthogonal detector Guidelines (SWGDOG). SWGDOG SC8 (2007). Substance Detector Dogs, Explosives.

Scientific Working Group on Dog and Orthogonal detector Guidelines (SWGDOG). SWGDOG SC2 (2009). General Guidelines.

Scientific Working Group on Dog and Orthogonal detector Guidelines (SWGDOG). SWGDOG SC7 (2010). Research and Technology.

Scientific Working Group on Dog and Orthogonal detector Guidelines (SWGDOG). SWGDOG SC1 (2011). Terminology.

Serpell, J.A. (2003). Anthropomorphism and Anthropomorphic Selection—Beyond the "Cute Response." *Society & Animals, 11(1),* 83–100.

Settle, R.H., Sommerville, B.A., McCormick, J., and Broom, D.M. (1994). Human Scent Matching Using Specially Trained Dogs. *Animal Behaviour, 48,* 1443–1448.

Shane, S. (October 29, 2002). FBI's Use of Bloodhounds in Anthrax Probe Disputed, 1A. *The Baltimore Sun.*

Shapira, I., Buchanan, F., and Brunton, D. (2011). Detection of Cage and Free-Ranging Norway Rats *Rattus norvegicus* by a Rodent Sniffing Dog on Browns Island, Auckland, New Zealand. *Conservation Evidence, 8*, 38–42.

Sharon, D., Gilad, Y., Glusman, G., Khen, M., Lancet, D., and Kalush, F. (2000). Identification and Characterization of Coding Single-Nucleotide Polymorphisms within a Human Olfactory Receptor Gene Cluster. *Gene, 260(1–2)*, 87–94.

Sharon, D., Glusman, G., Pilpel, Y., Horn-Saban, S., and Lancet, D. (1998). Genome Dynamics, Evolution, and Protein Modeling in the Olfactory Receptor Gene Superfamily. *Annals of the New York Academy of Sciences, 855*, 182–193.

Shen, Y., and Zelen, M. (2001). Screening Sensitivity and Sojourn Time from Breast Cancer Early Detection Clinical Trials: Mammograms and Physical Examinations. *Journal of Clinical Oncology, 19(15)*, 3490–3499.

Shepherd, G. (1994). Discrimination of Molecular Signals by the Olfactory Receptor Neuron. *Neuron, 13*, 771–790.

Shepherd, G.M., Greer, C.A., Mazzarello, P., and Sassoè-Pognetto, M. (2011). The First Images of Nerve Cells: Golgi on the Olfactory Bulb 1875. *Brain Research Reviews, 66(1–2)*, 92–105.

Sherman, R.A., Hall, M.J.R., and Thomas, S. (2000). Medicinal Maggots: An Ancient Remedy for Some Contemporary Afflictions. *Annual Review of Entomology, 45*, 55–81.

Shipley, M.T., and Ennis, M. (1996). Functional Organization of Olfactory System. *Journal of Neurobiology, 30(1)*, 123–176.

Shipman, P. (1981). *Life History of a Fossil: An Introduction to Taphonomy and Paleoecology*. Cambridge, Massachusetts: Harvard University Press.

Shipman, P. (2015). *The Invaders: How Humans and Their Dogs Drove Neanderthals to Extinction*. Cambridge, Massachusetts: Belknap Press of Harvard University Press.

Shirasu, M., and Touhara, K. (2011). The Scent of Disease: Volatile Organic Compounds of the Human Body Related to Disease and Disorder. *The Journal of Biochemistry, 150(3)*, 257–266.

Shoebotham, L.A. (2009). Has the Fourth Amendment Gone to the Dogs?: Unreasonable Expansion of Canine Sniff Doctrine to Include Sniffs of the Home. *Oregon Law Review, 88*, 829.

Shoebotham, L.A. (2012). Off the Fourth Amendment Leash?: Law Enforcement Incentives to Use Unreliable Drug-Detection Dogs, *Loyola Journal of Public Interest Law, 14*, 251.

Shwiff, S.A., Gebhardt, K., Kirkpatrick, K.N., and Shwiff, S.S. (2010). Potential Economic Damage from Introduction of Brown Tree Snakes, *Boiga irregularis* (Reptilia: Colubridae), to the Islands of Hawai'i. *Pacific Science, 64(1)*, 1–10.

Simsek, G., Bayar Muluk, N., Arikan, O.K., Ozcan Dag, Z., Simsek, Y., and Dag, E. (2014). Marked Changes in Olfactory Perception during Early Pregnancy: A Prospective Case-Control Study. *European Archives of Oto-Rhino-Laryngology, 272(3)*, 627–630.

Siniscalchi, M., and Quaranta, A. (2014). Wagging to the Right or to the Left: Lateralisation and What It Tells of the Dog's Social Brain, pp. 373–393, in *The Social Dog: Behavior and Cognition* (Kaminski, J., and Marshall-Pescini, S., eds.). Boston: Academic Press.

Siniscalchi, M., Franchini, D., Pepe, A.M., Sasso, R., Dimatteo, S., Vallortigara, G., and Quaranta, A. (2011a). Volumetric Assessment of Cerebral Asymmetries in Dogs. *Laterality, 16(5)*, 528–536.

Siniscalchi, M., Lusito, R., Sasso, R., and Quaranta, A. (2012). Are Temporal Features Crucial Acoustic Cues in Dog Vocal Recognition? *Animal Cognition, 15(5)*, 815–821.

Siniscalchi, M., Lusito, R., Vallortigara, G., and Quaranta, A. (2013). Seeing Left- or Right-Asymmetric Tail Wagging Produces Different Emotional Responses in Dogs. *Current Biology, 23(22)*, 2279–2282.

Siniscalchi, M., Padalino, B., Aube, L., and Quaranta, A. (2015). Right Nostril Use During Sniffing at Arousing Stimuli Produces Higher Cardiac Activity in Jumper Horses. *Laterality, 20(4)*, 483–500.

Siniscalchi, M., Quaranta, A., and Rogers, L. J. (2008). Hemispheric Specialization in Dogs for Processing Different Acoustic Stimuli. *PloS/ONE, 3(10)*, e3349.

Siniscalchi, M., Sasso, R., Pepe, A.M., Dimatteo, S., Vallortigara, G., and Quaranta, A. (2011b). Sniffing with Right Nostril: Lateralization of Response to Odour Stimuli by Dogs. *Animal Behaviour, 82(2)*, 399–404.

Siniscalchi, M., Sasso, R., Pepe, A.M., Vallortigara, G., and Quaranta, A. (2010). Dogs Turn Left to Emotional Stimuli. *Behavioural Brain Research, 208(2)*, 516–521.

Sinn, D.L., Gosling, S.D., and Hilliard, S. (2010). Personality and Performance in Military Working Dogs: Reliability and Predictive Validity of Behavioral Tests. *Applied Animal Behaviour Science, 127*, 51–65.

Skender, L., Karacic, V., Brcic, I., and Bagaric, A. (2002). Quantitative Determination of Amphetamines, Cocaine, and Opiates in Human Hair by Gas Chromatography/Mass Spectrometry. *Forensic Science International, 125(2)*, 120–126.

Skinner, A.P.C., Pachnicke, S., Lakatos, A., Franklin, R.J.M., and Jeffery, N.D. (2005). Nasal and Frontal Sinus Mucosa of the Adult Dog Contain Numerous Olfactory Sensory Neurons and Ensheathing Glia. *Research in Veterinary Science, 78(1)*, 9–15.

Skinner, B.F. (1953). *Science and Human Behavior*. New York: Simon and Schuster.

Skinner, B.F. (1956). A Case History in Scientific Method. *American Psychologist, 11(5)*, 221–233.

Skinner, B.F. (1974). *About Behaviorism*. New York: Knopf Doubleday.

Skinner, M., and Lazenby, R.A. (1983). *Found! Human Remains: A Field Manual for the Recovery of the Recent Human Skeleton*. Burnaby, B.C., Canada: Archaeology Press Simon Fraser University.

Sklar, P.B., Anholt, R.R., and Snyder, S.H. (1986). The Odorant-Sensitive Adenylate Cyclase of Olfactory Receptor Cells. Differential Stimulation by Distinct Classes of Odorants. *Journal of Biological Chemistry, 261(33)*, 15538–15543.

Skoog, D.A., Holler, F.J., and Crouch, S.R. (6th ed., 2006). *Principles of Instrumental Analysis*. Boston: Cengage Learning.

Slabbert, J.M., and Odendaal, J.S.J. (1999). Early Prediction of Adult Police Dog Efficiency—A Longitudinal Study. *Applied Animal Behaviour Science, 64(4)*, 269–288.

Slabbert, J.M., and Rasa, O.A.E. (1997). Observational Learning of an Acquired Maternal Behaviour Pattern by Working Dog Pups: An Alternative Training Method? *Applied Animal Behaviour Science, 53(4)*, 309–316.

Sleeman, R., Burton, F., Carter, J., Roberts, D., and Hulmston, P. (2000). Drugs on Money. *Analytical Chemistry, 72(11)*, 397A–403A.

Slensky, K., Drobatz, K., Downend, A., and Otto, C. (2004). Deployment Morbidity Among Search and Rescue Dogs from 9/11. *Journal of the American Veterinary Medical Association, 225(6)*, 868–873.

Slotnick, B., Cockerham, R., and Pickett, E. (2004). Olfaction in Olfactory Bulbectomized Rats. *The Journal of Neuroscience, 24(41)*, 9195–9200.

Smith, C.H. *Dogs, Vol. I* (1839), in the Naturalists Library, Mammalia. London: Hengry G. Bohn.

Smith, D.A., Ralls, K., Hurt, A., Adams, B., Parker, M., Davenport, B., Smith, M.C., and Maldonado, J.E. (2003). Detection and Accuracy Rates of Dogs Trained to Find Scats of San Joaquin Kit Foxes (*Vulpes macrotis mutica*). *Animal Conservation, 6*, 339–346.

Smith, D.A., Ralls, K., Cypher, B.L., Clark, Jr., H.O., Kelly, P.A., Williams, D.F., and Maldonado, J.E. (2006). Relative Abundance of Endangered San Joaquin Kit Foxes (*Vulpes macrotis mutica*) Based on Scat-Detection Dog Surveys. *The Southwestern Naturalist, 51(2)*, 210–219.

Smith, K., and Sines, J.O. (1960). Demonstration of a Peculiar Odor in the Sweat of Schizophrenic Patients. *AMA Archives of General Psychiatry, 2(2)*, 184–188.

Smith, M.C., Coleman, S.R., and Gormezano, I. (1969). Classical Conditioning of the Rabbit's Nictitating Membrane Response at Backward, Simultaneous, and Forward CS–US Intervals. *Journal of Comparative and Physiological Psychology, 69(2)*, 226–231.

Smith, M.E. (2009). The Thirteenth Annual Frankel Lecture: Comment: Going to the Dogs: Evaluating the Proper Standard for Narcotic Detector Dog Searches of Private Residences. *Houston Law Review, 46*, 103.

Smith, P.A. (2012). Person-Portable Gas Chromatography: Rapid Temperature Program Operation through Resistive Heating of Columns with Inherently Low Thermal Mass Properties. *Journal of Chromatography A, 1261*, 37–45.

Smith, P.A., Lepage, C.R.J., Kock, D., Wyatt, H.D.M., Hook, G.L., Betsinger, G., Erickson, R.P., and Eckenrode, B.A. (2004). Detection of Gas-Phase Chemical Warfare Agents Using Field-Portable Gas Chromatography–Mass Spectrometry Systems: Instrument and Sampling Strategy Considerations. *Trends in Analytical Chemistry, 23(4)*, 296–306.

Smith, P.M., Lakatos, A., Barnett, S.C., Jeffery, N.D., and Franklin, R.J. (2002). Cryopreserved Cells Isolated from the Adult Canine Olfactory Bulb Are Capable of Extensive Remyelination Following Transplantation into the Adult Rat CNS. *Experimental Neurology, 176(2)*, 402–406.

Smith, T.S., Partidge, S.T., Amstrup, S.C., and Schliebe, S. (2007). Post-Den Emergence Behavior of Polar Bears (*Ursus maritimus*) in Northern Alaska. *Arctic, 60(2)*, 187–194.

Smith-Bindman, R. (2010). Is Computed Tomography Safe? *New England Journal of Medicine, 363*, 1–4.

Smolinska, A., Klaasen, E.M.M., Dallinga, J.W., van de Kant, K.D.G., Jobsis, Q., Moonen, E.J.C., van Schayck, O.C.P., Dompeling, E., and van Schooten, F.J. (2014). Profiling of Volatile Organic Compounds in Exhaled Breath as a Strategy to Find Early Predictive Signatures of Asthma in Children. *PLoS/ONE, 9(4)*, e95668.

Sommerville, B.A., Green, M.A., and Gee, D.J. (1990). Using Chromatography and a Dog to Identify Some of the Compounds in Human Sweat which Are Under Genetic Influence, pp. 634–639, in *Chemical Signals in Vertebrate*s (MacDonald, D.W., Müller-Schwarze, D., Natynczuk, S.E., eds.). Oxford: Oxford University Press.

Sommerville, B.A., Settle, R.H., Darling, F.M., and Broom, D.M. (1993). The Use of Trained Dogs to Discriminate Human Scent. *Animal Behaviour, 46(1)*, 189–190.

Sonoda, H., Kohnoe, S., Yazamato, T., Satoh, Y., Morizono, G., Shokata, K., Morita, M. et al. (2011). Colorectal Cancer Screening with Odour Material by Canine Scent Detection. *Gut* (BMJ Gastroenterology), *60(6)*, 814–819.

Soproni, K., Miklósi, Á., Topál, J., and Csányi, V. (2002). Dogs' (*Canis familiaris*) Responsiveness to Human Pointing Gestures. *Journal of Comparative Psychology, 116(1)*, 27–34.

Soria-Gomez, E., Bellocchio, L., Reguero, L., Lepousez, G., Martin, C., Bendahmane, M., Ruehle, S. et al. (2014). The Endocannabinoid System Controls Food Intake via Olfactory Processes. *Nature Neuroscience, 17(3)*, 407–415.

Soroker, V., Suma, P., La Pergola, A., Cohen, Y., Alchanatis, O., Golomb, O., Goldstein, E. et al. (2013). Early Detection and Monitoring of Red Palm Weevil: Approaches and Challenges. Palm Pest Mediterranean Conference. Nice, France (January 16–18, 2013).

Southwest Research Institute (1974). Olfactory Acuity in Selection Animals Conducted During the Period of June 1972–September 1974. Report AD787495, Southwest Research Institute, San Antonio, Texas, U.S.A.

Spady, T.C., and Ostrander, E.A. (2008). Canine Behavioral Genetics: Pointing Out the Phenotypes and Herding up the Genes. *The American Journal of Human Genetics, 82(1)*, 10–18.

Spehr, M., Gisselmann, G., Poplawski, A., Riffell, J.A., Wetzel, C.H., Zimmer, R.K., and Hatt, H. (2003). Identification of a Testicular Odorant Receptor Mediating Human Sperm Chemotaxis. *Science, 299*, 2054–2058.

Spence, K.W., and Norris, E.B. (1950). Eyelid Conditioning as a Function of the Inter-Trial Interval. *Journal of Experimental Psychology, 40(6)*, 716–720.

Spencer, D.C. (2007). Understanding Seizure Dogs. *Neurology, 68*, E2–E3.

Spitzbarth, I., Bock, P., Haist, V., Stein, A., Tipold, A., Wewetzer, K., Baumgartner, W., and Beineke, A. (2011). Prominent Microglial Activation in the Early Proinflammatory Immune Response in Naturally Occurring Canine Spinal Cord Injury. *Journal of Neuropathology & Experimental Neurology, 70(8)*, 703–714.

Springer, K., and Carmichael, N. (2012). *Non-Target Species Management for the Macquarie Island Pest Eradication Project*. Proc. 25th Vertebrate Pests Conference (Timm, R.M., ed.), University of California, Davis.

St. John, J.A., Clarris, H.J., and Key, B. (2002). Multiple Axon Guidance Cues Establish the Olfactory Topographic Map: How Do These Cues Interact? *The International Journal of Developmental Biology, 46(4)*, 639–647.

St. John, J.A., Clarris, H.J., McKeown, S., Royal, S., and Key, B. (2003). Sorting and Convergence of Primary Olfactory Axons Are Independent of the Olfactory Bulb. *Journal of Comparative Neurology, 464(2)*, 131–140.

Stadler, S., Stefanuto, P.-H., Byer, J.D., Broki, M., Forbes, S., and Focant, J.-F. (2012). Analysis of Synthetic Canine Training Aids by Comprehensive Two-Dimensional Gas Chromatography-Time of Flight Mass Spectrometry. *Journal of Chromatography A, 1255*, 202–206.

Stahl, B., Distel, H., and Hudson, R. (1990). Effects of Reversible Nare Occlusion on the Development of the Olfactory Epithelium in the Rabbit Nasal Septum. *Cell and Tissue Research, 259*, 275–281.

Starling, M.J., Branson, N., Cody, D., and McGreevy, P.D. (2013). Conceptualising the Impact of Arousal and Affective State on Training Outcomes of Operant Conditioning. *Animals, 3*, 300–317.

Starovoitev, V.I. (2013). Nuzhno li sovershenstvovat' chutye sobak-detektorov? [Should we perfect the olfactory capabilities of detection dogs?] *Kriminalistichniy Visnik, 2(20)*, 175–183.

Statheropoulos, M., Agapiou, A., Spiliopoulos, C., Pallis, G.C., and Sianos, E. (2007). Environmental Aspects of VOCs Evolved in Early Stages of Human Decomposition. *Science of the Total Environment, 385*, 221–227.

Statheropoulos, M., Pallis, G.C., Mikedi, K., Gannoukos, S., Agapiou, A., Pappa, A., Cole, A., Vautz, W., and Thomas, C.L.P. (2014). Dynamic Vapor Generator That Simulates Transient Odor Emissions of Victims Entrapped in the Voids of Collapsed Buildings. *Analytical Chemistry, 86*, 3887–3894.

Statheropoulos, M., Spiliopoulos, C., and Agapiou, A. (2005). A Study of Volatile Organic Compounds Evolved from the Decaying Human Body. *Forensic Science International, 153*, 147–155.

Steen, J.M., Mohus, I., Kveesetberg, T., and Walloe, L. (1996). Olfaction in Bird Dogs during Hunting. *Acta Physiologica Scandinavica, 157*, 115–119.

Stefanuto, P.-H., Perrault, K., Stadler, S., Pesesse, R., LeBlanc, H.N., Forbes, S.L., and Focant, J.-F. (2015). GCxGC-TOFMS and Supervised Multivariate Approaches to Study Human Cadaveric Decomposition Olfactive Signatures. *Analytical and Bioanalytical Chemistry, 407(16)*, 4767–4778.

Steffen, G.S., and Candelaria, S.M. (2003). *Drug Interdiction: Partnerships, Legal Principles, and Investigative Methodologies for Law Enforcement*. Boca Raton: Taylor & Francis/CRC Press.

Steinbach, S., Reindl, W., Dempfle, A., Schuster, A., Wolf, P., Hundt, W., and Huber, W. (2013). Smell and Taste in Inflammatory Bowel Disease. *PLoS/ONE, 8(9)*, 73454.

Steiss, J.E. (2002). Muscle Disorders and Rehabilitation in Canine Athletes. *Veterinary Clinics of North America: Small Animal Practice, 32(1)*, 267–285.

Stejskal, S.M. (2013). *Death, Decomposition, and Detector Dogs: From Science to Scene*. Boca Raton: Taylor & Francis/CRC Press.

Stern, C.E., Sherman, S.J., Kirchhoff, B.A., and Hasselmo, M.E. (2001). Medial Temporal and Prefrontal Contributions to Working Memory Tasks with Novel and Familiar Stimuli. *Hippocampus, 11(4)*, 337–346.

Stettler, D.D., and Axel, R. (2009). Representations of Odor in the Piriform Cortex. *Neuron, 63(6)*, 854–864.

Stevenson, D.J., Ravenscroft, K.R., Zappalorti, R.T., Ravenscroft, M.D., Weigley, S.W., and Jenkins, C.L. (2010). Using a Wildlife Detector Dog for Locating Eastern Indigo Snakes (*Drymarchon couperi*). *Herpetological Review, 41(4)*, 437–442.

Steventon, B., Mayor, R., and Streit, A. (2014). Neural Crest and Placode Interaction during the Development of the Cranial Sensory System. *Developmental Biology, 389*, 28–38.

Stewart, T.D. (ed.) (1970). *Personal Identification in Mass Disasters*. Washington, District of Columbia: Smithsonian Institution Press.

Stewart, T.D. (1979). *Essentials of Forensic Anthropology, Especially as Developed in the United States*. Springfield, Illinois: Charles C. Thomas.

Steyn, P. (2015, March 26). Can Elephants' Amazing Sense of Smell Help Sniff Out Bombs? *National Geographic*. Available at http://news.nationalgeographic.com/2015/03/150326-army-nation-animals-elephants-bombs-science/.

Stockham, R.A., Slavin, D.L., and Kift, W. (2004). Specialized Use of Human Scent in Criminal Investigations. *Forensic Science Communications, 6(3)*. Washington, DC: FBI.

Stokke, T. (2014). The Effect of Reward Type and Reward Preferences on the Performance of Detection Dogs. MS thesis, Norwegian University of Life Sciences. Available at http://brage.bibsys.no/xmlui/handle/11250/277712.

Strobel, R., Noll, R., and Kury, J. (2001). Nitromethane K-9 Detection Limit. In 7th International Symposium on the Analysis and Detection of Explosives, Edinburgh.

Strong, V., and Brown, S.W. (1999). Seizure-Alert Dogs—Fact or Fiction? *Seizure, 8*, 62–65.

Strong, V., and Brown, S.W. (2000). Should People with Epilepsy Have Untrained Dogs as Pets? *Seizure, 9*, 427–430.

Strong, V., Brown, S., Huyton, M., and Coyle, H. (2002). Effect of Trained Seizure Alert Dogs® on Frequency of Tonic–Clonic Seizures. *Seizure, 11*, 402–405.

Strotmann, J., and Breer, H. (2006). Formation of Glomerular Maps in the Olfactory System. *Seminars in Cell & Developmental Biology, 17*, 402–410.

Strotmann, J., Levai, O., Fleischer, J., Schwarzenbacher, K., and Breer, H. (1994a). Olfactory Receptor Proteins in Axonal Processes of Chemosensory Neurons. *The Journal of Neuroscience, 24(35)*, 7754–7761.

Strotmann, J., Wanner, I., Helfrich, T., Beck, A., Meinken, C., Kubick, S., and Breer, H. (1994b). Olfactory Neurones Expressing Distinct Odorant Receptor Subtypes Are Spatially Segregated in the Nasal Neuroepithelium. *Cell Tissue Research, 276(3)*, 429–438.

Su, N.-Y., and Scheffrahn, R.H. (1990). Economically Important Termites in the United States and Their Control. *Sociobiology, 17*, 77–94.

Suder, P., and Silberring, J. (2006). *Mass Spectrometry* (in Polish). Kradow: Wydawnictwo Uniwersytetu Jagiellońskiego. Available at http://ptsm.ibch.poznan.pl/index.php?option=com_content&view=article&id=103:silberring&catid=47:podrczniki&Itemid=121.

Suh, K.S., Kim, S.Y., Bae, Y.C., Ronnett, G.V., and Moon, C. (2006). Effects of Unilateral Naris Occlusion on the Olfactory Epithelium of Adult Mice. *NeuroReport, 17(11)*, 1139–1142.

Sulimov, K.T. (1995). Kinologicheskaya identifikaciya individuma po obonyatel'nym signalam [Identifying individuals through olfactory cues using dogs] (Doctoral dissertation from the Institut Problem Ekologii i Evolucii imini A. N. Severtsova [A. N. Severtsov Institute of Ecology and Evolution]). Available at DisserCat accession number 03.00.08, http://www.dissercat.com/content/kinologicheskaya-identifikatsiya-individuuma-po-obonyatelnym-signalam.

Suma, P., La Pergola, A., Longa, S., and Soroker, V. (2014). The Use of Sniffing Dogs for the Detection of *Rhynchophorus ferrugineus*. *Phytoparasitica, 42*, 269–274.

Suter, U., Welcher, A.A., and Snipes, G.J. (1993). Progress in the Molecular Understanding of Hereditary Peripheral Neuropathies Reveals New Insights into the Biology of the Peripheral Nervous System. *Trends in Neurosciences, 16(2)*, 50–56.

Sutter, N.B., and Ostrander, E.A. (2004). Dog Star Rising: The Canine Genetic System. *Nature Reviews: Genetics, 5,* 900–910.

Suzuki, Y. (2007). Apoptosis and the Insulin-Like Growth Factor Family in the Developing Olfactory Epithelium. *Anatomical Science International, 82,* 200–206.

Suzuki, Y., Takeda, M., and Farbman, A.I. (1996). Supporting Cells as Phagocytes in the Olfactory Epithelium after Bulbectomy. *Journal of Comparative Neurology, 376(4),* 509–517.

Svartberg, K. (2002). Shyness–Boldness Predicts Performance in Working Dogs. *Applied Animal Behaviour Science, 79(2),* 157–174.

Svobodova, I., Vapeník, P., Pinc, L., and Bartos, L. (2008). Testing German shepherd Puppies to Assess Their Chances of Certification. *Applied Animal Behaviour Science, 113(1),* 139–149.

Symes, S.A., L'Abbe, E.N., Pokines, J.T., Yuzwa, T., Messer, D., Stromquist, A., and Keough, N. (2014). Thermal Alteration to Bone, pp. 367–402, in *Manual of Forensic Taphonomy* (Pokines, J.T., and Symes, S.A., eds.). Boca Raton: Taylor & Francis/CRC Press.

Syrotuck, W. (1972, reprinted 2000). *Scent and the Scenting Dog.* Mechanicsburg, Pennsylvania: Barkleigh Productions, Inc.

Szetei, V., Miklosi, A., Topal, J., and Csanyi, V. (2003). When Dogs Seem to Lose Their Nose: An Investigation on the Use of Visual and Olfactory Cues in Communicative Context Between Dog and Owner. *Applied Animal Behaviour Science, 83(2),* 141–152.

Tacher, S., Quignon, P., Rimbault, M., Dreano, S., Andre, C., and Galibert, F. (2005). Olfactory Receptor Sequence Polymorphism within and between Breeds of Dogs. *Journal of Heredity, 96(7),* 812–816.

Tachi, S., Tanie, K., Komoriya, K., Hosoda, Y., and Abe, M. (1981). Guide Dog Robot—Its Basic Plan and Some Experiments with Meldog Mark I. *Mechanism and Machine Theory, 16(1),* 21–29.

Tamari, K., Takeuchi, H., Kobayashi, M., Kurahashi, T., and Yamamoto, T. (2013). Suppression and Recovery of Voltage-Gated Currents after Cocaine Treatments of Olfactory Receptor Cells. *Auris Nasus Larynx, 40(1),* 66–70.

Tan, U., and Caliskan, S. (1987a). Asymmetries in the Cerebral Dimensions and Fissures of the Dog. *International Journal of Neuroscience, 32(3–4),* 943–952.

Tan, U., and Caliskan, S. (1987b). Allometry and Asymmetry in the Dog Brain: The Right Hemisphere Is Heavier Regardless of Paw Preference. *International Journal of Neuroscience, 35(3–4),* 189–194.

Tapp, P.D., Head, K., Head, E., Milgram, N.W., Muggenburg, B.A., and Su, M.Y. (2006). Application of an Automated Voxel-Based Morphometry Technique to Assess Regional Gray and White Matter Brain Atrophy in a Canine Model of Aging. *NeuroImage, 29(1),* 234–244.

Taslitz, A. (1990). Does the Cold Nose Know? The Unscientific Myth of the Dog Scent Lineup. *Hastings Law Journal, 42,* 15–134.

Tasmania, National Parks and Reserves Management Act 2002 (No. 62 of 2002, Royal Assent 19 December 2002). Available at http://www5.austlii.edu.au/au/legis/tas/consol_act/nparma2002361/; reserve listing at http://www.parks.tas.gov.au/file.aspx?id=28768.

Tataruca, S.-C. (2011). The Formation and Improvement of the Conditioned Reflexes of the Working Dog with the Purpose of Processing the Tracks of Human Scent, Drugs and Explosives. Presented at the 5th International Conference Balnimalcon 2011. Romania, Centrul Chilogic SIBIU.

Taveggia, C., Zanazzi, G., Petrylak, A., Yano, H., Rosenbluth, J., Einheber, S., Xu, X. et al. (2005). Neuregulin-1 Type III Determines the Ensheathment Fate of Axons. *Neuron, 47(5),* 681–694.

Taverna, G., Tidu, L., Grizzi, F., Giuisti, G., Seveso, M., Benetti, A., Hurle, R. et al. (2014). Prostate Cancer Urine Detection through Highly-Trained Dogs' Olfactory System: A Real Clinical Opportunity. *The Journal of Urology, 191(4)(Supplement),* e546.

Taverna, G., Tidu, L., Grizzi, F., Torri, V., Mandressi, A., Sardella, P., La Torre, G. et al. (2015). Olfactory System of Highly Trained Dogs Detects Prostate Cancer in Urine Samples. *The Journal of Urology, 193(4),* 1382–1387.

Taylor, B.W. (1955). *The Flora, Vegetation and Soils of Macquarie Island.* ANARE Reports, B(2), No. 19, Botany, 190.

Taylor, R.H. (1979). How the Macquarie Island Parakeet Became Extinct. *New Zealand Journal of Ecology, 2,* 42–45.

Techangamsuwan, S., Imbschweiler, I., Kreutzer, R., Kreutzer, M., Baumgartner, W., and Wewetzer, K. (2008). Similar Behaviour and Primate-Like Properties of Adult Canine Schwann Cells and Olfactory Ensheathing Cells in Long-Term Culture. *Brain Research, 1240,* 31–38.

Terauds, A. (2009). *Changes in Rabbit Numbers on Macquarie Island 1974–2008.* Report for the Tasmania Parks and Wildlife Service. Hobart, Tasmania.

Terauds, A., Doube, J., McKinlay, J., and Springer, K. (2014). Using Long-Term Population Trends of an Invasive Herbivore to Quantify the Impact of Management Actions in the Sub-Antarctic. *Polar Biology, 37(6)*, 833–843.

Terra, V.C., Sakamoto, A.C., Machado, H.R., Martins, L.D., Cavalheiro, E.A., Arida, R.M., Stollberger, C., Finsterer, J., and Scorza, F.A. (2012). Do Pets Reduce the Likelihood of Sudden Unexplained Death in Epilepsy? *Seizure 21(8)*, 649–651.

Tetzlaff, W., Okon, E.B., Karimi-Abdolrezaee, S., Hill, C.E., Sparling, J.S., Plemel, J.R., Plunet, W.T. et al. (2011). A Systematic Review of Cellular Transplantation Therapies for Spinal Cord Injury. *Journal of Neurotrauma, 28(8)*, 1611–1682.

Theobald, S., and Cheyne, J. (2006). *Predator Dog Best Practice Manual—Part I* Training. Department of Conservation, New Zealand.

Theobald, S., and Coad, N. (2002). Den Control of Stoats (*Mustela erminea*) in Trounson Kauri Park, Northland. *DOC Science Internal Series 90*. Department of Conservation, Wellington.

Thesen, A., Steen, J.B., and Doving, K.B. (1993). Behaviour of Dogs during Olfactory Tracking. *Journal of Experimental Biology, 180*, 247–251.

Thomas, E.K., Drobatz, K.J., and Mandell, D.C. (2014). Presumptive Cocaine Toxicosis in 19 Dogs: 2004–2012. *Journal of Veterinary Emergency and Critical Care (San Antonio, Tex.: 2001), 24(2)*, 201–207.

Thomas, W.B., and Dewey, C.W. (2003). Seizures and Narcolepsy, pp. 237–255, in *A Practical Guide to Canine and Feline Neurology* (Dewey, C.W., ed.). Ames, Iowa: Iowa State University Press.

Thompson, B.S., and Gordon, F.L. (2014). *Archaeological and Remote Sensing Investigations at the Ancestral Weissinger Home Site (1PE280) Associated with the Alabama Museum of Natural History's 36th Expedition Near Hamburg in Northeast Perry County, Alabama*. OAR Project Number: 14-050. Office of Archaeological Research, University of Alabama, Moundville, Alabama. (A copy of this publication may be obtained from the Laboratory for Human Osteology at the Alabama Museum of Natural History of the University of Alabama, Moundville, Alabama.)

Thompson, C.M., Royle, J.A., and Garner, J.D. (2012). A Framework for Inference about Carnivore Density from Unstructured Spatial Sampling of Scat Using Detector Dogs. *Journal of Wildlife Management, 76(4)*, 863–871.

Thorndike, E.L. (1988). Animal Intelligence: An Experimental Study of the Associate Processes in Animals. *American Psychologist, 53(10)*, 1125–1127 (an excerpt from Thorndike's 1911 volume, *Animal Intelligence: Experimental Studies*).

Thurber, D.K., McClain, W.R., and Whitmore, R.C. (1994). Indirect Effects of Gypsy Moth Defoliation on Nest Predation. *The Journal of Wildlife Management, 58*, 493–500.

Tian, H., and Ma, M. (2004). Molecular Organization of the Olfactory Septal Organ. *The Journal of Neuroscience, 24*, 8383–8390.

Tipple, C.A., Caldwell, P.T., Kile, B.M., Beussman, D.J., Rushing, B., Mitchell, N.J., Whitchurch, C.J., Grime, M., Stockham, R., and Eckenrode, B.A. (2014). Comprehensive Characterization of Commercially Available Canine Training Aids. *Forensic Science International, 242*, 242–254.

Tiscione, N.B., Alfor, I., Yeatman, D.T., and Shan, X. (2011). Ethanol Analysis by Headspace Gas Chromatography with Simultaneous Flame-Ionization and Mass Spectrometry Detection. *Journal of Analytical Toxicology, 35(7)*, 502–511.

Todes, D.P. (2014). *Ivan Pavlov: A Russian Life in Science*. Oxford: Oxford University Press.

Toll, P.W., and Reynolds, A.J. (2000). The Canine Athlete, pp. 662–668, in *Small Animal Clinical Nutrition IV*. Topeka, Kansas: Mark Morris Assoc.

Tom, B.M. (2012). A Comparison of Noninvasive Survey Methods for Monitoring Mesocarnivore Populations in Kentucky (MS thesis). University of Kentucky.

Tomashefski, J.F., and Felo, J.A. (2004). The Pulmonary Pathology of Illicit Drug and Substance Abuse. *Diagnostic Histopathology, 10(5)*, 413–426.

Topal, J., Byrne, R.W., Miklosi, A., and Csanyi, V. (2006). Reproducing Human Actions and Action Sequences: "Do as I Do!" in a Dog. *Animal Cognition, 9*, 355–367.

Topal, J., Miklosi, A., and Csanyi, V. (1997). Dog–Human Relationship Affects Problem Solving Behavior in the Dog. *Anthrozoos, 10(4)*, 214–224.

Tortora, G., and Grabowski, S. (2002). *Principles of Anatomy and Physiology* (10th ed.). New York: Wiley.

Treleven, E. (2008). Zapata Admits Killing Wife, Gets 5 Years: The Former Madison Man Pleads Guilty to the 1976 Murder (February 19, 2008), posted on Madison.com (February 19, 2008). Available at http://host.madison.com/news/zapata-admits-killing-wife-gets-years-the-former-madison-man/article_3f7a7f4f-cb83-5869-b9c6-23532bc49a4e.html.

Tswett, M.S. (1905). Trudy Varshavskogo Obshchestva Estestvoispytatelei Otdelenie Biologii (English: On a New Category of Adsorption Phenomena and Their Application in Biochemical Analysis). Included in *Chromatographic Adsorption Analysis: Selected Works of M.S. Tswett* (Berezkin, V.G., ed., 1990). New York: Ellis Horwood.

Tuccori, M., Lapi, F., Testi, A., Ruggiero, E., Moretti, U., Vannacci, A., Bonaiuti, R. et al. (2011). Drug-Induced Taste and Smell Alterations: A Case-on-Case Evaluation of an Italian Database of Spontaneous Adverse Drug Reaction Reporting. *Drug Safety, 34(10)*, 849–859.

Udell, M.A.R., Dorey, N.R., and Wynne, C.D.L. (2008a). Wolves Outperform Dogs in Following Human Social Cues. *Animal Behaviour, 76(6)*, 1767–1773.

Udell, M.A.R., Dorey, N.R., and Wynne, C.D.L. (2011). Can Your Dog Read Your Mind? Understanding the Causes of Canine Perspective Taking. *Learning and Behavior, 39(4)*, 289–302.

Udell, M.A.R., Giglio, R.F., and Wynne, C.D.L. (2008b). Domestic Dogs (*Canis familiaris*) Use Human Gestures but not Nonhuman Tokens to Find Hidden Food. *Journal of Comparative Psychology, 122(1)*, 84–93.

Udell, M.A.R., and Wynne, C.D.L. (2009). Ontogeny and Phylogeny: Both Are Essential to Human-Sensitive Behaviour in the Genus *Canis*. *Animal Behaviour, 79(2)*, e9–e14.

Ulrich, R., Imbschweiler, I., Kalkuhl, A., Lehmbecker, A., Ziege, S., Kegler, K., Becker, K., Deschl, U., Wewetzer, K., and Baumgärtner, W. (2014). Transcriptional Profiling Predicts Overwhelming Homology of Olfactory Ensheathing Cells, Schwann Cells and Schwann-Like Glia. *Glia, 62(10)*, 1559–1581.

Upadhyay, U.D., and Holbrook, E.H. (2004). Olfactory Loss as a Result of Toxic Exposure. *Otolaryngologic Clinics of North America, 37(6)*, 1185–1207.

U.S. Air Force (2015). AFI31-126: DOD Military Working Dog (MWD) Program. Washington, District of Columbia: Headquarters, Department of the Air Force.

U.S. Army (2005). *Field Manual 3-19.17: Military Working Dogs*. Washington, District of Columbia: Headquarters, Department of the Army.

U.S. Department of Agriculture (USDA) (2010). Gypsy Moth Program Manual. USDA. Available at http://www.aphis.usda.gov/import_export/plants/manuals/domestic/downloads/gypsy_moth.pdf.

U.S. Department of Agriculture (USDA) (2012). *National Detector Dog Manual* (updated periodically). Washington, District of Columbia: Animal and Plant Health Inspection Service. Plant Protection and Quarantine Programs. Available at http://www.aphis.usda.gov/import_export/plants/manuals/ports/downloads/detector_dog.pdf.

U.S. Fish & Wildlife Service (2011). Protocol for Surveying Management Activities That May Impact Northern Spotted Owls. Available at http://www.fws.gov/yreka/ES/2012RevisedNSOprotocol-2-15-12.pdf.

U.S. Fish & Wildlife Service (2011). Revised Recovery Plan for the Mojave Population of the Desert Tortoise (*Gopherus agassizii*). Available at http://www.fws.gov/nevada/desert_tortoise/documents/recovery_plan/RRP%20for%20the%20Mojave%20Desert%20Tortoise%20-%20May%202011.pdf. USFWS Pacific Southwest Region, Sacramento, California (The Recovery Plan notes that domestic "and feral free-roaming dogs are documented threats to captive and wild tortoises.")

U.S. Fish & Wildlife Service (2012). Mexican Spotted Owl Survey Protocol. Available at http://www.fws.gov/mountain-prairie/endspp/protocols/MexicanSpottedOwlSurveyProtocol2012.pdf.

U.S. Fish & Wildlife Service (2013). Recovery Plan for the Black-Footed Ferret (*Mustela nigripes*), Second Revision. USFWS Mountain-Prairie Region, Denver. Available at http://ecos.fws.gov/docs/recovery_plan/20131108%20BFF%202nd%20Rev.%20Final%20Recovery%20Plan.pdf.

U.S. Preventive Services Task Force (August 2011). Bladder Cancer in Adults: Screening. August 2011 recommendation for asymptomatic adults. Available at www.uspreventiveservicestaskforce.org/.

Usinger, R.L. (1966). *Monograph of Cimicidae (Hemiptera-Heteroptera)*. College Park, MD: Entomological Society of America.

Vallortigara, G. (2000). Comparative Neuropsychology of the Dual Brain: A Stroll through Animals' Left and Right Perceptual Worlds. *Brain and Language, 73(2)*, 189–219.

Vallortigara, G., and Andrew, R.J. (1994). Olfactory Lateralization in the Chick. *Neuropsychologia, 32(4)*, 417–423.

Vallortigara, G., Chiandetti, C., and Sovrano, V.A. (2011). Brain Asymmetry (Animal). *Wiley Interdisciplinary Reviews: Cognitive Science, 2*, 146–157.

Vallortigara, G., Rogers, L.J., and Bisazza, A. (1999). Possible Evolutionary Origins of Cognitive Brain Lateralization. *Brain Research Reviews, 30(2)*, 164–175.

van Berkel, J.J., Dallinga, J.W., Moller, G.M., Godschalk, R.W., Moonen, E., Wouters, E.F., and van Schooten, F.J. (2008). Development of Accurate Classification Method Based on the Analysis of Volatile Organic Compounds from Human Exhaled Air. *Journal of Chromatography, B: Analytical Technology in the Biomedical and Life Sciences, 861(1)*, 101–107.

van Bommel, L. (2010). *Guardian Dogs: Best Practice Manual for the use of Livestock Guardian Dogs.* Canberra: Invasive Animals Cooperative Research Centre.

van Bramer, S.E. (1997). *An Introduction to Mass Spectrometry.* Chester, PA: Widener University. Available at http://science.widener.edu/svb/massspec/massspec.pdf.

van der Zee, C.E., Nielander, H.B., Vos, J.P., Lopes da Silva, S., Verhaagen, J., Oestreicher, A.B., Schrama, L.H., Schotman, P., and Gispen, W.H. (1989). Expression of Growth-Associated Protein B-50 (GAP43) in Dorsal Root Ganglia and Sciatic Nerve during Regenerative Sprouting. *Journal of Neuroscience, 9(10)*, 3505–3512.

van De Werfhorst, L.C., Murray, J.L.S., Reynolds, S., Reynolds, K., and Holden, P.A. (2014). Canine Scent Detection and Microbial Source Tracking of Human Waste Contamination in Storm Drains. *Water Environment Research, 86(6)*, 550–558.

van Huis, A. (2013). Potential of Insects as Food and Feed in Assuring Food Security. *Annual Review of Entomology, 58*, 563–583.

van Huis, A., van Itterbeck, J., Harmke, K., Mertens, E., Halloran, A., Muir, G., and Vantomme, P. (2013). Edible Insects: Future Prospects for Food and Feed Security. Food and Agriculture Organization of the United Nations, Rome, Italy. FAO Forestry Paper 171. 187 pp. Available at http://www.fao.org/docrep/018/i3253e/i3253e.pdf.

van Kesteren, R.E., Mason, M.R., Macgillavry, H.D., Smit, A.B., and Verhaagen, J. (2011). A Gene Network Perspective on Axonal Regeneration. *Frontiers in Molecular Neuroscience, 4*, Article 46, 1–6.

van Smith (2014). Faking Drug-Dog Certification Puts Baltimore Drug-Money Forfeiture at Risk. *City Paper* (July 23, 2014). Available at http://www.citypaper.com/blogs/the-news-hole/bcp-faked-drugdog-certification-puts-baltimore-drugmoney-forfeiture-at-risk-20140723,0,610347.story.

Vanderhaeghen, P., Schurmans, S., Vassart, G., and Parmentier, M. (1993). Olfactory Receptors Are Displayed on Dog Mature Sperm Cells. *Journal of Cell Biology, 123(6; Part 1)*, 1441–1452.

Vanderhaeghen, P., Schurmans, S., Vassart, G., and Parmentier, M. (1997). Specific Repertoire of Olfactory Receptor Genes in the Male Germ Cells of Several Mammalian Species. *Genomics, 39(3)*, 239–246.

Varian, Inc. (2010). *Consumables and Supplies Catalog.* Posted at http://www.crawfordscientific.com/downloads/pdf_new/Varian-Catalogue-2010.pdf.

Vas, J., Topal, J., Gacsi, M., Miklosi, A., and Csanyi, V. (2005). A Friend or an Enemy? Dogs' Reaction to an Unfamiliar Person Showing Behavioural Cues of Threat and Friendliness at Different Times. *Applied Animal Behaviour Science, 94(1)*, 99–115.

Vass, A.A. (2001). Beyond the Grave—Understanding Human Decomposition. *Microbiology Today, 28*, 190–192.

Vass, A.A. (2012). Odor Mortis. *Forensic Science International, 222(1–3)*, 234–241.

Vass, A.A., Smith, R.R., Thompson, C.V., Burnett, M.N., Dulgerian, N., and Eckenrode, B.A. (2008). Odor Analysis of Decomposing Buried Human Remains. *Journal of Forensic Sciences, 53*, 384–392.

Vass, A.A., Smith, R.R., Thompson, C.V., Burnett, M.N., Wolf, D.A., Synstelien, J.A., Eckenrode, B.A., and Dulgerian, N. (2004). Decompositional Odor Analysis Database. *Journal of Forensic Sciences, 49*, 760–769.

Verhaagen, J., Greer, C.A., and Margolis, F.L. (1990). B-50/GAP43 Gene Expression in the Rat Olfactory System during Postnatal Development and Aging. *European Journal of Neuroscience, 2(5)*, 397–407.

Verhaagen, J., Oestreicher, A.B., Gispen, W.H., and Margolis, F.L. (1989). The Expression of the Growth Associated Protein B50/GAP43 in the Olfactory System of Neonatal and Adult Rats. *The Journal of Neuroscience, 9(2)*, 683–691.

Veseley, D.G. (2008). Training of Conservation Detection Dogs to Locate Kincaid's Lupine (*Lupinus sulphureu ssp. kincaidi*): Final Report—August 18, 2008. Prepared for U.S. Fish & Wildlife Service, Oregon State Office.

Vicars, S.M., Miquel, C.F., and Sobie, J.L. (2014). Assessing Preference and Reinforcer Effectiveness in Dogs. *Behavioural Processes, 103*, 75–83.

Vice, D.S., and Engeman, R.M. (2000). Brown Tree Snake Discoveries during Detector Dog Inspections Following Supertyphoon Paka. *Micronesia, 33(1/2)*, 105–110.

Vice, D.S., Engeman, R.M., Hall, M.A., and Clark, C.S. (2009). Working Dogs: The Last Line of Defense for Preventing Dispersal of Brown Treesnakes from Guam. In *Canine Ergonomics: The Science of Working Dogs* (Helton, W.S., ed.) Boca Raton: CRC Press.

Vickers, N.J. (2000). Mechanisms of Animal Navigation in Odor Plumes. *The Biological Bulletin, 198(2)*, 203–212.

Villamor, J.L., Bermejo, A.M., Fernandez, P., and Tabernero, M.J. (2005). A New GC-MS Method for the Determination of Five Amphetamines in Human Hair. *Journal of Analytical Toxicology, 29(2)*, 135–139.

Vincent, A.J., Taylor, J.M., Choi-Lundberg, D.L., West, A.K., and Chuah, M.I. (2005a). Genetic Expression Profile of Olfactory Ensheathing Cells Is Distinct from That of Schwann Cells and Astrocytes. *Glia, 51(2)*, 132–147.

Vincent, A.J., West, A.K., and Chuah, M.I. (2005b). Morphological and Functional Plasticity of Olfactory Ensheathing Cells. *Journal of Neurocytology, 34(1–2)*, 65–80.

Viranyi, Z., Gacsi, M., Kubinyi, E., Topal, J., Belenyi, B., Ujfalussy, D., and Miklosi, A. (2008). Comprehension of Human Pointing Gestures in Young Human-Reared Wolves (*Canis lupus*) and Dogs (*Canis familiaris*). *Animal Cognition, 11(3)*, 373–387.

Vitta, C.R., Bohman, B., Unelius, C.R., and Lorenzo, M.G. (2009). Behavioral and Electrophysiological Responses of *Triatoma brasiliensis* Males to Volatiles Produced in Metasternal Glands of Females. *Journal of Chemical Ecology, 35*, 1212–1221.

Vogel, S. (1994). *Life in Moving Fluids: The Physical Biology of Flow*. Princeton, NJ: Princeton University Press.

von Stephanitz (1923). *The German Shepherd Dog in Word and Picture*. Jena, Germany: Anton Kampfe.

vonHoldt, B.M., Pollinger, J.P., Lohmueller, K.E., Han, E., Parker, H.G., Quignon, P. et al. (2010). Genome-Wide SNP Haplotype Analyses Reveal a Rich History Underlying Dog Domestication. *Nature, 464(7290)*, 898–902.

Vu, D.T. (2001). SPME/GC-MS Characterization of Volatiles Associated with Methamphetamine: Toward the Development of a Pseudomethamphetamine Training Material. *Journal of Forensic Sciences, 46(5)*, 1014–1024.

Vynne, C., Machado, R.B., Marinho-Filho, J., and Wasser, S.K. (2009). Scat-Detection Dogs Seek Out New Locations of *Priodontes maximus* and *Mymecophaga tridactyla* in Central Brazil. *Edentata, 8–10*, 13–14.

Vynne, C., Skalski, J.R., Machado, R.B., Groom, M.J., Jacomo, A.T.A., Marinho-Filho, J., Ramos Neto, M.B. et al. (2011). Effectiveness of Scat-Detection Dogs in Determining Species Presence in a Tropical Savanna Landscape. *Conservation Biology, 25(1)*, 154–162.

Vyplelova, P., Vokalek, V., Pinc, L., Pacakova, Z., Bartos, L., Santariova, M., and Captkova, Z. (2014). Individual Human Odor Fallout as Detected by Trained Canines. *Forensic Science International, 234*, 13–15.

Waggoner, L.P., Johnston, J.M., Williams, Jackson, M.J., Jones, M., Boussom, T., and Petrousky, J.A. (1997). Canine Olfactory Sensitivity to Cocaine Hydrochloride and Methyl Benzoate, *SPIE*, 2937, 216–226.

Waggoner, L.P., Jones, M.H., Williams, M., Johnston, J.M., Edge, C.C., and Petrousky, J.A. (1998, December). Effects of Extraneous Odors on Canine Detection, pp. 355–362, in *Enabling Technologies for Law Enforcement and Security*. Bellingham, WA: International Society for Optics and Photonics.

Waguespack, A.M., Reems, M.R., Butman, M.L., Cherry, J.A., and Coppola, D.M. (2005). Naris Occlusion Alters Olfactory Marker Protein Immunoreactivity in Olfactory Epithelium. *Brain Research, 1044(1)*, 1–7.

Walczak, M. (2009). *Operant Conditioning of Dogs for Detection of Odor Markers of Cancer Diseases* (Ph.D. thesis in Polish). Jastrzębiec, Poland. Institute of Genetics and Animal Breeding of the Polish Academy of Sciences.

Walczak, M., Jezierski, T., Górecka-Bruzda, A., Sobczyńska, M., and Ensminger, J. (2012). Impact of Individual Training Parameters and Manner of Taking Breath Odor Samples on the Reliability of Canines as Cancer Screeners. *Journal of Veterinary Behavior: Clinical Applications and Research, 7(5)*, 283–294.

Walker, D.B., Walker, J.C., Cavnar, P.J., Taylor, J.L., Pickel, D.H., Hall, S.B., and Suarez, J.C. (2006). Naturalistic Quantification of Canine Olfactory Sensitivity. *Applied Animal Behaviour Science, 97(2–4)*, 241–254.

Wallner, W.E., and Ellis, T.L. (1976). Olfactory Detection of Gypsy Moth Pheromone and Egg Masses by Domestic Canines. *Journal of Economic Entomology, 5*, 563–565.

Walter, C., Oertel, B.G., Ludyga, D., Ultsch, A., Hummel, T., and Lötsch, J. (2014). Effects of 20 mg Oral Δ9-tetrahydrocannabinol on the Olfactory Function of Healthy Volunteers. *British Journal of Clinical Pharmacology, 78(5)*, 961–969.

Wang, C., and Sahay, P. (2009). Breath Analysis Using Laser Spectroscopic Techniques: Breath Biomarkers, Spectral Fingerprints, and Detection Limits. *Sensors, 9(10)*, 8230–8262.

Wang, F., Nemes, A., Mendelsohn, M., and Axel, R. (1998). Odorant Receptors Govern the Formation of a Precise Topographic Map. *Cell, 93(1)*, 47–60.

Wang, Z.J., Sun, L., and Heinbockel, T. (2012). Cannabinoid Receptor-Mediated Regulation of Neuronal Activity and Signaling in Glomeruli of the Main Olfactory Bulb. *Journal of Neuroscience, 32(25)*, 8475–8479.

Wasser, S.K., Davenport, B., Ramage, E.R., Hunt, K.E., Parker, M., Clarke, C., and Stenhouse, G. (2004). Scat Detection Dogs in Wildlife Research and Management: Application to Black Bears in the Yellowhead Ecosystem, Alberta, Canada. *Canadian Journal of Zoology, 82*, 475–492.

Wasser, S.K., Hayward, L.S., Hartman, J., Booth, R.K., Broms, K., Berg, J., Seely, E., Lewis, L., and Smith, H. (2012). Using Detection Dogs to Conduct Simultaneous Surveys of Northern Spotted (*Strix occidentalis caurina*) and Barred Owls (*Strix varia*). *PLoS/ONE, 7(8)*, e42892.

Wasser, S.K., Keim, J.L., Taper, M.L., and Lele, S.R. (2011). The Influences of Wolf Predation, Habitat Loss, and Human Activity on Caribou and Moose in the Alberta Oil Sands. *Frontiers in Ecology and the Environment, 9(10)*, 546–551.

Wasser, S.K., Smith, H., Madden, L., Marks, N., and Vynne, C. (2009). Scent-Matching Dogs Determine Number of Unique Individuals from Scat. *Journal of Wildlife Management, 73(7)*, 1233–1240.

Wasserman, E.A. (1973). Pavlovian Conditioning with Heat Reinforcement Produces Stimulus-Directed Pecking in Chicks. *Science, 181(4102)*, 875–877.

Waters, J., O'Connor, S., Park, K., and Goulson, D. (2011). Testing a Detection Dog to Locate Bumblebee Colonies and Estimate Nest Density. *Apidologie, 42(2)*, 200–205.

Weilenmann, A., and Juhlin, O. (2011). Understanding People and Animals: The Use of a Positioning System in Ordinary Human–Canine Interaction, pp. 2631–2640, in *Proceedings of the SIGCHI Conference on Human Factors in Computing Systems*. ACM.

Weiler, E., and Farbman, A. (1998). Supporting Cell Proliferation in the Olfactory Epithelium Decreases Postnatally. *Glia, 22(4)*, 315–328.

Weiss, E. (2002). Selecting Shelter Dogs for Service Dog Training. *Journal of Applied Animal Welfare Science, 5(1)*, 43–62.

Welch, J.B. (1990). A Detector Dog for Screwworms (Diptera: Callifphoridae). *Journal of Economic Entomology, 83(5)*, 1932–1934.

Welge-Luessen, A., and Wolfensberger, M. (2003). Reversible Anosmia after Amikacin Therapy. *Archives of Otolaryngology—Head and Neck Surgery, 129(12)*, 1331–1333.

Wells, D.L., and Hepper, P.G. (2000). The Discrimination of Dog Odours by Humans. *Perception, 29*, 111–115.

Wells, D.L., and Hepper, P.G. (2003). Directional Tracking in the Domestic Dog, *Canis familiaris*. *Applied Animal Behaviour Science, 84*, 297–305.

Wells, D.L., Lawson, S.W., and Siriwardena, A.N. (2008). Canine Responses to Hypoglycemia in Patients with Type 1 Diabetes. *The Journal of Alternative and Complementary Medicine, 14(10)*, 1235–1241.

Wells, J.D., and Greenberg, B. (1994). Effect of the Red Imported Fire Ant (Hymenoptera: Formicidae) and Carcass Type on the Daily Occurrence of Postfeeding Carrion-Fly Larvae (Diptera: Calliphoridae, Sarcophagidae). *Journal of Medical Entomology, 31(1)*, 171–174.

Wemelsfelder, F. (1985). Animal Boredom: Is a Scientific Study of the Subjective Experiences of Animals Possible?, pp. 115–154, in *Advances in Animal Welfare Science 1984*. Springer: Netherlands.

Wendelburg, K.L. (1998). Disorders of the Hip Joint in the Canine Athlete, pp. 174–195, in *Canine Sports Medicine and Surgery* (Bloomberg, M.S., Dee, J.F., and Taylor, R.A., eds.) Philadelphia: Saunders.

Wesson, D.W., Borkowski, A.H., Landreth, G.E., Nixon, R.A., Levy, E., and Wilson, D.A. (2011). Sensory Network Dysfunction, Behavioral Impairments, and Their Reversibility in an Alzheimer's ß-amyloidosis Mouse Model. *Journal of Neuroscience, 31(44)*, 15962–15971.

Westmoreland, D.G., and Rhodes, G.R. (1989). Analytical Techniques for Trace Organic Compounds-II: Detectors for Gas Chromatography. *Pure and Applied Chemistry, 61(6)*, 1147–1160.

Wewetzer, K., and Brandes, G. (2006). Axonal Signalling and the Making of Olfactory Ensheathing Cells: A Hypothesis. *Neuron Glia Biology, 2(3)*, 217–224.

Wewetzer, K., Kern, N., Ebel, C., Radtke, C., and Brandes, G. (2005). Phagocytosis of O4+ Axonal Fragments in Vitro by p75[NTR] Neonatal Olfactory Ensheathing Cells. *Glia, 49(4)*, 577–587.

Wewetzer, K., Radtke, C., Kocsis, J., and Baumgartner, W. (2011). Species-Specific Control of Cellular Proliferation and the Impact of Large Animal Models for the Use of Olfactory Ensheathing Cells and Schwann Cells in Spinal Cord Repair. *Experimental Neurology, 229(1)*, 80–87.

Wewetzer, K., Verdu, E., Angelov, D.N., and Navarro, X. (2002). Olfactory Ensheathing Glia and Schwann Cells: Two of a Kind? *Cell and Tissue Research, 309(3)*, 337–345.

Wheelwright, P. (1959). *Heraclitus*. Princeton, NJ: Princeton University Press.

Widacki, J. (1999). Neither Randomness nor Certainty. On one of the Methods for Determination of Diagnostic Value of Osmological Identification (in Polish). *Problemy Kryminalistyki, 225*, 62–63.

Widacki, J. (2000). Which image of scent identification examinations is the true one? (in Polish) *Problemy Kryminalistyki* 229, 46–47.

Wieland, G. (1938). Uber die Größe des Riechfeldes beim Hunde (Ein Beitrag zur Methodik derartiger Untersuchungen). *Zeitschrift für Hundeforschung, Bd. XII*, Heft 3, S. 1–23.

Williams, H., and Pembroke, A. (1989, April 1). Sniffer Dogs in the Melanoma Clinic? *The Lancet, 333(8640)*, 734.

Williams, M., and Johnston, J.M. (2002). Training and Maintaining the Performance of Dogs (*Canis familiaris*) on an Increasing Number of Odor Discriminations in a Controlled Setting. *Applied Animal Behaviour Science, 78*, 55–65.

Williams, M., Johnston, J.M., Waggoner, L.P., Cicoria, M., Hallowell, S.F., and Petrousky, J.A. (2001). *Canine Substance Detection: Operational Capabilities.* Institute for Biological Detection Systems, Auburn University.

Williams, S.K., Franklin, R.J., and Barnett, S.C. (2004). Response of Olfactory Ensheathing Cells to the Degeneration and Regeneration of the Peripheral Olfactory System and the Involvement of Neuregulins. *Journal of Comparative Neurology, 470(1),* 50–62.

Willis, C.M., Church, S.M., Guest, C.M., Cook, A.W., McCarthy, N., Bransbury, A.J., Church, M.R.T., and Church, J.C.T. (2004). Olfactory Detection of Human Bladder Cancer by Dogs: Proof of Principle Study. *British Medical Journal, 329,* 712–715.

Wilson, A.D. (2015). Advances in Electronic-Nose Technologies for the Detection of Volatile Biomarker Metabolites in the Human Breath. *Metabolites, 5,* 140–163.

Wilson, D.A. (2000). Comparison of Odor Receptive Field Plasticity in the Rat Olfactory Bulb and Anterior Piriform Cortex. *Journal of Neurophysiology, 84(6),* 3036–3042.

Wilson, D.A., and Stevenson, R.J. (2006). *Learning to Smell: Olfactory Perception from Neurobiology to Behavior.* Baltimore, Maryland: The Johns Hopkins University Press.

Wilsson, E., and Sinn, D.L. (2012). Are There Differences between Behavioral Measurement Methods? A Comparison of the Predictive Validity of Two Ratings Methods in a Working Dog Program. *Applied Animal Behaviour Science, 141(3),* 158–172.

Wilsson, E., and Sundgren, P.-E. (1997). The Use of a Behaviour Test for Selection of Dogs for Service and Breeding. II. Heritability for Tested Parameters and Effect of Selection Based on Service Dog Characteristics. *Applied Animal Behaviour Science, 54(2–3),* 235–241.

Wiltrout, C., Dogra, S., and Linster, C. (2003). Configurational and Nonconfigurational Interactions between Odorants in Binary Mixtures. *Behavioral Neuroscience, 117(2),* 236–245.

Wirth, T.C., Later, J.B., Oliphant, J.L., Lee, E.D., and Later, D.W. (2012a). Person-Portable GC-MS for Rapid On-Site Environmental Screening of Contaminants in Drinking Water. *American Laboratory* (online July 31, 2012). Available at http://www.americanlaboratory.com/914-Application-Notes/118159-Person-Portable-GC-MS-for-Rapid-On-Site-Environmental-Screening-of-Contaminants-in-Drinking-Water/.

Wirth, T.C., Sadowski, C.S., and Later, D.W. (2012b). Rapid On-Site Screening of Environmental VOCs in Soil Using Solid Phase Microextraction and a Person-Portable GC-MS. LG-GC Solutions for Separation Scientists: *The Application Notebook.* Available at http://www.chromatographyonline.com/rapid-site-screening-environmental-vocs-soil-using-solid-phase-microextractio-and-person-portable-gc?rel = canonical.

Witkiewicz, Z., and Hetper, J. (2001). *Chromatografia Gazowa* (English: *Gas Chromatography*). Warsaw: Wydawnictwo Naukowo-Techniczne.

Wojcikiewicz, J. (1999). Dog Scent Line-Ups as Scientific Evidence. 15th IAFS Triennial Meeting, August 1999: Los Angeles.

Wood, W.R., and Johnson, D.L. (1982). A Survey of Disturbance Processes in Archaeological Site Formation, pp. 539–605, in *Advances in Archaeological Method and Theory: Selections for Students from Volumes 1 through 4* (Schiffer, M.B., ed.). New York: Academic Press.

Woodford, W.J. (1981). U.S. Patent 4,260,517. "Available Odor of Cocaine." April 7, 1981.

Woollett, D.A., Hurt, A., and Richards, N. (2014). The Current and Future Roles of Free-Ranging Detection Dogs in Conservation Efforts, pp. 239–264, in *Free-Ranging Dogs & Wildlife Conservation* (Gompper, M.E., ed.). Oxford, UK: Oxford University Press.

World Health Organization. Fact sheet N°297, Updated February 2015. Available at http://www.who.int/mediacentre/factsheets/fs297/en/.

Wright, G.A., Kottcamp, S.M., and Thomson, M.G.A. (2008). Generalization Mediates Sensitivity to Complex Odor Features in the Honeybee. *Plos/ONE, 3(2),* e1704.

Wynne, C.D.L. (2007). What Are Animals? Why Anthropomorphism Is Still Not a Scientific Approach to Behavior. *Comparative Cognition & Behavior Reviews, 2,* 125–135.

Xu, T., and Oppenheim, F.G. (1993). Salivary Antimicrobials: Where Are We?, pp. 117–131, in *Cariology for the Nineties* (Bowen. W.H., and Tabak, L.A., eds.). Rochester, New York: University of Rochester Press.

Xu, Y., Gong, F., Dixon, S.J., and Abrereton, R.G. (2007). Application of Dissimilarity Indices, Principal Coordinates Analysis, and Rank Tests to Peak Tables in Metabolomics of the Gas Chromatography/Mass Spectrometry of Human Sweat. *Analytical Chemistry, 79,* 5633–5641.

Yadav, L., and Jayanand (2014). Non-Invasive Biosensor for Diabetes Monitoring. *World Journal of Medical Sciences, 11(1),* 82–89.

Yamamoto, M., Kikusui, T., and Ohta, M. (2009). Influence of Delayed Timing of Owners' Timing Actions on the Behaviors of Their Dogs, *Canis familiaris. Journal of Veterinary Behavior: Clinical Applications and Research, 4(1),* 11–18.

Yamazaki, K., Boyse, E.A., Bard, J., Curran, M., Kim, D., Ross, S.R., and Beauchamp, G.K. (2002). Presence of Mouse Mammary Tumor Virus Specifically Alters the Body Odor of Mice. *Proceedings of the National Academy of Sciences USA, 99(8)*, 5512–5515.

Yee, K.K., and Wysocki, C.J. (2001). Odorant Exposure Increases Olfactory Sensitivity: Olfactory Epithelium Is Implicated. *Physiology and Behavior, 72(5)*, 705–711.

Young, J.M., Endicott, R.M., Parghi, S.S., Walker, M., Kidd, J.M., and Trask, B.J. (2008). Extensive Copy-Number Variation of the Human Olfactory Receptor Gene Family. *The American Journal of Human Genetics, 83(2)*, 228–242.

Young, J.M., Kambere, M., Trask, B.J., and Lane, R.P. (2005). Divergent V1R Repertoires in Five Species: Amplifications in Rodents, Decimation in Primates, and a Surprisingly Small Repertoire in Dogs. *Genome Research, 15(2)*, 231–240.

Young, J.M., Massa, H.F., Hsu, L., and Trask, B.J. (2010). Extreme Variability among Mammalian V1R Gene Families. *Genome Research, 20(1)*, 10–18.

Young, J.M., Shykind, B.M., Lane, R.P., Tonnes-Priddy, L., Ross, J.A., Walker, M., Williams, E.M., and Trask, B.J. (2003). Odorant Expressed Sequence Tags Demonstrate Olfactory Expression of Over 400 Genes, Extensive Alternate Splicing and Unequal Expression Levels. *Genome Biology, 4(11)*, R71.

Young, J.M., and Trask, B.J. (2002). The Sense of Smell: Genomics of Vertebrate Odorant Receptors. *Human Molecular Genetics, 11(10)*, 1153–1160.

Young, J.M., and Trask, B.J. (2007). V2R Gene Families Degenerate in Primates, Dog and Cow, but Expanded in Opossum. *Trends in Genetics, 23(5)*, 212–215.

Yu, H., Xu, P., and Wang, P. (2005). Solid Phase Microextraction for Analysis of Alkanes and Aromatic Hydrocarbons in Human Breath. *Journal of Chromatography B, 826(1–2)*, 69–74.

Zahid, I., Grgurinovic, C., Zaman, T., De Keyzer, R., and Cayzer, L. (2012). Assessment of Technologies and Dogs for Detecting Insect Pests in Timber and Forest Products. *Scandinavian Journal of Forest Research, 27*, 492–502.

Zhang, H.-H., Wei, Q.-G., Zhang, H.-X., and Chen, L. (2011). Comparison of the Fraction of Olfactory Receptor Pseudogenes in Wolf (*Canis lupus*) with Domestic Dog (*Canis familiaris*). *Journal of Forestry Research, 22(2)*, 275–280.

Zhang, X., De la Cruz, O., Pinto, J.M., Nicolae, D., Firestein, S., and Gilad, Y. (2007). Characterizing the Expression of the Human Olfactory Receptor Gene Family Using a Novel DNA Microarray. *Genome Biology, 8*, R86.

Zhang, X., and Firestein, S. (2002). The Olfactory Receptor Gene Superfamily of the Mouse. *Nature Neuroscience, 5*, 124–133.

Zhang, X., Marcucci, F., and Firestein, S. (2010). High-Throughout Microarray Detection of Vomeronasal Receptor Gene Expression in Rodents. *Frontiers in Neuroscience, 4*, 164.

Zhang, X., Rogers, M., Tian, H., Zhang, X., Zou, D.-J., Liu, J., Ma, M., Shepherd, G.M., and Firestein, S.J. (2004). High-Throughout Microarray Detection of Olfactory Receptor Gene Expression in the Mouse. *Proceedings of the National Academy of Sciences USA, 101(39)*, 14168–14173.

Zhu, J. (1999). The Influence of Stability Class on Downwind Odor Concentration Predicted by Air Dispersion Models. *Journal of Environmental Science & Health Part A, 34(10)*, 1919–1931.

Zhu, M., and Ahlberg, P.E. (2004). The Origin of the Internal Nostril of Tetrapods. *Nature, 432*, 94–97.

Ziege, S., Baumgartner, W., and Wewetzer, K. (2013). Toward Defining the Regenerative Potential of Olfactory Mucosa: Establishment of Schwann Cell-Free Adult Canine Olfactory Ensheathing Cell Preparations Suitable for Transplantation. *Cell Transplantation, 22(2)*, 355–367.

Zimen, E. (1981). *The Wolf: A Species in Danger*. New York: Delacorte.

Zink, M.C., and Schlehr, M.R. (1997). *Peak Performance: Coaching the Canine Athlete*. Baltimore: Canine Sports Productions.

Zink, M.C., and Van Dyke, J.B. (2013). *Canine Sports Medicine and Rehabilitation*. Oxford: Wiley-Blackwell.

Zozulya, S., Echeverri, F., and Nguyen, T. (2001). The Human Olfactory Receptor Repertoire. *Genome Biology, 2(6)*. Research 0018.

Zucchi, R., Chiellini, G., Scanlan, T.S., and Grandy, D.K. (2006). Trace Amine-Associated Receptors and Their Ligands. *British Journal of Pharmacology, 149(8)*, 967–978.

Zuo, Y., Zhang, K., Wu, J., Rego, C., and Fritz, J. (2008). An Accurate and Nondestructive GC Method for Determination of Cocaine on U.S. Paper Currency. *Journal of Separation Science, 31*, 2444–2450.

Index

This index covers the preface. Page numbers followed by b, f, and t indicate boxes, figures, and tables, respectively.

9781482260236